Den of Vipers
Central Banks & the Fake Economy

by

Cynthia F. Hodges, JD, LLM, MA

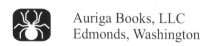

Auriga Books, LLC
Edmonds, Washington

Description

Central banks have wrested control of national economies from elected officials and have hijacked financial policy-making. This book paints a bleak picture of the economic landscape in an effort to warn investors and other interested parties of the potential dangers that lie ahead. Well into the so-called "booming economic times," stress fractures in the foundation are becoming increasingly apparent. Eventually, the financial house of cards will collapse. Anyone who is caught unaware risks losing everything.

Unlike some doom and gloom books, *Den of Vipers* offers doable solutions to economic woes created by a secretive clique of banking insiders. Strategies on how to protect one's assets and even profit from a systemic breakdown are also explored.

Anyone who is concerned about their financial future and is not convinced by the empty assurances of the mainstream media would benefit from reading this book.

About the Author

Cynthia F. Hodges holds a Juris Doctor from South Texas College of Law in Houston, Texas and an LLM in Environmental Law from Lewis & Clark Law School in Portland, Oregon. She also has a BA and an MA in Germanic Studies from the University of Texas at Austin.

Hodges is an experienced gold and silver investor, as well as a successful stock and options trader. As the manager of the investment portfolio of Scott Free Investments, LLC, she made an impressive 40% return on investment (ROI) for the company in 2017.

Hodges, a practicing attorney, is a member of the Washington State Bar Association. She has a number of law review articles published by the Animal Law Center at Michigan State University. She is the author of *5 Easy Ways to Promote Your Book Online* and has translated several books on horse-training theory (dressage) from German to English. More information is available at her website, cynthiahodges.com.

The banking problem "is the most important subject intelligent persons can investigate and reflect upon. It is so important that our present civilization may collapse unless it becomes widely understood and the defects are remedied very soon."

~ Robert H. Hemphill[1] ~

---

[1] Credit Manager, Federal Reserve Bank in Atlanta in the foreword to a book by Irving Fisher entitled *100% Money* (1935). Libertytree.ca. "Quotation by Robert Hemphill." *LibertyQuotes*, libertytree.ca/quotes/ Robert.Hemphill.Quote.CA66.

Contents

Chapter 1

The New World Economic Order

President Woodrow Wilson once said, "Some of the biggest men in the U.S., in the field of commerce and manufacturing, are afraid of somebody, are afraid of something. They know that there is a power somewhere so organized, so subtle, so watchful, so interlocked, so complete, so pervasive, that they had better not speak above their breath when they speak in condemnation of it."[2] "[T]he influence of bankers over governments…was not something about which anyone talked freely…"[3]

"Hundreds of years ago, bankers…became the financiers and financial advisers of governments…"[4] According to author Carroll Quigley, "The powers of financial capitalism had [a] far-reaching aim, nothing less than to create a world system of financial control in private hands able to dominate the political system of each country and the economy of the world as a whole. This system was to be controlled in a feudalist fashion by the central banks of the world acting in concert, by secret agreements arrived at in frequent private meetings and conferences."[5]

---

[2] From *The New Freedom*, 1913. "Woodrow Wilson > Quotes > Quotable Quote." *Goodreads*, Goodreads, www.goodreads.com/quotes/162688-since-i-entered-politics-i-have-chiefly-had-men-s-views.

[3] "History of Banking and Money Key Excerpts From Carroll Quigley's Tragedy and Hope." *Wanttoknow.info*, www.wanttoknow.info/articles/quigley_carroll.tragedy_hope_banking_money_history.

[4] *Id.*

[5] To achieve global financial control, the elites need to establish central bank domination of national economies worldwide (Federal Reserve in the USA), then centralize regional economies (European Monetary Union, NAFTA), then centralize the world economy (World Central Bank). *Id.*

The bankers "used their power and influence to…get all monetary matters out of the control of governments and political authority, on the ground that they would be handled better by private banking interests…"[6] William Gladstone, Prime Minister of the United Kingdom (UK) and Chancellor of the Exchequer, explained in 1852, "The hinge of the whole situation was this: the government itself was not to be a substantive power in matters of Finance, but was to leave the Money Power supreme and unquestioned."[7] I n the 1920's, for example, Montagu Norman (Governor of the Bank of England) and Benjamin Strong (Governor of the Federal Reserve Bank of New York) "were determined to use the financial power of Britain and of the United States to force all the major countries of the world to go on the gold standard and to operate it through central banks free from all political control, with all questions of international finance to be settled by agreements by such central banks without interference from governments."[8]

"The influence of financial capitalism and of the international bankers who created it was exercised both on business and on governments, but could have done neither if it had not been able to persuade both these to accept two 'axioms' of its own ideology. Both of these were based on the assumption that politicians were too weak and too subject to temporary popular pressures to be trusted

---

[6] "History of Banking and Money Key Excerpts From Carroll Quigley's Tragedy and Hope." *Wanttoknow.info*, www.wanttoknow.info/articles/quigley_carroll.tragedy_hope_banking_money_history.

[7] *Id.*

[8] *Id.* "[T]he gold standard is a monetary system in which the value of money is determined by a physical commodity—mainly gold because gold has been the most precious and trusted metal to convey trades." Van, Germinal G. "The Gold Standard Didn't Create the Great Depression, the Federal Reserve Did." *FEE Freeman Article*, Foundation for Economic Education, 25 May 2019, fee.org/articles/the-gold-standard-didn-t-create-the-great-depression-the-federal-reserve-did/?fbclid=IwAR0vrzpM7GgbTDRu2mqA0EM_1vSSK_JaYKWsCWX7BlDGZ6PUxZhjt8niybw.

with control of the money system."[9] Alexander Hamilton, the first Secretary of the United States Treasury, promulgated this argument in his proposal for the First Bank of the United States. "In studying other great banks of issue, such as the Bank of England and Bank of Amsterdam, he had concluded that a national bank must be shielded from political interference."[10] "Hamilton stressed the importance of a quasi-public structure for the bank. It would serve the national interest, but under the control of private individuals, not government officials."[11] "General Hamilton, in his report on this subject, so far from considering the bank a public institution, connected with, or controlled by, the government, holds it to be indispensable that it should not be so. It must be, says he, under private, not public, direction; under the guidance of individual interest, not public policy."[12] Likewise, "Congress made the [Federal Reserve] independent on the theory neither the legislative nor executive branches could be trusted with the money supply."[13]

"The substantive financial powers of the world were in the hands of these investment bankers (also called 'international' or 'merchant' bankers) who remained largely behind the scenes in their

---

[9] "History of Banking and Money Key Excerpts From Carroll Quigley's Tragedy and Hope." *Wanttoknow.info*, www.wanttoknow.info/articles/ quigley_carroll.tragedy_hope_banking_money_history.

[10] Davies, Phil. "The Bank That Hamilton Built." *Federal Reserve Bank of Minneapolis*, 1 Sept. 2007, www.minneapolisfed.org/article/2007/the-bank-that-hamilton-built.

[11] *Id.*

[12] "Still, he adds, the state may be holder of part of its stock; and consequently (what? it becomes a public property? no!), a sharer of the profits..." *M'Culloch v. Maryland*, 17 US 316 (1819).

[13] May, Donald H. "Reagan Blasts Fed's Control of Money Supply." *UPI*, 9 Feb. 1982, www.upi.com/Archives/1982/02/09/Reagan-blasts-Feds-control-of-money-supply/3386382078800/.

own unincorporated private banks."[14] Thus, "a relatively small number of bankers were in positions of immense influence in European and American economic life."[15] Walter Rathenau, who had inherited from his father control of the German General Electric Company, revealed in 1909 that "[t]hree hundred men, all of whom know one another, direct the economic destiny of Europe and choose their successors from among themselves."[16] The names of the big banking families included Raring, Lazard, Erlanger, Warburg, Schroder, Seligman, the Speyers, Mirabaud, Mallet, Fould, Morgan, and Rothschild.[17]

The greatest banking dynasty was that of Meyer Amschel Rothschild (1744-1812) (original surname was Bauer) of Frankfurt, Germany.[18] His five sons established branches in Vienna, London, Naples, Paris, and Frankfurt.[19] "Amshel had four sons, and they were all trained in the skills of creating money and finance. Amshel's sons were sent to various destinations throughout Europe to open family-owned banks. The oldest son, Amshel Mayer, remained in Frankfurt to preside over the hometown bank. The second son, Solomon, was sent to Vienna, Austria. In 1798, the third son, Nathan, was sent to London, and the fourth son, Karl, opened a bank in Naples, Italy. Finally, the fifth son was sent to Paris,

---

[14] "History of Banking and Money Key Excerpts From Carroll Quigley's Tragedy and Hope." *Wanttoknow.info*, www.wanttoknow.info/articles/ quigley_carroll.tragedy_hope_banking_money_history.

[15] *Id.*

[16] Circa 1909. *Id.*

[17] Originally Bauer, the adopted name, "Rothschild" or Red Shield, derived from the red shield that hung over the door to advertise the business. "History of Banking and Money Key Excerpts From Carroll Quigley's Tragedy and Hope." *Wanttoknow.info*, www.wanttoknow.info/articles/ quigley_carroll.tragedy_hope_banking_money_history.

[18] *Id.*

[19] *Id.*

France."[20] "By the mid 1800s, the Rothschilds dominated European banking, and were the wealthiest family on earth."[21]

The banking families "formed a system of international cooperation and national dominance which was more private, more powerful, and more secretive than that of their agents in the central banks."[22] They "were…devoted to secrecy and the secret use of financial influence in political life."[23] "This persistence as private firms continued because it ensured the maximum of anonymity and secrecy to persons of tremendous public power who dreaded public knowledge of their activities."[24] U.S. Supreme Court Justice Felix Frankfurter revealed, "The real rulers in Washington are invisible and exercise their power from behind the scenes."[25]

"The international bankers…on many occasions, placed their own members in official posts…"[26] "It must not be felt that these heads of the world's chief central banks were themselves substantive powers in world finance. They were not. Rather, they were the

---

[20] "They were so active that they could control and manipulate the entire British economy. These were not bankers per se. However, the goldsmiths were in reality the first bankers." Jones, Stack. "An Essay On The History Of Banking." *The Banking Swindle*, 1 Jan. 2018, criminalbankingmonopoly.wordpress.com/.

[21] *Id.*

[22] "History of Banking and Money Key Excerpts From Carroll Quigley's Tragedy and Hope." *Wanttoknow.info*, www.wanttoknow.info/articles/quigley_carroll.tragedy_hope_banking_money_history.

[23] *Id.*

[24] *Id.*

[25] In 1952. "New World Order: 37 Quotes on The New World Order, One-World Government and One-World Religion." *End Times Prophecy Report*, 8 Aug. 2018, endtimesprophecyreport.com/2013/06/05/new-world-order-37-quotes-on-the-new-world-order/.

[26] "History of Banking and Money Key Excerpts From Carroll Quigley's Tragedy and Hope." *Wanttoknow.info*, www.wanttoknow.info/articles/quigley_carroll.tragedy_hope_banking_money_history.

technicians and agents of the dominant investment bankers of their own countries, who had raised them up and were perfectly capable of throwing them down."[27] "By remaining behind the scenes, they (the Rothschilds [for example]) were able to avoid the brunt of public anger which was directed, instead, at the political figures which they largely controlled. This is a technique which has been practiced by financial manipulators ever since, and it is fully utilized by those who operate the Federal Reserve System today."[28] As English Prime Minister Benjamin Disraeli noted in 1844, "The world is governed by very different personages from what is imagined by those who are not behind the scenes."[29]

"The central machine of capital" extended its dominion over America, in that seven men controlled "a great share of the fundamental industry and resources of the United States. Three of the seven men, J. P. Morgan, James J. Hill, and George E Baker, head of the First National Bank of New York, belong to the so-called Morgan group; four of them, John D. and William Rockefeller, James Stiliman, head of the National City Bank, and Jacob H. Schiff of the private banking firm of Kuhn, Loeb Company, to the so-called

---

[27] *Id.*

[28] Quote by G. Edward Griffin. "The International Bankers: Famous Quotes." *ConspiracyAnalyst.org*, 23 Dec. 2019, conspiracyanalyst.org/ 2013/03/01/the-international-bankers-famous-quotes/.

[29] "Quotation by Benjamin Disraeli." *LibertyQuotes*, Libertytree.ca, 6 Dec. 2019, libertytree.ca/quotes/Benjamin.Disraeli.Quote.2E3D.

Standard Oil City Bank group..."[30]   John C. Calhoun, 7th Vice President and U.S. Senator, noted, "A power has risen up in the government greater than the people themselves, consisting of many and various powerful interests, combined in one mass, and held together by the cohesive power of the vast surplus in banks."[31] According to President Franklin D. Roosevelt, this "financial element in the large centers has owned the government of the U.S. since the days of Andrew Jackson."[32]

"The most powerful men in the United States were themselves answerable to another power, a foreign power, and a power which had been steadfastly seeking to extend its control over the young republic of the United States since its very inception. This power was the financial power of England, centered in the London Branch

---

[30] "The House of Rothschild Excerpted from the Book The Secrets of the Federal Reserve by Eustace Mullins Bankers Research Institute, 1983, Paperback." *Third World Traveler*, www.thirdworldtraveler.com/Banks/ House_Rothschild_TSOTFR.html. In the December 1912 issue of "Truth," magazine, George R. Conroy states of banker Jacob Schiff: "Mr Schiff is head of the great private banking house of Kuhn, Loeb, and co, which represents the Rothschilds interests on this side of the Atlantic. He has been described as financial strategist and has been for years the financial minister of the great impersonal power known as Standard Oil. He was hand in glove with the Harrimans, the Goulds, and the Rockefellers in all their railroad enterprises and has become the dominant power in the railroad and financial power of America." Hitchcock, Andrew. "Historical Timeline of the Rothschild Dynasty - Part 4." *The Sirius Report*, 18 Aug. 2016, www.thesiriusreport.com/geopolitics/historical-timeline-rothschild-dynasty-part-4/.

[31] John C. Calhoun, Vice President (1825-1832) and U.S. Senator, from a speech given on May 27, 1836. "The International Bankers: Famous Quotes." *ConspiracyAnalyst.org*, 23 Dec. 2019, conspiracyanalyst.org/ 2013/03/01/the-international-bankers-famous-quotes/.

[32] Andrew Jackson was president of the United States from 1829 to 1837. U.S. President Franklin D. Roosevelt in a letter written Nov. 21, 1933 to Colonel E. Mandell House. "A Quote by Franklin D. Roosevelt." *Goodreads*, Goodreads, www.goodreads.com/quotes/162689-the-real-truth-of-the-matter-is-as-you-and.

of the House of Rothschild."[33]   For example, "The ten largest bank holding companies in the United States are firmly in the hands of certain banking houses, all of which have branches in London. They are J. P. Morgan Company, Brown Brothers Harriman, Warburg, Kuhn, Loeb and J. Henry Schroder. All of them maintain close relationships with the House of Rothschild, principally through the Rothschild control of international money markets through its manipulation of the price of gold...Although these firms are ostensibly American firms...these banking houses actually take their direction from London..."[34]   "The fact was that [by] 1910, the United States was for all practical purposes being ruled from England..."[35]

The power of investment bankers over governments depends on a number of factors, but mainly on their control of credit and of the money supply.[36]   "Ancient goldsmiths discovered that extra profits could be made by growing the economy between easy money and tight money. When goldsmiths made money easy to borrow, money in circulation expanded, and people took out more loans to expand their businesses. Money changers would then tighten the money supply, and make money difficult to obtain. Goldsmiths knew that certain borrowers would not be able to repay loan debts. Goldsmiths would not allow these 'loan defaulters' to take out new

---

[33] "The House of Rothschild Excerpted from the Book The Secrets of the Federal Reserve by Eustace Mullins Bankers Research Institute, 1983, Paperback." *Third World Traveler*, www.thirdworldtraveler.com/Banks/House_Rothschild_TSOTFR.html.

[34] *Id.*

[35] *Id.*

[36] "History of Banking and Money Key Excerpts From Carroll Quigley's Tragedy and Hope." *Wanttoknow.info*, www.wanttoknow.info/articles/quigley_carroll.tragedy_hope_banking_money_history.

loans to repay the old ones. This led to bankruptcy, ruin, and the selling off of assets to goldsmiths for pennies on the dollar."[37]

According to the second President of the United States, John Adams, "There are two ways to conquer and enslave a nation. One is by the sword. The other is by debt."[38] Napoléon Bonaparte explained, "When a government is dependent upon bankers for money, they and not the leaders of the government control the situation…"[39] Henry Ford said, "The one aim of these financiers is world control by the creation of inextinguishable debts."[40] Reginald McKenna, former Chancellor of the Exchequer, understood that "[t]hey who control the credit of the nation direct the policy of Governments and hold in the hollow of their hands the destiny of the people."[41] Former U.S. Secretary of State, Henry Kissinger, put it more bluntly: "Who controls the money, controls the world."[42]

---

[37] "They were so active that they could control and manipulate the entire British economy. These were not bankers per se. However, the goldsmiths were in reality the first bankers." Jones, Stack. "An Essay On The History Of Banking." *The Banking Swindle*, 1 Jan. 2018, criminalbankingmonopoly.wordpress.com/.

[38] "Quote by John G. Adams." *Goodreads*, Goodreads, www.goodreads.com/quotes/697421-there-are-two-ways-to-conquer-and-enslave-a-nations.

[39] "Quote: Napoleon Bonaparte: When a Government Is Dependent upon Bankers." *Truth11.Com*, 8 Aug. 2009, truth11.com/2009/08/08/quote-napoleon-bonaparte-when-a-government-is-dependent-upon-bankers/.

[40] "A Quote by Henry Ford." *Goodreads*, Goodreads, www.goodreads.com/quotes/852618-the-one-aim-of-these-financiers-is-world-control-by.

[41] In 1924. "History of Banking and Money Key Excerpts From Carroll Quigley's Tragedy and Hope." *Wanttoknow.info*, www.wanttoknow.info/articles/quigley_carroll.tragedy_hope_banking_money_history.

[42] Circa 1995, Council on Foreign Relations. "The International Bankers: Famous Quotes." *ConspiracyAnalyst.org*, 23 Dec. 2019, conspiracyanalyst.org/2013/03/01/the-international-bankers-famous-quotes/.

For this reason, President Thomas Jefferson considered "public debt as the greatest of dangers to be feared. To preserve our independence, we must not let our rulers load us with public debt. We must make our choice between economy and liberty or confusion and servitude."[43] Unfortunately, from the time that the National Banking Act of 1863 was passed, "the entire US money supply would be created out of debt by bankers buying US government bonds and issuing them from reserves for bank notes."[44]

The National Bank Act of 1863 established new banks that "would operate under a tax-free status, and collectively have exclusive monopoly power to create the new form of money, bank notes…Most importantly, the entire U.S. money supply would be created out of debt where bankers would be buying U.S. government bonds, and issuing them for reserves for bank notes. John Kenneth Galbraith wrote, 'In numerous years following the war, the federal government ran a heavy surplus. It could not however, pay off its debt, retire its securities, because to do so meant there would be no

---

[43] "Jefferson on the Economy." *American Policy Roundtable*, web.archive.org/web/20170608041633/www.aproundtable.org/tps2.cfm?ID=1028&issuecode=taxes.

[44] "The History of Money Part 2." *XAT3*, www.xat.org/xat/usury.html. Salmon P. Chase, Chief Justice of the U. S. Supreme Court and Advisor to President Abraham Lincoln, later regretted his support of the Act, saying in 1864, "My agency, in promoting the passage of the National Bank Act, was the greatest mistake in my life. It has built up a monopoly which affects every interest in the country. It should be repealed, but before that can be accomplished, the people should be arrayed on one side, and the banks on the other, in a contest such as we have never seen before in this country." "Money Quotes: What The Experts Say About Money." *Midas Gold Group*, 27 Aug. 2020, www.midasgoldgroup.com/money-quotes/. "The National Bank Act of 1863 was designed to create a national banking system, float federal war loans, and establish a national currency." "National Bank Act of 1863." *Encyclopedia.com*, Encyclopedia.com, www.encyclopedia.com/history/encyclopedias-almanacs-transcripts-and-maps/national-bank-act-1863.

bonds to back the national bank notes. To pay off the debt was to destroy the money supply.'"[45]

The "dominance of investment bankers was based on their control over the flows of credit and investment funds in their own countries and throughout the world. They could dominate the financial and industrial systems of their own countries by their influence over the flow of current funds through bank loans, the discount rate, and the re-discounting of commercial debts; they could dominate governments by their control over current government loans and the play of the international exchanges...."[46] "Each central bank, in the hands of men like Montagu Norman of the Bank of England, Benjamin Strong of the New York Federal Reserve Bank, Charles Rist of the Bank of France, and Hjalmar Schacht of the Reichsbank, sought to dominate its government by its ability to control Treasury loans, to manipulate foreign exchanges, to influence the level of economic activity in the country, and to influence cooperative politicians by subsequent economic rewards in the business world..."[47] "Sir Drummond Fraser, vice-president of the Institute of Bankers, stated, 'The Governor of the Bank of England must be the autocrat who dictates the terms upon which alone the Government can obtain borrowed money.'"[48]

U.S. President James Madison complained, "History records that the money changers have used every form of abuse, intrigue, deceit, and violent means possible to maintain their control over

---

[45] Jones, Stack. "An Essay On The History Of Banking." *The Banking Swindle*, 1 Jan. 2018, criminalbankingmonopoly.wordpress.com/.

[46] "In this system the Rothschilds had been preeminent during much of the nineteenth century, but, at the end of that century, they were being replaced by J. P. Morgan whose central office was in New York..." "History of Banking and Money Key Excerpts From Carroll Quigley's Tragedy and Hope." *Wanttoknow.info*, www.wanttoknow.info/articles/quigley_carroll.tragedy_hope_banking_money_history.

[47] *Id.*

[48] In 1924. *Id.*

governments by controlling money and its issuance."[49] For example, "[b]y the end of the 1600s, England was in financial ruin…Frantic government officials met with the money changers and begged for the money necessary to pursue political purposes. The price was a government sanctioned, privately owned bank, which could issue money created out of nothing. The Bank of England would be the first privately owned central bank. It was deceptively called the Bank of England, as is the U.S. Federal Reserve, to make it appear to the general population that it was a branch of the government…[T]he bank was chartered in 1694, and began loaning out several times the amount of money it was supposed to have on reserve, all at interest. The new bank would lend politicians as much money as they needed, so long as those politicians secured the debt through taxation of the British people. As a result, the formation of the Bank of England became a form of legal counterfeiting of the national currency for private gain."[50] William Cobbett, a member of Parliament, reflects on the bank: "I set to work to read the Act of Parliament by which the Bank of England was created in 1694. The inventors knew well what they were about. Their design was to mortgage by degrees the whole of the country, all the lands, all the houses, and all other property, and even all labor, to those who would lend their money to the State — the scheme, the crafty, the cunning, the deep scheme has produced what the world never saw before — starvation in the midst of plenty."[51]

---

[49] James Madison, 1751-1836. "The International Bankers: Famous Quotes." *ConspiracyAnalyst.org*, 23 Dec. 2019, conspiracyanalyst.org/2013/03/01/the-international-bankers-famous-quotes/.

[50] "They were so active that they could control and manipulate the entire British economy. These were not bankers per se. However, the goldsmiths were in reality the first bankers." Jones, Stack. "An Essay On The History Of Banking." *The Banking Swindle*, 1 Jan. 2018, criminalbankingmonopoly.wordpress.com/.

[51] "Money Quotes: What The Experts Say About Money." *Midas Gold Group*, 27 Aug. 2020, www.midasgoldgroup.com/money-quotes/.

For their part, the Rothschilds understood well how to subjugate a nation. Meyer Amschel Rothschild "learned that loaning money to governments, and kings was more profitable than loaning to private individuals. Not only were the loans larger, but they would be secured through national taxation schemes, which meant the average citizen had to pay the debt."[52] He boasted in 1828, "Allow me to issue and control the money of a nation, and I care not who writes the laws."[53]

Baron Nathan Mayer de Rothschild (1777-1836) cared "not what puppet is placed upon the throne of England to rule the Empire on which the sun never sets. The man that controls Britain's money supply controls the British Empire, and I control the British money supply."[54] UK Prime Minister, Benjamin Disraeli, characterized Nathan Mayer Rothschild as "[t]he Lord and Master of the money markets of the world, and of course virtually Lord and Master of everything else. He literally held the revenues of Southern Italy in pawn…"[55]

"By 1850, James Rothschild [1792-1868], the heir of the French Rothschild family, was said to be worth 600 million French Franks. 150 million more than all of the other bankers in Europe

---

[52] "They were so active that they could control and manipulate the entire British economy. These were not bankers per se. However, the goldsmiths were in reality the first bankers." Jones, Stack. "An Essay On The History Of Banking." *The Banking Swindle*, 1 Jan. 2018, criminalbankingmonopoly.wordpress.com/.

[53] "Quotes On The New World Order." *Jesus-Is-Savior.com*, www.jesus-is-savior.com/False%20Religions/Illuminati/quotes_on_the_new_world_order.htm.

[54] "The House of Rothschild Excerpted from the Book The Secrets of the Federal Reserve by Eustace Mullins Bankers Research Institute, 1983, Paperback." *Third World Traveler*, www.thirdworldtraveler.com/Banks/House_Rothschild_TSOTFR.html.

[55] Hitchcock, Andrew. "Historical Timeline of the Rothschild Dynasty - Part 3." *The Sirius Report*, 17 Aug. 2015, www.thesiriusreport.com/geopolitics/historical-timeline-rothschild-dynasty-3/.

combined…"[56] "Only one man in France possessed more. That was the King, whose wealth was 800 million…This naturally gave him [Rothschild] untold powers, even to the extent of unseating governments whenever he chose to do so…"[57]

"In addition to their power over government based on government financing and personal influence, bankers could steer governments in ways they wished them to go by other pressures. Since most government officials felt ignorant of finance, they sought advice from bankers whom they considered to be experts in the field."[58] For example, British Prime Minister Benjamin Disraeli wrote of Nathan Mayer Rothschild: "Monarchs and Ministers of all countries courted his advice and were guided by his suggestions."[59] Mayer Amschel Rothschild's 1773 plan of action for his World Revolutionary Movement stipulated that "[c]andidates for public office should be servile and obedient to our commands, so that they may readily be used…"[60] Often, "politicians are manipulated

---

[56] "They were so active that they could control and manipulate the entire British economy. These were not bankers per se. However, the goldsmiths were in reality the first bankers." Jones, Stack. "An Essay On The History Of Banking." *The Banking Swindle*, 1 Jan. 2018, criminalbankingmonopoly.wordpress.com/.

[57] "The House of Rothschild Excerpted from the Book The Secrets of the Federal Reserve by Eustace Mullins Bankers Research Institute, 1983, Paperback." *Third World Traveler*, www.thirdworldtraveler.com/Banks/ House_Rothschild_TSOTFR.html.

[58] "History of Banking and Money Key Excerpts From Carroll Quigley's Tragedy and Hope." *Wanttoknow.info*, www.wanttoknow.info/articles/ quigley_carroll.tragedy_hope_banking_money_history.

[59] Hitchcock, Andrew. "Historical Timeline of the Rothschild Dynasty - Part 3." *The Sirius Report*, 17 Aug. 2015, www.thesiriusreport.com/ geopolitics/historical-timeline-rothschild-dynasty-3/.

[60] "The House of Rothschild Excerpted from the Book The Secrets of the Federal Reserve by Eustace Mullins Bankers Research Institute, 1983, Paperback." *Third World Traveler*, www.thirdworldtraveler.com/Banks/ House_Rothschild_TSOTFR.html.

'without their even knowing it.'"[61]   "Such advice could be enforced if necessary by manipulation of exchanges, gold flows, discount rates, and even levels of business activity…"[62] Unfortunately, "[t]he history of the last century shows…that the advice given to governments by bankers… was consistently good for bankers, but was often disastrous for governments, businessmen, and the people generally."[63]   For example in 1907, Jacob Schiff (a Rothschild) threatened, "Unless we have a Central Bank with adequate control of credit resources, this country is going to undergo the most severe and far reaching money panic in its history."[64]   Shortly thereafter, America found itself in a Rothschild-engineered financial crisis.[65]

"On the whole, in the period up to 1931, bankers, especially the Money Power controlled by the international investment bankers, were able to dominate both business and government."[66] Governor of the Bank of England, Vincent Vickers, disclosed, "Since 1919, the monetary policy of the Government has been the policy of the Bank of England and the policy of the Bank of England

---

[61] In *Coningsby*. "The Illuminati Plan to Enslave Americans (1969)." *HenryMakow.com*, 10 May 2016, www.savethemales.ca/confirmedrockefeller_plan_to_g.html.

[62] "History of Banking and Money Key Excerpts From Carroll Quigley's Tragedy and Hope." *Wanttoknow.info*, www.wanttoknow.info/articles/quigley_carroll.tragedy_hope_banking_money_history.

[63] *Id.*

[64] The head of Kuhn, Loeb and Co. in a speech to the New York Chamber of Commerce. Hitchcock, Andrew. "Historical Timeline of the Rothschild Dynasty - Part 4." *The Sirius Report*, 18 Aug. 2016, www.thesiriusreport.com/geopolitics/historical-timeline-rothschild-dynasty-part-4/.

[65] *Id.*

[66] "History of Banking and Money Key Excerpts From Carroll Quigley's Tragedy and Hope." *Wanttoknow.info*, www.wanttoknow.info/articles/quigley_carroll.tragedy_hope_banking_money_history.

has been the policy of Mr. Montagu Norman."[67] "On November 1, 1927, the *Wall Street Journal* called Mr. Norman 'the currency dictator of Europe...' Mr. Norman is reported to have said, 'I hold the hegemony of the world.'"[68]

The bankers gloated about their success in the August 25, 1924 edition of USA Banker's Magazine: "When, through a process of law, the common people lose their homes they will become more docile and more easily governed through the influence of the strong arm of government, applied by a central power of wealth under control of leading financiers. This truth is well known among our principal men now engaged in forming an imperialism of Capital to govern the world. By dividing the voters through the political party system, we can get them to expend their energies in fighting over questions of no importance. *Thus by discreet action, we can secure for ourselves what has been so well planned and so successfully accomplished*" (emphasis added).[69]

U.S. President James Garfield divulged, "Whoever controls the volume of money in any country is absolute master of all industry and commerce. And when you realize that the entire system is very easily controlled, one way or another by a few powerful men at the top, you will not have to be told how periods of inflation and depression originate."[70] *The Financial Times* wrote, "Half a dozen

---

[67] "On November 11, 1927, the *Wall Street Journal* called Mr. Norman 'the currency dictator of Europe.'" *Id.*

[68] *Id.*

[69] "The Bankers' Manifesto of 1892." *Pathway to Ascension*, www.pathwaytoascension.com/manifesto.htm.

[70] Garfield made this statement in 1881, and was assassinated just weeks later. "The History of Money Part 2." *XAT3*, www.xat.org/xat/usury.html.

men at the top of the Big Five Banks could upset the whole fabric of government finance by refraining from renewing Treasury Bills."[71]

Robert H. Hemphill, Credit Manager of the Federal Reserve Bank in Atlanta, lamented, "We are completely dependent on the commercial banks. Someone has to borrow every dollar we have in circulation, cash, or credit. If the banks create ample synthetic money we are prosperous; if not, we starve. We are absolutely without a permanent money system. When one gets a complete grasp of the picture, the tragic absurdity of our hopeless position is almost incredible, but there it is."[72]

One example of when credit was tightened occurred in the late 19th century. An American Bankers Association memo from 1891 instructed, "On September 1st, 1894, we will not renew our loans under any consideration. On September 1st, we will demand our money. We will foreclose and become mortgagees in possession. We can take two-thirds of the farms west of the Mississippi as well, at our own price...Then the farmers will become tenants, as in England."[73]

Pope Pius XI lamented, "In the first place, then, it is patent that in our days, not wealth alone is accumulated, but immense power and despotic economic domination are concentrated in the hands of the few, who for the most part are not the owners but only the trustees and directors of invested funds, which they administer at their own good pleasure. This domination is most powerfully exercised by those who, because they hold and control money, also govern credit and determine its allotment, for that reason supplying so to speak, the life blood of the entire economic body, and grasping

---

[71] On September 26, 1921. "History of Banking and Money Key Excerpts From Carroll Quigley's Tragedy and Hope." *Wanttoknow.info*, w w w . w a n t t o k n o w . i n f o / a r t i c l e s / quigley_carroll.tragedy_hope_banking_money_history.

[72] Circa 1939. "Central Banks Quotes." *AZ Quotes*, www.azquotes.com/ quotes/topics/central-banks.html.

[73] Recorded as testimony in the Congressional Record, April 29, 1913. "The History of Money Part 2." *XAT3*, www.xat.org/xat/usury.html.

in their hands, as it were, the very soul of production, so that no one can breathe against their will."[74]

General Douglas MacArthur was "concerned for the security of our great nation; not so much because of any threat from without, but because of the insidious forces working from within."[75] Indeed, Senator George W. Malone (R-NV) warned that there was a "preconceived plan to destroy the economic and social independence of the United States."[76] Unfortunately, "[w]e have a well-organized political-action group in this country, determined to destroy our Constitution and establish a one-party state…It operates secretly, silently, continuously to transform our Government…This ruthless power-seeking elite is a disease of our century…This group… is answerable neither to the President, the Congress, nor the courts. It is practically irremovable."[77]

President Woodrow Wilson's national campaign vice-chairman, William McAdoo, wrote in *Crowded Years* (1912), "The fact is that there is a serious danger of this country becoming a Pluto-democracy; that is, a sham republic with the real government in the hands of a small clique of enormously wealthy men, who

---

[74] "Prominent Quotes." *The Liberty Dollar*, libertydollar.org/ld/press-kit/prominent-quotes.htm.

[75] "Quotes On The New World Order." *Jesus-Is-Savior.com*, www.jesus-is-savior.com/False%20Religions/Illuminati/quotes_on_the_new_world_order.htm.

[76] Malone said this in 1957, Senator Barry Goldwater wrote in his book, *With No Apologies,* "The Trilateral Commission is intended to be the vehicle for multinational consolidation of the commercial and banking interests by seizing control of the political government of the United States. It represents a skillful, coordinated effort to seize control and consolidate the four centers of power--Political, Monetary, Intellectual, and Ecclesiastical." *Id.*

[77] "The International Bankers: Famous Quotes." *ConspiracyAnalyst.org*, 23 Dec. 2019, conspiracyanalyst.org/2013/03/01/the-international-bankers-famous-quotes/.

speak through their money, and whose influence, even today, radiates to every corner of the United States."[78]

John Hylan, mayor of New York City, warned in 1922, "The real menace to our republic is this invisible government which spreads its tentacles like a giant octopus and sprawls its slimy length over city, state and nation. It seizes in its long and powerful tentacles our executive officers, our legislative bodies, our schools, our courts, our newspapers and every agency created for the public protection…at the head of this octopus are the Rockefeller-Standard Oil interests and a small group of powerful banking houses generally referred to as the international bankers. The little coterie of powerful international bankers virtually run the United States government for their own selfish purposes. They practically control both parties, write political platforms, make cat's-paws of party leaders, use the leading men of private organizations, and resort to every device to place in nomination for high public office only such candidates as will be amenable to the dictates of corrupt big business."[79]

Senator William Jenner said in a 1954 speech, "Today the path of total dictatorship in the United States can be laid by strictly legal means, unseen and unheard by the Congress, the President, or the people. Outwardly, we have a Constitutional government. We have operating within our government and political system, another body representing another form of government – a bureaucratic elite."[80] U.S. Senator Daniel K. Inouye confirmed in 1977 that "[t]here exists a shadowy government, with its own Air Force, its own Navy, its own fundraising mechanism, and the ability to pursue its own ideas

---

[78] *Id.*

[79] *Id.*

[80] "New World Order: 37 Quotes on The New World Order, One-World Government and One-World Religion." *End Times Prophecy Report*, 8 Aug. 2018, endtimesprophecyreport.com/2013/06/05/new-world-order-37-quotes-on-the-new-world-order/.

of national interest, free from all the checks and balances, and free from the law itself."[81]

Curtis Dall, son-in-law of President Franklin Delano Roosevelt, wrote in *My Exploited Father-in-Law* (1970), "The One World Government leaders and their ever close bankers have now acquired full control of the money and credit machinery of the U.S. via the creation of the privately owned Federal Reserve Bank."[82]

Major General J. F. C. Fuller, a British military historian, wrote, "The government of the Western nations, whether monarchical or republican, had passed into the invisible hands of a plutocracy, international in power and grasp. It was, I venture to suggest, this semioccult power which...pushed the mass of the American people into the cauldron of World War I."[83]

British Prime Minister, Winston Churchill, explained that it was the globalists that had also taken over Russia: "From the days of Spartacus-Weishaupt to those of Karl Marx,...this world wide conspiracy for the overthrow of civilization and for the reconstitution of society on the basis of arrested development, of envious malevolence and impossible equality, has been steadily growing. It played a definitely recognizable role in the tragedy of the French Revolution. It has been the mainspring of every subversive movement during the nineteenth century, and now at last this band of extraordinary personalities from the underworld of the great cities of Europe and America have gripped the Russian people

---

[81] *Id.*

[82] "Quotes By Curtis Bean Dall." *AZ Quotes*, www.azquotes.com/author/ 41348-Curtis_Bean_Dall.

[83] This quote was from 1941. "New World Order: 37 Quotes on The New World Order, One-World Government and One-World Religion." *End Times Prophecy Report*, 8 Aug. 2018, endtimesprophecyreport.com/ 2013/06/05/new-world-order-37-quotes-on-the-new-world-order/.

by the hair of their heads, and have become practically the undisputed masters of that enormous empire."[84]

This also happened to Germany, according to Rep. Lewis T. McFadden (D-PA), Chairman of the House Banking and Currency Committee. In 1931, he said, "After WWI, Germany fell into the hands of the German International Bankers. Those bankers bought her and they now own her, lock, stock and barrel. They purchased her industries, they have mortgages on her soil, they control her production; they control all her public utilities. The International German Bankers have subsidized the present government of Germany and they have also supplied every dollar of the money Adolf Hitler has used in his lavish campaign to build up a threat to the government of Bruening. When Bruening fails to obey the orders of the German International Bankers, Hitler is brought forth to scare the Germans into submission."[85]

Ultimately, the Elite plan to establish a totalitarian new world order in which wealth and power is consolidated in their hands. According to Congressman Larry P. McDonald (D-GA), "The Rockefellers and their allies have, for at least fifty years, been carefully following a plan to use their economic power to gain political control of first America, and then the rest of the world…"[86]

The American Mercury Magazine (December 1957) warned, "The invisible Money Power is working to control and enslave

---

[84] Writing on "Zionism versus Bolshevism" in the Illustrated Sunday Herald, February 1920. "The Churchill You Didn't Know." *The Guardian*, Guardian News and Media, 27 Nov. 2002, www.theguardian.com/theguardian/2002/nov/28/features11.g21.

[85] Quote dated 1931. "The International Bankers: Famous Quotes." *ConspiracyAnalyst.org*, 23 Dec. 2019, conspiracyanalyst.org/2013/03/01/the-international-bankers-famous-quotes/.

[86] McDonald wrote this in the introduction to the book, *The Rockefeller File* (1975). Unfortunately, Congressman McDonald was killed in the Korean Airlines 747 that was shot down by the Soviets in 1983. "The New World Order and the United States of America." *Philadelphians.50megs.Com*, philadelphians.50megs.com/nwo-us.html.

mankind. It financed Communism, Fascism, Marxism, Zionism, Socialism. All of these are directed to making the United States a member of a World Government..."[87]   Rep. Larry P. MacDonald said, "The drive of the Rockefellers and their allies is to create a one-world government combining supercapitalism and Communism under the same tent, all under their control..."[88]

The New World Order (NWO) is Mayer Amschel Rothschild's dream of a global totalitarian government.   Rothschild called a meeting of other wealthy and influential men in Frankfurt in 1773.[89] "His purpose was to convince them that if they agreed to pool their resources, they could then finance and control the World Revolutionary Movement and use it as their Manual of Action to win ultimate control of the wealth, natural resources, and manpower

---

[87] American Mercury magazine, December 1957, pg. 92. "Quotes On The New World Order." *Jesus-Is-Savior.com*, www.jesus-is-savior.com/False%20Religions/Illuminati/quotes_on_the_new_world_order.htm.

[88] McDonald said this in 1976. He was killed on Korean Air Lines 007 in 1983. "New World Order: 37 Quotes on The New World Order, One-World Government and One-World Religion." *End Times Prophecy Report*, 8 Aug. 2018, endtimesprophecyreport.com/2013/06/05/new-world-order-37-quotes-on-the-new-world-order/.

[89] According to William Guy Carr's book, *Pawns In The Game.* "The House of Rothschild Excerpted from the Book The Secrets of the Federal Reserve by Eustace Mullins Bankers Research Institute, 1983, Paperback." *Third World Traveler*, www.thirdworldtraveler.com/Banks/House_Rothschild_TSOTFR.html.

of the entire world…"[90]   Author H. G. Wells, a member of the Fabian Society, a British organization that advances democratic socialism, explained that the term "new world order" is a synonym for a technocratic world state and a planned economy.[91]   Thus, "NWO" is "code for 'global governance' and, eventually, world government…"[92]

Dr. Lawrence Dunegan reported that, on March 20, 1969, Dr. Richard Day, the National Medical Director of the Rockefeller-sponsored "Planned Parenthood," told a meeting of the Pittsburgh Pediatric Society that "a New World System" would permanently transform the world.[93]   John Prukop of the Coalition of a Constitutional Washington revealed, "The 'plan' is to control all resources, human and natural. The control is not by elected public

---

[90] *Id.* In 1891, the British Labour leader said of the Rothschilds: "This blood-sucking crew has been the cause of untold mischief and misery in Europe during the present century, and has piled up its prodigious wealth chiefly through fomenting wars between States which ought never to have quarreled. Whenever there is trouble in Europe, wherever rumours of war circulate and men's minds are distraught with fear of change and calamity you may be sure that a hook-nosed Rothschild is at his games somewhere near the region of the disturbance." Hitchcock, Andrew. "Historical Timeline of the Rothschild Dynasty - Part 4." *The Sirius Report*, 18 Aug. 2016, www.thesiriusreport.com/geopolitics/historical-timeline-rothschild-dynasty-part-4/.

[91] Levis, Nick. "New World Disorder: Why Geithner's IMF SDR Plan For A Global Currency Looks a Bit Like High Treason." *Business Insider*, Business Insider, 20 Jul. 2011, www.businessinsider.com/new-world-disorder-why-geithners-imf-sdr-plan-for-a-global-currency-is-high-treason-2011-7.

[92] Jasper, William F. "Joe Biden on Creating a 'New World Order.'" *The New American*, 8 Apr. 2013, www.thenewamerican.com/usnews/politics/item/15036-joe-biden-on-creating-a-new-world-order?fbclid=IwAR1NnFrzxnXBi1mJKf94lRmSQQMCaoWo6ndOCvAlRB2JX mGWWBnV0OAyxlw.

[93] "New Order of Barbarians - Transcript of Tapes I-III." *100777.Com*, 22 May 2003, 100777.com/nwo/barbarians.

officials, but by a self-appointed oligarchy."[94]   Karol Wojtyla (Pope John Paul II) predicted that "we will live under the first One World Government…a government with absolute authority to decide the basic issues of survival. One world government is inevitable."[95]

Alternative media journalist, Alex Jones, elaborated on the NWO model: "[T]he New World Order…is a private, corporate take-over of the nation states of the governments of the world. And then these private corporations bring in a tyrannical form of neo-feudalism that they call corporatism — or fascism. Mussolini said that fascism should properly be called corporatism. And that's what it is, and they create the socialism to get control of the wealth, and to control society, then they pipe the profits to themselves. So they socialize the general public to take control of us, but it's private above us. It's basically just slavery."[96]

According to the globalists' viewpoint, "a larger and more powerful (and stifling) central government is the ideal government."[97]   "Authoritarian China has been lauded by many globalists such as the late David Rockefeller as a model for the New

---

[94] "Bankers Manifesto of 1892." *Frank-Webb.com*, web.archive.org/web/20190227170038/www.frank-webb.com/bankers-manifesto-of-1892.html.

[95] *TIME*, July 1992. "New World Order: 37 Quotes on The New World Order, One-World Government and One-World Religion." *End Times Prophecy Report*, 8 Aug. 2018, endtimesprophecyreport.com/2013/06/05/new-world-order-37-quotes-on-the-new-world-order/.

[96] "Aaron Russo: Reflections and Warnings - Full Transcript." *Matt Prather*, sites.google.com/site/themattprather/Reading/aaron-russo/reflections-and-warnings-full-transcript.

[97] Clabough, Raven. "George Soros Touts China as Leader of New World Order." *The New American*, 17 Nov. 2010, www.thenewamerican.com/world-news/north-america/item/10605-george-soros-touts-china-as-leader-of-new-world-order?fbclid=IwAR0lckBm-INZafvOcqeuUC9acGuyvLeoKR8otZP6073BqbLv3GyP5IieH3U#.

World Order."[98]   It has also emerged as the world's strongest proponent of globalization.[99]   "Chinese president Xi Jinping has vowed for the first time that China should take the lead in shaping the 'new world order...' Xi had on numerous occasions called for China to play an important part in building the new world order...News outlets dubbed Xi's new approach the 'Two Guides' (两个引导) policy, with the 'two' referring to the new world order and international security."[100]   Xi said, "The overall trend of world multi-polarization, economic globalization, and democratization of international relations remains unchanged. We should guide the international community to jointly build a more just and reasonable new world order."[101]

"Like the Chinese Communists, [Jyrki] Katainen, the vice-president of the EU's ruling and unelected European Commission, advocates for a multilateral world order in which both the EU and Communist China are leaders, making the rules and overseeing their

---

[98] Freeman, Makia. "7 NWO Agendas Accompanying the Coronavirus Outbreak." *Activist Post*, 21 Feb. 2020, www.activistpost.com/2020/02/7-nwo-agendas-accompanying-the-coronavirus-outbreak.html?fbclid=IwAR07E5b6kYhq6hsL9N2raQ5zRCQvR2BkSlzptepMUAO9l0u-eZ_bnqAdmP4. "China's communist surveillance state model is a beta test for the type of centralization that the UN wants for the entire planet." "Globalists Look To Exploit Coronavirus In Push For Global Government." *Prophecy News Watch*, www.prophecynewswatch.com/article.cfm?recent_news_id=3869&fbclid=IwAR2uc7HdPmGIuKsqSQ7Ayl8pB2K09hWJnBNtTSnZBbKFEM6LVFslmsp-EuE.

[99] Huang, Zheping. "Chinese President Xi Jinping Has Vowed to Lead the 'New World Order.'" *Quartz*, Quartz, 22 Feb. 2017, qz.com/916382/chinese-president-xi-jinping-has-vowed-to-lead-the-new-world-order/?fbclid=IwAR3uEWMJb4jsExoUgiSFrffjwwFFOJTvnewTkCSNL5Pl4dbGDWu4KeQmaNs.

[100] *Id.*

[101] *Id.*

[new] world order."[102] Leftist billionaire, George Soros, also thinks that China should be one of the global leaders.[103] He insisted, "Today, China has not only a more vigorous economy, but actually a better functioning government than the United States."[104] The incredible claim is that "the government of China — the same that suppresses dissension, forces abortions on its citizens, and tortures members of the Falun Gong faith — is a better functioning government than that of the United States."[105]

Senator Dianne Feinstein (D-CA) has also praised the Chinese Communist Party of China (CCP), "claiming the communist country is 'growing into a respectable nation…'"[106] Secretary of State Mike Pompeo criticized her for this, saying, "I talked…about this not being a battle about China but about authoritarianism and freedom… I was struck by Dianne Feinstein because didn't she have a driver for 20 years that…was a Chinese spy…? You'll recall, she meets with some frequency with Foreign Minister Zarif [Iran] there too… And this is not consistent with America's national security in either case. These are adversaries that intend harm for her state of

---

[102] Gomez, Christian. "EU Globalists and Chinese Communists Team Up To Protect NWO." *The New American*, 25 Jun. 2018, www.thenewamerican.com/world-news/europe/item/29379-eu-globalists-and-chinese-communists-team-up-to-protect-nwo#disqus_thread.

[103] Clabough, Raven. "George Soros Touts China as Leader of New World Order." *The New American*, 17 Nov. 2010, www.thenewamerican.com/world-news/north-america/item/10605-george-soros-touts-china-as-leader-of-new-world-order?fbclid=IwAR01ckBm-INZafvOcqeuUC9acGuyvLeoKR8otZP6073BqbLv3GyP5IieH3U#.

[104] *Id.*

[105] *Id.*

[106] Greenberg, Jay. "Pompeo: 'Something Not Quite Right' About Feinstein Praising China." *Neon Nettle*, Neon Nettle, 3 Aug. 2020, neonnettle.com/news/12194-pompeo-something-not-quite-right-about-feinstein-praising-china.

California and I wish she would not engage in this kind of rhetoric and these kinds of meetings…'"[107]

"Now a military expert is urging the free world to unite against China's expansionist agenda and make stopping the communists the top foreign policy objective…The military containment 'of Chinese expansionism and Communist Party Chairman Xi Jinping's stated goal of world domination needs to be the highest foreign policy priority of the Free World…'"[108]

"[P]roposals and references to a 'new world order' invariably are tied to efforts to erode national sovereignty and lead toward world government through steady political and economic merger on regional and global levels…"[109] H. G. Wells proclaimed, "It is the system of nationalist individualism that has to go…We are living in the end of the sovereign states…In the great struggle to evoke a Westernized World Socialism, contemporary governments may vanish…"[110] Strobe Talbot, Deputy Secretary of State, said, "In the

---

[107] *Id.*

[108] WND Staff. "'Free World' Needs to Blockade China's Expansionist Agenda." *WND*, WND, 9 Aug. 2020, www.wnd.com/2020/08/free-world-needs-blockade-chinas-expansionist-agenda/?fbclid=IwAR3Lt3ZjEEHmdM8boMkpvAW3NF7T0Ia0j-MO68vcEUGHLUMJEwUeJBmCXC0.

[109] Jasper, William F. "Joe Biden on Creating a 'New World Order.'" *The New American*, 8 Apr. 2013, www.thenewamerican.com/usnews/politics/item/15036-joe-biden-on-creating-a-new-world-order?fbclid=IwAR1NnFrzxnXBi1mJKf94lRmSQQMCaoWo6ndOCvAlRB2JXmGWWBnV0OAyxlw.

[110] H.G. Wells from his book, *The New World Order*, 1940. "Quotes On The New World Order And One-World Government." *American Freedom Party*, 29 June 2014, web.archive.org/web/20200201152435/american3rdposition.com/quotes-new-world-order/.

next century, nations as we know it will be obsolete; all states will recognize a single, global authority."[111]

Internationalists have been eroding U.S. national sovereignty to make us subservient to a global EU-like governing entity.[112] They are doing "an end run around national sovereignty, eroding it piece by piece..."[113] British historian, Arnold Toynbee, admitted, "We are at present working discreetly with all our might to wrest this mysterious force called sovereignty out of the clutches of the local nation states of the world."[114]

American journalist and political commentator, Walter Lippman, wrote, "What is being arranged in Washington these days is really a gigantic experiment in internationalism. We are witnessing the creation of a supranational control of the world's

---

[111] *TIME*, July 1992. "New World Order: 37 Quotes on The New World Order, One-World Government and One-World Religion." *End Times Prophecy Report*, 8 Aug. 2018, endtimesprophecyreport.com/2013/06/05/ new-world-order-37-quotes-on-the-new-world-order/.

[112] Greenley, Larry. "Next Step to World Government: Atlantic Union." *The New American*, 9 Mar. 2020, www.thenewamerican.com/print-magazine/item/34944-next-step-to-world-government-atlantic-union? f b c l i d = I w A R 2 u 5 W q O k - netjF2WHw3U0kIuZBLFk8jXgW_6eUrs2lUdyJ0olEVD0rMi0A.

[113] Richard N. Gardner, former deputy assistant Secretary of State for International Organisations under Kennedy and Johnson, and a member of the Trilateral Commission, wrote this in the April 1974 issue of the Council on Foreign Relation's (CFR) journal, Foreign Affairs (p. 558). "New World Order: 37 Quotes on The New World Order, One-World Government and One-World Religion." *End Times Prophecy Report*, 8 Aug. 2018, endtimesprophecyreport.com/2013/06/05/new-world-order-37-quotes-on-the-new-world-order/.

[114] Address to the 1931 Copenhagen conference as published in International Affairs: Journal of the Royal Institute of International Affairs (November 1931). "Arnold J. Toynbee." *Wikiquote*, Wikimedia Foundation, Inc., en.wikiquote.org/wiki/Arnold_J._Toynbee.

necessities. The old notions of sovereignty no longer govern the facts."[115]

"The means by which our planetary rulers plan to attain their long prized agenda is through such Rockefeller-Rothschild created entities as the Council on Foreign Relations."[116]   According to Carroll Quigley, "The Council on Foreign Relations (CFR) is the American Branch of a society which originated in England... (and)...believes national boundaries should be obliterated and one-world rule established."[117] "The CFR was founded for "the purpose of promoting disarmament and submergence of U.S. sovereignty and national independence into an all-powerful one-world government."[118]

"[T]he most glaring treasonous agenda of all that the Council on Foreign Relations has consistently maintained for near an entire century is the destruction of the United States as an independent,

---

[115] April 1917. "New World Order: 37 Quotes on The New World Order, One-World Government and One-World Religion." *End Times Prophecy Report*, 8 Aug. 2018, endtimesprophecyreport.com/2013/06/05/new-world-order-37-quotes-on-the-new-world-order/.

[116] Hagopian, Joachim. "One World Governance and the Council on Foreign Relations. 'We Shall Have World Government...by Conquest or Consent.'" *Global Research*, 24 Jan. 2021, www.globalresearch.ca/one-world-governance-and-the-council-on-foreign-relations-we-shall-have-world-government-by-conquest-or-consent/5541363.

[117] "Quotes On The New World Order." *Jesus-Is-Savior.com*, www.jesus-is-savior.com/False%20Religions/Illuminati/quotes_on_the_new_world_order.htm.

[118] Harper's, July 1958. "New World Order: 37 Quotes on The New World Order, One-World Government and One-World Religion." *End Times Prophecy Report*, 8 Aug. 2018, endtimesprophecyreport.com/2013/06/05/new-world-order-37-quotes-on-the-new-world-order/.

sovereign nation."[119]   "They [CFR] want to bring about the surrender of the sovereignty and the national independence of the U.S. They want to end national boundaries and racial and ethnic loyalties supposedly to increase business and ensure world peace."[120]   In 1975, powerful CFR insider and former Judge Advocate General of the US Navy, Admiral Chester Ward, wrote in his book entitled *Kissinger on the Couch* about the ultimate aim of the Council on Foreign Relations: "[The CFR has as a goal] submergence of US sovereignty and national independence into an all-powerful one-world government...this lust to surrender the sovereignty and independence of the United States is pervasive throughout most of the membership..."[121]

---

[119] Hagopian, Joachim. "One World Governance and the Council on Foreign Relations. 'We Shall Have World Government...by Conquest or Consent.'" *Global Research*, 24 Jan. 2021, www.globalresearch.ca/one-world-governance-and-the-council-on-foreign-relations-we-shall-have-world-government-by-conquest-or-consent/5541363.

[120] Harper's, July 1958. "New World Order: 37 Quotes on The New World Order, One-World Government and One-World Religion." *End Times Prophecy Report*, 8 Aug. 2018, endtimesprophecyreport.com/2013/06/05/new-world-order-37-quotes-on-the-new-world-order/.

[121] Hagopian, Joachim. "One World Governance and the Council on Foreign Relations. 'We Shall Have World Government...by Conquest or Consent.'" *Global Research*, 24 Jan. 2021, www.globalresearch.ca/one-world-governance-and-the-council-on-foreign-relations-we-shall-have-world-government-by-conquest-or-consent/5541363. "The main reason Trump was elected was for his promise to reject globalism and put 'America first...' Trump, the Brexit campaign, and other "nationalistic" movements around the world were a rejection of globalism in favor of nationalism economic policies." Dmitry, Baxter. "Soros and His Minions Are FURIOUS As Trump Uses COVID-19 To End Globalism & Bring Jobs Back To US." *News Punch*, 21 Mar. 2020, newspunch.com/soros-and-minions-furious-trump-uses-covid-19-end-globalism-bring-jobs-back-us/?fbclid=IwAR2OwnwijZrabO8EWe-uMKhEQ9w0LhgOPV50UrytfsyhITBiSFa2pG7ZuDg.

"The CFR has always envisioned and been working persistently towards a totalitarian one world government…"[122] Rep. John R. Rarick (D-LA) said, "The Council on Foreign Relations (CFR) is dedicated to one-world government, financed by a number of the largest tax exempt foundation (i.e. Rockefeller), and wielding such power and influence over our lives in the areas of finance, business, labor, military, education, and mass communication media, that it should be familiar to every American concerned with good government and with preserving and defending the US Constitution and our free-enterprise system…Not only does it have influence and power in key decision-making positions at the highest levels of government to apply pressure from above, but it also finances and uses individuals and groups to bring pressure from below, to justify the high level decisions for converting the US from a sovereign Republic into a servile member of a one-world dictatorship."[123] Dr. Johannes Koeppl, former German Ministry for Defense (*Verteidigungsministerium*) official and advisor to NATO, said in 2001, "The interests behind the Bush administration, such as the CFR, the Trilateral Commission…and the Bilderberg Group have prepared for and are now moving to implement open world dictatorship within the next five years."[124]   "What they [CFR] strive for would inevitably lead to dictatorship and loss of freedoms by the people."[125]

---

[122] Hagopian, Joachim. "One World Governance and the Council on Foreign Relations. 'We Shall Have World Government…by Conquest or Consent.'" *Global Research*, 24 Jan. 2021, www.globalresearch.ca/one-world-governance-and-the-council-on-foreign-relations-we-shall-have-world-government-by-conquest-or-consent/5541363.

[123] "150+ New World Order Globalist Agenda Quotes." *Wake Up New Zealand*, www.wakeupkiwi.com/nwo-globalist-agenda-quotes.shtml.

[124] *Inconvenient Truths*, www.inconvenienttruths.net/.

[125] Harper's, July 1958. "New World Order: 37 Quotes on The New World Order, One-World Government and One-World Religion." *End Times Prophecy Report*, 8 Aug. 2018, endtimesprophecyreport.com/2013/06/05/new-world-order-37-quotes-on-the-new-world-order/.

Council on Foreign Relations (CFR) member, Richard N. Gardner, provided this route to world government in 1974: "In short, the 'house of world order' will have to be built from the bottom up rather than from the top down. It will look like a great 'booming, buzzing confusion,' to use William James' famous description of reality, but an end run around national sovereignty, eroding it piece by piece, will accomplish much more than the old-fashioned frontal assault..."[126] "In 1995, former National Security Advisor Zbigniew Brzezinski, a longtime CFR member, revealed just how closely globalists were pursuing a bottom-up strategy for building a world government: 'We cannot leap into world government in one quick step,' he said. 'In brief, the precondition for eventual globalization — genuine globalization — is progressive regionalization, because thereby we move toward larger, more stable, more cooperative units.'"[127]

Gary Allen explained in his book, *The Rockefeller File*, "The master planners devised the strategy of a merger — a Great Merger — among nations."[128] For example, "[w]hile ostensibly opposed to one another during the Cold War — with the United States leading the free world and the then-Soviet Union ruling the enslaved communist world behind the Iron Curtain — leaders in the highest echelons of both societies (from politics, business, media, labor, Wall Street, and tax-exempt foundations) shared the common goal of

---

[126] "The Hard Road to World Order," published in the CFR house organ, *Foreign Affairs*, in April 1974. *Convergence*, www.channelingreality.com/ TTT/Intro/Convergence.htm.

[127] Greenley, Larry. "Next Step to World Government: Atlantic Union." *The New American*, 9 Mar. 2020, www.thenewamerican.com/print-magazine/item/34944-next-step-to-world-government-atlantic-union? f b c l i d = I w A R 2 u 5 W q O k - netjF2WHw3U0kIuZBLFk8jXgW_6eUrs2lUdyJ0olEVD0rMi0A.

[128] Repp, John M. "Opinion: UN Report Says US Is a 'Shithole Country.'" *Common Dreams*, 15 June 2018, www.commondreams.org/views/ 2 0 1 8 / 0 6 / 1 5 / u n - r e p o r t - s a y s - u s - s h i t h o l e - c o u n t r y ? utm_campaign=shareaholic&fbclid=IwAR3i8n-44579Pge2vqxSV65e6H9 p_UMNzgCbAdB0TFeQaFi7UGxwMauQ-uc.

'converging,' or merging, both societies under a single unified global economy and international regime often referred to by its architects as the 'New World Order.'"[129]   However, "before such a merger can be consummated, and the United States becomes just another province in a New World Order, there must at least be the semblance of parity among the senior partners in the deal. How does one make the nations of the world more nearly equal? The Insiders determined that a two-prong approach was needed; use American money and know-how to build up your competitors, while at the same time use every devious strategy you can devise to weaken and impoverish this country. The goal is not to bankrupt the United States. Rather, it is to reduce our productive might, and therefore our standard of living, to the meager subsistence level of the socialized nations of the world. The plan is not to bring the standard of living in less developed countries up to our level, but to bring ours down to meet theirs coming up...It is your standard of living which must be sacrificed on the altar of the New World Order."[130]   Their plan is succeeding.   According to a 2018 United Nations (UN) report, 40 million U.S. citizens "live in poverty. Five million live in the absolute deprivation we usually associate with the developing world. Four in ten Americans are so broke that they could not cover an

---

[129] Gomez, Christian. "EU Globalists and Chinese Communists Team Up To Protect NWO." *The New American*, 25 Jun. 2018, www.thenewamerican.com/world-news/europe/item/29379-eu-globalists-and-chinese-communists-team-up-to-protect-nwo#disqus_thread.

[130] Banerji, Rishabh. "These Are The 13 Families In The World That Apparently Control Everything." *India Times*, 9 Mar. 2018, www.indiatimes.com/culture/who-we-are/these-are-the-13-families-in-the-world-that-apparently-control-everything-from-politics-to-terrorism-257642.html?fbclid=IwAR1csUuCsRdOuzyAJRA3hUnL0K_EWRzTCIwj3EuJ2R2Rq3dIHcFO_sDyvOo.

emergency expense of $400 without selling something or borrowing."[131]

"The stated plan was that different parts of the world would be assigned different roles of industry and commerce in a unified global system. The continued pre-eminence of the United States and the relative independence and self-sufficiency of the United States would have to be changed... The United States was to be kept strong in information, communications, high technology, education and agriculture... [but] heavy industry would be transported out..."[132] In 1930, Representative McFadden correctly predicted that "[t]he United States under present conditions will be transformed from the most active of manufacturing nations into a consuming and importing nation with a balance of trade against it."[133]

---

[131] Repp, John M. "Opinion: UN Report Says US Is a 'Shithole Country.'" *Common Dreams*, 15 June 2018, www.commondreams.org/views/2018/06/15/un-report-says-us-shithole-country?utm_campaign=shareaholic&fbclid=IwAR3i8n-44579Pge2vqxSV65e6H9p_UMNzgCbAdB0TFeQaFi7UGxwMauQ-uc.

[132] "New Order of Barbarians - Transcript of Tapes I-III." *100777.Com*, 22 May 2003, 100777.com/nwo/barbarians. "The failings of centralization have caused numerous problems long before it led to a potential pandemic. The pandemic simply clarifies the issue. For example, the breakdown in the global supply chain is becoming a bigger threat by the day. The Baltic Dry Index a measure of shipping rates as well as global demand for goods, has essentially collapsed...Globalism has led to interdependent economies and nation states that no longer have redundancies in production. We have been forced to rely on production centers on the other side of the world for a vast majority of our goods." "Global Centralization Is the Cause of Crisis - Not the Cure." *NaturalNews.com*, 20 Feb. 2020, www.naturalnews.com/2020-02-20-global-centralization-cause-of-crisis.html.

[133] "Quotation by Louis McFadden." *LibertyQuotes*, libertytree.ca/quotes/Louis.McFadden.Quote.B24B.

"In the entire CFR lexicon, there is no term of revulsion carrying a meaning so deep as 'America First...'"[134]   President Donald Trump described his America First policy: "I hold up the American model as an example to the world of a working system of free enterprise that will produce the most benefits for the most people in the 21st century and beyond. A pro-worker, pro-citizen, pro-family agenda demonstrates how a nation can thrive when its communities, its companies, its government, and its people work together for the good of the whole nation..."[135] "European Union leaders announced that officials from the EU and China were coming together to strengthen and protect their international trade relations from Trump's 'America First' agenda."[136]

According to Aaron Russo, the ultimate goal of the private bankers in over-throwing the United States is "to create a one-world government, run by the banking industry. Run by the bankers. And they're doing it in sections — the European currency, the euro, and the European Constitution. There's one part of it. Now they're trying

---

[134] Hagopian, Joachim. "One World Governance and the Council on Foreign Relations. 'We Shall Have World Government...by Conquest or Consent.'" *Global Research*, 24 Jan. 2021, www.globalresearch.ca/one-world-governance-and-the-council-on-foreign-relations-we-shall-have-world-government-by-conquest-or-consent/5541363; Dmitry, Baxter. "Soros and His Minions Are FURIOUS As Trump Uses COVID-19 To End Globalism & Bring Jobs Back To US." *News Punch*, 21 Mar. 2020, newspunch.com/soros-and-minions-furious-trump-uses-covid-19-end-globalism-bring-jobs-back-us/?fbclid=IwAR2OwnwijZrabO8EWe-uMKhEQ9w0LhgOPV50UrytfsyhITBiSFa2pG7ZuDg.

[135] Trump, Donald. "Remarks by President Trump at the World Economic Forum." *U.S. Embassy in Switzerland and Liechtenstein*, 21 Jan. 2020, ch.usembassy.gov/remarks-by-president-trump-at-the-world-economic-forum/.

[136] Gomez, Christian. "EU Globalists and Chinese Communists Team Up To Protect NWO." *The New American*, 25 June 2018, www.thenewamerican.com/world-news/europe/item/29379-eu-globalists-and-chinese-communists-team-up-to-protect-nwo#disqus_thread.

to do it in America with the North American Union."[137]   Thus, European Union-style blocs are the first step. After World War II, the "Marshall Plan funds were designed by globalists in the United States to help their European counterparts begin building what we now know as the EU from day one. And trade agreements were the main tool used by the American and European globalists to consolidate political and economic power under the European Union..."[138]   "The formation of a U.S.-EU trading bloc would be a steppingstone toward a new U.S.-EU regional government, often referred to as an Atlantic Union...Proposals for an Atlantic Union regional government were popularized by Clarence Streit, beginning with his 1939 book *Union Now*. Streit's idea...was to create a union of the United States, Canada, and a dozen or so European nations. Streit explicitly declared that the purpose of creating an Atlantic Union was to lead to a world government...."[139]

"The historical record clearly shows that the globalists on both sides who [negotiate] trade deals have a track record of creating trade agreements that continually move our nation and the nations we negotiate with toward regional governments as steppingstones toward a world government under the UN."[140]   For example, the NAFTA trade agreement between the United States, Mexico, and Canada that went into effect in 1994 was a first step toward the establishment of the North American Union (NAU) as a regional

---

[137] "Aaron Russo: Reflections and Warnings - Full Transcript." *Matt Prather*, sites.google.com/site/themattprather/Reading/aaron-russo/reflections-and-warnings-full-transcript.

[138] Greenley, Larry. "Next Step to World Government: Atlantic Union." *The New American*, 9 Mar. 2020, www.thenewamerican.com/print-magazine/item/34944-next-step-to-world-government-atlantic-union?fbclid=IwAR2u5WqOk-netjF2WHw3U0kIuZBLFk8jXgW_6eUrs2lUdyJ0olEVD0rMi0A.

[139] *Id.*

[140] *Id.*

government for North America.[141] "In the nearly 25 years after NAFTA, the United States lost 1 in 4 manufacturing jobs, including nearly 1 in 4 vehicle-manufacturing jobs. It was an incentive to leave the country. The NAFTA agreement exemplified the decades-long failures of the international trading system. The agreement shifted wealth to the hands of a few, promoted massive outsourcing, drove down wages, and shuttered plants and factories by the thousands. The plants would leave our country, make the product, sell it into our country. We ended up with no jobs and no taxes..."[142] President Trump said, "When I took office three years ago [2017], America's economy was in a rather dismal state. Under the previous administration, nearly 200,000 manufacturing jobs had vanished..."[143] Luckily, he "ended the NAFTA disaster...and replaced it with the incredible new trade deal, the USMCA — that's Mexico and Canada."[144] The new agreements "represent a new model of trade for the 21st century — agreements that are fair, reciprocal, and that prioritize the needs of workers and families..."[145]

The John Birch Society (JBS) "has warned that the goal of elite globalist insiders was to converge the freedom-loving, market-based republics of the Western world with the captive, totalitarian

---

[141] *Id.*

[142] Trump, Donald. "Remarks by President Trump at the World Economic Forum." *U.S. Embassy in Switzerland and Liechtenstein*, 21 Jan. 2020, ch.usembassy.gov/remarks-by-president-trump-at-the-world-economic-forum/.

[143] *Id.*

[144] *Id.*

[145] *Id.*

communist-bloc nations."[146]   One way this can be achieved is via the U.N.[147] "CFR members calling themselves the Informal Agenda Group drafted the UN proposal that FDR signed...establishing the UN as a world governance precursor in 1945..."[148] "When the U.S. Senate ratified the UN Charter on July 28, 1945, the United States signed away its national sovereignty to the United Nations. For example, Article 25 of the UN Charter states: 'The Members of the United Nations agree to accept and carry out the decisions of the Security Council in accordance with the present Charter...'"[149] U.N. Secretary-General Antonio Guterres (former Prime Minister of Portugal (Socialist Party) from 1995 to 2002) said, "'[O]nly one thing is certain...: '[A] new model of global governance' is coming and the globalist body is doing all it can to hurry its arrival...' His solution to...disorder is more big government, and more bureaucratic institutions in more places, delivered via the U.N. and

---

[146] Gomez, Christian. "EU Globalists and Chinese Communists Team Up To Protect NWO." *The New American*, 25 Jun. 2018, www.thenewamerican.com/world-news/europe/item/29379-eu-globalists-and-chinese-communists-team-up-to-protect-nwo#disqus_thread.

[147] *Id.*

[148] Hagopian, Joachim. "One World Governance and the Council on Foreign Relations. 'We Shall Have World Government...by Conquest or Consent.'" *Global Research*, 24 Jan. 2021, www.globalresearch.ca/one-world-governance-and-the-council-on-foreign-relations-we-shall-have-world-government-by-conquest-or-consent/5541363.

[149] Greenley, Larry. "Next Step to World Government: Atlantic Union." *The New American*, 9 Mar. 2020, www.thenewamerican.com/print-magazine/item/34944-next-step-to-world-government-atlantic-union?fbclid=IwAR2u5WqOk-netjF2WHw3U0kIuZBLFk8jXgW_6eUrs2lUdyJ0olEVD0rMi0A. International treaties become federal law when ratified, and are thus, subordinate to the U.S. Constitution. Kirgis, Frederic L. "International Agreements and U.S. Law." *Insights*, American Society of International Law, 27 May 1997, www.asil.org/insights/volume/2/issue/5/international-agreements-and-us-law.

its multiple agencies all funded by the contributions of taxpayers around the world."[150]

"In 2015,…the UN took a giant step towards the global government…They issued a document entitled 'Transforming Our World: the 2030 Agenda for Sustainable Development…'"[151] As the UN 2030 document makes clear, "international socialism is needed to battle inequality even 'among' countries [Goal 20]. 'By 2030, ensure that all men and women, in particular the poor and the vulnerable, have equal rights to economic resources,' the document demands…The UN document also calls on government to seize control over 'production and consumption.'"[152] "The overlay of Marxist talk about 'meeting needs' has moved to center stage. The UN has assigned itself a time frame for moving forward in its plan for planetary hegemony."[153]

"At a meeting hosted by the highly influential World Economic Forum [WEF] earlier in June [2020], powerful officials from nonprofits, government, business, academia, labor unions and

[150] Kent, Simon. "U.N.'s Guterres Warns a 'New Model for Global Governance' Is Coming." *Breitbart*, 21 Jul. 2020, www.breitbart.com/politics/2020/07/21/u-n-s-guterres-warns-new-model-for-global-governance-is-coming-to-redistribute-power-and-wealth/?fbclid=IwAR3iWpHvEbWjTz0adZkF0QBtiAnj8AmI-k0GD2bYlQaDLFVVF7B8z7edC6A.

[151] Ludwig, E. Jeffrey. "The UN Wants to Be Our World Government By 2030." *American Thinker*, 27 Oct. 2018, www.americanthinker.com/articles/2018/10/the_un_wants_to_be_our_world_government_by_2030.html.

[152] Newman, Alex. "UN-Backed 'Great Reset' to Usher in New World Order." *The New American*, 15 July 2020, www.thenewamerican.com/world-news/europe/item/36379-un-backed-great-reset-to-usher-in-new-world-order?fbclid=IwAR20CLmHQsrwV0V7dk46O5yT2KjetreQXYFIivnu-wJa8YRevNaUz5A16Bw.

[153] Ludwig, E. Jeffrey. "The UN Wants to Be Our World Government By 2030." *American Thinker*, 27 Oct. 2018, www.americanthinker.com/articles/2018/10/the_un_wants_to_be_our_world_government_by_2030.html.

activist groups announced their plan for a 'Great Reset' of global capitalism..."[154]   The "globalist group of powerful Deep State elites" (including António Guterres, the secretary-general of the United Nations, and Prince Charles of England) "aims to fundamentally re-engineer industries, societies, education, agriculture, and more."[155]   "The purpose of the Great Reset isn't merely to enact policies that would lead to additional wealth redistribution, but rather to completely overhaul the world's existing structures and institutions..."[156]

"Instead of traditional capitalism, the high-profile group said the world should adopt more socialistic policies, such as wealth taxes, additional regulations and massive Green New Deal-like government programs..."[157]   "[T]he general principles of the plan are clear: The world needs massive new government programs and far-reaching policies comparable to those offered by American

---

[154] Hawkins, Justin. "Al Gore, UN Secretary-General, others now demanding 'Great Reset''of global capitalism." *Fox Business,* 24 Jun. 2020, www.foxbusiness.com/markets/al-gore-un-secretary-general-great-reset-global-capitalism?fbclid=IwAR18gs71dBfqNO0dqMKpi0uM-pRdMlU8yL2qaF_F_n5n2Xo6usxpzcuo37Q.

[155] Newman, Alex. "UN-Backed 'Great Reset' to Usher in New World Order." *The New American*, 15 July 2020, www.thenewamerican.com/world-news/europe/item/36379-un-backed-great-reset-to-usher-in-new-w   o   r   l   d   -   o   r   d   e   r   ?fbclid=IwAR20CLmHQsrwV0V7dk46O5yT2KjetreQXYFIivnu-wJa8YRevNaUz5A16Bw.

[156] Hawkins, Justin. "Al Gore, UN Secretary-General, others now demanding 'Great Reset''of global capitalism." *Fox Business,* 24 Jun. 2020, www.foxbusiness.com/markets/al-gore-un-secretary-general-great-reset-global-capitalism?fbclid=IwAR18gs71dBfqNO0dqMKpi0uM-pRdMlU8yL2qaF_F_n5n2Xo6usxpzcuo37Q.

[157] Haskins, Justin. "Introducing the 'Great Reset,' World Leaders' Radical Plan to Transform the Economy." *MSN*, MSN, 25 June 2020, www.msn.com/en-us/news/politics/introducing-the-great-reset-world-leaders-radical-plan-to-transform-the-economy/ar-BB15XGsU?fbclid=IwAR0nHYaWwbRdVMkSXaHZtrRXG7XbRMRBS55XWIzGC MR6InTtHuuQAn8iiu0.

socialists such as Sen. Bernie Sanders (I-Vt.), and Rep. Alexandria Ocasio-Cortez (D-N.Y.) in their Green New Deal plan. Or, put another way, we need a form of socialism…"[158]

"At the…meeting, one speaker after another cited climate change and environmental sustainability as the key justifications for radical economic changes that would include massive new regulations and restrictions on economic activity, wealth taxes and expansive government programs comparable to the Green New Deal…"[159] For example, Prince Charles claimed, "Systems and pathways must be redesigned to advance net zero transitions globally. Carbon pricing can provide a critical pathway to a sustainable market."[160] "IMF boss Kristalina Georgieva boasted of the 'massive fiscal stimulus' being 'injected' into the global economy. This massive infusion of cash looted from humanity must be used to forcibly restructure the economy so it can be rebuilt…'more fairer' [sic] in the future. For instance, she said governments and international organizations could put in place 'incentives' such as 'carbon prices' to force companies to do what the globalist establishment wants. 'Carbon prices,' of course, is just code language for literally taxing the gas exhaled by human beings, CO2. She also demanded more government 'social programs' to

---

[158] *Id.*

[159] Hawkins, Justin. "Al Gore, UN Secretary-General, others now demanding 'Great Reset''of global capitalism." *Fox Business,* 24 Jun. 2020, www.foxbusiness.com/markets/al-gore-un-secretary-general-great-reset-global-capitalism?fbclid=IwAR18gs71dBfqNO0dqMKpi0uM-pRdMlU8yL2qaF_F_n5n2Xo6usxpzcuo37Q.

[160] Inman, Phillip. "Pandemic is chance to reset global economy, says Prince Charles." *The Guardian,* 3 Jun. 2020, www.theguardian.com/uk-news/2020/jun/03/pandemic-is-chance-to-reset-global-economy-says-p r i n c e - c h a r l e s ? CMP=share_btn_fb&fbclid=IwAR2lvjSEa2foRKfNLamD0uZlwCKQr3W sdZg58AZ7lLRbjURrukz7puuscjM.

'take care of people.'"[161] "Other 'stakeholders' involved in the scheme include the CEO of Mastercard [Ajay Banga], which is funding Deep State efforts to eliminate cash in a move toward a cashless society. The president of Microsoft, which recently filed patent WO2020-060606 for implantable crypto-currency technology, is also a key booster," as well as Bernard Looney, CEO of BP, and Gina Gopinath, the chief economist at the International Monetary Fund (IMF).[162]

"In short, what remains of the tattered free-market system is set to be tossed out — along with the vibrant middle class it sustained. In its place will rise technocratic governance based on nebulous 'social' and 'environmental' goals set by the technocrats..."[163]

WEF organizer, Klaus Schwab, insisted that "[e]very country, from the United States to China, must participate, and every industry, from oil and gas to tech, must be transformed," calling for

---

[161] Newman, Alex. "UN-Backed 'Great Reset' to Usher in New World Order." *The New American*, 15 July 2020, www.thenewamerican.com/world-news/europe/item/36379-un-backed-great-reset-to-usher-in-new-w o r l d - o r d e r ? fbclid=IwAR20CLmHQsrwV0V7dk46O5yT2KjetreQXYFIivnu-wJa8YRevNaUz5A16Bw.

[162] *Id*. Hawkins, Justin. "Al Gore, UN Secretary-General, others now demanding 'Great Reset''of global capitalism." *Fox Business,* 24 Jun. 2020, www.foxbusiness.com/markets/al-gore-un-secretary-general-great-reset-global-capitalism?fbclid=IwAR18gs71dBfqNO0dqMKpi0uM-pRdMlU8yL2qaF_F_n5n2Xo6usxpzcuo37Q.

[163] Newman, Alex. "UN-Backed 'Great Reset' to Usher in New World Order." *The New American*, 15 July 2020, www.thenewamerican.com/world-news/europe/item/36379-un-backed-great-reset-to-usher-in-new-w o r l d - o r d e r ? fbclid=IwAR20CLmHQsrwV0V7dk46O5yT2KjetreQXYFIivnu-wJa8YRevNaUz5A16Bw.

even "stronger and more effective government."[164]　He warns that "there is no other choice but to submit..."[165]

"These are truly dangerous times for those who support individual liberty and free markets."[166]　Chris Talgo with the Heartland Institute "called on humanity to resist the Great Reset agenda for global government 'at all costs.'"[167]　"For those of us who support free markets, the Great Reset is nothing short of terrifying. Our current crony capitalist system has many flaws, to be sure, but granting more power to the government agents who created that crony system and eroding property rights is not the best way forward. America is the world's most powerful, prosperous nation precisely because of the very market principles the Great Reset supporters loathe, not in spite of them..."[168]　President Trump promised, "We will never let radical socialists destroy our economy,

---

[164] *Id.*

[165] *Id.*

[166] Hawkins, Justin. "Al Gore, UN Secretary-General, others now demanding 'Great Reset"of global capitalism." *Fox Business,* 24 Jun. 2020, www.foxbusiness.com/markets/al-gore-un-secretary-general-great-reset-global-capitalism?fbclid=IwAR18gs71dBfqNO0dqMKpi0uM-pRdMlU8yL2qaF_F_n5n2Xo6usxpzcuo37Q.

[167] Newman, Alex. "UN-Backed 'Great Reset' to Usher in New World Order." *The New American,* 15 July 2020, www.thenewamerican.com/world-news/europe/item/36379-un-backed-great-reset-to-usher-in-new-w　o　r　l　d　-　o　r　d　e　r　? fbclid=IwAR20CLmHQsrwV0V7dk46O5yT2KjetreQXYFlivnu-wJa8YRevNaUz5A16Bw.

[168] Haskins, Justin. "Introducing the 'Great Reset,' World Leaders' Radical Plan to Transform the Economy." *MSN,* MSN, 25 June 2020, www.msn.com/en-us/news/politics/introducing-the-great-reset-world-leaders-radical-plan-to-transform-the-economy/ar-BB15XGsU?fbclid=IwAR0nHYaWwbRdVMkSXaHZtrRXG7XbRMRBS55XWIzGC MR6InTtHuuQAn8iiu0.

wreck our country, or eradicate our liberty. America will always be the proud, strong, and unyielding bastion of freedom."[169]

Kofi Annan, former U.N. Secretary General, threatened, "A world government can intervene militarily in the internal affairs of any nation when it disapproves of their activities."[170] "On October 20, 2011, the West took it upon itself to use NATO to overthrow Libyan leader Muammar al-Gaddafi... because his planned roll-out of a new [gold-backed] currency to be used across Africa posed a palpable existential threat to central banks at the heart of the Western financial and political system...Citing a U. N. Security Council resolution to invoke a nefarious no-fly zone over Libya to 'protect civilians,' the United States, U.K., France, and others began a bombing campaign on March 19 — in actuality, of course, that protection was of the central bank monopoly and, in particular,

---

[169] Trump, Donald. "Remarks by President Trump at the World Economic Forum." *U.S. Embassy in Switzerland and Liechtenstein*, 21 Jan. 2020, ch.usembassy.gov/remarks-by-president-trump-at-the-world-economic-forum/.

[170] "New World Order: 37 Quotes on The New World Order, One-World Government and One-World Religion." *End Times Prophecy Report*, 8 Aug. 2018, endtimesprophecyreport.com/2013/06/05/new-world-order-37-quotes-on-the-new-world-order/. Kofi Annan became Secretary General to the United Nations in 1997. "He is married to Nane Lagergren, a Rothschild, whom he wed in 1984." Hitchcock, Andrew. "Historical Timeline of the Rothschild Dynasty – Part 6 (final)." *The Sirius Report,* 20 Aug. 2016, www.thesiriusreport.com/geopolitics/historical-timeline-rothschild-dynasty-6/.

France's financial interests in the historically French-colonial region…"[171]

"[I]f the U.N. can violate the Sovereignty of Haiti, Iraq and other countries, it can violate ours…The United States may not be the top dog 15 years from now. U. N. security council resolutions, backed by say Chinese soldiers, could be aimed at us."[172]   A troubling development occurred in June 2020 when "[t]he United Nations tweeted in support of Antifa…— the anti-government, radical leftist organization that has incited and perpetuated violence and widespread rioting following the death of George Floyd at the hands of the Minneapolis Police Department. The UN Geneva Twitter account tweeted: 'UN #HumanRights experts express profound concern over a recent statement by the US Attorney-General describing #Antifa and other anti-fascist activists as domestic terrorists, saying it undermines the rights to freedom of expression and of peaceful assembly in the country…' Antifa is notorious for causing mayhem and destruction around the US, which

---

[171] "Qaddafi's government holds 143 tons of gold, and a similar amount in silver. Sidney Blumenthal wrote the secretary of state Clinton on April 2, 2011, under the heading, 'France's client & Qaddafi's gold…' This gold was accumulated prior to the current rebellion and was intended to be used to establish a pan-African currency based on the Libyan golden Dinar. This plan was designed to provide, the Francophone African Countries with an alternative to the French franc (CFA). (Source Comment: According to knowledgeable individuals this quantity of gold and silver is valued at more than $7 billion. French intelligence officers discovered this plan shortly after the current rebellion began, and this was one of the factors that influenced President Nicolas Sarkozy's decision to commit France to the attack on Libya." Bernish, Claire. "8 Years Ago Today, The US Helped Murder Gaddafi to Stop the Creation of Gold-Backed Currency." *The Free Thought Project,* 20 Oct. 2017, thefreethoughtproject.com/8-years-ago-us-killed-gaddafi-gold/?fbclid=IwAR2i8YWZQmdUCYggA-vWrFUgoEB55CZq4qtj2HPxwj1nFotrlTLISVAt2es.

[172] Quote by columnist, Charley Reese. *Orlando Sentinel.* "Quotes On The New World Order." *Jesus-Is-Savior.com,* www.jesus-is-savior.com/False%20Religions/Illuminati/quotes_on_the_new_world_order.htm.

is why President Donald Trump intends to designate the group as a terrorist organization."[173]

"At the two-day founding meeting of the JBS [John Birch Society] in December 1958, founder Robert Welch issued a very far-sighted warning about the UN: 'There are three possible methods by which the Communists might take us over...[The] third method...is one which they are clearly relying on most heavily...A part of that plan, of course, is to induce the gradual surrender of American sovereignty, piece by piece and step by step, to various international organizations — of which the United Nations is the outstanding but far from the only example...'"[174] Another example is the World Trade Organization (WTO): "The Final Act of the Uruguay Round, marking the conclusion of the most ambitious trade negotiation of our century, will give birth – in Morocco – to the World Trade Organization, the third pillar of the New World Order, along with the United Nations and the International Monetary Fund."[175]

Unfortunately, many heads of state have signed on to this new world order.   David Rockefeller, "the most conspicuous representative today of the ruling class" (according to journalist, Bill Moyers), thought, "The supranational sovereignty of an intellectual elite and world bankers is surely preferable to the National auto

---

[173] Jones, Collin. "United Nations comes out in support of Antifa." *The Post Millenial*, 20 Jun. 2020, thepostmillennial.com/un-comes-out-in-support-of-antifa?fbclid=IwAR2-Euv-btLPRgi0CcKwKvqdkViWhpkOGnlsSauTXTxnXK-s4jMwyyaynA0.

[174] Greenley, Larry. "Next Step to World Government: Atlantic Union." *The New American*, 9 Mar. 2020, www.thenewamerican.com/print-magazine/item/34944-next-step-to-world-government-atlantic-union?fbclid=IwAR2u5WqOk-netjF2WHw3U0kIuZBLFk8jXgW_6eUrs2lUdyJ0olEVD0rMi0A.

[175] Government of Morocco, advertisement, *New York Times*, April 1994. "New World Order: 37 Quotes on The New World Order, One-World Government and One-World Religion." *End Times Prophecy Report*, 8 Aug. 2018, endtimesprophecyreport.com/2013/06/05/new-world-order-37-quotes-on-the-new-world-order/.

determination practiced in past centuries."[176]   He admitted to working toward NWO in his autobiography, *Memoirs:* "For more than a century ideological extremists…have seized upon well-publicized incidents…to attack the Rockefeller family for the inordinate influence they claim we wield over American political and economic institutions. Some even believe we are part of a secret cabal working against the best interests of the United States, characterizing my family and me as 'internationalists' and of conspiring with others around the world to build a more integrated global political and economic structure – one world, if you will. If that's the charge, I stand guilty, and I am proud of it."[177]   Other examples include Joe Biden ("The 'affirmative task' before us is to 'create a New World Order'"), Mikhail Gorbachev ("We are moving toward a new world order, the world of communism. We shall never turn off that road"), Henry Kissinger ("I think that his [Obama's] task will be to develop an overall strategy for America in this period, when really a New World Order can be created"), President Richard Nixon ("Each of us has the hope to build a New World Order"), King Edward VIII ("Whatever happens, whatever the outcome, New World Order is going to come into the world…It will be buttressed with police power…)" and George H. W. Bush ("Out of these

---

[176] Baden-Baden, Germany, 1991 "New World Order: 37 Quotes on The New World Order, One-World Government and One-World Religion." *End Times Prophecy Report*, 8 Aug. 2018, endtimesprophecyreport.com/2013/06/05/new-world-order-37-quotes-on-the-new-world-order/; "Quotes On The New World Order." *Jesus-Is-Savior.com*, www.jesus-is-savior.com/False%20Religions/Illuminati/quotes_on_the_new_world_order.htm.

[177] "Quotes On The New World Order." *Jesus-Is-Savior.com*, www.jesus-is-savior.com/False%20Religions/Illuminati/quotes_on_the_new_world_order.htm.

troubled times, our fifth objective — a new world order — can emerge.")[178]

David Rockefeller believed, "We are on the verge of a global transformation. All we need is the right major crisis, and the nation will accept the NWO."[179] According to Milton Friedman, "Only a crisis—actual or perceived—produces real change."[180] Yuri Bezmenov, a former Soviet KGB agent who defected to the United States, offered some insight into what they meant.[181] He explained that one of the stages involved in bringing down a nation state is destabilization.[182] For example, economic instability can cause a crisis that leads to the desired outcome, i.e. NWO.[183] British politician, Denis Healey, informed us that "[w]orld events do not occur by accident. They are made to happen, whether it is to do with national issues or commerce; and most of them are staged and

---

[178] Speech at Import Export Bank, April 5, 2013. "New World Order: 37 Quotes on The New World Order, One-World Government and One-World Religion." *End Times Prophecy Report*, 8 Aug. 2018, endtimesprophecyreport.com/2013/06/05/new-world-order-37-quotes-on-the-new-world-order/. Hangzhou, China, February 1972. Edward VIII became King on January 20, 1936, and abdicated eleven months later. He became the Duke of Windsor, and in July, 1940, he became the governor of the Bahamas. "Bush 'Out of these troubled times— a new world order.'" *The Washington Post,* www.washingtonpost.com/archive/politics/1990/09/12/bush-out-of-these-troubled-times-a-new-world-order/b93b5cf1-e389-4e6a-84b0-85f71bf4c946/.

[179] "Quotes On The New World Order." *Jesus-Is-Savior.com*, www.jesus-is-savior.com/False%20Religions/Illuminati/quotes_on_the_new_world_order.htm.

[180] "Milton Friedman > Quotes > Quotable Quote." *Good Reads,* www.goodreads.com/quotes/110844-only-a-crisis---actual-or-perceived---produces-real.

[181] At 1:09:00. Federaljacktube. "Former KGB Agent Yuri Bezmenov Explains How to Brainwash a Nation (Full Length)." *Youtube,* 28 Dec. 2012, www.youtube.com/watch?v=5It1zarINv0.

[182] *Id.*

[183] *Id.*

managed by those who hold the purse strings."[184] "[T]he major events are not random, but are steps towards the goal."[185] The insider, Dr. Richard Day, admitted "that, indeed, there was an organized power, force, group of men, who wielded enough influence to determine major events involving countries around the world…so that an entirely new world-wide system would be in operation before the turn of the century.'"[186]

Banker and "Father of the Federal Reserve," James Warburg, promised, "We shall have world government, whether or not we like it. The question is only whether world government will be achieved by consent or by conquest."[187] "If the New World Order agenda is not realized by the terrorist attacks on America and if American's don't agree to give up their weapons and relinquish their sovereignty to the New World Order, the next attack will be the use of chemical, biological and/or atomic warfare against the American people. The architects of the New World Order will not hesitate to use as a last resort an atomic or hydrogen bomb in a major American city."[188] Indeed, Dr. Richard Day revealed that "the new system would be

---

[184] "Denis Healey > Quotes > Quotable Quote." *Good Reads*, www.goodreads.com/quotes/40800-world-events-do-not-occur-by-accident-they-are-made.

[185] "The COVID-19 Trojan Horse Is Pushing Us Towards A One World Government." *Revelation Timeline Decoded*, revelationtimelinedecoded.com/covid-19-trojan-horse/?fbclid=IwAR1p1Z4zfiOrSB0oUYGoex-A4Kfz1pJLeWsC1KWUwceRtYPuecHg1f0Aw0c.

[186] "New Order of Barbarians - Transcript of Tapes I-III." *100777.Com*, 22 May 2003, 100777.com/nwo/barbarians.

[187] James Warburg was the son of CFR [Council on Foreign Relations] founder Paul Warburg, testimony before the Senate Foreign Relations Committee on February 7, 1950. "New World Order: 37 Quotes on The New World Order, One-World Government and One-World Religion." *End Times Prophecy Report*, 8 Aug. 2018, endtimesprophecyreport.com/2013/06/05/new-world-order-37-quotes-on-the-new-world-order/.

[188] Reference Op Ed page of the New York Times 9/24/01. *Id.*

brought in, if not by peaceful cooperation — everybody willingly yielding national sovereignty — then by bringing the nation to the brink of nuclear war. And everybody would be so fearful as hysteria is created by the possibility of nuclear war that there would be a strong public outcry to negotiate a public peace and people would willingly give up national sovereignty in order to achieve peace, and thereby this would bring in the New International Political System..."[189]

Belarusian President Alexander Lukashenko is concerned that powerful interests may use the coronavirus pandemic to reshape the world to their own advantage.[190] He warned, "America has the [dollar] printing press – they've thrown in $2 trillion and plan to spend $2 trillion more. My friend [UN Secretary-General] Antonio Guterres…has proposed printing money worth ten percent of global GDP. Even as things are, the dollar is gradually losing its value, and here it will just drop, giving rise to inflation. And then, having printed out this 10 percent of global GDP, those who stay on their feet will come to us and say, 'here is a little for you, but now you will do what we say.' That's how the world can be reshaped."[191]

Former UK prime minister, Gordon Brown, "has urged world leaders to create a temporary form of global government to tackle the twin medical and economic crises caused by the Covid-19

---

[189] "New Order of Barbarians - Transcript of Tapes I-III." *100777.Com*, 22 May 2003, 100777.com/nwo/barbarians.

[190] Tsukanov, Ilya. "Belarus's President Warns Global Elites Using COVID-19 Crisis to Try to Reshape World Order." *Sputnik*, 3 Apr. 2020, sputniknews.com/europe/202004031078824468-belaruss-president-warns-global-elites-using-covid-19-crisis-to-try-to-reshape-world-order/?fbclid=IwAR2WWNitdFQVyOjMaP42h94LhgN2fj_gsG2MzES2SUjvErSWzxm63EOl9wM.

[191] *Id.*

pandemic."[192]   He claimed that "there was a need for a taskforce involving world leaders, health experts and the heads of the international organisations that would have executive powers to coordinate the response,   which would include the UN security council."[193]   Gordon claims that "[t]his is not something that can be dealt with in one country."[194]

Henry Kissinger is another who believes that "[n]o country, not even the US, can in a purely national effort overcome the [corona] virus."[195]   He "warned that the United States will have to join a global program to overcome the damage wrought by the coronavirus pandemic" and that "[c]oping effectively with the political and societal damage will take international collaboration."[196]   Kissinger maintained that, "If the US doesn't couple its efforts to rebuild its own economy with the first steps

---

[192] Gordon also wanted more money for the World Bank and IMF, saying, "The World Bank and the International Monetary Fund needed an increase in their financial firepower to cope with the impact of the crisis on low- and middle-income countries." "Gordon Brown calls for global government to tackle coronavirus." *The Guardian*, www.theguardian.com/politics/2020/mar/26/gordon-brown-calls-for-global-government-to-tackle-coronavirus?fbclid=IwAR2tWJfhjwJ7VjVG4gSorvxAJOrCaNYGNXTGr1XUsgzIxNkrfOWZSMSVCMg.

[193] *Id.*

[194] *Id.*

[195] Buyniski, Helen. "Kissinger says 'even US' can't defeat Covid-19 alone. His solution? Global NWO government, of course." *RT,* 6 Apr. 2020, www.rt.com/op-ed/485127-kissinger-new-order-defeat-coronavirus/?fbclid=IwAR17vlVJHtqtx3kOOCMpeyMzWv1QsJmQJffn1YClUXKeKCtCPD-ZweMVBwM.

[196] McClean, Dorothy Cummings. "Kissinger: Failure to establish post-COVID new world order 'could set the world on fire.'" *Lifesite,* 7 Apr. 2020, www.lifesitenews.com/news/kissinger-failure-to-establish-post-covid-new-world-order-could-set-the-world-on-fire?fbclid=IwAR0lKwPV5QHTzd5qNdoauCAkk36U5W6mAHGq6Sd9-QRCorzF_DH-AA5wQZI.

toward creating a global government, humanity is doomed."[197] Analyst Anthony Wile at *The Daily Bell* explained, "Dr. Kissinger and his backers want more comprehensive global government."[198]

On the other hand, the Covid-19 "pandemic has exposed the weaknesses of the globalist system..."[199] "Globalization not only left the U.S. highly dependent on China for manufactured goods, but also spawned efficient but vulnerable supply chains...The coronavirus's disruption of supply chains not only unhinges U.S. imports, but also raises national security concerns."[200] Alexander Hamilton advised, "Every nation ought to endeavour to possess

---

[197] Buyniski, Helen. "Kissinger says 'even US' can't defeat Covid-19 alone. His solution? Global NWO government, of course." *RT,* 6 Apr. 2020, www.rt.com/op-ed/485127-kissinger-new-order-defeat-coronavirus/?fbclid=IwAR17vlVJHtqtx3kOOCMpeyMzWv1QsJmQJffn1YClUXKeKCtCPD-ZweMVBwM.

[198] Newman, Alex. "Globalist Henry Kissinger Outlines 'New World Order.'" *The New American*, 1 Sept. 2014, www.thenewamerican.com/world-news/item/19030-globalist-henry-kissinger-outlines-new-world-order?fbclid=IwAR1AaSLqFfNV2ROqwV7bo5slhsdSVSJwYoGX3U7VRYo0FbMmTvTS8DkYFoM#.

[199] Kissinger, Henry A. "The Coronavirus Pandemic Will Forever Alter the World Order." *The Wall Street Journal*, 3 Apr. 2020, www.henryakissinger.com/articles/the-coronavirus-pandemic-will-forever-alter-the-world-order/?fbclid=IwAR0TppEvo0h7SnGzo7ajGdasG46qNlS-AIIFjeXy6PKPfLrYux-z0vzKvcU. Buyniski, Helen. "Kissinger says 'even US' can't defeat Covid-19 alone. His solution? Global NWO government, of course." *RT,* 6 Apr. 2020, www.rt.com/op-ed/485127-kissinger-new-order-defeat-coronavirus/?fbclid=IwAR17vlVJHtqtx3kOOCMpeyMzWv1QsJmQJffn1YClUXKeKCtCPD-ZweMVBwM.

[200] Schilling, A. Gary. "Globalists May Soon Become an Extinct Species." *Bloomberg,* 16 Mar. 2020, www.bloomberg.com/opinion/articles/2020-03-16/coronavirus-globalists-may-soon-become-an-extinct-species?fbclid=IwAR2MunBPhH4ejTZQR_hltyUrAjHvV_Tx-MDCD4h1mfVRbD6DXtVAKmByVlU.

within itself all the essentials of national supply."[201] Thus, if supply chains break down overseas, then the nation can still feed itself. "Even after the virus scare subsides, look for more pressure from Washington for more reliable sources of goods, among other protectionist measures. Domestic producers will benefit…"[202]

In addition, the pandemic illustrated the potential dangers of unregulated immigration, which is encouraged by NWOers. "Philippe Legrain, founder of the Open Political Economy Network (OPEN) says that the spread of COVID-19…has 'highlighted the downsides of extensive international integration while fanning fears of foreigners and providing legitimacy for national restrictions on global trade and flows of people…'"[203]

Part of the NWO plan to destroy national sovereignty involves taking control of the world's financial system, which is the focus of this book.[204] One way politicians have furthered this agenda is by making it possible for the private banking corporations to control the money supply.[205] "In the world as a whole, the power of the central

---

[201] Buchanan, Patrick. "Kissinger Still Pushing The Myth Of A Happy New World Order." *The American Conservative*, 7 Apr. 2020, www.theamericanconservative.com/buchanan/kissinger-still-pushing-the-myth-of-a-happy-new-world-order/?fbclid=IwAR2AASuPu9gr8zyv4d1-OhkWIMJ1js-9ku89cIue8KL8z-2ZNSO8wbE8e0U.

[202] Schilling, A. Gary. "Globalists May Soon Become an Extinct Species." *Bloomberg,* 16 Mar. 2020, www.bloomberg.com/opinion/articles/2020-03-16/coronavirus-globalists-may-soon-become-an-extinct-species?fbclid=IwAR2MunBPhH4ejTZQR_h1tyUrAjHvV_Tx-MDCD4h1mfVRbD6DXtVAKmByVlU.

[203] Watson, Paul Joseph. "Think Tank Complains 'Coronavirus Is Killing Globalization as We Know It.'" *Summit News*, 13 Mar. 2020, summit.news/2020/03/13/think-tank-complains-coronavirus-is-killing-globalization-as-we-know-it/.

[204] Miupiu. "15 Quotes About New World Order - #1." *Steemit*, steemit.com/quotes/@miupiu/15-quotes-about-new-world-order-part-1.

[205] *Id.*

bankers rested very largely on their control of loans and of gold flows."[206]   Aaron Russo said, "[T]he Bank of England and the Federal Reserve are partners. And the Bank of England's a private bank, and so's the Bundesbank in Germany. All the banks of the G8 countries are all private banks, private central banks."[207]   The European Central Bank is also independent.[208]

"The apex of the system was to be the Bank for International Settlements [BIS] in Basel, Switzerland, a private bank owned and controlled by the world's central banks which were themselves

---

[206] "History of Banking and Money Key Excerpts From Carroll Quigley's Tragedy and Hope." *Wanttoknow.info*, www.wanttoknow.info/articles/ quigley_carroll.tragedy_hope_banking_money_history.

[207] "Aaron Russo: Reflections and Warnings - Full Transcript." *Matt Prather*, sites.google.com/site/themattprather/Reading/aaron-russo/ reflections-and-warnings-full-transcript.

[208] Former Chancellor of Germany, Gerhard Schroder, said, "We made a decision that monetary policy will be made by an independent European Central Bank." "Central Bank Quotes." *Brainy Quote*, www.brainyquote.com/quotes/gerhard_schroder_239484? src=t_central_bank.

private corporations..."[209] "It was intended to be the world cartel of ever-growing national financial powers by assembling the nominal heads of these national financial centers."[210]

Aaron Russo explained, "[A]ll the central banks of the world are working together, through the Bank of International Settlements in Switzerland — which is the central bank for all central banks. And how they all work together to create this one-world government..."[211] In 1930, Representative McFadden revealed, "The Federal Reserve Bank of New York is eager to enter into close relationship with the Bank for International Settlements...The conclusion is impossible to escape that the State and Treasury Departments are willing to pool the banking system of Europe and

---

[209] "1930: The first Rothschild world bank, the "Bank for International Settlements (BIS)" is established in Basel, Switzerland." Hitchcock, Andrew. "Historical Timeline of the Rothschild Dynasty – Part 5." *The Sirius Report*, 19 Aug. 2016, www.thesiriusreport.com/geopolitics/historical-timeline-rothschild-dynasty-5/. "The B.I.S.'... remote origins go back to the creation of the Bank of England in 1694 and the Bank of France in 1803..."The B.I.S. as a private institution was owned by the seven chief central banks and was operated by the heads of these, who together formed its governing board. Each of these kept a substantial deposit at the B.I.S., and periodically settled payments among themselves (and thus between the major countries of the world) by bookkeeping in order to avoid shipments of gold. They made agreements on all the major financial problems of the world, as well as on many of the economic and political problems, especially in reference to loans, payments, and the economic future of the chief areas of the globe." "History of Banking and Money Key Excerpts From Carroll Quigley's Tragedy and Hope." *Wanttoknow.info*, www.wanttoknow.info/articles/quigley_carroll.tragedy_hope_banking_money_history.

[210] "History of Banking and Money Key Excerpts From Carroll Quigley's Tragedy and Hope." *Wanttoknow.info*, www.wanttoknow.info/articles/quigley_carroll.tragedy_hope_banking_money_history.

[211] "Aaron Russo: Reflections and Warnings - Full Transcript." *Matt Prather*, sites.google.com/site/themattprather/Reading/aaron-russo/reflections-and-warnings-full-transcript.

America, setting up a world financial power independent of and above the Government of the United States..."[212]

"[I]f global financial elites have their way, America will move quickly toward accepting a planetary fiat currency issued by a world central bank."[213] (Nicholas Rockefeller allegedly revealed to Aaron Russo that the banking elite "want to create a new currency called the 'amero.'"[214]) "The United Nations would like the dollar, euro, yen, and other national currencies to be succeeded by a new 'global currency.' That recommendation appears in a U.N. report..., which suggests the dollar's outsize role in international finance has ended -- and says that it's time to invent a successor currency that would be managed by a 'Global Reserve Bank...'"[215]

"There are two ways in which the dollar's role in the international monetary system can be reduced. One possibility is a gradual, market-determined erosion of the dollar as a reserve currency in favor of the euro...However, 'With the dollar's hegemony unlikely to be seriously undermined by market forces, at least in the short and medium-term, the only way to bring about a

[212] "Louis Thomas McFadden Quotes," *AZ Quotes*, www.azquotes.com/ quote/615209.

[213] Newman, Alex. "Waking up to a World Currency." *The New American*, 15 Sept. 2010, www.thenewamerican.com/economy/economics/item/4498- waking-up-to-a-world-currency.

[214] "Aaron Russo: Reflections and Warnings - Full Transcript." *Matt Prather*, sites.google.com/site/themattprather/Reading/aaron-russo/ reflections-and-warnings-full-transcript.

[215] McCullagh, Declan. "United Nations Proposes New 'Global Currency.'" *CBS News*, 9 Sept. 2009, www.cbsnews.com/news/united- nations-proposes-new-global-currency/? fbclid=IwAR1g6IOfuRyddIBwcHaLVJfzNzB3d9zujpQKzpoh4- Yimk_MvTuVGkBO6Oo.

major reduction in its role as a reserve currency is by international agreement.'"[216]

On October 10, 1988, *The Economist* magazine predicted that, in 30 years, the world would be "ready for a new world currency."[217] The "cover featured a phoenix standing over a burning stack of paper currencies from around the world. In front of that phoenix was a plaque saying 'October 10, 2018.' *The Economist* was hinting that a 'phoenix' global currency would rise from the ashes of today's fiat currencies. The Economist was also predicting that today's national fiat currencies would be destroyed via hyperinflation.'"[218] "Fiat money is currency that a government has declared to be legal tender, but it is not backed by a physical commodity."[219] "One of the biggest reasons we need a global currency, according to *The Economist*, is because national boundaries 'are slowly dissolving.'"[220]

In April 2009, the G20 leaders reported that "[t]he world is a step closer to a global currency, backed by a global central bank,

---

[216] Marshall, Andrew Gavin. "The Bilderberg Plan for 2009: Remaking the Global Political Economy." *Global Research,* 26 May 2009, www.globalresearch.ca/the-bilderberg-plan-for-2009-remaking-the-global-political-economy/13738.

[217] Bit Coin Exchange Guide News Team. "Economist's 30-Year Old Prediction for a Global Currency Arrives: is Crypto Going to Rule World?" *Bit Coin Exchange Guide,* 10 Oct. 2018, bitcoinexchangeguide.com/economists-30-year-old-prediction-for-a-global-currency-arrives-is-crypto-going-to-rule-world/.

[218] *Id.*

[219] Jones, Stack. "An Essay On The History Of Banking." *The Banking Swindle*, 1 Jan. 2018, criminalbankingmonopoly.wordpress.com/.

[220] Bit Coin Exchange Guide News Team. "Economist's 30-Year Old Prediction for a Global Currency Arrives: is Crypto Going to Rule World?" *Bit Coin Exchange Guide,* 10 Oct. 2018, bitcoinexchangeguide.com/economists-30-year-old-prediction-for-a-global-currency-arrives-is-crypto-going-to-rule-world/.

running monetary policy for all humanity."[221]   This involves SDRs, which "are Special Drawing Rights, a synthetic paper currency issued by the International Monetary Fund…"[222]   In 2011, US Secretary of the Treasury, "Tim Geithner called for the IMF's Special Drawing Rights to be issued and used more frequently…The SDR would soon replace the dollar with a fixed exchange rate to all other currencies and this peg will devalue the dollar by some 50% or so from current levels."[223]   By issuing SDRs, the IMF is "in effect acting as if it were the world's central bank."[224]   "Essentially, 'they are putting a de facto world currency into play. It is outside the control of any sovereign body.'"[225]   Eventually, "[o]ur policy will not be made in Washington but by the IMF (and the people who run it behind the curtain) who will be in control of our finances and therefore our politics."[226]

---

[221] Marshall, Andrew Gavin. "The Bilderberg Plan for 2009: Remaking the Global Political Economy." *Global Research,* 26 May 2009, www.globalresearch.ca/the-bilderberg-plan-for-2009-remaking-the-global-political-economy/13738.

[222] *Id.*

[223] Levis, Nick. "New World Disorder: Why Geithner's IMF SDR Plan For A Global Currency Looks a Bit Like High Treason." *Business Insider,* Business Insider, 20 Jul. 2011, www.businessinsider.com/new-world-disorder-why-geithners-imf-sdr-plan-for-a-global-currency-is-high-treason-2011-7.

[224] Marshall, Andrew Gavin. "The Bilderberg Plan for 2009: Remaking the Global Political Economy." *Global Research,* 26 May 2009, www.globalresearch.ca/the-bilderberg-plan-for-2009-remaking-the-global-political-economy/13738.

[225] *Id.*

[226] Levis, Nick. "New World Disorder: Why Geithner's IMF SDR Plan For A Global Currency Looks a Bit Like High Treason." *Business Insider,* Business Insider, 20 Jul. 2011, www.businessinsider.com/new-world-disorder-why-geithners-imf-sdr-plan-for-a-global-currency-is-high-treason-2011-7.

According to Aaron Russo, "The elites'…final objective is to finalize a cashless, RFID microchipped society under the absolute tyranny and control of an entrenched one world government."[227] He said, "And what they want to do is control the American people, control the people of the world, put RFID chips in everybody, so everybody's a slave to these central banks."[228] Russo claimed that he got this information from Nicholas Rockefeller, who allegedly told him that "the whole agenda is to create a one-world government where everybody has an RFID chip implanted in them. All money is to be in those chips — there'll be no more cash…And all money will be in your chips. And so, instead of having cash, any time you have money in your chip, they can take out whatever they want to take out whenever they want to. If they say 'you owe us this much money in taxes,' they just deduct it out of your chip, digitally…And they control people — and you become a slave, you become a serf to these people. That's their goal, that's their intentions…"[229]

Dr. Richard Day said, "They do want to implant a chip in us so they can find and identify us, as well as monitor and control our purchases."[230] He explained, "Money would become predominately credit. It was already…money is primarily a credit thing but exchange of money would be not cash or palpable things but electronic credit signal…Any purchase of any significant amount

---

[227] Hagopian, Joachim. "One World Governance and the Council on Foreign Relations. 'We Shall Have World Government…by Conquest or Consent.'" *Global Research*, 24 Jan. 2021, www.globalresearch.ca/one-world-governance-and-the-council-on-foreign-relations-we-shall-have-world-government-by-conquest-or-consent/5541363.

[228] "Aaron Russo: Reflections and Warnings - Full Transcript." *Matt Prather*, sites.google.com/site/themattprather/Reading/aaron-russo/reflections-and-warnings-full-transcript.

[229] *Id.*

[230] "The Illuminati Plan to Enslave Americans (1969)." *HenryMakow.com*, 1 0 M a y 2 0 1 6 , w w w . s a v e t h e m a l e s . c a / confirmedrockefeller_plan_to_g.html.

would be done electronically. Earnings would be electronically entered into your account. It would be a single banking system. May have the appearance of being more than one but ultimately and basically it would be one single banking system, so that when you got paid, your pay would be entered for you into your account balance and then when you purchased anything at the point of purchase, it would be deducted from your account balance and you would actually carry nothing with you. Also computer records can be kept on whatever it was you purchased so that if you were purchasing too much of any particular item and some official wanted to know what you were doing with your money they could go back and review your purchases and determine what you were buying. There was a statement that any purchase of significant size like an automobile, bicycle, a refrigerator, a radio or television or whatever might have some sort of identification on it so it could be traced, so that very quickly anything which was either given away or stolen — whatever — authorities would be able to establish who purchased it and when."[231]

Dr. Day elaborated on the method of payment: "Electronic payments initially would all be based on different kinds of credit cards...But people would have credit cards with the electronic strip on it and once they got used to that then it would be pointed out the advantage of having all of that combined into a single credit card, serving a single monetary system and then they won't have to carry around all that plastic...So the next step would be the single card and then the next step would be to replace the single card with a skin implant. The single card could be lost or stolen, give rise to problems; could be exchanged with somebody else to confuse identify. The skin implant on the other hand would be not losable or counterfeitable or transferrable to another person so you and your accounts would be identified without any possibility of error. And

[231] Recollections of Dr. Lawrence Dunegan regarding a lecture by Dr. Day - an insider of the "Order" - he attended on March 20, 1969 at a meeting of the Pittsburgh Pediatric Society. "New Order of Barbarians - Transcript of Tapes I-III." *100777.Com*, 22 May 2003, 100777.com/nwo/barbarians.

the skin implants would have to be put some place that would be convenient to the skin; for example your right hand or your forehead."[232]

Dr. Day said that, in this system, "Nobody has any wealth. You own nothing of value except access to electronic impulses which are beyond your control. A cashless society. So when your reward for working is [nothing more than] impulses on the computer and the only claim you have is these impulses and the people who run the system can give or take them as they choose…But with this cashless society, I believe this is the first time in the history of the human race where the entire population of the world can be controlled economically so that somebody can say, 'I pushed the right buttons and I know how much credit you have electronically; I know where you spend your money electronically; and you cannot buy, you cannot sell unless you get on my computer.'"[233] "If you don't sign up, then you can't get any electric impulses in your banking account and you won't have any electric impulses with which to pay your electric, or your mortgage or your food, and when your electric impulses are gone, then you have no means of livelihood…"[234]

"Cash has been the target of the banking and financial elites for years."[235]   For example, in November "2016, the Indian government decided to demonetize the 500- and 1,000- rupee notes, the two biggest denominations in its currency system; these notes accounted for 86 percent of the country's circulating cash. With little warning, India's Prime Minister Narendra Modi announced to the citizenry on Nov. 8, 2016 that those notes were worthless, effective

---

[232] *Id.*

[233] *Id.*

[234] *Id.*

[235] Hankoff, Nick. "Coronavirus Being Used to Scare You Away From Using Cash." *Advocate,* 24 Mar. 2020, www.theadvocates.org/2020/03/coronavirus-being-used-to-scare-you-away-from-using-cash/?fbclid=IwAR3iYN4Niwu8AawMIhSH8kbohngSlHRUmgK_gOdFAE-LFIz0RR3xRu5-Awg.

immediately – and they had until the end of the year to deposit or exchange them for newly introduced 2000 rupee and 500 rupee bills…"[236]   Economist Norbert Häring elaborated, "Prime Minister Narendra Modi went on TV declaring all but the smallest denomination banknotes 'demonetised' with only 4 hours' notice. This meant you could not pay with them anymore. You had to bring them to the bank. This led to days of chaos and months of extreme dearth of cash in a country where half the population does not even have a bank account and 90 percent of payments are done in cash."[237]   One of the government's goals (and rationale for the abrupt announcement) was to promote a cashless society.[238]

Norbert Häring tells us that the drive to go cashless "is a successful but slow process in most rich countries with functioning democracies, because people care a lot about their right to use cash. Because of this resistance of the population, they can only use indirect measures, like regulations for banks that make cash more inconvenient and expensive for them, a cost which they pass on to customers. There has even been a paper by the IMF that recommends such indirect measures to get around the resistance of the population…"[239]

---

[236] Chappelow, Jim. "Demonetization." *Investopedia,* 20 Mar. 2020, www.investopedia.com/terms/d/demonetization.asp.

[237] Elmaazi, Mohammed. "Bill Gates and His 'War Against Cash' Are a Threat to Our Liberty, Economist Warns." *Sputnik News,* 9 May 2020, sputniknews.com/amp/analysis/202005071079213583-bill-gates-and-his-war-against-cash-are-a-threat-to-our-liberty-economist-warns/?fbclid=IwAR0z0XbSa6efxLY10IKmklyX48piXi4XK66l8f0kWvR8syY4S4iADgTWH5k.

[238] Chappelow, Jim. "Demonetization." *Investopedia,* 20 Mar. 2020, www.investopedia.com/terms/d/demonetization.asp.

[239] Elmaazi, Mohammed. "Bill Gates and His 'War Against Cash' Are a Threat to Our Liberty, Economist Warns." *Sputnik News,* 9 May 2020, sputniknews.com/amp/analysis/202005071079213583-bill-gates-and-his-war-against-cash-are-a-threat-to-our-liberty-economist-warns/?fbclid=IwAR0z0XbSa6efxLY10IKmklyX48piXi4XK66l8f0kWvR8syY4S4iADgTWH5k.

"Now, the coronavirus pandemic is being used to frighten the masses into accepting a cashless society."[240] COVID-19 and "The Great Lockdown" further the cashless agenda by some suggesting "that paper money be removed from the system because it is a viral spreader."[241] "The World Health Organisation (WHO) has advised people to use contactless technology instead of cash as banknotes may be spreading coronavirus. The infectious COVID-19 virus could be carried on the surface of banknotes for several days, the WHO warned...To stop the spread of the disease, people should use contactless payments where possible and wash their hands after handling cash, a WHO spokesman said. The Bank of England also recognised that banknotes 'can carry bacteria or viruses...' When possible it would also be advisable to use contactless payments to reduce the risk of transmission."[242]

Although "[m]any fear that coronavirus may be transmitted via cash[,] the Bank of England and the World Health Organisation (WHO) have said the risk is no greater than with other items."[243]

---

[240] Hankoff, Nick. "Coronavirus Being Used to Scare You Away From Using Cash." *Advocate,* 24 Mar. 2020, www.theadvocates.org/2020/03/coronavirus-being-used-to-scare-you-away-from-using-cash/?fbclid=IwAR3iYN4Niwu8AawMIhSH8kbohngSlHRUmgK_gOdFAE-LFIz0RR3xRu5-Awg.

[241] Durden, Tyler. "WHO Urges People To Go Cashless Because 'Dirty Banknotes Can Spread The Virus.'" *Activist Post*, 4 Mar. 2020, www.activistpost.com/2020/03/who-urges-people-to-go-cashless-because-dirty-banknotes-can-spread-the-virus.html.

[242] Sangster, Kalila. "Banknotes may be spreading coronavirus, World Health Organisation warns." *Yahoo Finance,* 3 Mar. 2020, finance.yahoo.com/news/who-world-health-organisation-coronavirus-banknotes-warning-111019361.html.

[243] O'Callaghan, Laura. "End of UK coins and banknotes? New measures mean Britain could be cashless in two years." *Express,* 6 May 2020, www.express.co.uk/news/uk/1278656/coronavirus-uk-cash-payments-stopped-cashless-society-two-years-atm-withdrawals?fbclid=IwAR2QnWDXKpMDOnkW38dYpGkX8wEoXEgBZpM-GijoIscUp9UdMHLj_ccluY8.

There is really no "evidence that the virus can be transmitted via cash. Most health experts say_that [cash] is not a relevant channel [for the virus]."[244] "Public officials and health experts have said that the risk of transferring the virus person-to-person through the use of banknotes is small...Other devices used to pay for items are just as likely to be vectors for disease transfer..."[245] "[T]he risk posed by handling a polymer note is no greater than touching any other common surface, such as handrails, doorknobs or credit cards."[246]

Nevertheless, as Norbert Häring revealed, "Banks are running mailing and internet campaigns, telling their customers that cash is dirty and cards or mobile payment solutions are not."[247] As a result, "[a] growing number of businesses and individuals worldwide have stopped using banknotes [for] fear that physical currency...could be

---

[244] Elmaazi, Mohammed. "Bill Gates and His 'War Against Cash' Are a Threat to Our Liberty, Economist Warns." *Sputnik News,* 9 May 2020, sputniknews.com/amp/analysis/202005071079213583-bill-gates-and-his-war-against-cash-are-a-threat-to-our-liberty-economist-warns/?fbclid=IwAR0z0XbSa6efxLY10IKmklyX48piXi4XK66l8f0kWvR8syY4S4iADgTWH5k.

[245] Sweet, Ken. "Filthy lucre: Paper money shunned for fear of virus sprea." *AP,* 20 Mar. 2020, apnews.com/167186097f44116220b757abebb49be3?fbclid=IwAR2-UVEZ7HPab0g9JHcEXEfCJ-Me3CjTVS0Y14CP8O4MFnSvLVl_GIWaXXk.

[246] Sangster, Kalila. "Banknotes may be spreading coronavirus, World Health Organisation warns." *Yahoo Finance,* 3 Mar. 2020, finance.yahoo.com/news/who-world-health-organisation-coronavirus-banknotes-warning-111019361.html.

[247] Elmaazi, Mohammed. "Bill Gates and His 'War Against Cash' Are a Threat to Our Liberty, Economist Warns." *Sputnik News,* 9 May 2020, sputniknews.com/amp/analysis/202005071079213583-bill-gates-and-his-war-against-cash-are-a-threat-to-our-liberty-economist-warns/?fbclid=IwAR0z0XbSa6efxLY10IKmklyX48piXi4XK66l8f0kWvR8syY4S4iADgTWH5k.

a vector for the spreading coronavirus."[248] "A survey conducted by Amaiz for Money Mail showed half of small business owners have either already gone cashless or plan to do so due to the epidemic…"[249] In Iran, "banks have announced that they will not accept cash from customers."[250] China is also pushing to end cash because it is a "virus spreader."[251]

"The Federal Reserve sent out a notice that they're stopping the printing of any paper currency 'this holiday season.'"[252] Journalist David Knight reported, "A listener sent me a notice that was sent to a credit union saying, 'Federal Reserve has suspended orders for new bills in 2020. During the holidays, members often request newly printed bills to give as gifts, unfortunately, this holiday season, newly printed bills will not be available due to COVID-19.'"[253] "This is all due to the virus, of course, because any

---

[248] Sweet, Ken. "Filthy lucre: Paper money shunned for fear of virus sprea." *AP*, 20 Mar. 2020, apnews.com/167186097f44116220b757abebb49be3?fbclid=IwAR2-UVEZ7HPab0g9JHcEXEfCJ-Me3CjTVS0Y14CP8O4MFnSvLV1_GIWaXXk.

[249] O'Callaghan, Laura. "End of UK coins and banknotes? New measures mean Britain could be cashless in two years." *Express,* 6 May 2020, www.express.co.uk/news/uk/1278656/coronavirus-uk-cash-payments-stopped-cashless-society-two-years-atm-withdrawals?fbclid=IwAR2QnWDXKpMDOnkW38dYpGkX8wEoXEgBZpM-GijoIscUp9UdMHLj_ccluY8.

[250] Sweet, Ken. "Filthy lucre: Paper money shunned for fear of virus sprea." *AP*, 20 Mar. 2020, apnews.com/167186097f44116220b757abebb49be3?fbclid=IwAR2-UVEZ7HPab0g9JHcEXEfCJ-Me3CjTVS0Y14CP8O4MFnSvLV1_GIWaXXk.

[251] Smith, Brandon. "Global Centralization Is The Cause Of Crisis – Not The Cure." *Activist Post,* 19 Feb. 2020, www.activistpost.com/2020/02/global-centralization-is-the-cause-of-crisis-not-the-cure.html.

[252] Knight, David. "Fed Introduces Cashless Society." *Info Wars,* 6 Oct. 2020, www.infowars.com/posts/fed-introduces-cashless-society/.

[253] *Id.*

new money they print could be contaminated. Just keep using old, clean, used currency…"[254] "The Federal Reserve is using this as an excuse to do what they've wanted to do for years…," i.e. not print money anymore.[255] They even urge customers to "take the digital route.'"[256]

"[C]hief executive John Howells warned if Britons continued with their current shopping habits, cash would be wiped out within a couple of years. 'If we do nothing, we could be in a virtually cashless society in two years' time,' he said…If his predictions come true, it will mean older shoppers may encounter difficulty. Many elderly Britons deal solely in cash and have never owned a credit card or bank card…"[257] In addition, "many of the measures that are taken to make cash inconvenient and hard to use are in violation of the status of euro banknotes and coins as legal tender…"[258]

"The war on cash is about imposing a new meta-narrative. As economist Joseph Salerno explains, the cashless society forces all payments to be made through the financial system…Being bound to computers for transactions kicks the door wide open to hardcore surveillance of personal activity and location data. Being eternally on the grid means relentless taxation and negative interest rates,

---

[254] *Id.*

[255] *Id.*

[256] *Id.*

[257] O'Callaghan, Laura. "End of UK coins and banknotes? New measures mean Britain could be cashless in two years." *Express,* 6 May 2020, www.express.co.uk/news/uk/1278656/coronavirus-uk-cash-payments-stopped-cashless-society-two-years-atm-withdrawals?fbclid=IwAR2QnWDXKpMDOnkW38dYpGkX8wEoXEgBZpM-GijoIscUp9UdMHLj_ccluY8.

[258] Elmaazi, Mohammed. "Bill Gates and His 'War Against Cash' Are a Threat to Our Liberty, Economist Warns." *Sputnik News,* 9 May 2020, sputniknews.com/amp/analysis/202005071079213583-bill-gates-and-his-war-against-cash-are-a-threat-to-our-liberty-economist-warns/?fbclid=IwAR0z0XbSa6efxLY10IKmklyX48piXi4XK66l8f0kWvR8syY4S4iADgTWH5k.

which the Federal Reserve is already gearing up for..."[259] "[W]e find ourselves in a cashless society in a matter of a year or two; which is what the globalists have been demanding for years. Everything goes digital, and thus even local economies become completely centralized as private trade dies."[260]

Sadly, a cashless society "would mean the death of what's left of our free society..."[261] Norbert Häring explained, "The interest of the financial sector in selling their own products instead of cash is obvious. The IT-companies want the data that [goes] with digitalisation [of cash] and the US-government wants the surveillance and sanctioning power that goes with digitalisation of payments. The other countries that co-operate also like the aspect of gaining more surveillance power over their populations...More importantly: everything that we pay [for] digitally is recorded, seen and stored by various service providers and ends up in our bank account information. If there is no possibility of using cash any more, our bank account information will be a near-complete log of our life. Anybody with the power to look into it, who develops an interest in us at any time, can see where we have been and what we did for every day and hour, decades into the past...Many people correctly think that nobody with the power to do this will ever develop enough of an interest in them. However, they have to realise

---

[259] Hankoff, Nick. "Coronavirus Being Used to Scare You Away From Using Cash." *Advocate,* 24 Mar. 2020, www.theadvocates.org/2020/03/ coronavirus-being-used-to-scare-you-away-from-using-cash/? fbclid=IwAR3iYN4Niwu8AawMIhSH8kbohngSlHRUmgK_gOdFAE-LFIz0RR3xRu5-Awg.

[260] Durden, Tyler. "WHO Urges People To Go Cashless Because 'Dirty Banknotes Can Spread The Virus.'" *Activist Post*, 4 Mar. 2020, www.activistpost.com/2020/03/who-urges-people-to-go-cashless-because-dirty-banknotes-can-spread-the-virus.html.

[261] Hankoff, Nick. "Coronavirus Being Used to Scare You Away From Using Cash." *Advocate,* 24 Mar. 2020, www.theadvocates.org/2020/03/ coronavirus-being-used-to-scare-you-away-from-using-cash/? fbclid=IwAR3iYN4Niwu8AawMIhSH8kbohngSlHRUmgK_gOdFAE-LFIz0RR3xRu5-Awg.

that it means something for them, too, if they have to live in a society, in which every person of any importance is totally transparent for the powerful and can thus be blackmailed or destroyed by them at will. This is inconsistent with democracy and a free society..."[262]

"Through monopolizing a centralized banking system of debt-based theft and global enslavement...[the] consolidation of power into fewer and fewer hands has eliminated competition in a closed, thoroughly insulated, anything but free, now stagnating global market...With the globalists wielding more power than ever before in human history, their centuries old, long sought after scheme of a one world government has never been closer at hand..."[263] Unfortunately, "the men in charge of our economy, laws, and justice system are handing our nation over to overlord bankers."[264] Rep. McFadden lamented, "They have created a super state controlled by international bankers and international industrialists acting together

---

[262] Elmaazi, Mohammed. "Bill Gates and His 'War Against Cash' Are a Threat to Our Liberty, Economist Warns." *Sputnik News,* 9 May 2020, sputniknews.com/amp/analysis/202005071079213583-bill-gates-and-his-war-against-cash-are-a-threat-to-our-liberty-economist-warns/?fbclid=IwAR0z0XbSa6efxLY10IKmklyX48piXi4XK66l8f0kWvR8syY4S4iADgTWH5k.

[263] Hagopian, Joachim. "One World Governance and the Council on Foreign Relations. 'We Shall Have World Government...by Conquest or Consent.'" *Global Research,* 24 Jan. 2021, www.globalresearch.ca/one-world-governance-and-the-council-on-foreign-relations-we-shall-have-world-government-by-conquest-or-consent/5541363.

[264] Levis, Nick. "New World Disorder: Why Geithner's IMF SDR Plan For A Global Currency Looks a Bit Like High Treason." *Business Insider,* Business Insider, 20 Jul. 2011, www.businessinsider.com/new-world-disorder-why-geithners-imf-sdr-plan-for-a-global-currency-is-high-treason-2011-7.

to enslave the world for their own pleasure."[265]   "If a one world system ever wins out, our rights as free citizens will vanish. It will be the end of freedom as we know it and the start of a new feudalism across the globe…"[266]

Not surprisingly, it has been necessary for the bankers "to conceal, or even to mislead, both governments and people about the nature of money and its methods of operation."[267] According to economist John Kenneth Galbraith, "The study of money, above all other fields in economics, is one in which complexity is used to disguise truth or to evade truth, not to reveal it."[268]   For example, "financial regulators baffle us with jargon…, making it barely intelligible to regular folks (cloaking it in such terms as 'clogged transmission mechanisms,' 'length of collateral chains')," etc.[269] One of the bankers' tools is the manipulation of the terms, "money" and "currency." This is the subject of the next chapter.

---

[265] McFadden said this in 1914. He was poisoned at a banquet before he could impeach Federal Reserve members. "Full text of 'Conspiracy Evidence Archives and Quotes.'" *Internet Archive*, archive.org/stream/ N W O Q u o t e s 1 4 / I n t e r n a t i o n a l % 2 0 B a n k e r s – famous%20quotes%20about%20international%20bankers%20wordpress.c om-13_djvu.txt.

[266] Levis, Nick. "New World Disorder: Why Geithner's IMF SDR Plan For A Global Currency Looks a Bit Like High Treason." *Business Insider*, Business Insider, 20 Jul. 2011, www.businessinsider.com/new-world-disorder-why-geithners-imf-sdr-plan-for-a-global-currency-is-high-treason-2011-7.

[267] "History of Banking and Money Key Excerpts From Carroll Quigley's Tragedy and Hope." *Wanttoknow.info*, www.wanttoknow.info/articles/ quigley_carroll.tragedy_hope_banking_money_history.

[268] Circa 1990. "The International Bankers: Famous Quotes." *ConspiracyAnalyst.org*, 23 Dec. 2019, conspiracyanalyst.org/2013/03/01/ the-international-bankers-famous-quotes/.

[269] Long, Caitlin. "The Real Story Of The Repo Market Meltdown, And What It Means For Bitcoin." *Forbes*, 25 Sept. 2019, www.forbes.com/ sites/caitlinlong/2019/09/25/the-real-story-of-the-repo-market-meltdown-and-what-it-means-for-bitcoin/#23f8ac237caa.

Chapter 2

Money vs. Currency

Distinguishing between currency and money is critical to understanding the current economic predicament and how to negotiate it.

"Money" is an economic unit of account that functions as a store of value and a medium of exchange.[270] As a unit of account, money makes "accounting for profit and loss of a business, balancing a budget, or valuing the total assets of a company... possible."[271]

"Money originates in the form of a commodity, having a physical property..."[272] It has certain characteristics, such as being fungible, durable, portable, recognizable, and stable.[273] Fungible means that the "[u]nits...should be of relatively uniform quality so that they are interchangeable with one another."[274] The physical character "should be durable enough to retain its usefulness in future exchanges and be reused multiple times."[275] Money is portable if it is "divisible into small quantities so that it can be conveniently carried or transported."[276] The authenticity and quantity should be

---

[270] Brock, Thomas. "Money." *Investopedia*, 25 Dec. 2020, www.investopedia.com/terms/m/money.asp. Justice Clifford's dissent. *Legal Tender Cases*, 79 U.S. 457 (1870).

[271] Brock, Thomas. "Money." *Investopedia*, 25 Dec. 2020, www.investopedia.com/terms/m/money.asp.

[272] *Id.*

[273] *Id.*

[274] *Id.*

[275] *Id.*

[276] *Id.*

readily recognizable so that users can easily agree to the terms of an exchange.[277]

Thus, to be useful as money, the commodity must be easily divisible into small portions, may be kept for an indefinite period without deteriorating, must possess great value in small bulk, and be capable of being easily transported.[278] In addition, a given denomination of money should always be equal in weight and quality, or fineness, to other pieces of money of the same denomination, and its value should be the same or as little subject to variation as possible.[279] Former Chair of the Federal Reserve, Alan Greenspan, summed it up: "Money is the common denominator of all economic transactions. It is that commodity which serves as a medium of exchange, is universally acceptable to all participants in an exchange economy as payment for their goods or services, and can, therefore, be used as a standard of market value and as a store of value, i.e., as a means of saving."[280']

"The process through which money is 'created' is not one of central planning, but rather one in which money is 'discovered' by markets."[281] "A metal is generally chosen because it is homogeneous and divisible: every unit is the same as every other

---

[277] *Id.*

[278] Justice Clifford's dissent. *Legal Tender Cases*, 79 U.S. 457 (1870).

[279] *Id.*

[280] Published in Ayn Rand's "Objectivist" newsletter in 1966, and reprinted in her book, *Capitalism: The Unknown Ideal*, in 1967. Greenspan, Alan. "Gold and Economic Freedom." *Constitution Society*, www.constitution.org/mon/greenspan_gold.htm.

[281] Cortez, JP. "Fake Money, Sound Money and Government Malfeasance." *Tenth Amendment Center*, 28 Aug. 2018, tenthamendmentcenter.com/2018/08/28/fake-money-sound-money-and-government-malfeasance/.

and it can be blended or formed in any quantity…"[282] Metals are also durable and have intrinsic value. "Historically, precious metals like gold and silver were adopted as these kinds of market-determined moneys" and "used as international media of exchange…"[283] "Gold and silver embodied the qualities desirable in money [to] a much greater degree than any other known commodity or substance…"[284] British economist, David Ricardo, said, "Gold and silver, like other commodities, have an intrinsic value, which is not arbitrary, but is dependent on their scarcity, the quantity of labour bestowed in procuring them, and the value of the capital employed in the mines which produce them."[285] Philosopher Karl Marx noted, "Although gold and silver are not by nature money, money is by nature gold and silver."[286]

Money should serve as a store of value, which "facilitates saving for the future."[287] This is one reason why it is important for its value in terms of other goods to be relatively stable or constant over time.[288] According to Chief Market Analyst at ITM Trading, Lynette Zang, "The true, fundamental value of a physical ounce of gold or silver is based upon the most important function that it

---

[282] Money may be kept for an indefinite period without deteriorating - paper can mold. Greenspan, Alan. "Gold and Economic Freedom." *Constitution Society*, www.constitution.org/mon/greenspan_gold.htm. Published in Ayn Rand's "Objectivist" newsletter in 1966, and reprinted in her book, *Capitalism: The Unknown Ideal*, in 1967.

[283] *Id.*

[284] Justice Clifford's dissent. *Legal Tender Cases*, 79 U.S. 457 (1870).

[285] "The 101 Best Gold Quotes From History – GoldSilver." *Gold Silver*, goldsilver.com/blog/101-best-gold-quotes-all-time/.

[286] *Id.*

[287] Brock, Thomas. "Money." *Investopedia*, 25 Dec. 2020, www.investopedia.com/terms/m/money.asp.

[288] *Id.*

performs, which is to hold its value over time..."[289]   Financial commentator, Peter A. Burshre, informs us, "Regardless of the dollar price involved, one ounce of gold would purchase a good-quality man's suit at the conclusion of the Revolutionary War, the Civil War, the presidency of Franklin Roosevelt and today."[290]   Indeed, gold and silver "are in themselves values, and being such,...are the only proper measures of value."[291]

Over time, gold has become the predominant monetary metal.[292]   "Gold, having both artistic and functional uses and being relatively scarce, has significant advantages over all other media of exchange."[293]   According to French statesman, Charles de Gaulle, "There can be no other criterion, no other standard than gold. Yes, gold which never changes, which can be shaped into ingots, bars, coins, which has no nationality and which is eternally and universally accepted as the unalterable fiduciary value par excellence."[294]   J. P. Morgan opined, "Gold is money. Everything else is credit."[295]

Author and speaker, Mark Nestmann, believes that "Gold is still the ultimate store of wealth. It's the world's only true money. And there isn't much of it to go around. All of it ever mined would fit into a small building — a 56-foot cube. The annual world

---

[289] At 27:30. ITM Trading, Inc. "And Central Banks Using Up Their Ammo." *Youtube,* 18 Dec. 2018, www.youtube.com/watch? v=NvWm6Qkp5gU.

[290] "The 101 Best Gold Quotes From History – GoldSilver." *Gold Silver*, goldsilver.com/blog/101-best-gold-quotes-all-time/.

[291] Justice Clifford's dissent. *Legal Tender Cases*, 79 U.S. 457 (1870).

[292] Greenspan, Alan. "Gold and Economic Freedom." *Constitution Society*, www.constitution.org/mon/greenspan_gold.htm.

[293] *Id.*

[294] "The 101 Best Gold Quotes From History – GoldSilver." *Gold Silver*, goldsilver.com/blog/101-best-gold-quotes-all-time/.

[295] *Id.*

production would fit into a 14-foot cube, roughly the size of an ordinary living room. If each Chinese citizen were to buy just one ounce, it would take up the annual supply for the next 200 years."[296]

"Humans have centuries of experience with basing their money on gold...The purpose of a 'gold standard system' is to maintain a currency of stable value..."[297] "After several millennia of being tested by market forces, gold and silver are undoubtedly sound money..."[298] "[S]ound money is money that is not prone to sudden appreciation or depreciation in purchasing power over the long term, aided by self-correcting mechanisms inherent in a free-market system..."[299]

Unfortunately, "goods that do not necessarily meet the five properties of optimal market-determined money...can be used to fulfill the functions of money in an economy."[300] "For generations, men had sought to avoid the one drawback of gold, its heaviness, by using pieces of paper to represent specific pieces of gold."[301] However, paper currency is not a store of value, because it gradually depreciates. Since it consistently loses value over time, it is not stable. Justice Clifford explained in his dissent in the Legal Tender Cases that "paper medium...possesses no value, is not money, either

---

[296] *Id.*

[297] Lewis, Nathan. "We Just Tested The Gold Standard -- It Still Works." *Forbes*, 8 Aug. 2019, www.forbes.com/sites/nathanlewis/2019/08/08/we-just-tested-the-gold-standard-it-still-works/#2044ef4c556b.

[298] Cortez, JP. "Fake Money, Sound Money and Government Malfeasance." *Tenth Amendment Center*, 28 Aug. 2018, tenthamendmentcenter.com/2018/08/28/fake-money-sound-money-and-government-malfeasance/.

[299] *Id.*

[300] Brock, Thomas. "Money." *Investopedia*, 25 Dec. 2020, www.investopedia.com/terms/m/money.asp.

[301] "History of Banking and Money Key Excerpts From Carroll Quigley's Tragedy and Hope." *Wanttoknow.info*, www.wanttoknow.info/articles/quigley_carroll.tragedy_hope_banking_money_history.

in the constitutional or commercial sense, but only a promise to pay money, is never worth par, and often much less, even as domestic exchange, and is always fluctuating…"[302]

Not surprisingly, paper currency has had many critics over the years. For example, Count Destutt de Tracy warned, "A theft of greater magnitude and still more ruinous, is the making of paper money; it is greater because in this money there is absolutely no real value; it is more ruinous because by its gradual depreciation during the time of its existence, it produces the effect which would be proration of the coins. All those iniquities are founded on the false idea the money is but a sign."[303] French philosopher, Voltaire, said, "Paper money eventually returns to its intrinsic value — zero."[304] Even the Federal Reserve Bank of Chicago admitted that paper currency is worthless (in *Modern Money Mechanics Workbook* (1975)): "Neither paper currency nor deposits have value as commodities, intrinsically; a 'dollar' bill is just a piece of paper. Deposits are merely book entries."[305]

"A new medium of exchange that does not serve any original non-money use as an economic good can be imposed to replace market-determined money by legal declaration. This type of legal tender can also be called fiat money. Fiat money becomes a medium of exchange through legal imposition on the market, rather than through the process of adoption by the market for easing

---

[302] Justice Clifford's dissent. *Legal Tender Cases*, 79 U.S. 457 (1870).

[303] Tracy lived 1754-1836. "The International Bankers: Famous Quotes." *ConspiracyAnalyst.org*, 23 Dec. 2019, conspiracyanalyst.org/2013/03/01/the-international-bankers-famous-quotes/.

[304] "Money Quotes: What The Experts Say About Money." *Midas Gold Group*, 27 Aug. 2020, www.midasgoldgroup.com/money-quotes/.

[305] "The International Bankers: Famous Quotes." *ConspiracyAnalyst.org*, 23 Dec. 2019, conspiracyanalyst.org/2013/03/01/the-international-bankers-famous-quotes/.

transactions."[306]   "Typically, this involves a legal mandate to use a specific good as money (known as a legal tender law)...Legal tender laws specify a certain good as legal money, which courts will recognize as a final means of payment in contracts and the legal means of settling tax bills."[307]   "Governmental currencies fall under the category of fiat money."[308]

G. Edward Griffin wrote in *The Creature From Jekyll Island,* "The American Heritage Dictionary defines fiat money as 'paper money decreed legal tender, not backed by gold or silver.' The two characteristics of fiat money, therefore, are (1) it does not represent anything of intrinsic value and (2) it is decreed legal tender. Legal tender simply means that there is a law requiring everyone to accept the currency in commerce. The two always go together because, since the money really is worthless, it soon would be rejected by the public in favor of a more reliable medium of exchange, such as gold or silver coin."[309]

"Fiat money often does not meet the general characteristics of money and the market-determined money that it replaces."[310] "Through market processes, the 'most marketable commodity,' as economist Ludwig von Mises described money, makes itself known. Money is not created by government decree, but rather by surviving the test of time and the pressures of market forces while maintaining

---

[306] Brock, Thomas. "Money." *Investopedia*, 25 Dec. 2020, www.investopedia.com/terms/m/money.asp.

[307] *Id.*

[308] *Id.*

[309] Wolverton II, JD, Joe. "Tennessee Considering Bills Restoring Gold and Silver as Sound Money." *The New American*, 2 Feb. 2019, www.thenewamerican.com/usnews/constitution/item/31369-tennessee-considering-bills-restoring-gold-and-silver-as-sound-money.

[310] Brock, Thomas. "Money." *Investopedia*, 25 Dec. 2020, www.investopedia.com/terms/m/money.asp.

its value…"[311] Henry Hazlitt believed, "The great merit of gold is precisely that it is scarce; that its quantity is limited by nature; that it is costly to discover, to mine and to process; and that it cannot be created by political fiat or caprice."[312] Most fiat currencies "consistently lose value over time…"[313] "Fiat moneys can lead to increased economic transaction costs, market distortions, and unintended consequences to the extent that they do not meet the characteristics that make a particular good suitable to serve as money."[314] Dennis Karnosky, Chief Economic Adviser at the St. Louis Federal Reserve Bank, admitted that a dollar (fiat currency) is "just something artificial we throw out there…what you're doing is you're fooling people."[315]

Early paper currencies were generally backed by gold, with every printed bill corresponding to an amount of gold held in a vault somewhere for which it could, technically, be exchanged (this rarely happened).[316] "Having a currency backed by an actual precious metal helped lend credibility to the governments that issue it. It facilitated the trust these institutions needed to make their currency system work. People accepted currencies because they knew their

---

[311] Cortez, JP. "Fake Money, Sound Money and Government Malfeasance." *Tenth Amendment Center*, 28 Aug. 2018, tenthamendmentcenter.com/2018/08/28/fake-money-sound-money-and-government-malfeasance/.

[312] "The 101 Best Gold Quotes From History – GoldSilver." *Gold Silver*, goldsilver.com/blog/101-best-gold-quotes-all-time/.

[313] Brock, Thomas. "Money." *Investopedia*, 25 Dec. 2020, www.investopedia.com/terms/m/money.asp.

[314] Fernando, Jason. "Inflation." *Investopedia*, 18 Nov. 2020, www.investopedia.com/terms/i/inflation.asp.

[315] "Money Quotes: What The Experts Say About Money." *Midas Gold Group*, 27 Aug. 2020, www.midasgoldgroup.com/money-quotes/.

[316] Brewer, Reuben Gregg. "The Beginner's Guide to Investing in Gold." *The Motley Fool*, 4 Sept. 2019, www.fool.com/investing/the-beginners-guide-to-investing-in-gold.aspx.

wealth was secured in (i.e., backed by) precious metals."[317] In the past, "[e]xchanges were stabilized on the gold standard because by law, in various countries, the monetary unit was made equal to a fixed quantity of gold, and the two were made exchangeable at that legal ratio. These relationships were established by the legal requirement that a person who brought gold, gold coins, or certificates to the public treasury (or other designated places) could convert any one of these into either of the others in unlimited amounts for no cost."[318]

This approach to paper money lasted well into the 20th century.[319] "Prior to World War I, the banking system in the United States (and in most of the world) was based on gold" and was "virtually the sole international standard of exchange."[320] Unfortunately, the link between gold and paper money has now been severed.[321] One exception is the Russian ruble, which is effectively back on a gold standard.[322] Sergey Glazyev, an advisor to Russian

---

[317] "Currency vs Money: What's the Difference?" *Schiff Gold*, 26 Oct. 2016, schiffgold.com/key-gold-news/currency-vs-money-whats-difference/.

[318] "History of Banking and Money Key Excerpts From Carroll Quigley's Tragedy and Hope." *Wanttoknow.info*, www.wanttoknow.info/articles/quigley_carroll.tragedy_hope_banking_money_history.

[319] Brewer, Reuben Gregg. "The Beginner's Guide to Investing in Gold." *The Motley Fool*, 4 Sept. 2019, www.fool.com/investing/the-beginners-guide-to-investing-in-gold.aspx.

[320] Greenspan, Alan. "Gold and Economic Freedom." *Constitution Society*, www.constitution.org/mon/greenspan_gold.htm.

[321] Brewer, Reuben Gregg. "The Beginner's Guide to Investing in Gold." *The Motley Fool*, 4 Sept. 2019, www.fool.com/investing/the-beginners-guide-to-investing-in-gold.aspx.

[322] Atlas Grinned. "Russian Stocks A Bargain With Ruble On De Facto Gold Standard." *Seeking Alpha,* 27 Jun. 2019, seekingalpha.com/article/4272351-russian-stocks-bargain-ruble-on-de-facto-gold-standard.

president, Vladimir Putin, said, "The ruble is the most gold-backed currency in the world."323

"A negative consequence of central bank control of money is the disconnect between the money supply and the demand for money."324 The relationship between goods and money — the price system — depends "upon five things: the supply and the demand for goods, the supply and the demand for money, and the speed of exchange between money and goods."325 "An increase in three of these (demand for goods, supply of money, speed of circulation) would move the prices of goods up and the value of money down."326 "[A] decrease in the...three items would be deflationary..."327

323 Rickards, James G. "New Gold Standard? Chaos." *Bullion Vault*, 1 Jan. 2020, www.bullionvault.com/gold-news/gold-standard-012120201.

324 Cortez, JP. "Fake Money, Sound Money and Government Malfeasance." *Tenth Amendment Center*, 28 Aug. 2018, tenthamendmentcenter.com/2018/08/28/fake-money-sound-money-and-government-malfeasance/.

325 "History of Banking and Money Key Excerpts From Carroll Quigley's Tragedy and Hope." *Wanttoknow.info*, www.wanttoknow.info/articles/quigley_carroll.tragedy_hope_banking_money_history.

326 *Id.*

327 Woods, Thomas E. Jr. "The Revolutionary War and the Destruction of the Continental." *Mises Institute*, 11 Oct. 2006, mises.org/library/revolutionary-war-and-destruction-continental. "Falling prices raise *real wages,* even when nominal wages don't rise. To put it in topical terms, if the price of toilet paper falls from $2 per roll to $1 dollar per roll, you can buy twice as much toilet paper without getting a raise." Mullen, Tom. "'Inflation is low': The Federal Reserve's Scam of the Century." *Tommullen.com*, 31 Mar. 2020, www.tommullen.net/featured/inflation-is-low-the-federal-reserves-scam-of-the-century/?fbclid=IwAR1As6UZbfSEJ6I0-s3g2LyrUf5QFsB0HJ5yrSdRMxE9TDTtYjwGUitZATc.

"The laws of supply and demand apply to money."[328] "Since most world currencies are fiat money, the money supply could increase rapidly for political reasons, resulting in inflation."[329] "Inflation is a quantitative measure of the rate at which the average price level of a basket of selected goods and services in an economy increases over a period of time. It is the constant rise in the general level of prices where a unit of currency buys less than it did in prior periods. Often expressed as a percentage, inflation indicates a decrease in the purchasing power of a nation's currency...Inflation is the rate at which the general level of prices for goods and services is rising and, consequently, the purchasing power of currency is falling...As prices rise, a single unit of currency loses value as it buys fewer goods and services."[330] Basically, inflation is when the price of goods goes up, and deflation is when the price of goods goes down.[331] "All of us experience the effects of inflation as the price of the goods and services we buy gradually goes up over time."[332]

As previously noted, an increase in the money supply can lead to inflation.[333] The more dollars in "circulation, the less the

---

[328] Borowski, Julie. "Top 10 Reasons to End the Federal Reserve." *FreedomWorks,* 1 Feb. 2012, www.freedomworks.org/content/top-10-reasons-end-federal-reserve.

[329] Fernando, Jason. "Inflation." *Investopedia,* 18 Nov. 2020, www.investopedia.com/terms/i/inflation.asp.

[330] *Id.*

[331] "The Inflation CPI Lie : BLS Posers..." *Signals Matter,* 2 Oct. 2017, www.signalsmatter.com/inflation-cpi/.

[332] "Indexing Income Taxes for Inflation: Why It Matters." *ITEP,* 22 Aug. 2016, itep.org/indexing-income-taxes-for-inflation-why-it-matters-1/.

[333] Fernando, Jason. "Inflation." *Investopedia,* 18 Nov. 2020, www.investopedia.com/terms/i/inflation.asp.

currency is worth."[334] In such cases, the money loses its purchasing power.[335] "If the supply of money in an economy is $1 billion, each unit of currency buys X (the purchasing power of each unit of currency). If the money supply is doubled without any expansion in the consumers' pool of goods and services, the purchasing power of each unit of currency falls in half. This reduction in the purchasing power of each unit of currency is called inflation."[336] "[H]igher prices are actually a direct consequence of inflation since increasing the supply of money decreases the purchasing power of the dollar."[337]

Inflation erodes the value of cash holdings, i.e., savings. "When prices rise excessively, cash, or savings deposited in banks decreases in value or becomes worthless since the money has far less purchasing power..."[338] "This loss of purchasing power impacts the general cost of living for the common public which ultimately leads to a deceleration in economic growth."[339] For example, "[i]magine your grandma stuffed a $10 bill in her old wallet in the year 1975 and then forgot about it. The cost of gasoline during that year was around $0.50 per gallon, which means she

[334] Borowski, Julie. "Top 10 Reasons to End the Federal Reserve." *FreedomWorks,* 1 Feb. 2012, www.freedomworks.org/content/top-10-reasons-end-federal-reserve.

[335] Fernando, Jason. "Inflation." *Investopedia*, 18 Nov. 2020, www.investopedia.com/terms/i/inflation.asp.

[336] Smith, Charles Hughes. "Modern Monetary Theory." *InflationData.com*, 5 Nov. 2019, inflationdata.com/articles/2019/11/05/modern-monetary-theory/.

[337] Borowski, Julie. "Top 10 Reasons to End the Federal Reserve." *FreedomWorks,* 1 Feb. 2012, www.freedomworks.org/content/top-10-reasons-end-federal-reserve.

[338] Kentoni, Will. "Hyperinflation." *Investopedia,* 8 Jul. 2018, www.investopedia.com/terms/h/hyperinflation.asp.

[339] Fernando, Jason. "Inflation." *Investopedia*, 18 Nov. 2020, www.investopedia.com/terms/i/inflation.asp.

could have then bought 20 gallons of gasoline with that $10 note. Twenty-five years later in the year 2000, the cost of gasoline was around $1.60 per gallon. If she finds the forgotten note in the year 2000 and then goes on to purchase gasoline, she would have bought only 6.25 gallons. Although the $10 note remained the same for its value, it lost its purchasing power by around 69 percent over the 25-year period."[340] "Those who save money are being robbed."[341]

When there was a gold standard, "[i]f a country exports more than it imports so that gold flows in to cover the difference, this gold will become the basis for an increased quantity of money, and this will cause a rise of prices within the country sufficient to reduce exports and increase imports."[342] "For example, following the Spanish conquest of the Aztec and Inca empires, massive amounts of gold and especially silver flowed into the Spanish and other European economies. Since the money supply had rapidly

---

[340] *Id.*

[341] Stewart Jones is a State Representative of South Carolina. Jones, Stewart. "The Founders Warned Us About Central Banking." *Ron Paul Liberty Report*, 10 Oct. 2019, www.ronpaullibertyreport.com/archives/the-founders-warned-us-about-central-banking?fbclid=IwAR1GtgHBthCfZDgqhObnuqCX2hO9116CjGntgnKJ75rw5KXrb5U3mKOVFKI.

[342] "History of Banking and Money Key Excerpts From Carroll Quigley's Tragedy and Hope." *Wanttoknow.info*, www.wanttoknow.info/articles/quigley_carroll.tragedy_hope_banking_money_history.

increased, prices spiked and the value of money fell, contributing to economic collapse."[343]

The money supply can also be increased by the monetary authorities either by printing more money, or by devaluing the currency.[344] For instance, "[t]he response to a depression is usually an increase in the money supply by the central bank. The extra money is designed to encourage banks to lend to consumers and businesses to create spending and investment."[345] "Our money supply has rapidly increased over the past century due to the Federal Reserve printing massive amounts of money..."[346] However, "if the increase in money supply is not supported by economic growth as measured by gross domestic product (GDP), the result can lead to

---

[343] "The spectacular postwar inflations in eastern Europe had intensified the traditional fear of inflation among bankers. In an effort to stop rises in prices which might become inflationary, bankers after 1919 increasingly sought to 'sterilize' gold when it flowed into their country. That is, they sought to set it aside so that it did not become part of the monetary system. As a result, the unbalance of trade which had initiated the flow of gold was not counteracted by price changes. Trade and prices remained unbalanced, and gold continued to flow. Somewhat similar was a spreading fear of decreasing gold reserves, so that when gold began to flow out of a country as a result of an unfavorable balance of international payments, bankers increasingly sought to hinder the flow by restrictions on gold exports." "History of Banking and Money Key Excerpts From Carroll Quigley's Tragedy and Hope." *Wanttoknow.info*, www.wanttoknow.info/articles/ quigley_carroll.tragedy_hope_banking_money_history; "Inflation." Fernando, Jason. "Inflation." *Investopedia*, 18 Nov. 2020, www.investopedia.com/terms/i/inflation.asp.

[344] Fernando, Jason. "Inflation." *Investopedia*, 18 Nov. 2020, www.investopedia.com/terms/i/inflation.asp.

[345] Kentoni, Will. "Hyperinflation." *Investopedia*, 8 Jul. 2018, www.investopedia.com/terms/h/hyperinflation.asp.

[346] Borowski, Julie. "Top 10 Reasons to End the Federal Reserve." *FreedomWorks*, 1 Feb. 2012, www.freedomworks.org/content/top-10-reasons-end-federal-reserve.

hyperinflation."[347]   If the free market is allowed to function, then balance will be restored. "Prices will rise to compensate for the increase in the money supply."[348]

"The idea that pumping new money stimulates the economy stems from the idea that *money* itself is what gives people purchasing power."[349]   For example, "[o]perating on the idea that purchasing power is money, the New Dealers simply printed more money in the hopes of restoring purchasing power to the underemployed masses. But this policy amounts to a trade in which money is exchanged not for goods, but for nothing at all."[350]   "The problem is that purchasing power is *not* merely money; it is, in fact, real goods or services. Ultimately, all exchanges are of goods for goods. In a money economy, goods are exchanged for money, and money is then exchanged for other goods. A shortage of purchasing power, then, is in fact a shortage of *goods*."[351]

"Flooding the economy with money that has not been traded for real goods introduces a whole set of temporary imbalances in the economy. There is a trade imbalance because the goods to be traded for other goods have not yet been produced. There is a price imbalance because prices are no longer in proportion to the money supply. There is a shortfall of *real* purchasing power (i.e., goods and services). In the wake of the credit expansion, there will be an imbalance of production, for many producers will be induced to increase their production, and even their facilities for production, for there are many willing buyers with the money, it seems, to pay for

---

[347] Kentoni, Will. "Hyperinflation." *Investopedia,* 8 Jul. 2018, www.investopedia.com/terms/h/hyperinflation.asp.

[348] "What Caused the Great Depression?" *FEE,* 2 Feb. 2018, fee.org/articles/what-caused-the-great-depression/.

[349] *Id.*

[350] *Id.*

[351] *Id.*

their wares."[352] "The problem is that trading with a *shortage of goods* is not a normal market phenomenon at all. It occurs only as a result of a large scale intervention in the market through credit expansion fueled by debt; this process is known as inflation. Monetized debt, or inflation, is based not on trading goods for goods, but on trading goods for the *promise* of goods that don't exist yet, but will be produced in the future. It is nothing other than a promise of future production."[353]

"Inflation is a natural consequence of loose government monetary policy. If those policies get too loose, hyperinflation can occur..."[354] "Hyperinflation is a term to describe rapid, excessive, and out-of-control price increases in an economy."[355] It "is measured in terms of exponential daily increases that can approach 5 to 10% a day."[356] Philip Cagan, Professor of Economics at Columbia University, defined hyperinflation as "an inflation rate of 50% or more in a single month..."[357]

"[H]yperinflation historically has one root cause: excessive money supply."[358] "Hyperinflation can occur in times of war and economic turmoil, followed by a central bank printing an excessive

---

[352] *Id.*

[353] *Id.*

[354] Clark, Jeff. "How Does Gold Fare During Hyperinflation?" *InflationData.com*, 25 Jun. 2012, inflationdata.com/articles/2012/06/25/gold-hyperinflation/.

[355] Kentoni, Will. "Hyperinflation." *Investopedia,* 8 Jul. 2018, www.investopedia.com/terms/h/hyperinflation.asp.

[356] *Id.*

[357] Clark, Jeff. "How Does Gold Fare During Hyperinflation?" *InflationData.com*, 25 Jun. 2012, inflationdata.com/articles/2012/06/25/gold-hyperinflation/.

[358] *Id.*

amount of money."[359] "Hyperinflation arises when the supply of goods and services — the output of the economy — remains roughly the same while the supply of currency skyrockets. As money increases but the sum of goods and services available for purchase remains flat, the value of existing money declines accordingly."[360]

"Hyperinflation can cause a surge in prices for basic goods — such as food and fuel..."[361] "Imagine the cost of food shopping going from $500 per week to $750 per week the next month, to $1,125 per week the next month and so on. If wages aren't keeping pace with inflation in an economy, the standard of living for the people goes down because they can't afford to pay for their basic needs and cost of living expenses."[362]

Eventually, "[d]ebts and deficits reach unsustainable levels, and politicians resort to diluting the currency to cover their expenses. A tipping point is reached, and investors lose confidence in the currency...Fiat money holds its purchasing power largely on the belief that it is stable and will preserve that power over time. Once this trust is broken, a flight from the currency ensues."[363] Thus, "hyperinflation often occurs when there is a loss of confidence in a country's currency and the central bank's ability to maintain its currency's value in the aftermath...If a government isn't managed

---

[359] Kentoni, Will. "Hyperinflation." *Investopedia,* 8 Jul. 2018, www.investopedia.com/terms/h/hyperinflation.asp.

[360] Smith, Charles Hughes. "Modern Monetary Theory." *InflationData.com,* 5 Nov. 2019, inflationdata.com/articles/2019/11/05/modern-monetary-theory/.

[361] Kentoni, Will. "Hyperinflation." *Investopedia,* 8 Jul. 2018, www.investopedia.com/terms/h/hyperinflation.asp.

[362] *Id.*

[363] Clark, Jeff. "How Does Gold Fare During Hyperinflation?" *InflationData.com,* 25 Jun. 2012, inflationdata.com/articles/2012/06/25/gold-hyperinflation/.

properly, citizens can also lose confidence in the value of their country's currency."[364]

"[P]aper money systems fail...because, inevitably, far too much credit is created under the paper system. There's no fundamental limit to credit. Sooner or later, people realize the debts can't be carried, much less repaid. At that point, the system collapses – and not because the money becomes more valuable (i.e., deflation). It collapses because people suddenly decide any other asset is better to hold than the money the banks keep printing."[365]

"During times of hyperinflation, people know the money will be worth less tomorrow so they exchange any cash they have for any physical good they can get their hands on (whether they need it or not)."[366] When the currency is perceived as having little or no value, "citizens spend the money as quickly as possible, typically buying tangible items in a desperate attempt to get rid of currency units before they lose value."[367] "After all, a bar of soap will still be a bar of soap tomorrow, but it may take twice as many dollars to buy it."[368] "This process increases the velocity of money, setting off a vicious cycle that destroys purchasing power faster and faster..."[369]

[364] Kentoni, Will. "Hyperinflation." *Investopedia,* 8 Jul. 2018, www.investopedia.com/terms/h/hyperinflation.asp.

[365] Stansberry, Porter. "How Paper Money Fails." *InflationData.com,* 11 Jul. 2010, inflationdata.com/articles/2010/07/11/how-paper-money-fails/.

[366] McMahon, Tim. "What is Hyperinflation?" *InflationData.com,* inflationdata.com/articles/hyperinflation/.

[367] Clark, Jeff. "How Does Gold Fare During Hyperinflation?" *InflationData.com,* 25 Jun. 2012, inflationdata.com/articles/2012/06/25/gold-hyperinflation/.

[368] McMahon, Tim. "What is Hyperinflation?" *InflationData.com,* inflationdata.com/articles/hyperinflation/.

[369] Clark, Jeff. "How Does Gold Fare During Hyperinflation?" *InflationData.com,* 25 Jun. 2012, inflationdata.com/articles/2012/06/25/gold-hyperinflation/.

"As prices begin to rise, basic goods — such as food and fuel — become scarce, sending prices in an upward spiral."[370] "In response, the government is forced to print even more money to try to stabilize prices and provide liquidity, which only exacerbates the problem."[371] "As the economy deteriorates further, companies charge more, consumers pay more, and the central bank prints more money — leading to a vicious cycle and hyperinflation."[372]

One famous case of "hyperinflation is the one that occurred in Germany during the Weimar Republic, from January 1919 until November 1923."[373] During that period, "the average price level increased by a factor of 20 billion, doubling every 28 hours."[374]

It all started when "[t]he nations that had been victorious in World War I demanded reparations from Germany, which could not be paid in German paper currency [*Reichsmarks*], as this was of suspect value due to government borrowing."[375] Because inflation makes it easier to pay off debts, "Germany attempted to print paper notes, buy foreign currency with them, and use that to pay their debts."[376]

---

[370] Kentoni, Will. "Hyperinflation." *Investopedia,* 8 Jul. 2018, www.investopedia.com/terms/h/hyperinflation.asp.

[371] *Id.*

[372] "Oftentimes, the lack of confidence is reflected in investment outflows leaving the country during times of economic turmoil and war. When these outflows occur, the country' currency value depreciates because investors are selling their country's investments in exchange for another country's investments. The central bank will often impose capital controls, which are bans on moving money out of the country." *Id.*

[373] Clark, Jeff. "How Does Gold Fare During Hyperinflation?" *InflationData.com,* 25 Jun. 2012, inflationdata.com/articles/2012/06/25/gold-hyperinflation/.

[374] *Id.*

[375] Fernando, Jason. "Inflation." *Investopedia,* 18 Nov. 2020, www.investopedia.com/terms/i/inflation.asp.

[376] *Id.*

"This policy led to the rapid devaluation of the German mark, and hyperinflation accompanied the development. German consumers exacerbated the cycle by trying to spend their money as fast as possible, expecting that it would be worth less and less the longer they waited. More and more money flooded the economy..."[377] "Prices rose not just by the day, but by the hour — or even the minute. If you had your morning coffee in a café, and you preferred drinking two cups rather than one, it was cheaper to order both cups at the same time."[378]

A German factory worker described payday (which was every day) as follows: "At eleven o'clock in the morning, a siren sounded and everybody gathered in the factory forecourt where a five-ton lorry [truck] was drawn up loaded brimful with paper money. The chief cashier and his assistants climbed up on top. They read out names and just threw out bundles of notes. As soon as you had caught one you made a dash for the nearest shop and bought just anything that was going..."[379]

"The flight from currency that had begun with the buying of diamonds, gold, country houses, and antiques now extended to minor and almost useless items — bric-a-brac, soap, hairpins..."[380] It got so bad that "dentists and doctors stopped asking for currency, seeking payment in butter or eggs instead."[381] One sad case involved the father of Walter Levy — a German-born oil consultant. "His father, a German lawyer, took out a life insurance policy in 1903. Every month he had made the payments faithfully. It was a

---

[377] *Id.*

[378] Litle, Justice. "Postcards From Weimar Germany." *InflationData.com*, 20 Sept. 2010, inflationdata.com/articles/2010/09/20/hyperinflation-in-weimar-germany/.

[379] *Id.*

[380] McMahon, Tim. "What is Hyperinflation?" *InflationData.com*, inflationdata.com/articles/hyperinflation/.

[381] *Id.*

twenty-year policy, and when it came due, he cashed it in and bought a single loaf of bread..."[382]

The *Reichsmark* collapsed to such an extent that people used "the worthless currency as wallpaper," and children glued "the notes together to make kites" or used "stacks of it as building blocks."[383]

Another episode "of hyperinflation occurred in the former Yugoslavia in the 1990s. On the verge of national dissolution, the country had already been experiencing inflation at rates that exceeded 75% annually. It was discovered that the leader of the then Serbian province, Slobodan Milosevic, had plundered the national treasury by having the Serbian central bank issue $1.4 billion of loans to his cronies. The theft forced the government's central bank to print excessive amounts of money so it could take care of its financial obligations. Hyperinflation quickly enveloped the economy, erasing what was left of the country's wealth, forcing its people into bartering for goods. The rate of inflation nearly doubled each day until it reached an unfathomable rate of 300 million percent a month. The central bank was forced to print more money just to keep the government running as the economy spiraled downward...Eventually, the government replaced its currency with the German mark, which helped to stabilize the economy."[384]

---

[382] Litle, Justice. "Postcards From Weimar Germany." *InflationData.com*, 20 Sept. 2010, inflationdata.com/articles/2010/09/20/hyperinflation-in-weimar-germany/.

[383] Woods, Thomas E. Jr. "The Revolutionary War and the Destruction of the Continental." *Mises Institute*, 11 Oct. 2006, mises.org/library/revolutionary-war-and-destruction-continental; Fernando, Jason. "Inflation." *Investopedia*, 18 Nov. 2020, www.investopedia.com/terms/i/inflation.asp.

[384] Kentoni, Will. "Hyperinflation." *Investopedia*, 8 Jul. 2018, www.investopedia.com/terms/h/hyperinflation.asp.

Zimbabwe "is a textbook case of how to create hyperinflation by thinking you can print all the money you want..."[385] The local currency has been rapidly devaluing, "fostering high inflation..."[386] "[B]y 2008, the (hyper)inflation rate had reached 2.2 million percent."[387] In 2009, Zimbabwe's currency collapsed under the weight of hyperinflation.[388] "Eggs sold for a million dollars each..."[389]

"Zimbabwean consumer George Bhamu of the eastern city of Mutare said inflation is making it impossible for families to afford basic commodities they need to live..."[390] "Hyperinflation is changing prices so quickly in Zimbabwe that what you see displayed on a supermarket shelf might change by the time you reach the checkout...In other shops, prices are only available at the checkout — and even then the cashier might stop a customer mid-payment to

---

[385] According to economist John Robertson, another cause was the government spending beyond its means." Mutsaka, Farai. "'It's a nightmare': Zimbabwe struggles with hyperinflation." *AP*, 10 Oct. 2019, apnews.com/1ce81eed4b064a529163513931b30178; Zulu, Blessing. "Zimbabwean Hyperinflation Officially Estimated At 2.2 Million Percent." *InflationData.com*, 15 Jul. 2008, inflationdata.com/articles/2008/07/16/zimbabwean-hyperinflation-officially-estimated-at-2-2-million-percent/.

[386] Mutsaka, Farai. "'It's a nightmare': Zimbabwe struggles with hyperinflation." *AP*, 10 Oct. 2019, apnews.com/1ce81eed4b064a529163513931b30178.

[387] McMahon, Tim. "What is Hyperinflation?" *InflationData.com*, inflationdata.com/articles/hyperinflation/.

[388] Mutsaka, Farai. "'It's a nightmare': Zimbabwe struggles with hyperinflation." *AP*, 10 Oct. 2019, apnews.com/1ce81eed4b064a529163513931b30178.

[389] McMahon, Tim. "What is Hyperinflation?" *InflationData.com*, inflationdata.com/articles/hyperinflation/.

[390] Zulu, Blessing. "Zimbabwean Hyperinflation Officially Estimated At 2.2 Million Percent." *InflationData.com*, 15 Jul. 2008, inflationdata.com/articles/2008/07/16/zimbabwean-hyperinflation-officially-estimated-at-2-2-million-percent/.

change prices…"[391]   Many people are forced into "001," which is the local slang for having to resort to eating only one meal a day.[392] "A Chivhu resident, who asked to be identified only as Innocent, said inflation is obliging many Zimbabweans to make a living by means that are sometimes less than reputable."[393]

"[T]he Zimbabwean government demonetized its dollar in 2015 as a way to combat the country's hyperinflation, which was recorded at 231,000,000 percent. The three-month process involved expunging the Zimbabwean dollar from the country's financial system and solidifying the U.S. dollar, the Botswana pula, and the South African rand as the country's legal tender in a bid to stabilize the economy."[394]

In Venezuela, the International Monetary Fund predicted that inflation would hit 720 per cent in 2016, but some local economic analysts expected "the rate to reach as high as 1,200 per cent…"[395] Im 2016, "the official exchange rate [was] 10 bolivars to the US dollar. But Venezuelans have so little faith in their currency — or the government's ability to fix the country's deepening economic crisis

---

[391] Mutsaka, Farai. "'It's a nightmare': Zimbabwe struggles with hyperinflation." *AP*, 10 Oct. 2019, apnews.com/1ce81eed4b064a529163513931b30178.

[392] *Id.*

[393] Zulu, Blessing. "Zimbabwean Hyperinflation Officially Estimated At 2.2 Million Percent." *InflationData.com*, 15 Jul. 2008, inflationdata.com/articles/2008/07/16/zimbabwean-hyperinflation-officially-estimated-at-2-2-million-percent/.

[394] Chappelow, Jim. "Demonetization." *Investopedia*, 20 Mar. 2020, www.investopedia.com/terms/d/demonetization.asp.

[395] Mogollon, Mery and Alexandra Zavis. "It costs $200 to buy a dozen eggs in Venezuela right now." *The Sydney Morning Herald*, 1 Jun. 2016, www.smh.com.au/world/it-costs-200-to-buy-a-dozen-eggs-in-venezuela-right-now-20160601-gp8qx5.html?fbclid=IwAR2HinM8aT4V1txOREInlXDg53S1xx77uIgcr94lyLVOj_sAYrOZgTrv1TE.

— that one US dollar can fetch upward of 1,000 bolivars (the equivalent of $139) on the black market…"[396]

The government does not publish data related to inflation, but the Finance Commission of the "National Assembly calculated that inflation for October 2019 was 20.7 percent and that cumulative inflation for 2019 was 4,035 percent…"[397] The IMF estimated that inflation in Venezuela would reach 200,000 percent in 2019.[398]

In 2020, inflation had hit "3,365% in the year through March… many goods were sold at prices beyond the reach of most Venezuelans."[399]

By 2019, few in Venezuela used bolivares — what was once one of the strongest economies in South America — "to buy goods or services. Most people have turned to US dollars, euros, cryptocurrencies or bartering to survive."[400] Instead, the now worthless bolivares are being used as materials to make arts and crafts. For example, Hector Cordero "weaves the currency into wallets and purses, which he sells to tourists in Colombia…[T]he artist incorporates 16 different denominations of Venezuelan currency into his crafts, many of them the discontinued bolivares soberanos. Cordero sells wallets made from hundreds or even

---

[396] *Id.*

[397] Held, Sergio. "Venezuela's currency: Worth more as craft paper than as money." *AJ Impact*, 24 Dec. 2019, www.aljazeera.com/ajimpact/venezuela-currency-worth-craft-paper-money-191224144545023.html.

[398] *Id.*

[399] Pons, Corina, et al. "Venezuela sets new price controls, with eggs costing more than a month's wages." *Reuters,* 30 Apr. 2020, www.reuters.com/article/us-venezuela-economy-idUSKBN22D41S?fbclid=IwAR1_kx90-m3ncyl1pv9nxXMCDZmrEENhFeemSCOhdvEUoYV11pzOwD2i7aI.

[400] Held, Sergio. "Venezuela's currency: Worth more as craft paper than as money." *AJ Impact*, 24 Dec. 2019, www.aljazeera.com/ajimpact/venezuela-currency-worth-craft-paper-money-191224144545023.html.

thousands of bills of the now valueless currency for about $8; the handbags go for about $12..."[401]

Due to the U.S. Founding Fathers' nasty experience with the Continental paper currency that had "provoked all manner of economic chaos and dislocation," they intended the money system to provide a permanent standard of value that would consist of gold and silver coin.[402]

Prior to the American Revolution (circa 1757), the colonies had distributed fiat "money known as Colonial Scrip. The endeavor was successful, and provided a reliable means of exchange and helped to provide a unity between the independent colonies. The Colonial Scrip was debt-free, printed in the public interest and was not backed by gold or silver coin...When officials in England asked [Benjamin] Franklin how he could account for the prosperity of the colonies, Franklin replied, 'In the colonies, we issue our own money. It is called Colonial Scrip. We issue it in proper proportion to the demands of trade, and industry to make the products pass easily from the producers to the consumers. In this manner, creating for ourselves our own paper money, we control its purchasing power, and we have no interest to pay to no one...' Parliament immediately passed the Currency Act of 1774. This prohibited colonial officials from issuing their own money and ordered them to pay all future taxes in gold or silver coins. This forced the colonies onto a gold and silver standard."[403]   Franklin later reflected, "The inability of the colonists to get power to issue their own money permanently out of

---

[401] *Id.*

[402] Woods, Thomas E. Jr. "The Revolutionary War and the Destruction of the Continental." *Mises Institute*, 11 Oct. 2006, mises.org/library/ revolutionary-war-and-destruction-continental.

[403] Jones, Stack. "An Essay On The History Of Banking." *The Banking Swindle*, 1 Jan. 2018, criminalbankingmonopoly.wordpress.com/.

the hands of George III and the international bankers was the prime reason for the Revolutionary War."[404]

By the time the first shots of the Revolution "were fired on April 19th, 1775, the colonies were drained of gold and silver coins through British taxation."[405] "Gold and silver coins had for years been flowing to Britain for purchases and they remained in such short supply that colonial trade was largely based on agricultural credit..."[406] The colonies were forced to fund "their armed resistance to increased British imperial control by issuing large amounts of paper money."[407] "The new government turned eagerly to the printing press to finance its military expenditures..."[408] Because the Continental Congress had little power to tax, it was forced to finance the war by borrowing and issuing paper currency known as "continentals."[409] Inflation eventually robbed them of all value.

---

[404] *Id.*

[405] *Id.*

[406] Narron, James and David Skeie. "Crisis Chronicles: Not Worth a Continental—The Currency Crisis of 1779 and Today's European Debt Crisis." *Liberty Street Economics,* 11 Apr. 2014, libertystreeteconomics.newyorkfed.org/2014/04/crisis-chronicles-not-worth-a-continentalthe-currency-crisis-of-1779-and-todays-european-debt-crisis.html.

[407] "Continental Currency." *Encyclopedia.com,* 7 Nov. 2019, www.encyclopedia.com/history/encyclopedias-almanacs-transcripts-and-maps/continental-currency.

[408] Rothbard, Murray N. "Not Worth a Continental." *Mises Institute,* 17 Dec. 2018, mises.org/library/not-worth-continental.

[409] Davies, Phil. "The Bank That Hamilton Built." *Federal Reserve Bank of Minneapolis,* 1 Sept. 2007, www.minneapolisfed.org/article/2007/the-bank-that-hamilton-built; Narron, James and David Skeie. "Crisis Chronicles: Not Worth a Continental—The Currency Crisis of 1779 and Today's European Debt Crisis." *Liberty Street Economics,* 11 Apr. 2014, libertystreeteconomics.newyorkfed.org/2014/04/crisis-chronicles-not-worth-a-continentalthe-currency-crisis-of-1779-and-todays-european-debt-crisis.html.

"On 22 June 1775, the Continental Congress voted to issue two million dollars in bills of credit," which were "to be redeemable, dollar for dollar, in specie [gold or silver]. In need of money quickly at the start of the emergency, Congress intended to print only this initial amount."[410] However, "a clamor arose for more and more issues of paper money. The public's confidence in the currency remained strong...The public seemed to enjoy the bonanza of new money. As a result, the Continental Congress stepped up the paper money issues."[411]

"For five years, Congress authorized ever-increasing amounts of paper money to meet the urgent demands of American forces for sustenance, clothing, pay, transportation, and every sort of military equipment, until the total, near the end of 1779, reached the unprecedented sum of $241,500,000..."[412]

"The delegates were fully aware that unsecured paper money would inflate rapidly..."[413] "When Congress first began printing bills of credit (irredeemable paper money that would be received as payment for taxes) in 1775, the idea was that the states would levy taxes and collect the bills in payment of the taxes, thereby retiring

---

[410] "Continental Currency." *Encyclopedia.com,* 7 Nov. 2019, www.encyclopedia.com/history/encyclopedias-almanacs-transcripts-and-maps/continental-currency; Rothbard, Murray N. "Not Worth a Continental." *Mises Institute,* 17 Dec. 2018, mises.org/library/not-worth-continental.

[411] Rothbard, Murray N. "Not Worth a Continental." *Mises Institute,* 17 Dec. 2018, mises.org/library/not-worth-continental.

[412] "Continental Currency." *Encyclopedia.com,* 7 Nov. 2019, www.encyclopedia.com/history/encyclopedias-almanacs-transcripts-and-maps/continental-currency.

[413] Rothbard, Murray N. "Not Worth a Continental." *Mises Institute,* 17 Dec. 2018, mises.org/library/not-worth-continental. The British were also aware of this fact. They counterfeited the continental to "undermine the nascent American economy" as part of their war strategy. Hatfield, Stuart. "Faking It: British Counterfeiting During the American Revolution." *Journal of the American Revolution,* 7 Oct. 2015, allthingsliberty.com/2015/10/faking-it-british-counterfeiting-during-the-american-revolution/.

them. Not only did the states not levy those taxes, but they also began printing paper money of their own. The result was that more and more paper continued to be printed…"[414] Adding to the problem was the British "counterfeiting [of] Congressional paper currency" to undermine the American economy and war effort.[415]

"Because Congress had no source of revenue apart from recommending that the states provide the means for redeeming Continental currency, this paper money in effect had little or no real backing."[416] "The result was a steady depreciation of the paper dollar…Prices rose rapidly, and continentals fell in value, as compared to the specie dollar."[417]

"As the war progressed, the value of the dollar fell dramatically for several reasons. One was the lack of any sort of backing to bolster its value. Paper money is basically a promise that it is worth what it says it is. Without massive gold and silver reserves backing it up, the dollar was subject to fluctuation that was based on the strength of the promise, and in this case the strength of the people making the promise, that is, Congress. As such, it was very much tied to the fortunes of the army. When the army had success, the value of the dollar rose, while failure caused it to plummet; with a few exceptions, the army had little success. This led to the devaluation of the currency, which made it hard to purchase supplies and necessities that the army needed to win the

---

[414] Woods, Thomas E. Jr. "The Revolutionary War and the Destruction of the Continental." *Mises Institute*, 11 Oct. 2006, mises.org/library/revolutionary-war-and-destruction-continental.

[415] Hatfield, Stuart. "Faking It: British Counterfeiting During the American Revolution." *Journal of the American Revolution,* 7 Oct. 2015, allthingsliberty.com/2015/10/faking-it-british-counterfeiting-during-the-american-revolution/.

[416] "Continental Currency." *Encyclopedia.com,* 7 Nov. 2019, www.encyclopedia.com/history/encyclopedias-almanacs-transcripts-and-maps/continental-currency.

[417] Rothbard, Murray N. "Not Worth a Continental." *Mises Institute,* 17 Dec. 2018, mises.org/library/not-worth-continental.

victories that could cause the currency to be worth something again…"[418] Thus, "[t]he Continentals proved to be a poor economic instrument: backed by nothing more than the promise of 'future tax revenues' and prone to rampant inflation, the notes ultimately had little fiscal value."[419]

"At the outset, the continental had circulated at par with a dollar of specie."[420] However, "by the end of 1777 in Philadelphia, it took nearly four dollars in paper money to buy one dollar in specie. By the end of 1778, it took nearly eight dollars in Continental currency to buy one dollar in specie."[421]

"Naturally, the depreciating continental…led to calls for economic controls in order to contain the upward pressure that the inflation was having on wages and prices."[422] "The Continental Congress and the state governments tried every coercive means available to prevent the persistent trend of rising prices."[423] For example, some "laws compelled creditors and merchants to accept

---

[418] "The Treaty of Alliance with France in 1778 went a long way to bolstering the confidence the people had in the Congress and the army, which helped prevent a war-ending panic." Hatfield, Stuart. "Faking It: British Counterfeiting During the American Revolution." *Journal of the American Revolution,* 7 Oct. 2015, allthingsliberty.com/2015/10/faking-it-british-counterfeiting-during-the-american-revolution/.

[419] History.com Editors. "Congress issues Continental currency." *A&E Television Networks*, 13 Nov. 2019, www.history.com/this-day-in-history/congress-issues-continental-currency.

[420] "Continental Currency." *Encyclopedia.com,* 7 Nov. 2019, www.encyclopedia.com/history/encyclopedias-almanacs-transcripts-and-maps/continental-currency.

[421] *Id.*

[422] Woods, Thomas E. Jr. "The Revolutionary War and the Destruction of the Continental." *Mises Institute*, 11 Oct. 2006, mises.org/library/revolutionary-war-and-destruction-continental.

[423] Rothbard, Murray N. "Not Worth a Continental." *Mises Institute,* 17 Dec. 2018, mises.org/library/not-worth-continental.

continentals on par with specie…"[424] "The New England states approved [stringent] price-control statutes in 1776 and early 1777. Other states followed…"[425] "[T]he price controls had all the predictable effects, including massive shortages, [and] disruption of the division of labor…"[426] "Price control, particularly in Pennsylvania and New England, led to acute shortages and widespread violations…"[427]

"Inflation, price controls, and legal tender laws combined to produce chaos and want. 'Stores were closed or pillaged,' wrote [Charles] Bullock, 'and merchants were mobbed, fined, or imprisoned; but such action merely drove men out of business, and tended to produce a real scarcity.' A June 1777 letter from Boston read, 'We are all starving here. [P]eople will not bring in provision, and we cannot procure the common necessaries of life.' Two years later, the same person wrote: 'We are likely to be starved thro'out Boston. Never such a scarcity of provisions…'"[428] "Statesman John Adams reasoned that the laws actually raised prices, since they created a scarcity of goods…"[429] "Within a couple of years, those experiments had been discontinued, partly at the behest of the very

---

[424] *Id.*

[425] Woods, Thomas E. Jr. "The Revolutionary War and the Destruction of the Continental." *Mises Institute*, 11 Oct. 2006, mises.org/library/ revolutionary-war-and-destruction-continental.

[426] *Id.*

[427] Rothbard, Murray N. "Not Worth a Continental." *Mises Institute,* 17 Dec. 2018, mises.org/library/not-worth-continental.

[428] Woods, Thomas E. Jr. "The Revolutionary War and the Destruction of the Continental." *Mises Institute*, 11 Oct. 2006, mises.org/library/ revolutionary-war-and-destruction-continental.

[429] Rothbard, Murray N. "Not Worth a Continental." *Mises Institute,* 17 Dec. 2018, mises.org/library/not-worth-continental.

Congress that had at one time enthusiastically urged them upon the states."[430]

"As the value [of the Continental] dropped, Congress had no choice but to print more money, driving the value down even further."[431] "As prices rose, the government found that it needed more and more dollars to finance its expenditures. More money was printed. This added supply of dollars led to further depreciation in the infamous spiral of inflation."[432] "By the end of the decade, inflation was nearly 50 percent, a suit cost a million Continentals"[433] "Shoes sold for 5,000 dollars a pair."[434] "As George Washington, the Patriots' commander in chief, complained at the time, 'A wagonload of currency will hardly purchase a wagonload of provisions.'"[435]

"By 1780, the bills were worth 1/40th of their face value. Congress struggled in vain to reform the currency by removing the

---

[430] Woods, Thomas E. Jr. "The Revolutionary War and the Destruction of the Continental." *Mises Institute*, 11 Oct. 2006, mises.org/library/ revolutionary-war-and-destruction-continental.

[431] Hatfield, Stuart. "Faking It: British Counterfeiting During the American Revolution." *Journal of the American Revolution,* 7 Oct. 2015, allthingsliberty.com/2015/10/faking-it-british-counterfeiting-during-the- american-revolution/.

[432] Rothbard, Murray N. "Not Worth a Continental." *Mises Institute,* 17 Dec. 2018, mises.org/library/not-worth-continental.

[433] Narron, James and David Skeie. "Crisis Chronicles: Not Worth a Continental—The Currency Crisis of 1779 and Today's European Debt Crisis." *Liberty Street Economics,* 11 Apr. 2014, libertystreeteconomics.newyorkfed.org/2014/04/crisis-chronicles-not- worth-a-continentalthe-currency-crisis-of-1779-and-todays-european-debt- crisis.html.

[434] Jones, Stack. "An Essay On The History Of Banking." *The Banking Swindle,* 1 Jan. 2018, criminalbankingmonopoly.wordpress.com/.

[435] Glass, Andrew. "Congress issues Continental currency, June 22, 1775." *Politico,* 22 Jun. 2018, www.politico.com/story/2018/06/22/congress- issues-continental-currency-june-22-1775-652244.

old bills from circulation and issuing new ones."[436] Also "[i]n 1780, Congress repudiated its solemn dollar-for-dollar promises and announced specie redemption at a rate of one specie dollar for forty dollars of continentals."[437]

At the start of 1781, "depreciation had reached 75 to 1 in most states, 100 to 1 in Philadelphia, 110 to 1 in Maryland, and 210 to 1 in North Carolina."[438] At one point in the year, "the exchange rate was $225 paper currency to $1 specie."[439] "In May [1781], the currency collapsed."[440]

"At the start of the war, the U.S. money supply [had been] 12 million dollars. By the end of the war, it was nearly 500 million."[441] "Without collateral to back them, millions of dollars in this currency

---

[436] *Id.*

[437] Rothbard, Murray N. "Not Worth a Continental." *Mises Institute,* 17 Dec. 2018, mises.org/library/not-worth-continental.

[438] "Continental Currency." *Encyclopedia.com,* 7 Nov. 2019, www.encyclopedia.com/history/encyclopedias-almanacs-transcripts-and-maps/continental-currency.

[439] Hatfield, Stuart. "Faking It: British Counterfeiting During the American Revolution." *Journal of the American Revolution,* 7 Oct. 2015, allthingsliberty.com/2015/10/faking-it-british-counterfeiting-during-the-american-revolution/.

[440] "Continental Currency." *Encyclopedia.com,* 7 Nov. 2019, www.encyclopedia.com/history/encyclopedias-almanacs-transcripts-and-maps/continental-currency.

[441] Jones, Stack. "An Essay On The History Of Banking." *The Banking Swindle,* 1 Jan. 2018, criminalbankingmonopoly.wordpress.com/.

had become nearly worthless..."[442] "The phrase 'not worth a Continental' became synonymous with worthless."[443]

"According to one contemporary, 'The annihilation was so complete that barber-shops were papered in jest with the bills; and the sailors, on returning from their cruise, being paid off in bundles of this worthless money, had suits of clothes made of it, and with characteristic light-heartedness turned their loss into a frolic by parading through the streets in decayed finery which in its better days had passed for thousands of dollars...'"[444] The following story appeared in the May 12, 1781 edition of the *Rivington's Royal Gazette*: "Last Saturday a large body of the inhabitants with paper dollars in their hats by way of cockades, paraded the streets of Philadelphia, carrying colors flying, with a dog tarred, and instead of the usual appendage and ornament of feathers, his back was congress covered with the Congress' paper dollars..."[445]

"Congress considered a number of remedies including devaluation, raising taxes, and tying currency issuance to future tax receipts — like a revenue bond — but ultimately elected to cease

---

[442] Davies, Phil. "The Bank That Hamilton Built." *Federal Reserve Bank of Minneapolis*, 1 Sept. 2007, www.minneapolisfed.org/article/2007/the-bank-that-hamilton-built.

[443] "Continental Currency." *Encyclopedia.com*, 7 Nov. 2019, www.encyclopedia.com/history/encyclopedias-almanacs-transcripts-and-maps/continental-currency.

[444] Woods, Thomas E. Jr. "The Revolutionary War and the Destruction of the Continental." *Mises Institute*, 11 Oct. 2006, mises.org/library/revolutionary-war-and-destruction-continental.

[445] Hatfield, Stuart. "Faking It: British Counterfeiting During the American Revolution." *Journal of the American Revolution*, 7 Oct. 2015, allthingsliberty.com/2015/10/faking-it-british-counterfeiting-during-the-american-revolution/.

issuing currency altogether…"[446]   As *The New York Herald* put it, the continental "expired…without a groan."[447]

By mid-1781, Continentals had effectively ceased to circulate as legal tender, and only hard money was used in the marketplace.[448] In Philadelphia, traders shut their shops and declined "to sell any more goods but for gold or silver."[449]   "The result of this ignominious end of the continental was a surprisingly quick return to a specie circulation, and a rapid fall of prices to a stable level…"[450]   Gold "is what people go back to. Many countries have been tempted to start counterfeiting their money and debasing their currency, but when it gets out of control, they go back to something people can trust…"[451]

---

[446] Narron, James and David Skeie. "Crisis Chronicles: Not Worth a Continental—The Currency Crisis of 1779 and Today's European Debt Crisis." *Liberty Street Economics,* 11 Apr. 2014, libertystreeteconomics.newyorkfed.org/2014/04/crisis-chronicles-not-worth-a-continentalthe-currency-crisis-of-1779-and-todays-european-debt-crisis.html.

[447] Circa in 1863. Woods, Thomas E. Jr. "The Revolutionary War and the Destruction of the Continental." *Mises Institute,* 11 Oct. 2006, mises.org/library/revolutionary-war-and-destruction-continental.

[448] Glass, Andrew. "Congress issues Continental currency, June 22, 1775." *Politico,* 22 Jun. 2018, www.politico.com/story/2018/06/22/congress-issues-continental-currency-june-22-1775-652244; "Continental Currency." *Encyclopedia.com,* 7 Nov. 2019, www.encyclopedia.com/history/encyclopedias-almanacs-transcripts-and-maps/continental-currency.

[449] *Rivington's Royal Gazette* (May 17, 1781). Hatfield, Stuart. "Faking It: British Counterfeiting During the American Revolution." *Journal of the American Revolution,* 7 Oct. 2015, allthingsliberty.com/2015/10/faking-it-british-counterfeiting-during-the-american-revolution/.

[450] Rothbard, Murray N. "Not Worth a Continental." *Mises Institute,* 17 Dec. 2018, mises.org/library/not-worth-continental.

[451] At 12. RonPaulLibertyReport. "Central Banking Is On The Ropes: Gold Will Survive & The Fed Will End." *Youtube,* 13 Dec. 2019, www.youtube.com/watch?v=Ndcb2SPRU7M.

"A courageous American contemporary wrote a fitting epitaph to the continentals: It becomes rulers to learn from the catastrophe of our Continental Currency, that money is upon a footing with commerce or religion. They all refuse to be the subject of law. It becomes the rulers of free men to learn further that money is property, and that the least attempt to lessen its value in our pockets and chests is taxing us without our consent. It is the highest act of tyranny..."[452] Indeed, "[i]nflation is the one form of taxation that can be imposed without legislation."[453] "Benjamin Franklin noted that the depreciation of the currency had, in effect, served as a tax that financed the war..."[454]

"Peletiah Webster, a discerning contemporary of the Revolution, summed up the effects of the American experiment with the continental. 'Paper money...polluted the equity of our laws, turned them into engines of oppression, corrupted the justice of our public administration, destroyed the fortunes of thousands who had confidence in it, enervated the trade, husbandry, and manufactures of our country, and went far to destroy the morality of our people.'"[455]

American revolutionary activist, Thomas Paine, wrote in *Common Sense*: "One of the evils of paper money is, that it turns the whole country into stock jobbers. The precariousness of its value and the uncertainty of its fate continually operate, night and day, to produce this destructive effect. Having no real value in itself it depends for support upon accident, caprice and party, and as it is the interest of some to depreciate and of others to raise its value, there is

---

[452] Rothbard, Murray N. "Not Worth a Continental." *Mises Institute,* 17 Dec. 2018, mises.org/library/not-worth-continental.

[453] "Milton Friedman Quotes." *Brainy Quote,* www.brainyquote.com/quotes/milton_friedman_101538.

[454] Glass, Andrew. "Congress issues Continental currency, June 22, 1775." *Politico,* 22 Jun. 2018, www.politico.com/story/2018/06/22/congress-issues-continental-currency-june-22-1775-652244.

[455] Rothbard, Murray N. "Not Worth a Continental." *Mises Institute,* 17 Dec. 2018, mises.org/library/not-worth-continental.

a continual invention going on that destroys the morals of the country...There are a set of men who go about making purchases upon credit, and buying estates they have not wherewithal to pay for; and having done this, their next step is to fill the newspapers with paragraphs of the scarcity of money and the necessity of a paper emission, then to have a legal tender under the pretense of supporting its credit, and when out, to depreciate it as fast as they can, get a deal of it for a little price, and cheat their creditors; and this is the concise history of paper money schemes...But the evils of paper money have no end. Its uncertain and fluctuating value is continually awakening or creating new schemes of deceit. Every principle of justice is put to the rack, and the bond of society dissolved...Of all the various sorts of base coin, paper money is the basest. It has the least intrinsic value of anything that can be put in the place of gold and silver. A hobnail or a piece of wampum far exceeds it. And there would be more propriety in making those articles a legal tender than to make paper so..."[456] "As to paper money, in any light it can be viewed, it is at best a bubble."[457]

President Thomas Jefferson also described paper money as a "bubble": "If the debt which the banking companies owe be a blessing to anybody, it is to themselves alone, who are realizing a solid interest of eight or ten per cent on it. As to the public, these companies have banished all our gold and silver medium, which, before their institution, we had without interest, which never could have perished in our hands, and would have been our salvation now in the hour of war; instead of which they have given us two hundred million of froth and bubble, on which we are to pay them heavy interest, until it shall vanish into air...We are warranted, then, in affirming that this parody on the principle of 'a public debt being a

---

[456] Dated January 10, 1776. Smith, George Ford. "Thomas Paine on Paper Money and Morality." *Mises Institute*, 29 Jan. 2019, mises.org/wire/ t h o m a s - p a i n e - p a p e r - m o n e y - a n d - m o r a l i t y ? fbclid=IwAR0W6lgaIIh5jxJ7gwTFzdRAa94LMpNXt0OJdGzxVvivyaxr9 GFbvGxxrwM.

[457] *Id.*

public blessing,' and its mutation into the blessing of private instead of public debts, is as ridiculous as the original principle itself. In both cases, the truth is, that capital may be produced by industry, and accumulated by economy; but jugglers only will propose to create it by legerdemain tricks with paper."[458]

Jefferson wrote that paper currency "has been, is, and for ever will be abused in every country in which it is permitted."[459] He thought that paper money "abuses also are inevitable and, by breaking up the measure of value, makes a lottery of all private property..."[460] Jefferson predicted that "[s]cenes are now to take place as will open the eyes of credulity and of insanity itself, to the dangers of a paper medium abandoned to the discretion of avarice and of swindlers."[461]

President George Washington condemned paper currency, for being "wicked."[462] He wrote, "Paper money has had the effect in your state that it will ever have, to ruin commerce, oppress the

---

[458] In a letter Jefferson wrote to John W. Eppes in 1813, he referred to a letter Alexander Hamilton had written a letter in 1781 to Robert Morris, the head of the Bank of North America, claiming, "A national debt, if it is not too excessive will be to us a national blessing." Jones, Stack. "An Essay On The History Of Banking." *The Banking Swindle*, 1 Jan. 2018, criminalbankingmonopoly.wordpress.com/.

[459] Letter to John Wayles Eppes, 6 November 1813. "Thomas Jefferson To John Wayles Eppes, 6 November 1813." Founders Online, *National Archives*, founders.archives.gov/documents/Jefferson/03-06-02-0458.

[460] Cortez, JP. "Fake Money, Sound Money and Government Malfeasance." *Tenth Amendment Center*, 28 Aug. 2018, tenthamendmentcenter.com/2018/08/28/fake-money-sound-money-and-government-malfeasance/.

[461] In a letter to Thomas Cooper, 1814. "Thomas Jefferson To Thomas Cooper, 10 September 1814." Founders Online, *National Archives*, founders.archives.gov/documents/Jefferson/03-07-02-0471.

[462] Cortez, JP. "Fake Money, Sound Money and Government Malfeasance." *Tenth Amendment Center*, 28 Aug. 2018, tenthamendmentcenter.com/2018/08/28/fake-money-sound-money-and-government-malfeasance/.

honest, and open the door to every species of fraud and injustice."[463] He warned, "If ever again our nation stumbles upon unfunded paper, it shall surely be like death to our body politic. This country will crash."[464]

Jefferson wrote, "The evils of this deluge of paper money are not to be removed until our citizens are generally and radically instructed in their cause and consequences, and silence by their authority the interested clamors and sophistry of speculating, shaving, and banking institutions. Till then, we must be content to return quoad hoc to the savage state, to recur to barter in the exchange of our property for want of a stable common measure of value, that now in use being less fixed than the beads and wampum of the Indian, and to deliver up our citizens, their property and their labor, passive victims to the swindling tricks of bankers and mountebankers."[465]

As a result of the bad experience with the continental, "[t]here was no interest in paper money in the early United States after the inflationary experiences of the Revolutionary War."[466] The framers of the Constitution knew "that paper promises…were utterly worthless as a standard of value for any practical purpose."[467] Number 44 of *The Federalist Papers* even maintains that "[p]aper

---

[463] In a letter to J. Bowen, Rhode Island, dated January 9, 1787. "George Washington Quote." *Liberty Tree*, libertytree.ca/quotes/ George.Washington.Quote.2BD2.

[464] "The International Bankers: Famous Quotes." *ConspiracyAnalyst.org*, 23 Dec. 2019, conspiracyanalyst.org/2013/03/01/the-international-bankers-famous-quotes/.

[465] Thomas Jefferson to John Adams, 1819. "Paper Money Collapse: The Folly of Elastic Money, 2nd Edition by Thomas Mayer, Detlev S. Schlichter." *O'Reilly*, www.oreilly.com/library/view/paper-money-collapse/9781118877364/xhtml/fm01.xhtml.

[466] Kaza, Greg. "The U.S. Presidents and the Money Issue." *FEE,* 1 Apr. 1996, fee.org/articles/the-us-presidents-and-the-money-issue/.

[467] Justice Clifford's dissent. *Legal Tender Cases*, 79 U.S. 457 (1870).

money may be deemed an aggression on the rights of the other states."[468]

Thomas Paine wanted to deny government the power to print paper currency. He wrote, "As to the assumed authority of any assembly in making paper money, or paper of any kind, a legal tender, or in other language, a compulsive payment, it is a most presumptuous attempt at arbitrary power. There can be no such power in a republican government: the people have no freedom, and property no security where this practice can be acted: and the committee who shall bring in a report for this purpose, or the member who moves for it, and he who seconds it merits impeachment, and sooner or later may expect it."[469] "The laws of a country ought to be the standard of equity, and calculated to impress on the minds of the people the moral as well as the legal obligations of reciprocal justice. But tender laws, of any kind, operate to destroy morality, and to dissolve, by the pretense of law, what ought to be the principle of law to support, reciprocal justice between man and man: and the punishment of a member who should move for such a law ought to be death…If anything had, or could have, a value equal to gold and silver, it would require no tender law: and if it had not that value it ought not to have such a law; and, therefore, all tender laws are tyrannical and unjust, and calculated to support fraud and oppression. Most of the advocates for tender laws are those who have debts to discharge, and who take refuge in such a law, to violate their contracts and cheat their creditors…"[470] "Considered as property, it is inconsistent to suppose that the breath of an assembly, whose authority expires with the year, can give to paper the value

---

[468] "Money Quotes: What The Experts Say About Money." *Midas Gold Group*, 27 Aug. 2020, www.midasgoldgroup.com/money-quotes/.

[469] Smith, George Ford. "Thomas Paine on Paper Money and Morality." *Mises Institute*, 29 Jan. 2019, mises.org/wire/thomas-paine-paper-money-and-morality?fbclid=IwAR0W6lgaIIh5jxJ7gwTFzdRAa94LMpNXt0OJdGzxVvivyaxr9GFbvGxxrwM.

[470] *Id.*

and duration of gold. They cannot even engage that the next assembly shall receive it in taxes. And by the precedent (for authority there is none), that one assembly makes paper money, another may do the same, until confidence and credit are totally expelled, and all the evils of depreciation acted over again. The amount, therefore, of paper money is this, that it is the illegitimate offspring of assemblies, and when their year expires, they leave a vagrant on the hands of the public."[471]

For such reasons, the Framers of the Constitution only granted to Congress in Article I, Section 8 the power to "coin Money, regulate the Value thereof, and of foreign Coin…"[472] This power to coin money and regulate the value of domestic and foreign coin was vested in the federal government to produce uniformity of value and to prevent a perpetually fluctuating and variable currency.[473]

The Founding Fathers established that "the official money of the United States would be precious metals – silver and gold."[474] "[T]he money unit of the United States is the coined dollar, described in the act establishing the mint."[475] On April 2, 1792, Congress "passed the act establishing a mint…, and made provision…that coins of gold and silver of certain fineness and weight and of certain denominations, value and descriptions, should be…struck and coined at the mint…silver coins, to-wit, 'DOLLARS OR UNITS,' each to contain 371 grains and 4/16ths parts of a grain

---

[471] *Id.*

[472] Congress has allowed the Federal Reserve to usurp its power to issue money and regulate its value.

[473] Unfortunately, "Probably no aspect of the American economy has strayed further from the Constitution than the monetary system," according to W. Cleon Skousen, *The Making of America*, p. 419. "The History of American Money." *CMI Gold $ Silver*, www.cmi-gold-silver.com/history-american-money/.

[474] *Id.*

[475] Justice Clifford's dissent. *Legal Tender Cases*, 79 U.S. 457 (1870).

of pure silver, or 416 grains of standard silver...".[476] "Coins of copper may also be minted for small fractional circulation," i.e., pennies and half pennies.[477] Thus, "[m]oney, in the constitutional sense, means coins of gold and silver fabricated and stamped by authority of law as a measure of value."[478]

"When we consider all of these constitutional provisions, it is easy to see that the Framers intended to establish a monetary system in which gold coins and silver coins were to be the official money of the United States."[479] Thomas Jefferson thought, "[s]pecie is the most perfect medium because it will preserve its own level; because, having intrinsic and universal value, it can never die in our hands, and it is the surest resource of reliance in time of war."[480] In contrast, he wrote, "Paper is poverty,...it is only the ghost of money,

---

[476] *Id.* 371 grains are equal to approx. 0.77 troy ounces of .999 fine silver. This would be about $20 worth of silver as of January 2021. "Silver Conversion." *Traditional Oven*, www.traditionaloven.com/metal/precious-metals/silver/convert-qty_371_25-grain-gr-of-silver-to-troy-ounce-tr-oz-silver.html.

[477] Justice Clifford's dissent. *Legal Tender Cases*, 79 U.S. 457 (1870).

[478] *Id.*

[479] Hornberger, Jacob. "Monetary Destruction in America." *Tenth Amendment Center*, 7 Jun. 2020, tenthamendmentcenter.com/2020/06/07/monetary-destruction-in-america/?fbclid=IwAR1qznHUtpPxV4SZfCJk0G9H9gTS2kepV1ZU5BKoX_o06DxBXusfHyCPK6s.

[480] In a letter to John Wayles Eppes in 1813. "Thomas Jefferson Quotes," *AZ Quotes*, www.azquotes.com/quote/650804.

and not money itself."481 James Madison believed that paper money was "unjust" and "unconstitutional."482

President Andrew Jackson agreed that real money was specie, and described gold coins as "a sound and portable currency."483 "Jackson believed that the nation's money supply should consist only of gold or silver coin minted by the Treasury and any foreign coin the Congress chose to accept."484 In 1836, Old Hickory signed the Specie Circular, which required "that payment for the purchase of public lands be made exclusively in gold or silver."485

"Paper money and what was coming in his day to be called commercial paper — bills of exchange, promissory notes, bank checks, and such — were to Jackson, just as they had been to John Adams...a form of fraud."486 In his farewell address, he warned, "The paper system...having of itself no intrinsic value...is liable to

---

481 In a letter to Edward Carrington in 1788. "Thomas Jefferson Quotes," *Your Dictionary*, quotes.yourdictionary.com/author/thomas-jefferson/166784.

482 Cortez, JP. "Fake Money, Sound Money and Government Malfeasance." *Tenth Amendment Center*, 28 Aug. 2018, tenthamendmentcenter.com/2018/08/28/fake-money-sound-money-and-government-malfeasance/.

483 Jackson, Andrew. "The Project Gutenberg EBook of State of the Union Addresses of Andrew Jackson." *Gutenberg.org*, 21 Nov. 2014, www.gutenberg.org/files/5016/5016-h/5016-h.htm.

484 "Second Bank of the United States (1816-1836)." *American History: From Revolution to Reconstruction and Beyond*, www.let.rug.nl/usa/essays/general/a-brief-history-of-central-banking/second-bank-of-the-united-states-(1816-1836).php.

485 Congress repealed the Specie Circular in 1838. The Editors of Encyclopedia Britannica. "Specie Circular." *Encyclopedia Britannica*, www.britannica.com/event/Specie-Circular.

486 Quote by John Steele Gordon. "History - Essays: Andrew Jackson, banks, and the Panic of." *The Lehrman Institute,* lehrmaninstitute.org/history/Andrew-Jackson-1837.html. (Citing H. W. Brands, *Andrew Jackson: His Life and Times*, p. 470).

great and sudden fluctuations, thereby rendering property insecure, and the wages of labor unsteady and uncertain."[487]

So deep was the public's distrust of government fiat currency due to the disastrous experiment with the Continental that it was not until the Civil War that paper money was again issued as legal tender in any substantial quantity.[488]

The next chapter discusses the history of central banks in the United States.

---

[487] Kaza, Greg. "The U.S. Presidents and the Money Issue." *FEE,* 1 Apr. 1996, fee.org/articles/the-us-presidents-and-the-money-issue/.

[488] Narron, James and David Skeie. "Crisis Chronicles: Not Worth a Continental—The Currency Crisis of 1779 and Today's European Debt Crisis." *Liberty Street Economics,* 11 Apr. 2014, libertystreeteconomics.newyorkfed.org/2014/04/crisis-chronicles-not-worth-a-continentalthe-currency-crisis-of-1779-and-todays-european-debt-crisis.html; Glass, Andrew. "Congress issues Continental currency, June 22, 1775." *Politico,* 22 Jun. 2018, www.politico.com/story/2018/06/22/congress-issues-continental-currency-june-22-1775-652244.

Chapter 3

A Brief History of Central Banks in USA

The First Bank of the United States

After the American Revolution, "the 1780s saw widespread economic disruption. The new nation's leaders had their work cut out for them: reestablishing commerce and industry, repaying war debt, restoring the value of the currency, and lowering inflation."[489] Secretary of the Treasury, Alexander Hamilton, had ambitious ideas about how to solve these problems. One of those was establishing a national bank.

"In December 1790, Hamilton submitted a report to Congress in which he outlined his proposal. Hamilton used the charter of the Bank of England as the basis for his plan. He argued that an American version of this institution could issue paper money (also called banknotes or currency), provide a safe place to keep public funds, offer banking facilities for commercial transactions, and act as the government's fiscal agent, including collecting the government's tax revenues and paying the government's debts."[490]

However, the United States Constitution made no provision for chartering federal corporations.[491] The Constitution "established a

---

[489] "The First Bank of the United States." *Federal Reserve History,* www.federalreservehistory.org/essays/first_bank_of_the_us.

[490] *Id.* Gold and silver were to be the basis of a paper circulation. *M'Culloch v. Maryland,* 17 US 316 (1819).

[491] Kaza, Greg. "The U.S. Presidents and the Money Issue." *FEE,* 1 Apr. 1996, fee.org/articles/the-us-presidents-and-the-money-issue/.

government of limited, enumerated powers. The federal government's powers were limited to those listed in the Constitution. If a power wasn't enumerated, it couldn't be exercised."[492] Thus, a liberal interpretation would be necessary to justify a national bank. "Hamilton believed that Article I, Section 8 of the Constitution, permitting the Congress to make laws that are necessary and proper for the government, empowered lawmakers to create a national bank."[493] This "'implied powers doctrine' postulated that 'the government has the right to employ any means necessary to execute its express powers under the Constitution.' In ringing phrases, Hamilton asserted that 'every power vested in a government is in its nature sovereign and includes, by force of the term, a right to employ all the means requisite and fairly applicable to the attainment of the ends of such power.'"[494] Hamilton claimed, "'Every power vested in a Government is in its nature sovereign, and includes by force of the term, a right to employ all the means requisite, and fairly applicable to the attainment of the ends of such power.' The incorporation of a bank was 'immediately relative' to 'the sovereign power of providing for the collection of taxes,' which, extended logically, necessarily included 'the right of granting a corporate capacity' to a national bank."[495]

---

[492] Hornberger, Jacob. "Monetary Destruction in America." *Tenth Amendment Center*, 7 Jun. 2020, tenthamendmentcenter.com/2020/06/07/monetary-destruction-in-america/?fbclid=IwAR1qznHUtpPxV4SZfCJk0G9H9gTS2kepV1ZU5BKoX_o06DxBXusfHyCPK6s.

[493] "The First Bank of the United States." *History, Art, and Archives,* history.house.gov/Historical-Highlights/1700s/1791_First_Bank/.

[494] Davies, Phil. "The Bank That Hamilton Built." *Federal Reserve Bank of Minneapolis*, 1 Sept. 2007, www.minneapolisfed.org/article/2007/the-bank-that-hamilton-built.

[495] Smock, Geoff. "John Marchall: Hamilton 2.0." *Journal of the American Revolution*, 30 Jun. 2020, allthingsliberty.com/2020/06/john-marshall-hamilton-2-0/.

Secretary of State, Thomas Jefferson, disagreed. He contended that the Constitution did not grant the government the authority to establish corporations, such as a national bank.[496]   Rather than a broad interpretation of the Constitution, he, along with other Anti-Federalists, favored "strict constructionism."[497]   "Jefferson argued in a written opinion to [President George] Washington that a national bank may be convenient, but not truly necessary or indispensable for the execution of the government's enumerated powers. Therefore, Hamilton's bank was unconstitutional…"[498]   He wrote in his "Opinion on the Constitutionality of a National Bank" (1791) the following: "It has been urged that a bank will give great facility or convenience in the collection of taxes. Suppose this were true: yet the Constitution allows only the means which are 'necessary,' not those which are merely 'convenient' for effecting the enumerated powers. If such a latitude of construction be allowed to this phrase as to give any non-enumerated power, it will go to everyone, for there is not one which ingenuity may not torture into a convenience in some instance or other, to some one of so long a list of enumerated powers. It would swallow up all the delegated powers, and reduce the whole to one power, as before observed. Therefore it was that the Constitution restrained them to the necessary means, that is to say, to those means without which the grant of power would be nugatory."[499]   "Nowhere in the Constitution was congress explicitly granted the authority to create a bank, and to "take a single step beyond the boundaries thus specially drawn around the powers

---

[496] "The First Bank of the United States." *Federal Reserve History*, www.federalreservehistory.org/essays/first_bank_of_the_us.

[497] Kaza, Greg. "The U.S. Presidents and the Money Issue." *FEE,* 1 Apr. 1996, fee.org/articles/the-us-presidents-and-the-money-issue/.

[498] Davies, Phil. "The Bank That Hamilton Built." *Federal Reserve Bank of Minneapolis*, 1 Sept. 2007, www.minneapolisfed.org/article/2007/the-bank-that-hamilton-built.

[499] Jefferson, Thomas. "Opinion on the Constitutionality of the Bill for Establishing a National Bank." *National Archives*, founders.archives.gov/documents/Jefferson/01-19-02-0051.

of Congress" would be for the national government "to take possession of a boundless field of power."[500] Jefferson also argued, "Since there was no power to issue paper money given to the federal government, it couldn't exercise such power."[501] Any "powers not expressly granted to Congress in the Constitution belonged to the states."[502]

James Madison of Virginia, "The Father of the Constitution," agreed with Jefferson and "added that a national bank would conflict with state interests under the Constitution by interfering with the right of states to charter and oversee their own banks of issue…"[503]

In addition to its unconstitutionality, Jefferson opposed the central bank because he believed that it catered to commercial and financial interests while hurting the agricultural sector.[504] "Thomas Jefferson was afraid that a national bank would create a financial monopoly that might undermine state banks and adopt policies that favored financiers and merchants, who tended to be creditors, over plantation owners and family farmers, who tended to be debtors."[505]

---

[500] Smock, Geoff. "John Marchall: Hamilton 2.0." *Journal of the American Revolution*, 30 Jun. 2020, allthingsliberty.com/2020/06/john-marshall-hamilton-2-0/.

[501] Hornberger, Jacob. "Monetary Destruction in America." *Tenth Amendment Center*, 7 Jun. 2020, tenthamendmentcenter.com/2020/06/07/monetary-destruction-in-america/?fbclid=IwAR1qznHUtpPxV4SZfCJk0G9H9gTS2kepV1ZU5BKoX_o06DxBXusfHyCPK6s.

[502] "The First Bank of the United States." *History, Art, and Archives,* history.house.gov/Historical-Highlights/1700s/1791_First_Bank/.

[503] Davies, Phil. "The Bank That Hamilton Built." *Federal Reserve Bank of Minneapolis*, 1 Sept. 2007, www.minneapolisfed.org/article/2007/the-bank-that-hamilton-built.

[504] Kaza, Greg. "The U.S. Presidents and the Money Issue." *FEE*, 1 Apr. 1996, fee.org/articles/the-us-presidents-and-the-money-issue/.

[505] "The First Bank of the United States." *History, Art, and Archives,* history.house.gov/Historical-Highlights/1700s/1791_First_Bank/.

Jefferson lamented that private bankers were empowered to "regulate according to their own interests, the quantum of circulating medium for the nation — to inflate, by deluges of paper, the nominal prices of property, and then to buy up that property at 1shilling. in the pound, having first withdrawn the floating medium which might endanger a competition in purchase…"[506]   Thus, he warned that "[t]he banks…have the regulation of the safety-valves of our fortunes, and…condense and explode them at their will."[507] Jefferson predicted, "If the American people ever allow private banks to control the issuance of their currency, first by inflation and then by deflation, the banks and corporations that will grow up around them will deprive the people of all their property until their children will wake up homeless on the continent their fathers conquered."[508]

Jefferson "sincerely believe[d] the banking institutions having the issuing power of money, are more dangerous to liberty than standing armies."[509]   He feared that the banking system was creating an aristocracy in the United States that was a threat to the Republic. "The bank mania…is raising up a moneyed aristocracy in our country which has already set the government at defiance, and although forced at length to yield a little on this first essay of their

---

[506] Jefferson, Thomas. "TJ: Plan for Reducing the Circulating Medium, 23 Nov. 1819, 23 November 2019." *Founders Online*, National Archives and Records Administration, founders.archives.gov/documents/Jefferson/ 98-01-02-0909.

[507] Thomas Jefferson to John Adams, 1819. Hodges, James P. PhD and Cynthia F. Hodges, JD, LLM, MA. "FED Up: Founding Fathers, the Banking System, and the Federal Reserve." *Leadership By George Washington*, 21 Apr. 2010, leadershipbygeorge.blogspot.com/2010/04/fed-up-founding-fathers-banking-system.html.

[508] In a letter to James Monroe, January 1, 1815. Deflation is "a general decline occurring in prices for goods and services when the inflation rate falls below 0%." Fernando, Jason. "Inflation." *Investopedia*, 18 Nov. 2020, www.investopedia.com/terms/i/inflation.asp.

[509] *Id.*

strength, their principles are unyielded and unyielding. These have taken deep root in the hearts of that class from which our legislators are drawn, and the sop to Cerberus from fable has become history. Their principles lay hold of the good, their pelf of the bad, and thus those whom the Constitution had placed as guards to its portals, are sophisticated or suborned from their duties."[510] Jefferson remarked, "It is a cruel thought, that, when we feel ourselves standing on the firmest ground in every respect, the cursed arts of our secret enemies, combining with other causes, should effect, by depreciating our money, what the open arms of a powerful enemy could not."[511] He "hope[d] we shall crush in its birth the aristocracy of the moneyed corporations which already dare to challenge our Government to a trial of strength and bid defiance to the laws of our country."[512]

Unfortunately, after much debate, Hamilton's bill creating the First Bank of the United States cleared both the House and the Senate. "The first congress created and incorporated a bank. Act of 5th February 1791, ch. 84."[513] President George Washington signed

---

[510] Thomas Jefferson to Josephus B. Stuart, 1817. "Thomas Jefferson." Quotes of Famous People, *Quote Park*, quotepark.com/quotes/1806450-thomas-jefferson-i-sincerely-believe-that-banking-institutions-are/.

[511] Thomas Jefferson to Richard Henry Lee, 1779. "From Thomas Jefferson to Richard Henry Lee, 17 June 1779." Founders Online, *National Archives*, founders.archives.gov/documents/Jefferson/01-02-02-0128.

[512] "Money Quotes: What The Experts Say About Money." *Midas Gold Group*, 27 Aug. 2020, www.midasgoldgroup.com/money-quotes/.

[513] *M'Culloch v. Maryland*, 17 US 316 (1819).

it into law on February 25, 1791.[514] The bank's charter was for 20 years.[515]

"The name of the bank was deliberately chosen to hide the fact that it was privately controlled, and like the Bank of England, the names of the private investors were never revealed. However, it was well-known that the Rothschild cartel was the driving power behind the Bank of the United States…"[516]

The Bank of the United States "was actually a private bank, but it functioned as a depository for the United States and collected taxes. It also issued redeemable bank notes which circulated as currency."[517] It "started with capitalization of $10 million, $2 million of which was owned by the government and the remaining $8 million by private investors. The size of its capitalization made

[514] "The First Bank of the United States." *Federal Reserve History*, www.federalreservehistory.org/essays/first_bank_of_the_us. "In McCullough, Marshall, writing for a Republican-dominated, unanimous court, would render it a fait accompli. Though the Constitution gave the congress no power to incorporate a bank per se, incorporation itself was a power that, by definition, emanated from other powers as it was 'a means by which other objects are accomplished.' The Constitution did give the congress the power to collect taxes, borrow money, regulate commerce, and to raise and support armies—all of which were enumerated powers which required congress to devise means for the management of public funds. Incorporating a bank, as Hamilton had argued two decades before, was one of those legitimate means. 'Let the end be legitimate, let it be within the scope of the Constitution, and all means which are appropriate, which are plainly adapted to that end, which are not prohibited…are constitutional.' The issue was at last settled: a national bank was constitutional…it is John Marshall, more than Hamilton himself, we have to thank—or to blame." Smock, Geoff. "John Marchall: Hamilton 2.0." *Journal of the American Revolution*, 30 Jun. 2020, allthingsliberty.com/2020/06/john-marshall-hamilton-2-0/.

[515] "The History of American Money." *CMI Gold $ Silver*, www.cmi-gold-silver.com/history-american-money/.

[516] Jones, Stack. "An Essay On The History Of Banking." *The Banking Swindle*, 1 Jan. 2018, criminalbankingmonopoly.wordpress.com/.

[517] "The History of American Money." *CMI Gold $ Silver*, www.cmi-gold-silver.com/history-american-money/.

the Bank not only the largest financial institution, but the largest corporation of any type in the new nation..."[518]

"In addition to its activities on behalf of the government, the Bank of the United States also operated as a commercial bank, which meant it accepted deposits from the public and made loans to private citizens and businesses..."[519] It did not regulate or act as a lender of last resort for other financial institutions, and it did not hold their reserves.[520] "To avoid inflation and the appearance of impropriety, the Bank was forbidden from buying US government bonds..."[521]

"Unlike modern central banks, the Bank of the United States did not set monetary policy as we know it today."[522] "Scholars such as Richard Timberlake, Jr., a former economics professor at the University of Georgia, have pointed out that neither Hamilton nor Congress intended the First Bank to control the size of the money stock — a defining function of the Fed and other modern central banks."[523] "Nevertheless, Timberlake contends that, over the course of several years, the bank took on that role..."[524] "Its prominence as one of the largest corporations in America and its branches' broad geographic position in the emerging American economy allowed it

[518] "Many of the initial investors were foreign, a fact that did not sit well with many Americans, even though the foreign shareholders could not vote..." "The First Bank of the United States." *History, Art, and Archives,* history.house.gov/Historical-Highlights/1700s/1791_First_Bank/.

[519] *Id.*

[520] "The First Bank of the United States." *Federal Reserve History,* www.federalreservehistory.org/essays/first_bank_of_the_us.

[521] "The First Bank of the United States." *History, Art, and Archives,* history.house.gov/Historical-Highlights/1700s/1791_First_Bank/.

[522] *Id.*

[523] Davies, Phil. "The Bank That Hamilton Built." *Federal Reserve Bank of Minneapolis,* 1 Sept. 2007, www.minneapolisfed.org/article/2007/the-bank-that-hamilton-built.

[524] *Id.*

to conduct a rudimentary monetary policy...By managing its lending policies and the flow of funds through its accounts, the bank could — and did — alter the supply of money and credit in the economy and hence the level of interest rates charged to borrowers..."[525] "To rein in credit, the bank promptly presented the state banknotes that passed through its offices for redemption in specie, reducing the lending capacity of the issuers. To ease credit, the bank lent more to businesses and banks and treated state banknotes with 'forbearance.'"[526] "In the course of business, the Bank would accumulate the notes of the state banks and hold them in its vault. When it wanted to slow the growth of money and credit, it would present the notes to banks for collection in gold or silver, thereby reducing state banks' reserves and putting the brakes on their ability to circulate new banknotes. To speed up the growth of money and credit, the Bank would hold on to the state banks' notes, thereby increasing state banks' reserves and allowing those banks to issue more banknotes by making loans..."[527]   "Timberlake sees this activity as an early form of open market operations — resented by many state banks — that acted as a check on inflation..."[528] "These actions, which had effects similar to today's monetary policy, can be seen most clearly in the Bank's interactions with state banks."[529]

---

[525] "The First Bank of the United States." *Federal Reserve History*, www.federalreservehistory.org/essays/first_bank_of_the_us.

[526] Davies, Phil. "The Bank That Hamilton Built." *Federal Reserve Bank of Minneapolis*, 1 Sept. 2007, www.minneapolisfed.org/article/2007/the-bank-that-hamilton-built.

[527] "The First Bank of the United States." *Federal Reserve History*, www.federalreservehistory.org/essays/first_bank_of_the_us.

[528] Davies, Phil. "The Bank That Hamilton Built." *Federal Reserve Bank of Minneapolis*, 1 Sept. 2007, www.minneapolisfed.org/article/2007/the-bank-that-hamilton-built.

[529] "The First Bank of the United States." *Federal Reserve History*, www.federalreservehistory.org/essays/first_bank_of_the_us.

"The bank had been presented as a way to stabilize the nations currency, and to control inflation. However, over the first five years, the U.S. government borrowed 8.5 million dollars from the Bank of the United States..."[530] Murray Rothbard wrote, "The First Bank of the United States promptly fulfilled its inflationary potential by issuing millions of dollars in paper money and demand deposits. The result of the outpouring of credit and paper money by the new bank of the United States was an increase in prices of 72% from 1791 to 1796."[531] Secretary of State, Thomas Jefferson, "watched the borrowing with sadness and frustration, unable to stop it. [He] wrote, 'I wish it were possible to obtain a single amendment to our Constitution taking from the federal government their power of borrowing.'"[532]

In an 1803 letter to Albert Gallatin, Thomas Jefferson wrote, "[The] Bank of the United States...is one of the most deadly hostility existing, against the principles and form of our Constitution...An institution like this, penetrating by its branches every part of the Union, acting by command and in phalanx, may, in a critical moment, upset the government. I deem no government safe which is under the vassalage of any self-constituted authorities, or any other authority than that of the nation, or its regular functionaries. What an obstruction could not this bank of the United States, with all its branch banks, be in time of war! It might dictate to us the peace we should accept, or withdraw its aids. Ought we then to give further growth to an institution so powerful, so hostile?"[533] He believed

---

[530] Jones, Stack. "An Essay On The History Of Banking." *The Banking Swindle*, 1 Jan. 2018, criminalbankingmonopoly.wordpress.com/.

[531] At 34:00 - 35:00. Misesmedia. "The Corrupt Origins of Central Banking in America | Thomas J. DiLorenzo." *Youtube*, 26 Jul. 2014, www.youtube.com/watch?v=1a9DrLOsrlA.

[532] Jones, Stack. "An Essay On The History Of Banking." *The Banking Swindle*, 1 Jan. 2018, criminalbankingmonopoly.wordpress.com/.

[533] "From Thomas Jefferson to Albert Gallatin, 13 December 1803." Founders Online, *National Archives*, founders.archives.gov/documents/Jefferson/01-42-02-0100.

that "the issuing power of money should be taken from banks and restored to Congress and the people to whom it belongs."[534]

Even Alexander Hamilton eventually turned against the central bank (circa 1798). "He felt that if currency or bank notes were to be issued and circulated as 'money,' it should have been done by Congress."[535] He warned, "To emit an unfunded paper as the sign of value ought not to continue a formal part of the Constitution, nor even hereafter to be employed; being, in its nature, pregnant with abuses, and liable to be made the engine of imposition and fraud; holding out temptations equally pernicious to the integrity of government and to the morals of the people."[536]

In 1811, a bill was introduced in Congress to renew the Bank of the U.S.' charter.[537] However, "[b]y 1811, the number of state banks had increased greatly, and those financial institutions feared both competition from a national bank and its power."[538] "The debate [in Congress] was heated, and representatives of Pennsylvania and Virginia passed resolutions asking Congress to abolish the bank. The press at that time openly called the bank a swindle, a vulture, a viper and a cobra. A congressman named P. B. Porter attacked the bank from the floor saying, 'If the bank's charter was renewed congress would have planted in the bosom of this

---

[534] In a letter to James Monroe, January 1, 1815. Deflation is "a general decline occurring in prices for goods and services when the inflation rate falls below 0%." Fernando, Jason. "Inflation." *Investopedia*, 18 Nov. 2020, www.investopedia.com/terms/i/inflation.asp.

[535] "The History of American Money." *CMI Gold $ Silver*, www.cmi-gold-silver.com/history-american-money/.

[536] "Money Quotes: What The Experts Say About Money." *Midas Gold Group*, 27 Aug. 2020, www.midasgoldgroup.com/money-quotes/.

[537] Jones, Stack. "An Essay On The History Of Banking." *The Banking Swindle*, 1 Jan. 2018, criminalbankingmonopoly.wordpress.com/.

[538] "The First Bank of the United States." *Federal Reserve History*, www.federalreservehistory.org/essays/first_bank_of_the_us.

constitution a viper, which one day or another would sting the liberty of this country to the heart.'"[539]

Despite Nathan Rothschild's threats "that the U.S. would find itself involved in a most disastrous war if the bank's charter were not renewed," the bill was "defeated by a single vote in the house, and was deadlocked in the senate."[540] At this point, James Madison (1809-1817) was in the White House.[541] "Madison, like Jefferson, was a staunch opponent of the bank; his vice president, George Clinton, broke the tie in the Senate, and sent the bank into oblivion."[542]

"Within five months, England attacked the U.S., and the War of 1812 was on. At that time, the British were still battling Napoleon, so the U.S. war ended in a draw in 1814. The money changers were down, but they were far from out. It would take merely two years to bring back the privately controlled banking system in the U.S. It would be bigger, and more powerful than ever before…"[543]

---

[539] Jones, Stack. "An Essay On The History Of Banking." *The Banking Swindle*, 1 Jan. 2018, criminalbankingmonopoly.wordpress.com/.

[540] *Id.*

[541] *Id.*

[542] *Id.*. Madison vetoed a bill rechartering the bank in 1815. Kaza, Greg. "The U.S. Presidents and the Money Issue." *FEE,* 1 Apr. 1996, fee.org/articles/the-us-presidents-and-the-money-issue/.

[543] Jones, Stack. "An Essay On The History Of Banking." *The Banking Swindle*, 1 Jan. 2018, criminalbankingmonopoly.wordpress.com/.

The Second Bank of the United States

After the War of 1812 concluded, "[m]any state-chartered banks had stopped redeeming their notes, which convinced Madison and his advisers that the time had come to move the country toward a more uniform, stable paper currency. In his annual report, [Alexander] Dallas [Secretary of the Treasury] called for the establishment of a national bank. After much debate..., Madison finally signed in April 1816 an act establishing the second Bank of the United States."[544]

"The Bank opened for business in Philadelphia in January 1817. It had much in common with its forerunner, including its functions and structure. It would act as fiscal agent for the federal government — holding its deposits, making its payments, and helping it issue debt to the public — and it would issue and redeem banknotes and keep state banks' issuance of notes in check. Also like its predecessor, the Bank had a twenty-year charter and operated as a commercial bank that accepted deposits and made loans to the public, both businesses and individuals. Its board consisted of twenty-five directors, with five appointed by the president and confirmed by the Senate. The capitalization for the second Bank was $35 million, considerably higher than the $10 million underwriting of the first Bank."[545] "The Bank's reach was far greater than that of its predecessor. Its branches eventually totaled twenty-five in number, compared to only eight for the first Bank."[546]

---

[544] "Six men figured prominently in establishing...the second Bank of the United States: the financiers John Jacob Astor, David Parish, Stephen Girard, and Jacob Barker; Alexander Dallas, who would become secretary of the Treasury in 1814; and Rep. John C. Calhoun of South Carolina." Hill, Andrew T. "The Second Bank of the United States." *Federal Reserve History*, 5 Dec. 2015, www.federalreservehistory.org/essays/ second_bank_of_the_us.

[545] *Id.*

[546] *Id.*

"The Bank served as a place in which the government could deposit federal funds, including tax revenues. The Bank was authorised to issue as many bank notes as the president and cashier were physically able to sign, but was required to be able to pay specie for currency on demand."[547] However, during its first three years, "[m]ore notes were issued than could be backed by specie."[548]

"In addition, the Bank was exempted from taxation by any state. In return, the Bank performed transactions for the government at no charge, and allowed the government to appoint five of its twenty-five directors. The Secretary of the Treasury had the right to remove any government deposits, after presenting the reasons for withdrawal to Congress."[549]

"Unlike modern central banks, the Bank did not set monetary policy…It also did not regulate, hold the reserves of, or act as a lender of last resort for other financial institutions. Nonetheless, its prominence as one of the largest US corporations and its branches' broad geographic position in the expanding economy allowed it to conduct a rudimentary monetary policy. The Bank's notes, backed by substantial gold reserves, gave the country a more stable national currency. By managing its lending policies and the flow of funds through its accounts, the Bank could — and did — alter the supply of money and credit in the economy and hence the level of interest rates charged to borrowers."[550]

"These actions, which had effects similar to today's monetary policy actions, can be seen most clearly in the national bank's interactions with state banks. In the course of business, it would accumulate the notes of the state banks and hold them in its vault.

---

[547] "Second Bank of the United States." *History Central*, www.historycentral.com/Ant/Economics/Second.html.

[548] *Id.*

[549] *Id.*

[550] Hill, Andrew T. "The Second Bank of the United States." *Federal Reserve History,* 5 Dec. 2015, www.federalreservehistory.org/essays/second_bank_of_the_us.

When it wanted to slow the growth of money and credit, it would present the notes for collection in gold or silver, thereby reducing state banks' reserves and putting the brakes on state banks' ability to circulate new banknotes (paper currency). To speed up the growth of money and credit, the Bank would hold on to the state banks' notes, thereby increasing state banks' reserves and allowing those banks to issue more banknotes through their loan-making process."[551]

"For its first three years in existence, the Second Bank was poorly run."[552] "The first president of the Bank was William Jones, a political appointee and a former secretary of the Navy who had gone bankrupt. Under Jones's leadership, the Bank first extended too much credit and then reversed that trend too quickly. The result was a financial panic that drove the economy into a steep recession."[553]

"[I]n 1819, shareholders elected Langdon Cheves, an attorney from South Carolina who had served as Speaker of the House of Representatives, as president of the Bank. Cheves cut in half the number of second Bank banknotes in circulation, made fewer loans, foreclosed on mortgages, and exerted more control over the Bank's branches. He presented state banknotes for specie, a request that sent many state-chartered financial institutions into bankruptcy because they did not have enough gold and silver on hand to cover the redemptions. Another depression, characterized by deflation and high unemployment, ensued…Public opinion started turning against the Bank as many believed it contributed to the recession."[554]

During this period, two attempts to have the bank struck down as unconstitutional failed. In *McCulloch v. Maryland,* 17 U.S. 316 (1819), the Supreme Court voted 9-0 to uphold the Second Bank as

---

[551] *Id.*

[552] "Second Bank of the United States." *History Central,* www.historycentral.com/Ant/Economics/Second.html.

[553] Hill, Andrew T. "The Second Bank of the United States." *Federal Reserve History,* 5 Dec. 2015, www.federalreservehistory.org/essays/second_bank_of_the_us.

[554] *Id.*

constitutional.[555]　The Court reaffirmed this opinion in *Osborn v. Bank of the United States*, 22 U.S. 738 (1824).[556]　Despite its legal victories, the Bank had many enemies.

"Opponents of the bank nominated a senator from Tennessee, Andrew Jackson, to run for president."[557]　"In 1828, Andrew Jackson, hero of the Battle of New Orleans and a determined foe of banks in general and the second Bank of the United States in particular, was elected president of the United States."[558] "Initially, no one [had given] Jackson a chance to win the presidency. The banks had long been able to control the political process with money. However, to the surprise and dismay of the money changers, Jackson was swept into office in 1828."[559]　"After twelve years of The Second Bank of the U.S. manipulating the American economy, the American people had had enough."[560]

"Jackson saw the national bank as a misuse of government funds and a dangerous financial apparatus just waiting to cause another financial panic like the one it had caused in 1819."[561]　Old Hickory, as he was known, agreed with Thomas Jefferson that a central bank was unconstitutional, especially insofar as it trampled

---

[555] "Second Bank of the United States (1816-1836)." *American History: From Revolution to Reconstruction and Beyond*, www.let.rug.nl/usa/ essays/general/a-brief-history-of-central-banking/second-bank-of-the-united-states-(1816-1836).php.

[556] *Id.*

[557] Jones, Stack. "An Essay On The History Of Banking." *The Banking Swindle*, 1 Jan. 2018, criminalbankingmonopoly.wordpress.com/.

[558] 7th President of the United States. Hill, Andrew T. "The Second Bank of the United States." *Federal Reserve History,* 5 Dec. 2015, www.federalreservehistory.org/essays/second_bank_of_the_us.

[559] Jones, Stack. "An Essay On The History Of Banking." *The Banking Swindle*, 1 Jan. 2018, criminalbankingmonopoly.wordpress.com/.

[560] *Id.*

[561] "James K. Polk: Battle of the Bank." *Spark Notes*, www.sparknotes.com/biography/polk/section4/.

on states' rights.562   In 1829, he said "[B]oth the constitutionality and the expediency of the law creating this bank are well questioned by a large portion of our fellow citizens..."563 Jackson believed, "If Congress has the right under the Constitution to issue paper money, it was given them to use themselves, not to be delegated to individuals or corporations."564

Jackson supported hard money and "believed specie — that is, gold and silver — was the most stable currency, not paper banknotes."565 His hatred for paper currency stemmed from a "land deal that had gone sour more than two decades before. In that deal, Jackson had accepted paper notes — essentially paper money — as payment for some land he had sold. When the buyers who had issued the notes went bankrupt, the paper he held became worthless. Although Jackson managed to save himself from financial ruin, he never trusted paper notes again. In Jackson's opinion, only specie — silver or gold coins — qualified as an acceptable medium for

---

562 Hill, Andrew T. "The Second Bank of the United States." *Federal Reserve History,* 5 Dec. 2015, www.federalreservehistory.org/essays/second_bank_of_the_us.

563 Jackson, Andrew. "December 8, 1829: First Annual Message to Congress." *UVA Miller Center,* 8 Dec. 1829, millercenter.org/the-presidency/presidential-speeches/december-8-1829-first-annual-message-congress.

564 "Money Quotes: What The Experts Say About Money." *Midas Gold Group,* 27 Aug. 2020, www.midasgoldgroup.com/money-quotes/. The Supreme Court ruled in *Briscoe v. Bank of Kentucky,* 36 U.S. 257 (1837) that state-chartered banks, state-owned banks, and the banknotes they created were also constitutional. "Second Bank of the United States (1816-1836)." *American History: From Revolution to Reconstruction and Beyond,* www.let.rug.nl/usa/essays/general/a-brief-history-of-central-banking/second-bank-of-the-united-states-(1816-1836).php.

565 Jackson was president from 1829-1837. McCollum, Jason. "Second Bank of the United States: Definition & Overview," *Study.com,* study.com/academy/lesson/second-bank-of-the-united-states-definition-overview.html.

transactions."[566] As a result, he "wanted to get rid of artificial paper money and stick to gold and silver coins."[567] Jackson argued that "loose credit and paper money hurt the poor and only led to economic downturns such as the Panic of 1819."[568]

Jackson also attacked central banks and fiat currency for undermining free institutions.[569] He depicted the Second Bank of the U.S. "as an institution which endangered the foundations of American liberty and democracy by encouraging an imbalance of power between the rich and the poor and threatened the Union by creating artificial distinctions."[570] Old Hickory accused the bank of being "a tool of the wealthy and a vehicle for special interests."[571] "To Jackson, the bank symbolized how a privileged class of businessmen oppressed the will of the common people of America."[572]

---

[566] Hill, Andrew T. "The Second Bank of the United States." *Federal Reserve History,* 5 Dec. 2015, www.federalreservehistory.org/essays/ second_bank_of_the_us.

[567] "Second Bank of the United States." *History Central,* www.historycentral.com/Ant/Economics/Second.html.

[568] McCollum, Jason. "Second Bank of the United States: Definition & Overview," *Study.com,* study.com/academy/lesson/second-bank-of-the-united-states-definition-overview.html.

[569] Jackson "signed the Specie Circular of 1836, which required gold payment of federal debt obligations..." Kaza, Greg. "The U.S. Presidents and the Money Issue." *FEE,* 1 Apr. 1996, fee.org/articles/the-us-presidents-and-the-money-issue/.

[570] "Second Bank of the United States." *History Central,* www.historycentral.com/Ant/Economics/Second.html.

[571] McCollum, Jason. "Second Bank of the United States: Definition & Overview," *Study.com,* study.com/academy/lesson/second-bank-of-the-united-states-definition-overview.html.

[572] History.com Editors. "Andrew Jackson shuts down Second Bank of the U.S." *History,* 16 Nov. 2009, www.history.com/this-day-in-history/ andrew-jackson-shuts-down-second-bank-of-the-u-s.

The president feared that the central bank would give special favors to the wealthy and connected, for which everyone else would have to pay. "Jackson believed the central bank created an alliance between Big Business and government that benefited a few while costing most Americans."[573] "[H]e felt that the Bank put too much power in the hands of too few private citizens — power that could be used to the detriment of the government."[574] "It is to be regretted," Jackson said, "that the rich and powerful too often bend the acts of government to their selfish purposes."[575] He cautioned, "It is not our own citizens only who are to receive the bounty of our government. More than eight millions of the stock of this bank are held by foreigners... Is there no danger to our liberty and independence in a bank that in its nature has so little to bind it to our country?...Controlling our currency, receiving our public moneys, and holding thousands of our citizens in dependence... would be more formidable and dangerous than a military power of the enemy."[576] Jackson warned, "The bold efforts that the present bank has made to control the government and the distress it has wantonly caused, are but premonitions of the fate which awaits the American people should they be deluded into a perpetuation of this institution or the establishment of another like it…"[577]

Jackson also objected to the fact that the Bank "lacked an effective system of regulation" and "congressional oversight over its

[573] Kaza, Greg. "The U.S. Presidents and the Money Issue." *FEE,* 1 Apr. 1996, fee.org/articles/the-us-presidents-and-the-money-issue/.

[574] Hill, Andrew T. "The Second Bank of the United States." *Federal Reserve History,* 5 Dec. 2015, www.federalreservehistory.org/essays/second_bank_of_the_us.

[575] Kaza, Greg. "The U.S. Presidents and the Money Issue." *FEE,* 1 Apr. 1996, fee.org/articles/the-us-presidents-and-the-money-issue/.

[576] Andrew Jackson, Veto of the Bank Bill, to the Senate, (1832). "The History of Money Part 2." *XAT3,* www.xat.org/xat/usury.html.

[577] "Money Quotes: What The Experts Say About Money." *Midas Gold Group*, 27 Aug. 2020, www.midasgoldgroup.com/money-quotes/.

business dealings."[578] "In other words, it was too far outside the jurisdiction of Congress, the president, and voters."[579]

Old Hickory remarked, "If the people only understood the rank injustice of our money and banking system, there would be a revolution before morning."[580] He believed, "[W]hen the law undertakes to...make the rich richer and the potent more powerful, the humble members of society — the farmers, mechanics and laborers...have a right to complain of the injustice of their government."[581]

For these reasons, Jackson considered central banking to be "the scourge of the people" and the banking elite to be "a den of vipers."[582] He vowed "to pay the national debt, to prevent a monied aristocracy from growing up around our administration that must bend to its views, and ultimately destroy the liberty of our country."[583] "He wanted to take control of the American monetary system to benefit the American people, not for the profiteering of the international bankers. Jackson pledged 'to put his foot upon the head

---

[578] Hill, Andrew T. "The Second Bank of the United States." *Federal Reserve History,* 5 Dec. 2015, www.federalreservehistory.org/essays/second_bank_of_the_us; History.com Editors. "Andrew Jackson shuts down Second Bank of the U.S." *History,* 16 Nov. 2009, www.history.com/this-day-in-history/andrew-jackson-shuts-down-second-bank-of-the-u-s.

[579] Hill, Andrew T. "The Second Bank of the United States." *Federal Reserve History,* 5 Dec. 2015, www.federalreservehistory.org/essays/second_bank_of_the_us.

[580] "The History of Money Part 2." *XAT3,* www.xat.org/xat/usury.html.

[581] Kaza, Greg. "The U.S. Presidents and the Money Issue." *FEE,* 1 Apr. 1996, fee.org/articles/the-us-presidents-and-the-money-issue/.

[582] *Id.*

[583] In 1835. Knutson, Lawrence L. "Jackson's Ghost Looms Over Debt." *CBS News,* 7 Feb. 2020, www.cbsnews.com/news/jacksons-ghost-looms-over-debt/.

of the monster [Bank of the U. S.] and crush him to the dust.'"584 He promised the central bankers, "By the Eternal God, I will rout you out!"585

"Jackson was determined to kill the bank at his first opportunity…However, the bank's twenty-year charter didn't come up for renewal until 1836. The last year of his second term, if he could survive that long."586 During his first term, he took the opportunity to root "out the banks minions from government service. Jackson fired 2,000 of the 11,000 employees of the federal government."587

"In 1832, with Jackson's reelection approaching, the banks struck an early blow, hoping Jackson would not want to stir up controversy. The banks asked Congress to sign a renewal bill. This was four years earlier than the bank's renewal was to come up. Congress complied, and sent the bill for Jackson to approve."588

In July 1832, Jackson vetoed the bill Congress had passed

---

584 McCollum, Jason. "Second Bank of the United States: Definition & Overview," *Study.com*, study.com/academy/lesson/second-bank-of-the-united-states-definition-overview.html.

585 "Quotes On The New World Order." *Jesus-Is-Savior.com*, www.jesus-is-savior.com/False%20Religions/Illuminati/quotes_on_the_new_world_order.htm.

586 Jones, Stack. "An Essay On The History Of Banking." *The Banking Swindle*, 1 Jan. 2018, criminalbankingmonopoly.wordpress.com/.

587 *Id.*

588 *Id.*

rechartering the Second Bank of the United States.[589] Congress was unable to override his veto.[590]

The reasons Old Hickory gave for vetoing the bill were that the central bank was incompatible with justice, sound policy, and the Constitution.[591] He wrote the following in his veto message: "A bank of the United States is in many respects convenient for the Government and for the people. Entertaining this opinion, and deeply impressed with the belief that some of the powers and privileges possessed by the existing bank are unauthorized by the Constitution, subversive of the rights of the States, and dangerous to the liberties of the people, I felt it my duty…to call to the attention of Congress to the practicability of organizing an institution combining its advantages and obviating these objections. I sincerely regret that in the act before me I can perceive none of those modifications of the bank charter which are necessary, in my opinion, to make it compatible with justice, with sound policy, or with the Constitution of our country."[592]

"The bank's charter was unfair, Jackson argued in his veto message, because it gave the bank considerable, almost monopolistic, market power, specifically in the markets that moved

---

[589] Kaza, Greg. "The U.S. Presidents and the Money Issue." *FEE*, 1 Apr. 1996, fee.org/articles/the-us-presidents-and-the-money-issue/. "President Jackson quietly vetoed it, Congress soon appeared to be moving toward over-riding the veto. Polk…almost single-handedly blocked the override." "James K. Polk: Battle of the Bank." *Spark Notes*, www.sparknotes.com/biography/polk/section4/.

[590] Jones, Stack. "An Essay On The History Of Banking." *The Banking Swindle*, 1 Jan. 2018, criminalbankingmonopoly.wordpress.com/.

[591] "Jackson Vetoes Re-Charter of the Second Bank of the US." *Museum of American Finance*, www.moaf.org/exhibits/checks_balances/andrew-jackson/broadsheet.

[592] "Second Bank of the United States (1816-1836)." *American History: From Revolution to Reconstruction and Beyond*, www.let.rug.nl/usa/essays/general/a-brief-history-of-central-banking/second-bank-of-the-united-states-(1816-1836).php.

financial resources around the country and into and out of other nations. That market power increased the bank's profits and thus its stock price, 'which operated as a gratuity of many millions [of dollars] to the stockholders,' who, Jackson claimed, were mostly 'foreigners' and 'our own opulent citizens.'"[593]

The bank's charter also "gave incorporated state banks better note redemption rights than those accorded to ordinary Americans and thereby created 'a bond of union among the banking establishments of the nation, erecting them into an interest separate from that of the people.' Second, it exempted foreign stockholders from taxation but contained a clause that would allow states to tax resident stockholders. The effect of the differential taxation, Jackson believed, would drive most of the stock overseas and thus 'make the American people debtors to aliens in nearly the whole amount due to this bank, and send across the Atlantic from two to five millions of specie every year to pay the bank dividends.' Because foreigners could not vote in corporate elections, the Bank would fall under the control of its few remaining citizen stockholders. 'It is easy to conceive,' Jackson argued, 'that great evils to our country and its institutions' would result 'from such a concentration of power in the hands of a few men irresponsible to the people.'"[594] "He suggested that it would be fairer to most Americans to create a wholly government-owned bank instead..."[595]

Another reason Jackson vetoed the bill was because "it has failed in the great end of establishing a uniform and sound

---

[593] "Jackson Vetoes Re-Charter of the Second Bank of the US." *Museum of American Finance*, www.moaf.org/exhibits/checks_balances/andrew-jackson/broadsheet.

[594] *Id.*

[595] "Jackson Vetoes Re-Charter of the Second Bank of the US." *Museum of American Finance*, www.moaf.org/exhibits/checks_balances/andrew-jackson/broadsheet.

currency."[596] Later, he "signed the Specie Circular of 1836, which required gold payment of federal debt obligations…"[597]

In 1832, Old Hickory's campaign slogan for his second term was "Jackson And No Bank!"[598] He "defeated the bank's main supporter, Henry Clay, by a margin of more than four-to-one…"[599] Thus, Jackson considered his re-election as evidence of popular anti-bank sentiment.[600] In his second term, he struck fatal blows to central banking.

Jackson "ordered the withdrawal of government deposits from the Second bank and instead had them put into safe banks."[601] "On September 10, 1833, Jackson removed all federal funds from the Second Bank of the U.S., redistributing them to various state banks…"[602] The president "deposited these funds, $10 million, in

---

[596] Jackson, Andrew. "December 8, 1829: First Annual Message to Congress." *UVA Miller Center*, 8 Dec. 1829, millercenter.org/the-presidency/presidential-speeches/december-8-1829-first-annual-message-congress.

[597] Kaza, Greg. "The U.S. Presidents and the Money Issue." *FEE*, 1 Apr. 1996, fee.org/articles/the-us-presidents-and-the-money-issue/.

[598] Hitchcock, Andrew. "Historical Timeline of the Rothschild Dynasty - Part 3." *The Sirius Report*, 17 Aug. 2015, www.thesiriusreport.com/geopolitics/historical-timeline-rothschild-dynasty-3/.

[599] "James K. Polk: Battle of the Bank." *Spark Notes*, www.sparknotes.com/biography/polk/section4/.

[600] Hill, Andrew T. "The Second Bank of the United States." *Federal Reserve History*, 5 Dec. 2015, www.federalreservehistory.org/essays/second_bank_of_the_us.

[601] "The History of Money Part 2." *XAT3*, www.xat.org/xat/usury.html.

[602] History.com Editors. "Andrew Jackson shuts down Second Bank of the U.S." *History*, 16 Nov. 2009, www.history.com/this-day-in-history/andrew-jackson-shuts-down-second-bank-of-the-u-s.

state banks."[603] "In addition, he announced that deposits to the bank would not be accepted after October 1."[604] "The loss of the federal government's deposits caused the Bank to shrink in both size and influence."[605]

"The immediate result...[was] that the country began to enjoy great prosperity. This sudden flow of cash caused an immediate expansion of the national economy, and the government paid off the entire national debt, leaving a surplus of $50 million in the Treasury."[606] "Jackson was the only president to ever pay off the debt. On January 8, 1835, Jackson paid off the final installment on the national debt, which had been necessitated by allowing the banks to issue currency for government bonds rather than issuing treasury bonds without such debt."[607]

"In April 1834, the House of Representatives voted 124-82 against rechartering the bank."[608] "Jackson had succeeded in

---

[603] "The House of Rothschild Excerpted from the Book The Secrets of the Federal Reserve by Eustace Mullins Bankers Research Institute, 1983, Paperback." *Third World Traveler*, www.thirdworldtraveler.com/Banks/House_Rothschild_TSOTFR.html.

[604] History.com Editors. "Andrew Jackson shuts down Second Bank of the U.S." *History*, 16 Nov. 2009, www.history.com/this-day-in-history/andrew-jackson-shuts-down-second-bank-of-the-u-s.

[605] Hill, Andrew T. "The Second Bank of the United States." *Federal Reserve History*, 5 Dec. 2015, www.federalreservehistory.org/essays/second_bank_of_the_us.

[606] "The House of Rothschild Excerpted from the Book The Secrets of the Federal Reserve by Eustace Mullins Bankers Research Institute, 1983, Paperback." *Third World Traveler*, www.thirdworldtraveler.com/Banks/House_Rothschild_TSOTFR.html.

[607] Jones, Stack. "An Essay On The History Of Banking." *The Banking Swindle*, 1 Jan. 2018, criminalbankingmonopoly.wordpress.com/.

[608] *Id.*

destroying the bank; its charter officially expired in 1836."[609] Shortly before his death in 1845, he was asked what he regarded to be his greatest achievement.[610] Jackson replied, "I killed the bank."[611]

The central bankers retaliated. On January 30, 1835, "Richard Lawrence, an unemployed house painter, approached Jackson…in the House chamber of the Capitol building and shot at him, but his gun misfired. A furious 67-year-old Jackson confronted his attacker, clubbing Lawrence several times with his walking cane. During the scuffle, Lawrence managed to pull out a second loaded pistol and pulled the trigger, but it also misfired."[612] The would-be assassin was found not guilty by reason of insanity, and "spent the rest of his life in a mental institution,"[613]

"Jackson was convinced that Lawrence had been hired by his Whig Party opponents to assassinate him. At the time, Jackson's Democrats and the Whigs were locked in battle over Jackson's attempt to dismantle the Bank of the United States."[614] Jackson said he knew the Rothschilds had been behind the assassination

---

[609] History.com Editors. "Andrew Jackson shuts down Second Bank of the U.S." *History*, 16 Nov. 2009, www.history.com/this-day-in-history/andrew-jackson-shuts-down-second-bank-of-the-u-s.

[610] Hitchcock, Andrew. "Historical Timeline of the Rothschild Dynasty - Part 3." *The Sirius Report*, 17 Aug. 2015, www.thesiriusreport.com/geopolitics/historical-timeline-rothschild-dynasty-3/.

[611] *Id.* "The History of Money Part 2." *XAT3*, www.xat.org/xat/usury.html.

[612] "A century later, Smithsonian Institute researchers conducted a study of Lawrence's derringers, during which both guns discharged properly on the test's first try. It was later determined that the odds of both guns misfiring during the assassination attempt were one in 125,000." History.com Editors. "Andrew Jackson narrowly escapes assassination." *History*, 16 Nov. 2009, www.history.com/this-day-in-history/andrew-jackson-narrowly-escapes-assassination.

[613] *Id.*

[614] *Id.*

attempt.[615]   It has been reported that Lawrence "later bragged that powerful people in Europe had hired him and promised to protect him if he were caught."[616]

The bankers' next move was to cause a depression, which they would blame on Jackson, in an effort to force Congress to restore the Second Bank of the United States. To that end, they contracted the money supply.[617]   Their agent was Nicholas Biddle, the third and last president of the Second Bank of the United States and a sworn enemy of Andrew Jackson.[618]   Biddle declared, "This worthy president thinks that because he has scalped Indians, and imprisoned Judges, he is to have his way with the Bank. He is mistaken."[619]

"Biddle threatened to cause a depression if the bank [were] not rechartered."[620]   He proclaimed in 1836, "Nothing but widespread suffering will produce any effect on Congress…Our only safety is in pursuing a steady course of firm restriction…such a course will ultimately lead to restoration of the currency and the re-charter of the bank."[621]   "Biddle clearly intended to use the money contraction power of the bank to cause a massive depression, until the U.S. gave

---

[615] Hitchcock, Andrew. "Historical Timeline of the Rothschild Dynasty - Part 3." *The Sirius Report*, 17 Aug. 2015, www.thesiriusreport.com/geopolitics/historical-timeline-rothschild-dynasty-3/.

[616] *Id.*

[617] *Id.*

[618] Nicholas Biddle was a member of a wealthy Philadelphia family who had become head of the Bank in 1823. Hill, Andrew T. "The Second Bank of the United States." *Federal Reserve History,* 5 Dec. 2015, www.federalreservehistory.org/essays/second_bank_of_the_us. "James K. Polk: Battle of the Bank." *Spark Notes*, www.sparknotes.com/biography/polk/section4/.

[619] Jones, Stack. "An Essay On The History Of Banking." *The Banking Swindle*, 1 Jan. 2018, criminalbankingmonopoly.wordpress.com/.

[620] *Id.*

[621] "The History of Money Part 2." *XAT3*, www.xat.org/xat/usury.html.

in…Biddle made good on his threat."[622] Biddle called in old loans and refused to issue new ones.[623] He announced that "the Bank would limit credit and call in loans. This contraction of credit, he believed, might create a backlash against Jackson and force the president to relent and redeposit government funds in the Bank, perhaps even renewing the charter."[624]

Predictably, "[a] financial panic ensued, followed by a deep depression…As a result, wages and prices plummeted, unemployment soared, and businesses went bankrupt."[625] Henry Clews, a banker, wrote in his book, *Twenty-Eight Years in Wall Street*, "that the Panic of 1837 was engineered because the charter of the Second Bank of the United States had run out in 1836…The Panic of 1837 was aggravated by the Bank of England when it in one day threw out all the paper connected with the United States… Why did the Bank of England…refuse to accept or discount any securities, bonds or other financial paper based in the United States? The purpose of this action was to create an immediate financial panic in the United States, cause a complete contraction of credit, halt further issues of stocks and bonds, and ruin those seeking to turn United States securities into cash…"[626] As promised, "Biddle blamed Jackson for the crash, saying it was caused by the

[622] Jones, Stack. "An Essay On The History Of Banking." *The Banking Swindle*, 1 Jan. 2018, criminalbankingmonopoly.wordpress.com/.

[623] "The History of Money Part 2." *XAT3*, www.xat.org/xat/usury.html.

[624] Hill, Andrew T. "The Second Bank of the United States." *Federal Reserve History*, 5 Dec. 2015, www.federalreservehistory.org/essays/second_bank_of_the_us.

[625] Jones, Stack. "An Essay On The History Of Banking." *The Banking Swindle*, 1 Jan. 2018, criminalbankingmonopoly.wordpress.com/.

[626] "The House of Rothschild Excerpted from the Book The Secrets of the Federal Reserve by Eustace Mullins Bankers Research Institute, 1983, Paperback." *Third World Traveler*, www.thirdworldtraveler.com/Banks/House_Rothschild_TSOTFR.html.

withdrawal of the federal funds from the bank…"[627]   "The nation newspapers blasted Jackson in editorials."[628]

Biddle "managed to convince many congressmen (partially through illegal loans and preferential treatment) that the bank needed to be rechartered…"[629] "Within months, Congress formed what was called, the Panic Session. Six months after Jackson had withdrawn federal money from the privately owned banks, he was officially censored. The resolution was passed 26-20, and was the first time a president had been censured by Congress."[630]

Ultimately, Biddle's strategy backfired because "it helped to support Jackson's claim that the Bank had been created to serve the interests of the wealthy, not to meet the nation's financial needs."[631] A committee was established "to investigate whether the bank had intentionally caused the crash. When the investigating committee, armed with a subpoena to examine the banks books, [arrived,] Biddle refused to give them up. [Neither] would he allow inspection of correspondence with members of congress, related to their personal loans, and advances Biddle had made to them. Biddle also refused to testify before the committee."[632]   "Biddle would later

---

[627] Jones, Stack. "An Essay On The History Of Banking." *The Banking Swindle*, 1 Jan. 2018, criminalbankingmonopoly.wordpress.com/.

[628] *Id.*

[629] "James K. Polk: Battle of the Bank." *Spark Notes*, www.sparknotes.com/biography/polk/section4/.

[630] "The banks threatened to withhold payments from politicians who refused to support the bank's position." Jones, Stack. "An Essay On The History Of Banking." *The Banking Swindle*, 1 Jan. 2018, criminalbankingmonopoly.wordpress.com/.

[631] Hill, Andrew T. "The Second Bank of the United States." *Federal Reserve History*, 5 Dec. 2015, www.federalreservehistory.org/essays/second_bank_of_the_us.

[632] Jones, Stack. "An Essay On The History Of Banking." *The Banking Swindle*, 1 Jan. 2018, criminalbankingmonopoly.wordpress.com/.

be arrested, and charged with fraud. Biddle was tried and acquitted, but died shortly thereafter while tied up in civil suits…"[633]

"Jackson's successor, Martin Van Buren (1837-1841), continued his policies. One of his first acts was to address the Panic of 1837, which was a mini-depression."[634] "Van Buren assigned the crisis' blame to the national bank and the national debt, arguing that both were not merely unnecessary, but in direct and deadly hostility to the principles of [the people's] Government, and to their own permanent welfare. Thus, Van Buren maintained that the best way to rectify the country's economy was to establish an independent organization to manage the government's funds, hence his creation of the Independent Treasury."[635] "Van Buren's solution: stand fast on gold and propose an independent Treasury to further wrest control of the federal government from central bank supporters. In 1840, Congress passed a bill establishing an independent Treasury, establishing independent treasury deposit offices separate from private or state banks to receive all government funds."[636] Van Buren hailed it as a "Second Declaration of Independence."[637]

"The advantages of a separation of bank and state were several. By removing its funds from state banks, the federal government would avoid association with institutions instrumental

---

[633] *Id.*

[634] Pinheiro, John C. "James K. Polk: Domestic Affairs." *UVA Miller Center,* millercenter.org/president/polk/domestic-affairs. Kaza, Greg. "The U.S. Presidents and the Money Issue." *FEE,* 1 Apr. 1996, fee.org/articles/the-us-presidents-and-the-money-issue/.

[635] "President Martin Van Buren's Independent Treasury Sparks Controversy within the Democratic Party." *The History Engine,* historyengine.richmond.edu/episodes/view/2190.

[636] Pinheiro, John C. "James K. Polk: Domestic Affairs." *UVA Miller Center,* millercenter.org/president/polk/domestic-affairs. Kaza, Greg. "The U.S. Presidents and the Money Issue." *FEE,* 1 Apr. 1996, fee.org/articles/the-us-presidents-and-the-money-issue/.

[637] Kaza, Greg. "The U.S. Presidents and the Money Issue." *FEE,* 1 Apr. 1996, fee.org/articles/the-us-presidents-and-the-money-issue/.

in bringing on the panic. The government would collect, store, and disburse public revenue through Treasury agents and postal employees and not be open to the charge that these funds were the basis for unchecked speculation."[638] Unfortunately, the Act was repealed the next year by the Whig-dominated Congress.[639]

President John Tyler (10th president, 1841-1845) vetoed two bills creating a new Bank of the United States for being "unconstitutional."[640]   After the second veto, Bank advocates demanded Tyler abide by the views of the Whig-controlled Congress and sign the bill, or resign the presidency.[641] Tyler refused.[642] As a result, he received hundreds of letters threatening him with assassination.[643]

President James K. Polk (Democrat, 1845-1849) "was opposed to centralized banks, much like his mentor, Andrew Jackson," and enacted the Independent Treasury Act of 1846.[644]

---

[638] "Martin Van Buren - The independent treasury." *World Biography: U.S. Presidents*, www.presidentprofiles.com/Washington-Johnson/Martin-Van-Buren-The-independent-treasury.html#ixzz6HdrZGav5.

[639] Pinheiro, John C. "James K. Polk: Domestic Affairs." *UVA Miller Center,* millercenter.org/president/polk/domestic-affairs.

[640] Hitchcock, Andrew. "Historical Timeline of the Rothschild Dynasty - Part 3." *The Sirius Report*, 17 Aug. 2015, www.thesiriusreport.com/geopolitics/historical-timeline-rothschild-dynasty-3/.

[641] Kaza, Greg. "The U.S. Presidents and the Money Issue." *FEE,* 1 Apr. 1996, fee.org/articles/the-us-presidents-and-the-money-issue/.

[642] *Id.*

[643] Hitchcock, Andrew. "Historical Timeline of the Rothschild Dynasty - Part 3." *The Sirius Report*, 17 Aug. 2015, www.thesiriusreport.com/geopolitics/historical-timeline-rothschild-dynasty-3/.

[644] "James K Polk." *ESRI,* www.arcgis.com/apps/Cascade/index.html?appid=e8e9072ed87e41e985e8add9a1f28969.

Polk considered the Central Bank to be an entity that had "set itself up as a great irresponsible rival power of the government."[645] As a congressman, he had "supported Jackson's plan to dismantle the Bank of the United States and replace it with a decentralized government banking system."[646] Polk had fought the bank's recharter as chairman of the House Ways and Means Committee.[647] When he summoned the bank's directors to testify in front of the committee, they "admitted widespread fraud and corruption."[648]

As president, Polk revived the Independent Treasury Act, which "entrusted the federal government with the exclusive management of government funds and required that disbursements be made in hard specie, such as gold or silver, or in paper backed by gold or silver."[649] "The act of Aug., 1846, provided that the public revenues be retained in the Treasury building and in subtreasuries… in various cities. The Treasury was to pay out its own funds and be completely independent of the banking and financial system of the nation; all payments by and to the government, moreover, were to be made in specie."[650]

---

[645] Akiboh, Alvita. "Who is James K. Polk?: The Most Important President You Don't Remember." *U.S. History Scene*, ushistoryscene.com/article/james-k-polk/. (Citing Mark E. Byrnes, *James K. Polk: A Biographical Companion*. Santa Barbara: ABC-CLIO, Inc., 2001: 9).

[646] History.com Editors. "James K. Polk." *History*, 29 Oct. 2009, www.history.com/topics/us-presidents/james-polk.

[647] Kaza, Greg. "The U.S. Presidents and the Money Issue." *FEE*, 1 Apr. 1996, fee.org/articles/the-us-presidents-and-the-money-issue/.

[648] "James K. Polk: Battle of the Bank." *Spark Notes*, www.sparknotes.com/biography/polk/section4/.

[649] Pinheiro, John C. "James K. Polk: Domestic Affairs." *UVA Miller Center*, millercenter.org/president/polk/domestic-affairs.

[650] "Independent Treasury System: Creation of the System." *Infoplease*, www.infoplease.com/encyclopedia/history/north-america/us/independent-treasury-system/creation-of-the-system.

The banking elite did not give up on their dreams of a central bank.

The Federal Reserve System

During the period when there was no central bank in the USA, corporations financed growth from profits, and not by taking out loans. In this way, they were becoming independent of the big banks. In November 1910, six of the world's leading bankers — Nelson Aldrich, A. Piatt Andrew, Henry Davison, Arthur Shelton, Frank Vanderlip and Paul Warburg — met secretly at Jekyll Island off of the coast of Georgia to remedy this situation.[651]

The bankers plotted to resurrect a privately owned central bank to regain economic control. "Aldrich and his colleagues had developed a plan for a Reserve Association of America, a single central bank with fifteen branches across the country."[652] The "mostly autonomous regional Reserve Banks...would be owned by commercial banks..."[653] "Each branch would be governed by boards of directors elected by the member banks in each district, with larger banks getting more votes. The branches would be responsible for holding the reserves of their member banks; issuing currency; discounting commercial paper; transferring balances between branches; and check clearing and collection. The national

---

[651] "A member of the exclusive Jekyll Island Club, most likely J.P. Morgan, arranged for the group to use the club's facilities. Founded in 1886, the club's membership boasted elites such as Morgan, Marshall Field, and William Kissam Vanderbilt I, whose mansion-sized "cottages" dotted the island." Richardson, Gary and Jessie Romero. "The Meeting at Jekyll Island." *Federal Reserve History*, 4 Dec. 2015, www.federalreservehistory.org/essays/jekyll_island_conference.

[652] *Id.*

[653] "Federal Reserve Act (1913)." *American History: From Revolution to Reconstruction and Beyond*, www.let.rug.nl/usa/essays/general/a-brief-history-of-central-banking/federal-reserve-act-(1913).php.

body would set discount rates for the system as a whole and buy and sell securities."[654]

This system was to consolidate the power to issue and regulate the nation's money into the banker's hands by making the Federal Reserve the only entity that could legally introduce U.S. paper currency into circulation. Although Article I, Section 8 of the United States Constitution grants Congress the power to "coin Money [and] regulate the Value thereof," "credit extended by the Federal Reserve banks ('paper reserves') could serve as legal tender…"[655]   The Fed would not only issue the nation's currency, but would also "charge interest against that currency."[656] "Aldrich knew their ties to Wall Street could arouse suspicion about their motives and threaten the bill's political passage. So he went to great lengths to keep the [Jekyll Island] meeting secret…"[657]

Senator Henry Cabot Lodge (R-MA) was opposed to the bank bill. On December 17, 1913, he confided in Senator Sinclair Weeks (R-MA) shortly before the bill's passage: "The powers vested in the Federal Reserve Board seen to me highly dangerous especially where there is political control of the Board…The bill as it stands seems to me to open the way to a vast inflation of the currency. I had hoped to support this bill, but I cannot vote for it because it seems to me to contain features and to rest upon principles in the highest

---

[654] Richardson, Gary and Jessie Romero. "The Meeting at Jekyll Island." *Federal Reserve History,* 4 Dec. 2015, www.federalreservehistory.org/essays/jekyll_island_conference.

[655] Greenspan, Alan. "Gold and Economic Freedom." *Constitution Society*, www.constitution.org/mon/greenspan_gold.htm.

[656] "The Fed accepts dollar reserves from foreign customers and sells them US government bonds in return. This is how the Federal Government borrows from foreign lenders." "The International Bankers: Famous Quotes." *ConspiracyAnalyst.org*, 23 Dec. 2019, conspiracyanalyst.org/2013/03/01/the-international-bankers-famous-quotes/.

[657] Richardson, Gary and Jessie Romero. "The Meeting at Jekyll Island." *Federal Reserve History,* 4 Dec. 2015, www.federalreservehistory.org/essays/jekyll_island_conference.

degree menacing to our prosperity, to stability in business, and to the general welfare of the people of the United States."[658]

Representative Charles A, Lindbergh (R-MN), an outspoken critic of the scheme, complained, "This [Federal Reserve Act] establishes the most gigantic trust on earth. When the President signs this bill, the invisible government of the monetary power will be legalized...the worst legislative crime of the ages is perpetrated by this banking and currency bill."[659]

The Glass-Owen Act establishing the Federal Reserve System was snuck through Congress on December 22, 1913.[660] "Many senators had already left for the holidays after being reassured by the leadership that nothing would be done on the bill until after they returned from their Christmas recess the following January."[661] At least 27 senators were absent when the act passed.[662] President Woodrow Wilson signed it into law on December 23, 1913.[663]

The Federal Reserve Act of 1913 created the Federal Reserve, which "is a privately owned central bank, owned by its shareholders, consisting of the major banks the make up each regional Fed

---

[658] Quinn, Jim. "The Federal Reserve Must Die." *HCP Live*, 25 Aug. 2009, www.mdmag.com/medical-news/federal_reserve_must_die.

[659] *Id.*

[660] AKA Federal Reserve Act or Currency Bill; "The House of Representatives passed the Federal Reserve Act by a vote of 298 to 60. The Senate also passed the measure 43 to 25." "Federal Reserve Act (1913)." *American History: From Revolution to Reconstruction and Beyond*, www.let.rug.nl/usa/essays/general/a-brief-history-of-central-banking/federal-reserve-act-(1913).php.

[661] "The International Bankers: Famous Quotes." *ConspiracyAnalyst.org*, 23 Dec. 2019, conspiracyanalyst.org/2013/03/01/the-international-bankers-famous-quotes/.

[662] *Id.*

[663] "Federal Reserve Act (1913)." *American History: From Revolution to Reconstruction and Beyond*, www.let.rug.nl/usa/essays/general/a-brief-history-of-central-banking/federal-reserve-act-(1913).php.

bank..."[664] Nicholas Rockefeller allegedly confided in Aaron Russo that "the New York Fed is the main controlling interest in the Federal Reserve System; they control the bulk of it. So, the New York Fed is really the Federal Reserve System, even though there are twelve different banks, it's run by the New York Fed, and the New York Fed *is* basically the Federal Reserve System..."[665] "Four of the largest shareowners of the New York Fed are...JPMorgan Chase, Citigroup, Goldman Sachs, and Morgan Stanley..."[666]

The Fed's mandate is "to provide for the establishment of Federal reserve banks, to furnish an elastic currency, to afford means of rediscounting commercial paper, to establish a more effective supervision of banking in the United States, and for other purposes."[667] The Fed's functions include "Conducting the nation's monetary policy by influencing the monetary and credit conditions in the economy in pursuit of maximum employment, stable prices, and moderate long-term interest rates; Supervising and regulating

---

[664] Marshall, Andrew Gavin. "The Bilderberg Plan for 2009: Remaking the Global Political Economy." *Global Research,* 26 May 2009, www.globalresearch.ca/the-bilderberg-plan-for-2009-remaking-the-global-political-economy/13738.

[665] "Aaron Russo: Reflections and Warnings - Full Transcript." *Matt Prather*, sites.google.com/site/themattprather/Reading/aaron-russo/reflections-and-warnings-full-transcript. Before Timothy Geithner became Treasury Secretary during the Obama administration, he was president of the New York Fed. Marshall, Andrew Gavin. "The Bilderberg Plan for 2009: Remaking the Global Political Economy." *Global Research*, 26 May 2009, www.globalresearch.ca/the-bilderberg-plan-for-2009-remaking-the-global-political-economy/13738.

[666] "One of JPMorgan Chase's primary regulators is (wait for it) the New York Fed..." Martens, Pam and Russ Martens. "The New York Fed, Owned by Multinational Banks, Is Nationalizing Capital Markets." *Wall Street on Parade*, 9 Apr. 2020, wallstreetonparade.com/2020/04/the-new-york-fed-owned-by-multinational-banks-is-nationalizing-capital-markets/?fbclid=IwAR00mmnOvw5SRN1mRcHQYLxaEihytz1NcYQHvEtGyp63NJn7AJ_Y9zxVtOo.

[667] Quinn, Jim. "The Federal Reserve Must Die." *HCP Live*, 25 Aug. 2009, www.mdmag.com/medical-news/federal_reserve_must_die.

banking institutions to ensure the safety and soundness of the nation's banking and financial system and to protect the credit rights of consumers; Maintaining the stability of the financial system and containing systemic risk that may arise in financial markets; Providing financial services to depository institutions, the U.S. government, and foreign official institutions, including playing a major role in operating the nation's payments system."[668]

The Federal Reserve organization consists of a Board of Governors, of which there are seven. This board supervises and regulates the operations of the Federal Reserve Banks. The board members are appointed by the President of the United States.[669] Consequently, the Federal Reserve is run by unelected bureaucrats who are unaccountable to the people.[670] As of January 2021, the chairman is Jerome Powell.

The members of the Board of Governors are part of the Federal Open Market Committee (FOMC). + They make decisions about interest rates and the growth of the United States' money supply. The FOMC includes five of the 12 regional bank presidents on a rotating basis.

"The Federal Reserve Banks, though heavily regulated, are l o c a l l y   c o n t r o l l e d   b y   t h e i r   m e m b e r   b a n k s ."[671]

---

[668] *Id.*

[669] "It is proposed that the Government shall retain sufficient power over the reserve banks to enable it to exercise a direct authority when necessary to do so, but that it shall in no way attempt to carry on through its own mechanism the routine operations and banking which require detailed knowledge of local and individual credit and which determine the funds of the community in any given instance. In other words, the reserve-bank plan retains to the Government power over the exercise of the broader banking functions, while it leaves to individuals and privately owned institutions the actual direction of routine." H.R. Report No. 69, 63 Cong. 1st Sess. 18-19 (1913). *Lewis v. United States*, 680 F.2d 1239 (1982).

[670] Borowski, Julie. "Top 10 Reasons to End the Federal Reserve." *FreedomWorks,* 1 Feb. 2012, www.freedomworks.org/content/top-10-reasons-end-federal-reserve.

[671] *Lewis v. United States*, 680 F.2d 1239 (1982).

The Federal Reserve Board regulates the Reserve Banks, but direct supervision and control of each Bank is exercised by its board of directors.[672] The stockholding commercial banks elect two-thirds of each Bank's nine member board of directors. The remaining three directors are appointed by the Federal Reserve Board. T h e directors enact by-laws regulating the manner of conducting general Bank business, and appoint officers to implement and supervise daily Bank activities.[673] These activities include collecting and clearing checks, making advances to private and commercial entities, holding reserves for member banks, discounting the notes of member banks, and buying and selling securities on the open market.[674] Incidentally, the Fed "pays no taxes on the trillions of dollars it makes."[675]

Importantly, the Federal Reserve System is not part of the government, but is rather a privately owned global banking consortium. The 12 private regional federal reserve banks are "independent, privately owned and locally controlled corporations… Each Federal Reserve Bank is a separate corporation owned by commercial banks in its region."[676] The name, "The Federal Reserve System," "is an open deception designed to give this private

---

[672] 12 U.S.C. s. 301.

[673] 12 U.S.C. s. 341.

[674] See 12 U.S.C. ss. 341-361. *Lewis v. United States*, 680 F.2d 1239 (1982).

[675] Jones, Stack. "An Essay On The History Of Banking." *The Banking Swindle*, 1 Jan. 2018, criminalbankingmonopoly.wordpress.com/.

[676] *Lewis v. United States*, 680 F.2d 1239 (1982).

bank the appearance that it is operating in the public's interest."[677] For example, the Federal Reserve is supposed to "further the nation's fiscal policy" with its dual mandate to maintain stable prices and achieve full employment (which is actually only 95%).[678]

"The fact that the Federal Reserve Board regulates the Reserve Banks does not make them federal agencies under the Act."[679] However, "[t]he Reserve Banks have properly been held to be federal instrumentalities for some purposes," such as "for purposes of immunity from state taxation" and "for purposes of the Service Contract Act, 41 U.S.C. s 351," but "not federal agencies for purposes of the Federal Tort Claims Act."[680]

---

[677] "Historically,…central banks were private, for-profit institutions… Printing money…turned out to be very profitable. But, in time people complained about this arrangement. During the twentieth century, central banks…officially took on a more public aspect…" "The History of Money Part 2." *XAT3*, www.xat.org/xat/usury.html; Lewis, Nathan. "The Problem With "Modern Monetary Theory" Is That It's True." *Forbes*, 21 Feb. 2019, www.forbes.com/sites/nathanlewis/2019/02/21/the-problem-with-modern-monetary-theory-is-that-its-true/#4fb22b0256fb.

[678] It does not operate "as a commercial bank, accepting deposits from and making loans to businesses and individuals." *Lewis v. United States*, 680 F.2d 1239 (1982); Davies, Phil. "The Bank That Hamilton Built." *Federal Reserve Bank of Minneapolis*, 1 Sept. 2007, www.minneapolisfed.org/article/2007/the-bank-that-hamilton-built.

[679] *Lewis v. United States*, 680 F.2d 1239 (1982).

[680] *Id. Brinks Inc. v. Board of Governors of the Federal Reserve System*, 466 F.Supp. 116 (D.D.C. 1979). Citing Federal Reserve Bank of Boston and Federal Reserve Bank of Minneapolis, the court applied the "important governmental function" test and concluded that the term "Federal Government" in the Service ContractAct must be "liberally construed to effectuate the Act's humanitarian purposes of providing minimum wage and fringe benefit protection to individuals performing contracts with the federal government." *Id. citing* 288 Mich. at 120, 284 N.W.2d 667.

Ronald Reagan observed, "The Federal Reserve System is autonomous…"[681] It functions independently of government control or oversight. "It is evident from the legislative history of the Federal Reserve Act that Congress did not intend to give the federal government direction over the daily operation of the Reserve Banks."[682] "Each Bank is statutorily empowered to conduct [its] activities without day to day direction from the federal government. Thus, for example, the interest rates on advances to member banks, individuals, partnerships, and corporations are set by each Reserve Bank and their decisions regarding the purchase and sale of securities are likewise independently made."[683] Thus, "[t]he Federal Reserve is answerable to no one."[684] "The bank's actions only have to be approved by the Fed's seven-member governing board in Washington…and the presidents of the 12 regional Federal Reserve Banks spread across the country."[685] "The Fed doesn't have to wait

---

[681] Fuerbringer, Jonathan. "Regan Criticizes Fed's Move." *The New York Times*, 20 Jan. 1982, www.nytimes.com/1982/01/20/business/reagan-criticizes-fed-s-move.html.

[682] "It is proposed that the Government shall retain sufficient power over the reserve banks to enable it to exercise a direct authority when necessary to do so, but that it shall in no way attempt to carry on through its own mechanism the routine operations and banking which require detailed knowledge of local and individual credit and which determine the funds of the community in any given instance. In other words, the reserve-bank plan retains to the Government power over the exercise of the broader banking functions, while it leaves to individuals and privately owned institutions the actual direction of routine." H.R. Report No. 69, 63 Cong. 1st Sess. 18-19 (1913). *Lewis v. United States*, 680 F.2d 1239 (1982).

[683] *Id.*

[684] "Ronald Reagan Quotes." *AZ Quotes*, www.azquotes.com/quote/1216586.

[685] Ullman, Owen. "An unsung hero of the coronavirus crisis: The Federal Reserve." *USA Today*, 24 Mar. 2020, www.usatoday.com/story/opinion/2020/03/24/unsung-hero-coronavirus-crisis-federal-reserve/2902681001/?fbclid=IwAR0SEFozSpmbHUjG7yUxgLSfPrg1i9kKHH37qCTXY_gNJlkOfNE774yjGfs.

for a vote in Congress to funnel $9 trillion in cumulative loans to Wall Street. It can create an unlimited amount of dollars electronically at the push of a button…"[686]

Throughout its 100-plus year history, the central bank has "operated under a veil of secrecy. The Federal Reserve has never been fully audited by any outside source. Our elected representatives in Congress have very little oversight over the central bank. It has continually resisted any kind of congressional oversight claiming that it would endanger its 'independence."[687] S e n a t o r B a r r y Goldwater (R-AZ) complained, "The accounts of the Federal Reserve System have never been audited. It operates outside the control of Congress and...manipulates the credit of the United States."[688]

During the 2008 financial crisis, the Congressional Budget Office reported that the bank bailout cost taxpayers $25 billion to help rescue struggling banks.[689] Bloomberg news columnist, David Reilly, complained about "a secretive group deploying billions of dollars to favored banks, operating with little oversight by the public or elected officials…The New York Fed is in the hot seat for its decision in November 2008 to buy out, for about $30 billion, insurance contracts AIG sold on toxic debt securities to banks,

---

[686] Martens, Pam and Russ Martens. "Fed's Balance Sheet Skyrockets to $4.7 Trillion." *Wall Street on Parade*, 19 Mar. 2020, wallstreetonparade.com/2020/03/feds-balance-sheet-skyrockets-to-4-7-t r i l l i o n / ? fbclid=IwAR2sB1L8ZLt0TTR04NQ8IbGBj3elYLb_W8xN4FHrMO3901 8KctJI9UoQs-A.

[687] Borowski, Julie. "Top 10 Reasons to End the Federal Reserve." *FreedomWorks,* 1 Feb. 2012, www.freedomworks.org/content/top-10-reasons-end-federal-reserve.

[688] In his 1964 book, *No Apologies.* "The History of Money Part 2." *XAT3*, www.xat.org/xat/usury.html.

[689] "CBO: Bank Bailout Cost Taxpayers $25 Billion." *CBN.com*, 30 Nov. 2010, web.archive.org/web/20110429163248/https://www1.cbn.com/cbnnews/finance/2010/november/cbo-tarp-bailout-cost-taxpayers-25-billion/.

including Goldman Sachs Group Inc., Merrill Lynch & Co., Societe Generale and Deutsche Bank AG, among others. That decision, critics say, amounted to a back-door bailout for the banks…"[690]

During testimony to Congress in 2009, then Fed Chairman Ben Bernanke refused to reveal to committee members the names of the institutions that had received up to $2 trillion of dollars in bailout money from the Federal Reserve.[691] "After promising a more transparent Fed, Bernanke has done the complete opposite. He continues to withhold the names of all financial institutions that have borrowed from the Fed and will not reveal the worthless collateral that they have put up for those loans. The Fed has lent in excess of $2.2 trillion to banks. The Fed has refused to reveal any information regarding these loans."[692] Bernanke also declined to disclose the identities of the foreign banks that were parties to sweetheart deals with the Federal Reserve.[693] Former Representative Ron Paul (R-TX) called for an audit of the Fed to find out the names of these banks, but none was conducted.[694] Alex

---

[690] "Secret Banking Cabal Emerges From AIG Shadows: David Reilly." *Bloomberg*, 28 Jan. 2010, www.bloomberg.com/news/2010-01-28/secret-banking-cabal-emerges-from-aig-shadows-david-reilly.html.

[691] These were called Term Auction Facility (TAF) loans. Amadeo, Kimberly. "Federal Reserve Chairman Ben Bernanke." *The Balance*, 26 Jan. 2021, www.thebalance.com/federal-reserve-chairman-ben-bernanke-3306152.

[692] Quinn, Jim. "The Federal Reserve Must Die." *HCP Live*, 25 Aug. 2009, www.mdmag.com/medical-news/federal_reserve_must_die.

[693] "Foreign central banks got $10 trillion of the $29 trillion in loans." Martens, Pam and Russ Martens. "The New York Fed, Owned by Multinational Banks, Is Nationalizing Capital Markets." *Wall Street on Parade*, 9 Apr. 2020, wallstreetonparade.com/2020/04/the-new-york-fed-owned-by-multinational-banks-is-nationalizing-capital-markets/?fbclid=IwAR00mmnOvw5SRN1mRcHQYLxaEihytz1NcYQHvEtGyp63NJn7AJ_Y9zxVtOo.

[694] Amadeo, Kimberly. "Federal Reserve Chairman Ben Bernanke." *The Balance*, 26 Jan. 2021, www.thebalance.com/federal-reserve-chairman-ben-bernanke-3306152.

Jones noted, "[T]he private Federal Reserve...arrogantly says it's above all U.S. laws, and above all three branches of government, and that no law enforcement can investigate them...Everybody else gets audited, nobody else is above the law, but them..."[695] "Investment Manager Ted Forstmann's opinion was, 'It's your money; it's not the Fed's money. Of course there should be transparency.'"[696]

"The sweeping Dodd-Frank legislation scaled back some powers of the Fed and Treasury."[697] The Dodd-Frank financial reform legislation of 2010 "eliminated the power of the Fed to secretly funnel trillions of dollars to domestic and foreign global banks while hiding the names and details from Congress and the public."[698]

"*Bloomberg News*...sued the Fed under the Freedom of Information Act to force them to reveal where $2.2 trillion of taxpayer money" had gone.[699] "The Federal Reserve Board of Governors hoped that the details of its negligence in turning over its

---

[695] "Aaron Russo: Reflections and Warnings - Full Transcript." *Matt Prather*, sites.google.com/site/themattprather/Reading/aaron-russo/reflections-and-warnings-full-transcript.

[696] Quinn, Jim. "The Federal Reserve Must Die." *HCP Live*, 25 Aug. 2009, www.mdmag.com/medical-news/federal_reserve_must_die.

[697] Long, Heather. "Federal Reserve slashes interest rates to zero as part of wide-ranging emergency intervention." *The Washington Post*, 15 Mar. 2020, www.washingtonpost.com/business/2020/03/15/federal-reserve-slashes-interest-rates-zero-part-wide-ranging-emergency-intervention/?fbclid=IwAR3ArnSj5NO2WPZw9qneawJhTKbW8Xqg3tspxLEkYlfmGJcKl4ZtHtx14FM.

[698] Martens, Pam and Russ Martens. "The Fed Has Pumped $9 Trillion into Wall Street Over the Past Six Months, But Mnuchin Says 'This Isn't Like the Financial Crisis.'" *Wall Street on Parade*, 14 Mar. 2020, wallstreetonparade.com/2020/03/the-fed-has-pumped-9-trillion-into-wall-street-over-the-past-six-months-but-mnuchin-says-this-isnt-like-the-financial-crisis/.

[699] Quinn, Jim. "The Federal Reserve Must Die." *HCP Live*, 25 Aug. 2009, www.mdmag.com/medical-news/federal_reserve_must_die.

infinite money creation to the New York Fed during the last financial crisis would never see the light of day. It battled media lawsuits to get the details of the sums loaned out and to whom for more than two years. When it lost at both the District Court and Appellate Court in New York, a group called the Clearing House Association, which included JPMorgan Chase and Citigroup, attempted to get the U.S. Supreme Court to overturn the public's right to know about the Fed's secret money spigot. The Supreme Court did not take the case and the scandalous details were revealed as a result of that as well as the Dodd-Frank financial reform legislation of 2010 mandating the release of the details of some of the programs by December 2010."[700]

"The Federal Reserve was ordered through a Freedom of Information Act request to release 28,000 pages of documents in March 2011. The documents exposed that one of the largest recipients of the Federal Reserve's money was foreign banks during the 2008 economic meltdown. The top foreign banks that received money were the Brussels and Paris based Dexia SA, the Dublin based Depfa Bank Plc, the Bank of China and Arab Banking Corp., according to Campaign for Liberty."[701]

In July 2011, due to a provision under the Dodd-Frank law, the nonpartisan investigative arm of Congress, the Government Accountability Office (GAO), "conducted a one-time, watered-down audit of the Federal Reserve."[702] "When the General Accountability Office (GAO), tallied up the cumulative total that the Federal

---

[700] Martens, Pam and Russ Martens. "The New York Fed, Owned by Multinational Banks, Is Nationalizing Capital Markets." *Wall Street on Parade*, 9 Apr. 2020, wallstreetonparade.com/2020/04/the-new-york-fed-owned-by-multinational-banks-is-nationalizing-capital-markets/?fbclid=IwAR00mmnOvw5SRN1mRcHQYLxaEihytz1NcYQHvEtGyp63NJn7AJ_Y9zxVtOo.

[701] Borowski, Julie. "Top 10 Reasons to End the Federal Reserve." *FreedomWorks,* 1 Feb. 2012, www.freedomworks.org/content/top-10-reasons-end-federal-reserve.

[702] *Id.*

Reserve had secretly sluiced to Wall Street from December 2007 through July 21, 2010, it came to $16.1 trillion."[703] "But the GAO did not include all of the programs that came out of the New York Fed."[704] This was perhaps because the "GAO investigators were not allowed to view most of the Federal Reserve's monetary policy decisions including discount window lending, open-market operations and details on its transactions with foreign governments and banks."[705]

One of the programs GAO did not include was the Primary Dealer Credit Facility (PDCF).[706] This "was one of a hodgepodge of programs set up by the Federal Reserve and administered by the New York Fed from December 2007 to at least July 2010."[707] "When those other programs are added, the Levy Economics Institute, using the Fed's own data, arrived at the tally of $19.559 trillion to the Wall Street trading houses and another $10 trillion in central bank liquidity swaps, bringing the bailout figure to over $29

---

[703] *Id.*

[704] Martens, Pam and Russ Martens. "Fed Repos Have Plowed $6.6 Trillion to Wall Street in Four Months; That's 34% of Its Feeding Tube During Epic Financial Crash." *Wall Street on Parade.* 27 Jan. 2020, wallstreetonparade.com/2020/01/fed-repos-have-plowed-6-6-trillion-to-wall-street-in-four-months-thats-34-of-its-feeding-tube-during-epic-financial-crash/.

[705] Borowski, Julie. "Top 10 Reasons to End the Federal Reserve." *FreedomWorks,* 1 Feb. 2012, www.freedomworks.org/content/top-10-reasons-end-federal-reserve.

[706] Martens, Pam and Russ Martens. "The Federal Reserve Now Owns 15 Percent of the U.S. Treasury Market; At Its Current Rate, It Could Own the Whole Market in Less than Two Years." *Wall Street on Parade*, 28 Mar. 2020, wallstreetonparade.com/2020/03/the-federal-reserve-now-owns-15-percent-of-the-u-s-treasury-market-at-its-current-rate-it-could-own-the-whole-market-in-less-than-two-years/.

[707] *Id.*

trillion…"[708]   A study by Better Markets entitled "Wall Street's Six Biggest Bailed-Out Banks: Their RAP Sheets & Their Ongoing Crime Spree" noted, "Of the more than $29 trillion in bailouts, just the six biggest banks in the country (the 'Six Megabanks') received more than $8.2 trillion in lifesaving support from American taxpayers during the 2008 financial crash, or nearly one-third of the total bailouts provided to the entire financial system. This was a massive transfer of wealth from Main Street to Wall Street to prevent the bankruptcy of just six banks, supposedly because they were vital to the economic security and prosperity of Main Street Americans."[709]   In other words, "the Fed shoveled out $29 trillion cumulatively through all of its programs to bail out Wall Street banks, their foreign derivative counterparties and foreign central banks."[710] "Citigroup received the largest bailout in global banking history, getting $2.5 trillion cumulatively in revolving loans from the Fed and billions more from taxpayers in the financial crisis of 2007

---

[708] Martens, Pam and Russ Martens. "Fed Repos Have Plowed $6.6 Trillion to Wall Street in Four Months; That's 34% of Its Feeding Tube During Epic Financial Crash." *Wall Street on Parade*. 27 Jan. 2020, wallstreetonparade.com/2020/01/fed-repos-have-plowed-6-6-trillion-to-wall-street-in-four-months-thats-34-of-its-feeding-tube-during-epic-financial-crash/.

[709] Martens, Pam and Russ Martens. "Bernie Sanders Hasn't Quite Captured What Wall Street Does: It's Actually a Fraud-Monetization System with a Money-Printing Unit Called the New York Fed." *Wall Street on Parade*, 21 Jan. 2020, wallstreetonparade.com/2020/01/bernie-sanders-hasnt-quite-captured-what-wall-street-does-its-actually-a-fraud-monetization-system-with-a-money-printing-unit-called-the-new-york-fed/.

[710] Martens, Pam and Russ Martens. "The Federal Reserve Now Owns 15 Percent of the U.S. Treasury Market; At Its Current Rate, It Could Own the Whole Market in Less than Two Years." *Wall Street on Parade*, 28 Mar. 2020, wallstreetonparade.com/2020/03/the-federal-reserve-now-owns-15-percent-of-the-u-s-treasury-market-at-its-current-rate-it-could-own-the-whole-market-in-less-than-two-years/.

to 2010."[711] The New York Fed provided the bulk of the $29 trillion in bailouts.[712]

"These bailouts happened without a single vote taking place in any chamber of Congress."[713] Neither Congress nor the public was even aware "of the staggering sums of money the Fed was pumping out."[714] They "only found out about the unchecked money spigot at the Fed when Senator Bernie Sanders attached an amendment to the Dodd-Frank financial reform legislation of 2010 that forced a release of the Fed data to the public and mandated an audit by the Government Accountability Office (GAO)."[715]

"That it took the New York Fed that long [December 2007 to July 21, 2010] and trillions of dollars to calm markets was indicative

---

[711] Martens, Pam and Russ Martens. "BlackRock Authored the Bailout Plan Before There Was a Crisis – Now It's Been Hired by three Central Banks to Implement the Plan." *Wall Street on Parade*, 5 Jun. 2020, wallstreetonparade.com/2020/06/blackrock-authored-the-bailout-plan-before-there-was-a-crisis-now-its-been-hired-by-three-central-banks-to-implement-the-plan/? fbclid=IwAR0GVrMUHztEuheKbZMYB56sZEc2DwIiAQEYSUIy9qSSf uzEqPoHz_u7wqQ.

[712] Martens, Pam and Russ Martens. "Bernie Sanders Hasn't Quite Captured What Wall Street Does: It's Actually a Fraud-Monetization System with a Money-Printing Unit Called the New York Fed." *Wall Street on Parade*, 21 Jan. 2020, wallstreetonparade.com/2020/01/bernie-sanders-hasnt-quite-captured-what-wall-street-does-its-actually-a-fraud-monetization-system-with-a-money-printing-unit-called-the-new-york-fed/.

[713] Borowski, Julie. "Top 10 Reasons to End the Federal Reserve." *FreedomWorks,* 1 Feb. 2012, www.freedomworks.org/content/top-10-reasons-end-federal-reserve.

[714] Martens, Pam and Russ Martens. "The Federal Reserve Now Owns 15 Percent of the U.S. Treasury Market; At Its Current Rate, It Could Own the Whole Market in Less than Two Years." *Wall Street on Parade*, 28 Mar. 2020, wallstreetonparade.com/2020/03/the-federal-reserve-now-owns-15-percent-of-the-u-s-treasury-market-at-its-current-rate-it-could-own-the-whole-market-in-less-than-two-years/.

[715] *Id.*

of just how incompetent it and other Federal regulators of Wall Street had been in reining in the wild gambles that were occurring in derivatives across Wall Street. The Fed's own negligent role in supervising the Wall Street banks may well explain why it battled in court for more than two years to keep the details of its loans a secret from Congress and the American people."[716]

An additional insult to American taxpayers was that during this time, "the banks continued to charge consumers double-digit interest rates on their credit cards as the banks borrowed significant sums from the Fed at less than one-half of one percent interest. A large part of the loans from the Fed went to the Wall Street banks' trading operations in London."[717]   "[T]he Fed loans were being made at ridiculously low rates of interest that would not even have been available to AAA-credit corporations. Many of these Wall Street trading houses were either insolvent or teetering on the verge of insolvency so the cheap loans (a significant portion of which were made at less than 1 percent interest) were a subsidy to Wall Street – a form of corporate welfare at a time when the same banks were charging consumers double-digit interest rates on their credit cards. *Bloomberg Markets* magazine reported in January 2012 that the

---

[716] Martens, Pam and Russ Martens. "Fed Repos Have Plowed $6.6 Trillion to Wall Street in Four Months; That's 34% of Its Feeding Tube During Epic Financial Crash." *Wall Street on Parade*. 27 Jan. 2020, wallstreetonparade.com/2020/01/fed-repos-have-plowed-6-6-trillion-to-wall-street-in-four-months-thats-34-of-its-feeding-tube-during-epic-financial-crash/.

[717] Martens, Pam and Russ Martens. "Fed Sets Off Panic with Plan to Eliminate Reserves at Wall Street's Mega Banks." *Wall Street on Parade,* 16 Mar. 2020, wallstreetonparade.com/2020/03/fed-sets-off-panic-with-plan-to-eliminate-reserves-at-wall-streets-mega-banks/.

underpriced loans amounted to $13 billion in extra income for the Wall Street banks."[718]

"Since the beginning of this bailout shebang [March 2020], the Fed created $1.5 trillion and handed it to Wall Street either as loans or to purchase financial instruments."[719] "Since the Fed turned on its latest money spigot to Wall Street [2020], it has refused to provide the public with the dollar amounts going to any specific banks. This has denied the public the ability to know which financial institutions are in trouble."[720] "According to Section 1101 of Dodd-Frank, both the House Financial Services Committee and the Senate Banking Committee are to be briefed on any emergency loans made by the Fed, including the names of the banks doing the borrowing. The section reads: 'The [Federal Reserve] Board shall provide to the Committee on Banking, Housing, and Urban Affairs of the Senate and the Committee on Financial Services of the House of Representatives, (i) not later than 7 days after the Board authorizes any loan or other financial assistance under this paragraph, a report that includes (I) the justification for the exercise of authority to provide such assistance; (II) the identity of the recipients of such assistance; (III) the date and amount of the assistance, and form in

---

[718] Martens, Pam and Russ Martens. "Fed Repos Have Plowed $6.6 Trillion to Wall Street in Four Months; That's 34% of Its Feeding Tube During Epic Financial Crash" *Wall Street on Parade*, 27 Jan. 2020, wallstreetonparade.com/2020/01/fed-repos-have-plowed-6-6-trillion-to-wall-street-in-four-months-thats-34-of-its-feeding-tube-during-epic-financial-crash/.

[719] Richter, Wolf. "$1.5 Trillion Helicopter Money for Wall Street in 3 Weeks of Fed Bailouts." *Wolf Street*, 2 Apr. 2020, wolfstreet.com/2020/04/02/helicopter-money-for-wall-street-1-5-trillion-in-3-weeks-of-fed-bailouts/?fbclid=IwAR0netP-VVmUMDmbNvCjD1J-MvMz3V9N0GmTymCv3IyyOYBl4qKhwACpqnI.

[720] Martens, Pam and Russ Martens. "The Fed Has Pumped $9 Trillion into Wall Street Over the Past Six Months, But Mnuchin Says 'This Isn't Like the Financial Crisis.'" *Wall Street on Parade*, 14 Mar. 2020, wallstreetonparade.com/2020/03/the-fed-has-pumped-9-trillion-into-wall-street-over-the-past-six-months-but-mnuchin-says-this-isnt-like-the-financial-crisis/.

which the assistance was provided; and (IV) the material terms of the assistance, including — (aa) duration; (bb) collateral pledged and the value thereof; (cc) all interest, fees, and other revenue or items of value to be received in exchange for the assistance; (dd) any requirements imposed on the recipient with respect to employee compensation, distribution of dividends, or any other corporate decision in exchange for the assistance; and (ee) the expected costs to the taxpayers of such assistance..."'[721] In January 2020, "[t]he Federal Reserve Bank of New York said it intervened twice via repurchase agreements, or repos [a type of short-term loan]. Eligible banks drew $47 billion in overnight liquidity from the central bank..."[722] "[A]s of February 6 [2020,] the Fed had not briefed the Senate Banking Committee on its repo loan operations..."[723] "The Fed, exactly as it did in 2008, has drawn a dark curtain around troubled banks and the public's right to know, while aiding and abetting a financial coverup of just how bad things are on Wall Street..."[724]

---

[721] *Id.*

[722] Derby, Michael S. "Fed Adds $82 Billion to Financial Markets." *The Wall Street Journal*, 14 Jan. 2020, www.wsj.com/articles/fed-adds-82-billion-to-financial-markets-11579016506.

[723] Martens, Pam and Russ Martens. "The Fed Has Pumped $9 Trillion into Wall Street Over the Past Six Months, But Mnuchin Says 'This Isn't Like the Financial Crisis.'" *Wall Street on Parade*, 14 Mar. 2020, wallstreetonparade.com/2020/03/the-fed-has-pumped-9-trillion-into-wall-street-over-the-past-six-months-but-mnuchin-says-this-isnt-like-the-financial-crisis/.

[724] *Id.*

Unfortunately, there are now calls to reverse Dodd-Frank.[725] Secretary of the Treasury Steve "Mnuchin suggested he might ask Congress to grant the Fed more tools to help the economy."[726] He "stated that the Trump administration would be going to Congress 'for authorities that they took away [with Dodd-Frank]...'"[727] "The text of the final bill was breathtaking in the breadth of new powers it bestowed on the Federal Reserve, including the Fed's ability to conduct secret meetings with no minutes provided to the American people..."[728]

In the late 1800s and early 1900s, "America began moving in the direction of socialism, interventionism, and imperialism..."[729] "The establishment of the Federal Reserve was consistent with the

[725] Long, Heather. "Federal Reserve slashes interest rates to zero as part of wide-ranging emergency intervention." *The Washington Post*, 15 Mar. 2020, www.washingtonpost.com/business/2020/03/15/federal-reserve-slashes-interest-rates-zero-part-wide-ranging-emergency-intervention/?fbclid=IwAR3ArnSj5NO2WPZw9qneawJhTKbW8Xqg3tspxLEkYlfmGJcKl4ZtHtx14FM.

[726] *Id.*

[727] Martens, Pam and Russ Martens. "The Fed Has Pumped $9 Trillion into Wall Street Over the Past Six Months, But Mnuchin Says 'This Isn't Like the Financial Crisis.'" *Wall Street on Parade*, 14 Mar. 2020, wallstreetonparade.com/2020/03/the-fed-has-pumped-9-trillion-into-wall-street-over-the-past-six-months-but-mnuchin-says-this-isnt-like-the-financial-crisis/.

[728] Martens, Pam and Russ Martens. "Stimulus Bill Allows Federal Reserve to Conduct Meetings in Secret; Gives Fed $454 Billion Slush Fund for Wall Street Bailouts." *Wall Street on Parade*, 26 Mar. 2020, wallstreetonparade.com/2020/03/stimulus-bill-allows-federal-reserve-to-conduct-meetings-in-secret-gives-fed-454-billion-slush-fund-for-wall-street-bailouts/.

[729] Hornberger, Jacob. "Monetary Destruction in America." *Tenth Amendment Center*, 7 Jun. 2020, tenthamendmentcenter.com/2020/06/07/monetary-destruction-in-america/?fbclid=IwAR1qznHUtpPxV4SZfCJk0G9H9gTS2kepV1ZU5BKoX_o06DxBXusfHyCPK6s.

overall trend toward socialism. The Fed was based on the socialist principle of central planning, in that it was given the power to centrally plan the amount of U.S. debt instruments being introduced into the economy. As with other socialist programs, the result [has been] a disaster."[730]

Essentially, through the Federal Reserve System, a few unelected bureaucrats are able to determine how taxpayer money is spent. Taxpayers are forced to bail out the "too big to fail" banks to the tune of billions, if not trillions of dollars. Thomas Jefferson felt that "[t]o compel a man to subsidize with His taxes the propagation of ideas which he Disbelieves and abhors is sinful and tyrannical."[731] "[W]hen unelected and unaccountable agencies pick banking winners while trying to end-run Congress, even as taxpayers are forced to lend, spend and guarantee about $8 trillion to prop up the financial system, our collective blood should boil."[732]

The next chapter will discuss how banks create money out of thin air.

---

[730] *Id.*

[731] "Thomas Jefferson > Quotes > Quotable Quote." *Goodreads,* www.goodreads.com/quotes/708734-to-compel-a-man-to-subsidize-with-his-taxes-the.

[732] "Secret Banking Cabal Emerges From AIG Shadows: David Reilly." *Bloomberg,* 28 Jan. 2010, www.bloomberg.com/news/2010-01-28/secret-banking-cabal-emerges-from-aig-shadows-david-reilly.html.

Chapter 4

Money for Nothing

In the past, banks used gold to extend credit and create bank notes (currency) and deposits.[733] Over time, they developed a system that replaced gold with credit instruments (bank notes and deposits).[734]

When the monetary system was based on the yellow metal, "[i]ndividual owners of gold [were] induced, by payments of interest, to deposit their gold in a bank (against which they [could] draw checks)."[735] These were called "'lodged deposits,' which were real claims left by a depositor in a bank, on which the depositor might receive interest, since such deposits were debts owed by the bank to the depositor."[736]

The first paper money was basically a receipt, i.e. "proof that gold and silver coins were left with the goldsmith to store in their

---

[733] Greenspan, Alan. "Gold and Economic Freedom." *Constitution Society*, www.constitution.org/mon/greenspan_gold.htm.

[734] *Id.*

[735] *Id.*

[736] "Lodged deposits as a form of savings are deflationary..." "History of Banking and Money Key Excerpts From Carroll Quigley's Tragedy and Hope." *Wanttoknow.info*, www.wanttoknow.info/articles/quigley_carroll.tragedy_hope_banking_money_history.

secured vaults."[737]   This gold certificate entitled "its bearer to exchange it for its piece of gold on demand."[738]

"Over time, paper money became the norm because it was more convenient to carry paper than…sacks of heavy gold and silver coins."[739]   "In view of the convenience of paper, only a small fraction of certificate holders ever demanded their gold."[740]   "Since it is rarely the case that all depositors want to withdraw all [of] their gold at the same time, the banker need keep only a fraction of his total deposits in gold as reserves."[741]   Thus, only the amount of gold required to cover the small number of certificates likely to be presented for payment needed to be held.

Goldsmiths/bankers started cheating the system; they figured out that "they could print more money than they had in actual gold" and lend it out.[742]   "A volume of certificates could be issued greater

---

[737] "They were so active that they could control and manipulate the entire British economy. These were not bankers per se. However, the goldsmiths were in reality the first bankers." Jones, Stack. "An Essay On The History Of Banking." *The Banking Swindle*, 1 Jan. 2018, criminalbankingmonopoly.wordpress.com/.

[738] Greenspan, Alan. "Gold and Economic Freedom." *Constitution Society*, www.constitution.org/mon/greenspan_gold.htm.

[739] "They were so active that they could control and manipulate the entire British economy. These were not bankers per se. However, the goldsmiths were in reality the first bankers." Jones, Stack. "An Essay On The History Of Banking." *The Banking Swindle*, 1 Jan. 2018, criminalbankingmonopoly.wordpress.com/.

[740] Greenspan, Alan. "Gold and Economic Freedom." *Constitution Society*, www.constitution.org/mon/greenspan_gold.htm.

[741] *Id.*

[742] "They were so active that they could control and manipulate the entire British economy. These were not bankers per se. However, the goldsmiths were in reality the first bankers." Jones, Stack. "An Essay On The History Of Banking." *The Banking Swindle*, 1 Jan. 2018, criminalbankingmonopoly.wordpress.com/; Greenspan, Alan. "Gold and Economic Freedom." *Constitution Society*, www.constitution.org/mon/greenspan_gold.htm.

than the volume of gold reserved for payment of demands against them."[743] In other words, they "loaned out that extra money, and collected interest on it…"[744] The "excess volume of paper claims against reserves" are called bank notes.[745]

The same thing could be done by deposit banks. "Deposit bankers discovered that orders and checks drawn against deposits by depositors and given to third persons were often not cashed by the latter, but were deposited to their own accounts. Thus, there were no actual movements of funds, and payments were made simply by bookkeeping transactions on the accounts. Accordingly, it was necessary for the banker to keep on hand in actual money (gold, certificates, and notes) no more than the fraction of deposits likely to be drawn upon and cashed; the rest could be used for loans, and if these loans were made by creating a deposit for the borrower, who in turn would draw checks upon it rather than withdraw it in money, such 'created deposits' or loans could also be covered adequately by retaining reserves to only a fraction of their value."[746] Essentially, "created deposits" are claims created by the bank out of nothing as loans from the bank to depositors who have to "pay interest on them,

---

[743] "History of Banking and Money Key Excerpts From Carroll Quigley's Tragedy and Hope." *Wanttoknow.info*, www.wanttoknow.info/articles/quigley_carroll.tragedy_hope_banking_money_history.

[744] "They were so active that they could control and manipulate the entire British economy. These were not bankers per se. However, the goldsmiths were in reality the first bankers." Jones, Stack. "An Essay On The History Of Banking." *The Banking Swindle*, 1 Jan. 2018, criminalbankingmonopoly.wordpress.com/.

[745] "History of Banking and Money Key Excerpts From Carroll Quigley's Tragedy and Hope." *Wanttoknow.info*, www.wanttoknow.info/articles/quigley_carroll.tragedy_hope_banking_money_history.

[746] *Id.*

since these represented debt from them to the bank…"[747] "[C]reated deposits, being an addition to the money supply, are inflationary."[748]

Throughout history, "banks have been required to hold reserves against their assets," i.e. loans and securities.[749] "[B]anks set aside a percentage of their assets as reserve and kept it in gold (for most of recorded history) or as cash at the Federal Reserve… Conceptually, the reserve gives depositors confidence that when they show up to take their money back, there will be cash to give them…"[750] "Reserves are concentrated in the largest banks, which have to keep a level of high-quality, liquid assets on their balance sheets…"[751] "The bank reserve requirement is the value of funds that banks must have on hand each night when they close their books."[752] "Total reserves include all the cash in banks' vaults, plus

---

[747] "[C]hecks could be drawn against such deposits to make payments to third parties…" *Id.*

[748] "History of Banking and Money Key Excerpts From Carroll Quigley's Tragedy and Hope." *Wanttoknow.info,* www.wanttoknow.info/articles/ quigley_carroll.tragedy_hope_banking_money_history.

[749] Haber, Bob. "The Fed Fires 'The Big One.'" *Forbes,* 16 Mar. 2020, www.forbes.com/sites/bobhaber/2020/03/16/the-fed-fires-the-big-one/? fbclid=IwAR0j5PP70PzRQM6lOpfHCaTaHkZQp4dYm4o1pNCazj2PX7a itN-uZ8mGmEU#6c90761e6aa8.

[750] *Id.*

[751] Tilford, Cale. "Repo: How the financial markets' plumbing got blocked." *Financial Times*, 25 Nov. 2019, ig.ft.com/repo-rate/.

[752] "Reserve requirements are amount of funds that a depository institution must hold in reserve against specified deposit liabilities." "Reserve Requirements." *Board of Governors of the Federal Reserve System,* www.federalreserve.gov/monetarypolicy/reservereq.htm.

banks' deposits at the Federal Reserve…"[753] It is "the percentage of outstanding loans that a fractional reserve bank must hold in federally guaranteed deposits."[754] "US Treasuries are the core asset used by every financial institution to satisfy its capital and liquidity requirements."[755]

"Reserves are what the banking system uses to construct the money supply. The money supply increases, not when reserves increase, but when banks loan out the additional reserves to customers."[756] "Banks engage in fractional reserve lending based on the amount of currency in their accounts."[757] Fractional reserve banking "is the practice of loaning out many times more money than the assets that are available on deposit. [it] is the principal of lending

---

[753] Davies, Antony and James P. Harrigan. "Massive Inflation May Be Coming, Because the US Government Has Cornered Itself into a Fiscal End Game." *FEE*, 21 May 2020, fee.org/articles/massive-inflation-may-be-coming-because-the-us-government-has-cornered-itself-into-a-fiscal-end-game/?fbclid=IwAR2EC1n-Wt7EXea4XZnzfkl3G9z8VtdguUeRjMqwCpjQJXZuVRnz6nairik.

[754] Klein, Peter G. "The Financial System Is Now Totally Dependent on Government Intervention." *Mises Institute,* 16 Mar. 2020, mises.org/power-market/financial-system-now-totally-dependent-government-intervention?fbclid=IwAR3eKYaKZMJqyM91joNY59D1nTY6LqHPhsz4iz1fQS2VowwbR5YGkAlOHPA.

[755] Long, Caitlin. "The Real Story Of The Repo Market Meltdown, And What It Means For Bitcoin." *Forbes*, 25 Sept. 2019, www.forbes.com/sites/caitlinlong/2019/09/25/the-real-story-of-the-repo-market-meltdown-and-what-it-means-for-bitcoin/#23f8ac237caa.

[756] Davies, Antony and James P. Harrigan. "Massive Inflation May Be Coming, Because the US Government Has Cornered Itself into a Fiscal End Game." *FEE*, 21 May 2020, fee.org/articles/massive-inflation-may-be-coming-because-the-us-government-has-cornered-itself-into-a-fiscal-end-game/?fbclid=IwAR2EC1n-Wt7EXea4XZnzfkl3G9z8VtdguUeRjMqwCpjQJXZuVRnz6nairik.

[757] Dirkmaat, Olav. "Do Not Worry about Gold Confiscation." *Gold Republic*, 16 Jun. 2015, www.goldrepublic.com/news/gold-confiscation.

at interest money that does not exist…"[758]   "Banks issue a larger (often much larger) quantity of money substitutes than the amount of physical currency entrusted to them by depositors."[759]   "By simultaneously issuing money substitutes corresponding to the same units of physical money to both the depositors and borrowers to whom the bank makes loans, in a process known as fractional reserve banking, banks can dramatically expand the supply of money available for transactions beyond the available supply of physical money."[760]

"The volume of deposits banks can create, like the amount of notes they can issue, depends upon the volume of reserves available to pay whatever fraction of checks are cashed rather than deposited."[761]   "By keeping more money within the banking system, banks can lend more credit by creating deposit currency."[762]   "They charge fees to lend that money. The less money is in their clients' accounts, the less money they can lend, and the fewer fees [and] interest they can collect."[763]

---

[758] "They were so active that they could control and manipulate the entire British economy. These were not bankers per se. However, the goldsmiths were in reality the first bankers." Jones, Stack. "An Essay On The History Of Banking." *The Banking Swindle*, 1 Jan. 2018, criminalbankingmonopoly.wordpress.com/.

[759] Brock, Thomas. "Money." *Investopedia*, 25 Dec. 2020, www.investopedia.com/terms/m/money.asp.

[760] *Id.*

[761] "History of Banking and Money Key Excerpts From Carroll Quigley's Tragedy and Hope." *Wanttoknow.info*, www.wanttoknow.info/articles/quigley_carroll.tragedy_hope_banking_money_history.

[762] Dirkmaat, Olav. "Do Not Worry about Gold Confiscation." *Gold Republic*, 16 Jun. 2015, www.goldrepublic.com/news/gold-confiscation.

[763] *Id.*

In Britain, the reserve requirement was "usually twenty times such reserves."[764] This was true in the United States, too, for the first 50 years of the Federal Reserve's existence.[765] Making use of the tool to manipulate reserve ratios, the central bank dropped it to "ten times reserves of notes and gold."[766] Thus, the Fed required most banks to keep just 10% of the deposits as reserves, either in cash in the banks' vaults or at the local Federal Reserve bank.[767] In other words, the banks could lend out 10 times more money than they had on reserve and charge interest on it.[768] For example, $1

---

[764] "History of Banking and Money Key Excerpts From Carroll Quigley's Tragedy and Hope." *Wanttoknow.info*, www.wanttoknow.info/articles/quigley_carroll.tragedy_hope_banking_money_history.

[765] Haber, Bob. "The Fed Fires 'The Big One.'" *Forbes*, 16 Mar. 2020, www.forbes.com/sites/bobhaber/2020/03/16/the-fed-fires-the-big-one/?fbclid=IwAR0j5PP70PzRQM6lOpfHCaTaHkZQp4dYm4o1pNCazj2PX7aitN-uZ8mGmEU#6c90761e6aa8.

[766] "History of Banking and Money Key Excerpts From Carroll Quigley's Tragedy and Hope." *Wanttoknow.info*, www.wanttoknow.info/articles/quigley_carroll.tragedy_hope_banking_money_history.

[767] Amadeo, Kimberly. "Reserve Requirement and How It Affects Interest Rates." *The Balance*, 10 Feb. 2019, www.thebalance.com/reserve-requirement-3305883. Kagan, Julia. "Fractional Reserve Banking." *Investopedia*, 18 Dec. 2020, www.investopedia.com/terms/f/fractionalreservebanking.asp; "Reserve Requirements." *Board of Governors of the Federal Reserve System*, www.federalreserve.gov/monetarypolicy/reservereq.htm. (Ranges from 0-10%.") "The central bank currently pays banks a 1.8% yield for cash held in Fed reserves." Winck. Ben. "The Fed has been injecting hundreds of billions into markets since September's rate crisis. Here's why it might not be enough to calm lending conditions." *Market Insider*, 30 Oct. 2019, markets.businessinsider.com/news/stocks/why-fed-repos-capital-injections-might-not-calm-liquidity-fears-2019-10-1028643549#a-bank-government-disconnect2.

[768] Misesmedia. "Money, Banking, and the Federal Reserve." *Youtube*, 22 Feb. 2006, www.youtube.com/watch?v=iYZM58dulPE&index=3&list=PLtft_2mpNiCvN-PRcAsLmGlMkUMhzjMuq.

million in bonds could be turned into $10 million in accounts (which is inflationary).[769]

Now, for the first time in history, the Fed has eliminated the reserve requirement.[770] Effective March 26, 2020, the Federal Reserve Board reduced reserve requirements for all depository institutions to 0%.[771] Banks "could lend an unlimited amount without having any assets or wealth to back it up."[772] "[B]anks could theoretically continue making loans to infinity."[773]

"The fractional reserve ruse is still used today to create the impression that bankers are lending something other than mere debt created with accounting entries on their books."[774] Reginald McKenna, former Chancellor of the Exchequer, said, "I am afraid

---

[769] *Id.*

[770] Klein, Peter G. "The Financial System Is Now Totally Dependent on Government Intervention." *Mises Institute,* 16 Mar. 2020, mises.org/power-market/financial-system-now-totally-dependent-government-i n t e r v e n t i o n ? fbclid=IwAR3eKYaKZMJqyM91joNY59D1nTY6LqHPhsz4iz1fQS2Vow wbR5YGkAlOHPA.

[771] "Fed reduces reserve requirement ratios to 0% - effective March 26." *Nexusnewsfeed.com,* www.nexusnewsfeed.com/article/geopolitics/fed-reduces-reserve-requirement-ratios-to-0-effective-march-26/? f b c l i d = I w A R 0 i - YjEgQ6HmkoohQjAuM9k68jijImT5GjpxccXF4weYvFs_UWJZBL2HD8.

[772] Macleod, Alan. "Big Banks Call for Wall Street Deregulation to 'Fight Coronavirus.'" *MPN News,* 6 Mar. 2020, www.mintpressnews.com/big-banks-call-wall-street-deregulation-fight-coronavirus/265558/? f b c l i d = I w A R 1 M t J p e 2 A _ - nxjKHjOSu8YP3vLuZwRjOMbXCjWlOjIxo9A82UBzGypfrLs.

[773] Haber, Bob. "The Fed Fires 'The Big One.'" *Forbes,* 16 Mar. 2020, www.forbes.com/sites/bobhaber/2020/03/16/the-fed-fires-the-big-one/? fbclid=IwAR0j5PP70PzRQM6lOpfHCaTaHkZQp4dYm4o1pNCazj2PX7a itN-uZ8mGmEU#6c90761e6aa8.

[774] Brown, Ellen. "Revive Lincoln's Monetary Policy: An Open Letter to President Obama." *The Web of Debt,* 8 Apr. 2009, www.webofdebt.com/articles/lincoln_obama.php.

the ordinary citizen will not like to be told that the banks can, and do, create money…"[775] The fact that banks fabricate money was admitted by William Paterson, who "upon obtaining the charter of the Bank of England in 1694…said, 'The Bank hath benefit of interest on all moneys which it creates out of nothing…'"[776] Ralph M. Hawtrey, former Secretary of Treasury in England, revealed, "Banks lend by creating credit. They create the means of payment out of nothing."[777]

This state of affairs was characterized by American economist, Irving Fisher, as the banks being able to "lend, not money, but promises to supply money they do not possess."[778] Major L.L.B. Angus reflected, "The modern banking system manufactures money out of nothing. The process is, perhaps, the most astounding piece of sleight of hand that was ever invented. Banks can in fact inflate, mint, and un-mint the modern ledger-entry currency."[779]

Both the Fed and the U.S. Government act complicity in the creation of money, as explained by financial planner and author, Kelsey Williams: "The U.S. Treasury, in conjunction with the Federal Reserve, continually expands the supply of money and credit by issuing Treasury Bonds, Notes, and Bills. The Federal Reserve receives the newly certified Treasury securities and then issues a credit to the U.S. Treasury reflecting the corresponding

---

[775] In 1924 "History of Banking and Money Key Excerpts From Carroll Quigley's Tragedy and Hope." *Wanttoknow.info*, www.wanttoknow.info/articles/quigley_carroll.tragedy_hope_banking_money_history.

[776] *Id.*

[777] "The International Bankers: Famous Quotes." *ConspiracyAnalyst.org*, 23 Dec. 2019, conspiracyanalyst.org/2013/03/01/the-international-bankers-famous-quotes/.

[778] *100% Money* (1935). Messamore, Wesley. "100 Reasons to End the Fed." *Young Americans for Liberty*, yaliberty.org/news/100-reasons-to-end-the-fed/.

[779] "Prominent Quotes." *The Liberty Dollar*, libertydollar.org/ld/press-kit/prominent-quotes.htm.

dollar amount."[780]   The process the central bank uses to create currency is by the FOMC first approving the purchase of United States bonds, then the Fed buys them.[781] It pays for the bonds with electronic credits, and the banks use the deposits as reserves.[782] Darryl R. Francis, former President of the Federal Reserve Bank of St. Louis, explained: "Since the direct method of printing money to finance government expenditures is prohibited in the United States, the monetization of government deficits has occurred indirectly…"[783] "In the current model, the federal government sells Treasury bonds and uses the proceeds to fund government spending. The Treasury pays interest on the bonds, and this mechanism — interest due on borrowed money — creates a 'governor' on spending: As borrowing rises, so do interest payments, and as interest payments rise, this crimps other government spending. The other mechanism in the current model is the central bank (Federal Reserve) can create currency out of thin air and buy Treasury bonds. This is a form of monetary stimulus, i.e., a way to inject new money into the financial system. When the central bank creates money out of thin air to buy newly issued Treasury bonds, this is called 'monetizing the debt': In effect, the central bank creates money out of thin air and transfers it to the government by buying Treasury bonds."[784]

---

[780] Williams, Kelsey. "Federal Reserve – Conspiracy Or Not?" *Kelsey's Gold Facts,* 22 Dec. 2018, www.kelseywilliamsgold.com/federal-reserve-conspiracy-or-not/.

[781] Brown, Ellen. "Revive Lincoln's Monetary Policy: An Open Letter to President Obama." *The Web of Debt,* 8 Apr. 2009, www.webofdebt.com/articles/lincoln_obama.php.

[782] *Id.*

[783] "Money Quotes: What The Experts Say About Money." *Midas Gold Group*, 27 Aug. 2020, www.midasgoldgroup.com/money-quotes/.

[784] Smith, Charles Hughes. "Modern Monetary Theory." *InflationData.com*, 5 Nov. 2019, inflationdata.com/articles/2019/11/05/modern-monetary-theory/.

In response to a question posed by *60 Minutes* correspondent, Scott Pelley, Jerome Powell said, "As a central bank, we have the ability to create money digitally. And we do that by buying treasury bills or bonds or other government guaranteed securities, and that actually increases the money supply. We also print actual currency and we distribute that through the Federal Reserve bank."[785]   In essence, these bonds are IOUs, i.e. debt, that the federal government borrows from the central bank.[786]   The terms of the loans are set by the Fed alone, and the Fed charges interest for this service.[787] "Credit extended by these banks is in practice...backed by the taxing power of the federal government."[788]   "By the end of the year [2020], the Fed is projected to have purchased $3.5 trillion in government securities with these newly created dollars..."[789]

---

[785] Shimron, Leeor. "Fed Chairman Powell 60 Minutes Interview Highlights Bitcoin's Value Proposition." *Forbes,* 18 May 2020, www.forbes.com/sites/leeorshimron/2020/05/18/fed-chairman-powell-60-minutes-interview-highlights-bitcoins-value-proposition/?fbclid=IwAR2JqJiGeYtrtZjiBz1_g0h1b3f0KEB2DIN1-U-kjFY5k0uxfdQvfkzBxsY#5938e6db4cdb.

[786] Brown, Ellen. "Revive Lincoln's Monetary Policy: An Open Letter to President Obama." *The Web of Debt,* 8 Apr. 2009, www.webofdebt.com/articles/lincoln_obama.php.

[787] *Id.*

[788] Greenspan, Alan. "Gold and Economic Freedom." *Constitution Society,* www.constitution.org/mon/greenspan_gold.htm.

[789] Schrotenboer, Brent. "US is `printing' money to help save the economy from the COVID-19 crisis, but some wonder how far it can go." *USA Today,* 13 May 2020, www.usatoday.com/in-depth/money/2020/05/12/coronavirushow-u-s-printing-dollars-save-economy-during-crisis-fed/3038117001/?fbclid=IwAR1QWoknShih2gZvREvMBumaWN4FU_AIxlfr9j4nuclqnLkrLWWMho7NXSA.

"The Treasury pays the Fed, and the Fed gives the money back to the Treasury."[790] "But where does the Federal Reserve get the money that it gives to the U.S. government? It is created out of nothing."[791] The "Fed can just push a button to create money."[792] "With a few strokes on a computer, the Federal Reserve can create dollars out of nothing, virtually 'printing' money and injecting it into the commercial banking system, much like an electronic deposit...'The way you and I have checking accounts in our banks, that's how all these other banks have accounts at the Fed,' said Pavlina Tcherneva, an economist at Bard College in New York. 'All the Fed does is literally credit them. They just type it in.'"[793] "This is functionally similar to if the Treasury simply ordered up $2.2 trillion in the form of $100 bills on forklift pallets, and used them to pay bills."[794] "When you or I write a check there must be sufficient funds in our account to cover the check, but when the Federal Reserve writes a check, there is no bank deposit on which that check is drawn. When the Federal Reserve writes a check, it is creating

---

[790] Lewis, Nathan. "The Problem With "Modern Monetary Theory" Is That It's True." *Forbes*, 21 Feb. 2019, www.forbes.com/sites/nathanlewis/2019/02/21/the-problem-with-modern-monetary-theory-is-that-its-true/#4fb22b0256fb.

[791] Williams, Kelsey. "Federal Reserve – Conspiracy Or Not?" *Kelsey's Gold Facts,* 22 Dec. 2018, www.kelseywilliamsgold.com/federal-reserve-conspiracy-or-not/.

[792] Schrotenboer, Brent. "US is `printing' money to help save the economy from the COVID-19 crisis, but some wonder how far it can go." *USA Today,* 13 May 2020, www.usatoday.com/in-depth/money/2020/05/12/coronavirushow-u-s-printing-dollars-save-economy-during-crisis-fed/3038117001/?fbclid=IwAR1QWoknShih2gZvREvMBumaWN4FU_AIxlfr9j4nuclqnLkrLWWMho7NXSA.

[793] *Id.*

[794] Lewis, Nathan. "The Problem With "Modern Monetary Theory" Is That It's True." *Forbes*, 21 Feb. 2019, www.forbes.com/sites/nathanlewis/2019/02/21/the-problem-with-modern-monetary-theory-is-that-its-true/#4fb22b0256fb.

money."[795] "'The United States can pay any debt it has because we can always print money to do that,' former Federal Reserve chairman Alan Greenspan said in 2011. 'So there is zero probability of default.'"[796]

H. L. Birum, Sr. wrote in *American Mercury* (August 1957), "The Federal Reserve Bank is nothing but a banking fraud and an unlawful crime against civilization. Why? Because they 'create' the money made out of nothing, and our Uncle Sap Government issues their 'Federal Reserve Notes' and stamps our Government approval with NO obligation whatever from these Federal Reserve Banks, Individual Banks or National Banks, etc."[797]

"Under a gold standard, the amount of credit that an economy can support is determined by the economy's tangible assets, since every credit instrument is ultimately a claim on some tangible asset."[798]   In the past, overly rapid credit expansion would periodically cause banks to become "loaned up to the limit of their gold reserves, interest rates rose sharply, new credit was cut off, and the economy went into a sharp, but short-lived recession…It was limited gold reserves that stopped the unbalanced expansions of business activity before they could develop into the post-World War

---

[795] *Putting It Simply,* 1984, Federal Reserve Bank of Boston. "Quotes," *Your Dictionary*, quotes.yourdictionary.com/author/Quote/556191.

[796] Schrotenboer, Brent. "US is `printing' money to help save the economy from the COVID-19 crisis, but some wonder how far it can go." *USA Today,* 13 May 2020, www.usatoday.com/in-depth/money/2020/05/12/coronavirushow-u-s-printing-dollars-save-economy-during-crisis-fed/3 0 3 8 1 1 7 0 0 1 / ? fbclid=IwAR1QWoknShih2gZvREvMBumaWN4FU_AIxlfr9j4nuclqnLkr LWWMho7NXSA.

[797] "The International Bankers: Famous Quotes." *ConspiracyAnalyst.org*, 23 Dec. 2019, conspiracyanalyst.org/2013/03/01/the-international-bankers-famous-quotes/.

[798] Greenspan, Alan. "Gold and Economic Freedom." *Constitution Society*, www.constitution.org/mon/greenspan_gold.htm.

I type of disaster."[799] "The readjustment periods were short and the economies quickly reestablished a sound basis to resume expansion. But the process of cure was misdiagnosed as the disease: if shortage of bank reserves was causing a business decline — argued economic interventionists — why not find a way of supplying increased reserves to the banks so they never need be short! If banks can continue to loan money indefinitely — it was claimed — there need never be any slumps in business."[800]

"The threat of gold redeemability imposes a constant check and limit on inflationary issues of government paper."[801] Thus, "government deficit spending under a gold standard is severely limited."[802] On the other hand, "[p]aper money has a history of being printed as bills of credit to finance runaway government."[803] "[G]overnment bonds are not backed by tangible wealth, only by the government's promise to pay out of future tax revenues, and cannot easily be absorbed by the financial markets."[804]

"If the government can remove the threat [of gold redeemability], it can expand and inflate without cease. And so it begins to emit propaganda, trying to persuade the public not to use

---

[799] *Id.*

[800] *Id.*

[801] Per economist Murray Rothbard. "History of Banking and Money Key Excerpts From Carroll Quigley's Tragedy and Hope." *Wanttoknow.info*, w w w . w a n t t o k n o w . i n f o / a r t i c l e s / quigley_carroll.tragedy_hope_banking_money_history.

[802] Greenspan, Alan. "Gold and Economic Freedom." *Constitution Society*, www.constitution.org/mon/greenspan_gold.htm.

[803] Jones, Stewart. "The Founders Warned Us About Central Banking." *Ron Paul Liberty Report*, 10 Oct. 2019, www.ronpaullibertyreport.com/ a r c h i v e s / t h e - f o u n d e r s - w a r n e d - u s - a b o u t - c e n t r a l - b a n k i n g ? fbclid=IwAR1GtgHBthCfZDgqhObnuqCX2hO9116CjGntgnKJ75rw5KXr b5U3mKOVFKI.

[804] Greenspan, Alan. "Gold and Economic Freedom." *Constitution Society*, www.constitution.org/mon/greenspan_gold.htm.

gold coins in their daily lives."[805] "If a government goes off the gold standard completely — that is, refuses to exchange certificates and notes for specie — the amount of notes and deposits can be increased indefinitely because these are no longer limited by limited amounts of gold reserves."[806]

"An almost hysterical antagonism toward the gold standard is one issue which unites statists of all persuasions..."[807] Alan Greenspan explained, "[T]he opposition to the gold standard in any form — from a growing number of welfare-state advocates — was prompted by...the realization that the gold standard is incompatible with chronic deficit spending (the hallmark of the welfare state)... [T]he welfare state is nothing more than a mechanism by which governments confiscate the wealth of the productive members of a society to support a wide variety of welfare schemes. A substantial part of the confiscation is effected by taxation. But the welfare statists were quick to recognize that if they wished to retain political power, the amount of taxation had to be limited and they had to resort to programs of massive deficit spending, i.e., they had to borrow money, by issuing government bonds, to finance welfare expenditures on a large scale."[808] "The central bank sham is in reality a hidden tax where nations sell bonds to the central banks to pay for things politicians don't have the political will to raise taxes to pay for. Those bonds are created by the central banks out of nothing. More money in circulation makes the money in circulation

[805] "The 101 Best Gold Quotes From History – GoldSilver." *Gold Silver*, goldsilver.com/blog/101-best-gold-quotes-all-time/.

[806] "History of Banking and Money Key Excerpts From Carroll Quigley's Tragedy and Hope." *Wanttoknow.info*, www.wanttoknow.info/articles/quigley_carroll.tragedy_hope_banking_money_history.

[807] Greenspan, Alan. "Gold and Economic Freedom." *Constitution Society*, www.constitution.org/mon/greenspan_gold.htm.

[808] *Id.*

worth less. The government then obtains as much money as it needs, and the people pay for it with inflation…"[809]

When the Federal Reserve replaced the national bank system in 1913, Federal Reserve notes were redeemable for gold.[810] In 1933, the United States abandoned the gold standard, in part, out "of a desire to free the economic system from the restricting influence of a gold-dominated financial system."[811]   Ludwig von Mises noted, "[T]he gold standard did not collapse. Governments abolished it in order to pave the way for inflation…"[812]

Alan Greenspan complained, "The abandonment of the gold standard made it possible for the welfare statists to use the banking system as a means to an unlimited expansion of credit. They have created paper reserves in the form of government bonds which…the banks accept in place of tangible assets and treat as if they were an actual deposit, i.e., as the equivalent of what was formerly a deposit of gold. The holder of a government bond or of a bank deposit created by paper reserves believes that he has a valid claim on a real asset. But the fact is that there are now more claims outstanding than real assets…As the supply of money (of claims) increases relative to the supply of tangible assets in the economy, prices must eventually rise. Thus the earnings saved by the productive members of the society lose value in terms of goods. When the economy's books are finally balanced, one finds that this loss in value represents the

---

[809] "They were so active that they could control and manipulate the entire British economy. These were not bankers per se. However, the goldsmiths were in reality the first bankers." Jones, Stack. "An Essay On The History Of Banking." *The Banking Swindle*, 1 Jan. 2018, criminalbankingmonopoly.wordpress.com/.

[810] "The History of American Money." *CMI Gold $ Silver*, www.cmi-gold-silver.com/history-american-money/.

[811] "History of Banking and Money Key Excerpts From Carroll Quigley's Tragedy and Hope." *Wanttoknow.info*, www.wanttoknow.info/articles/quigley_carroll.tragedy_hope_banking_money_history.

[812] "The 101 Best Gold Quotes From History – GoldSilver." *Gold Silver*, goldsilver.com/blog/101-best-gold-quotes-all-time/.

goods purchased by the government for welfare or other purposes with the money proceeds of the government bonds financed by bank credit expansion. In the absence of the gold standard, there is no way to protect savings from confiscation through inflation. There is no safe store of value. If there were, the government would have to make its holding illegal, as was done in the case of gold. If everyone decided, for example, to convert all his bank deposits to silver or copper or any other good, and thereafter declined to accept checks as payment for goods, bank deposits would lose their purchasing power and government-created bank credit would be worthless as a claim on goods. The financial policy of the welfare state requires that there be no way for the owners of wealth to protect themselves. This is the shabby secret of the welfare statists' tirades against gold. Deficit spending is simply a scheme for the confiscation of wealth. Gold stands in the way of this insidious process. It stands as a protector of property rights. If one grasps this, one has no difficulty in understanding the statists' antagonism toward the gold standard."[813]

Economist Murray Rothbard of the Austrian School of Economics said, "Unlike the days of the gold standard, it is impossible for the Federal Reserve to go bankrupt; it holds the legal monopoly of counterfeiting (of creating money out of thin air) in the entire country."[814] "The Fed can create unlimited amounts of dollars — that's right, trillions, if required — to ensure that banks have enough funds to make emergency loans to businesses large and small, as well as state and local governments that are running out of funds…"[815]

---

[813] Greenspan, Alan. "Gold and Economic Freedom." *Constitution Society*, www.constitution.org/mon/greenspan_gold.htm.

[814] "Murray Rothbard Quotes." *AZ Quotes*, www.azquotes.com/quote/962764.

[815] Ullman, Owen. "An unsung hero of the coronavirus crisis: The Federal Reserve." *USA Today*, 24 Mar. 2020, www.usatoday.com/story/opinion/2020/03/24/unsung-hero-coronavirus-crisis-federal-reserve/2902681001/?fbclid=IwAR0SEFozSpmbHUjG7yUxgLSfPrg1i9kKHH37qCTXY_gNJlkOfNE774yjGfs.

"The floodgates were now open for unrestrained federal spending for socialist, imperialism, and interventionist programs. The constraints that the Framers had placed on the federal government were gone — and without even the semblance of constitutional amendments. The finest monetary system in history was destroyed, and the federal government became one gigantic engine of plunder and looting of American taxpayers, both directly through the progressive income tax and indirectly through the inflationary policies of the Federal Reserve."[816]

"[A]n unstated, practical result of the Fed's bond purchases is that it creates money to finance the gigantic debt run up by Congress..."[817] "The Federal Reserve is the printing press that has financed the creation of the largest government to ever exist. Endless welfare and endless military spending are both made possible by the Federal Reserve. The Fed can just print the money for whatever the US establishment wants..."[818] "The Federal Reserve is largely responsible for the out-of-control spending by Congress. The federal government can only obtain money through taxation, printing or borrowing money. Printing money has become the federal government's preferred method. This is also the most

---

[816] Hornberger, Jacob. "Monetary Destruction in America." *Tenth Amendment Center*, 7 Jun. 2020, tenthamendmentcenter.com/2020/06/07/ m o n e t a r y - d e s t r u c t i o n - i n - a m e r i c a / ? fbclid=IwAR1qznHUtpPxV4SZfCJk0G9H9gTS2kepV1ZU5BKoX_o06D xBXusfHyCPK6s.

[817] Schrotenboer, Brent. "US is `printing' money to help save the economy from the COVID-19 crisis, but some wonder how far it can go." *USA Today*, 13 May 2020, www.usatoday.com/in-depth/money/2020/05/12/ coronavirushow-u-s-printing-dollars-save-economy-during-crisis-fed/ 3 0 3 8 1 1 7 0 0 1 / ? fbclid=IwAR1QWoknShih2gZvREvMBumaWN4FU_AIxlfr9j4nuclqnLkr LWWMho7NXSA.

[818] Paul, Ron. "Ron Paul: 'Forget the Russians: It's the Federal Reserve Seeking to Meddle in Our Elections.'" *The Free Thought Project*, 3 Sept. 2019, thefreethoughtproject.com/ron-paul-end-federal-reserve/? fbclid=IwAR1nGlN-ywVH6dp-4yR2CGmdisX6qSZxeBCo9nTDg- qmZ53-AvddeYuUpGw.

destructive method since the federal government is able to simply print more money as needed to finance its drunken spending spree. It has become a never-ending cycle of spending and printing more money."[819]   G. Edward Griffin observed, "It is the ability of governments to acquire money without direct taxation that makes modern warfare possible, and a central bank has become the preferred method of accomplishing that."[820]

In 2020, "[g]overnment-ordered business shutdowns... [caused] a steep drop in tax revenue for state and local governments. To ensure the flow of credit to these cash-strapped governments, the Federal Reserve has embarked on a previously unthinkable act: creating up to $500 billion in new fiat currency and lending it directly to states, cities, and counties through its Municipal Liquidity Facility...For now, this staves off default by local governments on existing debt and allows government services to continue uninterrupted. However, this marks a dramatic departure from the Federal Reserve's traditional role of equipping solvent financial institutions with the liquidity necessary to meet credit demands... spending (lending) by the central bank of newly created fiat money is far less politically problematic. Cranking up the printing presses to fund a bailout requires no immediate tax hikes, minimal official federal spending increases, and little legislative involvement. It therefore more easily slips under the political radar...For instance, Congress facilitated the municipal bailout now underway by simply allocating $35 billion to a Special Purpose Vehicle ('SPV') to backstop the $500 billion in new fiat currency lent by the Federal Reserve. Ironically, the SPV itself was financed indirectly by the central bank which purchases government debt in exchange for newly created fiat money...Perhaps most importantly, this program implements the infrastructure for a future massive bailout of poorly

---

[819] Borowski, Julie. "Top 10 Reasons to End the Federal Reserve." *FreedomWorks,* 1 Feb. 2012, www.freedomworks.org/content/top-10-reasons-end-federal-reserve.

[820] "Central Bank Quotes." *Brainy Quote,* www.brainyquote.com/quotes/g_edward_griffin_852221?src=t_central_bank.

managed governments…Large increases in real per capita spending along with underfunded public sector pension plans constitute financial time bombs. Only a combination of higher taxes, pension reform, or diminished essential government services — such as emergency medical responses and functioning mass transit — will defuse the situation unless local politicians can shift these burdens onto the shoulders of unsuspecting citizens elsewhere…"[821]

"The federal government ran its first trillion-dollar deficits in response to the housing crisis. Politicians defended the massive spending because all manner of things were 'too big to fail.' But, after the crisis passed, the government didn't reduce its spending back to pre-2008 levels. The increased spending had become the new normal…"[822] "The Congressional Budget Office has estimated that the fiscal deficit will rise to about $3.7 trillion this fiscal year [2020] or about 18% of GDP."[823]

The United States Treasury funds deficit spending by selling more debt, which the banks and other investors buy.[824] "Deficits

---

[821] Griffith, Joel. "A Backdoor Central Bank Bailout of State Governments." *Real Clear Markets*, 2 May 2020, www.realclearmarkets.com/articles/2020/05/02/a_backdoor_central_bank_bailout_of_state_governments_490609.html?fbclid=IwAR2ram3WBD1YDtA-phyhdAVkT1c8kageamzMChCjYT3r4duZ2iMWycBEYOY.

[822] Davies, Antony and James P. Harrigan. "Massive Inflation May Be Coming, Because the US Government Has Cornered Itself into a Fiscal End Game." *FEE*, 21 May 2020, fee.org/articles/massive-inflation-may-be-coming-because-the-us-government-has-cornered-itself-into-a-fiscal-end-game/?fbclid=IwAR2EC1n-Wt7EXea4XZnzfkl3G9z8VtdguUeRjMqwCpjQJXZuVRnz6nairik,

[823] Oh, Sunny. "Former IMF chief economist says Fed's bond-buying is 'smoke and mirrors,' doesn't solve U.S. debt problems" *Market Watch*, 20 May 2020, www.marketwatch.com/story/former-imf-chief-economist-says-feds-bond-buying-is-smoke-and-mirrors-doesnt-solve-us-debt-problems-2020-05-20?siteid=yhoof2&yptr=yahoo.

[824] Tilford, Cale. "Repo: How the financial markets' plumbing got blocked." *Financial Times*, 25 Nov. 2019, ig.ft.com/repo-rate/.

have gotten so enormous that the Federal Reserve simply prints the money the government needs...”[825] “[T]he funding required to support that level of borrowing will require the Federal Reserve to monetize the deficit, at least partially, by increasing the money supply.”[826] “[C]ontinued deficit spending [will] paint the Federal Reserve into a corner wherein monetary policy would become a slave to fiscal policy. To avoid government default, confiscatory taxes, government shutdown, or a combination of all three, the Federal Reserve has reached a point wherein it has little choice but to monetize federal deficits.”[827] Darryl R. Francis, seventh president of the Federal Reserve Bank of St. Louis, wrote, “Government debt is ultimately being financed by the creation of new money...I can find no benefits accruing to the whole of society from debt monetization, but the risks are very serious and can be expressed in one word, inflation.”[828] “Inflation occurs when the money supply grows faster than the economy.”[829] Sooner or later, Fed policies will yield “sustained and significant inflation...”[830]

---

[825] Davies, Antony and James P. Harrigan. “Massive Inflation May Be Coming, Because the US Government Has Cornered Itself into a Fiscal End Game.” *FEE*, 21 May 2020, fee.org/articles/massive-inflation-may-be-coming-because-the-us-government-has-cornered-itself-into-a-fiscal-end-game/?fbclid=IwAR2EC1n-Wt7EXea4XZnzfkl3G9z8VtdguUeRjMqwCpjQJXZuVRnz6nairik.

[826] *Id.*

[827] *Id.*

[828] “Money Quotes: What The Experts Say About Money.” *Midas Gold Group*, 27 Aug. 2020, www.midasgoldgroup.com/money-quotes/.

[829] Davies, Antony and James P. Harrigan. “Massive Inflation May Be Coming, Because the US Government Has Cornered Itself into a Fiscal End Game.” *FEE*, 21 May 2020, fee.org/articles/massive-inflation-may-be-coming-because-the-us-government-has-cornered-itself-into-a-fiscal-end-game/?fbclid=IwAR2EC1n-Wt7EXea4XZnzfkl3G9z8VtdguUeRjMqwCpjQJXZuVRnz6nairik.

[830] *Id.*

"By a continuing process of inflation," according to economist John Maynard Keynes, "Governments can confiscate, secretly and unobserved, an important part of the wealth of their citizens."[831] Economist Friedrich August von Hayek opined, "With the exception only of the period of the gold standard, practically all governments of history have used their exclusive power to issue money to defraud and plunder the people."[832]

Admittedly, this state of affairs is maddening. Adding insult to injury is the federal income tax — the topic of the next section.

---

[831] "Money Quotes: What The Experts Say About Money." *Midas Gold Group*, 27 Aug. 2020, www.midasgoldgroup.com/money-quotes/.

[832] "The 101 Best Gold Quotes From History – GoldSilver." *Gold Silver*, goldsilver.com/blog/101-best-gold-quotes-all-time/.

Working for the Fed

"A big problem with a shift toward socialism and imperialism was expense. Socialism and imperialism are expensive. If the federal government were to go down that road, it would require significant increases in federal taxes, which posed a big problem for federal officials because America had no federal income tax."[833]

Karl Marx' *Communist Manifesto* contained ten planks for socializing a country; the second plank was the introduction of a progressive income tax.[834] In 1848, Marx and Engels proposed that progressive taxation be used "to wrest, by degrees, all capital from the bourgeois, to centralize all instruments of production in the hands of the state."[835] Senator Nelson Aldrich, one of the conspirators responsible for the Federal Reserve, had once denounced the federal income tax as "communistic and socialistic."[836]

---

[833] Hornberger, Jacob. "Monetary Destruction in America." *Tenth Amendment Center*, 7 Jun. 2020, tenthamendmentcenter.com/2020/06/07/monetary-destruction-in-america/?fbclid=IwAR1qznHUtpPxV4SZfCJk0G9H9gTS2kepV1ZU5BKoX_o06DxBXusfHyCPK6s.

[834] *None Dare Call It Conspiracy* by Gary Allen with Larry Abraham, 1971. "None Dare Call It Conspiracy." *Whale.to*, www.whale.to/b/allen_b1.html#chapter4.

[835] Dorn, James A. "Ending Tax Socialism." *CATO Institute*, 13 Sept. 1996, www.cato.org/publications/commentary/ending-tax-socialism.

[836] Aldrich was the maternal grandfather of Nelson Aldrich Rockefeller. Lundberg says that "When Aldrich spoke, newsmen understood that although the words were his, the dramatic line was surely approved by 'Big John [D. Rockefeller]...'" *None Dare Call It Conspiracy* by Gary Allen with Larry Abraham, 1971. "None Dare Call It Conspiracy." *Whale.to*, www.whale.to/b/allen_b1.html#chapter4.

The federal income tax serves as a mechanism to collect the funds to pay the interest on the national debt.[837]   Most of the national debt, which is almost $28 trillion, is owed to the Federal Reserve System.[838]   This fact was confirmed in 1984, when the Reagan Grace Commission found that all of the federal income tax is used to pay the national debt.   "100% of what is collected is absorbed solely by interest on the Federal Debt...all individual income tax revenues are gone before one nickel is spent on the services taxpayers expect from government."[839]

Thus, all monies paid as income taxes to the Internal Revenue Service (IRS), the Fed's private tax collector, go directly into the hands of the central bankers. The tax essentially redistributes Americans' wealth to the banking elite.   This money is then spent however the bankers deem fit. For example, according to Representative Louis T. McFadden, "Through the Federal Reserve Board, over thirty billions of dollars was pumped into Germany [after World War I]...modernistic dwellings, her great planetariums, her gymnasiums, her swimming pools, her fine public highways, her perfect factories...All this was done with our money. All this was given to Germany through the Federal Reserve Board. The Federal Reserve Board has pumped so many billions of dollars into Germany that they dare not name the total."[840]   In addition, certain projects in the former USSR were "built with funds unlawfully

---

[837] *Id.*

[838] "US Debt Clock." *usdebtclock.org*, www.usdebtclock.org.

[839] Report submitted to President Ronald Reagan on January 15, 1984. "Famous Grace Commission Quote." *Liberty Tree*, quotes.liberty-tree.ca/quote_blog/Grace.Commission.Quote.C455.

[840] Rep. Lewis T. McFadden (D PA), Chairman of the House Banking and Currency Committee, 1931. "The International Bankers: Famous Quotes." *ConspiracyAnalyst.org*, 23 Dec. 2019, conspiracyanalyst.org/2013/03/01/the-international-bankers-famous-quotes/.

taken from the US Treasury by the corrupt and dishonest Federal Reserve Board and the Federal Reserve Banks."[841]

Another point of the tax is to limit people's ability to save. "'Taxing profits is tantamount to taxing success,' famed free-market economist Ludwig Von Mises once wrote. 'Progressive taxation of income and profits means that precisely those parts of the income which people would have saved and invested are taxed away.'"[842] Ferdinand Lundberg penned in *The Rich* And *The Super-Rich,* "What it [the income tax] became, finally, was a siphon gradually inserted into the pocketbooks of the general public. Imposed to popular huzzas as a class tax, the income tax was gradually turned into a mass tax in a jiujitsu turnaround."[843]

Why would the rulers do this? Because wealth represents power, and if it is in the hands of ordinary citizens, it is detrimental for the ruling class. "[B]asically the idea [is] to prevent people from accumulating any wealth which might have long range disruptive influence on the system."[844]

---

[841] Fox, F. Earle. "Conspiracy Theory: Fact or Fictionregarding the Federal Reserve & the IRS?" *Internet Archive Wayback Machine,* 17 July 2010, web.archive.org/web/20170406104258/http://www.theroadtoemmaus.org/RdLb/21PbAr/Pl/Consp-Fed&IRS.htm.

[842] Polumbo, Brad. "New Stanford Study Suggests Biden's Agenda Will Have 4 Devastating Economic Consequences." *Fee,* 19 Oct. 2020, fee.org/articles/new-stanford-study-suggests-bidens-agenda-will-have-4-devastating-economic-consequences/?fbclid=IwAR2rOrrbZGkhEeuAq8hp0pBLBGW6Bi-7N0msiCAfX7oBL-dVDHkxtglswWg.

[843] Hodges, James P. PhD. "Federal Income Tax: 2nd Plank of Communism." *Leadership By George Washington,* 12 Nov. 2011, leadershipbygeorge.blogspot.com/2011/11/federal-income-tax-2nd-plank-of.html.

[844] Recollections of Dr. Lawrence Dunegan regarding a lecture by Dr. Day - an insider of the "Order" - he attended on March 20, 1969 at a meeting of the Pittsburgh Pediatric Society. "New Order of Barbarians - Transcript of Tapes I-III." *100777.Com,* 22 May 2003, 100777.com/nwo/barbarians.

Aaron Russo explained, "[I]n 1913, they bring the Federal Reserve System into being. Now they have this Federal Reserve System which in 1913 got the right to create money for the government, when before that the government could create its own money. Now the government, when it needed money, had to borrow from this private bank called the Federal Reserve, which is a private bank, owned by individuals, incorporated in Delaware. And so what happens is, now the government borrows money from them to fund the government, then the government says, 'Well, we have to pay these people interest. How are we going to pay them interest? Let's impose a tax on the labor of the American people —' which never existed before '— to pay the interest to the bankers...' But the point I'm trying to make is that by creating this Federal Reserve System, the government now became dependent on these private banks for money. And they started taxing us...So what's happened is that through the implementation of the Federal Reserve System, the government has become vested in these bankers, and they get their money from the bankers, and so then they impose a tax on us, which makes us more slaves, and makes it more difficult for us to survive."[845]

The Supreme Court of the United States had previously found income tax laws on labor to be unconstitutional. Aldrich, with the support of President Taft, proposed an amendment to the Constitution empowering Congress to lay income taxes. The 16th Amendment, which was enacted as an attempt to circumvent prior rulings, reads: "The Congress shall have power to lay and collect taxes on incomes, from whatever source derived, without apportionment among the several States, and without regard to any census or enumeration."

However, the 16th Amendment was not ratified by the required 3/4 of states, and thus, it may not be valid. "A proposed amendment becomes part of the Constitution as soon as it is ratified

---

[845] "Aaron Russo: Reflections and Warnings - Full Transcript." *Matt Prather*, sites.google.com/site/themattprather/Reading/aaron-russo/reflections-and-warnings-full-transcript.

by three-fourths of the States (38 of 50 States)."⁸⁴⁶ In this case, only "the states of Delaware, Wyoming, and New Mexico approved the 16th Amendment to the U.S. Constitution, ratifying it into law," on February 3, 1913.⁸⁴⁷ U.S. District Court Judge James C. Fox opined in *Sullivan v. United States* (2003), "I think if you were to go back and try to find and review the ratification of the 16th amendment, which was the internal revenue, the income tax, I think

---

⁸⁴⁶ "The authority to amend the Constitution of the United States is derived from Article V of the Constitution…After Congress proposes an amendment, the Archivist of the United States, who heads the National Archives and Records Administration (NARA), is charged with responsibility for administering the ratification process under the provisions of 1 U.S.C. 106b…" "Constitutional Amendment Process." *National Archives*, 15 Aug. 2016, www.archives.gov/federal-register/ constitution; Leachman, Michael and David A. Super. "States Likely Could Not Control Constitutional Convention on Balanced Budget Amendment or Other Issues." *Center on Budget and Policy Priorities,* 18 Jan. 2017, www.cbpp.org/research/states-likely-could-not-control-constitutional-convention-on-balanced-budget-amendment-or. (Article V of the Constitution provides for two methods of enacting constitutional amendments. Congress may, by a two-thirds vote in each chamber, propose a specific amendment; if at least three-fourths of the states (38 states) ratify it, the Constitution is amended. Alternatively, the states may call on Congress to form a constitutional convention to propose amendments. Congress *must* act on this call if at least two-thirds of the states (34 states) make the request. The convention would then propose constitutional amendments. Under the Constitution, such amendments would take effect if ratified by at least 38 states…In part because the only constitutional convention in U.S. history — the one in 1787 that produced the current Constitution — went far beyond its mandate, Congress and the states have never called another one. Every amendment to the Constitution since 1787 has resulted from the first process.)

⁸⁴⁷ "The Ratification of the 16th Amendment." *History, Art & Archives: United States House of Representatives,* history.house.gov/Historical-Highlights/1901-1950/The-ratification-of-the-16th-Amendment/.

if you went back and examined that carefully, you would find that a sufficient number of states never ratified that amendment."[848]

In addition, it is a tenet of constitutional law that "a law repugnant to the Constitution is void," which was Chief Justice John Marshall's holding in *Marbury v. Madison*, 5 U.S. 137 (1803).[849] He explained, "If two laws conflict with each other, the Court must decide on the operation of each. If courts are to regard the Constitution, and the Constitution is superior to any ordinary act of the legislature, the Constitution, and not such ordinary act, must govern the case to which they both apply."[850] Thus, "[a]n unconstitutional act is not a law; it confers no rights; it imposes no duties; it affords no protection; it creates no office; it is in legal contemplation as inoperative as though it had never been passed."[851] As we shall see, the federal income tax is applied unconstitutionally in many cases.

Legally, the federal income tax only applies to "taxable income" per the Internal Revenue Code, 26 U.S.C. § 1 ("There is hereby imposed on the taxable income of..."). [852] Taxable income is income that is within the federal government's authority to tax.

"Income" is defined as a "profit gained through a sale conversion of capital assets..."[853] The definition of income "[conveys] the idea of gain or increase arising from corporate activities."[854] Thus, income is "a gain, a profit, something of

---

[848] "Motion for Temporary Restraining Order Hearing Before the Honorable James C. Fox Senior United States District Court Judge." *Sullivan v. United States*, 03-1611 (4th Cir. 2003). www.whatreallyhappened.com/WRHARTICLES/SullivanVUSA.pdf.

[849] *Marbury v. Madison*, 5 U.S. 137 (1803).

[850] *Id.*

[851] *Norton v. Shelby County*, 118 U.S. 425 (1886).

[852] 26 U.S. Code §1.

[853] *Eisner v. Macomber*, 252 U.S. 189, 207 (1920).

[854] *Doyle v. Mitchell Bros. Co.*, 247 U.S. 179, 185 (1918).

exchangeable value...severed from the capital however invested or employed and coming in, being 'derived,' that is received or drawn by the recipient for his separate use, benefit and disposal — that is the income derived from property..."[855]

The federal government may impose two types of taxes: direct taxes and indirect taxes.

A direct tax is laid on a person or on property, including income from real estate and personal property. "[D]irect taxes have been limited to taxes on land and appurtenances and taxes on polls or capitation taxes."[856]

Direct taxes are subject to apportionment. The U.S. Constitution Article I, § 2, cl. 3 mandates that "direct Taxes shall be apportioned among the several States...according to their respective Numbers..." In addition, Article I, § 9, cl. 4 stipulates that "[n]o Capitation, or other direct, Tax shall be laid, unless in Proportion to the Census or Enumeration herein before directed to be taken..."

In contrast, "indirect taxes are levied upon the happening of an event or an exchange."[857] It is voluntary upon and avoidable by the citizen, i.e. the tax can be avoided if one chooses not to engage in the taxed activity. "[T]he requirement to pay such taxes [excises (indirect tax)] involves the exercise of privileges, and the element of absolute and unavoidable demand is lacking."[858] An excise tax is a tax "laid upon the manufacture, sale or consumption of commodities within the country, upon licenses to pursue certain occupations, and upon corporate privileges."[859]

Indirect taxes, including excise taxes, are required to be uniformly laid. Article I, § 8, cl. 1 of the Constitution reads: "The

---

[855] *Eisner v. Macomber*, 252 U.S. 189 (1920).

[856] *Pollock v. Farmers' Loan and Trust Company*, 157 U.S. 429, 633 (1895).

[857] *Knowlton v. Moore*, 178 U.S. 41, 47 (1900).

[858] *Flint v. Stone Tracy Co.*, 220 U.S. 107, 151-152 (1911).

[859] *Id.*

Congress shall have Power To lay and collect Taxes...and Excises...but all...Excises shall be uniform throughout the United States..." "Uniformity of taxation" is defined as "[a] general principle that taxes should be levied in accord with some reasonable system of apportionment...it means that such taxes may only be levied with geographical uniformity...requiring the same plan and the same method to be operative throughout the United States."[860]

The Supreme Court of the United States has rejected the broad contention that all receipts — everything that comes in — are income within the proper definition of the term "gross income," and that "the entire proceeds of a conversion of capital assets should be treated as gross income."[861] "[A] mere conversion of capital assets [is] not to be treated as income."[862]

A tax on gross revenue, such as the federal income tax, taxes both capital and income, and is, therefore, not technically an income tax, because capital is not income.[863] Insofar as it taxes capital, it is a direct tax that must be apportioned, the 16th Amendment notwithstanding.

"[T]he Sixteenth Amendment did not confer any additional authority to tax on the federal government; It did not extend the taxing power to new subjects."[864] "[I]ts sole purpose and effect was to preclude the consideration of the source of income in order to reclassify the tax as a direct tax, requiring apportionment."[865] "The

---

[860] *Knowlton v. Moore*, 178 U.S. 41, 47 (1900).

[861] *See Doyle v. Mitchell Bros. Co.*, 247 U.S. 179 (1918).

[862] *Id.* at 185.

[863] *O'Gilvie v. United States*, 519 U.S. 79, 84 (1996). ("[A] restoration of capital was not income; hence it fell outside the definition of 'income' upon which the law imposed a tax.")

[864] *Brushaber v. Union P. R. Co.*, 240 U.S. 1 (1916).

[865] Cryer, Tommy K. JD. "The Memorandum." *Internet Archive,* 2006, a r c h i v e . o r g / s t r e a m / p d f y - u l z 6 h P C b - i F D 2 x H K / THE_MEMORANDUM%20IRS%20INCOME%20TAX%20_djvu.txt.

provisions…simply prohibited the previous complete and plenary power of income taxation possessed by Congress…from being taken out of the category of indirect taxation to which it inherently belonged and being placed in the category of direct taxation subject to apportionment by a consideration of the sources from which the income was derived…"[866]

Technically, the federal income tax is an indirect tax, but the 16th Amendment made it a direct tax. The 16th Amendment only authorizes a particular character of direct tax without apportionment, and therefore, if a tax is levied under its assumed authority which does not partake of the characteristics exacted by the 16th Amendment, it is outside of the Amendment and is void as a direct tax in the general constitutional sense because it is not apportioned.[867] Insofar as it taxes capital and not income (gain or profit), it has to be apportioned. The federal government has no authority to lay an unapportioned direct tax, which is how the federal income tax is applied in many cases. Such a tax is not constitutional, and thus, not legal.

Consequently, examples of "taxable income" are state bond interest and net revenue of a corporation involved in international shipping.[868]

Income that is not taxable includes that from labor because to work is a fundamental right.[869] Thus, the 16th Amendment does not authorize a tax on a salary (this includes a tax on the salary of

---

[866] *Stanton v. Baltic Mining Co.*, 240 U.S. 103 (1916).

[867] *Brushaber* at 11.

[868] *South Carolina v. Baker*, 485 U.S. 505, 524 (1988); *Peck & Co. v. Lowe*, 247 U.S. 165 (1918).

[869] *Butchers' Union Co. v. Crescent City Co.*, 111 U.S. 746, 4 S.Ct. 652 (1884); *Yick Wo v. Hopkins*, 118 U.S. 356 (1886); *Meyer v. Nebraska*, 262 U.S. 390, 43 S.Ct. 625 (1923).

federal judges).[870]   A person's labor is his property, or the capital. The purchase price for the labor, which requires time and energy, is his wage. The wage-earner trades a wage in return for labor. This is a quid pro quo exchange and not a "profit." Peter Gibbons, a tax attorney, agreed, "There is no constitutional basis for a tax on the wages of Americans living and working in the 50 states of the union. Period, end of argument."[871]

Neither can the federal government tax the employment of children, because those activities are under the sole and exclusive realm of the States.[872]   Another area that is exclusively within the jurisdiction of the State is the practice of law.   Tom Cryer was an attorney in Shreveport, Louisiana who defeated the IRS in federal court. "Cryer stopped filing and paying income tax unless and until the government could show him it had the legal right to demand he do either."[873]   "Tommy had not filed a 1040 'Return' because he believed that the law does not require Tommy to pay income taxes on his labor."[874]   "He was charged with two counts of…failure to

---

[870] *Evans v. Gore*, 253 U.S. 245, 263 (1920) (Overruled in part by *United States v. Hatter*, 532 U.S. 557 (2001) (Hatter overrules "Evans insofar as it holds that the Compensation Clause forbids Congress to apply a generally applicable, nondiscriminatory tax to the salaries of federal judges.")

[871] "America: Freedom to Fascism Quotes." *Quotes.net.* STANDS4 LLC, 2020, www.quotes.net/mquote/970882.

[872] The Tenth Amendment helps to define the concept of federalism, the relationship between Federal and state governments: "The powers not delegated to the United States by the Constitution, nor prohibited by it to the states, are reserved to the states respectively, or to the people." *Bailey v. Drexel Furniture Company*, 259 U.S. 20, 42 S.Ct. 449 (1922).

[873] "Tax Hero: Tommy Cryer Passes at 62." *Republic Magazine*, 2014, web.archive.org/web/20170729063103/http://www.republicmagazine.com/news/tax-hero-tommy-cryer-passes-at-62.html.

[874] "Attorney Tommy Cryer Beats the IRS in court; Jury says not guilty!" *Freedom Law School*, 12 Jul. 2007, web.archive.org/web/20170425083913/http://freedomlawschool.org/victories/attorney-beats-irs.html.

file."[875]   On July 12, 2007, the "Louisiana Federal Jury found Cryer NOT GUILTY of 2 counts of willful failure to file an income tax return…"[876]

Stock dividends are also not taxable income because they are a conversion of capital from one form to another. "[N]either under the Sixteenth Amendment nor otherwise has Congress power to tax without apportionment a true stock dividend…, or the accumulated profits behind it, as income of the stockholder."[877]

"While it is true that IRS is an agency of the privately owned Federal Reserve System and therefore is not part of the US government, until financial reforms are in place…, it would be advisable to comply with all current policies and laws to avoid the complications that some have encountered."[878]

Filmmaker, Aaron Russo, suggested, "Since making that movie [*From Freedom to Fascism*], many people have come to me and asked should they pay their income taxes or not? And I never advised people not to pay…I said: Look. I've done a lot of research. The Supreme Court has ruled that the IRS has no authority. The Sixteenth Amendment did not give the IRS the authority to tax your labor and your wages. That's a fact. The Supreme Court is the law of the land, and the IRS does not trump the Supreme Court. However, that being the case, the fact is if the mafia would come to you and say, 'We want $2,000 a month or we're going to hurt you…' I would not advise you not to pay them. Because you may get hurt by not paying them. Whether it's legal or not doesn't necessarily matter.

---

[875] "Tax Hero: Tommy Cryer Passes at 62." *Republic Magazine*, 2014, web.archive.org/web/20170729063103/http://www.republicmagazine.com/news/tax-hero-tommy-cryer-passes-at-62.html.

[876] "Attorney Tommy Cryer Beats the IRS in court; Jury says not guilty!" *Freedom Law School*, 12 Jul. 2007, web.archive.org/web/20170425083913/http://freedomlawschool.org/victories/attorney-beats-irs.html.

[877] *Eisner v. Macomber*, 252 U.S. 189, 40 S.Ct. 189 (1920).

[878] "February 3, 2007." *Matthew Books*, 3 Feb. 2007, www.matthewbooks.com/february-3-2007/.

You're gonna get hurt if you don't. It's the same thing with the IRS. They can hurt you. They can put you in jail. They can torture you. So if you don't pay them, you may get hurt. So I never advise people not to pay. I tell people 'Yeah, pay your taxes.'"[879]

Those who have chosen to fight the IRS have successfully used the 5th Amendment in their defense. "The Fifth Amendment privilege against self-incrimination is a cornerstone protection guaranteed by the United States Constitution. It provides, among other things, that no person 'shall be compelled in any criminal case to be a witness against himself...'"[880]

For example, Loren C. Troescher (in *United States v. Troescher*, 99 F.3d 933 (9th Cir. 1996)) appealed "an order of the district court compelling him to appear before the Internal Revenue Service to answer questions and produce documents. The IRS issued the summons after Troescher apparently failed to file income tax returns for several years. Troescher argue[d] that the district court erred in rejecting his assertion of the Fifth Amendment's privilege against self-incrimination."[881] The 9th Circuit district court agreed with the defendant.[882] It stated, "The individual may stand upon his constitutional rights as a citizen...He owes no duty to the state or to his neighbors to divulge his business, or to open his doors to an investigation, so far as it may tend to criminate him. He owes no such duty to the state, since he receives nothing therefrom, beyond the protection of his life and property. His rights are such as existed by the law of the land long antecedent to the organization of the state, and can only be taken from him by due process of law, and in

---

[879] "Aaron Russo: Reflections and Warnings - Full Transcript." *Matt Prather*, sites.google.com/site/themattprather/Reading/aaron-russo/reflections-and-warnings-full-transcript.

[880] Todd, Timothy M. "A Win For The 5th Amendment At The Tax Court." *Forbes*, 16 Nov. 2015, www.forbes.com/sites/timtodd/2015/11/16/a-win-for-the-5th-amendment-at-the-tax-court/#55257b616ecd.

[881] *United States v. Troescher*, 99 F.3d 933, 936 (9th Cir. 1996).

[882] *Id.*

accordance with the Constitution. Among his rights are a refusal to incriminate himself."[883] "The caselaw in this circuit [9th circuit] is clear that the Fifth Amendment may be validly invoked when the taxpayer fears prosecution for tax crimes."[884] "There is no general 'Tax-Crime Exception' to the Fifth Amendment..."[885]

The next chapter goes into how the Fed uses its power to influence the money supply, and thus, control the economy.

---

[883] *Hale v. Henkel*, 201 U.S. 43, 74 (1906).

[884] *United States v. Troescher*, 99 F.3d 933, 936 (9th Cir. 1996).

[885] *Id.*

Chapter 5

Monetary Meddling

"Central banks across the world manipulate money ostensibly to 'grow,' or 'stabilize,' or otherwise achieve their desired interventionist goals for the economy."[886] To achieve their goals, central banks such as the Federal Reserve try to "control liquidity in the financial system."[887] "Central banks can usually vary the amount of money in circulation by 'open market operations' or by influencing the discount rates of lesser banks."[888]

"The Fed has inordinate power over the direction of the economy by pulling the levers of monetary policy...."[889] "The Federal Reserve influences the banks' rates through its open market operations."[890] "In open market operations, a central bank buys or

---

[886] Cortez, JP. "Fake Money, Sound Money and Government Malfeasance." *Tenth Amendment Center*, 28 Aug. 2018, tenthamendmentcenter.com/2018/08/28/fake-money-sound-money-and-government-malfeasance/.

[887] Amadeo, Kimberly. "Reserve Requirement and How It Affects Interest Rates." *The Balance*, 10 Feb. 2019, www.thebalance.com/reserve-requirement-3305883.

[888] "History of Banking and Money Key Excerpts From Carroll Quigley's Tragedy and Hope." *Wanttoknow.info*, www.wanttoknow.info/articles/quigley_carroll.tragedy_hope_banking_money_history.

[889] Shimron, Leeor. "Fed Chairman Powell 60 Minutes Interview Highlights Bitcoin's Value Proposition." *Forbes*, 18 May 2020, www.forbes.com/sites/leeorshimron/2020/05/18/fed-chairman-powell-60-minutes-interview-highlights-bitcoins-value-proposition/?fbclid=IwAR2JqJiGeYtrtZjiBz1_g0h1b3f0KEB2DIN1-U-kjFY5k0uxfdQvfkzBxsY#5938e6db4cdb.

[890] Amadeo, Kimberly. "Reserve Requirement and How It Affects Interest Rates." *The Balance*, 10 Feb. 2019, www.thebalance.com/reserve-requirement-3305883.

sells government bonds in the open market. If it buys, it releases money into the economic system; if it sells, it reduces the amount of money in the community..."[891]   "For example, if the Federal Reserve Bank buys government securities in the open market, it pays for these by check which is soon deposited in a bank. It thus increases this bank's reserves with the Federal Reserve Bank."[892]
The Fed reduces the money supply by selling bonds to the public, which causes money to come out of accounts (which is deflationary).

The quantity of money can also be adjusted "by changing reserve requirements..."[893]   "When the Fed reduces the reserve requirement, it's exercising expansionary monetary policy. That creates more money in the banking system. When the Fed raises the reserve requirement, it's executing contractionary policy. That reduces liquidity and slows economic activity."[894]   "Increasing the reserve requirement takes money out of the economy, while

---

[891] "Since banks are permitted to issue loans for several times the value of their reserves with the Federal Reserve Bank, such a transaction permits them to issue loans for a much larger sum." "History of Banking and Money Key Excerpts From Carroll Quigley's Tragedy and Hope." *Wanttoknow.info*, www.wanttoknow.info/articles/quigley_carroll.tragedy_hope_banking_money_history.

[892] *Id.*

[893] *Id.*

[894] Amadeo, Kimberly. "Reserve Requirement and How It Affects Interest Rates." *The Balance*, 10 Feb. 2019, www.thebalance.com/reserve-requirement-3305883.

decreasing the reserve requirement puts money into the economy."[895]

"The Fed controls the fed-funds rate to influence the overall cost of borrowing in the U.S. economy as part of its efforts to achieve the job and inflation goals set for it by Congress."[896] "If the fed funds rate is high, it costs more for banks to lend to each other overnight. That has the same effect as raising the reserve requirement. Conversely, when the Fed wants to loosen monetary policy and increase liquidity, it lowers the fed funds rate target. That makes lending fed funds cheaper. It has the same effect as lowering the reserve requirement..."[897] "The Fed buys securities, usually Treasury notes, from member banks when it wants the fed funds rate to fall. The Fed adds credit to the bank's reserve in exchange for the security. Since the bank wishes to put this extra reserve to work, it will try to lend it to other banks. Banks cut their interest rates to do so. The Fed will sell securities to banks when it wants to increase the fed funds rate."[898] "The Fed Funds Rate has

---

[895] "Changing the reserve requirements as a method by which central banks can influence the credit policies of other banks is possible only in those places (like the United States) where there is a statutory limit on reserves. Increasing reserve requirements curtails the ability of lesser banks to grant credit, while decreasing it expands that ability." "History of Banking and Money Key Excerpts From Carroll Quigley's Tragedy and Hope." *Wanttoknow.info*, www.wanttoknow.info/articles/ quigley_carroll.tragedy_hope_banking_money_history. Kagan, Julia. "Fractional Reserve Banking." *Investopedia*, 18 Dec. 2020, www.investopedia.com/terms/f/fractionalreservebanking.asp.

[896] Derby, Michael S,. "Fed's $100 Billion Repo Intervention Falls Short Of Bank Demand." *The Wall Street Journal,* 4 Mar. 2020, www.wsj.com/ articles/feds-100-billion-repo-intervention-falls-short-of-bank- demand-11583332932?fbclid=IwAR1J- Zph20xp456s6uBSTArVVWXeV52Pd6EINx3Yqn4wRKS3cpZPD9EaU1 Q.

[897] Amadeo, Kimberly. "Reserve Requirement and How It Affects Interest Rates." *The Balance,* 10 Feb. 2019, www.thebalance.com/reserve- requirement-3305883.

[898] *Id.*

plotted a path of extremes over the decades, ranging from 0% to 19%, not exactly stable."[899] "President Richard Nixon's disastrous pressure on former Fed Chair Arthur Burns to keep rates low…is seen as one of the reasons for the inflation of the 1970s."[900]

"Central banks can also change the quantity of money by influencing the credit policies of other banks. This can be done by various methods, such as changing the re-discount rate…"[901] "By changing the re-discount rate, we mean the interest rate which central banks charge lesser banks for loans backed by commercial paper or other security which these lesser banks have taken in return for loans. By raising the re-discount rate, the central bank forces the lesser bank to raise its discount rate in order to operate at a profit; such a raise in interest rates tends to reduce the demand for credit and thus the amount of deposits (money). Lowering the re-discount rate permits an opposite result."[902]

"[A] paradox of banking practice arose from the fact that bankers, who loved deflation, often acted in an inflationary fashion from their eagerness to lend money at interest. Since they make money out of loans, they are eager to increase the amounts of bank credit on loan. But this is inflationary."[903] "Rising prices benefit debtors and injure creditors, while falling prices do the opposite."[904]

---

[899] Quinn, Jim. "The Federal Reserve Must Die." *HCP Live*, 25 Aug. 2009, www.mdmag.com/medical-news/federal_reserve_must_die.

[900] Bryan, Bob. "Trump's attacks on the Fed may be intense, but they're nothing compared to a wild new story about Ronald Reagan from former Fed Chairman Paul Volcker." *Business Insider,.* 24 Oct. 2018, www.businessinsider.com/ronald-reagan-fed-chair-volcker-trump-2018-10.

[901] "History of Banking and Money Key Excerpts From Carroll Quigley's Tragedy and Hope." *Wanttoknow.info*, www.wanttoknow.info/articles/quigley_carroll.tragedy_hope_banking_money_history.

[902] *Id.*

[903] *Id.*

[904] *Id.*

Inflation is good for debtors because it makes it easier to pay back money owed to lenders.[905] "A debtor called upon to pay a debt at a time when prices are higher than when he contracted the debt must yield up [fewer] goods and services than he obtained at the earlier date, on a lower price level when he borrowed the money. A creditor, such as a bank, which has lent money — equivalent to a certain quantity of goods and services — on one price level, gets back the same amount of money — but a smaller quantity of goods and services — when repayment comes at a higher price level, because the money repaid is then less valuable."[906]

When the Continental currency collapsed, John Witherspoon, a New Jersey clergyman who signed the Declaration of Independence, related, "For two or three years we constantly saw and were informed of creditors running away from their debtors, and the debtors pursuing them in triumph, and paying them without mercy…In Rhode Island, sources tell us of creditors 'leaping from rear windows of their houses or hiding themselves in their attics' in order to avoid debtors…"[907]

"The conflict between the deflationary ideas and inflationary practices of bankers had profound repercussions on business. The bankers made loans to business so that the volume of money increased faster than the increase in goods. The result was inflation. When this became clearly noticeable, the bankers would flee to notes or specie by curtailing credit and raising discount rates. This was beneficial to bankers in the short run (since it allowed them to foreclose on collateral held for loans), but it could be disastrous to them in the long run (by forcing the value of the collateral below the

---

[905] "Greenbacks: Definition & History." *Study.com*, study.com/academy/lesson/greenbacks-definition-lesson.html.

[906] "History of Banking and Money Key Excerpts From Carroll Quigley's Tragedy and Hope." *Wanttoknow.info*, www.wanttoknow.info/articles/quigley_carroll.tragedy_hope_banking_money_history.

[907] Woods, Thomas E. Jr. "The Revolutionary War and the Destruction of the Continental." *Mises Institute*, 11 Oct. 2006, mises.org/library/revolutionary-war-and-destruction-continental.

amount of the loans it secured). But such bankers' deflation was destructive to business and industry…"[908]

In addition, the Federal Reserve's manipulation of the interest rates has caused massive economic distortions.[909] "Some economists believe that the (over)issuance of a fiduciary is to blame for business cycles and economic recessions."[910] "In all countries, the demand for and volume of such credit was larger in time of a boom and less in time of a depression."[911] "The resulting fluctuation in the supply of money, chiefly deposits, was a prominent aspect of the 'business cycle.'"[912] They create a boom-bust cycle by dropping interest rates artificially low, which creates a massive "everything bubble."[913] "A bubble is an economic cycle characterized by the rapid escalation of asset prices followed by a contraction. It is created by a surge in asset prices unwarranted by the fundamentals of the asset and driven by exuberant market behavior."[914]

[908] "History of Banking and Money Key Excerpts From Carroll Quigley's Tragedy and Hope." *Wanttoknow.info*, www.wanttoknow.info/articles/quigley_carroll.tragedy_hope_banking_money_history.

[909] At 6. Schiff, Peter. "Powell resurrecting the high inflation Volcker buried." *Youtube*, 11 Dec. 2019, www.youtube.com/watch?v=lWcLQFap2sQ.

[910] Brock, Thomas. "Money." *Investopedia*, 25 Dec. 2020, www.investopedia.com/terms/m/money.asp.

[911] "History of Banking and Money Key Excerpts From Carroll Quigley's Tragedy and Hope." *Wanttoknow.info*, www.wanttoknow.info/articles/quigley_carroll.tragedy_hope_banking_money_history.

[912] *Id.*

[913] At 15. Gammon, George. "CPI Tax Scam: YOU'RE GOING TO LOSE A LOT OF MONEY! (Discover How)." *Youtube*, 11 Dec. 2019, www.youtube.com/watch?v=RA8PX_T1Suw.

[914] Kenton, Will. "Bubble." *Investopedia*, 30 June 2019, www.investopedia.com/terms/b/bubble.asp.

"Some policy makers have repeatedly warned that ultra-low rates encourage 'bubbles' in asset prices and risky lending."[915] Reducing interest rates lowers the acquisition cost of money and adds liquidity to the economy.[916] "High liquidity means there's a lot of capital…A liquidity glut develops when there is too much capital looking for too few investments. That leads to inflation. As cheap money chases fewer and fewer profitable investments, then the prices of those assets increase. It doesn't matter whether it's houses, gold, or high-tech companies. That leads to 'irrational exuberance.' Investors only think that the prices will rise. Everyone wants to buy so they don't miss out on tomorrow's profit. They create an asset bubble."[917]   "Central bank policies have inflated asset bubbles in the stock, bond, property, and credit markets."[918]

"Eventually, a liquidity glut means more of this capital becomes invested in bad projects. As the ventures go defunct and don't pay out their promised return, investors are left holding worthless assets."[919] "When no more investors are willing to buy at the elevated price, a massive sell-off occurs, causing the bubble to

---

[915] Randow, Jana and Yuko Takeo. "Negative Interest Rates." *Bloomberg,* 1 Nov. 2019, www.bloomberg.com/quicktake/negative-interest-rates.

[916] Patton, Mike. "Trump Administration Considers Reducing Payroll Tax To Zero." *Forbes*, 10 Mar. 2020, www.forbes.com/sites/mikepatton/2020/03/10/trump-administration-considers-reducing-payroll-tax-to-zero/?fbclid=IwAR2wNkXGZSe8bdjXd95Lis-NO3hO0b6neY0149LJBJGR6z0_mlcjnzQvQj0#1825e5473188.

[917] Amadeo, Kimberly. "Liquidity: Its Gluts, Traps, Ratios, and How the Fed Manages It." *The Balance*, 30 Dec. 2020,   www.thebalance.com/liquidity-definition-ratios-how-its-managed-3305939.

[918] "The Great Economic Depression of 2020: No lessons learned as central banks' bazookas dribble or misfire." *RT*, 23 Mar. 2020, www.rt.com/op-ed/483845-great-economic-depression-2020/.

[919] Amadeo, Kimberly. "Liquidity: Its Gluts, Traps, Ratios, and How the Fed Manages It." *The Balance*, 30 Dec. 2020,   www.thebalance.com/liquidity-definition-ratios-how-its-managed-3305939.

deflate."[920]   "When the artificial boom implodes, the result is dramatic – and deflationary. As with a collapsing star, the relationship of available credit to the functioning real economy goes from 'massive overabundance' to 'massive shortage' in the space of a market crash. Where banks would lend to anyone before, suddenly they lend to no one. Where investors were brazen before, suddenly they are terrified. During a supernova collapse, trillions of dollars in private credit flows evaporate into the ether – the result of loans being extinguished in a panic but not replaced..."[921]   "Panic ensues, resulting in a withdrawal of investment money. Prices plummet, as investors scramble madly to sell before prices drop further...This phase of the business cycle is called an economic contraction. It usually leads to a recession."[922]   In fact, Nobel Prize-winning economist, Milton Friedman, noted, "I know of no severe depression, in any country or any time, that was not accompanied by a sharp decline in the stock of money and equally of no sharp decline in the stock of money that was not accompanied by a severe depression."[923]

Milton Friedman opined, "The stock of money, prices and output was decidedly more unstable after the establishment of the Federal Reserve System than before. The most dramatic period of instability in output was...the period between the two [world] wars, which includes the severe [monetary] contractions of 1920-21, 1929-33, 1937-38. No other 20 year period in American history

---

[920] Kenton, Will. "Bubble." *Investopedia*, 30 June 2019, www.investopedia.com/terms/b/bubble.asp.

[921] Mercenary Trader. "Weekender: The Trouble With Modern Monetary Theory (MMT)." *Business Insider*, 19 Dec. 2010, www.businessinsider.com/weekender-the-trouble-with-modern-monetary-theory-mmt-2011-1.

[922] Amadeo, Kimberly. "Liquidity: Its Gluts, Traps, Ratios, and How the Fed Manages It." *The Balance*, 30 Dec. 2020, www.thebalance.com/liquidity-definition-ratios-how-its-managed-3305939.

[923] "Milton Friedman Quotations." *Memorablequotations.com*, www.memorablequotations.com/friedman.htm.

contains as many as three such severe contractions. This evidence persuades me that at least a third of the price rise during and just after World War I is attributable to the establishment of the Federal Reserve System and that the severity of each of the major contractions —1920-1, 1929-33 and 1937-8 is directly attributable to acts of commission and omission by the Reserve authorities."[924]

For example, Alan Greenspan explained how disastrous was "the Federal Reserve's attempt to assist Great Britain who had been losing gold to us because the Bank of England refused to allow interest rates to rise when market forces dictated (it was politically unpalatable). The reasoning of the authorities involved was as follows: if the Federal Reserve pumped excessive paper reserves into American banks, interest rates in the United States would fall to a level comparable with those in Great Britain; this would act to stop Britain's gold loss and avoid the political embarrassment of having to raise interest rates. The 'Fed' succeeded; it stopped the gold loss, but it nearly destroyed the economies of the world in the process. The excess credit which the Fed pumped into the economy spilled over into the stock market, triggering a fantastic speculative boom. Belatedly, Federal Reserve officials attempted to sop up the excess reserves and finally succeeded in braking the boom. But it was too late: by 1929 the speculative imbalances had become so overwhelming that the attempt precipitated a sharp retrenching and a consequent demoralizing of business confidence. As a result, the American economy collapsed. Great Britain fared even worse, and rather than absorb the full consequences of her previous folly, she abandoned the gold standard completely in 1931, tearing asunder what remained of the fabric of confidence and inducing a world-wide series of bank failures. The world economies plunged into the

---

[924] *Id.*

Great Depression of the 1930's."[925]   Thus, mis-pricing gold was a catalyst for the Great Depression.[926]

Rep. Charles Lindbergh, Sr. (R-MN) warned, "To cause high prices, all the Federal Reserve Board will do will be to lower the rediscount rate producing an expansion of credit and rising stock market, then when business men are adjusted to these conditions, it can check prosperity in mid career by raising the rate of interest. It can cause the pendulum of a rising and falling market to swing gently back and forth by slight changes in the discount rate, or cause violent fluctuations by greater rate variation and in either case, it will possess inside information as to financial conditions and advanced knowledge of the coming change, either up or down. This is the strangest and most dangerous advantage ever placed in the hands of a special privilege class by any government that ever existed. The system is private, conducted for the sole purpose of obtaining the greatest possible profits from the use of other peoples' money. They know in advance when to create panics to their

---

[925] Greenspan, Alan. "Gold and Economic Freedom." *Constitution Society*, www.constitution.org/mon/greenspan_gold.htm.

[926] At 14. Gammon, George. "Jim Rickards: His Gold Price Prediction Explained...($50,000+ IS POSSIBLE!!)" *Youtube*, 6 Dec. 2019, www.youtube.com/watch?v=HpqJ-sFScxA.

advantage, and they also know when to stop panic. Inflation and deflation work equally well for them when they control finance."[927]

This monetary manipulation could be used to serve a political agenda. Lindbergh predicted in 1912: "The Aldrich plan is the Wall Street Plan. It means another panic, if necessary, to intimidate the people…"[928] This is the tactic Rothschild used to further his goals: "Panics and financial depressions would ultimately result in World Government, a new order of one world government."[929]

For example, during the 1920s, the bankers were displeased with Presidents Harding and Coolidge, who were against the League of Nations, had cut the Federal Income Tax, had increased tariffs on

---

[927] "Famous Quotes About International Bankers, the Federal Reserve and America." *4closurefraud.com*, 13 Mar. 2012, 4closurefraud.org/2012/03/13/famous-quotes-about-international-bankers-the-federal-reserve-and-america/. The discount rate is the interest rate charged to commercial banks and other depository institutions on loans they receive from their regional Federal Reserve Bank's lending facility--the discount window. "One of the men who has benefitted dramatically from the booming stock market over the past decade is Jerome Powell himself. According to his previous and most recent financial disclosure form, he has tens of millions of dollars invested in the stock market." Martens, Pam and Russ Martens. "Fed Chair Powell Attempts to Blame U.S. Inequality on Globalization – Gets Smacked Down by Bloomberg Reporter." *Wall Street on Parade*, 11 Jun. 2020, wallstreetonparade.com/2020/06/fed-chair-powell-attempts-to-blame-u-s-inequality-on-globalization-gets-smacked-down-by-bloomberg-reporter/.

[928] "Charles Lindbergh Jr. Lucky Lindy Son of Congressman Charles Lindbergh Sr. (R-MN) Speech in Iowa on 9/11 September 11th 1941." *Americanbuilt.us*, americanbuilt.us/patriots/charles-lindbergh.shtml.

[929] Number 14. "The House of Rothschild Excerpted from the Book The Secrets of the Federal Reserve by Eustace Mullins Bankers Research Institute, 1983, Paperback." *Third World Traveler*, www.thirdworldtraveler.com/Banks/House_Rothschild_TSOTFR.html.

imports, and had reduced the national debt.[930] As punishment, the bankers decided to crash the economy. "Sir Montagu Norman was the organizer of these 'informal talks' between heads of central banks in 1927, which led directly to the Great Stockmarket Crash of 1929…"[931]

The opening salvo began with the Federal Reserve first flooding the United States with easy money, increasing the volume by up to 62%.[932] "In 1924,…the Reserve banks suddenly created some $500 million in new credit, which led to a bank credit expansion of over $4 billion in less than one year."[933] Businesses borrowed a lot of money and became heavily indebted.

"The Federal Reserve System launched a further burst of inflation in 1927, the result being that total currency outside banks plus demand and time deposits in the United States increased from $44.51 billion at the end of June 1924 to $55.17 billion in 1929. The volume of farm and urban mortgages expanded from $16.8 billion in 1921 to $27.1 billion in 1929. Similar increases occurred in industrial, financial, and state and local government indebtedness. This expansion of money and credit was accompanied by rapidly rising real estate and stock prices. Prices for industrial securities, according to Standard & Poor's common stock index, rose from 59.4

---

[930] *See* Hendrickson, John. "Budget and Tax Lessons from President Calvin Coolidge." *Calvin Coolidge Presidential Foundation,* 10 Dec. 2014, www.coolidgefoundation.org/blog/budget-and-tax-lessons-from-president-calvin-coolidge/. History.com Editors. "Calvin Coolidge." *History,* 27 Oct. 2009, www.history.com/topics/us-presidents/calvin-coolidge.

[931] "The House of Rothschild Excerpted from the Book The Secrets of the Federal Reserve by Eustace Mullins Bankers Research Institute, 1983, Paperback." *Third World Traveler,* www.thirdworldtraveler.com/Banks/House_Rothschild_TSOTFR.html.

[932] Jones, Stack. "An Essay On The History Of Banking." *The Banking Swindle,* 1 Jan. 2018, criminalbankingmonopoly.wordpress.com/.

[933] "What Caused the Great Depression?" *FEE,* 2 Feb. 2018, fee.org/articles/what-caused-the-great-depression/.

in June of 1922 to 195.2 in September of 1929. Railroad stock climbed from 189.2 to 446.0, while public utilities rose from 82.0 to 375. The flood of easy money drove interest rates down, pushed the stock market to dizzy heights, and thus gave birth to the 'Roaring Twenties.'"[934]

In April 1929, Paul Warburg sent a secret memo to his friends advising them of the impending stock market crash and depression.[935]   Joseph P. Kennedy forwarded the warning to his friend, father of Ed Kerrigan, saying, "Sell all of your stock now. Don't ask any questions."[936]   Thus, it was no "coincidence" that Rockefeller, J. P. Morgan, and the like got out of the stock market and bought gold just in time.[937]

The Federal Reserve then sought to "force prices downward by limiting the supply of money," i.e. creating deflation.[938]   To that end, it began to tighten the money supply in 1929.[939]   "[T]he monetary authorities…slowed the growth of the money supply…the Federal Reserve System…sold government securities and thereby halted the bank credit expansion. It raised its discount rate to 6% in

---

[934] *Id.*

[935] Jones, Stack. "An Essay On The History Of Banking." *The Banking Swindle*, 1 Jan. 2018, criminalbankingmonopoly.wordpress.com/.

[936] JPK's worth grew from $4 million in 1929 to over $100 million in 1935 right before the crash. During the Great Depression, Joseph P. Kennedy's worth grew from four million dollars in 1929 to over 100 million dollars in 1935. Apparently he had insider information and knew what the Federal Reserve intended to do. "The International Bankers: Famous Quotes." *ConspiracyAnalyst.org*, 23 Dec. 2019, conspiracyanalyst.org/2013/03/01/the-international-bankers-famous-quotes/.

[937] Jones, Stack. "An Essay On The History Of Banking." *The Banking Swindle*, 1 Jan. 2018, criminalbankingmonopoly.wordpress.com/.

[938] "History of Banking and Money Key Excerpts From Carroll Quigley's Tragedy and Hope." *Wanttoknow.info*, www.wanttoknow.info/articles/quigley_carroll.tragedy_hope_banking_money_history.

[939] Jones, Stack. "An Essay On The History Of Banking." *The Banking Swindle*, 1 Jan. 2018, criminalbankingmonopoly.wordpress.com/.

August 1929. Time-money rates rose to 8%, commercial paper rates to 6%, and call rates to the panic figures of 15% and 20%...It choked off the money supply, raised interest rates, and for the next three years, presided over a money supply that shrank by 30%. This deflation following the inflation wrenched the economy from tremendous boom to colossal bust."[940]

On October 24, 1929 ("Black Thursday"), the big New York bankers called in their 24-hour broker margin call loans.[941] This forced the brokers and stock-holders to sell at any price, which caused the stock market to crash.[942] Thus began the Great Depression. "[B]etween 1930 and 1933, the contraction assumed catastrophic proportions never experienced before or since in the United States."[943] Only when President Franklin D. Roosevelt enacted bank reform laws that gave the Federal Reserve even more power did the central bank put more money into circulation, which eased the suffering.[944]

Unfortunately, "Franklin Roosevelt blamed the economic crisis on the failure of America's 'free enterprise' system rather than place responsibility where it lay — with the Federal Reserve."[945] "The Federal Reserve caused the Great Depression through its easy

---

[940] "What Caused the Great Depression?" *FEE,* 2 Feb. 2018, fee.org/articles/what-caused-the-great-depression/.

[941] Jones, Stack. "An Essay On The History Of Banking." *The Banking Swindle*, 1 Jan. 2018, criminalbankingmonopoly.wordpress.com/.

[942] *Id.*

[943] "What Caused the Great Depression?" *FEE,* 2 Feb. 2018, fee.org/articles/what-caused-the-great-depression/.

[944] "An Essay On The History Of Banking." *The Banking Swindle,* criminalbankingmonopoly.wordpress.com/banking-essay/.

[945] Hornberger, Jacob. "Monetary Destruction in America." *Tenth Amendment Center*, 7 Jun. 2020, tenthamendmentcenter.com/2020/06/07/monetary-destruction-in-america/?fbclid=IwAR1qznHUtpPxV4SZfCJk0G9H9gTS2kepV1ZU5BKoX_o06DxBXusfHyCPK6s.

money policies during the 1920's."⁹⁴⁶   "[T]he Fed over-issued federal debt instruments, creating an artificial economic boom during the 'roaring 20s.'"⁹⁴⁷ "The expansion of the money supply led to an unsustainable credit-driven boom."⁹⁴⁸

Dr. Murray Rothbard, who was a strong proponent of laissez-faire economics, once said: "The guilt for the Great Depression must, at long last, be lifted from the shoulders of the free-market economy and placed where it properly belongs: at the doors of politicians, bureaucrats, and the mass of enlightened economists. And in any other depression, past or future, the story will be the same."⁹⁴⁹   Economist Milton Friedman agreed, asserting, "The Federal Reserve definitely caused the Great Depression by contracting the amount of money in circulation by one-third from 1929 to 1933."⁹⁵⁰   Former Federal Reserve Chairman, Ben Bernanke, admitted that the Fed had been responsible. He said, "I would like to say to Milton [Friedman] and Anna [Jacobson

⁹⁴⁶ Quinn, Jim. "The Federal Reserve Must Die." *HCP Live*, 25 Aug. 2009, www.mdmag.com/medical-news/federal_reserve_must_die.

⁹⁴⁷ Hornberger, Jacob. "Monetary Destruction in America." *Tenth Amendment Center*, 7 Jun. 2020, tenthamendmentcenter.com/2020/06/07/monetary-destruction-in-america/?fbclid=IwAR1qznHUtpPxV4SZfCJk0G9H9gTS2kepV1ZU5BKoX_o06DxBXusfHyCPK6s.

⁹⁴⁸ Quinn, Jim. "The Federal Reserve Must Die." *HCP Live*, 25 Aug. 2009, www.mdmag.com/medical-news/federal_reserve_must_die.

⁹⁴⁹ Van, Gerninal G. "The Gold Standard Didn't Create the Great Depression, the Federal Reserve Did." *FEE,* 25 May 2019, fee.org/articles/the-gold-standard-didn-t-create-the-great-depression-the-federal-reserved-i-d/?fbclid=IwAR0vrzpM7GgbTDRu2mqA0EM_1vSSK_JaYKWsCWX7BlDGZ6PUxZhjt8niybw.

⁹⁵⁰ "Milton Friedman Quotations." *Memorablequotations.com,* www.memorablequotations.com/friedman.htm.

Schwartz]: Regarding the Great Depression. You're right, we did it."[951]

Representative McFadden also blamed the bankers for the crash, saying, "It was not accidental. It was a carefully contrived occurrence…The international bankers sought to bring about a condition of despair here so that they might emerge as rulers of us all."[952] He also accused the international bankers of causing the crash to reacquire the "gold stock which Europe lost to America as the result of WWI."[953]

Franklin D. Roosevelt's son-in-law, Curtis Dall, alleged, "The depression was the calculated 'shearing' of the public by the World Money powers, triggered by the planned sudden shortage of supply of call money in the New York money market…"[954] As a result, approximately $40 billion was consolidated into fewer hands.[955]

The Federal Reserve's policy of maintaining low interest rates throughout the early 2000s, which resulted in cheaper mortgages, was seen as a major factor in the housing bubble that led to the

---

[951] "Let me end my talk by abusing slightly my status as an official representative of the Federal Reserve. I would like to say to Milton and Anna: Regarding the Great Depression. You're right, we did it. We're very sorry. But thanks to you, we won't do it again."…Remarks by Governor Ben S. Bernanke (At the Conference to Honor Milton Friedman, University of Chicago - Chicago, Illinois November 8, 2002). Pongracic, Ivan Jr. "The Great Depression According to Milton Friedman." *FEE*, 1 Sept. 2007, fee.org/articles/the-great-depression-according-to-milton-friedman/; Williams, Kelsey. "Federal Reserve – Conspiracy Or Not?" *Kelsey's Gold Facts,* 22 Dec. 2018, www.kelseywilliamsgold.com/federal-reserve-conspiracy-or-not/.

[952] Jones, Stack. "An Essay On The History Of Banking." *The Banking Swindle*, 1 Jan. 2018, criminalbankingmonopoly.wordpress.com/.

[953] *Id.*

[954] *My Exploited Father-in-Law,* 1970. Jones, Stack. "An Essay On The History Of Banking." *The Banking Swindle*, 1 Jan. 2018, criminalbankingmonopoly.wordpress.com/.

[955] Jones, Stack. "An Essay On The History Of Banking." *The Banking Swindle*, 1 Jan. 2018, criminalbankingmonopoly.wordpress.com/.

2007-2008 financial crisis. Stanford economist, John Taylor, has argued that the Fed's loose monetary policy in the early 2000s likely exacerbated housing price inflation (i.e. prices were driven to all-time highs), thus spurring the subsequent collapse of the subprime mortgage market.[956]

"The worldwide financial system experienced a 6.8 magnitude earthquake in September 2008. The very foundations of our economy were shaken to their core. The fear exhibited by government officials, politicians, and the public was palpable and real. For a few weeks there was the distinct possibility that the system would come crashing down. A massive printing of dollars by the Federal Reserve, the clandestine buying up of toxic assets by the Federal Reserve, behind the scenes deals with the biggest banks, covert currency swap deals with foreign Central Banks, and forcing the FASB to change accounting rules to allow banks to fraudulently value bad loans, temporarily staved off the final chapter in the 96-year-old diabolical experiment in currency manipulation."[957]

"[D]espite the Fed secretly throwing $29 trillion cumulatively to bail out Wall Street banks and their derivatives following the crash of 2008, the United States has never actually returned to a self-sustaining economy."[958]   "When the World Health Organization announced on February 24th [2020] that it was time to prepare for a global pandemic, the stock market plummeted. Over the following week, the Dow Jones Industrial Average dropped by more than 3,500 points or over 10%. In an attempt to contain the damage, on

---

[956] Dokko, Jane, et al. "Monetary Policy and the Housing Bubble." *Federalreserve.gov*, 22 Dec. 2009, www.federalreserve.gov/pubs/feds/2009/200949/200949pap.pdf.

[957] Quinn, Jim. "The Federal Reserve Must Die." *HCP Live*, 25 Aug. 2009, www.mdmag.com/medical-news/federal_reserve_must_die.

[958] Martens, Pam and Russ Martens. "Demand for Fed's Repo Loans Surges Past $100 Billion a Day as 10-Year Treasury Hits Lowest Rate in 149 Years." *Wall Street on Parade*, 5 Mar. 2020, wallstreetonparade.com/2020/03/demand-for-feds-repo-loans-surges-past-100-billion-a-day-as-10-year-treasury-hits-lowest-rate-in-149-years/.

March 3rd, the Federal Reserve slashed the fed funds rate from 1.5% to 1.0%, in their first emergency rate move and biggest one-time cut since the 2008 financial crisis. But rather than reassuring investors, the move fueled another panic sell-off."[959] Wall Street "suffered its worst trading day since 1987 despite a massive liquidity injection by the Federal Reserve...The Dow Jones Industrial average was down 2,352.75 points, or 9.99 percent, to 21,200.47 at the closing bell on [March 12, 2020]. It was the index's largest percentage drop since the Black Monday crash of 1987, and its largest point drop of all time..."[960]

"The Fed has signaled it is willing to flood the economy with newly minted dollars and has kept true to its word."[961] To prop up liquidity on Wall Street, the Federal Reserve Board of Governors announced that it "has reduced reserve requirement ratios to zero percent effective on March 26, [2020]...This action eliminates

[959] Brown, Ellen. "The Fed's baffling response to the Coronavirus explained." *Nexusnewsfeedf.com*, 12 Mar. 2020, www.nexusnewsfeed.com/article/geopolitics/the-fed-s-baffling-response-to-the-coronavirus-explained/?fbclid=IwAR3KdMgB13LT98gK8-5bQvXUM5mm5zjEiCDl6MIQ_4t74a d9X_V05lU8ajY.

[960] Griffith, Keith. "Dow plunges 10% in Wall Street's worst trading day since 1987 despite Fed pumping $1.5 TRILLION into bond markets amid panic over Trump's European travel ban." *Dailymail.com*, 12 Mar. 2020, www.dailymail.co.uk/news/article-8104731/Dow-set-fall-1-200-points-S-P-500-points-bear-territory.html?fbclid=IwAR02Prew4tzJHUM_6MmzNhg7am1Fsw3HucIHfY98rMIifhE 9OzcA3jZeiM0.

[961] Shimron, Leeor. "Fed Chairman Powell 60 Minutes Interview Highlights Bitcoin's Value Proposition." *Forbes,* 18 May 2020, www.forbes.com/sites/leeorshimron/2020/05/18/fed-chairman-powell-60-minutes-interview-highlights-bitcoins-value-proposition/?fbclid=IwAR2JqJiGeYtrtZjiBz1_g0h1b3f0KEB2DIN1-U-kjFY5k0uxfdQvfkzBxsY#5938e6db4cdb.

reserve requirements for thousands of depository institutions…"[962] "The Fed's bizarre action in removing reserve requirements at a time when public confidence in the banks is critical, raises concerns across Wall Street that at least some of these banks may desperately need access to those reserves to post collateral on derivative trades."[963]

Monetary authorities "take exceptional measures in extreme conditions of the economy."[964] That is the focus of the next section.

---

[962] Martens, Pam and Russ Martens. "Fed Sets Off Panic with Plan to Eliminate Reserves at Wall Street's Mega Banks." *Wall Street on Parade,* 16 Mar. 2020, wallstreetonparade.com/2020/03/fed-sets-off-panic-with-plan-to-eliminate-reserves-at-wall-streets-mega-banks/. Cheung, Brian. "Federal Reserve slashes rates to zero, restarts QE." *Yahoo Finance,* 16 Mar. 2020, finance.yahoo.com/news/federal-reserve-cuts-rates-to-zero-restarts-quantitative-easing-qe-210001968.html; Torres, Craig and Rich Miller. "Fed Cuts Main Interest Rate to Near Zero, to Boost Assets by $700 Billion." *Bloomberg*, 15 Mar. 2020, www.bloomberg.com/news/articles/2020-03-15/fed-cuts-main-rate-to-near-zero-to-boost-assets-by-700-billion? fbclid=IwAR0w3K1m_1_Hu_grpBM9r9WHlxy31AvzCQO3FQeBXA7-le6bWAmdEMpiFCw; O'Halloran, Suzanne. "Dow drops 2,999 points on word coronavirus crisis could extend until August." *Fox Business*, 16 Mar. 2020, www.foxbusiness.com/markets/us-stocks-march-16-2020? fbclid=IwAR0SNQD4jbEe-BAjk1aR2HK3-xyaxoocArng4mpLYTRxeHxKL0Zqrtkwaus.

[963] Martens, Pam and Russ Martens. "Fed Sets Off Panic with Plan to Eliminate Reserves at Wall Street's Mega Banks." *Wall Street on Parade,* 16 Mar. 2020, wallstreetonparade.com/2020/03/fed-sets-off-panic-with-plan-to-eliminate-reserves-at-wall-streets-mega-banks/.

[964] Weinberg, John. "The Great Recession and its Aftermath." *Federal Reserve History,* 22 Nov. 2013, www.federalreservehistory.org/essays/great-recession-and-its-aftermath.

Easy Money

The "ability of the Fed to manipulate the currency...gives the Fed's Board of Governors...huge amounts of power over the entire economy, including setting the price of just about everything indirectly..."[965]

"During deflationary periods, people and businesses hoard money [i.e. save] instead of spending and investing. The result is a collapse in aggregate demand, which leads to prices falling even further, a slowdown or halt in real production and output, and an increase in unemployment. A loose or expansionary monetary policy is usually employed to deal with such economic stagnation."[966]   By making borrowing as cheap as possible, the central bank hopes businesses and individuals will have ready access to nearly interest-free cash to invest and spend.[967]   However, economics commentator, George Gammon, cautions: "The main focus of central banks — their pinnacle of success — is spending. They think the more the consumer spends, the more debt they go into, the richer our society will be."[968]   The central banks believe that currency in and of itself creates consumption.[969]   Gammon warns, "They are trying to

---

[965] Haskins, Justin. "The Fed is pushing America dangerously close to socialism." *Glennbeck.com*, 23 Mar. 2020, www.glennbeck.com/blog/the-fed-is-pushing-america-dangerously-close-to-socialism.

[966] Hayes, Adam. "Negative Interest Rate Policy (NIRP) Definition." *Investopedia*, 7 May 2019, www.investopedia.com/terms/n/negative-interest-rate-policy-nirp.asp.

[967] Bayly, Lucy. "Federal Reserve cuts rates to near zero in emergency action," *NBC News,* 16 Mar. 2020, www.nbcnews.com/business/economy/federal-reserve-cuts-rates-near-zero-emergency-action-n1159691?cid=sm_npd_nn_fb_np&fbclid=IwAR1vJryRucDUBNTzpbUGIUYzex1MRGoIdYVa-f3V0KiwMLkY4XPquv3PBuE.

[968] At 5:50. Gammon, George. "Quantitative Easing: Will It Cause Hyperinflation? (ANSWER REVEALED)." *Youtube*, 19 Dec. 2019, www.youtube.com/watch?v=b7KafSma3xQ.

[969] At 1:35. *Id.*

deceive you into believing that currency equals consumption...[but] production equals consumption."[970]

"In past decades, the Fed has been reluctant to create too many dollars for fear of creating high inflation, as occurred in the 1970s in the U.S. and more recently by foreign governments that allowed their central banks to create unlimited amounts of their currencies to cover domestic debts."[971]   However, Alan "Greenspan initiated a series of interest cuts that brought the Federal Funds rate down to 1% in 2004 and left it at that level for over a year. He purposely created a housing bubble in order to artificially prop up the American economy after the huge stock market losses. The excess liquidity unleashed by Greenspan caused lending standards to deteriorate resulting in the housing bubble of 2004-2006 and the market meltdown beginning in 2008. His loose monetary policy resulted in a plunging dollar, surging commodity prices and humungous trade deficits."[972]

After the housing bubble burst, "there was the 2008 financial collapse on Wall Street – which produced the largest economic collapse in the U.S. since the Great Depression."[973]   The Fed lowered interest rates to zero in what was called ZIRP — a zero

---

[970] *Id.*

[971] Ullman, Owen. "An unsung hero of the coronavirus crisis: The Federal Reserve." *USA Today*, 24 Mar. 2020, www.usatoday.com/story/opinion/2020/03/24/unsung-hero-coronavirus-crisis-federal-reserve/2902681001/?fbclid=IwAR0SEFozSpmbHUjG7yUxgLSfPrg1i9kKHH37qCTXY_gNJlkOfNE774yjGfs.

[972] Quinn, Jim. "The Federal Reserve Must Die." *HCP Live*, 25 Aug. 2009, www.mdmag.com/medical-news/federal_reserve_must_die.

[973] Martens, Pam and Russ Martens. "The Fed Is Killing the Two Main Functions of Wall Street: Price Discovery and Prudent Capital Allocation." *Wall Street on Parade*, 11 Apr. 2020, wallstreetonparade.com/2020/04/the-fed-is-killing-the-two-main-functions-of-wall-street-price-discovery-and-prudent-capital-allocation/.

interest rate policy.[974]   The Federal Open Market Committee "lowered borrowing costs to near zero from above 5 percent in the 2007-09 downturn…"[975]   "The greater the supply of money in an economy, the lower the corresponding interest rates are. In turn, lower rates allow banks to make more loans."[976]   An IMF study observed, "[s]evere recessions have historically required 3 to 6 percentage points cut in policy rates."[977]

The Fed also pursued an unconventional bond-buying program called "quantitative easing" to stimulate the economy.[978] "Quantitative easing (QE) is an expansion of the open market

---

[974] Weinberg, John. "The Great Recession and its Aftermath." *Federal Reserve History*, 22 Nov. 2013, www.federalreservehistory.org/essays/great-recession-and-its-aftermath.

[975] Smialek, Jeanne. "Bonds Hit Historic Lows, Prompting Fed to Ponder: What More Can We Do?" *The New York Times*, 6 Mar. 2020, web.archive.org/web/20200307035222/https://www.nytimes.com/2020/03/06/business/economy/fed-coronavirus-rate-cut-limited-ammunition.html?fbclid=IwAR3SK_H_SWIXSpNx1zwSJBw9PaIGqhYqinfg3OhbzANEZM_qY1OeWkN1-o4.

[976] Amadeo, Kimberly. "Explaining Quantitative Easing – QE." *The Balance*, 3 Sept. 2019, www.thebalance.com/what-is-quantitative-easing-definition-and-explanation-3305881.

[977] "Banning cash so you pay the bank to hold your money is what the IMF wants." *MSN*, 25 Aug. 2019, www.msn.com/en-au/money/personalfinance/banning-cash-so-you-pay-the-bank-to-hold-your-money-is-what-the-imf-wants/ar-AAGjopy?fbclid=IwAR3azKMt8SEjVWBYhS_p6u0ZQIaY-IcLekCFi5K_A8CEThzwrEWGwugJnrc.

[978] Weinberg, John. "The Great Recession and its Aftermath." *Federal Reserve History*, 22 Nov. 2013, www.federalreservehistory.org/essays/great-recession-and-its-aftermath. Chappelow, Jim. "Quantitative Easing." *Investopedia*, 6 Sept. 2019, www.investopedia.com/terms/q/quantitative-easing.asp.

operations of a country's central bank."[979] When implementing QE, the central bank purchases government bonds or other securities from the market.[980] Using "QE methods, the central bank will buy mortgage-backed securities and Treasurys from its member banks which causes an added liquidity in the flow of money in capital markets."[981] This increases the money supply, provides banks with more liquidity, and encourages lending and investment.[982] "Quantitative easing is…adopted…to increase money supply in the economy in order to further increase lending by commercial banks and spending by consumers. The central bank infuses a pre-determined quantity of money into the economy by buying financial assets from commercial banks and private entities. This leads to an increase in banks' reserves."[983] According to the president of the Federal Reserve Bank of Boston, Eric Rosengren, "Bond-buying by the central bank bolsters the economy by lowering rates on long-term debt, making borrowing cheaper and encouraging

---

[979] Amadeo, Kimberly. "Explaining Quantitative Easing – QE." *The Balance*, 3 Sept. 2019, www.thebalance.com/what-is-quantitative-easing-definition-and-explanation-3305881.

[980] Chappelow, Jim. "Quantitative Easing." *Investopedia*, 6 Sept. 2019, www.investopedia.com/terms/q/quantitative-easing.asp.

[981] Amadeo, Kimberly. "Explaining Quantitative Easing – QE." *The Balance*, 3 Sept. 2019, www.thebalance.com/what-is-quantitative-easing-definition-and-explanation-3305881.

[982] Chappelow, Jim. "Quantitative Easing." *Investopedia*, 6 Sept. 2019, www.investopedia.com/terms/q/quantitative-easing.asp.

[983] "Definition of 'Quantitative Easing.'" *The Economic Times,* economictimes.indiatimes.com/definition/quantitative-easing.

spending."[984]   Thus, QE increases the money supply by making it easier to borrow money.[985]

   "To carry out QE, central banks create money by buying securities, such as government bonds, from banks with electronic cash that did not exist before."[986]   "'Through the purchase of [usually government] debt by a bank, fiat money is injected into the economy,' Gary North writes. 'The asset purchases are done by the trading desk at the New York Federal Reserve Bank. No funds change hands, but the central bank issues a credit to the banks' reserves as it buys the securities.'"[987]   "Where do central banks get the funds to purchase these assets? They simply create it out of thin air. This is what financial media speaks of when they refer to the Federal Reserve printing money. In the United States, only the central bank has this unique power."[988]   "The Fed...doesn't buy securities directly from the U.S. Treasury. Instead, it purchases previously issued Treasury securities through commercial banks...the Fed – is creating dollars to buy government debt in the

---

[984] Smialek, Jeanne. "Bonds Hit Historic Lows, Prompting Fed to Ponder: What More Can We Do?" *The New York Times*, 6 Mar. 2020, web.archive.org/web/20200307035222/https://www.nytimes.com/2020/03/06/business/economy/fed-coronavirus-rate-cut-limited-a m m u n i t i o n . h t m l ? fbclid=IwAR3SK_H_SWIXSpNx1zwSJBw9PaIGqhYqinfg3OhbzANEZM_qY1OeWkN1-o4.

[985] Chappelow, Jim. "Quantitative Easing." *Investopedia,* 6 Sept. 2019, www.investopedia.com/terms/q/quantitative-easing.asp. Amadeo, Kimberly. "Explaining Quantitative Easing – QE." *The Balance*, 3 Sept. 2019, www.thebalance.com/what-is-quantitative-easing-definition-and-explanation-3305881.

[986] R. A. "What is quantitative easing?" *The Economist,* 9 Mar. 2015, www.economist.com/the-economist-explains/2015/03/09/what-is-quantitative-easing.

[987] Amadeo, Kimberly. "Explaining Quantitative Easing – QE." *The Balance*, 3 Sept. 2019, www.thebalance.com/what-is-quantitative-easing-definition-and-explanation-3305881.

[988] *Id.*

form of securities previously issued by the U.S. Treasury. The Treasury then pays the Fed what it owes in interest on those securities. In turn, the Fed is required by law to return to the Treasury the profit it makes from the Treasury off of these securities…"[989] "The new money swells the size of bank reserves in the economy by the quantity of assets purchased — hence 'quantitative' easing. That raises stock prices and lowers interest rates, which in turn boosts investment…."[990] Former IMF chief economist, Ken Rogoff, said, "It's absolute smoke and mirrors."[991]

"QE is usually used when interest rates are already near 0 percent…"[992] "When the Great Recession hit [2008], the Fed slashed interest rates to stimulate the economy."[993] "[T]he Fed lowered the fed funds rate to zero. Interest rates were as low as they

---

[989] Schrotenboer, Brent. "US is `printing' money to help save the economy from the COVID-19 crisis, but some wonder how far it can go." *USA Today,* 13 May 2020, www.usatoday.com/in-depth/money/2020/05/12/coronavirushow-u-s-printing-dollars-save-economy-during-crisis-fed/3 0 3 8 1 1 7 0 0 1 / ? fbclid=IwAR1QWoknShih2gZvREvMBumaWN4FU_AIxlfr9j4nuclqnLkr LWWMho7NXSA.

[990] R. A. "What is quantitative easing?" *The Economist,* 9 Mar. 2015, www.economist.com/the-economist-explains/2015/03/09/what-is-quantitative-easing.

[991] Oh, Sunny. "Former IMF chief economist says Fed's bond-buying is 'smoke and mirrors,' doesn't solve U.S. debt problems" *Market Watch,* 20 May 2020, www.marketwatch.com/story/former-imf-chief-economist-says-feds-bond-buying-is-smoke-and-mirrors-doesnt-solve-us-debt-problems-2020-05-20?siteid=yhoof2&yptr=yahoo.

[992] Chappelow, Jim. "Quantitative Easing." *Investopedia,* 6 Sept. 2019, www.investopedia.com/terms/q/quantitative-easing.asp.

[993] Chorpenning, Ashley. "What Is Quantitative Tightening?" *Yahoo Finance,* 13 Nov. 2019, finance.yahoo.com/news/quantitative-tightening-211917762.html.

could be."[994]   However, "it was evident that wasn't nearly enough to stave off crisis."[995]   "[B]anks were reluctant to lend. They had so many bad loans on their books that they wanted to conserve cash to write off the bad debt. They were also hesitant to take on more potentially risky debt."[996]   "So, the Fed provided another jolt of stimulus..."[997]   The Fed "massively expand[ed] its open market operations with the quantitative easing program."[998]   It purchased "Treasury bonds, mortgage-backed securities and other assets in huge volume..."[999]   The Fed engaged in three separate rounds of Quantitative Easing (QE1, QE2, and QE3) in which it

[994] Amadeo, Kimberly. "Reserve Requirement and How It Affects Interest Rates." *The Balance*, 10 Feb. 2019, www.thebalance.com/reserve-requirement-3305883.

[995] Chorpenning, Ashley. "What Is Quantitative Tightening?" *Yahoo Finance*, 13 Nov. 2019, finance.yahoo.com/news/quantitative-tightening-211917762.html.

[996] Amadeo, Kimberly. "Reserve Requirement and How It Affects Interest Rates." *The Balance*, 10 Feb. 2019, www.thebalance.com/reserve-requirement-3305883.

[997] Chorpenning, Ashley. "What Is Quantitative Tightening?" *Yahoo Finance*, 13 Nov. 2019, finance.yahoo.com/news/quantitative-tightening-211917762.html.

[998] Amadeo, Kimberly. "Reserve Requirement and How It Affects Interest Rates." *The Balance*, 10 Feb. 2019, www.thebalance.com/reserve-requirement-3305883.

[999] *Id.* "The Fed also removed some unprofitable mortgage-backed securities from its member banks." Chorpenning, Ashley. "What Is Quantitative Tightening?" *Yahoo Finance*, 13 Nov. 2019, finance.yahoo.com/news/quantitative-tightening-211917762.html.

bought an estimated $4 trillion dollars of bonds and other securities from 2008 to 2014 to prop up the economy.[1000]

"At the November 25, 2008 Federal Open Market Committee meeting, the Fed announced QE1. It would purchase $800 billion in bank debt, U.S. Treasury notes, and mortgage-backed securities from member banks."[1001]   "The FED acquired various forms of Government and even private debt and added it to its books as 'assets.'"[1002]   "The asset side of the Fed's balance sheet grew significantly as it purchased bonds, mortgages, and other assets. The Fed's liabilities, primarily reserves at U.S. banks, grew by the same amount…"[1003]

"The Fed terminated QE1 in March 2010 because the economy was growing again. Just two months later, the economy started to falter, so the Fed renewed the program. It bought $30

[1000] McMahon, Tim. "What is Quantitative Tightening?" *InflationData.com*, inflationdata.com/articles/quantitative-tightening/. Martens, Pam and Russ Martens. "Demand for Fed's Repo Loans Surges Past $100 Billion a Day as 10-Year Treasury Hits Lowest Rate in 149 Years." *Wall Street on Parade*, 5 Mar. 2020, wallstreetonparade.com/2020/03/demand-for-feds-repo-loans-surges-past-100-billion-a-day-as-10-year-treasury-hits-lowest-rate-in-149-years/; Belz, Sage and David Wessel. "Quantitative easing lowered interest rates. Why isn't quantitative tightening lifting them more?" Brookings, 3 Dec. 2018, www.brookings.edu/blog/up-front/2018/12/03/quantitative-easing-lowered-interest-rates-why-isnt-quantitative-tightening-lifting-them-more/; Chappelow, Jim. "Quantitative Easing." *Investopedia,* 6 Sept. 2019, www.investopedia.com/terms/q/quantitative-easing.asp; Amadeo, Kimberly. "Explaining Quantitative Easing – QE." *The Balance*, 3 Sept. 2019, www.thebalance.com/what-is-quantitative-easing-definition-and-explanation-3305881.

[1001] Amadeo, Kimberly. "Explaining Quantitative Easing – QE." *The Balance*, 3 Sept. 2019, www.thebalance.com/what-is-quantitative-easing-definition-and-explanation-3305881.

[1002] McMahon, Tim. "What is Quantitative Tightening?" *InflationData.com*, inflationdata.com/articles/quantitative-tightening/.

[1003] Chappelow, Jim. "Quantitative Easing." *Investopedia,* 6 Sept. 2019, www.investopedia.com/terms/q/quantitative-easing.asp.

billion a month in longer-term Treasurys to keep its holdings at around $2 trillion...On November 3, 2010, the Fed announced it would increase its purchases with QE2. It would buy $600 billion of Treasury securities by the end of the second quarter of 2011."[1004]

"On September 13, 2012, the Fed announced QE3. It agreed to buy $40 billion in MBS [Mortgage Backed Securities] and continue Operation Twist, adding a total $85 billion of liquidity a month. The Fed...[a]nnounced it would keep the fed funds rate at zero until 2015...In December 2012, the Fed announced QE4, effectively ending QE3. It intended to buy a total of $85 billion in long-term Treasurys and MBS..."[1005]

Not surprisingly, "QE exploded the Fed's balance sheet, which is a tally of the bank's liabilities and assets."[1006] "Prior to the crisis, the balance sheet totaled about $925 billion. With all the purchased debt, which the Fed categorized as assets, the balance sheet ballooned to $4.5 trillion by 2017."[1007] These "assets" consisted mainly of U.S. Treasuries and Mortgage Backed Securities.[1008]

Several years after the financial crisis had peaked, "the Fed decided to shrink its balance sheet by shedding some of its accumulated assets, effectively reversing QE. That reversal is quantitative tightening."[1009] "Quantitative Tightening (QT) is a

---

[1004] Amadeo, Kimberly. "Explaining Quantitative Easing – QE." *The Balance*, 3 Sept. 2019, www.thebalance.com/what-is-quantitative-easing-definition-and-explanation-3305881.

[1005] *Id.*

[1006] Chorpenning, Ashley. "What Is Quantitative Tightening?" *Yahoo Finance*, 13 Nov. 2019, finance.yahoo.com/news/quantitative-tightening-211917762.html.

[1007] *Id.*

[1008] McMahon, Tim. "What is Quantitative Tightening?" *InflationData.com*, inflationdata.com/articles/quantitative-tightening/.

[1009] Chorpenning, Ashley. "What Is Quantitative Tightening?" *Yahoo Finance*, 13 Nov. 2019, finance.yahoo.com/news/quantitative-tightening-211917762.html.

contractionary monetary policy, i.e. the opposite of Quantitative Easing (QE)."[1010]   Under QT, interest rates are increased and the money supply in circulation is decreased "by retiring some of the Fed's debt holdings..."[1011]

"QT was the Fed's attempt to reduce its holdings after it bought huge amounts of debt during the 2008 Great Recession..."[1012]   "QE had poured money into the economy, and through quantitative tightening, the Fed planned to take some of that money out again. First it raised interest rates, which had plummeted to zero during the financial crisis. Then, it began retiring some of the debt it held by paying off maturing bonds...The Fed began to 'normalize' its balance sheet by raising interest rates in December 2015, the first hike in nearly a decade."[1013]

In October 2017, the Fed started unwinding its balance sheet.[1014] "In October 2017, it began to reduce its hoard of bonds by as much as $50 billion per month..."[1015]

"Beginning in 2018, the Fed decided that the economy was healthy enough that they could begin retiring some of that debt. Rather than selling their debt on the open market, the Fed decided to simply let the Government Debt it held expire and not issue new debt to replace it. This creates downward pressure on the money

---

[1010] McMahon, Tim. "What is Quantitative Tightening?" *InflationData.com*, inflationdata.com/articles/quantitative-tightening/.

[1011] Chorpenning, Ashley. "What Is Quantitative Tightening?" *Yahoo Finance*, 13 Nov. 2019, finance.yahoo.com/news/quantitative-tightening-211917762.html.

[1012] *Id.*

[1013] *Id.*

[1014] Tilford, Cale. "Repo: How the financial markets' plumbing got blocked." *Financial Times*, 25 Nov. 2019, ig.ft.com/repo-rate/.

[1015] Chorpenning, Ashley. "What Is Quantitative Tightening?" *Yahoo Finance*, 13 Nov. 2019, finance.yahoo.com/news/quantitative-tightening-211917762.html.

supply."[1016] "By March 2019, the cap on reductions reduced from $30 billion a month to $15 billion."[1017]

The Federal Reserve had been "steadily raising interest rates as the U.S. economy picked up steam after years of near-zero rates following the Great Recession of 2007-09."[1018] Former Fed Chair, Janet Yellen, who presided when the balance sheet reduction operation began in October 2017, remarked that the QT process would "run in the background" and be "like watching paint dry."[1019] However, many investors worried "that quantitative tightening would negatively impact markets."[1020] "During the past decade, returns have shown a relatively high correlation with the Fed's purchases."[1021] "[I]f quantitative easing (QE) made the stock market go up, QT will make it go down."[1022] "Stock prices are positively influenced by super low interest rates because it makes their dividend yields, typically two or three percent on blue chip stocks,

[1016] McMahon, Tim. "What is Quantitative Tightening?" *InflationData.com*, inflationdata.com/articles/quantitative-tightening/.

[1017] Chorpenning, Ashley. "What Is Quantitative Tightening?" *Yahoo Finance*, 13 Nov. 2019, finance.yahoo.com/news/quantitative-tightening-211917762.html.

[1018] Davidson, Paul. "Trump wants Fed to cut interest rates to zero or below. Here's what it could mean for you." *USA Today*, 12 Sept. 2019, www.usatoday.com/story/money/2019/09/12/interest-rates-what-zero-negative-rates-would-mean-you/2293676001/.

[1019] Cox, Jeff. "Worries grow over the Fed's efforts to fix funding issues: 'This is all likely to get much worse.'" *CNBC*, 18 Oct. 2019, www.cnbc.com/2019/10/22/fed-repo-worries-continue-over-the-efforts-to-fix-funding-issues.html.

[1020] Chorpenning, Ashley. "What Is Quantitative Tightening?" *Yahoo Finance*, 13 Nov. 2019, finance.yahoo.com/news/quantitative-tightening-211917762.html.

[1021] *Id.*

[1022] Chambers, Clem. "How Quantitative Tightening Affects The Market." *Forbes*, 28 Feb. 2019, www.forbes.com/sites/investor/2019/02/28/how-quantitative-tightening-affects-the-market/#540069a0763c.

more attractive to those seeking income. Conversely, that is why the stock market sells off when the Fed goes on a path of raising interest rates (called 'tightening' in Fed lingo)..."[1023]   Indeed, "the Fed's selloff of assets was a contributing factor to the market dip in late 2018, which left the S&P 500 about 20% below its top price..."[1024]

"Some Fed officials...think the central bank hurt the economy by taking interest rates from barely above zero in 2015 to nearly 2.5 percent by December 2018."[1025]   In what has been dubbed the "Powell Pivot," Fed Chairman, Jerome Powell, admitted on January 4, 2019 that the December 2018 rate hike had been a "miscalculation."[1026]   "December's [2018] near crash suddenly turned around in sync with the Federal Reserve Chairman changing his QT tune from hawkish to dovish..."[1027]   "The Fed lowered the interest rate in July, September and October [2019] in an effort to calm recession fears on Wall Street...The benchmark U.S. interest

---

[1023] Martens, Pam and Russ Martens. "Fed Chair Powell Attempts to Blame U.S. Inequality on Globalization – Gets Smacked Down by Bloomberg Reporter." *Wall Street on Parade,* 11 Jun. 2020, wallstreetonparade.com/2020/06/fed-chair-powell-attempts-to-blame-u-s-inequality-on-globalization-gets-smacked-down-by-bloomberg-reporter/.

[1024] Chorpenning, Ashley. "What Is Quantitative Tightening?" *Yahoo Finance,* 13 Nov. 2019, finance.yahoo.com/news/quantitative-tightening-211917762.html.

[1025] Long, Heather. "2019: The year the Federal Reserve admitted it was wrong." *Washington Post,* 11 Dec. 2019, www.washingtonpost.com/business/2019/12/11/year-federal-reserve-admitted-it-was-wrong/.

[1026] *Id.*

[1027] Chambers, Clem. "How Quantitative Tightening Affects The Market." *Forbes,* 28 Feb. 2019, www.forbes.com/sites/investor/2019/02/28/how-quantitative-tightening-affects-the-market/#540069a0763c.

rate [was] just shy of 1.75 percent, down from nearly 2.5 percent a year [before]…"[1028]

In September 2019, the repo market flashed warning signs regarding the solvency of the financial system.[1029] On September 17, 2019, "the overnight borrowing rate in the repo market went from its typical 2 percent to 10 percent."[1030] "Repos are short-term operations in which financial institutions provide high-quality collateral in exchange for cash reserves they use to operate…"[1031] "Typically, banks, hedge funds and money market funds are the counterparties on these repo loans. The spike to a 10 percent interest rate on a collateralized loan seemed to be signaling that there was a growing worry about one or more of these players defaulting and

---

[1028] Long, Heather. "Federal Reserve predicts no interest rate cuts in 2020, ignoring Trump's calls to boost the economy." *The Washington Post,* 11 Dec. 2019, www.washingtonpost.com/business/2019/12/11/federal-reserve-predicts-no-interest-rate-cuts-ignoring-trumps-calls-boost-economy/?wpisrc=al_news__alert-economy--alert-national&wpmk=1.

[1029] Long, Caitlin. "The Real Story Of The Repo Market Meltdown, And What It Means For Bitcoin." *Forbes,* 25 Sept. 2019, www.forbes.com/sites/caitlinlong/2019/09/25/the-real-story-of-the-repo-market-meltdown-and-what-it-means-for-bitcoin/#23f8ac237caa.

[1030] Martens, Pam and Russ Martens. "The Man Who Advises the New York Fed Says It and Other Central Banks Are 'Fueling a Ponzi Market.'" *Wall Street on Parade,* 22 Jan. 2020, wallstreetonparade.com/2020/01/the-man-who-advises-the-new-york-fed-says-it-and-other-central-banks-are-fueling-a-ponzi-market/.

[1031] Cox, Jeff. "Fed to pump in more than $1 trillion in dramatic ramping up of market intervention amid coronavirus meltdown." *CNBC,* 12 Mar. 2020, www.cnbc.com/2020/03/12/fed-to-pump-more-than-500-billion-into-short-term-bank-funding-expand-types-of-security-purchases.html?__source=iosappshare%7Ccom.apple.UIKit.activity.PostToFacebook&fbcl id=IwAR15uK1dO3bybc49XFX90ozIhLhZTroLUrUDsr_gEnJJ1tQL1voo 1TkiwGA.

lenders were backing away from making the loans."[1032] It appeared that the "banks [did] not want to lend to each other because the risk that they [saw] in the system demand[ed] more than a 1.75% interest rate regardless of how much money they [had] to lend."[1033]

On September 17, 2019, the Federal Reserve intervened in the repo market "for the first time since the financial crisis [2008], injecting billions into the nation's financial system."[1034] "A repo operation is an effort to keep interest rates in the Fed's preferred range."[1035] "[F]rom September 17 through September 24 [2019] – the New York Fed cumulatively plowed $373.9 billion into the

[1032] Martens, Pam and Russ Martens. "The Man Who Advises the New York Fed Says It and Other Central Banks Are 'Fueling a Ponzi Market.'" *Wall Street on Parade*, 22 Jan. 2020, wallstreetonparade.com/2020/01/the-man-who-advises-the-new-york-fed-says-it-and-other-central-banks-are-fueling-a-ponzi-market/.

[1033] At 9:45. Gammon, George. "Repo Market Update: Is The Entire Financial System Broken? (ANSWERED)." *Youtube*, 18 Dec. 2019, www.youtube.com/watch?v=vw6fymmI9B0.

[1034] "Why the repo market went awry…and how the Fed should fix it." *The Economist*, 2 Nov. 2019, www.economist.com/finance-and-economics/2019/11/02/why-the-repo-market-went-awry; Winck, Ben. "The Fed's recent repo crisis was the fault of big banks and hedge funds, new study finds." *Markets Insider*, 9 Dec. 2019, markets.businessinsider.com/news/stocks/fed-repo-crisis-fault-banks-hedge-funds-new-study-finds-2019-12-1028748492.

[1035] Bomey, Nathan. "New York Federal Reserve injects $1.5 trillion into markets amid coronavirus chaos for stocks." *USA Today*, 12 Mar. 2020, www.usatoday.com/story/money/2020/03/12/coronavirus-new-york-federal-reserve-stock-market-liquidity/5032970002/?fbclid=IwAR3fKK3v5WH_miBv3irfIxdseJsUm5jRy5zelLOhEh8Crmy-MgDGCl_DfoM.

trading houses of Wall Street using repo loans."[1036] From September 17, 2019 to the end of January 2020, the New York Fed used repo loans to "funnel a cumulative total of $6.6 trillion to some of the 24 trading houses on Wall Street that are known as its 'primary dealers...'"[1037] Repos work differently from QE.[1038] "Under these repurchase agreements, the Fed offers to buy securities, and if there is not enough demand for cash, or not enough collateral to cover this much cash, then the repo auction will be undersubscribed..."[1039]

[1036] Martens, Pam and Russ Martens. "Fed Repos Have Plowed $6.6 Trillion to Wall Street in Four Months; That's 34% of Its Feeding Tube During Epic Financial Crash." *Wall Street on Parade*. 27 Jan. 2020, wallstreetonparade.com/2020/01/fed-repos-have-plowed-6-6-trillion-to-wall-street-in-four-months-thats-34-of-its-feeding-tube-during-epic-financial-crash/.

[1037] "By the end of January 2020, the Fed's balance and repo market spreadsheets had indicated the central bank injected $6.6 trillion to private institutions..." Martens, Pam and Russ Martens. "Fed Repos Have Plowed $6.6 Trillion to Wall Street in Four Months; That's 34% of Its Feeding Tube During Epic Financial Crash." *Wall Street on Parade*. 27 Jan. 2020, wallstreetonparade.com/2020/01/fed-repos-have-plowed-6-6-trillion-to-wall-street-in-four-months-thats-34-of-its-feeding-tube-during-epic-financial-crash/; Redman, Jamie. "Data Shows the US Economy Was Collapsing 5 Months Before the Coronavirus Outbreak." *Bitcoin.com,* 3 May 2020, news.bitcoin.com/data-shows-the-us-economy-was-collapsing-5-months-before-the-coronavirus-outbreak/?fbclid=IwAR3cgTDBLMYGIYpRAO_pGNc7V-boxoJX-FHsWpJYCoJ3UOxdU6DmCN3hh-Q.

[1038] "So that total amount of cash that will actually get poured into the system may only be a small fraction of the theoretical $4.5 trillion offered over the next four weeks. It may turn out to be just a guarantee by the Fed that there will be enough if there is enough demand for it, and enough collateral to cover it." Richter, Wolf. "As Everything Bubble Implodes, Frazzled Fed Rolls Out Fastest Mega-Money Printer Ever, up to $4.5 Trillion in Four Weeks." *Wolf Street,* 12 Mar. 2020, wolfstreet.com/2020/03/12/frazzled-fed-rolls-out-fastest-mega-money-printer-ever-up-to-4-5-trillion-in-four-weeks/?fbclid=IwAR0E7v8G2QZf2rVqoEUuYYAesDUZLOTEogiq6C2JvYmrjzVLbmeM53FhlQc.

[1039] *Id.*

Some speculate that "[t]he Fed was doing this because a financial institution or institutions were in bad shape and desperate for capital..."[1040] "Repricing risk is...what the free market attempted to do...That's exactly how free markets are supposed to function. They are supposed to accurately price risk. But the New York Fed killed that pricing mechanism by jumping into the market. It is currently offering this repo money at a fictitiously priced 1.55 percent."[1041]

"By October 2019, the Fed announced it would once again start expanding its balance sheet by buying up to $60 billion in Treasury bills a month."[1042] This was done "to build up banks' reserves and increase the amount of cash in the financial system" and "to keep [the Fed's] key interest rate within an intended

---

[1040] "By bad shape I mean 'Lehman Brothers' type failure... The fact that even $1.5 TRILLION in repos didn't fix this issue means it's truly a systemic problem." Phoenix Capital Research. "We Are Now Approaching the 'Lehman' Event...Prepare NOW!" *ZeroHedge.com,* 17 Mar. 2020, www.zerohedge.com/news/2020-03-17/we-are-now-approaching-lehman-event-prepare-now.

[1041] Martens, Pam and Russ Martens. "The Man Who Advises the New York Fed Says It and Other Central Banks Are 'Fueling a Ponzi Market.'" *Wall Street on Parade,* 22 Jan. 2020, wallstreetonparade.com/2020/01/the-man-who-advises-the-new-york-fed-says-it-and-other-central-banks-are-fueling-a-ponzi-market/.

[1042] Chorpenning, Ashley. "What Is Quantitative Tightening?" *Yahoo Finance,* 13 Nov. 2019, finance.yahoo.com/news/quantitative-tightening-211917762.html.

range."[1043]   "[T]he Fed's action effectively stopped quantitative tightening…"[1044]

"[T]he Fed insisted this was not another round of quantitative easing. Some market observers reacted to that announcement with skepticism."[1045]   George Gammon said, "The Fed can't admit that they are doing QE4…because the economy is built on asset prices, debt, and confidence, and that would destroy confidence."[1046]   He believed that, if the Fed announced that they are doing QE4, that would destroy confidence because over the last 10 years, confidence has hinged on the Fed's perceived ability to manage the economy, and part of that management system was quantitative easing.[1047]   If it were to become apparent that QE does not actually work, then the house of cards would collapse.[1048]

Economist Peter Schiff, CEO and chief global strategist of Euro Pacific Capital Inc., correctly predicted that the Fed would continue to lower interest rates, expand its balance sheet, and print

---

[1043] Tilford, Cale. "Repo: How the financial markets' plumbing got blocked." *Financial Times*, 25 Nov. 2019, ig.ft.com/repo-rate/. Winck. Ben. "The Fed has been injecting hundreds of billions into markets since September's rate crisis. Here's why it might not be enough to calm lending conditions." *Market Insider*, 30 Oct. 2019, markets.businessinsider.com/news/stocks/why-fed-repos-capital-injections-might-not-calm-liquidity-fears-2019-10-1028643549#a-bank-government-disconnect2.

[1044] Chorpenning, Ashley. "What Is Quantitative Tightening?" *Yahoo Finance*, 13 Nov. 2019, finance.yahoo.com/news/quantitative-tightening-211917762.html.

[1045] *Id.*

[1046] At 3:30. Gammon, George. "Repo Market: Will Year End Doomsday Trigger DOLLAR COLLAPSE?!?." *Youtube*, 27 Dec. 2019, www.youtube.com/watch?v=7jXN42_GxNQ.

[1047] *Id.*

[1048] At 4. Gammon, George. "Repo Market Update: Is The Entire Financial System Broken? (ANSWERED)." *Youtube*, 18 Dec. 2019, www.youtube.com/watch?v=vw6fymmI9B0.

money in order to prop up the bond market, stock market, and even the government.[1049]

Jerome Powell suggested to lawmakers in December 2019 that low interest rates might be a permanent part of the economic landscape.[1050] "Fed Chairman Jerome Powell said there was essentially no limit to the Fed's emergency lending ability. 'We can continue to make loans, and the point of all that is to support the flow of credit in the economy to households and businesses,' he said. The Fed is only limited by how much backstop it gets from the Treasury Department. 'We're required to get full security for our loans so we don't lose money,' he said."[1051]

"[T]he Fed has cut rates by 150 basis points to near zero and run through its entire 2008 crisis handbook. That wasn't enough to calm markets, though."[1052] Bloomberg Opinion columnist and chief economic adviser at Allianz SE, Mohamed A. El-Erian, said, "Not only did the spike in the repo rate come as a surprise to the New York Fed, but they also haven't been able to normalize it as quickly as they thought they could. It hasn't proven to be temporary. It hasn't proven to be reversible without massive injections of

---

[1049] At 1:20. Schiff, Peter. "Ep. 520: Volcker Dies as Inflation Comes Back to Life." *Youtube*, 11 Dec. 2019, www.youtube.com/watch?v=bJrq2SA8PCw.

[1050] Hamilton, Jesse and Rich Miller. "Fed Warns Prolonged Low Interest Rates Could Spark Instability." *Bloomberg*, 15 Nov. 2019, www.bloomberg.com/news/articles/2019-11-15/fed-warns-prolonged-low-interest-rates-could-spark-instability.

[1051] Robb, Greg. "Fed balance sheet hits record, as Powell says there is no limit to lending power." *Market Watch*, 27 Mar. 2020, www.marketwatch.com/story/fed-balance-sheet-hits-record-as-powell-says-there-is-no-limit-to-lending-power-2020-03-26?reflink=mw_share_facebook&fbclid=IwAR0xKgkn7vsS1QNY3i_ntdw10HBWey-VfdGgoya_avJqEy-xLN6BApHWhcE.

[1052] "At this rate, the Fed will own two-thirds of the Treasury market in a year…" Bianco, Jim. "The Fed's Cure Risks Being Worse Than the Disease." *Yahoo Finance*, 27 Mar. 2020, finance.yahoo.com/news/feds-cure-risks-being-worse-110052807.html.

liquidity. Which means that structural issues are playing a role..."[1053]

As a result of Fed money printing, stocks had climbed to record highs.[1054] However, on March 12, 2020, the markets plunged into turmoil. "As fear swept through markets and fueled unprecedented volatility, liquidity — the ability to trade without causing significant price moves — deteriorated in Treasuries to its worst since the 2008 financial crisis."[1055]

Major central banks (People's Bank of China (PBOC), European Central Bank (ECB), Fed, etc.) had pumped more than $150 billion a month into the economy.[1056] As a result, there was "no lack of monetary stimulus in the economy. Global money supply has soared to $81 trillion, an all-time high..."[1057] Yet, "[t]he Federal Reserve Bank of New York...took steps to inject more than $1.5

[1053] McCormick, Liz. "Repo Blowup Was Fueled by Big Banks and Hedge Funds, BIS Says." *Bloomberg,* 8 Dec. 2019, www.bloomberg.com/news/articles/2019-12-08/repo-blowup-was-fueled-by-big-banks-and-hedge-funds-bis-says.

[1054] Long, Heather. "Federal Reserve predicts no interest rate cuts in 2020, ignoring Trump's calls to boost the economy." *The Washington Post,* 11 Dec. 2019, www.washingtonpost.com/business/2019/12/11/federal-reserve-predicts-no-interest-rate-cuts-ignoring-trumps-calls-boost-economy/?wpisrc=al_news__alert-economy--alert-national&wpmk=1.

[1055] Spratt, Stephen and Liz Capo McCormick. "Fed's New Repo Measures Followed a $100 Billion Treasury Exodus." *Yahoo Finance,* 1 Apr. 2020, finance.yahoo.com/news/over-100-billion-treasuries-dumped-171106252.html.

[1056] Lacalle, Daniel. PhD. "The Fed Panicked, and Its Rate Cut Is Making the Economy Worse." *Mises Institute,* 9 Mar. 2020, mises.org/wire/fed-panicked-and-its-rate-cut-making-economy-worse?fbclid=IwAR31Z6Qs6p8b9dRJ-_YZBaEuHz4Pq0SQoLzOH7W2TJlQ3G4vboe6ViwOuMI#.XmbHfDyEiq4.twitter.

[1057] *Id.*

trillion into the markets in a bid to calm investors…"[1058] "[T]he Fed announced it [was] restarting the crisis-era program of bond purchases known as 'quantitative easing,' in which the central bank buys hundreds of billions of dollars in bonds to further push down rates…"[1059]

In March 2020, the Fed announced a major asset purchase program: The U.S. central bank would buy $500 billion of Treasury notes and $200 billion of mortgage securities.[1060] It would expand its purchases to include Treasury securities of all types and maturities, not just T-Bills.[1061] The New York Fed announced that its $60 billion purchase of Treasury bills (up to a one-year maturity) would be expanded to include "purchases across a range of maturities to roughly match the maturity composition of Treasury

---

[1058] Bomey, Nathan. "New York Federal Reserve injects $1.5 trillion into markets amid coronavirus chaos for stocks." *USA Today*, 12 Mar. 2020, www.usatoday.com/story/money/2020/03/12/coronavirus-new-york-federal-reserve-stock-market-liquidity/5032970002/?fbclid=IwAR3fKK3v5WH_miBv3irfIxdseJsUm5jRy5zelLOhEh8Crmy-MgDGCl_DfoM.

[1059] Long, Heather. "Federal Reserve slashes interest rates to zero as part of wide-ranging emergency intervention." *The Washington Post*, 15 Mar. 2020, www.washingtonpost.com/business/2020/03/15/federal-reserve-slashes-interest-rates-zero-part-wide-ranging-emergency-intervention/?fbclid=IwAR3ArnSj5NO2WPZw9qneawJhTKbW8Xqg3tspxLEkYlfmGJcKl4ZtHtx14FM.

[1060] Bayly, Lucy. "Federal Reserve cuts rates to near zero in emergency action," *NBC News,* 16 Mar. 2020, www.nbcnews.com/business/economy/federal-reserve-cuts-rates-near-zero-emergency-action-n1159691?cid=sm_npd_nn_fb_np&fbclid=IwAR1vJryRucDUBNTzpbUGIUYzex1MRGoIdYVa-f3V0KiwMLkY4XPquv3PBuE.

[1061] Richter, Wolf. "As Everything Bubble Implodes, Frazzled Fed Rolls Out Fastest Mega-Money Printer Ever, up to $4.5 Trillion in Four Weeks." *Wolf Street,* 12 Mar. 2020, wolfstreet.com/2020/03/12/frazzled-fed-rolls-out-fastest-mega-money-printer-ever-up-to-4-5-trillion-in-four-weeks/?fbclid=IwAR0E7v8G2QZf2rVqoEUuYYAesDUZLOTEogiq6C2JvYmrjzVLbmeM53FhlQc.

securities outstanding."[1062]   Up to this point, Treasury purchases "had been confined to short-term T-bills. Under the new regime, the Fed will extend its purchases…to include bills, notes, Treasury Inflation-Protected Securities and…coupon-bearing securities…"[1063] The Fed's Open Market Desk planned to make "purchases across eleven sectors, including nominal coupons, bills, Treasury Inflation-Protected Securities, and Floating Rate Notes."[1064]   The Fed intended to pump at least another $700 billion into the U.S. economy.[1065]

"In total, this would amount to nearly $4.5 trillion through April 13 [2020] that the Fed is offering to create to bail out Wall Street, repo market participants, the asset holders, the banks, and Corporate America. It would more than double the already re-ballooned balance sheet (currently $4.3 trillion). It could push the

---

[1062] Martens, Pam and Russ Martens. "Federal Reserve Announces Unprecedented $1.5 Trillion in Loans to Wall Street Today and Tomorrow." *Wall Street on Parade*, 12 Mar. 2020, wallstreetonparade.com/ 2020/03/federal-reserve-announces-unprecedented-1-5-trillion-in-loans-to-wall-street-today-and-tomorrow. David, Javier E. "Stock market news live: Dow pares losses after Fed announces $500 billion in short-term bank funding." *Yahoo Finance*, 12 Mar. 2020, finance.yahoo.com/news/stock-market-news-live-march-12-013620137.html.

[1063] Cox, Jeff. "Fed to pump in more than $1 trillion in dramatic ramping up of market intervention amid coronavirus meltdown." *CNBC*, 12 Mar. 2020, www.cnbc.com/2020/03/12/fed-to-pump-more-than-500-billion-into-short-term-bank-funding-expand-types-of-security-purchases.html? __source=iosappshare%7Ccom.apple.UIKit.activity.PostToFacebook&fbcl id=IwAR15uK1dO3bybc49XFX90ozIhLhZTroLUrUDsr_gEnJJ1tQL1voo 1TkiwGA.

[1064] Martens, Pam and Russ Martens. "Federal Reserve Announces Unprecedented $1.5 Trillion in Loans to Wall Street Today and Tomorrow." *Wall Street on Parade*, 12 Mar. 2020, wallstreetonparade.com/ 2020/03/federal-reserve-announces-unprecedented-1-5-trillion-in-loans-to-wall-street-today-and-tomorrow.

[1065] Haskins, Justin. "The Fed is pushing America dangerously close to socialism." *Glennbeck.com*, 23 Mar. 2020, www.glennbeck.com/blog/the-fed-is-pushing-america-dangerously-close-to-socialism.

balance sheet to nearly $9 trillion by April 13."[1066] "Such big purchases of securities by the Fed also effectively increase the money supply and drive down interest rates..."[1067] "[T]he Federal Reserve...inflated its balance sheet by 14 percent to almost all-time highs..., completely reversing the virtually nonexistent prior normalization."[1068]

The Federal Reserve also reduced its benchmark interest rate (the rate at which commercial banks lend to each other) to near zero.[1069] "[T]he policy-setting Federal Open Market Committee

---

[1066] Richter, Wolf. "As Everything Bubble Implodes, Frazzled Fed Rolls Out Fastest Mega-Money Printer Ever, up to $4.5 Trillion in Four Weeks." *Wolf Street,* 12 Mar. 2020, wolfstreet.com/2020/03/12/frazzled-fed-rolls-out-fastest-mega-money-printer-ever-up-to-4-5-trillion-in-four-weeks/? fbclid=IwAR0E7v8G2QZf2rVqoEUuYYAesDUZLOTEogiq6C2JvYmrjz VLbmeM53FhlQc.

[1067] Schrotenboer, Brent. "US is `printing' money to help save the economy from the COVID-19 crisis, but some wonder how far it can go." *USA Today,* 13 May 2020, www.usatoday.com/in-depth/money/2020/05/12/ coronavirushow-u-s-printing-dollars-save-economy-during-crisis-fed/ 3 0 3 8 1 1 7 0 0 1 / ? fbclid=IwAR1QWoknShih2gZvREvMBumaWN4FU_AIxlfr9j4nuclqnLkr LWWMho7NXSA.

[1068] Lacalle, Daniel. PhD. "The Fed Panicked, and Its Rate Cut Is Making the Economy Worse." *Mises Institute,* 9 Mar. 2020, mises.org/wire/fed-panicked-and-its-rate-cut-making-economy-worse? fbclid=IwAR31Z6Qs6p8b9dRJ-_YZBaEuHz4Pq0SQoLzOH7W2TJlQ3G4vboe6ViwOuMI#.XmbHfDyEi q4.twitter.

[1069] Torres, Craig and Rich Miller. "Fed Cuts Main Interest Rate to Near Zero, to Boost Assets by $700 Billion." *Bloomberg*, 15 Mar. 2020, www.bloomberg.com/news/articles/2020-03-15/fed-cuts-main-rate-to-near-zero-to-boost-assets-by-700-billion? fbclid=IwAR0w3K1m_1_Hu_grpBM9r9WHlxy31AvzCQO3FQeBXA7-le6bWAmdEMpiFCw. Long, Heather. "Federal Reserve slashes interest rates to zero as part of wide-ranging emergency intervention." *The Washington Post*, 15 Mar. 2020, www.washingtonpost.com/business/ 2020/03/15/federal-reserve-slashes-interest-rates-zero-part-wide-ranging-emergency-intervention/.

announced its first emergency interest rate cut — and its biggest one-time move — since 2008…The swift action lowered interest rates to a range of 1 percent to 1.25 percent…"[1070] "The target for the benchmark federal funds rate was cut to 0–0.25 percent and the discount window (the interest rate at which the Fed loans money… to commercial banks) was slashed to 0.25 percent."[1071] The Fed said it would keep interest rates near zero "until it is confident that the economy has weathered recent events and is on track to achieve its maximum employment and price stability goals."[1072] Apparently, the U.S. economy could not handle anything much above 0% interest rates.

On the day the Fed announced its planned actions [March 12, 2020], "[s]tocks briefly pared their steep losses…But the extremely volatile market activity continued: The Dow Jones industrial average

---

[1070] Smialek, Jeanne. "Bonds Hit Historic Lows, Prompting Fed to Ponder: What More Can We Do?" *The New York Times*, 6 Mar. 2020, web.archive.org/web/20200307035222/https://www.nytimes.com/2020/03/06/business/economy/fed-coronavirus-rate-cut-limited-ammunition.html?fbclid=IwAR3SK_H_SWIXSpNx1zwSJBw9PaIGqhYqinfg3OhbzANEZM_qY1OeWkN1-o4.

[1071] Klein, Peter G. "The Financial System Is Now Totally Dependent on Government Intervention." *Mises Institute,* 16 Mar. 2020, mises.org/power-market/financial-system-now-totally-dependent-government-intervention?fbclid=IwAR3eKYaKZMJqyM91joNY59D1nTY6LqHPhsz4iz1fQS2VowwbR5YGkAlOHPA.

[1072] Torres, Craig and Rich Miller. "Fed Cuts Main Interest Rate to Near Zero, to Boost Assets by $700 Billion." *Bloomberg*, 15 Mar. 2020, www.bloomberg.com/news/articles/2020-03-15/fed-cuts-main-rate-to-near-zero-to-boost-assets-by-700-billion?fbclid=IwAR0w3K1m_1_Hu_grpBM9r9WHlxy31AvzCQO3FQeBXA7-le6bWAmdEMpiFCw.

and S&P 500 index were down" about 7.5%.[1073] This betrayed the fact that central banks have no effective tools with which to increase confidence.[1074] "As Wall Street recognizes the Fed's limited ammunition and the growing risks, investors are increasingly pessimistic…"[1075]

Shortly thereafter, the Federal Reserve decided to buy corporate debt and "exchange-traded funds that track the corporate bond market, a first for the U.S. central bank…"[1076] The Fed "announced it [would] be engaging in outright purchases of

---

[1073] Bomey, Nathan. "New York Federal Reserve injects $1.5 trillion into markets amid coronavirus chaos for stocks." *USA Today*, 12 Mar. 2020, www.usatoday.com/story/money/2020/03/12/coronavirus-new-york-federal-reserve-stock-market-liquidity/5032970002/?fbclid=IwAR3fKK3v5WH_miBv3irfIxdseJsUm5jRy5zelLOhEh8Crmy-MgDGCl_DfoM.

[1074] Lacalle, Daniel. PhD. "The Fed Panicked, and Its Rate Cut Is Making the Economy Worse." *Mises Institute,* 9 Mar. 2020, mises.org/wire/fed-panicked-and-its-rate-cut-making-economy-worse?fbclid=IwAR31Z6Qs6p8b9dRJ-_YZBaEuHz4Pq0SQoLzOH7W2TJlQ3G4vboe6ViwOuMI#.XmbHfDyEiq4.twitter.

[1075] Smialek, Jeanne. "Bonds Hit Historic Lows, Prompting Fed to Ponder: What More Can We Do?" *The New York Times*, 6 Mar. 2020, web.archive.org/web/20200307035222/https://www.nytimes.com/2020/03/06/business/economy/fed-coronavirus-rate-cut-limited-ammunition.html?fbclid=IwAR3SK_H_SWIXSpNx1zwSJBw9PaIGqhYqinfg3OhbzANEZM_qY1OeWkN1-o4.

[1076] "There is a total of $10 trillion of corporate debt in America from bonds to loans." Vardi, Nathan. "The Federal Reserve Moves To Buy Corporate Debt." *Forbes*, 23 Mar. 2020, www.forbes.com/sites/nathanvardi/2020/03/23/the-federal-reserve-moves-to-buy-corporate-debt/?fbclid=IwAR3v93Orsu2lTli0X0TpRNsG_E0fpFwqMsJLT7oUPe5xufkCPuPfIInQtyM#fab35304c47f. Riquier, Andrea. "The Fed is going to buy ETFs. What does it mean?" *Market Watch*, 28 Mar. 2020, www.marketwatch.com/story/the-fed-is-going-to-buy-etfs-what-does-it-mean-2020-03-23?siteid=yhoof2&yptr=yahoo.

corporate bonds in both the primary and secondary markets, exchange traded funds, asset-backed commercial paper along with its ongoing purchases of Treasury securities and agency mortgage-backed securities...”[1077] “Under the program, it plans to make both outright purchases of corporate bonds as well as ETFs invested in the asset class, including potentially some sub-investment grade debt...”[1078]

“‘The Fed will buy IG [investment grade] corp bonds including the $1 trillion of ‘fallen angels' IG bonds that are 1 step from being downgraded to junk bonds,’ tweeted Nouriel Roubini, an economist at New York University...‘Most of such fallen angels are bound 2 junk downgrade. So the Fed takes a reckless credit & [market] risk.’”[1079] “The Fed surprised the market...with the stunning announcement that it was going to start buying up junk bonds from the markets after they had been cratering for most of the month of March [2020]...”[1080] On April 9, 2020, “the Federal Reserve announced that it would allow two of its emergency lending programs to begin buying junk bonds. Those are bonds with less

---

[1077] Martens, Pam and Russ Martens. “The New York Fed, Owned by Multinational Banks, Is Nationalizing Capital Markets.” *Wall Street on Parade*, 9 Apr. 2020, wallstreetonparade.com/2020/04/the-new-york-fed-owned-by-multinational-banks-is-nationalizing-capital-markets/?fbclid=IwAR00mmnOvw5SRN1mRcHQYLxaEihytz1NcYQHvEtGyp63NJn7AJ_Y9zxVtOo.

[1078] Boesler, Matthew. “Fed Has Purchased $1.8 Billion of Corporate-Bond ETFs So Far.” *Yahoo Finance,* 21 May 2020, finance.yahoo.com/news/fed-purchased-1-8-billion-204012560.html.

[1079] Vardi, Nathan. “The Federal Reserve Moves To Buy Corporate Debt.” *Forbes*, 23 Mar. 2020, www.forbes.com/sites/nathanvardi/2020/03/23/the-federal-reserve-moves-to-buy-corporate-debt/?fbclid=IwAR3v93Orsu2lTli0X0TpRNsG_E0fpFwqMsJLT7oUPe5xufkCPuPfIInQtyM#fab35304c47f.

[1080] Martens, Pam and Russ Martens. “Fed Chair Powell Tells Whoppers This Morning on the Brookings Institution Webcast.” *Wall Street on Parade*, 9 Apr. 2020, wallstreetonparade.com/2020/04/fed-chair-powell-tells-whoppers-this-morning-on-the-brookings-institution-webcast/.

than an investment-grade credit rating, meaning they have a greater likelihood of defaulting...A U.S. Treasury note has the unconditional guarantee of the U.S. government to make the timely payment of interest every six months and pay the principal at maturity. Junk bonds are backed by nothing more than deeply-indebted corporations, which can, and do, frequently file for bankruptcy protection, making their bonds sometimes sell for pennies on the dollar...The two Fed programs that will be allowed to buy junk bonds along with investment grade bonds are called the Primary Market Corporate Credit Facility (PMCCF) and the Secondary Market Corporate Credit Facility (SMCCF)..."[1081]

"The Fed's sweeping new loan programs unveiled [April 9, 2020] will provide $2 trillion in additional aid to small, medium and large companies as well as cash-strapped states and cities."[1082] "The Fed plans to start purchasing up to $500 billion in short-term bonds from all 50 states, the District of Columbia and large cities with more than a million people..."[1083]

[1081] Martens, Pam and Russ Martens. "The Fed Is Killing the Two Main Functions of Wall Street: Price Discovery and Prudent Capital Allocation." *Wall Street on Parade*, 11 Apr. 2020, wallstreetonparade.com/2020/04/the-fed-is-killing-the-two-main-functions-of-wall-street-price-discovery-and-prudent-capital-allocation/.

[1082] Long, Heather. "Fed Chair Powell says U.S. economy deteriorating with alarming speed." *The Washington Post*, 9 Apr. 2020, www.msn.com/en-us/news/us/fed-chair-powell-says-us-economy-deteriorating-with-alarming-speed/ar-BB12o0Ak?fbclid=IwAR1Jkd_mpgI3SL_nuwrXPsW3uQ8SRlr2MV5KnzeF6SAeVv6ZIMYUVmWAH1w.

[1083] *Id.*

The Federal Reserve has given a no-bid contract to BlackRock to buy corporate bonds and commercial mortgages.[1084] "[T]he BlackRock-run program will get $75 billion of the $454 billion in taxpayers' money to eat the losses on its corporate bond purchases, which will include its own ETFs, which the Fed is allowing it to buy in the program…"[1085] "The Fed began buying ETFs through its so-called Secondary Market Corporate Credit Facility on May 12 [2020]."[1086] "Federal Reserve purchases of exchanged-traded funds invested in corporate debt totaled $1.8 billion in the first six days of the program…"[1087]

[1084] "Essentially, Blackrock will oversee $27 trillion and is now considered the most powerful business in the U.S…" Redman, Jamie. "Data Shows the US Economy Was Collapsing 5 Months Before the Coronavirus Outbreak." *Bitcoin.com,* 3 May 2020, news.bitcoin.com/data-shows-the-us-economy-was-collapsing-5-months-before-the-coronavirus-outbreak/? fbclid=IwAR3cgTDBLMYGIYpRAO_pGNc7V-boxoJX-FHsWpJYCoJ3UOxdU6DmCN3hh-Q; Martens, Pam and Russ Martens. "BlackRock Authored the Bailout Plan Before There Was a Crisis – Now It's Been Hired by three Central Banks to Implement the Plan." *Wall Street on Parade*, 5 Jun. 2020, wallstreetonparade.com/2020/06/blackrock-authored-the-bailout-plan-before-there-was-a-crisis-now-its-been-hired-by-three-central-banks-to-implement-the-plan/? fbclid=IwAR0GVrMUHztEuheKbZMYB56sZEc2DwIiAQEYSUIy9qSSf uzEqPoHz_u7wqQ.

[1085] Martens, Pam and Russ Martens. "BlackRock Authored the Bailout Plan Before There Was a Crisis – Now It's Been Hired by three Central Banks to Implement the Plan." *Wall Street on Parade*, 5 Jun. 2020, wallstreetonparade.com/2020/06/blackrock-authored-the-bailout-plan-before-there-was-a-crisis-now-its-been-hired-by-three-central-banks-to-implement-the-plan/? fbclid=IwAR0GVrMUHztEuheKbZMYB56sZEc2DwIiAQEYSUIy9qSSf uzEqPoHz_u7wqQ.

[1086] Boesler, Matthew. "Fed Has Purchased $1.8 Billion of Corporate-Bond ETFs So Far." *Yahoo Finance*, 21 May 2020, finance.yahoo.com/news/fed-purchased-1-8-billion-204012560.html.

[1087] *Id.*

"Buying corporate bonds, of course, means the Fed will be taking market risks."[1088]   In addition to assuming risk, adding assets of private companies to its already large balance sheet would give the Fed direct control over the economy.[1089]   "[T]he Federal Reserve has been buying up mortgage bonds worth hundreds of millions of dollars, and according to Mish Shedlock, the Fed now owns nearly a third of that entire market…"[1090] As of May 2020, the Fed had purchased more than $2 trillion of Treasurys and asset backed securities.[1091]

"The Fed has pumped over $1 trillion [in]to the system in recent weeks, with its chair Jerome Powell promising never before seen levels of money printing and so-called quantitative easing to

---

[1088] Vardi, Nathan. "The Federal Reserve Moves To Buy Corporate Debt." *Forbes*, 23 Mar. 2020, www.forbes.com/sites/nathanvardi/2020/03/23/the-federal-reserve-moves-to-buy-corporate-debt/?fbclid=IwAR3v93Orsu2lTli0X0TpRNsG_E0fpFwqMsJLT7oUPe5xufkCPuPflInQtyM#fab35304c47f.

[1089] Haskins, Justin. "The Fed is pushing America dangerously close to socialism." *Glennbeck.com*, 23 Mar. 2020, www.glennbeck.com/blog/the-fed-is-pushing-america-dangerously-close-to-socialism.

[1090] "The Fed has snapped up $1 trillion of mortgage bonds since March. It bought around $300 billion of the bonds in each of March and April, and since then has been buying about $100 billion a month.   The Fed now owns almost a third of bonds backed by home loans in the U.S. Buying the securities has pushed mortgage rates lower, with the average 30-year rate falling to 2.91% as of last week from 3.3% in early February." Durden, Tyler. "If You Feel Like Something Really, Really Bad Is About To Happen, You're Definitely Not Alone." *Zero Hedge*, 11 Sept. 2020, www.zerohedge.com/personal-finance/if-you-feel-something-really-really-bad-about-happen-youre-definitely-not-alone?utm_campaign=&utm_content=ZeroHedge%3A%20The%20Durden%20Dispatch&utm_medium=email&utm_source=zh_newsletter&fbclid=IwAR0GcPMLmadUb8gu1UkFCgGEXlCdoA06CObVf2Mp7jf-WX5aWJIpGjEjd-s.

[1091] Robb, Greg. "The Fed and Congress may need to do more to support economy, Clarida says." *Market Watch*, 21 May 2020, www.marketwatch.com/story/the-fed-and-congress-may-need-to-do-more-to-support-economy-clarida-says-2020-05-21?siteid=yhoof2&yptr=yahoo.

infinity through an unlimited bond-buying program…"[1092]   The Fed announced that it will "buy assets 'in the amounts needed' to support smooth market functioning and effective transmission of monetary policy."[1093]   Neel Kashkari, President of the Federal Reserve Bank of Minneapolis, said, "There's an infinite amount of cash at the Federal Reserve. We will do whatever we need to do to make sure there's enough cash in the banking system."[1094]   "In its monetary policy decision, the Fed…telegraphed that its pace of asset purchases would remain at minimum at the current rate" through 2022.[1095]

As a result of its asset purchases, "[t]he Federal Reserve's balance sheet topped \$5 trillion for the first time amid the U.S. central bank's aggressive efforts to cushion debt markets…through

[1092] Bambrough, Billy. "Donald Trump And The Fed Are Destroying The U.S. Dollar." *Forbes*, 28 Mar. 2020, www.forbes.com/sites/billybambrough/2020/03/28/donald-trump-and-the-fed-are-destroying-the-u s - d o l l a r / ? fbclid=IwAR0FVSZWzVX5vEiMO6JUKf9DUyHAIM9Hbr3mPA2ECTJxMTkz4c80Xz8NRlE#36964d106ebc.

[1093] Robb, Greg. "Fed announces unlimited QE and sets up several new lending programs." *Market Watch*, 23 Mar. 2020, www.marketwatch.com/story/fed-announces-unlimited-qe-and-sets-up-several-new-lending-p r o g r a m s - 2 0 2 0 - 0 3 - 2 3 ? reflink=mw_share_facebook&fbclid=IwAR1ZuxKWVmG2oXcIZ8icAOkTG-w7aMpCqLIcIAK4ifd1EHELVjN6tyCMzxs.

[1094] Said on March 22, 2020. Frost, Liam. "The Federal Reserve is printing \$1 million every second." *Decrypt.com*, 27 Mar. 2020, decrypt.co/23805/the-federal-reserve-is-printing-1-million-every-second?fbclid=IwAR1D2kiJSMK8jcF2S0GprjdcMnVxZx5YKNrDZTNeMo7u6nF0nffvx7-q47Q.

[1095] McCormick, Emily. "Stock market news: Dow plunges 1,861 points, or 7%, for worst day since mid-March." *Yahoo Finance,* 11 Jun. 2020, finance.yahoo.com/news/stock-market-news-live-june-11-2020-222011316.html.

large-scale bond-buying programs."[1096]   "The Federal Reserve's
balance sheet expanded to a record $5.3 trillion in the week ended
March 25 [2020] from $4.7 trillion in the prior week…"[1097]   This
was up drastically from the year before: "On May 29, 2019, the
Federal Reserve's balance sheet stood at $3.9 trillion."[1098]
"Throughout and in the aftermath of the global financial crisis the
Fed grew its balance sheet by a paltry $3.7 trillion…"[1099]   "This
means that on average, the Fed has been printing roughly $970,000
every second during that time period [March 18–25, 2020] in its
efforts to keep the market alive…"[1100]   "As of…May 27, 2020, the
Fed's balance sheet had skyrocketed to $7.145 trillion, an increase

[1096] Boesler, Matthew. "Federal Reserve's Balance Sheet Tops $5 Trillion
for First Time." *Yahoo Finance*, 26 Mar. 2020, finance.yahoo.com/news/
federal-balance-sheet-tops-5-210123506.html.

[1097] Robb, Greg. "Fed balance sheet hits record, as Powell says there is no
limit to lending power." *Market Watch*, 27 Mar. 2020,
www.marketwatch.com/story/fed-balance-sheet-hits-record-as-powell-
says-there-is-no-limit-to-lending-power-2020-03-26?
reflink=mw_share_facebook&fbclid=IwAR0xKgkn7vsS1QNY3i_ntdw10
HBWey-VfdGgoya_avJqEy-xLN6BApHWhcE.

[1098] Martens, Pam and Russ Martens. "U.S. Debt Crisis Comes into View
as Fed's Balance Sheet Explodes Past $7 Trillion." *Wall Street on Parade*,
29 May 2020, wallstreetonparade.com/2020/05/u-s-debt-crisis-comes-into-
view-as-feds-balance-sheet-explodes-past-7-trillion/.

[1099] Bambrough, Billy. "Donald Trump And The Fed Are Destroying The
U.S. Dollar." *Forbes*, 28 Mar. 2020, www.forbes.com/sites/
billybambrough/2020/03/28/donald-trump-and-the-fed-are-destroying-the-
u s - d o l l a r / ?
fbclid=IwAR0FVSZWzVX5vEiMO6JUKf9DUyHAIM9Hbr3mPA2ECTJ
xMTkz4c80Xz8NRlE#36964d106ebc.

[1100] Frost, Liam. "The Federal Reserve is printing $1 million every
second." *Decrypt.com*, 27 Mar. 2020, decrypt.co/23805/the-federal-
reserve-is-printing-1-million-every-second?
fbclid=IwAR1D2kiJSMK8jcF2S0GprjdcMnVxZx5YKNrDZTNeMo7u6n
F0nffvx7-q47Q.

of 83 percent in one year's time..."[1101] "Much of this increase was driven by the Fed's open-ended buying of U.S. government bonds..."[1102] "This...dramatic expansion of the Fed's balance sheet to support Wall Street [has occurred] without one vote, or debate, or hearing occurring in Congress..."[1103]

"The Fed's balance sheet is expected to continue to expand as the central bank steps in to try to keep credit flowing in all corners of the financial market, including Treasurys, commercial paper and municipal bonds...."[1104] Wall Street veteran and founder of Wyoming-based crypto bank Avanti, Caitlin Long, "expects the U.S.

[1101] Martens, Pam and Russ Martens. "U.S. Debt Crisis Comes into View as Fed's Balance Sheet Explodes Past $7 Trillion." *Wall Street on Parade*, 29 May 2020, wallstreetonparade.com/2020/05/u-s-debt-crisis-comes-into-view-as-feds-balance-sheet-explodes-past-7-trillion/.

[1102] Robb, Greg. "Fed balance sheet hits record, as Powell says there is no limit to lending power." *Market Watch*, 27 Mar. 2020, www.marketwatch.com/story/fed-balance-sheet-hits-record-as-powell-says-there-is-no-limit-to-lending-power-2020-03-26?reflink=mw_share_facebook&fbclid=IwAR0xKgkn7vsS1QNY3i_ntdw10HBWey-VfdGgoya_avJqEy-xLN6BApHWhcE.

[1103] Martens, Pam and Russ Martens. "Federal Reserve Announces Unprecedented $1.5 Trillion in Loans to Wall Street Today and Tomorrow." *Wall Street on Parade*, 12 Mar. 2020, wallstreetonparade.com/2020/03/federal-reserve-announces-unprecedented-1-5-trillion-in-loans-to-wall-street-today-and-tomorrow/.

[1104] Robb, Greg. "Fed balance sheet hits record, as Powell says there is no limit to lending power." *Market Watch*, 27 Mar. 2020, www.marketwatch.com/story/fed-balance-sheet-hits-record-as-powell-says-there-is-no-limit-to-lending-power-2020-03-26?reflink=mw_share_facebook&fbclid=IwAR0xKgkn7vsS1QNY3i_ntdw10HBWey-VfdGgoya_avJqEy-xLN6BApHWhcE.

Federal Reserve's balance sheet to top $10 trillion before the coronavirus crisis is over..."[1105]

"For the first time in the history of the Federal Reserve, it has signed on to a plan with Congress to nationalize the unmanageable debts of global banks and other multinational corporations and put the U.S. taxpayer on the hook for the losses..."[1106] "[T]he nationalization of bad debts will work like this: the U.S. Treasury will hand $454 billion of taxpayers' money to the Federal Reserve. The Fed will, in turn, hand the bulk of this money to the New York Fed. The New York Fed will then create Special Purpose Vehicles (SPVs) using the $454 billion as loss absorbing capital (equity) to leverage its purchases of bad debts to $4.54 trillion...according to the text of the stimulus bill, the Treasury is simply the provider of the taxpayer cash to the Fed...This is exactly what happened during the last financial crisis: the New York Fed was put in charge of the bailout programs and then farmed them out to multinational banks like Goldman Sachs and JPMorgan Chase – who are among the largest share owners of the New York Fed..."[1107]

"[T]he U.S. Congress handed over $454 billion of taxpayers' money to the Fed, without any meaningful debate, to eat losses on

---

[1105] Bambrough, Billy. "Donald Trump And The Fed Are Destroying The U.S. Dollar." *Forbes*, 28 Mar. 2020, www.forbes.com/sites/billybambrough/2020/03/28/donald-trump-and-the-fed-are-destroying-the-u s - d o l l a r / ? fbclid=IwAR0FVSZWzVX5vEiMO6JUKf9DUyHAIM9Hbr3mPA2ECTJxMTkz4c80Xz8NRlE#36964d106ebc.

[1106] Martens, Pam and Russ Martens. "The New York Fed, Owned by Multinational Banks, Is Nationalizing Capital Markets." *Wall Street on Parade*, 9 Apr. 2020, wallstreetonparade.com/2020/04/the-new-york-fed-owned-by-multinational-banks-is-nationalizing-capital-markets/?fbclid=IwAR00mmnOvw5SRN1mRcHQYLxaEihytz1NcYQHvEtGyp63NJn7AJ_Y9zxVtOo.

[1107] "(Before the last financial crisis, U.S. national debt stood at $11 trillion. It has more than doubled in a dozen years to the current $24 trillion. Much of that growth resulted from fiscal stimulus measures to shore up the U.S. economy that multinational banks on Wall Street destroyed in 2008.)" *Id.*

toxic assets produced by the Wall Street banks it supervises. The Fed plans to leverage the $454 billion into a $4.54 trillion bailout plan, 'going direct' with bailouts to the commercial paper market, money market funds, and a host of other markets."[1108]   "[T]he Fed is allowing Wall Street's fat cats to privatize profits and socialize losses. This can also be expressed as an institutionalized wealth transfer scheme to the 1 percent…The losses in the SPVs [Special Purpose Vehicles] will be borne by the U.S. taxpayer – up to a total of $454 billion thus far. That's the amount that the current stimulus bill (CARES Act) allocated to these SPVs…"[1109]

"Before January of 2009, the Federal Reserve had never before purchased Mortgage-Backed Securities. Before September 14, 2008, the Fed had never in its history made loans against stocks as collateral. Before May 12, 2020, the Federal Reserve had never before purchased corporate bonds or junk bonds. Today, the Fed is doing all of these things and numerous aspects of what it is doing are likely illegal under its statutory legislation known as the Federal

---

[1108] Martens, Pam and Russ Martens. "BlackRock Authored the Bailout Plan Before There Was a Crisis – Now It's Been Hired by three Central Banks to Implement the Plan." *Wall Street on Parade*, 5 Jun. 2020, wallstreetonparade.com/2020/06/blackrock-authored-the-bailout-plan-before-there-was-a-crisis-now-its-been-hired-by-three-central-banks-to-i m p l e m e n t - t h e - p l a n / ? fbclid=IwAR0GVrMUHztEuheKbZMYB56sZEc2DwIiAQEYSUIy9qSSf uzEqPoHz_u7wqQ.

[1109] Martens, Pam and Russ Martens. "The Fed Is Killing the Two Main Functions of Wall Street: Price Discovery and Prudent Capital Allocation." *Wall Street on Parade*, 11 Apr. 2020, wallstreetonparade.com/2020/04/the-fed-is-killing-the-two-main-functions-of-wall-street-price-discovery-and-prudent-capital-allocation/.

Reserve Act."[1110] "Such a policy," the president of the Federal Reserve Bank of Boston, Eric Rosengren, noted, "would require a change in the Federal Reserve Act."[1111] "[T]he Fed is legally limited to government-backed debt, like mortgage-backed securities and Treasury notes. Buying other asset classes would require opening legislation that empowers the Fed, as Mr. Rosengren noted…"[1112]

Following suit with the Fed's quantitative easing policies, "[t]he central banks of Poland, Colombia, the Philippines and South Africa have all begun to buy government and private sector bonds on secondary markets, while the central banks of Brazil and the Czech Republic have asked for new laws to allow them to do so."[1113]

The European Central Bank (ECB) also "agreed to pump more liquidity into the financial system and joined other central

---

[1110] The Fed is "making trillions of dollars in revolving loans to multinational trading houses against collateral that includes stocks…" Martens, Pam and Russ Martens. "U.S. Debt Crisis Comes into View as Fed's Balance Sheet Explodes Past $7 Trillion." *Wall Street on Parade*, 29 May 2020, wallstreetonparade.com/2020/05/u-s-debt-crisis-comes-into-view-as-feds-balance-sheet-explodes-past-7-trillion/; Martens, Pam and Russ Martens. "The New York Fed, Owned by Multinational Banks, Is Nationalizing Capital Markets." *Wall Street on Parade*, 9 Apr. 2020, wallstreetonparade.com/2020/04/the-new-york-fed-owned-by-multinational-banks-is-nationalizing-capital-markets/?fbclid=IwAR00mmnOvw5SRN1mRcHQYLxaEihytz1NcYQHvEtGyp63NJn7AJ_Y9zxVtOo.

[1111] Smialek, Jeanne. "Bonds Hit Historic Lows, Prompting Fed to Ponder: What More Can We Do?" *The New York Times*, 6 Mar. 2020, web.archive.org/web/20200307035222/https://www.nytimes.com/2020/03/06/business/economy/fed-coronavirus-rate-cut-limited-ammunition.html?fbclid=IwAR3SK_H_SWIXSpNx1zwSJBw9PaIGqhYqinfg3OhbzANEZM_qY1OeWkN1-o4.

[1112] *Id.*

[1113] Wheatley, Jonathan. "Emerging market central banks embark on radical stimulus policies." *Yahoo Finance*, 29 Mar. 2020, finance.yahoo.com/m/0475597d-5a09-3b22-b535-b561236876fc/emerging-market-central-banks.html.

banks in a bid to ease a funding squeeze."[1114] "[T]he European Central Bank launched a 750 billion euro ($820 billion) debt-buying program to keep borrowing costs in check as countries prepare to increase spending to counter the impact of the coronavirus…"[1115] "The measures include buying public and private-sector securities until at least the end of 2020."[1116] Taking a page out of the Federal Reserve's book, it will also buy commercial-paper.[1117] "The program brings the total of the ECB's planned bond purchases this year to 1.1 trillion euros, its biggest annual amount ever…"[1118] "The decision to consider raising the limits on QE holdings could be controversial. The caps, set at the start of the program in 2015, are meant to address concerns the central bank would breach European Union law by financing governments."[1119]

"Critics of the historic stimulus measures have warned about the possibility of inflation.."[1120] Dr. Judy Shelton, President Trumps' nominee to the Federal Reserve in 2020, has criticized

---

[1114] Randow, Jana. "Europe Bonds Soar as Lagarde Pledges No Limits to ECB Action." *Bloomberg*, 18 Mar. 2020, www.bloomberg.com/news/articles/2020-03-18/ecb-announces-750-billion-euro-pandemic-bond-buying-program?cmpid=socialflow-facebook-business&utm_campaign=socialflow-organic&utm_source=facebook&utm_content=business&utm_medium=social&fbclid=IwAR2CYk9i5qj7xuvo0p7ROUw5k8HroHCHGhXrW2JVMQaYWf9CQ-GuBHMfzfc.

[1115] *Id.*

[1116] *Id.*

[1117] *Id.*

[1118] *Id.*

[1119] *Id.*

[1120] Bambrough, Billy. "Donald Trump And The Fed Are Destroying The U.S. Dollar." *Forbes*, 28 Mar. 2020, www.forbes.com/sites/billybambrough/2020/03/28/donald-trump-and-the-fed-are-destroying-the-u-s-dollar/?fbclid=IwAR0FVSZWzVX5vEiMO6JUKf9DUyHAIM9Hbr3mPA2ECTJxMTkz4c80Xz8NRlE#36964d106ebc.

"'Quantitative Easing,' which is basically a term designed to conceal the fact that the central bank is creating debt-backed currency out of thin air and then using it to buy U.S. Treasury bonds that taxpayers will have to repay with taxes…"[1121] She also "slammed the ultra-low interest rates supposedly designed to 'stimulate' the economy back to prosperity."[1122] "The error of taking extreme monetary measures in an epidemic is to assume that the problem of the economy is an excess of unjustified savings and a lack of demand that must be created artificially via interventionism."[1123]

"[L]ower rates are likely to generate two dangerous side effects: a disproportionate increase in refinancing of already nonperforming loans and a credit crunch in the profitable economy. Banks will be forced to refinance and keep bad existing loans as well as finance governments at ultralow rates while seeing no alternative but to cut loans to new customers and small enterprises…"[1124] "At the same time as the bank loans out money at very low interest rates, it also pays lower interest rates on any money that is deposited."[1125] Lower interest "means savers get less

---

[1121] Newman, Alex. "Trump Nominates Gold Advocate to Federal Reserve." *New American*, 7 Feb. 2020, www.thenewamerican.com/usnews/politics/item/34831-trump-nominates-gold-advocate-to-federal-reserve?fbclid=IwAR3wJ8NEBE-t0FNu6_UqzJ0bg2HrFwliT-0vFNfDJPC8MjiPxXQx83ON9Zs.

[1122] *Id.*

[1123] Lacalle, Daniel. PhD. "The Fed Panicked, and Its Rate Cut Is Making the Economy Worse." *Mises Institute,* 9 Mar. 2020, mises.org/wire/fed-panicked-and-its-rate-cut-making-economy-worse?fbclid=IwAR31Z6Qs6p8b9dRJ-_YZBaEuHz4Pq0SQoLzOH7W2JlQ3G4vboe6ViwOuMI#.XmbHfDyEiq4.twitter.

[1124] *Id.*

[1125] Joanne Im, a high school student from New Jersey, was a champ on her school's economics team. "9 Insights About Negative Interest Rates." *Knowledge@Wharton High School,* kwhs.wharton.upenn.edu/2019/09/9-insights-negative-interest-rates.

in monthly interest on the money they keep in savings accounts at banks. Many retirees have complained the Fed is hurting them by keeping rates down…"[1126]   "This decade of unprecedentedly low interest rates deprived savers (people who cannot afford the risk of the stock market) of the 4 and 5 percent interest they had been able to earn on safe instruments like Treasury notes and federally-insured Certificates of Deposit before the financial crisis. Millions of Americans had to start depleting savings in order to make ends meet…"[1127]

"In its monetary policy decision, the Fed projected interest rates would remain near zero through 2022…"[1128]   "Chairman Jerome Powell said the central bank wasn't even 'thinking about thinking about' raising interest rates."[1129]   As a result, people are forced to look for yield elsewhere, such as on the stock market.

[1126] Long, Heather. "Federal Reserve predicts no interest rate cuts in 2020, ignoring Trump's calls to boost the economy." *The Washington Post,* 11 Dec. 2019, www.washingtonpost.com/business/2019/12/11/federal-reserve-predicts-no-interest-rate-cuts-ignoring-trumps-calls-boost-economy/?wpisrc=al_news__alert-economy--alert-national&wpmk=1.

[1127] Martens, Pam and Russ Martens. "Fed Chair Powell Attempts to Blame U.S. Inequality on Globalization – Gets Smacked Down by Bloomberg Reporter." *Wall Street on Parade,* 11 Jun. 2020, wallstreetonparade.com/2020/06/fed-chair-powell-attempts-to-blame-u-s-inequality-on-globalization-gets-smacked-down-by-bloomberg-reporter/.

[1128] McCormick, Emily. "Stock market news: Dow plunges 1,861 points, or 7%, for worst day since mid-March." *Yahoo Finance,* 11 Jun. 2020, finance.yahoo.com/news/stock-market-news-live-june-11-2020-222011316.html.

[1129] Goldstein, Steve. "Swift market reaction to Fed may be more about what it didn't do than what it did, analysts say." *Market Watch,* 11 Jun. 2020, www.marketwatch.com/story/swift-market-reaction-to-fed-may-be-more-about-what-it-didnt-do-than-what-it-did-analysts-say-2020-06-11?siteid=yhoof2&yptr=yahoo.

QE has created several asset bubbles, including in stocks.[1130] "[S]ince the stock market has set repeated new highs since the program launched, some veteran market watchers believe the Fed is fueling a Ponzi-like rally in stocks..."[1131] The Fed used market repurchase agreements (repos) and Treasury bill purchases to pump "billions of dollars of emergency funding into the financial system..." and money markets.[1132] The financial institutions take that money and invest it in the stock market, which drives prices up higher and expands the asset bubble.[1133] "The way QE has worked to push up stock market assets is that banks get lent money on the cheap and they then stuff that money into assets like stocks that will bring them a higher return than the borrowing charge."[1134] As a

---

[1130] Amadeo, Kimberly. "Explaining Quantitative Easing – QE." *The Balance*, 3 Sept. 2019, www.thebalance.com/what-is-quantitative-easing-definition-and-explanation-3305881.

[1131] Martens, Pam and Russ Martens. "Fed Repos Have Plowed $6.6 Trillion to Wall Street in Four Months; That's 34% of Its Feeding Tube During Epic Financial Crash." *Wall Street on Parade*. 27 Jan. 2020, wallstreetonparade.com/2020/01/fed-repos-have-plowed-6-6-trillion-to-wall-street-in-four-months-thats-34-of-its-feeding-tube-during-epic-financial-crash/.

[1132] Ashworth, Marcus. "What Is Really to Blame for the Repo Market Blowup." *The Washington Post*, 9 Dec. 2019, www.washingtonpost.com/business/what-is-really-to-blame-for-the-repo-market-blowup/2019/12/09/38d68258-1a83-11ea-977a-15a6710ed6da_story.html; Winck. Ben. "The Fed has been injecting hundreds of billions into markets since September's rate crisis. Here's why it might not be enough to calm lending conditions." *Market Insider*, 30 Oct. 2019, markets.businessinsider.com/news/stocks/why-fed-repos-capital-injections-might-not-calm-liquidity-fears-2019-10-1028643549#a-bank-government-disconnect2.

[1133] At 8. Gammon, George. "Asset Bubbles Explained: Simple And Fast! (COLLABORATION VIDEO)." *Youtube*, 13 Dec. 2019, www.youtube.com/watch?v=eyz7SeSIbqc.

[1134] Chambers, Clem. "How Quantitative Tightening Affects The Market." *Forbes*, 28 Feb. 2019, www.forbes.com/sites/investor/2019/02/28/how-quantitative-tightening-affects-the-market/#540069a0763c.

result of those injections, the stock market was driven to all time highs.

The Fed will only allow the stock market to go down a certain amount before injecting new liquidity (called "the Fed put").[1135] (At least, "The Bank of England admits that the reason they are doing QE is to boost asset prices..."[1136]) "Stocks are a great place to stuff free money, especially if you can hedge the trade and lock in a profit."[1137] Consequently, companies would rather put excess money into the stock market (or real estate or corporate bond market) to earn a risk-reduced return rather than invest in productivity.[1138] This results in less productivity, less income, less spending, and an asset bubble.[1139]

In sum, "The Fed spent a decade laying plans to 'normalize' monetary policy after the 2007-2009 crisis. For a brief time it even raised interest rates and shed some of the trillions of dollars in bonds it had bought to support the economy. Interest rates are back to zero, and the Fed has restarted bond buying. The central bank's asset holdings topped a record $5 trillion [as of March 28, 2020], and could be on pace to even double that, perhaps hitting a level

---

[1135] Gammon, George. "Quantitative Easing Exposed: Discover How It DESTROYS A SOCIETY!" *Youtube*, 9 Dec. 2019, www.youtube.com/watch?v=d-ifzjfGTkM.

[1136] At 3:50. Gammon, George. "Quantitative Easing: Will It Cause Hyperinflation? (ANSWER REVEALED)." *Youtube*, 19 Dec. 2019, www.youtube.com/watch?v=b7KafSma3xQ.

[1137] Chambers, Clem. "How Quantitative Tightening Affects The Market." *Forbes*, 28 Feb. 2019, www.forbes.com/sites/investor/2019/02/28/how-quantitative-tightening-affects-the-market/#540069a0763c.

[1138] Gammon, George. "Quantitative Easing: Will It Cause Hyperinflation? (ANSWER REVEALED)." *Youtube*, 19 Dec. 2019, www.youtube.com/watch?v=b7KafSma3xQ.

[1139] *Id.*

equivalent to 50% of GDP or more."[1140]   "The Fed increased its balance sheet by $2.8 trillion, or 60%, just since February of [2020] …"[1141] "Introducing trillions of new dollars into the economy can… create inflation, devaluing dollars and encouraging consumers to spend as quickly as possible, rather than save, introducing lots of additional economic distortions…"[1142]   "It is hard to envision a scenario in which such a large supply dump of dollars does not lead to inflation…"[1143]

The dollar has weakened across the board as a result of the Fed's policies.[1144]   "When the Fed introduces trillions of new dollars into an economy to spur demand, rather than as a reaction to market forces, it devalues everyone's currency, discouraging people

---

[1140] Schneider, Howard. "As virus threatens, U.S. embraces big government, for now." *MSN*, 28 Mar. 2020, www.msn.com/en-us/news/ politics/as-virus-threatens-us-embraces-big-government-for-now/ar-BB11PDTL?ocid=sf2.

[1141] Shimron, Leeor. "Fed Chairman Powell 60 Minutes Interview Highlights Bitcoin's Value Proposition." *Forbes,* 18 May 2020, www.forbes.com/sites/leeorshimron/2020/05/18/fed-chairman-powell-60-minutes-interview-highlights-bitcoins-value-proposition/? fbclid=IwAR2JqJiGeYtrtZjiBz1_g0h1b3f0KEB2DIN1-U-kjFY5k0uxfdQvfkzBxsY#5938e6db4cdb.

[1142] Haskins, Justin. "The Fed is pushing America dangerously close to socialism." *Glennbeck.com*, 23 Mar. 2020, www.glennbeck.com/blog/the-fed-is-pushing-america-dangerously-close-to-socialism.

[1143] Shimron, Leeor. "Fed Chairman Powell 60 Minutes Interview Highlights Bitcoin's Value Proposition." *Forbes,* 18 May 2020, www.forbes.com/sites/leeorshimron/2020/05/18/fed-chairman-powell-60-minutes-interview-highlights-bitcoins-value-proposition/? fbclid=IwAR2JqJiGeYtrtZjiBz1_g0h1b3f0KEB2DIN1-U-kjFY5k0uxfdQvfkzBxsY#5938e6db4cdb.

[1144] Torres, Craig and Rich Miller. "Fed Cuts Main Interest Rate to Near Zero, to Boost Assets by $700 Billion." *Bloomberg*, 15 Mar. 2020, www.bloomberg.com/news/articles/2020-03-15/fed-cuts-main-rate-to-near-zero-to-boost-assets-by-700-billion? fbclid=IwAR0w3K1m_1_Hu_grpBM9r9WHlxy31AvzCQO3FQeBXA7-le6bWAmdEMpiFCw.

from saving."[1145]   As the markets tanked in the spring of 2020, "the greenback surged as investors sought refuge in the world's primary reserve currency..."[1146]   "'In short-term, [there was] huge dollar demand because [of] short-covering, but it won't last,' Wall Street veteran and founder of Wyoming-based crypto bank Avanti, Caitlin Long, said...predicting the dollar's eventual crash..."[1147]

The central bankers "are going to continue to engage in exceedingly reckless manipulation of the markets, and that is going to have very serious long-term implications."[1148]   Ron "Paul, the former Texas congressman and author of *End the Fed*, anticipates that such money creation will lead to disaster. He says it will cause overheated financial bubbles fueled by too much easy money in the system – a bubble that could burst with painful fallout.

[1145] Haskins, Justin. "The Fed is pushing America dangerously close to socialism." *Glennbeck.com*, 23 Mar. 2020, www.glennbeck.com/blog/the-fed-is-pushing-america-dangerously-close-to-socialism.

[1146] Spratt, Stephen and Liz Capo McCormick. "Fed's New Repo Measures Followed a $100 Billion Treasury Exodus." *Yahoo Finance*, 1 Apr. 2020, finance.yahoo.com/news/over-100-billion-treasuries-dumped-171106252.html.

[1147] Bambrough, Billy. "Donald Trump And The Fed Are Destroying The U.S. Dollar." *Forbes*, 28 Mar. 2020, www.forbes.com/sites/billybambrough/2020/03/28/donald-trump-and-the-fed-are-destroying-the-u s - d o l l a r / ? fbclid=IwAR0FVSZWzVX5vEiMO6JUKf9DUyHAIM9Hbr3mPA2ECTJxMTkz4c80Xz8NRlE#36964d106ebc.

[1148] Durden, Tyler. "If You Feel Like Something Really, Really Bad Is About To Happen, You're Definitely Not Alone." *Zero Hedge*, 11 Sept. 2020, www.zerohedge.com/personal-finance/if-you-feel-something-really-really-bad-about-happen-youre-definitely-not-alone? utm_campaign=&utm_content=ZeroHedge%3A%20The%20Durden%20Dispatch&utm_medium=email&utm_source=zh_newsletter&fbclid=IwAR0GcPMLmadUb8gulUkFCgGEX1CdoA06CObVf2Mp7jf-WX5aWJlpGjEjd-s.

Creating too much money that chases too few goods also leads to price inflation, decreasing the purchasing power of the dollar…"[1149]

"Potential risks of the combined cross-party rescue bill and Fed's biggest-ever bazooka include out-of-control inflation, the dollar's displacement as the world's funding currency, and the complete destabilization of the U.S. financial system."[1150]

To make matters worse, the Fed is threatening to embark on a negative rate interest policy, which is the topic of the next section.

[1149] Schrotenboer, Brent. "US is `printing' money to help save the economy from the COVID-19 crisis, but some wonder how far it can go." *USA Today,* 13 May 2020, www.usatoday.com/in-depth/money/2020/05/12/coronavirushow-u-s-printing-dollars-save-economy-during-crisis-fed/3038117001/?fbclid=IwAR1QWoknShih2gZvREvMBumaWN4FU_AIxlfr9j4nuclqnLkr LWWMho7NXSA.

[1150] Bambrough, Billy. "Donald Trump And The Fed Are Destroying The U.S. Dollar." *Forbes*, 28 Mar. 2020, www.forbes.com/sites/billybambrough/2020/03/28/donald-trump-and-the-fed-are-destroying-the-us-dollar/?fbclid=IwAR0FVSZWzVX5vEiMO6JUKf9DUyHAIM9Hbr3mPA2ECTJ xMTkz4c80Xz8NRlE#36964d106ebc.

How Low Can the Fed Go?

During the 2008 global financial crisis, central banks reduced interest rates. Now, "[t]here's growing talk of pushing rates…below zero."[1151] "A negative interest rate policy (NIRP) is an unusual monetary policy tool in which nominal target interest rates are set with a negative value, below…zero percent."[1152] Negative interest rates are "seen as an experimental measure after traditional policy options proved ineffective in reviving economies damaged by the 2008 financial crisis and recession…"[1153] Negative interest rates indicate a desperate attempt to boost economic growth through financial manipulation.[1154]

"Negative interest rate policy, or NIRP, is the most recently deployed weapon of central bankers in their long campaign of financial repression — a deliberate policy of depressing interest rates in order to transfer wealth from savers (private citizens) to debtors (largely governments)."[1155] "Negative rates work by effectively paying borrowers to take out loans and requiring people and businesses that deposit money to pay a fee rather than earn

[1151] Davidson, Paul. "Trump wants Fed to cut interest rates to zero or below. Here's what it could mean for you." *USA Today*, 12 Sept. 2019, www.usatoday.com/story/money/2019/09/12/interest-rates-what-zero-negative-rates-would-mean-you/2293676001/.

[1152] "Negative Interest Rate Definition." *Investopedia*, 17 Aug. 2019, www.investopedia.com/terms/n/negative-interest-rate.asp.

[1153] Randow, Jana and Yuko Takeo. "Negative Interest Rates." *Bloomberg*, 1 Nov. 2019, www.bloomberg.com/quicktake/negative-interest-rates.

[1154] "Negative Interest Rate Definition." *Investopedia*, 17 Aug. 2019, www.investopedia.com/terms/n/negative-interest-rate.asp.

[1155] Brightman, Chris. "Negative Rates Are Dangerous to Your Wealth." *Research Affiliates*, Apr. 2016, www.researchaffiliates.com/en_us/publications/articles/542_negative_rates_are_dangerous_to_your_wealth.html.

interest..."[1156] "Instead of receiving money on deposits in the form of interest, depositors must pay regularly to keep their money with the bank..."[1157]

"An example of a negative interest rate policy would be to set the key rate at -0.2 percent, such that bank depositors would have to pay two-tenths of a percent on their deposits instead of receiving any sort of positive interest."[1158] As a result of NIRP, "some banking customers in European markets where lending rates are negative are actually paying interest to their banks!"[1159]

In a negative interest rate environment, "banks and other financial firms would have to pay to keep their excess reserves stored at the central bank rather than receive positive interest income..."[1160] Charging negative interest is intended to goad "banks to lend money more freely and businesses and individuals to invest, lend, and spend money rather than pay a fee to

---

[1156] Long, Heather. "Federal Reserve slashes interest rates to zero as part of wide-ranging emergency intervention." *The Washington Post*, 15 Mar. 2020, www.washingtonpost.com/business/2020/03/15/federal-reserve-slashes-interest-rates-zero-part-wide-ranging-emergency-intervention/?fbclid=IwAR3ArnSj5NO2WPZw9qneawJhTKbW8Xqg3tspxLEkYlfmGJcKl4ZtHtx14FM.

[1157] "Negative Interest Rate Definition." *Investopedia*, 17 Aug. 2019, www.investopedia.com/terms/n/negative-interest-rate.asp.

[1158] Hayes, Adam. "Negative Interest Rate Policy (NIRP) Definition." *Investopedia*, 7 May 2019, www.investopedia.com/terms/n/negative-interest-rate-policy-nirp.asp.

[1159] Williams, Sean. "3 Dangers of a Negative Interest Rate Policy." *The Motley Fool*, 20 Feb. 2016, www.fool.com/investing/general/2016/02/20/3-dangers-of-a-negative-interest-rate-policy.aspx.

[1160] "Negative Interest Rate Definition." *Investopedia*, 17 Aug. 2019, www.investopedia.com/terms/n/negative-interest-rate.asp.

keep it in a bank account.[1161] The goal is to encourage lending, spur inflation, reinvigorate economic growth, and ward off deflation.[1162] The theory is that NIRP will "encourage consumers and businesses to spend rather than save their money. Presumably, a bank would rather lend, even at a low interest rate, than pay to keep its money at a central bank…"[1163] "Negative rates punish banks that are playing it safe by hoarding cash."[1164]

Banks would pass those interest costs and loss of income on to customers by charging for deposits.[1165] Cash deposited at a bank incurs "a storage charge, rather than the opportunity to earn interest income…"[1166] JPMorgan Chase CEO, Jamie Dimon, said bank

---

[1161] Hayes, Adam. "Negative Interest Rate Policy (NIRP) Definition." *Investopedia*, 7 May 2019, www.investopedia.com/terms/n/negative-interest-rate-policy-nirp.asp; Kuepper, Justin. "What Negative Interest Rates Mean for Investors." *The Balance,* 30 Nov. 2019, www.thebalance.com/what-negative-interest-rates-mean-for-investors-1978886.

[1162] Kuepper, Justin. "What Negative Interest Rates Mean for Investors." *The Balance,* 30 Nov. 2019, www.thebalance.com/what-negative-interest-rates-mean-for-investors-1978886; Randow, Jana and Yuko Takeo. "Negative Interest Rates." *Bloomberg,* 1 Nov. 2019, www.bloomberg.com/quicktake/negative-interest-rates.

[1163] Davidson, Paul. "Trump wants Fed to cut interest rates to zero or below. Here's what it could mean for you." *USA Today*, 12 Sept. 2019, www.usatoday.com/story/money/2019/09/12/interest-rates-what-zero-negative-rates-would-mean-you/2293676001/.

[1164] Randow, Jana and Yuko Takeo. "Negative Interest Rates." *Bloomberg,* 1 Nov. 2019, www.bloomberg.com/quicktake/negative-interest-rates.

[1165] Davidson, Paul. "Trump wants Fed to cut interest rates to zero or below. Here's what it could mean for you." *USA Today*, 12 Sept. 2019, www.usatoday.com/story/money/2019/09/12/interest-rates-what-zero-negative-rates-would-mean-you/2293676001/; "9 Insights About Negative Interest Rates." *Knowledge@Wharton High School,* kwhs.wharton.upenn.edu/2019/09/9-insights-negative-interest-rates.

[1166] "Negative Interest Rate Definition." *Investopedia*, 17 Aug. 2019, www.investopedia.com/terms/n/negative-interest-rate.asp.

executives have discussed imposing certain fees on consumers if rates fall to zero or below.[1167] Some of the fees may include "[m]onthly charges for maintaining a checking account, higher fees for wire transfers and overdrafts, fees for out-of-network ATM usage, and even fees to see a teller as opposed to using an ATM."[1168] Money market mutual funds would also likely charge consumers for deposits.[1169]

"On the personal side, you may find it more lucrative to restructure all your loans into negative interest rate loans, then defer any repayment until the due date. Can you say 'goodbye student loan crisis?'"[1170] Donald Trump put it this way: "Got to pay back your loan? Oh, how much am I getting?"[1171] NIRP would also

---

[1167] Davidson, Paul. "Trump wants Fed to cut interest rates to zero or below. Here's what it could mean for you." *USA Today*, 12 Sept. 2019, www.usatoday.com/story/money/2019/09/12/interest-rates-what-zero-negative-rates-would-mean-you/2293676001/.

[1168] Williams, Sean. "3 Dangers of a Negative Interest Rate Policy." *The Motley Fool*, 20 Feb. 2016, www.fool.com/investing/general/2016/02/20/3-dangers-of-a-negative-interest-rate-policy.aspx.

[1169] Davidson, Paul. "Trump wants Fed to cut interest rates to zero or below. Here's what it could mean for you." *USA Today*, 12 Sept. 2019, www.usatoday.com/story/money/2019/09/12/interest-rates-what-zero-negative-rates-would-mean-you/2293676001/.

[1170] Carosa, Chris. "What Are 'Negative' Interest Rates And How Can You Make Money From Them?" *Forbes*, 20 Aug. 2019, www.forbes.com/sites/chriscarosa/2019/08/20/what-are-negative-interest-rates-and-how-can-you-make-money-from-them/#4766600a409b.

[1171] Trump, Donald. "Remarks by President Trump at the World Economic Forum." *U.S. Embassy in Switzerland and Liechtenstein*, 21 Jan. 2020, ch.usembassy.gov/remarks-by-president-trump-at-the-world-economic-forum/.

allow the federal government to refinance its massive debt at a lower cost.[1172]

Former Federal Reserve chairman, Alan Greenspan, suggested that negative interest rates were on their way to the U.S.[1173] "The Fed has not (yet) deployed NIRP but is actively discussing it."[1174] Former Fed Chairman, Janet Yellen, said that the Fed "would consider all options to stimulate U.S. economic growth…"[1175] She indicated that the Fed is "taking a look at them…"[1176]

President Donald Trump, who thinks "the Fed should cut and the Fed should stimulate," "has urged the Fed to make the nation's interest rates negative, something that has never happened before in

---

[1172] Davidson, Paul. "Trump wants Fed to cut interest rates to zero or below. Here's what it could mean for you." *USA Today*, 12 Sept. 2019, www.usatoday.com/story/money/2019/09/12/interest-rates-what-zero-negative-rates-would-mean-you/2293676001/.

[1173] "9 Insights About Negative Interest Rates." *Knowledge@Wharton High School,* kwhs.wharton.upenn.edu/2019/09/9-insights-negative-interest-rates.

[1174] Brightman, Chris. "Negative Rates Are Dangerous to Your Wealth." *Research Affiliates*, Apr. 2016, www.researchaffiliates.com/en_us/p u b l i c a t i o n s / a r t i c l e s / 542_negative_rates_are_dangerous_to_your_wealth.html.

[1175] Williams, Sean. "3 Dangers of a Negative Interest Rate Policy." *The Motley Fool*, 20 Feb. 2016, www.fool.com/investing/general/2016/02/20/3-dangers-of-a-negative-interest-rate-policy.aspx.

[1176] Brightman, Chris. "Negative Rates Are Dangerous to Your Wealth." *Research Affiliates*, Apr. 2016, www.researchaffiliates.com/en_us/p u b l i c a t i o n s / a r t i c l e s / 542_negative_rates_are_dangerous_to_your_wealth.html.

the United States…"[1177] He has tweeted that the Fed "should get our interest rates down to ZERO, or less."[1178]

Some places have already implemented negative interest rates. "Denmark's Nationalbank introduced negative rates in July 2012."[1179] The European Central Bank cut benchmark lending rates below zero in 2014 to as low as -0.40%.[1180] Central banks in Sweden, Switzerland, and Japan have also had negative rates for

---

[1177] Smialek, Jeanne. "Bonds Hit Historic Lows, Prompting Fed to Ponder: What More Can We Do?" *The New York Times*, 6 Mar. 2020, web.archive.org/web/20200307035222/https://www.nytimes.com/2020/03/06/business/economy/fed-coronavirus-rate-cut-limited-ammunition.html?fbclid=IwAR3SK_H_SWIXSpNx1zwSJBw9PaIGqhYqinfg3OhbzANEZM_qY1OeWkN1-o4; Long, Heather. "Federal Reserve slashes interest rates to zero as part of wide-ranging emergency intervention." *The Washington Post*, 15 Mar. 2020, www.washingtonpost.com/business/2020/03/15/federal-reserve-slashes-interest-rates-zero-part-wide-ranging-emergency-intervention/?fbclid=IwAR3ArnSj5NO2WPZw9qneawJhTKbW8Xqg3tspxLEkYlfmGJcKl4ZtHtx14FM.

[1178] Davidson, Paul. "Trump wants Fed to cut interest rates to zero or below. Here's what it could mean for you." *USA Today*, 12 Sept. 2019, www.usatoday.com/story/money/2019/09/12/interest-rates-what-zero-negative-rates-would-mean-you/2293676001/.

[1179] Scott, David. "There's a big problem with the last tool in the arsenal of the world's central banks." *Business Insider*, 17 Feb. 2016, www.businessinsider.com/theres-a-big-problem-with-negative-interest-rates-2016-2.

[1180] Randow, Jana and Yuko Takeo. "Negative Interest Rates." *Bloomberg*, 1 Nov. 2019, www.bloomberg.com/quicktake/negative-interest-rates. Chang, Ellen. "How Do Negative Interest Rates Work?" *The Street*, 23 Feb. 2018, www.thestreet.com/how-to/how-negative-interest-rates-work-14492328.

several years.[1181] The deposit rate in Switzerland is -0.75%, Sweden -0.35% and at the Bank of Japan, it is -0.10%.[1182]

The coronavirus brought a "first to U.S. financial markets — negative yields on government debt."[1183] "Yields on both the one-month and three-month Treasury bills dipped below zero" on March 25, 2020.[1184] In addition, high inflation means the "US 10-Year Treasury bond is producing significantly negative inflation-adjusted returns…"[1185]

Government bonds issued by governments with a NIRP policy, and some corporate bonds in those markets, already trade at negative yields.[1186] "In Germany,…all government fixed income instruments except the 30-year bond [carried] rates below zero. Denmark, France and Sweden are among other European nations also in the

---

[1181] Davidson, Paul. "Trump wants Fed to cut interest rates to zero or below. Here's what it could mean for you." *USA Today*, 12 Sept. 2019, www.usatoday.com/story/money/2019/09/12/interest-rates-what-zero-negative-rates-would-mean-you/2293676001/.

[1182] Chang, Ellen. "How Do Negative Interest Rates Work?" *The Street*, 23 Feb. 2018, www.thestreet.com/how-to/how-negative-interest-rates-work-14492328.

[1183] Cox, Jeff. "Negative rates come to the US: 1-month and 3-month Treasury bill yields are now below zero." *CNBC*, 25 Mar. 2020, www.cnbc.com/2020/03/25/negative-rates-come-to-the-us-1-month-and-3-month-treasury-bill-yields-are-now-negative.html?fbclid=IwAR2H7UYRDpI2yY35p104gy6Z63Eda4pWaswcKCOXdqNSgQo1CqT3vrRzIZ8.

[1184] *Id.*

[1185] "The Inflation CPI Lie : BLS Posers…" *Signals Matter*, 2 Oct. 2017, www.signalsmatter.com/inflation-cpi/.

[1186] Brightman, Chris. "Negative Rates Are Dangerous to Your Wealth." *Research Affiliates*, Apr. 2016, www.researchaffiliates.com/en_us/publications/articles/542_negative_rates_are_dangerous_to_your_wealth.html.

category."[1187]   On May 20, 2020, the U.K. sold "bonds at negative interest rates, showing investor demand for government securities is so high that some are willing to pay for the privilege. According to the Debt Management Office, the U.K. auctioned £3.75 billion ($4.6 billion) of 3-year TMBMKGB-03Y, 0.008% notes at an average rate of -0.003%."[1188]

"Negative yields are largely a function of demand, as prices and yields move in opposite direction for bonds. Investors pay a large premium above par on the bonds and can receive less than their initial investment at maturity."[1189]   "That means investors buying those securities won't get all of their money back…"[1190] Ric Edelman, co-founder of Edelman Financial Engine, explains, "Ordinarily, when you buy a bond, the issuer pays you interest in exchange for the rights to use your money for a period of time. But

---

[1187] Cox, Jeff. "Negative rates come to the US: 1-month and 3-month Treasury bill yields are now below zero." *CNBC*, 25 Mar. 2020, www.cnbc.com/2020/03/25/negative-rates-come-to-the-us-1-month-and-3-month-treasury-bill-yields-are-now-negative.html?fbclid=IwAR2H7UYRDpI2yY35p104gy6Z63Eda4pWaswcKCOXdqNSgQo1CqT3vrRzIZ8.

[1188] Goldstein, Steve. "Britain sells its first bonds at a negative interest rate." *Market Watch*, 20 May 2020, www.marketwatch.com/story/britain-sells-its-first-bonds-at-a-negative-interest-rate-2020-05-20?siteid=yhoof2&yptr=yahoo.

[1189] Cox, Jeff. "Negative rates come to the US: 1-month and 3-month Treasury bill yields are now below zero." *CNBC*, 25 Mar. 2020, www.cnbc.com/2020/03/25/negative-rates-come-to-the-us-1-month-and-3-month-treasury-bill-yields-are-now-negative.html?fbclid=IwAR2H7UYRDpI2yY35p104gy6Z63Eda4pWaswcKCOXdqNSgQo1CqT3vrRzIZ8.

[1190] Randow, Jana and Yuko Takeo. "Negative Interest Rates." *Bloomberg*, 1 Nov. 2019, www.bloomberg.com/quicktake/negative-interest-rates.

when rates fall below zero, you're actually paying the issuer to hold your cash for you."[1191]

Unfortunately, it is difficult for investors to find yields in a negative rate environment.[1192] "Zero real interest rates predict zero real returns, and negative real interest rates predict negative real returns."[1193] Consequently, negative interest rates hurt companies that rely on loaning money.[1194] NIRP also hurts people who rely on interest income. Positive interest rates reward investors for risking the money they lend, but with negative interest rates, "savers are penalized and borrowers get paid to borrow money."[1195] For example, when one buys a new car, the dealer gives you the option to pay with cash or credit. When rates are above zero, buying a car on credit will cost more because one must pay interest on the loan. When interest rates are negative, it is cheaper to buy the car on

---

[1191] Carosa, Chris. "What Are 'Negative' Interest Rates And How Can You Make Money From Them?" *Forbes*, 20 Aug. 2019, www.forbes.com/sites/ chriscarosa/2019/08/20/what-are-negative-interest-rates-and-how-can-you-make-money-from-them/#4766600a409b.

[1192] Kuepper, Justin. "What Negative Interest Rates Mean for Investors." *The Balance,* 30 Nov. 2019, www.thebalance.com/what-negative-interest-rates-mean-for-investors-1978886.

[1193] Brightman, Chris. "Negative Rates Are Dangerous to Your Wealth." *Research Affiliates*, Apr. 2016, www.researchaffiliates.com/en_us/ p u b l i c a t i o n s / a r t i c l e s / 542_negative_rates_are_dangerous_to_your_wealth.html.

[1194] Carosa, Chris. "What Are 'Negative' Interest Rates And How Can You Make Money From Them?" *Forbes*, 20 Aug. 2019, www.forbes.com/sites/ chriscarosa/2019/08/20/what-are-negative-interest-rates-and-how-can-you-make-money-from-them/#4766600a409b.

[1195] Randow, Jana and Yuko Takeo. "Negative Interest Rates." *Bloomberg,* 1 Nov. 2019, www.bloomberg.com/quicktake/negative-interest-rates.

credit than with cash.[1196] "It's more than free money. You're actually getting paid to borrow money."[1197] "Homeowners in Denmark are currently receiving checks each month because their mortgages have negative interest rates."[1198]

"If investors can't generate any return on investment by parking their money in CDs or savings accounts, they may grow more desperate for sources of income appreciation... What might happen is a considerable rise in risk-taking among investors, which could correlate to an increase in volatility in equity prices."[1199]

"Continuing low interest rates could dent U.S. bank profits and push bankers into riskier behavior that might threaten the nation's financial stability."[1200] A recent report from the Fed "highlighted the rate squeeze facing banks and insurers, noting that it could erode lending standards. If interest rates were to remain low for a prolonged period, the profitability of banks, insurers, and other financial intermediaries could come under stress and spur reach-for-yield behavior, thereby increasing the vulnerability of the financial sector to subsequent shocks."[1201] "Fed Governor Lael Brainard said...that the low-for-long environment and the associated

---

[1196] Carosa, Chris. "What Are 'Negative' Interest Rates And How Can You Make Money From Them?" *Forbes*, 20 Aug. 2019, www.forbes.com/sites/chriscarosa/2019/08/20/what-are-negative-interest-rates-and-how-can-you-make-money-from-them/#4766600a409b.

[1197] *Id.*

[1198] Chang, Ellen. "How Do Negative Interest Rates Work?" *The Street*, 23 Feb. 2018, www.thestreet.com/how-to/how-negative-interest-rates-work-14492328.

[1199] Williams, Sean. "3 Dangers of a Negative Interest Rate Policy." *The Motley Fool*, 20 Feb. 2016, www.fool.com/investing/general/2016/02/20/3-dangers-of-a-negative-interest-rate-policy.aspx.

[1200] Hamilton, Jesse and Rich Miller. "Fed Warns Prolonged Low Interest Rates Could Spark Instability." *Bloomberg*, 15 Nov. 2019, www.bloomberg.com/news/articles/2019-11-15/fed-warns-prolonged-low-interest-rates-could-spark-instability.

[1201] *Id.*

incentives to reach for yield and take on additional debt could increase financial vulnerabilities."[1202] With $14 trillion in negative-yielding bonds and $81 trillion in global money supply, the combination of a panic-induced fall in asset prices and massively leveraged bets could generate a rapid financial shock…"[1203]

However, when cash is available, "cutting rates significantly into negative territory becomes impossible. Cash has the same purchasing power as bank deposits, but at zero nominal interest…. Therefore, instead of paying negative interest, one can simply hold cash at zero interest. Cash is a free option on zero interest, and acts as an interest rate floor…"[1204] "Consumers facing fees to have cash in an account may decide to take the money out of the financial system altogether (called a bank run)…"[1205] Nominal interest rates "can fall to −1.00% or more before savers will abandon their bank accounts for physical cash."[1206] People may invest that cash in other

---

[1202] *Id.*

[1203] Lacalle, Daniel. PhD. "The Fed Panicked, and Its Rate Cut Is Making the Economy Worse." *Mises Institute,* 9 Mar. 2020, mises.org/wire/fed-panicked-and-its-rate-cut-making-economy-worse? f b c l i d = I w A R 3 1 Z 6 Q s 6 p 8 b 9 d R J - _YZBaEuHz4Pq0SQoLzOH7W2TJlQ3G4vboe6ViwOuMI#.XmbHfDyEi q4.twitter.

[1204] Agarwai, Ruchir and Signe Krogstrup. "Cashing In: How to Make Negative Interest Rates Work." *IMF Blog,* 5 Feb. 2019, blogs.imf.org/ 2019/02/05/cashing-in-how-to-make-negative-interest-rates-work/.

[1205] Kuepper, Justin. "What Negative Interest Rates Mean for Investors." *The Balance,* 30 Nov. 2019, www.thebalance.com/what-negative-interest-rates-mean-for-investors-1978886.

[1206] Brightman, Chris. "Negative Rates Are Dangerous to Your Wealth." *Research Affiliates,* Apr. 2016, www.researchaffiliates.com/en_us/ p u b l i c a t i o n s / a r t i c l e s / 542_negative_rates_are_dangerous_to_your_wealth.html.

assets such as gold and real estate, which "could lead to bubbles that eventually pop."[1207]

Therefore, "negative interest rates would require the assistance of outlawing cash, so that banking customers don't cheat by simply drawing out on their accounts."[1208] "Kenneth Rogoff... wrote that a cashless society would offer such benefits as 'greater flexibility for the Federal Reserve to stimulate the economy when necessary.'"[1209]

An IMF study proposed that central banks make "cash as costly as bank deposits with negative interest rates, thereby making deeply negative interest rates feasible while preserving the role of cash...The proposal is for a central bank to divide the monetary base into two separate local currencies — cash and electronic money (e-money). E-money would be issued only electronically and would pay the policy rate of interest, and cash would have an exchange rate — the conversion rate — against e-money...When setting a negative interest rate on e-money, the central bank would let the conversion rate of cash in terms of e-money depreciate at the same rate as the negative interest rate on e-money. The value of cash would thereby fall in terms of e-money. To illustrate, suppose your bank announced a negative 3 percent interest rate on your bank deposit of 100 dollars today. Suppose also that the central bank announced that cash-dollars would now become a separate currency that would depreciate against e-dollars by 3 percent per year. The conversion rate of cash-dollars into e-dollars would hence change from 1 to

---

[1207] Davidson, Paul. "Trump wants Fed to cut interest rates to zero or below. Here's what it could mean for you." *USA Today*, 12 Sept. 2019, www.usatoday.com/story/money/2019/09/12/interest-rates-what-zero-negative-rates-would-mean-you/2293676001/.

[1208] Hankoff, Nick. "Coronavirus Being Used to Scare You Away From Using Cash." *Advocate*, 24 Mar. 2020, www.theadvocates.org/2020/03/coronavirus-being-used-to-scare-you-away-from-using-cash/?fbclid=IwAR3iYN4Niwu8AawMIhSH8kbohngSlHRUmgK_gOdFAE-LFIz0RR3xRu5-Awg.

[1209] *Id.*

0.97 over the year. After a year, there would be 97 e-dollars left in your bank account. If you instead took out 100 cash-dollars today and kept it safe at home for a year, exchanging it into e-money after that year would also yield 97 e-dollars. At the same time, shops would start advertising prices in e-money and cash separately, just as shops in some small open economies already advertise prices both in domestic and in bordering foreign currencies. Cash would thereby be losing value both in terms of goods and in terms of e-money, and there would be no benefit to holding cash relative to bank deposits. This dual local currency system would allow the central bank to implement as negative an interest rate as necessary for countering a recession, without triggering any large-scale substitutions into cash."[1210] "In a cashless world, there would be no lower bound on interest rates. A central bank could reduce the policy rate from, say, 2 percent to minus 4 percent…The interest rate cut would transmit to bank deposits, loans, and bonds. Without cash, depositors would have to pay the negative interest rate to keep their money with the bank…"[1211]   In other words, IMF wants to ban cash to make negative interest rates feasible because cash acts as a floor for interest rates.[1212]   This is because no one will pay a bank to keep cash if they can just withdraw it.

"[T]he Federal Government in Australia has moved to ban cash transactions above $10,000" with the threat of two years in jail to give authorities greater control during recessions.[1213]   "A number

---

[1210] Agarwai, Ruchir and Signe Krogstrup. "Cashing In: How to Make Negative Interest Rates Work." *IMF Blog*, 5 Feb. 2019, blogs.imf.org/2019/02/05/cashing-in-how-to-make-negative-interest-rates-work/.

[1211] *Id.*

[1212] "Banning cash so you pay the bank to hold your money is what the IMF wants." *MSN,* 25 Aug. 2019, www.msn.com/en-au/money/personalfinance/banning-cash-so-you-pay-the-bank-to-hold-your-money-is-what-the-imf-wants/ar-AAGjopy?fbclid=IwAR3azKMt8SEjVWBYhS_p6u0ZQIaY-IcLekCFi5K_A8CEThzwrEWGwugJnrc.

[1213] *Id.*

of other countries have already imposed limits — France has banned cash transactions above 1,000 euros; Spain above 2,500 euros; Italy above 3,000 euros..."[1214]

Some experts are skeptical that NIRP will work. K.C. Ma, director of the Roland George investments program at Stetson University in Deland, Fla, said, "Consumers will not take out loans to buy new cars or homes just because the financing term is attractive. The notion that negative interest rates will produce loans and generate economic growth is just wishful thinking."[1215] "No economic agent is going to consume more or invest more because of an interest rate cut."[1216]

In addition, banks may be less likely to lend. "Banks may be reluctant to pass on the cost of negative interest rates to their customers because doing so may encourage them to move their assets. In these cases, negative interest rates would lower the profits of banks and discourage them from lending."[1217] "Banks are not

---

[1214] *Id.*

[1215] Chang, Ellen. "How Do Negative Interest Rates Work?" *The Street,* 23 Feb. 2018, www.thestreet.com/how-to/how-negative-interest-rates-work-14492328. In a few cases, negative interest rates have stimulated some additional lending, but largely at the margins. Davidson, Paul. "Trump wants Fed to cut interest rates to zero or below. Here's what it could mean for you." *USA Today,* 12 Sept. 2019, www.usatoday.com/story/money/2019/09/12/interest-rates-what-zero-negative-rates-would-mean-you/2293676001/.

[1216] Lacalle, Daniel. PhD. "The Fed Panicked, and Its Rate Cut Is Making the Economy Worse." *Mises Institute,* 9 Mar. 2020, mises.org/wire/fed-panicked-and-its-rate-cut-making-economy-worse?fbclid=IwAR31Z6Qs6p8b9dRJ-_YZBaEuHz4Pq0SQoLzOH7W2TJlQ3G4vboe6ViwOuMI#.XmbHfDyEiq4.twitter.

[1217] Kuepper, Justin. "What Negative Interest Rates Mean for Investors." *The Balance,* 30 Nov. 2019, www.thebalance.com/what-negative-interest-rates-mean-for-investors-1978886.

going to lend more into a supply shock and even less at lower rates."[1218]

For example, in the Eurozone, negative interest rates drove down what banks earned on money they lent, but they still "had to pay customers for their deposits. The resulting squeeze on profits left many European banks complaining that the ECB was making it harder for them to lend, not easier… "[1219]

"The new era of negative rates is now the subject of a debate about whether the policy has distorted financial markets, crippled banks and threatened pensions…"[1220] "A member of the New York Fed's Investor Advisory Committee on Financial Markets, Scott Minerd, published a critique which he headlined as follows: 'Global Central Banks Fueling a Ponzi Market…' The thrust of the article is that central banks (which include the New York Fed's Wall Street money spigot that was launched on September 17, 2019) are creating a Ponzi scheme of liquidity that is hiding the true state of risk in both the stock and bond markets. The implication is that without the Fed's cheap money flooding markets, interest rates on questionable debt would be much higher, thus providing a red flag for investors…"[1221]

[1218] Lacalle, Daniel. PhD. "The Fed Panicked, and Its Rate Cut Is Making the Economy Worse." *Mises Institute,* 9 Mar. 2020, mises.org/wire/fed-panicked-and-its-rate-cut-making-economy-worse?fbclid=IwAR31Z6Qs6p8b9dRJ-_YZBaEuHz4Pq0SQoLzOH7W2TJlQ3G4vboe6ViwOuMI#.XmbHfDyEiq4.twitter.

[1219] Randow, Jana and Yuko Takeo. "Negative Interest Rates." *Bloomberg,* 1 Nov. 2019, www.bloomberg.com/quicktake/negative-interest-rates.

[1220] *Id.*

[1221] Martens, Pam and Russ Martens. "The Man Who Advises the New York Fed Says It and Other Central Banks Are 'Fueling a Ponzi Market.'" *Wall Street on Parade,* 22 Jan. 2020, wallstreetonparade.com/2020/01/the-man-who-advises-the-new-york-fed-says-it-and-other-central-banks-are-fueling-a-ponzi-market/.

NIRP would also devalue the country's currency.[1222] "Most investors will be looking outside of the United States for opportunities if the rates are dropped into the negative."[1223] When investors search for better returns in foreign markets, it decreases the value of their nation's currency.[1224] This makes U.S. exports less expensive overseas.[1225] "If more and more central banks use negative rates as a stimulus tool, the policy might ultimately lead to a currency war of competitive devaluations...[that] may prove difficult to reverse."[1226]

Lynette Zang predicted, "When the central banks default, when they lose control, they will print money and introduce global negative interest rates. And that will bring hyperinflation and it will be game over. They are talking about 'hotter' inflation because they know it is coming."[1227] Inflation is the subject of the next chapter.

[1222] Davidson, Paul. "Trump wants Fed to cut interest rates to zero or below. Here's what it could mean for you." *USA Today*, 12 Sept. 2019, www.usatoday.com/story/money/2019/09/12/interest-rates-what-zero-negative-rates-would-mean-you/2293676001/.

[1223] Kuepper, Justin. "What Negative Interest Rates Mean for Investors." *The Balance*, 30 Nov. 2019, www.thebalance.com/what-negative-interest-rates-mean-for-investors-1978886.

[1224] *Id.*

[1225] Davidson, Paul. "Trump wants Fed to cut interest rates to zero or below. Here's what it could mean for you." *USA Today*, 12 Sept. 2019, www.usatoday.com/story/money/2019/09/12/interest-rates-what-zero-negative-rates-would-mean-you/2293676001/.

[1226] Randow, Jana and Yuko Takeo. "Negative Interest Rates." *Bloomberg*, 1 Nov. 2019, www.bloomberg.com/quicktake/negative-interest-rates.

[1227] At 31. ITM Trading, Inc. "And Central Banks Using Up Their Ammo." *Youtube*, 18 Dec. 2018, www.youtube.com/watch?v=NvWm6Qkp5gU.

Chapter 6

Some Like It Hot

With quantitative easing and other policies, the central bank essentially prints money and injects it into the economy. Increasing the money supply can lead to high levels of inflation. "Inflation is the increase in the supply of money, especially artificially..."[1228] The Bureau of Labor Statistics (BLS) defines inflation "as a process of continuously rising prices or equivalently, of a continuously falling value of money."[1229] Basically, inflation is when the price of goods goes up.

"The more money that's created and put into circulation, the less valuable it becomes."[1230] "The single most important contributor to high inflation right now is the trillions of dollars central bankers around the world have pumped into the financial system since the crisis began in late 2007. Never mind that the crisis was caused by too much money to begin with..."[1231]

"In practice, the central bank buys U.S. Treasury bonds on the open market with newly created money. It holds those bonds on its balance sheet and the newly minted dollars go into circulation. This

---

[1228] At 8. RonPaulLibertyReport. "Central Banking Is On The Ropes: Gold Will Survive & The Fed Will End." *Youtube*, 13 Dec. 2019, www.youtube.com/watch?v=Ndcb2SPRU7M.

[1229] Boring, Perianne. "If You Want To Know The Real Rate Of Inflation, Don't Bother With The CPI." *Forbes*, 3 Feb. 2014, www.forbes.com/sites/perianneboring/2014/02/03/if-you-want-to-know-the-real-rate-of-inflation-dont-bother-with-the-cpi/#5f1504b9200b.

[1230] "M2 measures the supply of US dollars, which includes cash, checking deposits, saving deposits, and money market mutual funds." *Id.*

[1231] "The U.S. Lies About Inflation: Here's The Inflation Secret The Government Doesn't Want You to Know." *Money Morning*, moneymorning.com/the-u-s-lies-about-inflation-heres-the-inflation-secret-the-government-doesnt-want-you-to-know/.

increases the money supply. An increase in the money supply is by definition inflation."[1232] "The Fed's unprecedented bond buying program, Quantitative Easing, created $116 million an hour for the entire year [2013]."[1233] During the week of March 18–25, 2020, the Fed printed approximately $970,000 every second.[1234]

"A core factor that influences economic and monetary policy is consumer price inflation, or the rate at which prices are rising."[1235] The Fed tries to maintain inflation at 2% per annum.[1236] Chairman Jerome Powell said in December 2019, "We are strongly committed to symmetrically and sustainably achieving our 2 percent inflation objective so that in making long-term plans, households and

---

[1232] Maharrey, Mike. "Enjoy That Stimulus: You're Going to Pay for It!" *Tenth Amendment Center*, 12 Jun. 2020, blog.tenthamendmentcenter.com/2020/06/enjoy-that-stimulus-youre-going-to-pay-for-it/?fbclid=IwAR19Z7wT2WimDrd0lKKYKML2cbNPnIAVfnN-0SlNoUC8WvjMQ7tuzdIpJqg.

[1233] "M2 measures the supply of US dollars, which includes cash, checking deposits, saving deposits, and money market mutual funds." Boring, Perianne. "If You Want To Know The Real Rate Of Inflation, Don't Bother With The CPI." *Forbes,* 3 Feb. 2014, www.forbes.com/sites/perianneboring/2014/02/03/if-you-want-to-know-the-real-rate-of-inflation-dont-bother-with-the-cpi/#5f1504b9200b.

[1234] Frost, Liam. "The Federal Reserve is printing $1 million every second." *Decrypt.com,* 27 Mar. 2020, decrypt.co/23805/the-federal-reserve-is-printing-1-million-every-second?fbclid=IwAR1D2kiJSMK8jcF2S0GprjdcMnVxZx5YKNrDZTNeMo7u6nF0nffvx7-q47Q.

[1235] Marstrand, Bob. "Lies, damned lies and CPI." *Of Wealth,* 11 Oct. 2016, www.ofwealth.com/lies-damned-lies-cpi/.

[1236] Amadeo, Kimberly. "Explaining Quantitative Easing – QE." *The Balance,* 3 Sept. 2019, www.thebalance.com/what-is-quantitative-easing-definition-and-explanation-3305881.

businesses can reasonably expect 2 percent inflation over time."[1237] Powell claims "we are way below the Fed's 2% target."[1238] "However, headline and core inflation are both running above 2% …"[1239]

The 2% inflation goal conflicts with the Fed's mandate to maintain price stability. "The mandate is stable prices. 'Stable' means the prices don't go up."[1240] A "2% increase per year is not stable but rather ever-escalating, so not within the mandate…"[1241] Therefore, "Federal Reserve redefines 'stable' to mean that prices always go up the 'target' inflation at 2%…"[1242] Lynette Zang said, "I know that the longer I hold onto the dollars, the less and less value they have. Particularly with the global central banks on a mission to create that 'elusive' inflation that they have been trying to generate…"[1243]

"In contrast to the mainstream view, Austrians argue that the goal of a monetary system is not 'stable prices.'…but prices

---

[1237] Cox, Jeff. "Powell says the Fed is 'strongly committed' to 2% inflation goal, a sign that rates are likely to hold steady." *CNBC*, 25 Nov. 2019, www.cnbc.com/2019/11/25/powell-says-the-fed-is-strongly-committed-to-meeting-its-inflation-goal.html.

[1238] At 1:20. Arcadia Economics. "Michael Pento: "Interest Rates Will Probably Never Be Raised Again In Our Lifetime." *Youtube*. 12 Dec. 2019, www.youtube.com/watch?v=X3KYNZcvioY.

[1239] At 7:40. Schiff, Peter. "Ep. 520: Volcker Dies as Inflation Comes Back to Life." *Youtube*, 11 Dec. 2019, www.youtube.com/watch?v=bJrq2SA8PCw.

[1240] At 6:50. *Id.*

[1241] At 21. *Id.*

[1242] At 10. Gammon, George. "CPI Tax Scam: YOU'RE GOING TO LOSE A LOT OF MONEY! (Discover How)." *Youtube*, 11 Dec. 2019, www.youtube.com/watch?v=RA8PX_T1Suw.

[1243] At 16:30. ITM Trading, Inc. "And Central Banks Using Up Their Ammo." *Youtube*, 18 Dec. 2018, www.youtube.com/watch?v=NvWm6Qkp5gU.

determined by market forces. Following a supply shock, we would expect prices to rise as markets work to allocate available stocks according to the subjective preferences and expectations of market participants…What the economy requires during a crisis is a monetary system in which market participants are free to negotiate and exchange; entrepreneurs can plan, experiment, and receive feedback; and resources can be allocated to their most highly valued uses…"[1244]

Worse still, it appears that the Fed really wants inflation to be over 2%.[1245] Some "Fed officials have said that a period of time above 2% would be fine."[1246] In fact, they are considering implementing a rule that would allow inflation to run above two per cent "to compensate for past periods of muted price increases."[1247] Federal Reserve Vice Chairman, Richard Clarida, claimed that such a plan to allow "makeup" inflation could help to "reverse past misses of the inflation objective."[1248] With this "inflation

---

[1244] Klein, Peter G. "The Financial System Is Now Totally Dependent on Government Intervention." *Mises Institute,* 16 Mar. 2020, mises.org/power-market/financial-system-now-totally-dependent-government-intervention?fbclid=IwAR3eKYaKZMJqyM91joNY59D1nTY6LqHPhsz4iz1fQS2VowwbR5YGkAlOHPA.

[1245] At 7:40. Schiff, Peter. "Ep. 520: Volcker Dies as Inflation Comes Back to Life." *Youtube,* 11 Dec. 2019, www.youtube.com/watch?v=bJrq2SA8PCw.

[1246] Cox, Jeff. "Powell says the Fed is 'strongly committed' to 2% inflation goal, a sign that rates are likely to hold steady." *CNBC,* 25 Nov. 2019, www.cnbc.com/2019/11/25/powell-says-the-fed-is-strongly-committed-to-meeting-its-inflation-goal.html.

[1247] Keoun, Bradly. "Fed Considers Letting Inflation Run Hot, Vice Chair Clarida Says." *The Street,* 24 Feb. 2019, www.thestreet.com/markets/fed-considers-letting-inflation-run-hot-vice-chair-clarida-says-14875204.

[1248] *Id.*

averaging," official inflation could go up to 4% to average out.[1249] "Goldman Sachs believes the central bank will decide to allow overshoots of its inflation goal next year. 'If implemented...this change would decrease the likelihood of further near-term policy tightening and lead to a small and gradual increase in both expected and realized price inflation,' says Goldman's equity strategist Ben Snider...The alternative approach encourages higher prices during expansions."[1250]

John Williams, President of the Federal Reserve Bank of New York, has warned of the danger of runaway inflation, saying, "We must remain vigilant regarding a sustained takeoff in inflation."[1251] "The Fed's tools for fighting inflation are raising interest rates and shrinking its balance sheet..."[1252] "However, Powell has intimated that the Fed will wait for inflation to get really bad before they do anything about it."[1253]

Some "doubt that central banks have the capacity to keep inflation in check if the money they have created begins circulating

---

[1249] At 9. Gammon, George. "Federal Reserve: Discover Lies & Secrets They're Hiding From YOU!" *Youtube*, 27 Nov. 2019, www.youtube.com/watch?v=ha_MFJadAzA.

[1250] Li, Yun. "The Fed may soon let inflation run a little hotter than usual, Goldman says." *CNBC*, 18 Mar. 2019, www.cnbc.com/2019/03/18/the-fed-may-soon-let-inflation-run-a-little-hotter-than-usual-goldman-says.html.

[1251] Keoun, Bradly. "Fed Considers Letting Inflation Run Hot, Vice Chair Clarida Says." *The Street*, 24 Feb. 2019, www.thestreet.com/markets/fed-considers-letting-inflation-run-hot-vice-chair-clarida-says-14875204.

[1252] At 17:30. Schiff, Peter. "Ep. 520: Volcker Dies as Inflation Comes Back to Life." *Youtube*, 11 Dec. 2019, www.youtube.com/watch?v=bJrq2SA8PCw.

[1253] At 1:20. Arcadia Economics. "Michael Pento: "Interest Rates Will Probably Never Be Raised Again In Our Lifetime." *Youtube*. 12 Dec. 2019, www.youtube.com/watch?v=X3KYNZcvioY.

more rapidly."[1254]   When inflation goes up, the Fed will have to increase interest rates and the economy will not be able to handle it. Peter Schiff maintained that "the Fed cannot act on inflation" because, if the Fed were to "raise interest rates high enough, it would cause everything to implode."[1255] For example, "[i]f the Fed had to jack up the interest rates to 7%, it would cause the economy to implode because of all of the debt."[1256] The result would be "an economic implosion that would dwarf 2007."[1257]

Indeed, the "Fed paused its effort to raise interest rates — the primary means by which officials try to keep inflation at bay — with the 'Powell Pivot' that ended QT."[1258] Michael Pento, President and Founder of Pento Portfolio Strategies, predicted that "interest rates will probably never be raised again in my lifetime…"[1259]   As a

---

[1254] R. A. "What is quantitative easing?" *The Economist,* 9 Mar. 2015, www.economist.com/the-economist-explains/2015/03/09/what-is-quantitative-easing.

[1255] At 17:30. Schiff, Peter. "Ep. 520: Volcker Dies as Inflation Comes Back to Life." *Youtube,* 11 Dec. 2019, www.youtube.com/watch?v=bJrq2SA8PCw.

[1256] At 4:20. Schiff, Peter. "Powell resurrecting the high inflation Volcker buried." *Youtube,* 11 Dec. 2019, www.youtube.com/watch?v=lWcLQFap2sQ.

[1257] At 17:30. Schiff, Peter. "Ep. 520: Volcker Dies as Inflation Comes Back to Life." *Youtube,* 11 Dec. 2019, www.youtube.com/watch?v=bJrq2SA8PCw.

[1258] Keoun, Bradly. "Fed Considers Letting Inflation Run Hot, Vice Chair Clarida Says." *The Street,* 24 Feb. 2019, www.thestreet.com/markets/fed-considers-letting-inflation-run-hot-vice-chair-clarida-says-14875204.

[1259] At 1:20. Arcadia Economics. "Michael Pento: "Interest Rates Will Probably Never Be Raised Again In Our Lifetime." *Youtube.* 12 Dec. 2019, www.youtube.com/watch?v=X3KYNZcvioY.

consequence, Schiff forecasts a "tsunami of inflation; we are going to have an inflationary depression."[1260]

Jerome Powell is helping to resurrect high inflation.[1261] In fact, "[t]here is a ton of inflation right now and they are scurrying around to try to hide it…"[1262] Some of the inflation is moving into consumer prices, but a "lot of it is in the stock market, it is in financial assets, in real estate, in bonds…that keeps a temporary lid on consumer prices."[1263] "History has shown that slightly higher inflation would lift stock valuations as funds tend to flow from cash to equities as inflation expectations rise."[1264] "There is a lag between this and consumer prices going up — longer than has been in [the] past."[1265] The true impact of Fed policies is not being captured by the Consumer Price Index (CPI) measure of inflation.[1266] "In other words, there's a lot at stake. And when there's a lot at stake, agencies, like people, do desperate things. Or

---

[1260] At 4:20. Schiff, Peter. "Powell resurrecting the high inflation Volcker buried." *Youtube*, 11 Dec. 2019, www.youtube.com/watch?v=lWcLQFap2sQ.

[1261] At 5:50. Schiff, Peter. "Ep. 520: Volcker Dies as Inflation Comes Back to Life." *Youtube*, 11 Dec. 2019, www.youtube.com/watch?v=bJrq2SA8PCw.

[1262] At 8. RonPaulLibertyReport. "Central Banking Is On The Ropes: Gold Will Survive & The Fed Will End." *Youtube*, 13 Dec. 2019, www.youtube.com/watch?v=Ndcb2SPRU7M.

[1263] At 13:50. Schiff, Peter. "Ep. 520: Volcker Dies as Inflation Comes Back to Life." *Youtube*, 11 Dec. 2019, www.youtube.com/watch?v=bJrq2SA8PCw.

[1264] Li, Yun. "The Fed may soon let inflation run a little hotter than usual, Goldman says." *CNBC*, 18 Mar. 2019, www.cnbc.com/2019/03/18/the-fed-may-soon-let-inflation-run-a-little-hotter-than-usual-goldman-says.html.

[1265] At 13:50. Schiff, Peter. "Ep. 520: Volcker Dies as Inflation Comes Back to Life." *Youtube*, 11 Dec. 2019, www.youtube.com/watch?v=bJrq2SA8PCw.

[1266] *Id.*

as one German finance minister admitted from the ECB: 'When the data gets too bad, we just lie.'"[1267]

[1267] "The Inflation CPI Lie : BLS Posers..." *Signals Matter*, 2 Oct. 2017, www.signalsmatter.com/inflation-cpi/.

The CPI Lie

"The measure of inflation is…the price measure of a basket of goods. This carefully controlled basket of goods is called the Consumer Price Index, or CPI…"[1268]   The Bureau of Labor Statistics calculates the CPI, which is the most widely used measure of the U.S. inflation rate.[1269] "The CPI is perhaps one of the most important government statistics because it affects a number of public programs and is used as a benchmark to set public policy."[1270] The federal government and the Federal Reserve use CPI to set tax, monetary, and fiscal policies.[1271]

"The methodology used to calculate the CPI has undergone numerous revisions."[1272]   In fact, "over the past 30 years, the government has changed the way it calculates inflation more than 20 times."[1273]

"Originally, the CPI was determined by comparing the price of a fixed basket of goods and services spanning two different periods.

[1268] "The Inflation CPI Lie : BLS Posers…" *Signals Matter*, 2 Oct. 2017, www.signalsmatter.com/inflation-cpi/.

[1269] Palmer, Barclay. "Why the Consumer Price Index Is Controversial." *Investopedia*, 25 Jun. 2019, www.investopedia.com/articles/07/consumerpriceindex.asp.

[1270] Boring, Perianne. "If You Want To Know The Real Rate Of Inflation, Don't Bother With The CPI." *Forbes*, 3 Feb. 2014, www.forbes.com/sites/perianneboring/2014/02/03/if-you-want-to-know-the-real-rate-of-inflation-dont-bother-with-the-cpi/#5f1504b9200b.

[1271] *Id.*

[1272] Palmer, Barclay. "Why the Consumer Price Index Is Controversial." *Investopedia*, 25 Jun. 2019, www.investopedia.com/articles/07/consumerpriceindex.asp.

[1273] Boring, Perianne. "If You Want To Know The Real Rate Of Inflation, Don't Bother With The CPI." *Forbes*, 3 Feb. 2014, www.forbes.com/sites/perianneboring/2014/02/03/if-you-want-to-know-the-real-rate-of-inflation-dont-bother-with-the-cpi/#5f1504b9200b.

In this case, the CPI was a cost of goods index (COGI)."[1274] Eventually, the U.S. Congress decided "that the CPI should reflect changes in the cost to maintain a constant standard of living."[1275] Consequently, the CPI has morphed into a cost of living index (COLI).[1276] Thus, the CPI does not measure inflation (rising prices), but rather it tracks consumer spending patterns that change as prices change.[1277]

The government assumes that consumer spending habits change as economic conditions change, including rising prices.[1278] "The new methodology takes into account changes in the quality of goods and substitution."[1279] "Substitution" is the premise that, as prices rise for one item, consumers will switch to similar items that have not risen in price as much.[1280] "Substitution, the change in purchases by consumers in response to price changes, changes the relative weighting of the goods in the basket."[1281] "The method used by the CPI calculators reduces the weighting of the faster rising

---

[1274] Palmer, Barclay. "Why the Consumer Price Index Is Controversial." *Investopedia*, 25 Jun. 2019, www.investopedia.com/articles/07/consumerpriceindex.asp.

[1275] *Id.*

[1276] *Id.*

[1277] Boring, Perianne. "If You Want To Know The Real Rate Of Inflation, Don't Bother With The CPI." *Forbes*, 3 Feb. 2014, www.forbes.com/sites/perianneboring/2014/02/03/if-you-want-to-know-the-real-rate-of-inflation-dont-bother-with-the-cpi/#5f1504b9200b.

[1278] *Id.*

[1279] Palmer, Barclay. "Why the Consumer Price Index Is Controversial." *Investopedia*, 25 Jun. 2019, www.investopedia.com/articles/07/consumerpriceindex.asp.

[1280] Marstrand, Bob. "Lies, damned lies and CPI." *Of Wealth,* 11 Oct. 2016, www.ofwealth.com/lies-damned-lies-cpi/.

[1281] Palmer, Barclay. "Why the Consumer Price Index Is Controversial." *Investopedia*, 25 Jun. 2019, www.investopedia.com/articles/07/consumerpriceindex.asp.

item, and increases the weighting of the slower rising one. The classic… example of this is that, if steak prices rise faster than hamburgers, then people are supposed to eat more hamburgers and less steak. Therefore, hamburgers are given more weight in CPI and steak less…"[1282]

"The first measure, the consumer price index for urban consumers [CPI], assumes you purchase the same quantity of each good in the CPI basket over time. In contrast, the C-CPI-U, or chained consumer price index for urban consumers [based on substitution], recognizes that individuals can shift their expenditure patterns toward cheaper goods in the same expenditure category… The prices in the C-CPI-U index increase at a slower rate because individuals can shift their purchases toward cheaper substitute goods…C-CPI-U implies smaller price increases than the CPI-U."[1283] Therefore, "if prices rise and consumers substitute products, the CPI formula could hold a bias that doesn't report rising prices."[1284] "The overall result tends to be a lower CPI."[1285]

"It's important to have an accurate measure of inflation because consumers, especially those on fixed incomes, are

[1282] Marstrand, Bob. "Lies, damned lies and CPI." *Of Wealth,* 11 Oct. 2016, www.ofwealth.com/lies-damned-lies-cpi/.

[1283] "This means the tax brackets will have smaller adjustments and more individuals will fall into the higher tax brackets and pay more taxes." "New tax code = new price index = new tax bracket adjustments." *The Fred Blog,* 25 Jan. 2018, fredblog.stlouisfed.org/2018/01/new-tax-code-new-price-index-new-tax-bracket-adjustments/.

[1284] Boring, Perianne. "If You Want To Know The Real Rate Of Inflation, Don't Bother With The CPI." *Forbes,* 3 Feb. 2014, www.forbes.com/sites/perianneboring/2014/02/03/if-you-want-to-know-the-real-rate-of-inflation-dont-bother-with-the-cpi/#5f1504b9200b.

[1285] Palmer, Barclay. "Why the Consumer Price Index Is Controversial." *Investopedia,* 25 Jun. 2019, www.investopedia.com/articles/07/consumerpriceindex.asp.

negatively impacted by rising prices."[1286]   Unfortunately, "[t]he different methods of measuring inflation [COGI vs. COLI] produce disparate indications of inflation for the same period."[1287] This has, in part, caused the new CPI's accuracy to be questioned.[1288] In fact, two government agencies, the BLS and the U.S. Department of Agriculture (USDA), do not agree on price inflation. "According to the BLS, the average price of beef and veal increased 20 percent over the past five years. However, according to the USDA, beef prices have increased 26 percent over the past five years."[1289]   A statistician at the BLS admitted, "I would expect those numbers to be a little closer together."[1290] "When even the federal government gets different numbers on the same products, how could this possibly be an accurate measurement of inflation?"[1291]

"For many years, [the] CPI 'scale' has been reporting inflation (i.e. the rising cost of goods) at around 2% a year..."[1292] "From the mid 1980s all the way to August of 2008, the money supply grew at an average annual rate of around 5 percent...[O]verall inflation (as measured by the implicit price deflator) averaged around 2 percent

---

[1286] Boring, Perianne. "If You Want To Know The Real Rate Of Inflation, Don't Bother With The CPI." *Forbes*, 3 Feb. 2014, www.forbes.com/sites/perianneboring/2014/02/03/if-you-want-to-know-the-real-rate-of-inflation-dont-bother-with-the-cpi/#5f1504b9200b.

[1287] Palmer, Barclay. "Why the Consumer Price Index Is Controversial." *Investopedia*, 25 Jun. 2019, www.investopedia.com/articles/07/consumerpriceindex.asp.

[1288] Boring, Perianne. "If You Want To Know The Real Rate Of Inflation, Don't Bother With The CPI." *Forbes*, 3 Feb. 2014, www.forbes.com/sites/perianneboring/2014/02/03/if-you-want-to-know-the-real-rate-of-inflation-dont-bother-with-the-cpi/#5f1504b9200b.

[1289] *Id.*

[1290] *Id.*

[1291] *Id.*

[1292] "The Inflation CPI Lie : BLS Posers..." *Signals Matter*, 2 Oct. 2017, www.signalsmatter.com/inflation-cpi/.

over this period…In an attempt to stimulate the economy following the 2008 housing crash, the federal government ran several trillion-dollar deficits…From the end of 2008 through February of 2020, the money supply grew at an average annualized rate of around 10 percent—about double the rate at which it grew prior to 2008…. [All] things [being] equal, this should have given us an annual inflation rate of around 8 percent."[1293]   In addition, "[i]t doesn't make sense that the BLS's measurement of inflation was only 1.5% [for 2018] while at the same time, monetary inflation grew 4.9%."[1294]

David Ranson is one economist who questions the official CPI's reliability as a measure of inflation.[1295]   He "believes that the CPI is a lagging indicator of inflation and is not a good indicator of current inflation."[1296]   Ranson suggested that "increases in the price of commodities are a better indicator of current inflation because inflation initially affects commodity prices, and it may take several

---

[1293] Davies, Antony and James P. Harrigan. "Massive Inflation May Be Coming, Because the US Government Has Cornered Itself into a Fiscal End Game." *FEE*, 21 May 2020, fee.org/articles/massive-inflation-may-be-coming-because-the-us-government-has-cornered-itself-into-a-fiscal-end-game/?fbclid=IwAR2EC1n-Wt7EXea4XZnzfkl3G9z8VtdguUeRjMqwCpjQJXZuVRnz6nairik.

[1294] "On 01/07/2013 M2 was $10.452 trillion. On 01/06/2014 M2 grew to $10.962 trillion. That's a 4.9% increase in the monetary base in just one year. Conversely, a 4.9% decrease in the value of the US dollar." Boring, Perianne. "If You Want To Know The Real Rate Of Inflation, Don't Bother With The CPI." *Forbes*, 3 Feb. 2014, www.forbes.com/sites/perianneboring/2014/02/03/if-you-want-to-know-the-real-rate-of-inflation-dont-bother-with-the-cpi/#5f1504b9200b.

[1295] Palmer, Barclay. "Why the Consumer Price Index Is Controversial." *Investopedia*, 25 Jun. 2019, www.investopedia.com/articles/07/consumerpriceindex.asp.

[1296] *Id.*

years for this commodity inflation to work its way through an economy and to be reflected in the CPI."[1297]

Other "critics view the methodological changes and the switch from a COGI to a COLI as a purposeful manipulation that allows the U.S. government to report a lower CPI..."[1298] The changes in how CPI is calculated could be a convenient way to include or exclude certain products to slant the results.[1299] "Government agencies like the BLS upon which the public so blindly relies purposely under-report the massive increases in the foregoing costs in order to reduce the reported level of inflation..."[1300] "The Fed or the government can measure inflation any way they want to...They measure things that don't go up and they take out the things that do."[1301] For instance, the BLS excludes the cost of particular items when considering the cost of living for average Americans, such as medical care, housing, food, education, and heat.[1302] Another example: In 2008, "as the money supply increased, the increase went largely into exchanges of financial assets rather than exchanges of goods and services...Because prices of financial assets are not included in inflation calculations, we would not observe an increase

---

[1297] "Ranson bases his inflation measure on a commodity basket of precious metals." *Id.*

[1298] *Id.*

[1299] Unfortunately, a lack of transparency makes it impossible to know. Boring, Perianne. "If You Want To Know The Real Rate Of Inflation, Don't Bother With The CPI." *Forbes*, 3 Feb. 2014, www.forbes.com/sites/perianneboring/2014/02/03/if-you-want-to-know-the-real-rate-of-inflation-dont-bother-with-the-cpi/#5f1504b9200b.

[1300] "The Inflation CPI Lie: BLS Posers..." *Signals Matter*, 2 Oct. 2017, www.signalsmatter.com/inflation-cpi/.

[1301] At 1:20. Arcadia Economics. "Michael Pento: "Interest Rates Will Probably Never Be Raised Again In Our Lifetime." *Youtube*. 12 Dec. 2019, www.youtube.com/watch?v=X3KYNZcvioY.

[1302] "The Inflation CPI Lie: BLS Posers..." *Signals Matter*, 2 Oct. 2017, www.signalsmatter.com/inflation-cpi/.

in the official inflation numbers..."[1303]   The Fed just redefines the terms to do whatever it wants.[1304]

Adding to suspicions is the fact that "the Bureau of Labor Statistics operates under a veil of secrecy. The raw data used to calculate the CPI is not available to the public."[1305] This "makes it impossible to audit their findings."[1306]   The excuse is "'so companies can't compare prices.' This makes very little sense because companies can easily compare prices with data openly available on the internet."[1307]

Some believe that officials are actually terrified of the real inflation rate, and so they are making up a fake one. "Bluntly put, most insiders recognize that the Fed and BLS are fictionalizing the CPI numbers to temporarily save their own hind-ends...Because they know that inflation, like hard liquor, is hard for an addicted market to control."[1308] They maintain "that the official numbers out of the BLS are distorting market truth with a financial propaganda

---

[1303] Davies, Antony and James P. Harrigan. "Massive Inflation May Be Coming, Because the US Government Has Cornered Itself into a Fiscal End Game." *FEE*, 21 May 2020, fee.org/articles/massive-inflation-may-be-coming-because-the-us-government-has-cornered-itself-into-a-fiscal-e n d - g a m e / ? f b c l i d = I w A R 2 E C 1 n - Wt7EXea4XZnzfkl3G9z8VtdguUeRjMqwCpjQJXZuVRnz6nairik.

[1304] At 21. Schiff, Peter. "Ep. 520: Volcker Dies as Inflation Comes Back to Life." *Youtube*, 11 Dec. 2019, www.youtube.com/watch?v=bJrq2SA8PCw.

[1305] Boring, Perianne. "If You Want To Know The Real Rate Of Inflation, Don't Bother With The CPI." *Forbes*, 3 Feb. 2014, www.forbes.com/sites/perianneboring/2014/02/03/if-you-want-to-know-the-real-rate-of-inflation-dont-bother-with-the-cpi/#5f1504b9200b.

[1306] *Id.*

[1307] *Id.*

[1308] "The Inflation CPI Lie: BLS Posers..." *Signals Matter*, 2 Oct. 2017, www.signalsmatter.com/inflation-cpi/.

machine that would make the Soviet-era Pravda reporting seem a step up in transparency and blunt-speak..."[1309]

For example, the official party line is that car prices have not changed.[1310] However, the most basic Ford F-150 model sells for $26,540 nowadays [2017], while the most basic F-150 sold for $14,995 in 1996.[1311] "That's a 20 year price increase of $11,545, or 77%. It works out that this popular workhorse has gone up in price by nearly 3% a year over the past couple of decades."[1312]

Unfortunately, "[r]ising prices are hitting U.S. consumers a lot harder than the U.S. Federal Reserve – or the U.S. government – would have us believe..."[1313] "By excluding food and energy prices...the CPI fails to convey the pain that rising prices are inflicting on American households."[1314] Since "1999, even the BLS reports show an 87% increase in medical costs, an 80% increase in energy costs, a 51% increase in food costs, a 53% increase in housing costs and a 115% increase in the costs of a college education."[1315] "College tuition (university fees) tripled in price over 20 years. Other big ticket items that more than doubled... include childcare (up around 120%) and healthcare (up about 105%)

[1309] *Id.*

[1310] Marstrand, Bob. "Lies, damned lies and CPI." *Of Wealth,* 11 Oct. 2016, www.ofwealth.com/lies-damned-lies-cpi/.

[1311] "The Inflation CPI Lie: BLS Posers..." *Signals Matter*, 2 Oct. 2017, www.signalsmatter.com/inflation-cpi/.

[1312] *Id.*

[1313] "The U.S. Lies About Inflation: Here's The Inflation Secret The Government Doesn't Want You to Know." *Money Morning*, moneymorning.com/the-u-s-lies-about-inflation-heres-the-inflation-secret-the-government-doesnt-want-you-to-know/.

[1314] *Id.*

[1315] "The Inflation CPI Lie: BLS Posers..." *Signals Matter*, 2 Oct. 2017, www.signalsmatter.com/inflation-cpi/.

..."[1316] "Meanwhile, US median household income is below 1999 levels..."[1317]

"Not since 1974 have grocery store prices surged 2.6 percent in just one month. That just happened in April [2020], according to new data released by the U.S. Bureau of Labor Statistics...Prices Americans paid for eggs, meat, cereal and milk all went higher in April...The largest increases were for meat and eggs. Consumers paid 4.3 percent more in April for meats, poultry, fish and eggs, 1.5 percent more for fruits and vegetables, and 2.9 percent more for cereals and bakery products, as well as nonalcoholic beverages."[1318]

"Alan Greenspan systematically encouraged changes to the CPI index that have understated it by 4% to 5% for two decades."[1319] "The fact is, inflation today, using the more honest CPI scale of the 1980's, before it was 'tweaked' by the current fiction team at the BLS, puts the real figures at well above 7%, not 2%."[1320] "Some people, such as John Williams at Shadow Government Statistics, think CPI could be understated by as much as 7% a year..."[1321] Shadow Stats said the real rate of inflation is 10%, if it were measured according to how it was done in the

[1316] Marstrand, Bob. "Lies, damned lies and CPI." *Of Wealth,* 11 Oct. 2016, www.ofwealth.com/lies-damned-lies-cpi/.

[1317] "The Inflation CPI Lie: BLS Posers..." *Signals Matter*, 2 Oct. 2017, www.signalsmatter.com/inflation-cpi/.

[1318] Davidson, Jordan. "April Grocery Prices Jumped the Most in 46 Years." *Eco Watch,* 13 May 2020, www.ecowatch.com/april-grocery-prices-coronavirus-2645989811.html?rebelltitem=2#rebelltitem2.

[1319] Quinn, Jim. "The Federal Reserve Must Die." *HCP Live*, 25 Aug. 2009, www.mdmag.com/medical-news/federal_reserve_must_die.

[1320] "The Inflation CPI Lie: BLS Posers..." *Signals Matter*, 2 Oct. 2017, www.signalsmatter.com/inflation-cpi/.

[1321] Marstrand, Bob. "Lies, damned lies and CPI." *Of Wealth,* 11 Oct. 2016, www.ofwealth.com/lies-damned-lies-cpi/.

1970s.[1322]   Others agree that the true rate of inflation is somewhere between 9% and 12%.[1323]

It is "in the self interest of the economic and financial establishment to understate inflation..."[1324]   "A lot of the establishment has a vested interest in underreporting the CPI rate most of the time. This includes governments, central banks, commercial banks and the entire investment industry."[1325]   For example, "commercial banks want lower CPI so they can pay less interest on bank deposits."[1326]

The government has several motives for hiding the real inflation rate and keeping the CPI statistic as low as possible.[1327] One is for political reasons.   Elected officials "know positive economic news, such as inflation that's under control, sound good in campaign speeches and can make the difference in a close election. In non-election years, fudging numbers like the CPI serves to avoid public pressure to do something to fix it. Government statistics that show inflation is not a problem keeps the issue off of the public

---

[1322] At 10. Gammon, George. "CPI Tax Scam: YOU'RE GOING TO LOSE A LOT OF MONEY! (Discover How)." *Youtube*, 11 Dec. 2019, www.youtube.com/watch?v=RA8PX_T1Suw.

[1323] "The U.S. Lies About Inflation: Here's The Inflation Secret The Government Doesn't Want You to Know." *Money Morning*, moneymorning.com/the-u-s-lies-about-inflation-heres-the-inflation-secret-the-government-doesnt-want-you-to-know/.

[1324] Marstrand, Bob. "Lies, damned lies and CPI." *Of Wealth*, 11 Oct. 2016, www.ofwealth.com/lies-damned-lies-cpi/.

[1325] *Id.*

[1326] *Id.*

[1327] Boring, Perianne. "If You Want To Know The Real Rate Of Inflation, Don't Bother With The CPI." *Forbes*, 3 Feb. 2014, www.forbes.com/sites/perianneboring/2014/02/03/if-you-want-to-know-the-real-rate-of-inflation-dont-bother-with-the-cpi/#5f1504b9200b.

radar, regardless of the reality."[1328] "It also gooses up the real GDP growth rate, so they can point to a stronger economy."[1329]

Another reason to fudge the inflation numbers is to save money. "Many government entitlements...are linked to the CPI."[1330] "The CPI is tied to the incomes of about 80 million Americans, specifically: Social Security beneficiaries, food stamp recipients, military and federal Civil Service retirees and survivors, and children on school lunch programs."[1331]

On the Social Security website, it states, "OASDI [Old Age, Survivors and Disability Insurance] benefits are indexed for inflation to protect beneficiaries from the loss of purchasing power implied by inflation. In the absence of such indexing, the purchasing power of Social Security benefits would be eroded as rising prices raise the cost of living."[1332] "If social security payments are linked

---

[1328] "The U.S. Lies About Inflation: Here's The Inflation Secret The Government Doesn't Want You to Know." *Money Morning*, moneymorning.com/the-u-s-lies-about-inflation-heres-the-inflation-secret-the-government-doesnt-want-you-to-know/.

[1329] Marstrand, Bob. "Lies, damned lies and CPI." *Of Wealth*, 11 Oct. 2016, www.ofwealth.com/lies-damned-lies-cpi/.

[1330] "The U.S. Lies About Inflation: Here's The Inflation Secret The Government Doesn't Want You to Know." *Money Morning*, moneymorning.com/the-u-s-lies-about-inflation-heres-the-inflation-secret-the-government-doesnt-want-you-to-know/.

[1331] Boring, Perianne. "If You Want To Know The Real Rate Of Inflation, Don't Bother With The CPI." *Forbes*, 3 Feb. 2014, www.forbes.com/sites/perianneboring/2014/02/03/if-you-want-to-know-the-real-rate-of-inflation-dont-bother-with-the-cpi/#5f1504b9200b.

[1332] At 6. Gammon, George. "CPI Tax Scam: YOU'RE GOING TO LOSE A LOT OF MONEY! (Discover How)." *Youtube*, 11 Dec. 2019, www.youtube.com/watch?v=RA8PX_T1Suw.

to the C-CPI-U, then social security payments will increase at a slower rate."[1333]

On the other hand, "lower official numbers mean lower payouts."[1334] "If the CPI is low, the less money the government needs to spend on cost of living adjustments, something seniors are acutely aware of."[1335] Shadow Stats' John "Williams says Social Security payments would be twice as high each month if the CPI formula had never been changed. It's no wonder so many seniors struggle to make ends meet."[1336] For example, if inflation were measured with C-PIU, then one would receive $1,000 per month, but if they measure it with C-CPI-U, then one would only receive $900/month.[1337] "The ploy has saved the debt-ridden U.S.

[1333] "New tax code = new price index = new tax bracket adjustments." *The Fred Blog*, 25 Jan. 2018, fredblog.stlouisfed.org/2018/01/new-tax-code-new-price-index-new-tax-bracket-adjustments/.

[1334] "The U.S. Lies About Inflation: Here's The Inflation Secret The Government Doesn't Want You to Know." *Money Morning*, moneymorning.com/the-u-s-lies-about-inflation-heres-the-inflation-secret-the-government-doesnt-want-you-to-know/.

[1335] Boring, Perianne. "If You Want To Know The Real Rate Of Inflation, Don't Bother With The CPI." *Forbes*, 3 Feb. 2014, www.forbes.com/sites/perianneboring/2014/02/03/if-you-want-to-know-the-real-rate-of-inflation-dont-bother-with-the-cpi/#5f1504b9200b.

[1336] "The U.S. Lies About Inflation: Here's The Inflation Secret The Government Doesn't Want You to Know." *Money Morning*, moneymorning.com/the-u-s-lies-about-inflation-heres-the-inflation-secret-the-government-doesnt-want-you-to-know/.

[1337] At 8:30. Gammon, George. "CPI Tax Scam: YOU'RE GOING TO LOSE A LOT OF MONEY! (Discover How)." *Youtube*, 11 Dec. 2019, www.youtube.com/watch?v=RA8PX_T1Suw.

government billions of dollars…"[1338]   Social Security is insolvent, and paying less to beneficiaries will delay the date of insolvency.[1339]

Thus, "[g]overnments want lower CPI because a lot of their payments increase in line with it. This includes things such as pension payments, welfare, and interest paid on inflation linked government bonds."[1340]   "The higher the CPI, the more money the government needs to spend on these income payments to keep pace with the cost of living."[1341]

In addition, inflation acts to increase the amount one pays in federal income tax. "A household's tax obligation depends on the income bracket for their earned income…"[1342]   "[A]s the cost of living goes up, our incomes often tend to rise as well in order to keep pace."[1343]   "As income increases to keep up with inflation, it moves individuals into higher tax brackets, which means that a

---

[1338] "The U.S. Lies About Inflation: Here's The Inflation Secret The Government Doesn't Want You to Know." *Money Morning*, moneymorning.com/the-u-s-lies-about-inflation-heres-the-inflation-secret-the-government-doesnt-want-you-to-know/.

[1339] At 7:30. Gammon, George. "CPI Tax Scam: YOU'RE GOING TO LOSE A LOT OF MONEY! (Discover How)." *Youtube*, 11 Dec. 2019, www.youtube.com/watch?v=RA8PX_T1Suw.

[1340] Marstrand, Bob. "Lies, damned lies and CPI." *Of Wealth,* 11 Oct. 2016, www.ofwealth.com/lies-damned-lies-cpi/.

[1341] Boring, Perianne. "If You Want To Know The Real Rate Of Inflation, Don't Bother With The CPI." *Forbes*, 3 Feb. 2014, www.forbes.com/sites/perianneboring/2014/02/03/if-you-want-to-know-the-real-rate-of-inflation-dont-bother-with-the-cpi/#5f1504b9200b.

[1342] "New tax code = new price index = new tax bracket adjustments." *The Fred Blog*, 25 Jan. 2018, fredblog.stlouisfed.org/2018/01/new-tax-code-new-price-index-new-tax-bracket-adjustments/.

[1343] "Indexing Income Taxes for Inflation: Why It Matters." *ITEP,* 22 Aug. 2016, itep.org/indexing-income-taxes-for-inflation-why-it-matters-1/.

larger percentage of their income is going to taxes."[1344] "If your income goes up, then you pay more or a higher percentage of your income in tax."[1345] "Nominally, you make more money, but do not have more purchasing power."[1346]

"Economists argue that the income brackets should be adjusted when prices change...This is referred to as indexing the tax brackets...The [Federal Income Tax] Act continues to adjust the tax brackets for price changes, as did the prior personal income tax legislation. The difference is the price index used to adjust those tax brackets. The previous tax code used the CPI-U measure to adjust the brackets, while the new code uses the C-CPI-U measure."[1347] This means that more individuals will now fall into higher tax brackets and pay more taxes than before.[1348]

Another bonus for government officials is that allowing inflation to devalue the dollar would help reduce the nation's debt burden.[1349] "As anyone who looks at the balance sheet knows, the

---

[1344] At 10. Gammon, George. "CPI Tax Scam: YOU'RE GOING TO LOSE A LOT OF MONEY! (Discover How)." *Youtube*, 11 Dec. 2019, www.youtube.com/watch?v=RA8PX_T1Suw.

[1345] At 4. *Id.*

[1346] At 10. *Id.*

[1347] "New tax code = new price index = new tax bracket adjustments." *The Fred Blog*, 25 Jan. 2018, fredblog.stlouisfed.org/2018/01/new-tax-code-new-price-index-new-tax-bracket-adjustments/.

[1348] At 1:20. Gammon, George. "CPI Tax Scam: YOU'RE GOING TO LOSE A LOT OF MONEY! (Discover How)." *Youtube*, 11 Dec. 2019, www.youtube.com/watch?v=RA8PX_T1Suw.

[1349] This refers to federal debt held by the public. "The U.S. Lies About Inflation: Here's The Inflation Secret The Government Doesn't Want You to Know." *Money Morning*, moneymorning.com/the-u-s-lies-about-inflation-heres-the-inflation-secret-the-government-doesnt-want-you-to-know/; Chappell, Bill. "U.S. National Debt Hits Record $22 Trillion." *NPR*, 13 Feb. 2019, www.npr.org/2019/02/13/694199256/u-s-national-debt-hits-22-trillion-a-new-record-thats-predicted-to-fall.

US is broke."[1350] Donald Trump said that, if the national debt topped $21 trillion by the end of President Obama's term in office, "Obama will have effectively bankrupted our country."[1351] "The debt of the federal government topped $26 trillion for the first time on [June 10, 2020]..."[1352] As of January 18, 2021, the U.S. national debt has grown to over $27.8 trillion.[1353] "The Congressional Budget Office (CBO) has predicted the national deficit will hit a record-breaking $3.7 trillion for just this federal fiscal year [2020] ..."[1354] "Over the next 10 years, annual federal deficits — when Congress spends more than it takes in through tax revenues — are expected to average $1.2 trillion..."[1355] The CBO estimates that debt will reach $28.7 trillion by 2029..."[1356] "As a share of the U.S.

[1350] "The Inflation CPI Lie : BLS Posers..." *Signals Matter*, 2 Oct. 2017, www.signalsmatter.com/inflation-cpi/.

[1351] Chappell, Bill. "U.S. National Debt Hits Record $22 Trillion." *NPR*, 13 Feb. 2019, www.npr.org/2019/02/13/694199256/u-s-national-debt-hits-22-trillion-a-new-record-thats-predicted-to-fall.

[1352] Jeffrey, Terence P. "Federal Debt Tops $26 Trillion for First Time; Jumps $2 Trillion in Just 63 Days." *CNS News*, 10 Jun. 2020, www.cnsnews.com/article/washington/terence-p-jeffrey/federal-debt-tops-26-trillion-first-time-jumps-2-trillion-just? fbclid=IwAR0I0e87psr963MMEXQboOmw8eIxy4fONPHhb8VsodVscY E1YN9PMEv897c.

[1353] "US Debt Clock." *usdebtclock.org*, www.usdebtclock.org.

[1354] Grzeszczzak, Jocelyn. "Under Trump's Watch, America's National Debt Has Increased by $6.6 Trillion." *Newsweek*, 29 Jul. 2020, www.newsweek.com/under-trumps-watch-americas-national-debt-has-increased-66-trillion-1521418? utm_term=Autofeed&utm_medium=Social&utm_source=Facebook&fbcli d=IwAR14ZF2HG9b1Xh-cF-TjIlG6PeU3Syf5l5xsXr8IVtgVkWDZcmm9aVD2JHc#Echobox=1596040 317.

[1355] Chappell, Bill. "U.S. National Debt Hits Record $22 Trillion." *NPR*, 13 Feb. 2019, www.npr.org/2019/02/13/694199256/u-s-national-debt-hits-22-trillion-a-new-record-thats-predicted-to-fall.

[1356] *Id.*

economy, the national debt stood at 78 percent of GDP in 2018. But the CBO says it will rise to 93 percent by the end of 2029..."[1357] Essentially, the federal government is insolvent, and only inflation can bail it out.[1358]

"The rise has been blamed on factors from the Great Recession to wars in Iraq and Afghanistan and rising costs of Social Security and Medicare..."[1359] "The CBO predicts federal spending will rise from 20.8 percent of GDP in 2019 to 23 percent in 2029, with programs such as Social Security and Medicare expected to spend more to cope with an aging population and rising health care costs."[1360] Combined with that is a lower corporate tax rate, which the Trump administration lowered in January 2018.[1361] Lower income in taxes for the US government means an even larger budget deficit.[1362]

"The idea that debt can grow faster than the ability to repay, until it unbalances a society, was well understood thousands of years ago, according to Michael Hudson, an economist and historian...'The fact is, debt causes instability for a society...'"[1363]

[1357] *Id.*

[1358] At 15. Gammon, George. "CPI Tax Scam: YOU'RE GOING TO LOSE A LOT OF MONEY! (Discover How)." *Youtube*, 11 Dec. 2019, www.youtube.com/watch?v=RA8PX_T1Suw.

[1359] Chappell, Bill. "U.S. National Debt Hits Record $22 Trillion." *NPR,* 13 Feb. 2019, www.npr.org/2019/02/13/694199256/u-s-national-debt-hits-22-trillion-a-new-record-thats-predicted-to-fall.

[1360] *Id.*

[1361] Tilford, Cale. "Repo: How the financial markets' plumbing got blocked." *Financial Times*, 25 Nov. 2019, ig.ft.com/repo-rate/.

[1362] *Id.*

[1363] Holland, Ben. "A 5,000-Year-Old Plan to Erase Debts Is Now a Hot Topic in America." *Bloomberg*, 10 Dec. 2019, www.bloomberg.com/news/articles/2019-12-10/a-5-000-year-old-plan-to-erase-debts-is-hot-topic-now-in-america?utm_campaign=pol&utm_medium=bd&utm_source=applenews.

"The politicians have no choice but to tax 'the living daylights' out of the poor and middle class to pay for the debt time bomb that the federal government has created, 23T in on-balance sheet debt, 100 T off-balance sheet debt and social security is insolvent, which goes back to the Federal Reserve."[1364]

The U.S. government is worried about deflation, because that increases the value of its debt burden.[1365] Thus, it would be in its best interest to increase inflation to devalue the dollar, which would decrease the value of its debt.[1366] "If they do not try to collapse the dollar, then the…overwhelming debt will completely consume the entire economy."[1367] Although Representative Paul Ryan believes, "There is nothing more insidious that a country can do to its people than to debase its currency," there is nothing new about devaluing the dollar.[1368] Franklin D. "Roosevelt took the gold from the people and debased the currency."[1369]

The Federal Reserve also has an interest in manipulating the numbers to hide its inflationary policies. The "quest for [2%] target inflation has been the official excuse/justification made by the Fed during the last 9 years for cranking down interest rates (ZIRP) and

---

[1364] At 15. Gammon, George. "CPI Tax Scam: YOU'RE GOING TO LOSE A LOT OF MONEY! (Discover How)." *Youtube*, 11 Dec. 2019, www.youtube.com/watch?v=RA8PX_T1Suw.

[1365] At 9. Gammon, George. "Federal Reserve: Discover Lies & Secrets They're Hiding From YOU!" *Youtube*, 27 Nov. 2019, www.youtube.com/watch?v=ha_MFJadAzA.

[1366] At 7. *Id.*

[1367] At 15:20. *Id.*

[1368] Krugman, Paul. "Abraham Lincoln, Inflationist." *The New York Times*, 10 Feb. 2011, www.nytimes.com/2011/02/11/opinion/11krugman.html.

[1369] At 16. RonPaulLibertyReport. "Central Banking Is On The Ropes: Gold Will Survive & The Fed Will End." *Youtube*, 13 Dec. 2019, www.youtube.com/watch?v=Ndcb2SPRU7M.

quintupling the US money supply (QE)..."[1370] Programs such as QE devalue the domestic currency.[1371] "Increasing the supply of money is similar to increasing supply of any other asset — it lowers the cost of money."[1372] "By increasing the money supply, QE keeps the value of the country's currency low..."[1373]

"Central banks want low CPI so they can demonstrate that they aren't destroying the value of a country's fiat currency too fast."[1374] "The Fed reports the consumer price inflation rate over the past ten years as ranging from about 1.5% to 2.4%, not counting a few outlying years. The average from 2010 – 2019 was 1.77%. The Fed then tells us that low number proves its massive inflation of the currency during the last decade 'hasn't resulted in inflation,' by which they mean a rise in the price of consumer goods. But it has. The key to this deception is its false premise: that one should compare the prices of goods and services this year to what they were last year. That's the wrong comparison. The correct comparison would be between what prices are today vs. what they would [have been] without quantitative easing."[1375] "Fed policies like quantitative easing and holding interest rates near zero should have

---

[1370] "The Inflation CPI Lie: BLS Posers..." *Signals Matter*, 2 Oct. 2017, www.signalsmatter.com/inflation-cpi/.

[1371] Chappelow, Jim. "Quantitative Easing." *Investopedia*, 6 Sept. 2019, www.investopedia.com/terms/q/quantitative-easing.asp.

[1372] Amadeo, Kimberly. "Explaining Quantitative Easing – QE." *The Balance*, 3 Sept. 2019, www.thebalance.com/what-is-quantitative-easing-definition-and-explanation-3305881.

[1373] *Id.*

[1374] Marstrand, Bob. "Lies, damned lies and CPI." *Of Wealth*, 11 Oct. 2016, www.ofwealth.com/lies-damned-lies-cpi/.

[1375] Mullen, Tom. "'Inflation is low': The Federal Reserve's Scam of the Century." *Tommullen.com*, 31 Mar. 2020, www.tommullen.net/featured/inflation-is-low-the-federal-reserves-scam-of-the-century/?fbclid=IwAR1As6UZbfSEJ6I0-s3g2LyrUf5QFsB0HJ5yrSdRMxE9TDTtYjwGUitZATc.

pushed inflation much higher – but the CPI's mutant methodology made sure that didn't happen. If the CPI were reported accurately, the Fed would be forced to raise interest rates, which in turn would slow the economy and slam the stock markets "[1376]

Low CPI gives the Fed "an excuse to print money to prop up bond and stock markets for their friends in the financial industry."[1377] "The Fed is using the 'target inflation' meme to justify the asset bubble created by QE 1-3 and the Zero Interest Rate Policy (ZIRP)..."[1378] "The Central Bank is about stimulating the markets, not a targeted CPI...Bernanke & Yellen were never aiming for a higher 'target CPI' to stop their post-08 QE/ZIRP keg party; instead, they've been coyly fudging the numbers of a bogus CPI to make it appear much lower than it really was. Or put more bluntly: the CPI is a canard and the 'target inflation' meme a smoke and mirror pose..."[1379]

Luke Gromen, a proponent of a dollar collapse end game theory, suggests that the Fed will print as much money as needed to make sure they keep the interest rates down.[1380] The Fed would print money to buy enough T bills to suppress interest rates.[1381] Such action would expand the Federal Reserve's balance sheet to $20 trillion, which would put a tremendous amount of downward

---

[1376] "The U.S. Lies About Inflation: Here's The Inflation Secret The Government Doesn't Want You to Know." *Money Morning*, moneymorning.com/the-u-s-lies-about-inflation-heres-the-inflation-secret-the-government-doesnt-want-you-to-know/.

[1377] Marstrand, Bob. "Lies, damned lies and CPI." *Of Wealth*, 11 Oct. 2016, www.ofwealth.com/lies-damned-lies-cpi/.

[1378] "The Inflation CPI Lie : BLS Posers..." *Signals Matter*, 2 Oct. 2017, www.signalsmatter.com/inflation-cpi/.

[1379] *Id.*

[1380] At 12. Gammon, George. "Repo Market: Will Year End Doomsday Trigger DOLLAR COLLAPSE?!?." *Youtube*, 27 Dec. 2019, www.youtube.com/watch?v=7jXN42_GxNQ.

[1381] *Id.*

pressure on the dollar.[1382]   Once the dollar goes low enough, other countries would be able to buy Treasuries.[1383]   This would put a bid on the Treasuries and that would decrease the amount of money that the Fed would have to print to keep those interest rates low.[1384] "The Fed has to expand its balance sheet until it can push the dollar down far enough to where it is attractive for foreign entities to buy our debt."[1385]   "Because America is broke and increasingly unable to actually produce real income (US GDP annualizes at around 1.9% and US manufacturing output has been shrinking at a 0.41% annual rate for the last decade), our pinched government has been doing what anyone with a Ferrari appetite and a bus-boy salary does: borrow, over-spend and eventually burn out…"[1386]   " T h e   U S … issues more Treasuries each year in the same way a broke college kid applies for more MasterCards to pay last month's Visa bills… because US now survives off debt, this also means we survive off Treasury bonds…Given this unfortunate reality, the Fed, along with the US Treasury, and of course the BLS, can all agree on this: they need to make those Treasury bonds look good – or at least not look bad…And nothing makes sovereign bonds look worse than high inflation. Currently, the 10-Year US Treasury produces a woefully modest yield of around 2.2%…But here's the rub, if the US 10 year is producing a paltry yield of 2.2%, and reported inflation, as of today's CPI projections is only around 2%, investors are barely scraping an inflation adjusted return. Needless to say, the Fed wants to make sure such figures don't get any worse…After all, if no one buys our bonds, we'd have to come up with a national economic plan that considered economic growth rather than issuing more debt

---

[1382] *Id.*

[1383] *Id.*

[1384] *Id.*

[1385] At 15:20. *Id.*

[1386] "The Inflation CPI Lie: BLS Posers…" *Signals Matter*, 2 Oct. 2017, www.signalsmatter.com/inflation-cpi/.

to stay alive…Moreover, if faith in our bonds sinks, then bond prices would sink, which in turn means our interest rates would rise, placing a massive (and unsustainable) burden on the US government's cost of borrowing…So if there ever came a day when honestly reported US inflation rates were higher than the yields of the US 10-Year, the demand for that bond would sink faster than the Titanic, and with it, our entire US economic house of cards…"[1387]

According to Luke Gromen, if the Fed has to come in on a permanent basis and inject more liquidity into the market, then that will be the catalyst for the dollar collapse, which can occur overnight.[1388] An example is the 1985 Plaza Accord, which involved secret monetary diplomacy.[1389] Finance ministers and central bankers of the G5 industrial nations reached an agreement to sell dollars on worldwide currency markets in an effort to devalue the dollar.[1390] The stated claim was to boost exports, but really it was to inflate away $23 trillion in debt and make off-sheet liabilities easier to handle.[1391] The dollar plummeted; it was down 4.29% the day after the Plaza Accord and down 55% against the Japanese yen a year later.[1392]

It is unlikely that such a scheme would work today because China, Japan, and the EU are trying to devalue their own currencies.[1393] Thus, they would not be willing to lower the value of

---

[1387] *Id.*

[1388] At 15:20. Gammon, George. "Repo Market: Will Year End Doomsday Trigger DOLLAR COLLAPSE?!?." *Youtube*, 27 Dec. 2019, www.youtube.com/watch?v=7jXN42_GxNQ.

[1389] At 3. Gammon, George. "Dollar Collapse: Can It Happen Overnight? (ANSWERED!)" *Youtube*, 29 Nov. 2019, www.youtube.com/watch?v=P0K-9EQk1PA.

[1390] At 3. *Id.*

[1391] At 7. *Id.*

[1392] At 3. *Id.*

[1393] At 7. *Id.*

the dollar now by increasing the value of their currency.[1394] However, the Fed could trap money in the US by "going cashless" and setting up capital controls.[1395] It could then print dollars to sell into the foreign exchange (FX) market, which would lower their value, even to the point of collapse.[1396]

Some have suggested that Modern Monetary Theory (MMT) will be the response to this situation, which could lead to massive inflation. This is the topic of the next section.

[1394] *Id.*

[1395] At 10. Gammon, George. "Dollar Collapse: Can It Happen Overnight? (ANSWERED!)" *Youtube*, 29 Nov. 2019, www.youtube.com/watch? v=P0K-9EQk1PA.

[1396] *Id.*

Modern Monetary Theory (MMT)

Author Thomas E. Woods, Jr. related the following story: "When I was a boy, my mother found it endearing that whenever my parents would say they needed money for this or that, I would simply recommend that they go to the bank and get some. But something like that is not far removed from the actual views of a great many people of influence…"[1397]

"Many of the nation's leading progressives and democratic socialists are big supporters of a fringe economic idea called Modern Monetary Theory [MMT], which directly calls for the Fed to print whatever amount of money the national government needs to control the economy."[1398]   Political leaders such as Alexandria Ocasio-Cortez and Bernie Sanders have espoused MMT, as well as economist Stephanie Kelton, who is Bernie Sanders' senior economic advisor.[1399]

MMT, developed by American economist Warren Mosler, is a heterodox macroeconomic theory that proposes that monetarily sovereign nations such as the U.S., U.K., Japan, and Canada are not constrained operationally by revenues when it comes to federal government spending.[1400]   It posits that a government can print money to pay its bills.[1401]   "MMT says that a government doesn't

---

[1397] Woods, Thomas E. Jr. "The Revolutionary War and the Destruction of the Continental." *Mises Institute*, 11 Oct. 2006, mises.org/library/revolutionary-war-and-destruction-continental.

[1398] Haskins, Justin. "The Fed is pushing America dangerously close to socialism." *Glennbeck.com*, 23 Mar. 2020, www.glennbeck.com/blog/the-fed-is-pushing-america-dangerously-close-to-socialism.

[1399] "Modern Monetary Theory (MMT)." *Investopedia*. 24 Sept. 2019, www.investopedia.com/modern-monetary-theory-mmt-4588060.

[1400] *Id.*

[1401] Lewis, Nathan. "The Problem With "Modern Monetary Theory" Is That It's True." *Forbes*, 21 Feb. 2019, www.forbes.com/sites/nathanlewis/2019/02/21/the-problem-with-modern-monetary-theory-is-that-its-true/#4fb22b0256fb.

need to sell bonds to borrow money, since that is money it can create on its own."[1402]   "In other words, such governments do not need taxes or borrowing for spending since they can print as much as they need and are the monopoly issuers of the currency."[1403]

The central tenet "of MMT is that a government that issues its own currency can always fund itself with that currency."[1404]   "The federal government can issue however much new currency it wants, so the government could fund large-scale socially useful projects if the political will to do so were present."[1405]   Such "governments with a fiat currency system can and should print (or create with a few keystrokes in today's digital age) as much money as they need to spend."[1406]

"The basic idea of MMT...bypasses both paying interest on newly issued money and the artifice of central bank monetization. Instead, the Treasury issues new currency directly. This removes the 'governor' of interest payments, freeing the Treasury to issue cost-free currency in virtually unlimited quantities."[1407]   It has been suggested that the federal government could pay off its debt to the Federal Reserve with debt-free Treasury notes.   The inventor, Thomas Edison, observed, "If our nation can issue a dollar bond, it

[1402] "The government sells bonds to drain excess reserves and hit its overnight interest rate target." *Id.*

[1403] "Modern Monetary Theory (MMT)." *Investopedia*. 24 Sept. 2019, www.investopedia.com/modern-monetary-theory-mmt-4588060.

[1404] Horan, Patrick. "5 Problems with MMT." *The Bridge*, 18 Mar. 2019, www.mercatus.org/bridge/commentary/5-problems-mmt.

[1405] Smith, Charles Hughes. "Modern Monetary Theory." *InflationData.com*, 5 Nov. 2019, inflationdata.com/articles/2019/11/05/modern-monetary-theory/.

[1406] "Modern Monetary Theory (MMT)." *Investopedia*. 24 Sept. 2019, www.investopedia.com/modern-monetary-theory-mmt-4588060.

[1407] Smith, Charles Hughes. "Modern Monetary Theory." *InflationData.com*, 5 Nov. 2019, inflationdata.com/articles/2019/11/05/modern-monetary-theory/.

can issue a dollar bill. The element that makes the bond good, makes the bill good, also. The difference between the bond and the bill is that the bond lets money brokers collect twice the amount of the bond and an additional 20%, whereas the currency pays nobody but those who contribute directly in some useful way. It is absurd to say that our country can issue $30 million in bonds and not $30 million in currency. Both are promises to pay, but one promise fattens the usurers and the other helps the people."[1408]

"At the end of the day, MMT's 'eye-opening revelation' is simply a technical observation that Uncle Sam has a printing press...that Uncle Sam can run that printing press whenever he wants...and that, therefore, Uncle Sam can always pay off debts issued in his own legal tender...The U.S. government is like the banker in Monopoly in that government issuance of currency and debt is a closed loop, with all U.S. debts payable by U.S. currency (which has no limits)..."[1409]

Despite claims, MMT is not actually a "new" theory. For instance, President Abraham Lincoln essentially engaged in MMT. During his administration (1861-1865), the Union needed money to fund the Civil War, but "the bankers [Chase Bank] were willing to lend it only under circumstances...involving staggering interest rates of 24 to 36 percent. President Abraham Lincoln saw that this would bankrupt the North..."[1410] He declined.

Colonel Dick Taylor of Illinois advised the president "that the Union had the power under the Constitution to solve its financing

[1408] Brown, Ellen. "Revive Lincoln's Monetary Policy: An Open Letter to President Obama." *The Web of Debt*, 8 Apr. 2009, www.webofdebt.com/articles/lincoln_obama.php.

[1409] Mercenary Trader. "Weekender: The Trouble With Modern Monetary Theory (MMT)." *Business Insider*, 19 Dec. 2010, www.businessinsider.com/weekender-the-trouble-with-modern-monetary-theory-mmt-2011-1.

[1410] Brown, Ellen. "Revive Lincoln's Monetary Policy: An Open Letter to President Obama." *The Web of Debt*, 8 Apr. 2009, www.webofdebt.com/articles/lincoln_obama.php.

problem by printing its money as a sovereign government. Taylor said: 'Just get Congress to pass a bill authorizing the printing of full legal tender treasury notes… and pay your soldiers with them and go ahead and win your war with them also. If you make them full legal tender…they will have the full sanction of the government and be just as good as any money; as Congress is given that express right by the Constitution.'"[1411]

Lincoln, agreeing with Colonel Taylor, said, "The government should create, issue and circulate all the currency and credit needed to satisfy the spending power of the government and the buying power of consumers…The privilege of creating and issuing money is not only the supreme prerogative of Government, but it is the Government's greatest creative opportunity. By the adoption of these principles, the long-felt want for a uniform medium will be satisfied. The taxpayers will be saved immense sums of interest, discounts and exchanges. The financing of all public enterprises, the maintenance of stable government and ordered progress, and the conduct of the Treasury will become matters of practical administration. The people can and will be furnished with a currency as safe as their own government. Money will cease to be the master and become the servant of humanity. Democracy will rise superior to the money power."[1412]

Pursuant to his plan, Lincoln persuaded Congress to enact the Legal Tender Act of 1862, which provided for the creation of Treasury notes.[1413] These notes were printed at no interest to the

---

[1411] *Id.*

[1412] "The History of Money Part 2." *XAT3*, www.xat.org/xat/usury.html.

[1413] "Greenbacks: Definition & History." *Study.com*, study.com/academy/lesson/greenbacks-definition-lesson.html.

federal government.[1414]   They were called "Greenbacks" because green dye was used on the back in the printing process to distinguish them from bank notes.[1415] Lincoln proclaimed, "We gave the people of this republic the greatest blessing they ever had, their own paper money to pay their own debts."[1416]   He hoped that "[b]y Government creation of money, the taxpayers will be saved immense sums of interest."[1417]

The federal government (Union) began printing greenbacks in 1862.[1418] "Initially limited to $150 million, a second $150 million issue was approved in July [1862] and a third $150 million issue passed in early 1863."[1419]   During the course of the Civil War

---

[1414] Jones, Stack. "An Essay On The History Of Banking." *The Banking Swindle*, 1 Jan. 2018, criminalbankingmonopoly.wordpress.com/. By April 1862, "$449,338,902 worth of Lincoln's debt free money has been printed and distributed." Hitchcock, Andrew. "Historical Timeline of the Rothschild Dynasty - Part 3." *The Sirius Report*, 17 Aug. 2015, www.thesiriusreport.com/geopolitics/historical-timeline-rothschild-dynasty-3/; "Greenback movement." *Encyclopedia Brittanica,* 6 Dec. 2019, www.britannica.com/event/Greenback-movement.

[1415] "Greenbacks: Definition & History." *Study.com*, study.com/academy/lesson/greenbacks-definition-lesson.html; Jones, Stack. "An Essay On The History Of Banking." *The Banking Swindle*, 1 Jan. 2018, criminalbankingmonopoly.wordpress.com/.

[1416] Hitchcock, Andrew. "Historical Timeline of the Rothschild Dynasty - Part 3." *The Sirius Report*, 17 Aug. 2015, www.thesiriusreport.com/geopolitics/historical-timeline-rothschild-dynasty-3/

[1417] Greenbacks were in circulation until 1994. Hodges, James P. PhD and Cynthia F. Hodges, JD, LLM, MA. "FED Up: Founding Fathers, the Banking System, and the Federal Reserve." *Leadership By George Washington*, 21 Apr. 2010, leadershipbygeorge.blogspot.com/2010/04/fed-up-founding-fathers-banking-system.html.

[1418] "The Greenback Question." *US History.com*, www.u-s-history.com/pages/h171.html.

[1419] Kaza, Greg. "The U.S. Presidents and the Money Issue." *FEE,* 1 Apr. 1996, fee.org/articles/the-us-presidents-and-the-money-issue/.

(1862-1865), nearly $450 million in greenbacks was printed.[1420] "With this new money, Lincoln paid the troops, and bought their supplies."[1421] About 15% of the war effort was funded by paper notes printed and backed by the government (and not specie).[1422]

Although the greenback was not backed by gold, it was backed by the government, and it could be used to pay public and private debts.[1423] "The original intention was for the greenbacks to hold the same value as regular gold-backed notes, but that result never occurred."[1424] "Since the debt instruments promised to pay people gold coins, people were willing to accept them in lieu of the actual gold coins. Problems arose when people realized that the Lincoln regime could not honor all of the debt instruments that it had put

---

[1420] Jones, Stack. "An Essay On The History Of Banking." *The Banking Swindle*, 1 Jan. 2018, criminalbankingmonopoly.wordpress.com/. By April 1862, "$449,338,902 worth of Lincoln's debt free money has been printed and distributed." Hitchcock, Andrew. "Historical Timeline of the Rothschild Dynasty - Part 3." *The Sirius Report*, 17 Aug. 2015, www.thesiriusreport.com/geopolitics/historical-timeline-rothschild-dynasty-3/; "Greenback movement." *Encyclopedia Brittanica,* 6 Dec. 2019, www.britannica.com/event/Greenback-movement.

[1421] Jones, Stack. "An Essay On The History Of Banking." *The Banking Swindle*, 1 Jan. 2018, criminalbankingmonopoly.wordpress.com/.

[1422] Brown, Ellen. "Revive Lincoln's Monetary Policy: An Open Letter to President Obama." *The Web of Debt*, 8 Apr. 2009, www.webofdebt.com/articles/lincoln_obama.php. "Greenback." *Investopedia,* 30 Apr. 2019, www.investopedia.com/terms/g/greenback.asp; "Greenback." *Museum of American Finance*, www.moaf.org/exhibits/checks_balances/abraham-lincoln/greenback.

[1423] "Greenbacks: Definition & History." *Study.com*, study.com/academy/lesson/greenbacks-definition-lesson.html.

[1424] "The Greenback Question." *US History.com*, www.u-s-history.com/pages/h171.html.

into circulation. That risk caused the Lincoln notes to begin trading at a discount."[1425]

"Issuing paper money led to inflation — the money itself was worth less (because when a product's supply rises, its worth declines)."[1426] "As always happens with paper money, the Greenbacks lost buying power."[1427] Rampant price inflation ensued because greenbacks were not backed by gold or silver.[1428] "Inflation was 14% in 1862 and 25% in 1863 and 1864."[1429] Overall, "[p]rices rose 110.9 percent from 1860 to war's end."[1430]

The greenback declined steadily in value, especially against gold.[1431] "By mid-1864, greenbacks were worth 35 cents in

---

[1425] Hornberger, Jacob. "Monetary Destruction in America." *Tenth Amendment Center*, 7 Jun. 2020, tenthamendmentcenter.com/2020/06/07/monetary-destruction-in-america/?fbclid=IwAR1qznHUtpPxV4SZfCJk0G9H9gTS2kepV1ZU5BKoX_o06DxBXusfHyCPK6s.

[1426] "Greenbacks: Definition & History." *Study.com*, study.com/academy/lesson/greenbacks-definition-lesson.html.

[1427] Cortez, JP. "Fake Money, Sound Money and Government Malfeasance." *Tenth Amendment Center*, 28 Aug. 2018, tenthamendmentcenter.com/2018/08/28/fake-money-sound-money-and-government-malfeasance/.

[1428] "Greenback Labor Party." *Ohio History Central*, ohiohistorycentral.org/w/Greenback_Labor_Party; "Greenback." *Investopedia*, 30 Apr. 2019, www.investopedia.com/terms/g/greenback.asp.

[1429] "Greenback." *Investopedia*, 30 Apr. 2019, www.investopedia.com/terms/g/greenback.asp; "Greenback." *Museum of American Finance*, www.moaf.org/exhibits/checks_balances/abraham-lincoln/greenback.

[1430] Kaza, Greg. "The U.S. Presidents and the Money Issue." *FEE*, 1 Apr. 1996, fee.org/articles/the-us-presidents-and-the-money-issue/.

[1431] "Greenback Labor Party." *Ohio History Central*, ohiohistorycentral.org/w/Greenback_Labor_Party; "Greenback." *Investopedia*, 30 Apr. 2019, www.investopedia.com/terms/g/greenback.asp.

gold."[1432]   According to H. W. Brand's book, *Greenback Planet: How the Dollar Conquered the World and Threatened Civilization as We Know It*, the greenback plummeted "to a value of 258 greenback to 100 gold (its lowest point) in 1864. When the war ended in 1865, the value of the greenback recovered to 150 greenback to 100 gold."[1433]   "But the rise in their value also increased the cost of everyday goods and supplies."[1434]   Lincoln tried to scapegoat "gold speculators" for the decline in the value of the greenback against gold.[1435] "Failing to regulate the gold market, he tried to destroy it by passing a Gold Bill in mid-1864 that prohibited all gold futures contracts and imposed severe penalties. Public opposition, however, forced the bill's repeal that year."[1436]

Legal tender laws made federal notes legal tender for all debts. This "allowed debtors who had borrowed money (gold or silver coin) before the Civil War to repay debts with Greenbacks that had less than half the buying power of the original loan."[1437]   For example, storeowners were "legally required to accept at face value the devalued notes of the Lincoln regime. [They] would have to accept a $10 bill when it was only worth, say, $7 in the

---

[1432] Kaza, Greg. "The U.S. Presidents and the Money Issue." *FEE,* 1 Apr. 1996, fee.org/articles/the-us-presidents-and-the-money-issue/.

[1433] "Greenback." *Investopedia,* 30 Apr. 2019, www.investopedia.com/terms/g/greenback.asp.

[1434] *Id.*

[1435] Kaza, Greg. "The U.S. Presidents and the Money Issue." *FEE,* 1 Apr. 1996, fee.org/articles/the-us-presidents-and-the-money-issue/.

[1436] *Id.*

[1437] Cortez, JP. "Fake Money, Sound Money and Government Malfeasance." *Tenth Amendment Center*, 28 Aug. 2018, tenthamendmentcenter.com/2018/08/28/fake-money-sound-money-and-government-malfeasance/.

marketplace…"[1438] "Creditors were understandably furious over this swindle…"[1439] "Pressure from business interests and creditors in the postwar period led to an effort to retire the greenbacks. These forces did not want to receive payments in cheap money and opposed any government policy that would lead to inflation."[1440] "In the late 1870s, the government announced that it would support all greenbacks with gold. This action stabilized the currency, [and] increased its value."[1441]

Even though it did not work out as hoped, Lincoln's monetary policy still constituted a threat to established interests and made him an enemy of powerful forces.[1442] The bankers' displeasure with Lincoln was first voiced in an editorial that appeared in the *Times of London* in 1862: "If this mischievous financial policy, which has its origins in North America, shall be endured down to a fixture, then that government will furnish its own money without cost. It will pay off its debt and be without debt. It will have all the money necessary to carry on its commerce. It will become prosperous without precedence in the history of the world. The brains and the wealth of

---

[1438] Hornberger, Jacob. "Monetary Destruction in America." *Tenth Amendment Center*, 7 Jun. 2020, tenthamendmentcenter.com/2020/06/07/monetary-destruction-in-america/?fbclid=IwAR1qznHUtpPxV4SZfCJk0G9H9gTS2kepV1ZU5BKoX_o06D xBXusfHyCPK6s.

[1439] Cortez, JP. "Fake Money, Sound Money and Government Malfeasance." *Tenth Amendment Center*, 28 Aug. 2018, tenthamendmentcenter.com/2018/08/28/fake-money-sound-money-and-government-malfeasance/.

[1440] "The Greenback Question." *US History.com*, www.u-s-history.com/pages/h171.html.

[1441] "Greenback Labor Party." *Ohio History Central*, ohiohistorycentral.org/w/Greenback_Labor_Party.

[1442] Brown, Ellen. "Revive Lincoln's Monetary Policy: An Open Letter to President Obama." *The Web of Debt*, 8 Apr. 2009, www.webofdebt.com/articles/lincoln_obama.php.

all countries will go to North America. That country must be destroyed or it will destroy every monarchy on the globe."[1443]

President Lincoln, aware of the danger, lamented, "I have two great enemies, the Southern Army in front of me and the bankers in the rear. Of the two, the one at my rear is my greatest foe."[1444] In 1864, he wrote, "I see in the near future a crisis approaching that unnerves me and causes me to tremble for the safety of my country. As a result of the war, corporations have been enthroned and an era of corruption in high places will follow, and the money power of the country will endeavor to prolong its reign by working upon the prejudices of the people until all wealth is aggregated in a few hands, and the Republic is destroyed. I feel at this moment more anxiety for the safety of my country than ever before, even in the midst of war."[1445]

"The banker's intention was to divide and conquer the nation through war, which they would finance…"[1446] Luckily, Lincoln had a friend in Tsar Alexander II of Russia, who was well aware of the money changers' scam. He refused to allow them to set up a central

---

[1443] "The History of Money Part 2." *XAT3*, www.xat.org/xat/usury.html. Brown, Ellen. "Revive Lincoln's Monetary Policy: An Open Letter to President Obama." *The Web of Debt*, 8 Apr. 2009, www.webofdebt.com/articles/lincoln_obama.php.

[1444] "Quotes by Abraham Lincoln." *myqualitywriting.com*, www.myqualitywriting.com/QuotesbyAbrahamLincoln1.html.

[1445] Abraham Lincoln – In a letter written to William Elkin, 1860 The quote can be found on page 954 of the second volume of "Abraham Lincoln: A New Portrait," a Lincoln biography written in 1931 by Emanuel Hertz. The quote appears in a letter from Abraham Lincoln to Col. William F. Elkins dated November 21, 1864. Buhler, Rich. "Abraham Lincoln Quote About Capitalism and Corruption-Correctly Attributed!" *Truthorfiction*, 26 Feb. 2016, www.truthorfiction.com/abraham-lincoln-quote-about-capitalism-and-corruption/. This quote has been correctly attributed to Lincoln.

[1446] Jones, Stack. "An Essay On The History Of Banking." *The Banking Swindle*, 1 Jan. 2018, criminalbankingmonopoly.wordpress.com/.

bank in Russia.[1447]   The Tsar warned France and Britain that, if they assisted the Confederacy against Lincoln's Union forces, then Russia would consider it to be an act of war.[1448]   "To show that he wasn't messing about, he sent part of his Pacific Fleet to port in San Francisco and another part to New York."[1449]   These actions helped Lincoln secure a victory in the Civil War.   Years later (in 1917), international bankers financed the Bolshevik Revolution to overthrow Tsar Nicholas II so that they could install a central bank in Russia.[1450]

The bankers were forced to use more covert means to deal with Lincoln's opposition. According to Gerald G. McGeer, John Wilkes Booth was hired by "international bankers" to kill the president: "Abraham Lincoln was assassinated through the machinations of a group representative of the international bankers who feared the United States President's national credit ambitions, and the plot was hatched in Toronto and Montreal. The bankers… had opposed Lincoln's national currency program, and had fought him throughout the entire Civil War, regarding his policy of green back currency."[1451]   "McGeer stated that the international bankers not only wanted to reestablish a federal central bank, but also

---

[1447] Hitchcock, Andrew. "Historical Timeline of the Rothschild Dynasty - Part 3." *The Sirius Report*, 17 Aug. 2015, www.thesiriusreport.com/ geopolitics/historical-timeline-rothschild-dynasty-3/.

[1448] "The History of Money Part 2." *XAT3*, www.xat.org/xat/usury.html.

[1449] Hitchcock, Andrew. "Historical Timeline of the Rothschild Dynasty - Part 3." *The Sirius Report*, 17 Aug. 2015, www.thesiriusreport.com/ geopolitics/historical-timeline-rothschild-dynasty-3/.

[1450] "Why did US bankers fund the Russian Revolution?" *Communism Made Easy,* communism-explained.blogspot.com/2010/05/why-did-us-bankers-fund-russian.html; "Who financed Lenin and Trotsky?" *Wildboar.net*, www.wildboar.net/multilingual/easterneuropean/russian/ literature/articles/whofinanced/whofinancedleninandtrotsky.htm.

[1451] According to an article of the Vancouver Sun, on May 2nd, 1934. Jones, Stack. "An Essay On The History Of Banking." *The Banking Swindle*, 1 Jan. 2018, criminalbankingmonopoly.wordpress.com/.

wanted to debase America's currency on the gold they controlled. What this meant was the bankers wanted to put America on a gold standard. Lincoln had done just the opposite when he issued green backs, which were based purely on the good faith and credit of the U.S. nation. McGeer wrote, 'They were the men interested in the establishment of the gold standard money system, and the right of the bankers to manage the currency and credit of every nation in the world.'"[1452] "Lincoln would certainly have killed off the national banks monopoly had he not been killed himself in 1865."[1453]

"With Lincoln out of the way, the bankers were able to proceed with their plans…Within eight years after Lincoln's assassination, silver was demonetized and the gold standard money system set up in the United States."[1454] "The Coinage Act of 1873 demonetized silver as the legal tender of the United States, in favor of fully adopting the gold standard…"[1455] Earnest Seyd, who was an agent for the Bank of England, disclosed in 1873, "I went to America in the winter of 1872-1873 to secure…the passage of a bill demonetizing silver. It was in the interest of those I represented – the governors of the Bank of England, to have it done. By 1873 gold coins were the only form of coin money."[1456] "The withdrawal of silver from the economy resulted in a contraction of the money supply, which contributed to a recession throughout the country. In

---

[1452] Jones, Stack. "An Essay On The History Of Banking." *The Banking Swindle*, 1 Jan. 2018, criminalbankingmonopoly.wordpress.com/.

[1453] "The History of Money Part 2." *XAT3*, www.xat.org/xat/usury.html; Brown, Ellen. "Revive Lincoln's Monetary Policy: An Open Letter to President Obama." *The Web of Debt*, 8 Apr. 2009, www.webofdebt.com/ articles/lincoln_obama.php.

[1454] "From the Book LINCOLN MONEY MARTYRED." *Cyberclass.net*, www.cyberclass.net/lincoln.htm.

[1455] Chappelow, Jim. "Demonetization." *Investopedia,* 20 Mar. 2020, www.investopedia.com/terms/d/demonetization.asp.

[1456] "The International Bankers: Famous Quotes." *ConspiracyAnalyst.org*, 23 Dec. 2019, conspiracyanalyst.org/2013/03/01/the-international-bankers-famous-quotes/.

response to the recession and political pressure from farmers and from silver miners and refiners, the Bland-Allison Act remonetized silver as legal tender in 1878."[1457]

"Not since Lincoln has the United States issued debt free notes...the 1994 Regal Act, actually authorized the replacement of Lincoln's green backs with debt-based notes. This meant that Lincoln's greenbacks were in circulation in the U.S. until 1994."[1458] "Every circulating FRN (Federal Reserve Note) represents a one dollar debt to the Federal Reserve System."[1459] "According to historian W. Cleon Skousen: Right after the Civil War, there was considerable talk about reviving Lincoln's brief experiment with the...monetary system. Had not the European money-trust intervened, it would have no doubt become an established institution."[1460] For example, James Buel of the American Bankers Association suggested in 1877: "It is advisable to do all in your power to sustain such prominent daily and weekly newspapers...as will oppose the Greenback issue of paper money and that you will also withhold patronage from all applicants (for loans) who are not willing to oppose the government issue of money...To repeal the act creating bank notes, or to restore to circulation the government issue of money will be to provide the people with money and will therefore seriously affect our individual profits as bankers and

---

[1457] Chappelow, Jim. "Demonetization." *Investopedia,* 20 Mar. 2020, www.investopedia.com/terms/d/demonetization.asp.

[1458] Jones, Stack. "An Essay On The History Of Banking." *The Banking Swindle,* 1 Jan. 2018, criminalbankingmonopoly.wordpress.com/.

[1459] *Money Facts,* circa 1970, House Banking and Currency Committee. "Quotes from International Bankers." *Stopthecrime.net,* 25 Feb. 2019, stopthecrime.net/wp/2019/02/25/quotes-from-international-bankers/.

[1460] Brown, Ellen. "Revive Lincoln's Monetary Policy: An Open Letter to President Obama." *The Web of Debt,* 8 Apr. 2009, www.webofdebt.com/articles/lincoln_obama.php.

lenders."[1461]   "The institution that became established instead was the Federal Reserve, a privately-owned central bank given the power in 1913 to print Federal Reserve Notes (or dollar bills) and lend them to the government" at interest.[1462]

Traditional economic theories hold that unlimited spending would be fiscally irresponsible as the debt would balloon and inflation would skyrocket, as was the case with the Continental and the Greenback.[1463]   According to MMT, however, "[d]ebt and deficits don't really matter..."[1464]   Officials do not need to worry about large debts, because the government cannot go broke or be insolvent unless a political decision to do so is made.[1465]   "[T]he only limit the government has when it comes to spending is the availability of real resources, like workers, construction supplies, etc."[1466]   This ignores the fact that "[t]he financial power of the

---

[1461]   In 1877. "The International Bankers: Famous Quotes." *ConspiracyAnalyst.org*, 23 Dec. 2019, conspiracyanalyst.org/2013/03/01/the-international-bankers-famous-quotes/.

[1462] Brown, Ellen. "Revive Lincoln's Monetary Policy: An Open Letter to President Obama." *The Web of Debt*, 8 Apr. 2009, www.webofdebt.com/articles/lincoln_obama.php.

[1463] "Modern Monetary Theory (MMT)." *Investopedia*. 24 Sept. 2019, www.investopedia.com/modern-monetary-theory-mmt-4588060.

[1464] Haskins, Justin. "The Fed is pushing America dangerously close to socialism." *Glennbeck.com*, 23 Mar. 2020, www.glennbeck.com/blog/the-fed-is-pushing-america-dangerously-close-to-socialism.

[1465] "Modern Monetary Theory (MMT)." *Investopedia*. 24 Sept. 2019, www.investopedia.com/modern-monetary-theory-mmt-4588060.

[1466] *Id.*

United States government is…inextricably linked to the productive power of the real U.S. economy…"[1467]

Economist Ludwig von Mises observed "that printing up additional green paper tickets does not increase the available resources in society…"[1468] "Most people are of the view that the government has some extra resources that can be employed in a time of crisis. Unfortunately, this is a dream. The government has no resources apart from those it takes from the private sector…Contrary to popular thinking, government bureaucrats are not trained to generate real wealth."[1469] "Real wealth is not created by a printing press or punched out by government decree. Real wealth is assets, savings, goods and services – the productive output of the underlying economy itself."[1470] "[U]ltimately, 'wealth' (as measured in new goods and services generated by capital and labor) is generated by increasing productivity, via investment in greater efficiencies… In other words, efficiency and productivity are core dynamics…"[1471]

[1467] Mercenary Trader. "Weekender: The Trouble With Modern Monetary Theory (MMT)." *Business Insider*, 19 Dec. 2010, www.businessinsider.com/weekender-the-trouble-with-modern-monetary-theory-mmt-2011-1.

[1468] Woods, Thomas E. Jr. "The Revolutionary War and the Destruction of the Continental." *Mises Institute*, 11 Oct. 2006, mises.org/library/revolutionary-war-and-destruction-continental.

[1469] Shostak, Frank. "The Bureaucrats Can't Fix This." *Mises Wire*, 2 Apr. 2020, mises.org/wire/bureaucrats-cant-fix?fbclid=IwAR2OMen14SwzJUDCyzsRcfiwXMu4TyXFXI1mBFkg-LykyllACwxQlhjMAXw.

[1470] Mercenary Trader. "Weekender: The Trouble With Modern Monetary Theory (MMT)." *Business Insider*, 19 Dec. 2010, www.businessinsider.com/weekender-the-trouble-with-modern-monetary-theory-mmt-2011-1.

[1471] Smith, Charles Hughes. "Modern Monetary Theory." *InflationData.com*, 5 Nov. 2019, inflationdata.com/articles/2019/11/05/modern-monetary-theory/.

Thus, "governments cannot fund themselves infinitely (except in a meaningless 'technical' sense). Credible access to underlying assets constrains them! The amount a government can leverage itself is linked to its 'collateral,' i.e. the size of the economy supporting it. A government's ability to 'self fund' in the MMT-described method, then, is bound by the outer limits of investor credibility...which, in turn, are impacted by the 'collateral' of taxable real assets at the government's disposal..."[1472]   "[I]f the government abuses its Monopoly privileges, investors can change their preferences and play a different game, i.e. rotate out of U.S. liabilities (bonds and currency) and into alternatives (hard assets, other currencies, E.M. [emerging markets] etc.).[1473]

Nobel Prize-winning economist, Paul Krugman, warned that the U.S. would see hyperinflation if MMT were put into practice and investors refused to buy U.S. bonds.[1474] He said, "Do the math, and it becomes clear that any attempt to extract too much from seigniorage — more than a few percent of GDP, probably — leads to an infinite upward spiral in inflation. In effect, the currency is destroyed."[1475]

"This is one common objection to MMT: the freedom to issue new currency is difficult to limit, as there will always be more demands for government spending. Without some 'governor' to limit the issuance of new currency to align with the expansion of goods and services, then governments tend to issue new currency far in excess of what the real economy is creating. This generates inflation,

---

[1472] Mercenary Trader. "Weekender: The Trouble With Modern Monetary Theory (MMT)." *Business Insider*, 19 Dec. 2010, www.businessinsider.com/weekender-the-trouble-with-modern-monetary-theory-mmt-2011-1.

[1473] *Id.*

[1474] "Modern Monetary Theory (MMT)." *Investopedia.* 24 Sept. 2019, www.investopedia.com/modern-monetary-theory-mmt-4588060.

[1475] Seigniorage is the difference between the face value of currency and the cost to produce it. *Id.*

which impoverishes everyone using the currency…"[1476] "In other words, it's inherently inflationary as it puts new money into the economy but doesn't increase the goods and services…"[1477]

Proponents of MMT admit that inflation is a possible outcome of such spending.[1478] "When government spending is too great with respect to the resources available, inflation can surge if decision-makers are not careful."[1479] However, MMT fans insist that inflation can be fought with fiscal policy.[1480] "There are two main levers in the public sector's arsenal to stimulate the U.S. economy: monetary policy and fiscal policy. The first is under the purview of the Federal Reserve and the second is the responsibility of the federal government…"[1481]

"MMT argues fiscal policy is more important than monetary policy in determining inflation, so raising taxes is the solution to high inflation."[1482] MMT supporters think that it should be up to the institution with authority over tax and budget policy — the U.S.

[1476] Smith, Charles Hughes. "Modern Monetary Theory." *InflationData.com*, 5 Nov. 2019, inflationdata.com/articles/2019/11/05/modern-monetary-theory/.

[1477] *Id.*

[1478] "Modern Monetary Theory (MMT)." *Investopedia*. 24 Sept. 2019, www.investopedia.com/modern-monetary-theory-mmt-4588060.

[1479] *Id.*

[1480] MMT proponent, Stephanie Kelton, called on fiscal policy to manage the business cycle. *Id.* Strain, Michael R. "'Modern Monetary Theory' Is a Joke That's Not Funny" *Bloomberg*, 17 Jan. 2019, www.bloomberg.com/opinion/articles/2019-01-17/modern-monetary-theory-would-sink-u-s-in-debt.

[1481] Patton, Mike. "Trump Administration Considers Reducing Payroll Tax To Zero." *Forbes*, 10 Mar. 2020, www.forbes.com/sites/mikepatton/2020/03/10/trump-administration-considers-reducing-payroll-tax-to-zero/?fbclid=IwAR2wNkXGZSe8bdjXd95Lis-NO3hO0b6neY0149LJBJGR6z0_mlcjnzQvQj0#1825e5473188.

[1482] Horan, Patrick. "5 Problems with MMT." *The Bridge*, 18 Mar. 2019, www.mercatus.org/bridge/commentary/5-problems-mmt.

Congress — to raise taxes to make prices stable and have a budget surplus.[1483]   Rather than primarily being a means to provide the government with money to spend to build infrastructure, fund social welfare programs, etc, "[t]axes…are a tool to take money out of an economy that is getting overheated."[1484]

"Unfortunately, the underlying model used in MMT is based on false assumptions about the inflation process."[1485]   Michael R. Strain, resident scholar at the American Enterprise Institute, has argued that MMT's proposal that taxes can be used to reduce inflation is flawed.[1486]   "Taxation tends to reduce the amount of money in a community and is usually a deflationary force; government spending tends to increase the amount of money in a community and is usually an inflationary force…"[1487]   "It is [actually] monetary policy that determines the price level, not fiscal policy…"[1488]

[1483] Presumably, this would entail the Fed raising interest rates, which it quickly bailed on when QT threatened to tank the stock market.   Strain, Michael R. "'Modern Monetary Theory' Is a Joke That's Not Funny" *Bloomberg*, 17 Jan. 2019, www.bloomberg.com/opinion/articles/2019-01-17/modern-monetary-theory-would-sink-u-s-in-debt.

[1484] "Modern Monetary Theory (MMT)." *Investopedia*. 24 Sept. 2019, www.investopedia.com/modern-monetary-theory-mmt-4588060.

[1485] Sumner, Scott. "Tax-and-spend progressives put faith in flawed policy theory." *The Hill,* 25 Jan. 2019, thehill.com/opinion/finance/426862-tax-and-spend-progressives-put-faith-in-flawed-policy-theory.

[1486] Horan, Patrick. "5 Problems with MMT." *The Bridge*, 18 Mar. 2019, www.mercatus.org/bridge/commentary/5-problems-mmt.

[1487] "History of Banking and Money Key Excerpts From Carroll Quigley's Tragedy and Hope." *Wanttoknow.info*, www.wanttoknow.info/articles/quigley_carroll.tragedy_hope_banking_money_history.

[1488] Sumner, Scott. "MMT is wrong." *The Library of Economics and Liberty,* www.econlib.org/mmt-is-wrong/.

In addition, MMT calls for tax increases in order to restrain inflation at a time when the economy is already slowing down.[1489] "Raising taxes would only make a downturn worse, increasing unemployment and further slowing the economy," according to Michael R. Strain.[1490] "How likely does it seem that Congress and the president would raise taxes during a period of high inflation when the public is already upset at rising prices? Not very likely…"[1491] "When households are being hit with price increases, the natural inclination of an elected representative might be to increase their disposable income by lowering taxes, not raising them…"[1492] "Without some real-world limit on the issuance of new money, money will be issued in surplus because the issuance isn't an economic process, it's a political process. This is a fatal flaw in MMT. Relying on politicians to impose limits on their own desire to win re-election is to deny human nature…"[1493]

For example, during the Covid-19 pandemic in March 2020, "President Trump called on Congress to enact a large tax cut and

---

[1489] Strain, Michael R. "'Modern Monetary Theory' Is a Joke That's Not Funny" *Bloomberg*, 17 Jan. 2019, www.bloomberg.com/opinion/articles/2019-01-17/modern-monetary-theory-would-sink-u-s-in-debt.

[1490] "Modern Monetary Theory (MMT)." *Investopedia*. 24 Sept. 2019, www.investopedia.com/modern-monetary-theory-mmt-4588060; Strain, Michael R. "'Modern Monetary Theory' Is a Joke That's Not Funny" *Bloomberg*, 17 Jan. 2019, www.bloomberg.com/opinion/articles/2019-01-17/modern-monetary-theory-would-sink-u-s-in-debt.

[1491] Horan, Patrick. "5 Problems with MMT." *The Bridge*, 18 Mar. 2019, www.mercatus.org/bridge/commentary/5-problems-mmt.

[1492] Strain, Michael R. "'Modern Monetary Theory' Is a Joke That's Not Funny" *Bloomberg*, 17 Jan. 2019, www.bloomberg.com/opinion/articles/2019-01-17/modern-monetary-theory-would-sink-u-s-in-debt.

[1493] Smith, Charles Hughes. "Modern Monetary Theory." *InflationData.com*, 5 Nov. 2019, inflationdata.com/articles/2019/11/05/modern-monetary-theory/.

pushed Democrats to support it."[1494]   Congress was "under enormous pressure to provide immediate assistance to workers and industries that [were] facing the prospect of mass layoffs and bankruptcies."[1495]   "President Trump want[ed] to send cash to Americans suffering financially from the coronavirus crisis immediately."[1496]   Politicians passed "a $1 trillion stimulus plan to combat the economic damage caused by the effort to control the coronavirus. The measure include[d] a plan to send $1,200 checks to individuals and $2,400 to couples earning below a certain income... It also provide[d] a cash infusion for small businesses, the airline

[1494] Macleod, Alan. "Big Banks Call for Wall Street Deregulation to 'Fight Coronavirus.'" *MPN News*, 6 Mar. 2020, www.mintpressnews.com/big-banks-call-wall-street-deregulation-fight-coronavirus/265558/?fbclid=IwAR1MtJpe2A_-nxjKHjOSu8YP3vLuZwRjOMbXCjWlOjIxo9A82UBzGypfrLs.

[1495] Ferrechio, Susan and Nihal Krishan. "Senate GOP unveils $1,200 direct cash payments in massive stimulus proposal." *Washington Examiner*, 19 Mar. 2020, www.washingtonexaminer.com/news/congress/senate-gop-unveils-1-200-direct-cash-payments-in-massive-stimulus-proposal?utm_source=WEX_Breaking+News+Alert_03%2F19%2F2020&utm_medium=email&utm_campaign=WEX_Breaking+News&rid=24098895&fbclid=IwAR3TJwtD_8r7Exl00wd4c2rniXXE6fe4bsW6hwPNn6vDehtS24kqjFX4CIw.

[1496] Earle, Geoff. "Trump wants IMMEDIATE cash handouts for Americans: Treasury Secretary Steven Mnuchin says everyone will get MORE THAN $1,000 within two weeks once he strikes Senate deal - and tax payments are deferred for 90 days too." *Daily Mail,* 17 Mar. 2020, www.dailymail.co.uk/news/article-8122293/Donald-Trump-wants-checks-Americans-IMMEDIATELY.html?fbclid=IwAR2x8DfHeY7Heu8dVKQN9U1B3IRvTyiTRo-TRohKhkJXj_o90xdw-_NfGn4.

industry, and healthcare providers…"[1497]   Airlines asked the government for over $50 billion in aid, and Trump promised "to back the airlines 100 percent."[1498]

"[L]awmakers have passed four massive stimulus packages totaling nearly $3 trillion to blunt the economic pain from the virus outbreak. That includes the $2.2 trillion CARES Act signed into law at the end of March" 2020.[1499]   The Coronavirus Aid, Relief, and Economic Security Act (CARES Act), the costliest stimulus plan in U.S. history, "will total $6 trillion…the package would include $4 trillion in lending power for the Federal Reserve as well as a $2

[1497] Ferrechio, Susan and Nihal Krishan. "Senate GOP unveils $1,200 direct cash payments in massive stimulus proposal." *Washington Examiner*, 19 Mar. 2020, www.washingtonexaminer.com/news/congress/ senate-gop-unveils-1-200-direct-cash-payments-in-massive-stimulus- p r o p o s a l ? utm_source=WEX_Breaking+News+Alert_03%2F19%2F2020&utm_med ium=email&utm_campaign=WEX_Breaking+News&rid=24098895&fbcli d=IwAR3TJwtD_8r7Exl00wd4c2rniXXE6fe4bsW6hwPNn6vDehtS24kqj FX4CIw.

[1498] "Here Come the Bailouts, Starting With the Airlines." *The New York Tims,* 17 Mar. 2020, www.nytimes.com/2020/03/17/business/dealbook/ c o r o n a v i r u s - a i r l i n e - b a i l o u t s . h t m l ? fbclid=IwAR0OsdRHoS5atSi4c6hYLNNIcFEiTo5c_fkTSxP2Kr_JY6QP3 AJhYG1ThNM.

[1499] Henney, Megan. "Fed's Powell warns coronavirus recovery could stretch through end of 2021." *Fox Business*, 17 May 2020, www.foxbusiness.com/markets/federal-reserve-jerome-powell- c o r o n a v i r u s - p a n d e m i c - e c o n o m i c - r e c o v e r y ? fbclid=IwAR1bTP1DicnDOcd3ZPq_OKM1B6IAWKwxijeD3rtxddezBG BHtwlbMJ6cYqw.

trillion aid package..."[1500]   "It include[d] checks for most Americans, boosted unemployment aid, help for small business as well as a massive loan fund for corporations..."[1501]   The plan sent

---

[1500] "The other $4 trillion will allow the Federal Reserve to make huge emergency bailouts of whatever entity it chooses — a measure that was used to prop up Wall Street firms from collapse during the 2008 financial crisis." Bowden, Ebony. "Coronavirus stimulus package to exceed $6T, Larry Kudlow says." *New York Post,* 24 Mar. 2020, nypost.com/ 2020/03/24/coronavirus-stimulus-package-to-exceed-6t-larry-kudlow-s a y s / ? f b c l i d = I w A R 1 q G g C n b I O r - I n - YRUiSRMRDXKQOlEjMC-10MPhbFKVX5WH_K1ocakkU_k. Rep. Thomas Massie of Kentucky, a Republican, objected on the basis that a quorum was not present. "I came here to make sure our republic doesn't die by unanimous consent in an empty chamber and I request a recorded vote," Massie said. Schultz, Marisa. "Congress OKs $2T stimulus in historic coronavirus response, as rep's objections sidelined." *Fox News,* 27 Mar. 2020, www.foxnews.com/politics/house-massie-bill-coronavirus? f b c l i d = I w A R 1 - r s 9 D P K V U Q m B e f H - YzfcctpSUcjaebg6S09RZV1-2hC3oenR43YAk5ME; Gomez, Christian. "Senate Coronavirus Stimulus Swells to $2 Trillion; Final Vote on Monday." *The New American*, 21 Mar. 2020, www.thenewamerican.com/ usnews/congress/item/35214-senate-coronavirus-stimulus-swells-to-2- t r i l l i o n - f i n a l - v o t e - o n - m o n d a y ? fbclid=IwAR1KJyfp2ynnXGGKePC0A2G3873eBSbYaOI7BNSlQeplgEq 2d1423WkLmBQ.

[1501] Schultz, Marisa. "Congress OKs $2T stimulus in historic coronavirus response, as rep's objections sidelined." *Fox News*, 27 Mar. 2020, www.foxnews.com/politics/house-massie-bill-coronavirus?fbclid=IwAR1-rs9DPKVUQmBefH-YzfcctpSUcjaebg6S09RZV1-2hC3oenR43YAk5ME. The progressive group "New Consensus is proposing that the government both scale up the stimulus and pay for it through non-debt monetary expansion, or simply having the government print more money." Relman, Eliza. "The Senate is about to pass the 'largest relief package in history' amid the coronavirus-induced economic crisis, but progressives say it isn't enough." *Business Insider*, 21 Mar. 2020, www.businessinsider.com/ coronavirus-progressives-say-13-trillion-stimulus-isnt-enough-2020-3? utm_source=yahoo.com&utm_medium=referral.

"payments totaling $500 billion directly to Americans."[1502]   "The bill provides specific sums that can be made as loans or loan guarantees to passenger airlines ($25 billion), cargo airlines ($4 billion), and loans and loan guarantees to businesses necessary to national security ($17 billion)..."[1503] The stimulus package injected $1 trillion into the economy — approximately $50 billion for the airline industry and up to $500 billion for small businesses.[1504] The progressive group, "New Consensus[,] is proposing that the government both scale up the stimulus and pay for it through non-debt monetary expansion, or simply having the government print more money."[1505]

[1502] Breuninger, Kevin. "Trump wants direct payments of $1,000 for adults, $500 for kids in coronavirus stimulus bill, Mnuchin says." *CNBC*, 19 Mar. 2020, www.cnbc.com/2020/03/19/coronavirus-trump-wants-payments-of-1000-for-adults-500-for-kids.html?fbclid=IwAR2SSdXREmF1PstXDgRUECgWplZjOSTDpoybLIOgwnCbA YmNZqUtzA5VOz8.

[1503] Martens, Pam and Russ Martens. "Stimulus Bill Allows Federal Reserve to Conduct Meetings in Secret; Gives Fed $454 Billion Slush Fund for Wall Street Bailouts." *Wall Street on Parade*, 26 Mar. 2020, wallstreetonparade.com/2020/03/stimulus-bill-allows-federal-reserve-to-conduct-meetings-in-secret-gives-fed-454-billion-slush-fund-for-wall-street-bailouts/.

[1504] Restuccia. Andrew, Andrew Duehren, and Lindsay Wise. "U.S. Seeks to Send Checks to Americans as Part of Stimulus Package." *The Wall Street Journal*, 17 Mar. 2020, www.wsj.com/articles/trump-administration-seeking-850-billion-stimulus-package-11584448802?mod=hp_lead_pos2.

[1505] Relman, Eliza. "The Senate is about to pass the 'largest relief package in history' amid the coronavirus-induced economic crisis, but progressives say it isn't enough." *Business Insider*, 21 Mar. 2020, www.businessinsider.com/coronavirus-progressives-say-13-trillion-stimulus-isnt-enough-2020-3?utm_source=yahoo.com&utm_medium=referral.

The CARES Act is projected to cause a net revenue loss of $591.1 billion over the next ten years.[1506]   At the same time, President Trump proposed fighting the economic fallout from the coronavirus by temporarily or permanently eliminating the payroll tax on workers' gross earnings.[1507]   "The payroll tax is the tax collected from employers and employees to fund the government's social insurance programs including Social Security and Medicare."[1508]   "Federal payroll taxes generated $1.17 trillion in fiscal year 2018…"[1509]   "Nearly 90% of Social Security's budget came from payroll taxes in 2018…Medicare, which provides 18% of the U.S. population with health insurance, was 36% funded from

---

[1506] Reilly, Peter J. "Stimulus' Tax Benefits Heavily Weighted To Ultrawealthy." *Forbes*, 27 Mar. 2020, www.forbes.com/sites/peterjreilly/ 2020/03/27/cares-bills-tax-benefit-heavily-weighted-to-ultrawealthy/? f b c l i d = I w A R 0 X G 5 9 - ZKf_PfHjiggIdKZEvNh-5REJKaJNVCpYEh7v2ZlQl4436h_0wuU#5696e 6c91c3c.

[1507] Schneider, Howard and Steve Holland. "Trump's coronavirus payroll tax cut would punch hole in Social Security, Medicare budgets." *Reuters*, 11 Mar. 2020, news.yahoo.com/trumps-radical-plan-waive-payroll-192517459.html; Breuninger, Kevin. "White House won't explain how it would pay for Trump's proposed payroll tax holiday." *CNBC Markets*, 10 Mar. 2020, www.cnbc.com/2020/03/10/white-house-wont-explain-how-it-would-pay-for-trumps-proposed-payroll-tax-holiday.html? fbclid=IwAR2tNNEKkY2lRaPuzzRjkg57AWcvLt8vhiYRxk52ojesigjP9U hKFABD9Dc.

[1508] Patton, Mike. "Trump Administration Considers Reducing Payroll Tax To Zero." *Forbes*, 10 Mar. 2020, www.forbes.com/sites/mikepatton/ 2020/03/10/trump-administration-considers-reducing-payroll-tax-to-zero/? f b c l i d = I w A R 2 w N k X G Z S e 8 b d j X d 9 5 L i s - NO3hO0b6neY0149LJBJGR6z0_mlcjnzQvQj0#1825e5473188.

[1509] O'Reilly, Andrew and John Roberts. "Trump floats temporarily eliminating payroll tax to boost economy amid coronavirus fears." *Fox News*, 10 Mar. 2020, www.foxnews.com/politics/trump-floats-temporarily-eliminating-payroll-tax-boost-economy-amid-coronavirus-fears? f b c l i d = I w A R 1 _ D G i G h 0 x D x m g V F Z N n O z A Q e 8 S - XOQMH_BfZAtlU7nLSs7Eo0DLp39Qku8.

payroll taxes in 2018...”[1510]   “During the most recent fiscal year (ending June 30, 2019), the payroll tax accounted for $1.243 trillion of the total $3.462 trillion collected. Thus, the payroll tax represented 35.9% of total federal revenue.”[1511] “U.S. workers and their employers each contribute 7.65% of the employees’ gross pay for Social Security and Medicare through the payroll tax... “[1512] “Trump proposed reducing the payroll tax for both employers and employees from 14.4 percent to zero...”[1513] “Trump would like to eventually make the payroll tax cut permanent and fund Social Security, Medicare and unemployment insurance from general revenues...”[1514]

[1510] Schneider, Howard and Steve Holland. “Trump’s coronavirus payroll tax cut would punch hole in Social Security, Medicare budgets.” *Reuters*, 11 Mar. 2020, news.yahoo.com/trumps-radical-plan-waive-payroll-192517459.html.

[1511] Patton, Mike. “Trump Administration Considers Reducing Payroll Tax To Zero.” *Forbes*, 10 Mar. 2020, www.forbes.com/sites/mikepatton/2020/03/10/trump-administration-considers-reducing-payroll-tax-to-zero/?fbclid=IwAR2wNkXGZSe8bdjXd95Lis-NO3hO0b6neY0149LJBJGR6z0_mlcjnzQvQj0#1825e5473188.

[1512] Schneider, Howard and Steve Holland. “Trump’s coronavirus payroll tax cut would punch hole in Social Security, Medicare budgets.” *Reuters*, 11 Mar. 2020, news.yahoo.com/trumps-radical-plan-waive-payroll-192517459.html.

[1513] Patton, Mike. “Trump Administration Considers Reducing Payroll Tax To Zero.” *Forbes*, 10 Mar. 2020, www.forbes.com/sites/mikepatton/2020/03/10/trump-administration-considers-reducing-payroll-tax-to-zero/?fbclid=IwAR2wNkXGZSe8bdjXd95Lis-NO3hO0b6neY0149LJBJGR6z0_mlcjnzQvQj0#1825e5473188.

[1514] O’Reilly, Andrew and John Roberts. “Trump floats temporarily eliminating payroll tax to boost economy amid coronavirus fears.” *Fox News*, 10 Mar. 2020, www.foxnews.com/politics/trump-floats-temporarily-eliminating-payroll-tax-boost-economy-amid-coronavirus-fears?fbclid=IwAR1_DGiGh0xDxmgVFZNnOzAQe8S-XOQMH_BfZAtlU7nLSs7Eo0DLp39Qku8.

"The rationale is to put more money in the hands of consumers so they will spend more and keep our economy strong..."[1515]   "An Obama administration 2011 payroll tax cut to counteract the Great Recession, for example, returned $109 billion to households by cutting 2 percentage points from the amount that employees pay the federal government...."[1516]   However, there is some fear that the cuts "could exacerbate funding shortfalls that the two popular programs already face in coming years, as the U.S. population ages and demand for healthcare increases..."[1517] There is also reluctance among some Republicans because it could explode the deficit, which is expected to top $1 trillion in 2020.[1518] "Cutting it to zero will reduce federal revenue, increase the deficit and add to the national debt."[1519]

[1515] Patton, Mike. "Trump Administration Considers Reducing Payroll Tax To Zero." *Forbes*, 10 Mar. 2020, www.forbes.com/sites/mikepatton/2020/03/10/trump-administration-considers-reducing-payroll-tax-to-zero/?fbclid=IwAR2wNkXGZSe8bdjXd95Lis-NO3hO0b6neY0149LJBJGR6z0_mlcjnzQvQj0#1825e5473188.

[1516] Schneider, Howard and Steve Holland. "Trump's coronavirus payroll tax cut would punch hole in Social Security, Medicare budgets." *Reuters*, 11 Mar. 2020, news.yahoo.com/trumps-radical-plan-waive-payroll-192517459.html.

[1517] *Id.*

[1518] O'Reilly, Andrew and John Roberts. "Trump floats temporarily eliminating payroll tax to boost economy amid coronavirus fears." *Fox News*, 10 Mar. 2020, www.foxnews.com/politics/trump-floats-temporarily-eliminating-payroll-tax-boost-economy-amid-coronavirus-fears?fbclid=IwAR1_DGiGh0xDxmgVFZNnOzAQe8S-XOQMH_BfZAtlU7nLSs7Eo0DLp39Qku8; Schneider, Howard and Steve Holland. "Trump's coronavirus payroll tax cut would punch hole in Social Security, Medicare budgets." *Reuters*, 11 Mar. 2020, news.yahoo.com/trumps-radical-plan-waive-payroll-192517459.html.

[1519] Patton, Mike. "Trump Administration Considers Reducing Payroll Tax To Zero." *Forbes*, 10 Mar. 2020, www.forbes.com/sites/mikepatton/2020/03/10/trump-administration-considers-reducing-payroll-tax-to-zero/?fbclid=IwAR2wNkXGZSe8bdjXd95Lis-NO3hO0b6neY0149LJBJGR6z0_mlcjnzQvQj0#1825e5473188.

"MMT's diagnosis is that a lack of currency is the primary problem. The MMT solution assumes the new currency can be efficiently invested within the existing political system without disrupting the increasingly precarious existing financial system..."[1520] "[W]hen a government declares, via various silly justifications, that it intends to use the printing press to finance itself, it typically finds that it cannot without a currency breakdown."[1521] This is despite the fact that "[t]axes create an ongoing demand for currency."[1522] For example, "In the third century, the Roman government started paying its bills by making coins with higher and higher denominations... [T]he value of the denarius eventually fell to less than a millionth of its original value."[1523]

MMT proponents think that "'There will always be demand for U.S. currency – because we need it for transactions and payroll and taxes!'...Therefore, [there is] permanent currency demand... [However,] the 'constant demand for the currency' argument in part stems from U.S. hegemony and the use of the $USD as the world's

---

[1520] Smith, Charles Hughes. "Modern Monetary Theory." *InflationData.com*, 5 Nov. 2019, inflationdata.com/articles/2019/11/05/modern-monetary-theory/.

[1521] Lewis, Nathan. "The Problem With "Modern Monetary Theory" Is That It's True." *Forbes*, 21 Feb. 2019, www.forbes.com/sites/nathanlewis/2019/02/21/the-problem-with-modern-monetary-theory-is-that-its-true/#ac9ed5956fb0.

[1522] "Modern Monetary Theory (MMT)." *Investopedia*. 24 Sept. 2019, www.investopedia.com/modern-monetary-theory-mmt-4588060.

[1523] Lewis, Nathan. "The Problem With 'Modern Monetary Theory' Is That It's True." *Forbes*, 21 Feb. 2019, www.forbes.com/sites/nathanlewis/2019/02/21/the-problem-with-modern-monetary-theory-is-that-its-true/#4fb22b0256fb.

reserve currency. But this is a situation that can change...”[1524] “Players like China and Russia are taking small but meaningful steps to cut the $USD out of their trading patterns.”[1525]

“MMT is presented as the solution to the ‘problem’ of insufficient government funding, but that’s not the real problem: The real problem is the purchasing power of the fiat currency that will be issued in the trillions of dollars. It’s a recipe for the collapse of money as we know it.”[1526]   “Adding more currency and capacity/‘growth’ doesn’t fix this problem, it actually makes it worse. If we look around at the trillions of dollars in recently issued currency floating around the world looking for a yield, the trillions poured into asset bubbles that only benefit the few at the top, the gargantuan waste of capital, it’s hard not to see MMT as a ‘green’ Band-Aid for a profoundly broken, wasteful, unsustainable system...”[1527]   “MMT is [just] another attempt to preserve a dysfunctional status quo by adding another layer of newly issued currency and ‘growth.’”[1528]

“If you start to rely on a flawed theory as a guide to policy, there will eventually come a time when it will lead policymakers astray, as happened when President [Lyndon B.] Johnson relied on an MMT-type theory and accidentally triggered the greatest

---

[1524] Mercenary Trader. “Weekender: The Trouble With Modern Monetary Theory (MMT).” *Business Insider*, 19 Dec. 2010, www.businessinsider.com/weekender-the-trouble-with-modern-monetary-theory-mmt-2011-1.

[1525] *Id.*

[1526] Smith, Charles Hughes. “Modern Monetary Theory.” *InflationData.com*, 5 Nov. 2019, inflationdata.com/articles/2019/11/05/modern-monetary-theory/.

[1527] *Id.*

[1528] *Id.*

peacetime inflation in American history."[1529] "In 1968, President Johnson raised taxes and balanced the budget, in the hope and expectation that this would hold down inflation. Instead, inflation got even worse, as monetary policy was still highly expansionary."[1530] "US consumer price inflation had peaked at 13.3% in 1979. By September 1981 it had fallen to 11%."[1531] The great inflation of 1966-1981 "only fell in the early 1980s when Fed Chair Paul Volcker reduced the growth of the money supply..." via a contractionary monetary policy.[1532] "Paul Volcker...raised rates more than anyone thought he would dare, [and] provoked a recession..."[1533]

"In the eighteenth century, people learned lessons from their wartime experience, and devotion to hard money was widespread in the years that followed. Today, the workings of the Federal Reserve are so obscure to most people that hardly anyone is even aware that there is a lesson to be learned in the first place. It is in just such an intellectual environment that government is able to get away with its

---

[1529] Sumner, Scott. "Tax-and-spend progressives put faith in flawed policy theory." *The Hill,* 25 Jan. 2019, thehill.com/opinion/finance/426862-tax-and-spend-progressives-put-faith-in-flawed-policy-theory. Sumner, Scott. "MMT is wrong." *The Library of Economics and Liberty,* www.econlib.org/mmt-is-wrong/.

[1530] *Id.*

[1531] Marstrand, Rob. "Where should you put your money?" *Of Wealth,* 29 Sept. 2016, www.ofwealth.com/where-should-you-put-your-money/#.V_0bXJMrK9Y.

[1532] Sumner, Scott. "Tax-and-spend progressives put faith in flawed policy theory." *The Hill,* 25 Jan. 2019, thehill.com/opinion/finance/426862-tax-and-spend-progressives-put-faith-in-flawed-policy-theory. Horan, Patrick. "5 Problems with MMT." *The Bridge,* 18 Mar. 2019, www.mercatus.org/bridge/commentary/5-problems-mmt.

[1533] Authers, John. "A Shift in the Global Financial Order Is Upon Us." *Bloomberg Opinion,* 8 Mar. 2020, www.bloomberg.com/opinion/articles/2020-03-09/crash-in-oil-prices-bond-yields-marks-shift-in-global-order.

greatest mischief."[1534] "Modern monetary theory is seductive in its promises...but if enacted, it could cause great harm to the U.S. economy."[1535]

The next chapter argues that the dangerous and destructive Federal Reserve System should be abolished.

[1534] Woods, Thomas E. Jr. "The Revolutionary War and the Destruction of the Continental." *Mises Institute*, 11 Oct. 2006, mises.org/library/ revolutionary-war-and-destruction-continental.

[1535] Strain, Michael R. "'Modern Monetary Theory' Is a Joke That's Not Funny" *Bloomberg*, 17 Jan. 2019, www.bloomberg.com/opinion/articles/ 2019-01-17/modern-monetary-theory-would-sink-u-s-in-debt.

Chapter 7

End the Fed

"A system of fractional reserve banking with fiat currency, an unaccountable central bank, and pervasive government control of bank lending policies (including reserve and capital requirements) and interest rates — along with equity markets dependent on an endless supply of Fed-supplied artificial credit — is extremely fragile…" and "unstable."[1536] "The system is winding down and the failures are becoming more evident."[1537] In the best case scenario, the system is 100% reliant on Quantitative Easing.[1538] In the worst case scenario, the system has been completely broken since 2008.[1539]

"In the most recent example of huge volatility and financial turmoil, the stock market dropped by one-third in three short

---

[1536] Klein, Peter G. "The Financial System Is Now Totally Dependent on Government Intervention." *Mises Institute,* 16 Mar. 2020, mises.org/power-market/financial-system-now-totally-dependent-government-intervention?fbclid=IwAR3eKYaKZMJqyM91joNY59D1nTY6LqHPhsz4iz1fQS2VowwbR5YGkAlOHPA; Long, Caitlin. "The Real Story Of The Repo Market Meltdown, And What It Means For Bitcoin." *Forbes,* 25 Sept. 2019, www.forbes.com/sites/caitlinlong/2019/09/25/the-real-story-of-the-repo-market-meltdown-and-what-it-means-for-bitcoin/#23f8ac237caa.

[1537] At 5:50. RonPaulLibertyReport. "Central Banking Is On The Ropes: Gold Will Survive & The Fed Will End." *Youtube,* 13 Dec. 2019, www.youtube.com/watch?v=Ndcb2SPRU7M.

[1538] At 9:45. Gammon, George. "Repo Market Update: Is The Entire Financial System Broken? (ANSWERED)." *Youtube,* 18 Dec. 2019, www.youtube.com/watch?v=vw6fymmI9B0.

[1539] At 13:40. *Id.*

weeks."[1540] "Despite emergency action from the Federal Reserve to shore up the economy by infusing markets and Main Street with easier access to cash," Wall Street crashed.[1541] "Wall Street shuddered during the market rout on March 12, 2020, otherwise known as 'Black Thursday.'"[1542] "It was worse than the initial crash of the stock market in 1929."[1543]

In "the worst week for markets since the 2008 financial crisis," "[a] sickening plunge in stocks sent markets down shortly after opening on Monday [March 9, 2020]…The market dropped more than 7 percent after trading started on the New York Stock Exchange, prompting the first suspension of trade since the financial

---

[1540] Williams, Kelsey. "Fed Action Accelerates Boom-Bust Cycle; Not A Virus Crisis." *Yahoo Finance*, 19 May 2020, finance.yahoo.com/news/fed-action-accelerates-boom-bust-065808585.html.

[1541] Bayly, Lucy. "Dow falls 2,200 points, trading halted, as rate cut fails to calm markets." *NBC News*, 16 Mar. 2020, www.nbcnews.com/business/markets/dow-falls-2-200-points-trading-halted-rate-cut-fails-n1160246?fbclid=IwAR24696MUcBAcdGR3gAIl6YRnUqAlJxZWSwerePFTWZai8lu68gJ7FjS1Nw.

[1542] Redman, Jamie. "Data Shows the US Economy Was Collapsing 5 Months Before the Coronavirus Outbreak." *Bitcoin.com,* 3 May 2020, news.bitcoin.com/data-shows-the-us-economy-was-collapsing-5-months-before-the-coronavirus-outbreak/?fbclid=IwAR3cgTDBLMYGIYpRAO_pGNc7V-boxoJX-FHsWpJYCoJ3UOxdU6DmCN3hh-Q.

[1543] Williams, Kelsey. "Fed Action Accelerates Boom-Bust Cycle; Not A Virus Crisis." *Yahoo Finance*, 19 May 2020, finance.yahoo.com/news/fed-action-accelerates-boom-bust-065808585.html.

crash of 2008."[1544] "The Dow Jones industrial average suffered its worst single-day point drop ever…as an oil price war rattled investors who have already been panicked over the coronavirus epidemic. The blue-chip index neared bear territory amid mounting fears about a global recession, plunging a record-breaking 2,013.76 points, or 7.8 percent, to close at 23,851.02."[1545] ("A bear market is confirmed when stocks reach 20 percent below record peak."[1546]) The Dow "closed over 2,000 points lower, coming back from a point drop of more than 2,150 points, or 8.2 percent, at session lows…"[1547] "By the end of the day Monday, the Dow [had] lost 2,999 points, a 12.94% drop…By percentage, the Dow had its second-largest drop in history, worse than any day during the crash

---

[1544] Bayly, Lucy. "Dow plummets, trading briefly suspended after Trump's coronavirus response sparks market sell-off." *NBC News*, 12 Mar 2020, www.nbcnews.com/business/markets/trading-wall-street-temporarily-suspended-after-trump-s-crisis-response-n1156406? fbclid=IwAR3SOc27oG8hUdoTBC2VIo_4k1Uh7DRKj88l3XMOM93Q8 6qZAcqHzgbFskI; Saunders, Joe. "Trading Halted Market-Wide as S&P Plummets 7% in Minutes." *The Western Journal*, 9 Mar. 2020, www.westernjournal.com/trading-halted-market-wide-sp-plummets-7-minutes/? utm_source=facebook&utm_medium=patriotupdate&utm_campaign=lmin etwork&utm_content=2020-03-09&fbclid=IwAR3x1TGvSy-NCnqsh4H0-2Pxmc5qXslI2XqsKv3TVSkWmngmSD3DuyaP2PI.

[1545] McEnery, Thornton. "Dow loses over 2,000 points, worst single-day drop ever, as oil prices crash." *New York Post*, 9 Mar. 2020, nypost.com/ 2020/03/09/dow-loses-over-2000-points-worst-single-day-drop-ever-as-oil-prices-crash/?fbclid=IwAR2nfX-r6e_9icqr1BqOxbfYSjFRZfxYxrxb5VjXG7jaG19Kbp5ZTYoHGss.

[1546] *Id.*

[1547] Garber, Jonathan. "Dow plunges over 2,000 points, oil collapses amid price war and coronavirus." *Fox Business*, 9 Mar. 2020, www.foxbusiness.com/markets/us-markets-march-9-2020? fbclid=IwAR3Nf-EknmtR5bQ-ISRm568hH-og7H8_Gq2K34gAa4plAWm2mMH2Ryi-aWM.

of 1929."[1548] "The S&P 500 plunged by 7 percent, triggering a circuit breaker, which halts all trading on the New York Stock Exchange for 15 minutes..."[1549] "The S&P 500 index lost 7.6 percent to close at 2,746.56 — its worst day since December 2008..."[1550] It was "about 18 percent below its all-time high set on Feb. 19 [2020]..."[1551] Meanwhile, "[t]he Nasdaq dropped 7.3 percent to 7,950.68."[1552]

On Thursday, March 12, 2020, "[t]he Dow Jones Industrial Average fell by 2,000 points...after...a massive sell-off on Wall Street."[1553] Trading was halted twice that day.[1554] "Trading in Wall

---

[1548] The Associated Press. "Dow drops nearly 3,000 points, worse than any day during 1929 crash." *KGUN9.com*, 16 Mar. 2020, www.kgun9.com/ news/national/coronavirus/world-markets-dow-futures-sliding-as-c o r o n a v i r u s - c o n t i n u e s - t o - s p r e a d ? fbclid=IwAR30tCDohTBWOoL3t5pq9Il7opi_Ygyf7u4m4030w_dbtuJS7 AeuyK6L-U0.

[1549] Bayly, Lucy. "Dow plummets, trading briefly suspended after Trump's coronavirus response sparks market sell-off." *NBC News*, 12 Mar 2020, www.nbcnews.com/business/markets/trading-wall-street-temporarily-s u s p e n d e d - a f t e r - t r u m p - s - c r i s i s - r e s p o n s e - n 1 1 5 6 4 0 6 ? fbclid=IwAR3SOc27oG8hUdoTBC2VIo_4k1Uh7DRKj88l3XMOM93Q8 6qZAcqHzgbFskI.

[1550] McEnery, Thornton. "Dow loses over 2,000 points, worst single-day drop ever, as oil prices crash." *New York Post*, 9 Mar. 2020, nypost.com/ 2020/03/09/dow-loses-over-2000-points-worst-single-day-drop-ever-as-o i l - p r i c e s - c r a s h / ? f b c l i d = I w A R 2 n f X - r6e_9icqr1BqOxbfYSjFRZfxYxrxb5VjXG7jaG19Kbp5ZTYoHGss.

[1551] *Id.*

[1552] *Id.*

[1553] Bayly, Lucy. "Dow plummets, trading briefly suspended after Trump's coronavirus response sparks market sell-off." *NBC News*, 12 Mar 2020, www.nbcnews.com/business/markets/trading-wall-street-temporarily-s u s p e n d e d - a f t e r - t r u m p - s - c r i s i s - r e s p o n s e - n 1 1 5 6 4 0 6 ? fbclid=IwAR3SOc27oG8hUdoTBC2VIo_4k1Uh7DRKj88l3XMOM93Q8 6qZAcqHzgbFskI.

[1554] *Id.*

Street futures was suspended after they fell by the 5% maximum allowed. Brent crude, the international oil standard, fell almost 10% while gold gained."[1555] Overall, "U.S. stocks were down about 30 percent in March [2020]…"[1556]

"Some say that fear and economic dislocation due to the COVID-19 pandemic was the culprit. I don't think so. All asset prices were artificially elevated due to previous Fed reflation efforts. A lack of fundamental underpinnings had left the stock market extremely vulnerable to a selloff of considerable magnitude, regardless of the specific trigger event."[1557] "The chaos [in markets] came just over 12 hours after the Fed unleashed a series of crisis response measures, slashing rates to almost zero…, injecting cash into Treasurys, and announcing coordinated efforts with central banks across the world to ensure liquidity…"[1558] The New York Federal Reserve increased "its daily cash injections into the banking

---

[1555] The Associated Press. "Dow drops nearly 3,000 points, worse than any day during 1929 crash." KGUN9.com, 16 Mar. 2020, www.kgun9.com/news/national/coronavirus/world-markets-dow-futures-sliding-as-coronavirus-continues-to-spread?fbclid=IwAR30tCDohTBWOoL3t5pq9Il7opi_Ygyf7u4m4030w_dbtuJS7AeuyK6L-U0.

[1556] Long, Heather. "Fed Chair Powell says U.S. economy deteriorating with alarming speed." The Washington Post, 9 Apr. 2020, www.msn.com/en-us/news/us/fed-chair-powell-says-us-economy-deteriorating-with-alarming-speed/ar-BB12o0Ak?fbclid=IwAR1Jkd_mpgI3SL_nuwrXPsW3uQ8SRlr2MV5KnzeF6SAeVv6ZIMYUVmWAH1w.

[1557] Williams, Kelsey. "Fed Action Accelerates Boom-Bust Cycle; Not A Virus Crisis." Yahoo Finance, 19 May 2020, finance.yahoo.com/news/fed-action-accelerates-boom-bust-065808585.html.

[1558] Bayly, Lucy. "Dow falls 2,200 points, trading halted, as rate cut fails to calm markets." NBC News, 16 Mar. 2020, www.nbcnews.com/business/markets/dow-falls-2-200-points-trading-halted-rate-cut-fails-n1160246?fbclid=IwAR24696MUcBAcdGR3gAIl6YRnUqAlJxZWSwerePFTWZai8lu68gJ7FjS1Nw.

system to $150 billion from $100 billion…"[1559]   It had taken such measures "in the hopes of boosting the economy amid the coronavirus outbreak…"[1560]

In response to the stock market drop, "the U.S. central bank fired its 'financial bazookas,' like allowing private dealers to operate without declaring any reserve status. The Fed cut the benchmark interest rate to zero and introduced 14 foreign currency swap lines and discount windows. The Fed also created a $450 billion slush fund for Wall Street execs and the Commercial Paper Funding Facility (CPFF), a Term Asset-Backed Securities Loan Facility (TALF), and a Secondary Market Corporate Credit Facility (SMCCF)."[1561]   "On top of the massive economic aid package, the Fed has been working hard to prop up plunging markets — with

---

[1559] "U.S. Treasurys were the beneficiary of the flight to safety with heavy buying pushing longer-dated yields lower by more than 30 basis points. Overnight, the benchmark 10-year yield fell to a record low of 0.38 percent before bouncing to 0.501 percent at the close. Likewise, the 30-year yield plunged below 1 percent for the first time ever, and was down 27.8 basis points to 0.938 percent…" Garber, Jonathan. "Dow plunges over 2,000 points, oil collapses amid price war and coronavirus." *Fox Business*, 9 Mar. 2020, www.foxbusiness.com/markets/us-markets-march-9-2020?fbclid=IwAR3Nf-EknmtR5bQ-ISRm568hH-og7H8_Gq2K34gAa4plAWm2mMH2Ryi-aWM.

[1560] The Associated Press. "Dow drops nearly 3,000 points, worse than any day during 1929 crash." *KGUN9.com*, 16 Mar. 2020, www.kgun9.com/news/national/coronavirus/world-markets-dow-futures-sliding-as-coronavirus-continues-to-spread?fbclid=IwAR30tCDohTBWOoL3t5pq9Il7opi_Ygyf7u4m4030w_dbtuJS7AeuyK6L-U0.

[1561] Redman, Jamie. "Data Shows the US Economy Was Collapsing 5 Months Before the Coronavirus Outbreak." *Bitcoin.com,* 3 May 2020, news.bitcoin.com/data-shows-the-us-economy-was-collapsing-5-months-before-the-coronavirus-outbreak/?fbclid=IwAR3cgTDBLMYGIYpRAO_pGNc7V-boxoJX-FHsWpJYCoJ3UOxdU6DmCN3hh-Q.

mixed results despite its shock-and-awe firepower."[1562] Despite its efforts, "Federal Reserve Chair Jerome H. Powell said [on April 9, 2020] the U.S. economy is in an emergency and is deteriorating 'with alarming speed.'"[1563]

"Xiao and Iaralov suggest that the risks for a more adverse market shock, referred to by BAML [Bank of America Merrill Lynch] as a tail risk, are building…Given the huge gains in asset prices seen in the years after the global financial crisis, largely fueled by an unprecedented wave of monetary-policy stimulus, should investors lose faith that increasingly innovative central-bank policy can help improve underlying economic conditions, there's very little — including fiscal policy — for markets to fall back on."[1564]

"[I]f there's a clear message from the extraordinary market events of [February and March 2020], it's that the current financial order no longer suffices to maintain the stability we've grown

---

[1562] Bambrough, Billy. "Donald Trump And The Fed Are Destroying The U.S. Dollar." *Forbes*, 28 Mar. 2020, www.forbes.com/sites/billybambrough/2020/03/28/donald-trump-and-the-fed-are-destroying-the-u s - d o l l a r / ? fbclid=IwAR0FVSZWzVX5vEiMO6JUKf9DUyHAIM9Hbr3mPA2ECTJ xMTkz4c80Xz8NRlE#36964d106ebc.

[1563] Long, Heather. "Fed Chair Powell says U.S. economy deteriorating with alarming speed." *The Washington Post*, 9 Apr. 2020, www.msn.com/en-us/news/us/fed-chair-powell-says-us-economy-deteriorating-with-a l a r m i n g - s p e e d / a r - B B 1 2 o 0 A k ? fbclid=IwAR1Jkd_mpgI3SL_nuwrXPsW3uQ8SRlr2MV5KnzeF6SAeVv6 ZIMYUVmWAH1w.

[1564] Scott, David. "There's a big problem with the last tool in the arsenal of the world's central banks." *Business Insider*, 17 Feb. 2016, www.businessinsider.com/theres-a-big-problem-with-negative-interest-rates-2016-2.

accustomed to expect."[1565] "[T]he Fed launched an unnecessary and panic-inducing emergency rate cut and caused the opposite effect of what they desired. Instead of calming markets, the Federal Reserve's 50–basis point cut sent a message of panic to market participants…"[1566] Heavy-handed central bank actions, such as more bond purchases, "raise concerns that the economy might be in worse shape than even many experts thought…"[1567] Chris Rupkey, Chief Financial Economist at MUFG Bank, said, "Sometimes the massive Fed interventions have generated even more panic selling in the markets as it shows the severity and concern of Fed officials of just how bad the risks are to the economy."[1568] For example, "[a]lthough the next meeting wasn't until March 17-18 [2020], the Fed held an emergency meeting March 3 and reduced its target interest rate by 0.50%. The stock market immediately sank on the

---

[1565] Authers, John. "New World Order Is Coming, Maybe in Helicopters." *Bloomberg*, 9 Mar. 2020, www.bloomberg.com/opinion/articles/2020-03-09/oil-crash-coronavirus-is-just-the-start-of-market-shocks?fbclid=IwAR2YtaU-DhkS0kI7-L6iJQzClEBvP7jXwE3M6uoLRXddmkFdUGWWUFuDACI.

[1566] Lacalle, Daniel. PhD. "The Fed Panicked, and Its Rate Cut Is Making the Economy Worse." *Mises Institute,* 9 Mar. 2020, mises.org/wire/fed-panicked-and-its-rate-cut-making-economy-worse?fbclid=IwAR31Z6Qs6p8b9dRJ-_YZBaEuHz4Pq0SQoLzOH7W2TJlQ3G4vboe6ViwOuMI#.XmbHfDyEiq4.twitter.

[1567] Long, Heather. "Federal Reserve slashes interest rates to zero as part of wide-ranging emergency intervention." *The Washington Post*, 15 Mar. 2020, www.washingtonpost.com/business/2020/03/15/federal-reserve-slashes-interest-rates-zero-part-wide-ranging-emergency-intervention/?fbclid=IwAR3ArnSj5NO2WPZw9qneawJhTKbW8Xqg3tspxLEkYlfmGJcKl4ZtHtx14FM.

[1568] *Id.*

news…"[1569]   Then, "the Federal Reserve announced [March 15, 2020] it [was] slashing interest rates to near-zero and reinstating its bond-buying program."[1570]   "Typically, when the Fed cuts rates this aggressively, it signals that the expected risk to the economy is serious. That's the message investors heard…"[1571]   "The efforts… were… interpreted by traders as a sign of desperation, or at least, an indication that things are worse than they had thought."[1572]   The Fed's emergency cut "tells market participants that the situation is much worse than it seems and that the Fed knows more than the rest of us about how dire everything can be."[1573]   "Far from calming

---

[1569] Patton, Mike. "Trump Administration Considers Reducing Payroll Tax To Zero." *Forbes*, 10 Mar. 2020, www.forbes.com/sites/mikepatton/2020/03/10/trump-administration-considers-reducing-payroll-tax-to-zero/?fbclid=IwAR2wNkXGZSe8bdjXd95Lis-NO3hO0b6neY0149LJBJGR6z0_mlcjnzQvQj0#1825e5473188.

[1570] English, Carleton and Nicholas Jasinski. "Dow Plunges 3,000 Points in Worst Selloff Since 1987." *Market Watch*, 16 Mar. 2020, www.marketwatch.com/articles/wall-street-is-bracing-for-another-day-of-big-losses-in-the-dow-51584362387?reflink=share_barrons_facebook&fbclid=IwAR0RysDhnM6rURO9b77u8oR7DsiSFRB6DeSLdaFwYYULAhEmnMPOiwrnVYE.

[1571] Patton, Mike. "Trump Administration Considers Reducing Payroll Tax To Zero." *Forbes*, 10 Mar. 2020, www.forbes.com/sites/mikepatton/2020/03/10/trump-administration-considers-reducing-payroll-tax-to-zero/?fbclid=IwAR2wNkXGZSe8bdjXd95Lis-NO3hO0b6neY0149LJBJGR6z0_mlcjnzQvQj0#1825e5473188.

[1572] English, Carleton and Nicholas Jasinski. "Dow Plunges 3,000 Points in Worst Selloff Since 1987." *Market Watch*, 16 Mar. 2020, www.marketwatch.com/articles/wall-street-is-bracing-for-another-day-of-big-losses-in-the-dow-51584362387?reflink=share_barrons_facebook&fbclid=IwAR0RysDhnM6rURO9b77u8oR7DsiSFRB6DeSLdaFwYYULAhEmnMPOiwrnVYE.

[1573] Lacalle, Daniel. PhD. "The Fed Panicked, and Its Rate Cut Is Making the Economy Worse." *Mises Institute,* 9 Mar. 2020, mises.org/wire/fed-panicked-and-its-rate-cut-making-economy-worse?fbclid=IwAR31Z6Qs6p8b9dRJ-_YZBaEuHz4Pq0SQoLzOH7W2TJlQ3G4vboe6ViwOuMI#.XmbHfDyEiq4.twitter.

market jitters, the Fed's constant thrashing around in the dark, attempting to push one button or another…reminds market participants that financial crisis and recession are always lurking around the corner…"[1574]

"Bankers' 'Whatever It Takes' bazookas are impotent and only dribble or misfire…Money printing, unlimited bailouts, central bank manipulations and 'buy the dip' no longer work."[1575] "[G]iven the massive monetary stimulus that's taken place since the financial crisis in 2008, there is nothing more the Fed can do. Easy money cannot be made much easier…"[1576] "Governments and central banks have exhausted all fiscal and monetary tools to generate a perceptible effect. The obsession with maintaining and increasing the bubble of sovereign bonds in times of growth has led central banks to a dead end. They are now forced to take even more useless measures and, on top of that, the confidence of financial agents diminishes."[1577] According to Mike O'Rourke, chief market

---

[1574] Klein, Peter G. "The Financial System Is Now Totally Dependent on Government Intervention." *Mises Institute,* 16 Mar. 2020, mises.org/power-market/financial-system-now-totally-dependent-government-i n t e r v e n t i o n ? fbclid=IwAR3eKYaKZMJqyM91joNY59D1nTY6LqHPhsz4iz1fQS2Vow wbR5YGkAlOHPA.

[1575] "The Great Economic Depression of 2020: No lessons learned as central banks' bazookas dribble or misfire." *RT,* 23 Mar. 2020, www.rt.com/op-ed/483845-great-economic-depression-2020/.

[1576] Klein, Peter G. "The Financial System Is Now Totally Dependent on Government Intervention." *Mises Institute,* 16 Mar. 2020, mises.org/power-market/financial-system-now-totally-dependent-government-i n t e r v e n t i o n ? fbclid=IwAR3eKYaKZMJqyM91joNY59D1nTY6LqHPhsz4iz1fQS2Vow wbR5YGkAlOHPA.

[1577] Lacalle, Daniel. PhD. "The Fed Panicked, and Its Rate Cut Is Making the Economy Worse." *Mises Institute,* 9 Mar. 2020, mises.org/wire/fed-p a n i c k e d - a n d - i t s - r a t e - c u t - m a k i n g - e c o n o m y - w o r s e ? f b c l i d = I w A R 3 1 Z 6 Q s 6 p 8 b 9 d R J - _YZBaEuHz4Pq0SQoLzOH7W2TJlQ3G4vboe6ViwOuMI#.XmbHfDyEi q4.twitter.

strategist at financial brokerage, JonesTrading, investors have begun to express concern that the Federal Reserve's "monetary policy has become impotent."[1578]   Societe Generale strategist, Kit Juckes, said, "The central banks threw the kitchen sink at it [Wall Street] yesterday evening, yet here we are. There is a great sense that central banks are going to get to grips with the issues of getting money flowing...But the human problem, the macro problem, there is nothing they can do about that."[1579]   Former Fed chairman, Ben Bernanke, admitted, "Most of the policies that support robust economic growth in the long run are outside the province of the central bank."[1580]

"The market now realizes its sum of all fear that the world's central banks are powerless to stop the market turmoil...investors are hunkering down for a severe global recession."[1581]   "Among Fed leaders, the growing consensus is the economic pain will be

---

[1578] Kilgore, Tomi. "'Bearmageddon' for stocks appears to be upon us, strategist says." *Market Watch*, 15 Mar. 2020, www.marketwatch.com/story/bearmageddon-for-stocks-appears-to-be-upon-us-strategist-says-2020-03-15?reflink=mw_share_facebook&fbclid=IwAR1v5viyQmNrbpheaogqtoBY8mq8C63Ma4nttdiyxO9A6xTWxJOqIVU3c-Q.

[1579] Bayly, Lucy. "Dow falls 2,200 points, trading halted, as rate cut fails to calm markets." *NBC News*, 16 Mar. 2020, www.nbcnews.com/business/markets/dow-falls-2-200-points-trading-halted-rate-cut-fails-n1160246?fbclid=IwAR24696MUcBAcdGR3gAIl6YRnUqAlJxZWSwerePFTWZai8lu68gJ7FjS1Nw.

[1580] "Central Bank Quotes." *Brainy Quote*, www.brainyquote.com/topics/central-bank-quotes.

[1581] Innes, Stephen. "Currency Carnage: FX Market's Unhinged." *Yahoo Finance*, 18 Mar. 2020, finance.yahoo.com/news/currency-carnage-fx-market-unhinged-222325310.html.

substantial, and the recovery will be slow..."[1582] "There is an important lesson to be learned from this episode: When we centralize great responsibility and power in one institution, its failure will have far-reaching and terrible consequences."[1583]

Ultimately, the problem is the Fed itself. Henry Hazlitt wrote, "The practices of the Fed distort the real-world market indicators of cost, future prices, investments and production."[1584] "As explained by Austrian business cycle theory, injections of fiat money (whether by interest rate or money supply channels) generate artificial booms, setting in motion the inevitable boom-bust cycle..."[1585] "The Austrian Business Cycle Theory explains why we see such wide fluctuations in the economy. The theory states that a false boom occurs when the Federal Reserve lowers interest rates below the market rate which increases the supply of money. Artificially low credit cost sends out misleading economic signals to producers. They are inclined to respond by greatly expanding their production

---

[1582] Long, Heather. "Fed Chair Powell says U.S. economy deteriorating with alarming speed." *The Washington Post*, 9 Apr. 2020, www.msn.com/en-us/news/us/fed-chair-powell-says-us-economy-deteriorating-with-alarming-speed/ar-BB12o0Ak?fbclid=IwAR1Jkd_mpgI3SL_nuwrXPsW3uQ8SRlr2MV5KnzeF6SAeVv6ZIMYUVmWAH1w.

[1583] Pongracic, Ivan Jr. "The Great Depression According to Milton Friedman." *FEE*, 1 Sept. 2007, fee.org/articles/the-great-depression-according-to-milton-friedman/.

[1584] Jones, Stewart. "The Founders Warned Us About Central Banking." *Ron Paul Liberty Report*, 10 Oct. 2019, www.ronpaullibertyreport.com/archives/the-founders-warned-us-about-central-banking?fbclid=IwAR1GtgHBthCfZDgqhObnuqCX2hO9116CjGntgnKJ75rw5KXrb5U3mKOVFKI.

[1585] Klein, Peter G. "The Financial System Is Now Totally Dependent on Government Intervention." *Mises Institute,* 16 Mar. 2020, mises.org/power-market/financial-system-now-totally-dependent-government-intervention?fbclid=IwAR3eKYaKZMJqyM91joNY59D1nTY6LqHPhsz4iz1fQS2VowwbR5YGkAlOHPA.

around the same time. In retrospect, these investment decisions called malinvestments are seen as a bad allocation of resources. Malinvestments will lead to wasted capital and economic losses. The expansion of credit cannot continue permanently which means that inevitable bust will follow a false boom created by the Federal Reserve."[1586] "The Federal Reserve has brought us endless boom-and-bust cycles. The U.S. economy was much more stable before the Federal Reserve came into existence. It bears significant responsibility for every financial crisis over the past century including the Great Depression, the stagflation of the 1970s and recent economic meltdown."[1587]

Dr. Ron Paul (R-TX) agreed that the central bankers have been "feeding the fire of inflation, distortion, and debt."[1588] He said, "The Fed has followed a consistent policy of flooding the economy with easy money, leading to a misallocation of resources and an artificial 'boom' followed by a recession or depression when the Fed-created bubble bursts."[1589] "The Federal Reserve has consistently set rates too low, leading to credit bubbles, which always end in recession or depression."[1590] For example, the Fed induced a "bubble surrounding stocks in the late nineties which was pricked in early 2000."[1591]

[1586] Borowski, Julie. "Top 10 Reasons to End the Federal Reserve." *FreedomWorks,* 1 Feb. 2012, www.freedomworks.org/content/top-10-reasons-end-federal-reserve.

[1587] *Id.*

[1588] At 2. RonPaulLibertyReport. "Central Banking Is On The Ropes: Gold Will Survive & The Fed Will End." *Youtube,* 13 Dec. 2019, www.youtube.com/watch?v=Ndcb2SPRU7M.

[1589] Quinn, Jim. "The Federal Reserve Must Die." *HCP Live,* 25 Aug. 2009, www.mdmag.com/medical-news/federal_reserve_must_die.

[1590] *Id.*

[1591] Williams, Kelsey. "Federal Reserve – Conspiracy Or Not?" *Kelsey's Gold Facts,* 22 Dec. 2018, www.kelseywilliamsgold.com/federal-reserve-conspiracy-or-not/.

"One of their [Federal Reserve] self-proclaimed objectives is to manage the economic cycle. What they really meant in proclaiming their ability to do this, is that they could 'manage' to avoid recessions and depressions and extend the prosperity phase of the cycle. How well have they done? The word *horrible* comes to mind. *Abysmal failure* is another. In their initial attempt at managing the economic cycle, the Fed ushered in the most severe depression in our country's history," which began "with the stock market crash in 1929."[1592]

The Great Depression "was not caused by unfettered market forces. There is nothing in the operation of free markets that would create depressions or even recessions."[1593] In fact, "[o]ne of the great attributes of the private-property market system is its inherent ability to overcome almost any obstacle. Through price and cost readjustment, managerial efficiency and labor productivity, new savings and investments, the market economy tends to regain its equilibrium and resume its service to consumers."[1594] "In capitalism, people and industries are resilient. The reason is simple. They are free to act on their reason and to seek a profit."[1595] Thus, "market economies are 'self-adjusting' and...cannot get stuck in a

---

[1592] Pongracic, Ivan Jr. "The Great Depression According to Milton Friedman." *FEE*, 1 Sept. 2007, fee.org/articles/the-great-depression-according-to-milton-friedman/; Williams, Kelsey. "Fed Action Accelerates Boom-Bust Cycle; Not A Virus Crisis." *Yahoo Finance*, 19 May 2020, finance.yahoo.com/news/fed-action-accelerates-boom-bust-065808585.html.

[1593] Pongracic, Ivan Jr. "The Great Depression According to Milton Friedman." *FEE*, 1 Sept. 2007, fee.org/articles/the-great-depression-according-to-milton-friedman/.

[1594] "What Caused the Great Depression?" *FEE,* 2 Feb. 2018, fee.org/articles/what-caused-the-great-depression/.

[1595] Weiner, Keith, PhD. "Flattening the Economy Because, Virus." *Keith Weiner Economics*, 18 Mar. 2020, keithweinereconomics.com/2020/03/18/flattening-the-economy-because-virus/.

recession for very long."[1596] By contrast, "[i]n socialism and central planning, there is no resiliency. The people starve if the crop yield is below quota, they drown if the tide rises, they suffer in darkness if an oil shipment is delayed. The reason is simple. They are not allowed to act, but must wait for orders from a central planner."[1597]

Milton Friedman concluded "that, had the Fed not been created, the downturn of 1929 would not have become a major depression."[1598] He elaborated: "Had the Federal Reserve System never been established, and had a similar series of runs started, there is little doubt that the same measures would have been taken as in 1907 — a restriction of payments. That would have been more drastic than what actually occurred in the final months of 1930. However, by preventing the draining of reserves from good banks, restriction would almost certainly have prevented the subsequent series of bank failures in 1931, 1932, and 1933, just as restriction in 1907 quickly ended bank failures then…The panic over, confidence restored, economic recovery would very likely have begun in early 1931, just as it had in early 1908. The existence of the Reserve System prevented the drastic therapeutic measure: directly, by reducing the concern of the stronger banks, who, mistakenly as it turned out, were confident that borrowing from the System offered them a reliable escape mechanism in case of difficulty; indirectly, by lulling the community as a whole, and the banking system in particular, into the belief that such drastic measures were no longer

---

[1596] Pongracic, Ivan Jr. "The Great Depression According to Milton Friedman." *FEE*, 1 Sept. 2007, fee.org/articles/the-great-depression-according-to-milton-friedman/.

[1597] Weiner, Keith, PhD. "Flattening the Economy Because, Virus." *Keith Weiner Economics*, 18 Mar. 2020, keithweinereconomics.com/2020/03/18/flattening-the-economy-because-virus/.

[1598] Pongracic, Ivan Jr. "The Great Depression According to Milton Friedman." *FEE*, 1 Sept. 2007, fee.org/articles/the-great-depression-according-to-milton-friedman/.

necessary now that the System was there to take care of such matters..."[1599]

Monetary economist, Lawrence H. White of the University of Missouri — St. Louis, wrote, "Friedman understood...that before the Federal Reserve Act, financial panics in the US were mitigated by the actions of private commercial bank clearinghouses. Friedman and [Anna] Schwartz's view of the 1930's was that the Fed, having nationalized the roles of the clearinghouse associations [CHAs], particularly the lender-of-last-resort role, did less to mitigate the panic than the CHAs had done in earlier panics like 1907 and 1893. In that sense, the economy would have been better off if the Fed had not been created."[1600]

Ben S. Bernanke admitted that the Fed had played a role in the Great Depression: "I would like to say to Milton and Anna: Regarding the Great Depression. You're right, we did it. We're very sorry..."[1601]   Bernanke then "engaged in irresponsible monetary behavior that helped trigger a massive financial meltdown and a

---

[1599] *Id.*

[1600] On the Division of Labour blog (March 12, 2007). Pongracic, Ivan Jr. "The Great Depression According to Milton Friedman." *FEE*, 1 Sept. 2007, fee.org/articles/the-great-depression-according-to-milton-friedman/.

[1601] Remarks by Governor Ben S. Bernanke at the Conference to Honor Milton Friedman, University of Chicago Chicago, Illinois November 8, 2002. Williams, Kelsey. "Fed Action Accelerates Boom-Bust Cycle; Not A Virus Crisis." *Yahoo Finance*, 19 May 2020, finance.yahoo.com/news/fed-action-accelerates-boom-bust-065808585.html.

subsequent recession."[1602] "Cheap credit and 'monopoly' money had blown bubbles in the debt markets that popped."[1603]

"[T]he Fed's failure in the early '30s shows the dangers of excessive centralization of important market functions that were previously dispersed among multiple private institutions."[1604]

"Today, it's understood by many that the recklessness of the Fed allowed for the subprime mortgages that caused the Great Recession of 2008."[1605] "It is the Fed money supply inflation and ultralow interest rates that caused the inevitable crisis in the first place."[1606]

"The Fed created the economic crisis with its more than a decade–long campaign of ultralow interest rates and quantitative easing policy that injected massive liquidity into financial markets. This unprecedented monetary policy caused companies to become more leveraged and to embark upon capital spending programs on a massive scale. This made an economic crisis inevitable…The truth is that 'monetary policy,' that is, inflation, cannot solve such

---

[1602] Anderson, William L. "The Costs Are Mounting in this Government-Imposed Economic Collapse." *Mises Institute*, 24 Mar. 2020, mises.org/wire/costs-are-mounting-government-imposed-economic-collapse?fbclid=IwAR1ggouFwQpu6uof_Wv_Ym_RPrzvgPkr5hoz7pXFE3MiK6RYNmIlJY2kqp0.

[1603] Williams, Kelsey. "Fed Action Accelerates Boom-Bust Cycle; Not A Virus Crisis." *Yahoo Finance*, 19 May 2020, finance.yahoo.com/news/fed-action-accelerates-boom-bust-065808585.html.

[1604] Pongracic, Ivan Jr. "The Great Depression According to Milton Friedman." *FEE*, 1 Sept. 2007, fee.org/articles/the-great-depression-according-to-milton-friedman/.

[1605] Jones, Stewart. "The Founders Warned Us About Central Banking." *Ron Paul Liberty Report*, 10 Oct. 2019, www.ronpaullibertyreport.com/archives/the-founders-warned-us-about-central-banking?fbclid=IwAR1GtgHBthCfZDgqhObnuqCX2hO9116CjGntgnKJ75rw5KXrb5U3mKOVFKI.

[1606] Thornton, Mark. "The Fed Can't Save Us." *Mises Institute*, 12 Mar. 2020, mises.org/power-market/fed-cant-save-us.

problems."[1607] The 2008 financial crisis was "built on the dung heap of faulty pricing and misallocation of capital. Wall Street's mega banks paid Moody's and Standard & Poor's big bucks to rate insanely structured pools of subprime mortgages and other bad debts and get AAA-rated credits to sell to investors, including public pension funds. These pools should have been rated junk from the beginning. The bad bets were packaged into Collateralized Loan Obligations (CLOs) and Collateralized Debt Obligations (CDOs). The Fed rewarded this behavior by secretly handing out $29 trillion cumulatively in below-market-rate loans to these corrupted global banks for more than two years — with not a single vote held in Congress or even the awareness by Congress that the Fed was pumping trillions of dollars into insolvent banks on Wall Street. Guess what the Fed is accepting today as collateral in its emergency loan program known as the Primary Dealer Credit Facility (PDCF): CLOs, CDOs, and stocks, as well as other toxic waste from the global banks that operate as trading houses on Wall Street."[1608]

"According to the U.S. Treasury, as of February 29, 2020, there was $16.9 trillion in marketable U.S. Treasury securities outstanding. Of that amount, at the end of February, the Federal Reserve held $2.47 trillion or 14.6 percent – making it, by far, the largest single holder of U.S. Treasuries anywhere in the world. [In March], the Fed's ownership of the Treasury market had increased to $3.12 trillion…And on March 23 [2020], the Fed announced that it would buy unlimited amounts of both Treasury securities and agency mortgage-backed securities 'to support smooth market functioning.' But exactly how can a so-called 'free market' function

---

[1607] *Id.*

[1608] Martens, Pam and Russ Martens. "The Fed Is Killing the Two Main Functions of Wall Street: Price Discovery and Prudent Capital Allocation." *Wall Street on Parade*, 11 Apr. 2020, wallstreetonparade.com/2020/04/the-fed-is-killing-the-two-main-functions-of-wall-street-price-discovery-and-prudent-capital-allocation/.

smoothly if the country's own central bank is cornering the market…"[1609]

Mike O'Rourke complained, "The central bank continues to intervene without ever giving markets an opportunity to clear. This will only extend the length of time it takes for the market to stabilize."[1610] "The last thing the economy needs is for state actors to 'step in' to rescue it…"[1611]

"[B]y flooding the economy with new money, expanding asset purchases, and facilitating Congress and the president's spending sprees, the Fed is exacerbating America's long-term economic problems. The Federal Reserve is unlikely to end these emergency measures after the government declares it is safe to resume normal life. Consumers, businesses, and (especially) the federal government are so addicted to low interest rates, quantitative easing, and other Federal Reserve interventions that any effort by the Fed to allow rates to rise or to stop creating new money will cause a severe recession. Eventually, the Federal Reserve-created consumer, business, and government debt bubbles will explode, leading to a major crisis that will dwarf the current coronavirus

---

[1609] Martens, Pam and Russ Martens. "The Federal Reserve Now Owns 15 Percent of the U.S. Treasury Market; At Its Current Rate, It Could Own the Whole Market in Less than Two Years." *Wall Street on Parade*, 28 Mar. 2020, wallstreetonparade.com/2020/03/the-federal-reserve-now-owns-15-percent-of-the-u-s-treasury-market-at-its-current-rate-it-could-own-the-whole-market-in-less-than-two-years/.

[1610] Kilgore, Tomi. "'Bearmageddon' for stocks appears to be upon us, strategist says." *Market Watch*, 15 Mar. 2020, www.marketwatch.com/story/bearmageddon-for-stocks-appears-to-be-upon-us-strategist-says-2020-03-15?reflink=mw_share_facebook&fbclid=IwAR1v5viyQmNrbpheaogqtoBY8mq8C63Ma4nttdiyxO9A6xTWxJOqIVU3c-Q.

[1611] Klein, Peter G. "The Financial System Is Now Totally Dependent on Government Intervention." *Mises Institute,* 16 Mar. 2020, mises.org/power-market/financial-system-now-totally-dependent-government-intervention?fbclid=IwAR3eKYaKZMJqyM91joNY59D1nTY6LqHPhsz4iz1fQS2VowwbR5YGkAlOHPA.

shutdown."[1612] "The truth is that the Fed is trying to doctor the stock and bond markets. So far it has not worked and could even be said to be backfiring…"[1613]

Christopher Whalen, founder of Whalen Global Advisors, said, "You're seeing the end game for monetary policy here, which is at a certain point you have to stop. Otherwise, you get grotesque asset bubbles like we saw, and the engine just runs out of fuel."[1614] Ultimately, the Fed is "trying to salvage an unworkable system."[1615]

"As a sign of just how brazen and disastrously broken the U.S. financial system has become, with no hearings in Congress…the New York Fed turned on its money spigot to Wall Street again on September 17, 2019…the New York Fed has been spewing hundreds of billions of dollars each week to Wall Street's trading houses… with no accountability to anyone or explanation as to why Wall

---

[1612] Paul, Ron. "Will Coronavirus End the Fed?" *Ron Paul Institute,* 30 Mar. 2020, www.ronpaulinstitute.org/archives/featured-articles/2020/ m a r c h / 3 0 / w i l l - c o r o n a v i r u s - e n d - t h e - f e d / ? fbclid=IwAR1_DnSktag1_IBqBrAw-pooprcz6AC8pikp2JA8npi-QGq5RtVRETCB5mc.

[1613] Thornton, Mark. "The Fed Can't Save Us." *Mises Institute*, 12 Mar. 2020, mises.org/power-market/fed-cant-save-us.

[1614] Cox, Jeff. "Fed to pump in more than $1 trillion in dramatic ramping up of market intervention amid coronavirus meltdown." *CNBC*, 12 Mar. 2020, www.cnbc.com/2020/03/12/fed-to-pump-more-than-500-billion-into-short-term-bank-funding-expand-types-of-security-purchases.html? __source=iosappshare%7Ccom.apple.UIKit.activity.PostToFacebook&fbcl id=IwAR15uK1dO3bybc49XFX90ozIhLhZTroLUrUDsr_gEnJJ1tQL1voo 1TkiwGA.

[1615] At 9. RonPaulLibertyReport. "Central Banking Is On The Ropes: Gold Will Survive & The Fed Will End." *Youtube*, 13 Dec. 2019, www.youtube.com/watch?v=Ndcb2SPRU7M.

Street needs or deserves this money."[1616]   "When the economy started to tank as governments shut things down in response to the coronavirus, the Federal Reserve fired up the printing press and created trillions of dollars out of thin air to monetize the debt."[1617] Author Chris Rosini tells us, "They are now printing more than they did in QE1...."[1618]

Ron Paul commented on the government spending and slashing of interest rates under the CARES Act: "It's impossible, it won't solve the problems, because we got into this by too much spending, too much debt, too much inflation, too much manipulation, too much drive for zero interest rates, and that's what they're doing. They're solving the problem by spending even more, printing even more, and get the interest rates below zero and they think that's going to solve the problem but it isn't."[1619]

"Such a bailout creates severe economic risks. Longer term, these newly created dollars threaten to increase inflation. The $500 billion spent on municipal debt multiplies into trillions of additional

---

[1616] Martens, Pam and Russ Martens. "Bernie Sanders Hasn't Quite Captured What Wall Street Does: It's Actually a Fraud-Monetization System with a Money-Printing Unit Called the New York Fed." *Wall Street on Parade*, 21 Jan. 2020, wallstreetonparade.com/2020/01/bernie-sanders-hasnt-quite-captured-what-wall-street-does-its-actually-a-fraud-monetization-system-with-a-money-printing-unit-called-the-new-york-fed/.

[1617] Maharrey, Mike. "Enjoy That Stimulus: You're Going to Pay for It!" *Tenth Amendment Center*, 12 Jun. 2020, blog.tenthamendmentcenter.com/2020/06/enjoy-that-stimulus-youre-going-to-pay-for-it/?fbclid=IwAR19Z7wT2WimDrd0lKKYKML2cbNPnIAVfnN-0SlNoUC8WvjMQ7tuzdIpJqg.

[1618] At 5. RonPaulLibertyReport. "Central Banking Is On The Ropes: Gold Will Survive & The Fed Will End." *Youtube*, 13 Dec. 2019, www.youtube.com/watch?v=Ndcb2SPRU7M.

[1619] Favocci, Christine. "Dr. Ron Paul hits nail on the head in no-nonsense coronavirus interview." *WND*, 30 Mar. 2020, www.wnd.com/2020/03/dr-ron-paul-hits-nail-head-no-nonsense-coronavirus-interview/?fbclid=IwAR1G9cb8BGg9RujH6DN7YqHkEjMRte5uRjoLceDDkl_-CZRrGi4sv2DInYo.

dollars as the funds are deposited at lending institutions and loaned to other borrowers. A greater quantity of money chases existing resources operates as a stealth tax by eroding real savings, diminishing real wages, and driving up the cost of living."[1620] "[I]f these massive demand-side programs are launched aggressively, the result in the medium term will be a new crisis. We already saw it in 2009 with the misguided response of the eurozone, spending almost 3 percent of GDP in white elephants and adding debt to a financial credit crunch problem. It triggered a worse crisis afterward."[1621]

"When you boil it all down, the Fed can't do anything other than print money. It doesn't manufacture any products or provide any services. It just creates inflation and devalues the dollars already in circulation. In effect, prices ultimately have to rise so the larger quantity of money can buy the same quantity of goods. This devaluation takes away the spending power of the dollars you already have. It punishes savers. And it ultimately serves as a stealth tax…When all is said and done, you will end up with a lower standard of living."[1622]

"It is becoming increasingly apparent that the 'PhD Standard' has not, and will never, provide a stable, reliable, and uniform

---

[1620] Griffith, Joel. "A Backdoor Central Bank Bailout of State Governments." *Real Clear Markets*, 2 May 2020, www.realclearmarkets.com/articles/2020/05/02/a_backdoor_central_bank_bailout_of_state_governments_490609.html?fbclid=IwAR2ram3WBD1YDtA-phyhdAVkT1c8kageamzMChCjYT3r4duZ2iMWycBEYOY.

[1621] Lacalle, Daniel. PhD. "The Fed Panicked, and Its Rate Cut Is Making the Economy Worse." *Mises Institute,* 9 Mar. 2020, mises.org/wire/fed-panicked-and-its-rate-cut-making-economy-worse?fbclid=IwAR31Z6Qs6p8b9dRJ-_YZBaEuHz4Pq0SQoLzOH7W2TJlQ3G4vboe6ViwOuMI#.XmbHfDyEiq4.twitter.

[1622] Maharrey, Mike. "Enjoy That Stimulus: You're Going to Pay for It!" *Tenth Amendment Center*, 12 Jun. 2020, blog.tenthamendmentcenter.com/2020/06/enjoy-that-stimulus-youre-going-to-pay-for-it/?fbclid=IwAR19Z7wT2WimDrd0lKKYKML2cbNPnIAVfnN-0SlNoUC8WvjMQ7tuzdIpJqg.

monetary system, upon which rational economic calculation and rising prosperity can be based."[1623] In fact, "Federal Reserve policy and actions are an abuse of fundamental economics. The effects of their actions are hugely volatile and unpredictable. Their actions and effects have spawned problems that are nearly insurmountable."[1624] "In 1980, Milton and Rose Friedman wrote of the Fed's record over the 45 years after the banking crisis of 1930–33: Since 1935, the [Federal Reserve] System has presided over — and greatly contributed to — a major recession of 1937–38, a wartime and immediate postwar inflation, and a roller coaster economy since, with alternate rises and falls in inflation and decreases and increases in unemployment. Each inflationary peak and each temporary inflationary trough has been at a higher and higher level, and the average level of unemployment has gradually increased. The System has not made the same mistake that it made in 1929–1933 — of permitting or fostering a monetary collapse — but it has made the opposite mistake, of fostering an unduly rapid growth in the quantity of money and so promoting inflation. In addition, it has continued, by swinging from one extreme to another, to produce not only booms but also recessions, some mild, some sharp."[1625]

"Almost all Federal Reserve activity is comprised of reactions to problems that resulted from their own actions. And it has been

---

[1623] Lewis, Nathan. "The World Gold Standard System Will Rise Again — But, Not Yet." *Forbes*, 6 Dec. 2019, www.forbes.com/sites/nathanlewis/2019/12/06/the-world-gold-standard-system-will-rise-again---but-not-yet/#5474426235e6.

[1624] Williams, Kelsey. "Fed Action Accelerates Boom-Bust Cycle; Not A Virus Crisis." *Yahoo Finance*, 19 May 2020, finance.yahoo.com/news/fed-action-accelerates-boom-bust-065808585.html.

[1625] Pongracic, Ivan Jr. "The Great Depression According to Milton Friedman." *FEE*, 1 Sept. 2007, fee.org/articles/the-great-depression-according-to-milton-friedman/.

that way ever since the Fed opened for business in 1913..."[1626] Unfortunately, "the PhD types seem to be getting ready to double down on the sort of silliness that hasn't worked very well thus far, and might lead to eventual disaster. These academics and central bankers with PhDs remain very eager to convince anyone who will listen why they really, really should be allowed to manage our monetary systems. Mostly, this is because their very, very good ideas will help to fix the problems left by the last generation of PhD-bearing money manipulators. These range from CPI targeting fans to the advocates of 'Modern Monetary Theory.'"[1627]

Dr. Judy Shelton "understand[s] the Fed's role in causing regular economic crises, and the manipulation of official inflation and GDP figures...Shelton directly blamed the Fed for the "devastating 2008 global meltdown" that sparked economic turmoil worldwide.[1628] In particular, she pointed the finger at the Fed's "influence over the creation of money and credit."[1629] She asked, "How can...slightly less [sic] than a dozen people meeting eight times a year decide what the cost of capital should be versus some kind of organically, market supply determined rate? The Fed is not omniscient. They don't know what the right rate should be. How could anyone? If the success of capitalism depends on someone

[1626] Williams, Kelsey. "Fed Action Accelerates Boom-Bust Cycle; Not A Virus Crisis." *Yahoo Finance*, 19 May 2020, finance.yahoo.com/news/fed-action-accelerates-boom-bust-065808585.html.

[1627] Lewis, Nathan. "The World Gold Standard System Will Rise Again — But, Not Yet." *Forbes*, 6 Dec. 2019, www.forbes.com/sites/nathanlewis/2019/12/06/the-world-gold-standard-system-will-rise-again---but-not-yet/#5474426235e6.

[1628] In a *Wall Street Journal* piece entitled, "The Case for Monetary Regime Change." Newman, Alex. "Trump Nominates Gold Advocate to Federal Reserve." *New American*, 7 Feb. 2020, www.thenewamerican.com/usnews/politics/item/34831-trump-nominates-gold-advocate-to-federal-reserve?fbclid=IwAR3wJ8NEBE-t0FNu6_UqzJ0bg2HrFwliT-0vFNfDJPC8MjiPxXQx83ON9Zs.

[1629] *Id.*

being smart enough to know what the rate should be on everything ...we're doomed. We might as well resurrect Gosplan."[1630] "Capitalism cherishes voluntary contracts and interest rates that are determined by savings, not credit creation by a central bank."[1631] Ultimately, "Mises proved that socialist planning is impossible, even if the planner is a wise, honest, caring genius."[1632]

"[A]s a result of the banking crisis of 1930–33, the Fed was granted more responsibilities and more control over banking. As is often the case in politics, failure was used to justify an expansion of power. That expansion of the Fed's power resulted in a great amount of economic destruction through the subsequent decades."[1633] "By any reasonable measure, the Federal Reserve has failed miserably in all their responsibilities. When organizations fail in a capitalist system, they are supposed to be replaced, not given more responsibility."[1634] Instead, "[t]he bankers who control the Federal Reserve along with their politician protectors have dramatically expanded the scope, authority, and influence of the Federal Reserve with each scientifically created crisis that has occurred in the last 96 years."[1635]

Rep. Lindbergh opined, "The financial system has been turned over to the Federal Reserve Board. That Board administers the

[1630] "Gosplan was the committee that centrally planned the failed Soviet economy." *Id.*

[1631] "Central Bank Quotes." *Brainy Quote*, www.brainyquote.com/quotes/ron_paul_396265?src=t_central_bank.

[1632] Weiner, Keith, PhD. "Flattening the Economy Because, Virus." *Keith Weiner Economics*, 18 Mar. 2020, keithweinereconomics.com/2020/03/18/flattening-the-economy-because-virus/.

[1633] Pongracic, Ivan Jr. "The Great Depression According to Milton Friedman." *FEE*, 1 Sept. 2007, fee.org/articles/the-great-depression-according-to-milton-friedman/.

[1634] Quinn, Jim. "The Federal Reserve Must Die." *HCP Live*, 25 Aug. 2009, www.mdmag.com/medical-news/federal_reserve_must_die.

[1635] *Id.*

finance system by authority of a purely profiteering group. The system is Private, conducted for the sole purpose of obtaining the greatest possible profits from the use of other people's money. From now on, depressions will be scientifically created."[1636] "[I]n fact, it is run solely to gain private profit for its select stock holders."[1637]

"The policies of the Federal Reserve hurt the average American. It benefits the privileged few at the expense of the rest of us. The Federal Reserve erodes most Americans' standard of living while enriching well-connected elites. The central bank serves big spending politicians, big bankers and their friends. Special interests receive access to money and credit before the harmful inflationary effects impact the entire economy."[1638] The Fed's policies "have only helped the 0.01 percent. What have record low rates achieved? Corporate plunder. The rate cuts and bailouts enabled corporations to borrow record amounts of cash and to conduct massive stock buyback programs. It allowed corporations to enrich CEO compensation packages at the expense of future growth and job creation, enabled malinvestment in billion-dollar zombie corporations that are all debt without earnings, and created a record wealth-inequality gap..."[1639] "Northman Trader author Sven Henrich proclaimed, 'Central banks have become the primary driver of wealth inequality. And they refuse to admit the self-evident... They are the driver of excess that primarily benefits the few. Central

---

[1636] "The History of Money Part 2." *XAT3*, www.xat.org/xat/usury.html.

[1637] *Id.*

[1638] Borowski, Julie. "Top 10 Reasons to End the Federal Reserve." *FreedomWorks,* 1 Feb. 2012, www.freedomworks.org/content/top-10-reasons-end-federal-reserve.

[1639] "The Great Economic Depression of 2020: No lessons learned as central banks' bazookas dribble or misfire." *RT*, 23 Mar. 2020, www.rt.com/op-ed/483845-great-economic-depression-2020/.

banking is socialism for the top 1%.'"[1640] "It's basically policy now that the Fed exists to bail out banks and the financial sector forever, no matter how much it costs other sectors of the economy…This is monetary policy that was built by bankers and exists for the benefit of bankers. Every solution involves helping bankers. The Fed has no other ideas."[1641]

Representative Ron Paul explained, "Though the Federal Reserve policy harms the average American, it benefits those in a position to take advantage of the cycles in monetary policy. The main beneficiaries are those who receive access to artificially inflated money and/or credit before the inflationary effects of the policy impact the entire economy. Federal Reserve policies also benefit big spending politicians who use the inflated currency created by the Fed to hide the true costs of the welfare-warfare state."[1642]

"When it comes to the central bank and its machinations, the fix is in. The Fed — ostensibly a non-profit organization — owns the mint, the money, and sets the terms of the loans it makes to the federal treasury. What's more, there is no product; there is nothing being loaned other than worthless paper that can never be traded in for anything of value because all that is used to secure the worth of the currency is now owned by the very bankers who control the

---

[1640] Redman, Jamie. "Data Shows the US Economy Was Collapsing 5 Months Before the Coronavirus Outbreak." *Bitcoin.com*, 3 May 2020, ews.bitcoin.com/data-shows-the-us-economy-was-collapsing-5-months-before-the-coronavirus-outbreak/?fbclid=IwAR3cgTDBLMYGIYpRAO_pGNc7V-boxoJX-FHsWpJYCoJ3UOxdU6DmCN3hh-Q.

[1641] McMaken, Ryan. "The Fed Announces Another Flood of Easy Money." *Mises Institute*, 12 Mar. 2020, mises.org/power-market/fed-announces-another-flood-easy-money.

[1642] Quinn, Jim. "The Federal Reserve Must Die." *HCP Live*, 25 Aug. 2009, www.mdmag.com/medical-news/federal_reserve_must_die.

Federal Reserve."[1643] "Real wealth is tangible things produced with tangible effort. Loans made out of thin-air 'money' require no effort and are entirely ephemeral. But if those loans are used to acquire real ownership of real assets, then something has been exchanged for nothing and one party is getting screwed."[1644] For example, "[t]he Fed has a whole story about why falling prices would be catastrophic. But falling prices are what naturally happens as society produces more per capita...Prices fell dramatically over the course of the 19th century [while on gold standard]. A basket of goods that cost $100 in 1800 cost only $48.94 in 1899. That means one could buy twice as much with the same wages in 1899 as one could in 1800. Falling prices are the natural result of a more productive economy. But as the Fed's inflation table shows, it has *always* overcome this natural tendency and made prices rise. That same basket of goods that fell from $100 in 1800 to $48.94 in 1899 cost $1,498.45 in 2019. It should cost something like $24.00, or even less considering accelerating innovation. Yes, monetary inflation eventually raises wages, too, but always more slowly than it raises consumer goods, making wage earners poorer while the beneficiaries of inflation – mostly in the financial sector – get richer. Get it yet? You're being ripped off on a massive scale..."[1645] Horace Greeley, founder and editor of *The New York Tribune*, revealed, "While boasting of our noble deeds, we are careful to control the ugly fact that by an iniquitous money system, we have

---

[1643] Wolverton, Joe, II, JD. "Tennessee Considering Bills Restoring Gold and Silver as Sound Money." *The New American*, 2 Feb. 2019, www.thenewamerican.com/usnews/constitution/item/31369-tennessee-considering-bills-restoring-gold-and-silver-as-sound-money.

[1644] "Banks Quotes." *Good Reads*, www.goodreads.com/quotes/tag/banks.

[1645] Mullen, Tom. "'Inflation is low': The Federal Reserve's Scam of the Century." *Tommullen.com*, 31 Mar. 2020, www.tommullen.net/featured/inflation-is-low-the-federal-reserves-scam-of-the-century/?fbclid=IwAR1As6UZbfSEJ6I0-s3g2LyrUf5QFsB0HJ5yrSdRMxE9TDTtYjwGUitZATc.

nationalized a system of oppression which, though more refined, is not less cruel than the old system of chattel slavery."[1646]

Rep. Ron Paul said while questioning Fed Chairman, Ben Bernanke, "The Federal Reserve in collaboration with the giant banks has created the greatest financial crisis the world has ever seen. The foolish notion that unlimited amounts of money and credit created out of thin air can provide sustainable economic growth has delivered this crisis to us. Instead of economic growth and stable prices, [the Federal Reserve] has given us a system of government and finance that now threatens the world financial and political institutions. Pursuing the same policy of excessive spending, debt expansion, and monetary inflation can only compound the problems that prevent the required corrections. Doubling the money supply didn't work, quadrupling it won't work either. Buying up the bad debt of privileged institutions and dumping worthless assets on the American people is morally wrong and economically futile."[1647]

The Fed "has helped enable trillion-dollar deficits and an exploding national debt. It has encouraged companies to issue more bonds, and a big chunk of marginal investment grade bonds (BBB) will soon be headed for junk bond status. It has also encouraged individual investors not to save or invest in safe assets and to put their money into riskier stocks because they cannot earn interest from banks or dividends from safe companies."[1648]

"By putting the nation into massive debt, the future growth of a 'natural' economy is being choked to death, forever reliant on

---

[1646] "Prominent Quotes." *The Liberty Dollar*, libertydollar.org/ld/press-kit/prominent-quotes.htm.

[1647] Quinn, Jim. "The Federal Reserve Must Die." *HCP Live*, 25 Aug. 2009, www.mdmag.com/medical-news/federal_reserve_must_die.

[1648] Thornton, Mark. "The Fed Can't Save Us." *Mises Institute*, 12 Mar. 2020, mises.org/power-market/fed-cant-save-us.

central bank stimulus."[1649]   Unfortunately, "[t]his mess will continue. They will have to keep feeding it with…more inflation and more intervention."[1650]   "There will be a breaking point…"[1651] "Any economist should see all these effects as bad for the economy. The Fed is the cause of the crisis, not the cure."[1652]

The financial situation will continue to deteriorate until the root causes are exposed and eradicated, namely that bankers have hijacked the economy for their own gain.   "There is no limit to the lengths global bankers will go to in order to control the economic policies that affect the entire population of the world."[1653]   Sir Josiah Stamp, Director of the Bank of England, admitted (circa 1940), "Banking was conceived in iniquity and was born in sin. The bankers own the earth. Take it away from them, but leave them the power to create deposits, and with a flick of the pen they will create. enough deposits to buy it back again. However, take it away from them, and all the great fortunes like mine will disappear and they ought to disappear, for this would be a happier and better world to

---

[1649] Anderson, Anthony. "New Dollar Backed by Gold Coming This October 2020?" *GSI Exchange*, 27 May 2020, gsiexchange.com/is-a-new-dollar-backed-by-gold-at-10000-per-ounce-coming-by-october-1st-2020/?fbclid=IwAR0JeJRf6pMwprbp4UUdETDxl4lQQg3Oek5XnXrk3CEAVjZdWUbay6W6m28.

[1650] At 9. RonPaulLibertyReport. "Central Banking Is On The Ropes: Gold Will Survive & The Fed Will End." *Youtube*, 13 Dec. 2019, www.youtube.com/watch?v=Ndcb2SPRU7M.

[1651] Anderson, Anthony. "New Dollar Backed by Gold Coming This October 2020?" *GSI Exchange*, 27 May 2020, gsiexchange.com/is-a-new-dollar-backed-by-gold-at-10000-per-ounce-coming-by-october-1st-2020/?fbclid=IwAR0JeJRf6pMwprbp4UUdETDxl4lQQg3Oek5XnXrk3CEAVjZdWUbay6W6m28.

[1652] Thornton, Mark. "The Fed Can't Save Us." *Mises Institute*, 12 Mar. 2020, mises.org/power-market/fed-cant-save-us.

[1653] Wolverton, Joe, II, JD. "Tennessee Considering Bills Restoring Gold and Silver as Sound Money." *The New American*, 2 Feb. 2019, www.thenewamerican.com/usnews/constitution/item/31369-tennessee-considering-bills-restoring-gold-and-silver-as-sound-money.

live in. But, if you wish to remain the slaves of the bankers and pay the cost of your own slavery, let them continue to create deposits."[1654] In other words, "[i]f you want to be slaves of bankers and pay the cost of your own slavery, then let the bankers control money and control credit."[1655]

Aaron Russo said, "[T]hese people control the money, so they make all the rules… And the truth is America has really become a socialistic, communistic country. And everybody says its a capitalistic country, it's not a capitalistic country. How can it be capitalistic when you have a central bank?…[I]t can't be! It's a planned economy…If they want to create prosperity, they just print dollars, they just make dollars, or put digits into the economy. And then now you have prosperity. You don't have real prosperity, you don't have real manufacturing, you just have money being injected in, it's an infusion of credit."[1656]

"By bailing out the nation's 'bad economic actors,' and forestalling the resetting process, the Fed is consigning the future of the United States to a weakened state."[1657] "Wall Street's mega banks and their primary regulator, the Federal Reserve, are no longer just a threat to the safety and soundness of the U.S. banking system — together they are an unparalleled and unprecedented threat to the

---

[1654] "Central Banks Quotes." *Good Reads*, www.goodreads.com/quotes/tag/central-banks.

[1655] Sir Josiah Stamp. "The International Bankers: Famous Quotes." *ConspiracyAnalyst.org*, 23 Dec. 2019, conspiracyanalyst.org/2013/03/01/the-international-bankers-famous-quotes/.

[1656] "Aaron Russo: Reflections and Warnings - Full Transcript." *Matt Prather*, sites.google.com/site/themattprather/Reading/aaron-russo/reflections-and-warnings-full-transcript.

[1657] Anderson, Anthony. "New Dollar Backed by Gold Coming This October 2020?" *GSI Exchange*, 27 May 2020, gsiexchange.com/is-a-new-dollar-backed-by-gold-at-10000-per-ounce-coming-by-october-1st-2020/?fbclid=IwAR0JeJRf6pMwprbp4UUdETDxl4lQQg3Oek5XnXrk3CEAVjZdWUbay6W6m28.

idea of democracy as we understand it."[1658] "[I]t's not overstating it to say that the Fed-facilitated out-of-control federal government spending constitutes the greatest threat to the American way of life in history."[1659] Milton Friedman explained, "Any system which gives so much power and so much discretion to a few men, so that mistakes — excusable or not — can have such far reaching effects, is a bad system. It is a bad system to believers in freedom just because it gives a few men such power without any effective check by the body politic — this is the key political argument against an independent central bank."[1660]

"Through manipulation of the amount of currency it creates, the Fed has power to swing an election. It did so in 1980 by creating a recession and damaging President Carter's reelection hopes. And it flooded the nation with freshly created currency in 1972 to help reelect Richard Nixon."[1661] Ex-New York Fed president, Bill Dudley. threatened "to use Fed monetary policy to affect the outcome of a US election": "Trump's re-election arguably presents a threat to the United States' and global economy, and if the goal of monetary policy is to achieve the best long-term economic outcome,

---

[1658] Martens, Pam and Russ Martens. "Stimulus Bill Allows Federal Reserve to Conduct Meetings in Secret; Gives Fed $454 Billion Slush Fund for Wall Street Bailouts." *Wall Street on Parade*, 26 Mar. 2020, wallstreetonparade.com/2020/03/stimulus-bill-allows-federal-reserve-to-conduct-meetings-in-secret-gives-fed-454-billion-slush-fund-for-wall-street-bailouts/.

[1659] Jones, Stewart. "The Founders Warned Us About Central Banking." *Ron Paul Liberty Report*, 10 Oct. 2019, www.ronpaullibertyreport.com/archives/the-founders-warned-us-about-central-banking?fbclid=IwAR1GtgHBthCfZDgqhObnuqCX2hO9116CjGntgnKJ75rw5KXrb5U3mKOVFKI.

[1660] "Milton Friedman Quotations." *Memorablequotations.com*, www.memorablequotations.com/friedman.htm.

[1661] McManus, John F. "The Power of the Federal Reserve." *The New American*, 27 Jun. 2020, www.thenewamerican.com/reviews/opinion/item/29397-the-power-of-the-federal-reserve.

the Fed's officials should consider how their decisions would affect the political outcome of 2020..."[1662]

Chris Martenson opined, "The bankers and financiers are badly overplaying their hands, again, and people are starting to catch on to the scam."[1663] "The Fed has come under increasing scrutiny in recent years following several waves of 'quantitative easing' — also known as printing new money — and its unprecedented, multi-trillion-dollar bailouts of foreign banks, big corporations, and other central banks. Its widespread manipulation of markets has also attracted fierce criticism and a bipartisan outcry to rein in the institution."[1664] Unfortunately, "There is no hope of regulating restraint. Power of this magnitude operates beyond the reach of regulations."[1665]

According to Alex Jones, "folks are starting to find out who the real enemy is: offshore, private banking corporations that have engaged in a hostile corporate take-over of the United States and almost every other nation on the planet. And the private Federal Reserve is their beach-head here in the United States."[1666] For

---

[1662] Paul, Ron. "Ron Paul: 'Forget the Russians: It's the Federal Reserve Seeking to Meddle in Our Elections.'" *The Free Thought Project*, 3 Sept. 2019, thefreethoughtproject.com/ron-paul-end-federal-reserve/?fbclid=IwAR1nGlN-ywVH6dp-4yR2CGmdisX6qSZxeBCo9nTDg-qmZ53-AvddeYuUpGw.

[1663] "Banks Quotes." *Good Reads*, www.goodreads.com/quotes/tag/banks.

[1664] Newman, Alex. "Washington State Considers Gold and Silver as Legal Tender." *The New American*, 31 Jan. 2012, www.thenewamerican.com/usnews/politics/item/9171-washington-state-considers-gold-and-silver-as-legal-tender.

[1665] Wolverton, Joe, II, JD,. "Tennessee Considering Bills Restoring Gold and Silver as Sound Money." *The New American*, 2 Feb. 2019, www.thenewamerican.com/usnews/constitution/item/31369-tennessee-considering-bills-restoring-gold-and-silver-as-sound-money.

[1666] "Aaron Russo: Reflections and Warnings - Full Transcript." *Matt Prather*, sites.google.com/site/themattprather/Reading/aaron-russo/reflections-and-warnings-full-transcript.

instance, Dr. Ron Paul asserted that the nation's economic "problem started…in 1913 with the creation of the Fed."[1667] Vice President of the Ludwig von Mises Institute, Joseph Salerno, wrote that "the very existence and function of the Fed is a destructive influence on the U.S. and global economy."[1668]

Judy Shelton came out as "a fierce critic of the Fed and its quasi-'central planning' schemes."[1669] She "exposed the fact that the Federal Reserve System has 'rigged'" the economy "in favor of Wall Street and the wealthiest 1 percent" via its "dangerous manipulation of interest rates."[1670] Shelton warned, "The Federal Reserve is not your friend. Loose monetary policy is bad for you and for your economic prospects."[1671] President Trump has also attacked "the Fed as the 'biggest risk' for the economy."[1672] Author Eustace Mullins even accused the Federal Reserve System of being "a criminal syndicate."[1673]

[1667] At 16:15. RonPaulLibertyReport. "Central Banking Is On The Ropes: Gold Will Survive & The Fed Will End." *Youtube*, 13 Dec. 2019, www.youtube.com/watch?v=Ndcb2SPRU7M.

[1668] Newman, Alex. "Trump Nominates Gold Advocate to Federal Reserve." *New American*, 7 Feb. 2020, www.thenewamerican.com/usnews/politics/item/34831-trump-nominates-gold-advocate-to-federal-reserve?fbclid=IwAR3wJ8NEBE-t0FNu6_UqzJ0bg2HrFwliT-0vFNfDJPC8MjiPxXQx83ON9Zs.

[1669] *Id.*

[1670] *Id.*

[1671] *Id.*

[1672] Bryan, Bob. "Trump's attacks on the Fed may be intense, but they're nothing compared to a wild new story about Ronald Reagan from former Fed Chairman Paul Volcker." *Business Insider,*. 24 Oct. 2018, www.businessinsider.com/ronald-reagan-fed-chair-volcker-trump-2018-10.

[1673] Mullins is author of *Secrets of the Federal Reserve*, 1991. "The International Bankers: Famous Quotes." *ConspiracyAnalyst.org*, 23 Dec. 2019, conspiracyanalyst.org/2013/03/01/the-international-bankers-famous-quotes/.

Representative Louis Thomas McFadden (R-PA), Chairman of the U.S. Banking Currency Commission for 22 years, declared, "We have in this country one of the most corrupt institutions the world has ever known. I refer to the Federal Reserve Board...This evil institution has impoverished...the people of the United States...and has practically bankrupted our Government. It has done this through...the corrupt practice of the moneyed vultures who control it."[1674] "There is not a man within the sound of my voice who does not know that this nation is run by the international bankers."[1675] "Sen. Dick Durbin...blurted out an obvious truth about Congress: ...'And the banks — hard to believe in a time when we're facing a banking crisis that many of the banks created -- are still the most powerful lobby on Capitol Hill. And they frankly own the place.' The blunt acknowledgment that the same banks that caused the financial crisis 'own' the U.S. Congress — according to one of

---

[1674] "The History of Money Part 2." *XAT3*, www.xat.org/xat/usury.html.

[1675] "Central Banks Quotes." *AZ Quotes*, www.azquotes.com/quotes/topics/central-banks.html.

that institution's most powerful members — demonstrates just how extreme this institutional corruption is."[1676]

Dr. Ron Paul complained, "Americans have been living under a corrupt and immoral monetary system ever since" the creation of the Federal Reserve.[1677] Jim McCarthy wrote, "Sneaky and underhanded, the Federal Reserve has been sucking the life blood out of the United States since 1913. Like a black widow spider, it weaves a web of corruption and deceit. Unknown to its prey, the Fed's bite is poisonous, deep, long-lasting and brings financial upheaval and misery to Americans."[1678]

Representative Wright Patman, Chairman of the House of Representatives Committee on Banking and Currency for 40 years,

---

[1676] "One might think it would be a big news story for the second most-powerful member of the U.S. Senate to baldly state that the Congress is 'owned' by the bankers who spawned the financial crisis and continue to dictate the government's actions. But it won't be. The leading members of the media work for the very corporations that benefit most from this process. Establishment journalists are integral and well-rewarded members of the same system and thus cannot and will not see it as inherently corrupt (instead, as *Newsweek*'s Evan Thomas said, their role, as 'members of the ruling class,' is to 'prop up the existing order,' 'protect traditional institutions' and 'safeguard the status quo'). That Congress is fully owned and controlled by a tiny sliver of narrow, oligarchical, deeply corrupted interests is simultaneously so obvious yet so demonized (only Unserious Shrill Fringe radicals, such as the IMF's former chief economist, use that sort of language) that even Durbin's explicit admission will be largely ignored. Even that extreme of a confession (Durbin elaborated on it with Ed Schultz last night) hardly causes a ripple." Greenwald, Glenn. "Top Senate Democrat: bankers 'own' the U.S. Congress." *Salon*, 30 Apr. 2009, www.salon.com/2009/04/30/ownership/.

[1677] Paul, Ron. "Ron Paul: 'Forget the Russians: It's the Federal Reserve Seeking to Meddle in Our Elections.'" *The Free Thought Project*, 3 Sept. 2019, thefreethoughtproject.com/ron-paul-end-federal-reserve/?fbclid=IwAR1nGlN-ywVH6dp-4yR2CGmdisX6qSZxeBCo9nTDg-qmZ53-AvddeYuUpGw.

[1678] Jim McCarthy, *The Money Spiders, the Ruin-NATION of the United States by the Federal Reserve.* "Federal Reserve Quotes." *Good Reads*, www.goodreads.com/quotes/tag/federal-reserve.

warned, "In the United States today, we have two governments. We have the duly constituted government and then we have an independent, uncontrolled and uncoordinated government in the Federal Reserve System operating the money powers which are reserved for Congress by the Constitution."[1679] As Lawrence Parks, Executive Director of Fame, noted, "Bypassing voters, taxpayers and the public at large, Congress has delegated to the Fed a power that the Congress itself does not have."[1680] "To make a law constitutional, nothing more is necessary than that it should be fairly adapted to carry into effect some specific power given to congress... the power of coining money implies the power of establishing a mint. The power of laying and collecting taxes implies the power of regulating the mode of assessment and collection, and of appointing revenue officers; but it does not imply the power of establishing a great banking corporation, branching out into every district of the country, and inundating it with a flood of paper-money...To derive such a tremendous authority from implication, would be to change the subordinate into fundamental powers; to make the implied powers greater than those which are expressly granted; and to change the whole scheme and theory of the government..."[1681]

"Today, the American economy operates under a monetary system which is completely outside the Constitution."[1682] According to W. Cleon Skousen, "Probably no aspect of the American economy has strayed further from the Constitution than the monetary

---

[1679] For 20 years, Patman continuously introduced legislation to repeal the Federal Reserve Banking Act of 1913. "Full text of 'The Deep State.'" *Internet Archive*, 4 Jul. 2017, archive.org/stream/TheDeepState/The%20Deep%20State_djvu.txt.

[1680] "Money Quotes: What The Experts Say About Money." *Midas Gold Group*, 27 Aug. 2020, www.midasgoldgroup.com/money-quotes/.

[1681] *M'Culloch v. Maryland*, 17 US 316 (1819).

[1682] "The History of American Money." *CMI Gold $ Silver*, www.cmi-gold-silver.com/history-american-money/.

system."[1683] "The United States Constitution grants to Congress the authority to coin money and regulate the value of the currency. The Constitution does not give Congress the authority to delegate control over monetary policy to a central bank."[1684] Representative Ron Paul declared, "America's Founders...had a remarkable understanding of the ideas of liberty. They understood that liberty cannot exist with a government that has access to a printing press. Sound money and liberty go hand-in-hand."[1685] Thomas Jefferson lamented, "Everything predicted by the enemies of banks, in the beginning, is now coming to pass. We are to be ruined now by the deluge of bank paper..."[1686]

"In a letter Gouvernor Morris wrote to James Madison on July 2nd, 1787, he revealed what was the true motivation of the banking cartel: "The rich will strive to establish their dominion and enslave the rest. They always did. They always will. They will have the same effect here as elsewhere, if we do not, by the power of government, keep them in their proper spheres."[1687]

Thomas Jefferson believed that "the issuing power of money should be taken from banks and restored to Congress and the people

---

[1683] From *The Making of America*, p. 419. *Id.*

[1684] Quinn, Jim. "The Federal Reserve Must Die." *HCP Live*, 25 Aug. 2009, www.mdmag.com/medical-news/federal_reserve_must_die.

[1685] Paul, Ron. "Ron Paul: 'Forget the Russians: It's the Federal Reserve Seeking to Meddle in Our Elections.'" *The Free Thought Project*, 3 Sept. 2019, thefreethoughtproject.com/ron-paul-end-federal-reserve/?fbclid=IwAR1nGlN-ywVH6dp-4yR2CGmdisX6qSZxeBCo9nTDg-qmZ53-AvddeYuUpGw.

[1686] Letters of Thomas Jefferson. "Banks Quotes." *Good Reads*, www.goodreads.com/quotes/tag/banks.

[1687] Jones, Stack. "An Essay On The History Of Banking." *The Banking Swindle*, 1 Jan. 2018, criminalbankingmonopoly.wordpress.com/.

to whom it belongs."[1688] He suggested that the legislature intervene to abolish the central bank (at that time, the First Bank of the United States), writing, "The evil has been produced by the error of their sanction of this ruinous machinery of banks; and justice, wisdom, duty, all require that they should interpose and arrest it before the schemes of plunder and spoilation desolate the country."[1689] Even Alexander Hamilton eventually turned against the central bank (circa 1798). "He felt that if currency or bank notes were to be issued and circulated as 'money,' it should have been done by Congress."[1690]

Senator John Danforth (circa 1980) regretted that the situation feared by Thomas Jefferson had since come to pass: "I have never seen more Senators express discontent with their jobs…I think the major cause is that, deep down in our hearts, we have been accomplices in doing something terrible and unforgivable to our wonderful country. Deep down in our heart, we know that we have given our children a legacy of bankruptcy…"[1691]

Even President Woodrow Wilson ultimately rued signing the Glass-Owen Act establishing the Federal Reserve. In 1916, he wrote, "I am a most unhappy man. I have unwittingly ruined my country. A great industrial nation is controlled by its system of credit. Our system of credit is concentrated. The growth of the

---

[1688] In a letter to James Monroe, January 1, 1815. Deflation is "a general decline occurring in prices for goods and services when the inflation rate falls below 0%." Fernando, Jason. "Inflation." *Investopedia*, 18 Nov. 2020, www.investopedia.com/terms/i/inflation.asp.

[1689] Letter to William C. Rives in 1819. Jefferson, Thomas. "TJ: Plan for Reducing the Circulating Medium, 23 Nov. 1819, 23 November 2019." *Founders Online*, National Archives and Records Administration, founders.archives.gov/documents/Jefferson/98-01-02-0909.

[1690] "The History of American Money." *CMI Gold $ Silver*, www.cmi-gold-silver.com/history-american-money/.

[1691] "The International Bankers: Famous Quotes." *ConspiracyAnalyst.org*, 23 Dec. 2019, conspiracyanalyst.org/2013/03/01/the-international-bankers-famous-quotes/.

Nation and all our activities are in the hands of a few men. We have come to be one of the worst ruled, one of the most completely controlled and dominated Governments in the world – no longer a Government of free opinion no longer a Government by conviction and vote of the majority, but a Government by the opinion and duress of small groups of dominant men…"[1692]

Rep. McFadden stated, "Every effort has been made by the Federal Reserve Board to conceal its power but the truth is the Federal Reserve Board has usurped the government of the United States. It controls everything here and it controls all our foreign relations. It makes and breaks governments at will. No man and no body of men is more entrenched in power than the arrogant credit monopoly which operates the Federal Reserve Board and the Federal Reserve banks. These evil-doers have robbed this country of more than enough money to pay the national debt. What the Government has permitted the Federal Reserve Board to steal from the people should now be restored to the people."[1693]

Alex Jones advised us to "research the private Federal Reserve for yourself, realize it is the main head on the hydra that we have to go after. Realize that we can fight the political parties all day, but until we go after the heart, the root, of the problem, nothing's going to get better."[1694] Aaron Russo suggested, "Shut down the Federal Reserve System…The real problem is the banking industry and the bankers in this country."[1695]

[1692] "Central Banks Quotes." *AZ Quotes*, www.azquotes.com/quotes/topics/central-banks.html.

[1693] Said in 1914. "The International Bankers: Famous Quotes." *ConspiracyAnalyst.org*, 23 Dec. 2019, conspiracyanalyst.org/2013/03/01/the-international-bankers-famous-quotes/.

[1694] "Aaron Russo: Reflections and Warnings - Full Transcript." *Matt Prather*, sites.google.com/site/themattprather/Reading/aaron-russo/reflections-and-warnings-full-transcript.

[1695] *Id.*

John Allison, the former CEO of the BB&T bank and of the Cato Institute, wrote, "I would get rid of the Federal Reserve because the volatility in the economy is primarily caused by the Fed. Sound money matters. When the Fed is radically changing the money supply, distorting interest rates, and over-regulating the financial sector, it makes rational economic calculation difficult. Markets do form bubbles, but the Fed makes them worse."[1696] Allison believes "that simply allowing the market to regulate itself would be preferable to the Fed harming the stability of the financial system."[1697] "In the face of a recession caused by massive supply-chain disruption, the US central bank has shown itself to be impotent…"[1698] "The Fed's desperate, yet impotent, attempts to counteract the COVID-19 scare show the need to replace central banking with a monetary and financial system based on market principles. Let market participants determine the value of money,

---

[1696] This quote appeared on p. 351 of Vol. 34, No. 2 (Spring/Summer 2014) issue of the Cato Journal. Allison, John A. "Market Discipline Beats Regulatory Discipline." *Cato Journal*, www.cato.org/sites/cato.org/files/serials/files/cato-journal/2014/5/cato-journal-v34n2-9.pdf.

[1697] Bryan, Bob. "Trump is meeting with an ex-bank CEO who wants to abolish the Federal Reserve and return to the gold standard." *Business Insider*, 28 Nov. 2016, www.businessinsider.com/trump-meeting-john-allison-bank-ceo-abolish-the-fed-gold-standard-2016-11? fbclid=IwAR1EQE7q7kSztggK0rGULdVV1RZYSXJ8ezHbl3DJOJ11eNe GOu7KvjNpqTk.

[1698] Brown, Ellen. "The Fed's baffling response to the Coronavirus explained." *Nexusnewsfeedf.com*, 12 Mar. 2020, www.nexusnewsfeed.com/article/geopolitics/the-fed-s-baffling-response-to-the-coronavirus-explained/? fbclid=IwAR3KdMgB13LT98gK8-5bQvXUM5mm5zjEiCDl6MIQ_4t74a d9X_V05lU8ajY.

interest rates, and the behavior and profitability of banks — as they do for other sectors of the economy."[1699]

Since 1958, the John Birch Society has demanded that "the Federal Reserve be not only audited but also abolished. [T]he group's position: The powers of Congress are described in Article I, Section 8 of the Constitution, and the creation of a central bank like the Federal Reserve is not listed as one of those powers. The Federal Reserve is charged with protecting the value of the dollar through managing our nation's monetary policy. However, since its inception in 1913, the dollar has lost 95 percent of its value under the Federal Reserve's monetary oversight. The John Birch Society advocates abolishing the Federal Reserve."[1700]

Another option would be to nationalize the Fed. Michael Hureaux-Perez opined, "As with the banking sector, they [the mega corporations] play games with the lives of millions, hysterically reject any kind of government intervention when the profits are rolling in, but are quick to pass the bill for the cleanup and the far-reaching consequences of these avoidable tragedies to the public when things go wrong. We have a straightforward proposal: if they want public money, we want public control..."[1701] Henry Makow, PhD wrote, "Our society and culture are a fraud based on one central fraud, the monopoly over government credit in the hands of Cabalist private bankers. They are using this power to extend their monopoly over every aspect of our lives by manipulating world events and

---

[1699] Klein, Peter G. "The Financial System Is Now Totally Dependent on Government Intervention." *Mises Institute,* 16 Mar. 2020, mises.org/power-market/financial-system-now-totally-dependent-government-intervention? fbclid=IwAR3eKYaKZMJqyM91joNY59D1nTY6LqHPhsz4iz1fQS2Vow wbR5YGkAlOHPA.

[1700] Wolverton II, JD, Joe. "Tennessee Considering Bills Restoring Gold and Silver as Sound Money." *The New American*, 2 Feb. 2019, www.thenewamerican.com/usnews/constitution/item/31369-tennessee-considering-bills-restoring-gold-and-silver-as-sound-money.

[1701] "Banks Quotes." *Good Reads*, www.goodreads.com/quotes/tag/banks.

social behavior. The only way to save civilization from failure is to nationalize the Central Banks."[1702]   Investment banker, Ziad K. Abdelnour, agreed that "100 years is enough: time to make the Fed a public utility."[1703]

"The US Congress created the Fed with legislation; it can also abolish the Fed with legislation…"[1704]   "Abolishing the Federal Reserve will allow Congress to reassert its constitutional authority over monetary policy."[1705]   Representative Ron Paul contended, "If we want to enjoy the blessings of Liberty, we must audit and then end the Federal Reserve!"[1706]   Paul offered a path forward: "Audit the Fed is a step toward restoring health to our economic system by ending the fiat money pandemic that facilitates the welfare-warfare state and the unstable, debt-based economy."[1707]   According to Paul Broun, "It's absolutely critical that we audit the Fed so the American people can see what's going on over there. Do it from top to bottom so that we can have transparency in this entity called the Federal

---

[1702] "The Illuminati Plan to Enslave Americans (1969)." *HenryMakow.com*, 10 May 2016, www.savethemales.ca/confirmedrockefeller_plan_to_g.html.

[1703] In *Economic Warfare: Secrets of Wealth Creation in the Age of Welfare Politics*. "Federal Reserve Quotes." *Good Reads*, www.goodreads.com/quotes/tag/federal-reserve.

[1704] Paul, Ron. "Ron Paul: 'Forget the Russians: It's the Federal Reserve Seeking to Meddle in Our Elections.'" *The Free Thought Project*, 3 Sept. 2019, thefreethoughtproject.com/ron-paul-end-federal-reserve/?fbclid=IwAR1nGlN-ywVH6dp-4yR2CGmdisX6qSZxeBCo9nTDg-qmZ53-AvddeYuUpGw.

[1705] Quinn, Jim. "The Federal Reserve Must Die." *HCP Live*, 25 Aug. 2009, www.mdmag.com/medical-news/federal_reserve_must_die.

[1706] Paul, Ron. "Ron Paul: 'Forget the Russians: It's the Federal Reserve Seeking to Meddle in Our Elections.'" *The Free Thought Project*, 3 Sept. 2019, thefreethoughtproject.com/ron-paul-end-federal-reserve/?fbclid=IwAR1nGlN-ywVH6dp-4yR2CGmdisX6qSZxeBCo9nTDg-qmZ53-AvddeYuUpGw.

[1707] *Id.*

Reserve. Hopefully, the American people will see that we need to go back to the gold standard...and get rid of the Fed."[1708]

President Andrew Jackson felt that, "[i]f Congress has the right under the constitution to issue paper money, it was given them to be used by themselves, not to be delegated to individuals or corporations."[1709]   After Jackson had abolished the second central bank, President Martin Van Buren proposed an independent Treasury to further wrest control of the federal government from central bank supporters, which Congress passed in 1840.[1710] The act established an independent treasury deposit offices separate from private or state banks to receive all government funds.[1711]   Van Buren hailed it as a "Second Declaration of Independence."[1712]   An independent treasury could be revived to replace the Fed.

At the very least, "Congress should proactively roll back the authority of the Federal Reserve to directly or indirectly provide credit to state and local governments. A good starting point would be consideration of the proposed State and Local Pensions Accountability and Security Act (HR 2126) which would prohibit

---

[1708] "The 101 Best Gold Quotes From History – GoldSilver." *Gold Silver*, goldsilver.com/blog/101-best-gold-quotes-all-time/.

[1709] "Central Banks Quotes." *Good Reads*, www.goodreads.com/quotes/tag/central-banks.

[1710] Kaza, Greg. "The U.S. Presidents and the Money Issue." *FEE*, 1 Apr. 1996, fee.org/articles/the-us-presidents-and-the-money-issue/.

[1711] Pinheiro, John C. "James K. Polk: Domestic Affairs." *UVA Miller Center*, millercenter.org/president/polk/domestic-affairs.

[1712] Kaza, Greg. "The U.S. Presidents and the Money Issue." *FEE*, 1 Apr. 1996, fee.org/articles/the-us-presidents-and-the-money-issue/.

the Federal Reserve from providing public pension bailouts or other financial assistance."[1713]

The next chapter discusses the benefits of returning to sound money, as prescribed by the U.S. Constitution.

[1713] Griffith, Joel. "A Backdoor Central Bank Bailout of State Governments." *Real Clear Markets*, 2 May 2020, www.realclearmarkets.com/articles/2020/05/02/a_backdoor_central_bank_bailout_of_state_governments_490609.html?fbclid=IwAR2ram3WBD1YDtA-phyhdAVkT1c8kageamzMChCjYT3r4duZ2iMWycBEYOY.

Chapter 8

Constitutional Money

"In addition to not-so-stellar management of the stages of the economic cycle, the Fed has managed to destroy the value of the U.S. dollar..."[1714]   The central bank's manipulations have "had a devastating impact on [the dollar's] purchasing power, which is now down to about 8 percent of its 1933 value. It has eroded the value of savings, insurance policies, retirement funds, and the fixed incomes of the elderly."[1715]   "Most people know intuitively that their purchasing power is diminishing, but don't know why," according to Jason Overstreet (R-WA).[1716]

"The U.S. dollar's loss of purchasing power is the result of inflation created by the Fed. The Fed creates inflation by expanding the supply of money and credit. The expansion of the supply of money and credit cheapens the value of all money in circulation. The inflation is intentional. And since the inflation is ongoing and cumulative, its effects are unpredictable and volatile."[1717]

For example, despite its mandate to keep prices stable, Federal Reserve officials try to maintain inflation at around 2% per

---

[1714] Williams, Kelsey. "Federal Reserve – Conspiracy Or Not?" *Kelsey's Gold Facts,* 22 Dec. 2018, www.kelseywilliamsgold.com/federal-reserve-conspiracy-or-not/.

[1715] "The History of American Money." *CMI Gold $ Silver,* www.cmi-gold-silver.com/history-american-money/.

[1716] Newman, Alex. "Washington State Considers Gold and Silver as Legal Tender." *The New American,* 31 Jan. 2012, www.thenewamerican.com/usnews/politics/item/9171-washington-state-considers-gold-and-silver-as-legal-tender.

[1717] Williams, Kelsey. "Federal Reserve – Conspiracy Or Not?" *Kelsey's Gold Facts,* 22 Dec. 2018, www.kelseywilliamsgold.com/federal-reserve-conspiracy-or-not/.

year.[1718]   Lynette Zang noted, "If something grows at 2% a year, it's not really very visible, and you don't really feel it that much. Over time,…2% — because it's compounding — turns into 4, 8, etc, but that's why they 'target' that 2%. You are still losing the value — the purchasing power value of your currency — but you don't notice it, and therefore, you don't complain about it."[1719]

Ben Bernanke said, "Like gold, U.S. dollars have value only to the extent that they are strictly limited in supply. But the U.S. government has a technology, called a printing press (or, today, its electronic equivalent), that allows it to produce as many U.S. dollars as it wishes at essentially no cost. By increasing the number of U.S. dollars in circulation, or even by credibly threatening to do so, the U.S. government can also reduce the value of a dollar in terms of goods and services, which is equivalent to raising the prices in dollars of those goods and services."[1720]   "With our fiat paper Federal Reserve note currency, every time the Federal Reserve prints another note, the value of existing notes is debased, ultimately driving prices higher and higher."[1721]   For instance, "[i]n 1913 (the year the Fed was founded) a bottle of Coke cost five cents. Today, a bottle of Coca-Cola costs an average of $1.79. While there are many factors (like supply and demand, cost of goods, etc.) that help set prices, inflation plays a critical part. At an average inflation rate of

---

[1718] "Federal Reserve issues FOMC statement of longer-run goals and policy strategy." *Board of Governors of the Federal Reserve System*, 25 Jun. 2012, www.federalreserve.gov/newsevents/pressreleases/monetary20120125c.htm.

[1719] At 15:15. ITM Trading, Inc. "Stocks, Cash, Debt… Q&A with Lynette Zang and Eric Griffin." *Youtube,* 2 Jan. 2020, www.youtube.com/watch?v=TMvw4jD0oO4.

[1720] Quinn, Jim. "The Federal Reserve Must Die." *HCP Live*, 25 Aug. 2009, www.mdmag.com/medical-news/federal_reserve_must_die.

[1721] Per Jason Overstreet. Newman, Alex. "Washington State Considers Gold and Silver as Legal Tender." *The New American*, 31 Jan. 2012, www.thenewamerican.com/usnews/politics/item/9171-washington-state-considers-gold-and-silver-as-legal-tender.

3.12% annually, inflation alone accounts for $1.30 of the actual cost of Coke."[1722]

Deutsche Bank macro strategist, Oliver Harvey, warned that "trying to keep spending at pre-lockdown levels while keeping lockdowns in place will lead to more money chasing much [fewer] goods and services, resulting in 'inflation, and a lot of it…' He notes that supply is inelastic, or fixed, this time around, resulting in higher prices…imposing tough supply constraints on the economy could result in hyperinflation, worsening people's living standards…"[1723]

Exacerbating the problem, "[t]he Fed pumped over $1 trillion into the system in [March 2020], with its chair Jerome Powell promising never before seen levels of money printing and so-called quantitative easing to infinity through an unlimited bond-buying program…The Fed has also cut its benchmark interest rate to near zero and made sure commercial banks will continue lending to companies, cities and states — all told the extraordinary measures are expected to grow the Fed's balance sheet by $4.5 trillion this year."[1724] By comparison, "[t]hroughout and in the aftermath of the global financial crisis the Fed grew its balance sheet by a paltry $3.7 trillion…"[1725]

[1722] Jones, Stewart. "The Founders Warned Us About Central Banking." *Ron Paul Liberty Report*, 10 Oct. 2019, www.ronpaullibertyreport.com/archives/the-founders-warned-us-about-central-banking?fbclid=IwAR1GtgHBthCfZDgqhObnuqCX2hO9116CjGntgnKJ75rw5KXrb5U3mKOVFKI.

[1723] Garber, Jonathan. "Coronavirus hyperinflation risk looms, buy gold: Peter Schiff." *Yahoo Finance*, 25 Mar. 2020, finance.yahoo.com/news/coronavirus-hyperinflation-looms-buy-gold-124257282.html.

[1724] Bambrough, Billy. "Donald Trump And The Fed Are Destroying The U.S. Dollar." *Forbes*, 28 Mar. 2020, www.forbes.com/sites/billybambrough/2020/03/28/donald-trump-and-the-fed-are-destroying-the-u s - d o l l a r / ? fbclid=IwAR0FVSZWzVX5vEiMO6JUKf9DUyHAIM9Hbr3mPA2ECTJxMTkz4c80Xz8NRlE#36964d106ebc.

[1725] *Id.*

As a result of the Fed's shenanigans, "purchasing power of the U.S. dollar has declined by more than 98 percent" since the Federal Reserve was established in 1913.[1726] In other words, "[t]he U.S. dollar today is worth less than 2 cents compared to its purchasing power in 1913..."[1727] In 1913, $1 would buy the equivalent of $26.42 in 2021.[1728] The dollar is still dropping in value.[1729]

The more money printing they do, the less value dollars have..."[1730] "Economic law cannot be repealed. Easy money leads to inflation in any century."[1731] "The US dollar is in a state of perpetual decline (by intention) which will ultimately end in complete repudiation..."[1732] "The only reason they [dollars] have

---

[1726] Williams, Kelsey. "Federal Reserve – Conspiracy Or Not?" *Kelsey's Gold Facts,* 22 Dec. 2018, www.kelseywilliamsgold.com/federal-reserve-conspiracy-or-not/; Wolverton, Joe, II, JD. "Tennessee Considering Bills Restoring Gold and Silver as Sound Money." *The New American,* 2 Feb. 2019, www.thenewamerican.com/usnews/constitution/item/31369-tennessee-considering-bills-restoring-gold-and-silver-as-sound-money.

[1727] Williams, Kelsey. "Fed Action Accelerates Boom-Bust Cycle; Not A Virus Crisis." *Yahoo Finance,* 19 May 2020, finance.yahoo.com/news/fed-action-accelerates-boom-bust-065808585.html.

[1728] "Inflation Calculator." *US Inflation Calculator,* www.usinflationcalculator.com.

[1729] At 29:18. ITM Trading, Inc. "And Central Banks Using Up Their Ammo." *Youtube,* 18 Dec. 2018, www.youtube.com/watch?v=NvWm6Qkp5gU.

[1730] *Id.*

[1731] Kaza, Greg. "The U.S. Presidents and the Money Issue." *FEE,* 1 Apr. 1996, fee.org/articles/the-us-presidents-and-the-money-issue/.

[1732] Williams, Kelsey. "Federal Reserve – Conspiracy Or Not?" *Kelsey's Gold Facts,* 22 Dec. 2018, www.kelseywilliamsgold.com/federal-reserve-conspiracy-or-not/.

any value is because most people still have confidence that they have value…"[1733]

"Potential risks of the…Fed's biggest-ever bazooka include out-of-control inflation, the dollar's displacement as the world's funding currency, and the complete destabilization of the U.S. financial system."[1734] "Some economists have even warned that the US is on the brink of the biggest bubble in world history — not just a correction of a business cycle or another recession, but a complete collapse of the US dollar."[1735] Wall Street veteran and founder of Wyoming-based crypto bank Avanti, Caitlin Long, "expects the U.S. Federal Reserve's balance sheet to top $10 trillion before the coronavirus crisis is over and predict[ed] the dollar's eventual crash…"[1736] "The 'free money' insanity…will result in rapid price inflation across America, putting us on the path toward a

---

[1733] At 29:18. ITM Trading, Inc. "And Central Banks Using Up Their Ammo." *Youtube,* 18 Dec. 2018, www.youtube.com/watch? v=NvWm6Qkp5gU.

[1734] Bambrough, Billy. "Donald Trump And The Fed Are Destroying The U.S. Dollar." *Forbes,* 28 Mar. 2020, www.forbes.com/sites/ billybambrough/2020/03/28/donald-trump-and-the-fed-are-destroying-the-u s - d o l l a r / ? fbclid=IwAR0FVSZWzVX5vEiMO6JUKf9DUyHAIM9Hbr3mPA2ECTJ xMTkz4c80Xz8NRlE#36964d106ebc.

[1735] Jones, Stewart. "The Founders Warned Us About Central Banking." *Ron Paul Liberty Report,* 10 Oct. 2019, www.ronpaullibertyreport.com/ archives/the-founders-warned-us-about-central-banking? fbclid=IwAR1GtgHBthCfZDgqhObnuqCX2hO9116CjGntgnKJ75rw5KXr b5U3mKOVFKI.

[1736] Bambrough, Billy. "Donald Trump And The Fed Are Destroying The U.S. Dollar." *Forbes,* 28 Mar. 2020, www.forbes.com/sites/ billybambrough/2020/03/28/donald-trump-and-the-fed-are-destroying-the-u s - d o l l a r / ? fbclid=IwAR0FVSZWzVX5vEiMO6JUKf9DUyHAIM9Hbr3mPA2ECTJ xMTkz4c80Xz8NRlE#36964d106ebc.

Venezuela-type scenario and more money printing goes to insane levels to bail out everybody and everything in the economy."[1737]

Economist Peter Schiff has "blamed the U.S. Federal Reserve and other central banks in part for the impending crisis. 'I think we are going to have a dollar crisis — you think the Turkish lira looks bad now, wait till you see when the dollar is imploding and we have a sovereign debt crisis in the U.S... The U.S. government is going to be given a choice between defaulting on the debt, or else massive runaway inflation."[1738]

"This progressive deterioration in the value of money through history is not an accident, and has had behind it two great driving forces – the impecuniosity of Governments and the superior political influence of the debtor class."[1739] Ben Bernanke concluded that, "under a paper-money system, a determined government can always generate...positive inflation."[1740] "[F]iat money is continually manipulated both in value and quantity."[1741]

[1737] Adams, Mike. "Urgent alert: Financial system collapsing, food supply collapsing, hyperinflation coming, guns and ammo wiped out, military martial law plans leaked... details." *Natural News*, 19 Mar. 2020, www.naturalnews.com/2020-03-19-urgent-alert-financial-system-collapsing-food-supply-hyperinflation.html.

[1738] Fearnow, Benjamin. "There Could Be a Financial Crash Before End of Trump's First Term, Experts Say, Citing Looming Debts." *Newsweek*, 23 Sept. 2018, www.newsweek.com/stock-market-1134867?fbclid=IwAR2qYXwuBp-gBoHWnz4O_28BsUBS4tVUldapK0ls2g5O0l3PrW202Lwb_G8.

[1739] "John Maynard Keynes Quotes – Keynes Said It." *John Maynard Keynes*, www.maynardkeynes.org/keynes-quotes.html.

[1740] Quinn, Jim. "The Federal Reserve Must Die." *HCP Live*, 25 Aug. 2009, www.mdmag.com/medical-news/federal_reserve_must_die.

[1741] At 12:40. Gammon, George. "Quantitative Easing: Will It Cause Hyperinflation? (ANSWER REVEALED)." *Youtube*, 19 Dec. 2019, www.youtube.com/watch?v=b7KafSma3xQ.

Ayn Rand warned, "Whenever destroyers appear among men, they start by destroying money, for money is men's protection and the base of a moral existence. Destroyers seize gold and leave to its owners a counterfeit pile of paper. This kills all objective standards and delivers men into the arbitrary power of an arbitrary setter of values. Gold was an objective value, an equivalent of wealth produced. Paper is a mortgage on wealth that does not exist, backed by a gun aimed at those who are expected to produce it. Paper is a check drawn by legal looters upon an account which is not theirs: upon the virtue of the victims. Watch for the day when it bounces, marked: 'Account Overdrawn.'"[1742]

According to economist John Maynard Keynes, Vladimir "Lenin...declared that the best way to destroy the Capitalist System was to debauch the currency. By a continuing process of inflation, governments can confiscate, secretly and unobserved, an important part of the wealth of their citizens. By this method they not only confiscate, but they confiscate arbitrarily; and, while the process impoverishes many, it actually enriches some. The sight of this arbitrary rearrangement of riches strikes not only at security, but at confidence in the equity of the existing distribution of wealth."[1743]

"In the United States, today's monetary system is antithetical to sound money. Money, including its supply, is controlled by unelected bureaucrats operating a government-backed banking cartel with no real constraints on its power..."[1744] "Washington seems to have lapsed into the hands of a quasi-financial oligarchy, bent on preserving stimulative asset inflation policies at all costs (regardless

---

[1742] "The 101 Best Gold Quotes From History – GoldSilver." *Gold Silver*, goldsilver.com/blog/101-best-gold-quotes-all-time/.

[1743] "John Maynard Keynes Quotes – Keynes Said It." *John Maynard Keynes*, www.maynardkeynes.org/keynes-quotes.html.

[1744] Cortez, JP. "Fake Money, Sound Money and Government Malfeasance." *Tenth Amendment Center*, 28 Aug. 2018, tenthamendmentcenter.com/2018/08/28/fake-money-sound-money-and-government-malfeasance/.

of the damage to the real economy)."[1745] "This creates the everything bubble that accomplishes only one thing — to create and exacerbate wealth inequality. It will cause a great discrepancy between haves and have-nots and wipe out the middle class."[1746]

Ohio attorney, Alfred Crozier, lamented in 1913 that the Glass-Owen bill establishing the Fed granted "just what Wall Street and the big banks for twenty-five years have been striving for — private instead of public control of currency. It...rob[s] the government and the people of all effective control over the public's money, and vest[s] in the banks exclusively the dangerous power to make money among the people scarce or plenty."[1747]

Aaron Russo maintained, "The Federal Reserve is poison to our country...Whoever makes the money makes the rules. Rothschild said that. And they make the money! Why are we allowing these private bankers to make the money for our country? It makes no sense! Why are we paying interest to these banks, to make money for us, when the government can do it itself without paying interest? And without all that debt. There's no answer to that question and it's the question no politician will raise. Everybody talks about 'America's debt' — how much debt we're in — we're in debt because we have to borrow money, and we don't have to borrow money...We can create the money and back it by gold so

---

[1745] Mercenary Trader. "Weekender: The Trouble With Modern Monetary Theory (MMT)." *Business Insider*, 19 Dec. 2010, www.businessinsider.com/weekender-the-trouble-with-modern-monetary-theory-mmt-2011-1.

[1746] At 11:40. Gammon, George. "Quantitative Easing: Will It Cause Hyperinflation? (ANSWER REVEALED)." *Youtube*, 19 Dec. 2019, www.youtube.com/watch?v=b7KafSma3xQ.

[1747] Jones, Stack. "An Essay On The History Of Banking." *The Banking Swindle*, 1 Jan. 2018, criminalbankingmonopoly.wordpress.com/.

they can't create too much of it, so you don't have the inflation, and do what the founding fathers gave us…"[1748]

"Before 1914, the global monetary system was based on the classical gold standard."[1749] "The pure and classical gold standard was effective from 1870 to 1914. Individuals used gold as commodity money because it guaranteed that the government would redeem any amount of paper money for its value in gold. Furthermore, the gold standard was mainly trusted as backed-commodity money because it kept inflation relatively low and sustainable…"[1750] "[T]he value of gold was set at $20.67 an ounce; therefore, one dollar was equal to one-twentieth of an ounce of gold."[1751]

"In 1914, the United States was engaged in World War I and could not subsidize its military expenditures by solely relying on the gold standard. President Woodrow Wilson took the United States economy off [of] the gold standard and used the Federal Reserve to print more money so the United States government could supply its military arsenal during the war."[1752]

[1748] "Aaron Russo: Reflections and Warnings - Full Transcript." *Matt Prather*, sites.google.com/site/themattprather/Reading/aaron-russo/reflections-and-warnings-full-transcript.

[1749] Rickards, James G. "New Gold Standard? Chaos." *Bullion Vault*, 1 Jan. 2020, www.bullionvault.com/gold-news/gold-standard-012120201.

[1750] Van, Germinal G. "The Gold Standard Didn't Create the Great Depression, the Federal Reserve Did." *FEE Freeman Article*, Foundation for Economic Education, 25 May 2019, fee.org/articles/the-gold-standard-didn-t-create-the-great-depression-the-federal-reserve-did/?fbclid=IwAR0vrzpM7GgbTDRu2mqA0EM_1vSSK_JaYKWsCWX7BlDGZ6PUxZhjt8niybw.

[1751] *Id.*

[1752] *Id.*

In 1944, "a new monetary system emerged at Bretton Woods..."[1753] "The Bretton Woods international monetary system invested the dollar, which then was defined as and (internationally) was legally convertible to gold at $35/oz, with global currency status."[1754] "Under the Bretton Woods system, all major currencies were pegged to the Dollar at a fixed exchange rate. The Dollar itself was pegged to gold at the rate of $35 per ounce. Indirectly, the other currencies had a fixed gold value because of their peg to the Dollar. Other currencies could devalue against the Dollar, and therefore against gold, if they received permission from the International Monetary Fund (IMF). However, the Dollar could not devalue, at least in theory. It was the keystone of the entire system – intended to be permanently anchored to gold. From 1950-1970 the Bretton Woods system worked fairly well. Trading partners of the US who earned Dollars could cash those Dollars into the US Treasury and be paid in gold at the fixed rate. In 1950, the US had about 20,000 tons of gold. By 1970, that amount had been reduced to about 9,000 tons. The 11,000-ton decline went to US trading partners, primarily Germany, France and Italy, who earned Dollars and cashed them in for gold..."[1755]

[1753] Rickards, James G. "New Gold Standard? Chaos." *Bullion Vault*, 1 Jan. 2020, www.bullionvault.com/gold-news/gold-standard-012120201.

[1754] Benko, Ralph. "President Trump: Replace The Dollar With Gold As The Global Currency To Make America Great Again." *Forbes*, 25 Feb. 2017, www.forbes.com/sites/ralphbenko/2017/02/25/president-trump-replace-the-dollar-with-gold-as-the-global-currency-to-make-america-great-again/amp/?__&fbclid=IwAR08UD15lTTTpxe9ovabRK3ps1n5Vw7gcBV-SnZZUMQl8dmSasktRMFeFqI.

[1755] Rickards, James G. "New Gold Standard? Chaos." *Bullion Vault*, 1 Jan. 2020, www.bullionvault.com/gold-news/gold-standard-012120201.

In 1971, President Richard Nixon ended this loose version of the gold standard.[1756] The president realized that gold "stood in the way of the expansionary fiscal policy he was hoping to adopt ahead of his re-election campaign."[1757] Therefore, "in 1971, the Nixon Administration suspended wages, issued price controls, and canceled dollar-to-gold convertibility, completing the final step in ending the 'gold standard.' This gave the central government planners — and the Federal Reserve — the power to print money without restraint. This is how the national debt has been able to reach the levels that it has…"[1758]

When Nixon ended the direct convertibility of the Dollar to gold in 1971, it was "the first time [that] the monetary system had no gold backing…"[1759] "The result was a huge shock to the world order."[1760] "[T]he decline of the dollar after it was severed from its

---

[1756] Authers, John. "New World Order Is Coming, Maybe in Helicopters." *Bloomberg*, 9 Mar. 2020, www.bloomberg.com/opinion/articles/2020-03-09/oil-crash-coronavirus-is-just-the-start-of-market-shocks?fbclid=IwAR2YtaU-DhkS0kI7-L6iJQzClEBvP7jXwE3M6uoLRXddmkFdUGWWUFuDACI.

[1757] Authers, John. "A Shift in the Global Financial Order Is Upon Us." *Bloomberg Opinion*, 8 Mar. 2020, www.bloomberg.com/opinion/articles/2020-03-09/crash-in-oil-prices-bond-yields-marks-shift-in-global-order.

[1758] Jones, Stewart. "The Founders Warned Us About Central Banking." *Ron Paul Liberty Report*, 10 Oct. 2019, www.ronpaullibertyreport.com/archives/the-founders-warned-us-about-central-banking?fbclid=IwAR1GtgHBthCfZDgqhObnuqCX2hO9116CjGntgnKJ75rw5KXrb5U3mKOVFKI.

[1759] Rickards, James G. "New Gold Standard? Chaos." *Bullion Vault*, 1 Jan. 2020, www.bullionvault.com/gold-news/gold-standard-012120201.

[1760] Authers, John. "A Shift in the Global Financial Order Is Upon Us." *Bloomberg Opinion*, 8 Mar. 2020, www.bloomberg.com/opinion/articles/2020-03-09/crash-in-oil-prices-bond-yields-marks-shift-in-global-order.

last links to gold in 1971 has affected all Americans, even if it has been ignored by most elected officials."[1761]

"With the gold peg gone, the financial system adopted a new anchor, which was oil."[1762] "For the next decade, the world was no longer anchored to the dollar, but to oil. With the tie to gold gone, oil producers needed to hike prices to keep their buying power constant. This they did. In dollar terms, oil suffered two immense shocks during the 1970s, which plunged the world into stagflation. But in gold terms, the oil price ended the decade more or less where it had started; oil producers had protected themselves against the falling purchasing power of the dollar:…This 'Oil Standard' era ended in the early 1980s, at a point when markets — and everyone else — had lost faith in the ability of central banks to control inflation."[1763]

"In 1982, Federal Reserve Chairman Paul Volcker formally abandoned the 'Monetarist experiment,' and adopted a loose and ad-hoc method that…aimed to stabilize the dollar's value vs. gold and other commodities, taming the wild swings of the 1970s and early 1980s. He was helped in this by the other governments of the world, who got together at the Plaza Accord in 1985 to deal with a dollar that was too strong (it was $300/oz. [gold] at the time), and again at the Louvre Accord in 1987 to deal with a dollar that was too weak

---

[1761] Kaza, Greg. "The U.S. Presidents and the Money Issue." *FEE,* 1 Apr. 1996, fee.org/articles/the-us-presidents-and-the-money-issue/.

[1762] Authers, John. "A Shift in the Global Financial Order Is Upon Us." *Bloomberg Opinion,* 8 Mar. 2020, www.bloomberg.com/opinion/articles/ 2020-03-09/crash-in-oil-prices-bond-yields-marks-shift-in-global-order.

[1763] Authers, John. "New World Order Is Coming, Maybe in Helicopters." *Bloomberg,* 9 Mar. 2020, www.bloomberg.com/opinion/articles/ 2020-03-09/oil-crash-coronavirus-is-just-the-start-of-market-shocks? f b c l i d = I w A R 2 Y t a U - D h k S 0 k I 7 - L6iJQzClEBvP7jXwE3M6uoLRXddmkFdUGWWUFuDACI.

($400/oz. [gold] at the time). The whole world was guiding the dollar into a rough band around $350/oz."[1764]

Journalist P. J. O'Rourke explained, "A U.S. dollar is an I.O.U. from the Federal Reserve Bank. It's not backed by gold or silver. It's a promissory note that doesn't actually promise anything."[1765]   As such, "[t]he dollar will eventually go to zero. There is a 100% chance that this will occur."[1766]   "The Dollar collapse has already begun and the need for a new monetary order will need to emerge."[1767]

"Jim Reid, 'Global Head of Thematic Research' at Deutsche Bank, recently suggested that fiat currencies might disappear before 2030."[1768]   "We think fiat money systems should be inherently unstable and prone to high inflation all other things being equal. Politically it is always too tempting to create money when nothing is backing it...The forces that have held the current fiat system together now look fragile and they could unravel in the 2020s. If so, that will start to lead to a backlash against fiat money and demand for alternative currencies, such as gold or crypto could soar."[1769]

[1764] Lewis, Nathan. "We Just Tested The Gold Standard -- It Still Works." *Forbes*, 8 Aug. 2019, www.forbes.com/sites/nathanlewis/2019/08/08/we-just-tested-the-gold-standard-it-still-works/#2044ef4c556b.

[1765] "The 101 Best Gold Quotes From History – GoldSilver." *Gold Silver*, goldsilver.com/blog/101-best-gold-quotes-all-time/.

[1766] Adams, Mike. "Analysis: Bitcoin could go to $100,000 as the fiat currency dollar collapses, but the 'value' won't be the fortune you're imagining." *Natural News*, 17 May 2020, www.naturalnews.com/2020-05-17-analysis-bitcoin-could-go-to-100000-as-fiat-currency-dollar-collapses.html.

[1767] Rickards, James G. "New Gold Standard? Chaos." *Bullion Vault*, 1 Jan. 2020, www.bullionvault.com/gold-news/gold-standard-012120201.

[1768] Lewis, Nathan. "The World Gold Standard System Will Rise Again — But, Not Yet." *Forbes*, 6 Dec. 2019, www.forbes.com/sites/nathanlewis/2019/12/06/the-world-gold-standard-system-will-rise-again---but-not-yet/#5474426235e6.

[1769] *Id.*

Peter Schiff warned, "[H]yperinflation, or extremely high and worsening inflation, is 'very much on the table,' and...a complete destruction of the U.S. currency would be accelerated if the world 'dumps the dollar as a reserve...'"[1770] "If we were to slip into hyperinflation, there will be disastrous consequences for those unprepared. Given that the US dollar is the world's reserve currency, the problems would spread to practically every country on earth. Hyperinflation will shake people's confidence not only in the US dollar, but in the paper currency system as a whole...What we do know is that the measures to cure hyperinflation include tying the currency to a hard asset or even replacing it with one."[1771]

"The decline of the Dollar as a reserve currency started in 2000 with the advent of the Euro and accelerated in 2010 with the beginning of a new currency war."[1772] The International Monetary Fund (IMF) has created Special Drawing Rights (SDR), which are "a form of 'world money,' created in 1969 as an alternative to the US dollar (in case the dollar somehow fails...) SDRs would eventually replace the U.S. dollar as the global reserve currency... Considering the potential damage that the Fed's QE will inflict on the dollar, weakening its status as the world's currency, the potential IMF move toward replacing greenbacks with SDRs would cause a massive devaluation of the dollar, possibly up to 80%..."[1773]

[1770] Garber, Jonathan. "Coronavirus hyperinflation risk looms, buy gold: Peter Schiff." *Yahoo Finance*, 25 Mar. 2020, finance.yahoo.com/news/coronavirus-hyperinflation-looms-buy-gold-124257282.html.

[1771] Clark, Jeff. "How Does Gold Fare During Hyperinflation?" *InflationData.com*, 25 Jun. 2012, inflationdata.com/articles/2012/06/25/gold-hyperinflation/.

[1772] Rickards, James G. "New Gold Standard? Chaos." *Bullion Vault*, 1 Jan. 2020, www.bullionvault.com/gold-news/gold-standard-012120201.

[1773] Anderson, Anthony. "New Dollar Backed by Gold Coming This October 2020?" *GSI Exchange*, 27 May 2020, gsiexchange.com/is-a-new-dollar-backed-by-gold-at-10000-per-ounce-coming-by-october-1st-2020/?fbclid=IwAR0JeJRf6pMwprbp4UUdETDxl4lQQg3Oek5XnXrk3CEAVjZdWUbay6W6m28.

According to Bob Chapman, International Forecaster, "The dollar has clearly been abandoned and foreigners are starting to bail from dollar-denominated assets in droves."[1774]

"Now we have reached a new juncture,…Some new financial order, to replace Bretton Woods and the system that Volcker built to replace it, is now needed. A decade of monetary expansion has delayed the issue. It is hard to see how it can be delayed much further."[1775] "We have leveraged our debt-based currency to the hilt and the die is cast," said Rep. Matt Shea (R-WA), a military veteran who supports honest money.[1776] Shea added, "The Federal Reserve is faced with the position of having to further inflate our currency or have the system start to disintegrate."[1777]

The current global system is imploding and a new system based on a sound foundation needs to replace it, such as a "hard-money system based on gold, silver, and copper coins, which had always been viewed as more dependable and stable than paper currency."[1778] "The monetary system will have to be rebuilt. This is just unsustainable…No one should have the capability to counterfeit money. And at that point, we can have sound money, and we already have a precedent for that for thousands of years, gold has been

---

[1774] Quote from 2008. "The International Bankers: Famous Quotes." *ConspiracyAnalyst.org*, 23 Dec. 2019, conspiracyanalyst.org/2013/03/01/the-international-bankers-famous-quotes/.

[1775] Authers, John. "A Shift in the Global Financial Order Is Upon Us." *Bloomberg Opinion*, 8 Mar. 2020, www.bloomberg.com/opinion/articles/2020-03-09/crash-in-oil-prices-bond-yields-marks-shift-in-global-order.

[1776] Newman, Alex. "Washington State Considers Gold and Silver as Legal Tender." *The New American*, 31 Jan. 2012, www.thenewamerican.com/usnews/politics/item/9171-washington-state-considers-gold-and-silver-as-legal-tender.

[1777] *Id.*

[1778] "Greenbacks: Definition & History." *Study.com*, study.com/academy/lesson/greenbacks-definition-lesson.html.

money…" and it cannot be counterfeited.[1779]   Thus, "[g]old should once again play a leading role…"[1780]

It is possible, if not likely, that the fiat currency will be "reset" to gold if and when it collapses.   Lynette Zang opined, "When they are ultimately forced to do that reset, it will be with fiat against gold…"[1781]

Jim Reid agreed "that gold — the 'Once and Future Money' — is a likely successor. 'We have lived in an era of fiat money since the early 1970s. Since then virtually all money in existence has only had a value based on trust and, in particular, trust in governments' ability to maintain its value. Prior to this period, most of the money in existence through history was backed by a commodity – usually a precious metal like gold or silver. When money broke loose from such an arrangement inflation tended to increase (often dramatically), and when money returned to it inflation was becalmed."[1782]

Gold "is what people go back to. Many countries have been tempted to start counterfeiting their money and debasing their currency, but when it gets out of control, they go back to something people can trust…"[1783]   Paul Singer advised, "If you want an

---

[1779] At 14. RonPaulLibertyReport. "Central Banking Is On The Ropes: Gold Will Survive & The Fed Will End." *Youtube*, 13 Dec. 2019, www.youtube.com/watch?v=Ndcb2SPRU7M.

[1780] Rickards, James G. "New Gold Standard? Chaos." *Bullion Vault*, 1 Jan. 2020, www.bullionvault.com/gold-news/gold-standard-012120201.

[1781] At 27:30. ITM Trading, Inc. "And Central Banks Using Up Their Ammo." *Youtube*, 18 Dec. 2018, www.youtube.com/watch?v=NvWm6Qkp5gU.

[1782] Lewis, Nathan. "The World Gold Standard System Will Rise Again — But, Not Yet." *Forbes*, 6 Dec. 2019, www.forbes.com/sites/nathanlewis/2019/12/06/the-world-gold-standard-system-will-rise-again---but-not-yet/#5474426235e6.

[1783] At 12. RonPaulLibertyReport. "Central Banking Is On The Ropes: Gold Will Survive & The Fed Will End." *Youtube*, 13 Dec. 2019, www.youtube.com/watch?v=Ndcb2SPRU7M.

alternative currency, check out gold. It has stood the test of thousands of years as a store of value and medium of exchange."[1784] "When creditability in fiat money dissipates, gold may be the only viable option left standing…"[1785]

"Gold and silver currency retains earned wealth in the hands of the people and has provided civil societies with a fair, honest, and reliable medium of exchange for over six thousand years."[1786] According to Lysander Spooner, "[T]here is no such thing as an inflation of prices, relatively to gold. There is such a thing as a depreciated paper currency."[1787]   In other words, per Lynette Zang, "A rising gold price is an indication of a failing currency…"[1788] Peter Schiff explained, "Gold has intrinsic value. The problem with the dollar is it has no intrinsic value. And if the Federal Reserve is going to spend trillions of them to buy up all these bad mortgages and all other kinds of bad debt, the dollar is going to lose all of its value. Gold will store its value, and you'll always be able to buy more food with your gold."[1789]

John Allison, the former CEO of the BB&T bank and of the Cato Institute, asserted, "We need a private, free-banking system

---

[1784] "The 101 Best Gold Quotes From History – GoldSilver." *Gold Silver*, goldsilver.com/blog/101-best-gold-quotes-all-time/.

[1785] Clark, Jeff. "How Does Gold Fare During Hyperinflation?" *InflationData.com*, 25 Jun. 2012, inflationdata.com/articles/2012/06/25/gold-hyperinflation/.

[1786] Newman, Alex. "Washington State Considers Gold and Silver as Legal Tender." *The New American*, 31 Jan. 2012, www.thenewamerican.com/usnews/politics/item/9171-washington-state-considers-gold-and-silver-as-legal-tender.

[1787] "The 101 Best Gold Quotes From History – GoldSilver." *Gold Silver*, goldsilver.com/blog/101-best-gold-quotes-all-time/.

[1788] At 27:30. ITM Trading, Inc. "And Central Banks Using Up Their Ammo." *Youtube,* 18 Dec. 2018, www.youtube.com/watch?v=NvWm6Qkp5gU.

[1789] "The 101 Best Gold Quotes From History – GoldSilver." *Gold Silver*, goldsilver.com/blog/101-best-gold-quotes-all-time/.

based on a market standard such as gold. If the United States had continued with the classical gold standard instead of having instituted a government money monopoly in 1913, we would have learned through experimentation, as all markets do, and would have a radically better financial system and higher economic growth today."[1790]

Ralph Waldo Emerson observed, "The desire of gold is not for gold. It is for the means of freedom and benefit."[1791] "Sound money is freedom," Representative Matthew Shea (R-WA) announced.[1792] William F. Rickenbacker said, "Gold would have value if for no other reason than that it enables a citizen to fashion his financial escape from the state."[1793] Alan Greenspan agreed, affirming that "gold and economic freedom are inseparable…"[1794] Indeed, as Norm Franz noted, "[g]old is the money of kings; silver is the money of gentlemen; barter is the money of peasants; but debt is the money of slaves."[1795]

[1790] This quote appeared on p. 351 of Vol. 34, No. 2 (Spring/Summer 2014) issue of the Cato Journal. Allison, John A. "Market Discipline Beats Regulatory Discipline." *Cato Journal*, www.cato.org/sites/cato.org/files/serials/files/cato-journal/2014/5/cato-journal-v34n2-9.pdf.

[1791] "The 101 Best Gold Quotes From History – GoldSilver." *Gold Silver*, goldsilver.com/blog/101-best-gold-quotes-all-time/.

[1792] Newman, Alex. "Washington State Considers Gold and Silver as Legal Tender." *The New American*, 31 Jan. 2012, www.thenewamerican.com/usnews/politics/item/9171-washington-state-considers-gold-and-silver-as-legal-tender.

[1793] "The 101 Best Gold Quotes From History – GoldSilver." *Gold Silver*, goldsilver.com/blog/101-best-gold-quotes-all-time/.

[1794] Greenspan, Alan. "Gold and Economic Freedom." *Constitution Society*, www.constitution.org/mon/greenspan_gold.htm.

[1795] "The 101 Best Gold Quotes From History – GoldSilver." *Gold Silver*, goldsilver.com/blog/101-best-gold-quotes-all-time/.

According to Rep. Jason Overstreet (R-WA), "[S]ound money is actually the key to an honest system of government."[1796] Ron "Paul pointed out that it's really about the size and scope of government. 'If you're for less government, you want sound money. The people who want big government, they don't want sound money. They want to deceive you and commit fraud. They want to print the money. They want a monopoly. They want to get you conditioned, as our schools have conditioned us, to the point where deficits don't matter.'"[1797] "Sound money, like gold and silver, acts as a check and balance on big government, a hedge against inflation, and a way to combat manipulation by the Fed..."[1798]

The U.S. Founding Fathers understood the dangers of centralized manipulation of the money supply, the hidden taxation of inflation, and the control of buying power.[1799] American revolutionary leader, Christopher Gadsden, wrote in September 1764, "The evils attending a wanton exercise of power, in some of the colonies, by issuing a redundancy of paper currency, has always been avoided by this province, by a proper attention to the dangerous consequences of such a practice, and the fatal influence it

---

[1796] Newman, Alex. "Washington State Considers Gold and Silver as Legal Tender." *The New American*, 31 Jan. 2012, www.thenewamerican.com/ usnews/politics/item/9171-washington-state-considers-gold-and-silver-as-legal-tender.

[1797] Boldin, Michael. "Signed by the Governor: Arizona Law Treats Gold and Silver as Money." *Tenth Amendment Center*, 23 May 2017, blog.tenthamendmentcenter.com/2017/05/signed-by-the-governor-arizona-law-treats-gold-and-silver-as-money/.

[1798] Jones, Stewart. "The Founders Warned Us About Central Banking." *Ron Paul Liberty Report*, 10 Oct. 2019, www.ronpaullibertyreport.com/ archives/the-founders-warned-us-about-central-banking? fbclid=IwAR1GtgHBthCfZDgqhObnuqCX2hO9116CjGntgnKJ75rw5KXr b5U3mKOVFKI.

[1799] *Id.*

must have upon public credit."[1800]

As a result, "[t]here is a glorious tradition of hard-money advocates in the history of the United States."[1801] Presidents George Washington, Thomas Jefferson, and Andrew Jackson believed that only gold and silver were "real" money. According to Representative Ron Paul, "A system of capitalism presumes sound money, not fiat money manipulated by a central bank."[1802] "Reviving that heritage is essential to our economic well-being."[1803]

"The federal government…was given the power to coin money, not print money, and to regulate the value of such money…'"[1804] Article I, Section 8 of the U.S. Constitution grants Congress the power to "coin Money [and] regulate the Value thereof." George Bancroft, United States Secretary of the Navy (1845–1846) wrote, "[James] Madison, agreeing with the journal of the convention, records that the grant of power to emit bills of credit was refused by a majority of more than four to one. The evidence is

[1800] Gadsen, Christopher. "The Stamp Act - A Letter from Christopher Gadsden." *The Royal Colony of South Carolina*, www.carolana.com/SC/ Royal_Colony/stamp_act_gadsden_letter.html.

[1801] Kaza, Greg. "The U.S. Presidents and the Money Issue." *FEE,* 1 Apr. 1996, fee.org/articles/the-us-presidents-and-the-money-issue/.

[1802] "Central Bank Quotes." *Brainy Quote*, www.brainyquote.com/quotes/ ron_paul_396265?src=t_central_bank.

[1803] Kaza, Greg. "The U.S. Presidents and the Money Issue." *FEE,* 1 Apr. 1996, fee.org/articles/the-us-presidents-and-the-money-issue/.

[1804] "Article 1, Section 8 of the Constitution also gave Congress the power 'To borrow Money on the credit of the United States…There is something important to realize about the federal government's debt instruments: It was understood that they were not money or 'legal tender,' but rather promises to pay money — i.e., promises to pay gold coins and silver coins." Hornberger, Jacob. "Monetary Destruction in America." *Tenth Amendment Center*, 7 Jun. 2020, tenthamendmentcenter.com/2020/06/07/ m o n e t a r y - d e s t r u c t i o n - i n - a m e r i c a / ? fbclid=IwAR1qznHUtpPxV4SZfCJk0G9H9gTS2kepV1ZU5BKoX_o06D xBXusfHyCPK6s.

perfect; no power to emit paper money was granted to the legislature of the United States."[1805]

Ron Paul asserted, "[T]he Constitution certainly does not empower the federal government to erode the American standard of living via an inflationary monetary policy. In fact, Congress' constitutional mandate regarding monetary policy should only permit currency backed by stable commodities such as silver and gold to be used as legal tender."[1806] Paul believed, "We in the Congress have a moral and constitutional obligation to protect the value of the dollar and to understand why it is so important to the economy that a central bank not be given the unbelievable power of inflating a currency at will and pretending that it knows how to fine-tune an economy through this counterfeit system of money."[1807] He maintained, "[A]bolishing the Federal Reserve and returning to a constitutional system will enable America to return to the type of monetary system envisioned by our nation's founders: One where the value of money is consistent because it is tied to a commodity such as gold. Such a monetary system is the basis of a true free-market economy."[1808] Paul said, "Stabilizing the currency will also give Americans new incentives to save as they will no longer have to fear inflation eroding their savings."[1809]

Aaron Russo opined, "Well, I think if you analyze the situation, and if you realize that since the Federal Reserve has come

---

[1805] United States Minister to the United Kingdom (November 12, 1846 – August 31, 1849), to Germany (August 28, 1867 – June 30, 1874). "George Bankcroft Quote." *Liberty Tree*, libertytree.ca/quotes/ George.Bancroft.Quote.2BD3.

[1806] Quinn, Jim. "The Federal Reserve Must Die." *HCP Live*, 25 Aug. 2009, www.mdmag.com/medical-news/federal_reserve_must_die.

[1807] "Central Banks Quotes." *AZ Quotes*, www.azquotes.com/quotes/ topics/central-banks.html.

[1808] Quinn, Jim. "The Federal Reserve Must Die." *HCP Live*, 25 Aug. 2009, www.mdmag.com/medical-news/federal_reserve_must_die.

[1809] *Id.*

into being in 1913,…they turned over the most important power that the American government has — the creation and issuance of money — to a private bank. Through that private bank issuing money, they have destroyed this country. They have destroyed the purchasing power of the money, in this country. They've created social programs that are destroying this country."[1810] He said, "You have to take the creation of money away from the private bankers and you'll solve 95 percent of your problems."[1811] Russo believed that, "if the American Government made the money, backed by gold, which limited the amount they could make, you wouldn't have debt and you wouldn't have inflation."[1812] He declared, "[T]he Federal Reserve System, these bankers, are responsible for the demise of America. And if we ever want to win this battle, you must shut down the Federal Reserve System. And we must shut down these bankers, and restore sound money to this country."[1813] Russo suggested, "Restore America's Republic to what it's supposed to be, get the bankers out of our government…until we do that, we're going to be slaves."[1814]

"The key to protecting the American way of life from the Federal Reserve's obliteration of our currency rests with the legislatures, but we must heed the lessons of history now."[1815] We can draw inspiration from the actions of our forefathers. For

---

[1810] "Aaron Russo: Reflections and Warnings - Full Transcript." *Matt Prather*, sites.google.com/site/themattprather/Reading/aaron-russo/reflections-and-warnings-full-transcript.

[1811] *Id.*

[1812] *Id.*

[1813] *Id.*

[1814] *Id.*

[1815] Jones, Stewart. "The Founders Warned Us About Central Banking." *Ron Paul Liberty Report*, 10 Oct. 2019, www.ronpaullibertyreport.com/archives/the-founders-warned-us-about-central-banking?fbclid=IwAR1GtgHBthCfZDgqhObnuqCX2hO9116CjGntgnKJ75rw5KXrb5U3mKOVFKI.

example, "[o]ne of the major planks in Democratic candidate James K. Polk's platform in 1844 was to re-create the Independent Treasury System. Congress reestablished the system in August 1846 to trade only in gold and silver coin..."[1816]   The Independent Treasury Act "entrusted the federal government with the exclusive management of government funds and required that disbursements be made in hard specie, such as gold or silver, or in paper backed by gold or silver."[1817]   Unfortunately, "[t]he Independent Treasury System ended in 1921."[1818]

Another attempt at monetary independence was made on June 4, 1963, when President John F. Kennedy signed Executive Order (EO) 11110.[1819] This EO gave the Treasury Department the power to issue silver certificates as the base for U.S. currency.[1820] The U.S. government regained the power to issue currency without going through the Rothschild-owned Federal Reserve.[1821] Perhaps learning from Lincoln's mistake of a purely fiat currency, Kennedy had the Treasury notes backed by silver. The theory was that, once enough silver certificates were in existence, they would eliminate the demand for Federal Reserve notes.   President Kennedy also

---

[1816] "Independent Treasury System." *Encyclopedia.com*, 29 Feb. 2020, www.encyclopedia.com/history/united-states-and-canada/us-history/independent-treasury-system.

[1817] Pinheiro, John C. "James K. Polk: Domestic Affairs." *UVA Miller Center*, millercenter.org/president/polk/domestic-affairs.

[1818] "Independent Treasury System." *Encyclopedia.com*, 29 Feb. 2020, www.encyclopedia.com/history/united-states-and-canada/us-history/independent-treasury-system.

[1819] Previously, the President could issue Silver Certificates on his own authority. Hitchcock, Andrew. "Historical Timeline of the Rothschild Dynasty – Part 6 (final)." *The Sirius Report,* 20 Aug. 2016, www.thesiriusreport.com/geopolitics/historical-timeline-rothschild-dynasty-6/.

[1820] *Id.*

[1821] *Id.*

announced on July 18, 1963: "I want to make it equally clear that this nation will maintain the dollar as good as gold, freely interchangeable with gold at $35 an ounce, the foundation-stone of the free world's trade and payments system."[1822]

A few months later, on November 22, 1963, President Kennedy was assassinated in Dallas, Texas, perhaps because he wanted to issue money for the American people, rather than for the benefit of the foreign banking elite.[1823] Author Jim Marrs speculated in his book, *Crossfire: The Plot That Killed Kennedy,* that JFK was trying to transfer power from the Federal Reserve to the United States Department of the Treasury, and that forces opposed to such action might have played some part in the assassination.

On the day Kennedy was shot, the new president, Lyndon B. Johnson, rescinded Executive Order 11110 whilst flying on Air Force One from Dallas to Washington, D.C.[1824] Less than a year later, "in October 1964, the Treasury ceased issuing Silver Certificates altogether."[1825] "On June 24, 1968, President Johnson issued a proclamation that henceforth Federal Reserve silver certificates were merely fiat legal tender and could not be redeemed in silver."[1826]

[1822] "Special Message to the Congress on Balance of Payments." *The American Presidency Project*, 18 Jul. 1963, www.presidency.ucsb.edu/documents/special-message-the-congress-balance-payments.

[1823] Hitchcock, Andrew. "Historical Timeline of the Rothschild Dynasty – Part 6 (final)." *The Sirius Report,* 20 Aug. 2016, www.thesiriusreport.com/geopolitics/historical-timeline-rothschild-dynasty-6/.

[1824] Hitchcock, Andrew. "Historical Timeline of the Rothschild Dynasty – Part 6 (final)." *The Sirius Report,* 20 Aug. 2016, www.thesiriusreport.com/geopolitics/historical-timeline-rothschild-dynasty-6/.

[1825] Griffin, G. Edward. "JFK And The Federal Reserve." *Freedom Force International*, 16 May 2017, freedomforceinternational.org/position-statements/jfk_and_fed/.

[1826] "The History of American Money." *CMI Gold $ Silver*, www.cmi-gold-silver.com/history-american-money/.

"The key to restoring sound money in the manner prescribed by the Constitution is for the people to call on Congress to abolish the Federal Reserve and to elect state legislators (all of whom took an oath to 'support the Constitution') committed to busting up the Fed's fiat money monopoly by enacting bills restoring gold and silver to their constitutional status."[1827] The "Constitutional Tender Act" could return monetary policy to constitutional tender provisions.[1828] "While this won't stop the Federal Reserve's destruction of the dollar, it will allow people to convert dollars to sound money before a collapse."[1829]

However, "[t]he best road back to a really well-functioning monetary system is through the states…exercising their monetary power as articulated in Article I, Section 10 of the [U.S.] Constitution to make nothing but gold and silver coin a payment in tender of debts," according to Utah attorney and businessman, Larry Hilton.[1830] The Constitution bans states from issuing their own currency, but Article I, Section 10 stipulates: "No State shall…make any Thing but gold and silver Coin a Tender in Payment of

---

[1827] Wolverton II, JD, Joe. "Tennessee Considering Bills Restoring Gold and Silver as Sound Money." *The New American*, 2 Feb. 2019, www.thenewamerican.com/usnews/constitution/item/31369-tennessee-considering-bills-restoring-gold-and-silver-as-sound-money.

[1828] It could abolish fractional reserve lending and raise the reserve requirement of banks from 10% to 100%. This would prevent the banks from inflating the money supply. "Constitutional Tender." *Tenth Amendment Center*, tenthamendmentcenter.com/legislation/constitutional-tender/.

[1829] Jones, Stewart. "The Founders Warned Us About Central Banking." *Ron Paul Liberty Report*, 10 Oct. 2019, www.ronpaullibertyreport.com/archives/the-founders-warned-us-about-central-banking?fbclid=IwAR1GtgHBthCfZDgqhObnuqCX2hO9116CjGntgnKJ75rw5KXrb5U3mKOVFKI.

[1830] Newman, Alex. "Washington State Considers Gold and Silver as Legal Tender." *The New American*, 31 Jan. 2012, www.thenewamerican.com/usnews/politics/item/9171-washington-state-considers-gold-and-silver-as-legal-tender.

Debts."[1831]   Thus, states have a constitutional duty to use gold and silver as legal tender.[1832] Any state that only accepts Federal Reserve Notes or coins of the U.S. Mint is in violation of this provision. "The responsibility is on the states to follow the constitution," Ron Paul noted.[1833]

A common theme in state initiatives to make gold and silver legal tender is to eliminate capital gains taxes. Rep. Mark Finchem (R-AZ) said, "What the IRS has figured out at the federal level is to target inflation as a gain. They call it capital gains."[1834] "Income taxes are one major way government bureaucrats penalize holders of precious metals. If you own gold to protect against the ongoing devaluation of America's paper currency (which results from the inflationary practices of the Federal Reserve), you may end up with

---

[1831] Ellis, Blake. "States seek currencies made of silver and gold." *CNN Money*, 3 Feb. 2012, money.cnn.com/2012/02/03/pf/states_currencies/index.htm.

[1832] Under the Constitution, the states "were to have whatever powers they wished to exercise, unless there was an express restriction on a particular power within the Constitution. That was why the Framers deemed it necessary to restrict the powers of the states when it came to money: no printing of paper money, no coining of money, and no making anything but gold coins and silver coins official money." Hornberger, Jacob. "Monetary Destruction in America." *Tenth Amendment Center*, 7 Jun. 2020, tenthamendmentcenter.com/2020/06/07/monetary-destruction-in-america/?fbclid=IwAR1qznHUtpPxV4SZfCJk0G9H9gTS2kepV1ZU5BKoX_o06DxBXusfHyCPK6s.

[1833] Boldin, Michael. "Signed by the Governor: Arizona Law Treats Gold and Silver as Money." *Tenth Amendment Center*, 23 May 2017, blog.tenthamendmentcenter.com/2017/05/signed-by-the-governor-arizona-law-treats-gold-and-silver-as-money/.

[1834] McHarrey, Mike. "Now in Effect: Arizona Law Treats Gold and Silver as Money." *Tenth Amendment Center*, 9 Aug. 2017, blog.tenthamendmentcenter.com/2017/08/now-in-effect-arizona-law-treats-gold-and-silver-as-money/.

a 'gain' on your gold when it's priced in dollars…"[1835] "For example, under current New Hampshire law, "gold and silver are subject to capital gains taxation when exchanged for Federal Reserve notes or when used in barter transactions."[1836] Dr. Paul explained, "Since inflation increases the value of precious metals, these taxes give the government one more way to profit from the Federal Reserve's currency debasement.'"[1837]

Some "state legislators across the country have started to recognize that paying taxes on nominal gains is beyond the pale."[1838] "Practically speaking, state laws that recognize gold and silver as money restore a government view of precious metals as the favored form of money – a currency rather than a piece of property or other asset. Using this logic, it would be inappropriate for a state to levy taxes when the precious metals are used or exchanged…"[1839] Louisiana, Utah, and Texas have passed legislation recognizing gold and silver as legal tender, which allows for transactions using precious metals in lieu of cash.[1840]

[1835] "Gold and Silver Bullion and Tax Laws in New Hampshire." *Sound Money Defense League*, www.soundmoneydefense.org/gold-silver-laws-new-hampshire.

[1836] *Id.*

[1837] Wolverton II, JD, Joe. "Tennessee Considering Bills Restoring Gold and Silver as Sound Money." *The New American*, 2 Feb. 2019, www.thenewamerican.com/usnews/constitution/item/31369-tennessee-considering-bills-restoring-gold-and-silver-as-sound-money.

[1838] "Gold and Silver Bullion and Tax Laws in New Hampshire." *Sound Money Defense League*, www.soundmoneydefense.org/gold-silver-laws-new-hampshire.

[1839] "Gold and Silver Bullion and Tax Laws in Washington." *Sound Money Defense League*, www.soundmoneydefense.org/gold-silver-laws-washington.

[1840] Louisiana (H.B. 682) was the second state to eliminate sales tax for gold and silver currency and bullion. Anderson, Anthony Allen. "States Where Gold and Silver Have Become Legal Tender." *GSI Exchange*, 25 Jul. 2019, gsiexchange.com/states-gold-silver-become-legal-tender/.

In the states that have passed gold and silver legal tender laws, if precious metals appreciate over time against the dollar, it is not viewed as a capital gain and is not taxed.[1841] "It is simply one form of money converted into another."[1842] "In other words, individuals buying gold or silver bullion, or utilizing gold and silver in a transaction, would no longer be subject to state taxes on the exchange."[1843] "As Rep. Mark Finchem (R-AZ) points out…the purchase of gold and silver coins with Federal Reserve notes — those dollar bills now printed by the government — is simply an exchange of one form of currency for another. To tax this exchange would be like taxing someone for exchanging two dimes and a nickel for a quarter…For example, if someone buys a 1 oz. Gold American Eagle Coin selling for $1,300 one year and sells it at a future date for a higher figure, 'that person has not experienced a capital gain,' argues Finchem, since it's the government-issued dollar bills that have dropped in buying power."[1844] In states without a state income tax, such as Washington, there is no taxation on capital gains on precious metals.[1845]

[1841] Williams, David Yoe. "Return to Tender: Why Arizona and Other States Are Choosing Gold." *Real Money*, 25 May 2017, realmoney.thestreet.com/articles/05/25/2017/return-tender-why-arizona-and-other-states-are-choosing-gold.

[1842] *Id.*

[1843] McHarrey, Mike. "Now in Effect: Arizona Law Treats Gold and Silver as Money." *Tenth Amendment Center*, 9 Aug. 2017, blog.tenthamendmentcenter.com/2017/08/now-in-effect-arizona-law-treats-gold-and-silver-as-money/.

[1844] USMR Staff. "More States Standing Up for Gold & Silver! Is Yours Next?" *U.S. Money*, 22 Jun. 2017, www.usmoneyreserve.com/blog/states-standing-up-for-gold-silver/.

[1845] "Gold and Silver Bullion and Tax Laws in Washington." *Sound Money Defense League*, www.soundmoneydefense.org/gold-silver-laws-washington.

"Arizona and Utah recently eliminated capital gains taxation on precious metals..."[1846] Utah, for example, approved a landmark law that recognized gold and silver as legal tender.[1847] "Utah became the first in recent times to officially accept gold and silver coins [issued by the U.S. Mint] as legal tender at their true value" with the Utah Legal Tender Act.[1848] "Under the law, the coins — which include American Gold and Silver Eagles — are treated the same as U.S. dollars for tax purposes, eliminating capital gains taxes. Since the face value of some U.S.-minted gold and silver coins — like the one-ounce, $50 American Gold Eagle coin — is so much less than the metal value [one ounce of gold is now worth more than $1,800], the new law allows the coins to be exchanged at their market value, based on weight and fineness."[1849] "In essence, the bill legalizes currency competition in Utah by removing punitive state taxes on individuals and businesses trading in precious-metal coins..."[1850]

"Rep. Ken Ivory (R) argues that the bill would reduce dependence on federal funding and help Utah avoid relying solely

---

[1846] "Gold and Silver Bullion and Tax Laws in New Hampshire." *Sound Money Defense League*, www.soundmoneydefense.org/gold-silver-laws-new-hampshire.

[1847] Newman, Alex. "Washington State Considers Gold and Silver as Legal Tender." *The New American*, 31 Jan. 2012, www.thenewamerican.com/usnews/politics/item/9171-washington-state-considers-gold-and-silver-as-legal-tender.

[1848] Newman, Alex. "Gold, Silver Now Legal Tender in Utah." *The New American*, 29 Mar. 2011, www.thenewamerican.com/economy/markets/item/4604-gold-silver-now-legal-tender-in-utah; Ellis, Blake. "States seek currencies made of silver and gold." *CNN Money*, 3 Feb. 2012, money.cnn.com/2012/02/03/pf/states_currencies/index.htm.

[1849] Ellis, Blake. "States seek currencies made of silver and gold." *CNN Money*, 3 Feb. 2012, money.cnn.com/2012/02/03/pf/states_currencies/index.htm.

[1850] Newman, Alex. "Gold, Silver Now Legal Tender in Utah." *The New American*, 29 Mar. 2011, www.thenewamerican.com/economy/markets/item/4604-gold-silver-now-legal-tender-in-utah.

on federal money during emergencies like bank failures, a currency collapse, or a currency war between countries."[1851] "Rep. Ken Ivory…explained…that the measure is 'a way for us to preserve for the citizens of Utah…the purchasing power of the money they hold.' He cited as evidence the ever-increasing purchasing power of 1960s half-dollar silver coins even as the Federal Reserve's paper currency continues to lose value…"[1852]

In Arizona, a bill (HB2014) introduced by Rep. Mark Finchem (R-Tucson) and signed into law by Governor Doug Ducey in May 2017, made gold and silver legal tender, and eliminated state capital gains taxes on specie (coins having precious metal content).[1853] "Arizona's HB2014 bolsters residents' ability to use precious metals to diversify away from paper currency, paves the way for the use of gold and silver as currency, and essentially acknowledges that precious metals can work as a hedge against inflation."[1854] "The freedom of choice expanded by HB2014 will help allow Arizona residents to secure the purchasing power of their money."[1855] "Dr. Paul praised the bill filed in Arizona for 'ensuring

---

[1851] USMR Staff. "More States Standing Up for Gold & Silver! Is Yours Next?" *U.S. Money*, 22 Jun. 2017, www.usmoneyreserve.com/blog/states-standing-up-for-gold-silver/.

[1852] Newman, Alex. "Gold, Silver Now Legal Tender in Utah." *The New American*, 29 Mar. 2011, www.thenewamerican.com/economy/markets/item/4604-gold-silver-now-legal-tender-in-utah.

[1853] Boldin, Michael. "Signed by the Governor: Arizona Law Treats Gold and Silver as Money." *Tenth Amendment Center*, 23 May 2017, blog.tenthamendmentcenter.com/2017/05/signed-by-the-governor-arizona-law-treats-gold-and-silver-as-money/.

[1854] USMR Staff. "More States Standing Up for Gold & Silver! Is Yours Next?" *U.S. Money*, 22 Jun. 2017, www.usmoneyreserve.com/blog/states-standing-up-for-gold-silver/.

[1855] Boldin, Michael. "Signed by the Governor: Arizona Law Treats Gold and Silver as Money." *Tenth Amendment Center*, 23 May 2017, blog.tenthamendmentcenter.com/2017/05/signed-by-the-governor-arizona-law-treats-gold-and-silver-as-money/.

that people are not punished by the taxman for rejecting Federal Reserve notes in favor of gold or silver."[1856] The Arizona law also takes a step towards fulfilling the constitutional requirement of Article I, Section 10, i.e. "No State shall…make any Thing but gold and silver Coin a Tender in Payment of Debts," which has been ignored for decades in every state.[1857]

"Texas appears to be a champion for sound money laws, with multiple pieces of legislation" aimed at returning monetary sovereignty to the state.[1858] In 2013, "HB78 eliminated the sales tax on purchases of gold, silver, and platinum bullion and numismatic coins."[1859] In 2015, the Lone Star State created a state bullion depository.[1860] House Bill 483 "allows for the nation's first state bullion depository to be established in Texas under the supervision of the state's comptroller's office."[1861] Upon signing the bill, Governor Greg Abbott said, "[W]ith the passage of this bill, the Texas Bullion Depository will become the first state-level facility of its kind in the nation, increasing the security and stability of our gold

---

[1856] Wolverton II, JD, Joe. "Tennessee Considering Bills Restoring Gold and Silver as Sound Money." *The New American*, 2 Feb. 2019, www.thenewamerican.com/usnews/constitution/item/31369-tennessee-considering-bills-restoring-gold-and-silver-as-sound-money.

[1857] Boldin, Michael. "Signed by the Governor: Arizona Law Treats Gold and Silver as Money." *Tenth Amendment Center*, 23 May 2017, blog.tenthamendmentcenter.com/2017/05/signed-by-the-governor-arizona-law-treats-gold-and-silver-as-money/.

[1858] USMR Staff. "More States Standing Up for Gold & Silver! Is Yours Next?" *U.S. Money*, 22 Jun. 2017, www.usmoneyreserve.com/blog/states-standing-up-for-gold-silver/.

[1859] *Id.*

[1860] *Id.*

[1861] "Gold and Silver Bullion and Tax Laws in Washington." *Sound Money Defense League*, www.soundmoneydefense.org/gold-silver-laws-washington.

reserves and keeping taxpayer funds from leaving Texas to pay for fees to store gold in facilities outside our state."[1862]

On June 4, 2014, Oklahoma Governor Mary Fallin signed into law Senate Bill 862, recognizing gold and silver US-minted coins as legal tender and exempt from state taxation.[1863] The bill reads, in part, "gold and silver coins issued by the United States government are legal tender in the State of Oklahoma."[1864]

In West Virginia, the "Legislature approved Senate Bill 502, originally introduced by Sen. Craig Blaire (R-Martinsburg), which called for the exemption of taxation on sales of investment metal bullion and investment coins...The law went into effect on July 1, 2019."[1865]

Constitutionalist icon, Ron Paul, approved of such legislation, saying, "The Federal Reserve's failure to reignite the economy with record-low interest rates since the last crash is a sign that we may soon see the dollar's collapse. It is therefore imperative that the law protect people's right to use alternatives to what may

---

[1862] *Id.*

[1863] Newman, Alex. "Washington State Considers Gold and Silver as Legal Tender." *The New American*, 31 Jan. 2012, www.thenewamerican.com/ usnews/politics/item/9171-washington-state-considers-gold-and-silver-as-legal-tender.

[1864] "Gold and Silver Bullion and Tax Laws in Washington." *Sound Money Defense League*, www.soundmoneydefense.org/gold-silver-laws-washington.

[1865] Anderson, Anthony Allen. "States Where Gold and Silver Have Become Legal Tender." *GSI Exchange*, 25 Jul. 2019, gsiexchange.com/ states-gold-silver-become-legal-tender/.

soon be virtually worthless Federal Reserve notes."[1866] In Paul's opinion, "Paper is not money, it's fraud."[1867]

Such legislation by the states sends a "powerful message…to the central bank. 'This proto-gold standard in the American west is a rebuke and challenge to the Fed, and a reminder that easy monetary policy since 2007 has won the central bank many more enemies than friends,' noted analyst James West…"[1868]

The laws may also help undermine the Federal Reserve's monopoly on money "by introducing competition into the monetary system."[1869] Matthew Shea said, "The free-market is about competition, and allowing competing currencies is just another extension of that time-honored principle."[1870] "[C]ompetition in currency would provide, among other benefits, greater security to the people…in protecting their property from inflation."[1871]

"The absence of competition from gold and silver currency,

[1866] Wolverton II, JD, Joe. "Tennessee Considering Bills Restoring Gold and Silver as Sound Money." *The New American*, 2 Feb. 2019, www.thenewamerican.com/usnews/constitution/item/31369-tennessee-considering-bills-restoring-gold-and-silver-as-sound-money.

[1867] McHarrey, Mike. "Now in Effect: Arizona Law Treats Gold and Silver as Money." *Tenth Amendment Center*, 9 Aug. 2017, blog.tenthamendmentcenter.com/2017/08/now-in-effect-arizona-law-treats-gold-and-silver-as-money/.

[1868] Newman, Alex. "Gold, Silver Now Legal Tender in Utah." *The New American*, 29 Mar. 2011, www.thenewamerican.com/economy/markets/item/4604-gold-silver-now-legal-tender-in-utah.

[1869] Boldin, Michael. "Signed by the Governor: Arizona Law Treats Gold and Silver as Money." *Tenth Amendment Center*, 23 May 2017, blog.tenthamendmentcenter.com/2017/05/signed-by-the-governor-arizona-law-treats-gold-and-silver-as-money/.

[1870] Newman, Alex. "Washington State Considers Gold and Silver as Legal Tender." *The New American*, 31 Jan. 2012, www.thenewamerican.com/usnews/politics/item/9171-washington-state-considers-gold-and-silver-as-legal-tender.

[1871] *Id.*

...exposes... citizens and businesses to more than a few problems including the 'chronic depreciation' of the Fed's fiat paper money and the accompanying loss of purchasing power. And measures must be taken to fix the problem, legislators and economists believe."[1872]

"If any state authorizes gold and silver as an alternative to Federal Reserve notes, economists say that the economy of such a state would stabilize and increase."[1873] "If sound money gains a foothold in the marketplace against Federal Reserve notes, the people would be able to choose the time-tested stability of gold and silver over the central bank's rapidly-depreciating paper currency."[1874] "A happy side effect of such a system would be the weakening of the Federal Reserve notes and a strengthening of the appeal of gold and silver. This genuine recovery (as opposed to the 'boom and bust' pseudo-recovery espoused by Bernanke) would obliterate the fiat money monopoly exercised by the Federal Reserve..."[1875]

Economics professor, William Greene, an expert on constitutional tender, "asserts that legislation to establish gold and silver as legal tender and to create a state bullion depository could undermine the Fed because people would favor gold and silver coins over Federal Reserve Notes. Over time, the state will attract more

---

[1872] *Id.*

[1873] Wolverton II, JD, Joe. "Tennessee Considering Bills Restoring Gold and Silver as Sound Money." *The New American*, 2 Feb. 2019, www.thenewamerican.com/usnews/constitution/item/31369-tennessee-considering-bills-restoring-gold-and-silver-as-sound-money.

[1874] Boldin, Michael. "Signed by the Governor: Arizona Law Treats Gold and Silver as Money." *Tenth Amendment Center*, 23 May 2017, blog.tenthamendmentcenter.com/2017/05/signed-by-the-governor-arizona-law-treats-gold-and-silver-as-money/.

[1875] Wolverton II, JD, Joe. "Tennessee Considering Bills Restoring Gold and Silver as Sound Money." *The New American*, 2 Feb. 2019, www.thenewamerican.com/usnews/constitution/item/31369-tennessee-considering-bills-restoring-gold-and-silver-as-sound-money.

banking business, its treasury will build real wealth, and people will abhor Federal Reserve Notes."[1876]

In addition, "when people in multiple states actually start using gold and silver instead of Federal Reserve Notes, it would effectively nullify the Federal Reserve and end the federal government's monopoly on money."[1877] Greene explained, "Over time, as residents of the State use both Federal Reserve Notes and silver and gold coins, the fact that the coins hold their value more than Federal Reserve Notes do will lead to a 'reverse Gresham's Law' effect, where good money (gold and silver coins) will drive out bad money (Federal Reserve Notes). As this happens, a cascade of events can begin to occur, including the flow of real wealth toward the State's treasury, an influx of banking business from outside of the State (as citizens residing in other States carry out their desire to bank with sound money), and an eventual outcry against the use of Federal Reserve Notes for any transactions. At that point, the Federal Reserve system will have become unwanted and irrelevant, and can be easily abolished by the people's elected Representatives in Washington, D.C."[1878]

"By placing the lion's share of the blame squarely at the feet of the federal government, particularly its unrepentant, unchecked, and (most importantly) unconstitutional manipulation of the monetary system of the United States through the creation and perpetuation of the Federal Reserve system, bills to restore the value of sound money...reassert the sovereignty of the states and re-

---

[1876] "Texas to Establish Bullion Depository with HB 3169." *Scottsdale Bullion & Coin*, 17 May 2017, www.sbcgold.com/blog/texas-establish-bullion-depository-hb-3169/; Boldin, Michael. "Signed by the Governor: Arizona Law Treats Gold and Silver as Money." *Tenth Amendment Center*, 23 May 2017, blog.tenthamendmentcenter.com/2017/05/signed-by-the-governor-arizona-law-treats-gold-and-silver-as-money/.

[1877] *Id.*

[1878] "Texas to Establish Bullion Depository with HB 3169." *Scottsdale Bullion & Coin*, 17 May 2017, www.sbcgold.com/blog/texas-establish-bullion-depository-hb-3169/.

enshrine the 10th Amendment to the Constitution wherein the Founding Fathers intended to erect an impregnable barricade, one that would protect the people from the usurpations they knew would be attempted by the general government. The only hope of a recovery lies where hope for liberty has always lain: with the people and the states."[1879] "Nullifying the Fed on a state by state level can get us there."[1880]

"The road to restoring a constitutional monetary system in America might be long and tough, but the alternatives, according to experts, are not pretty — a destruction of the currency, economic upheaval, and maybe worse. There is even a very real possibly that a global monetary regime with the power to print world money could be erected, at least if the system's powerful proponents get their way...' noted Rep. Overstreet."[1881]

If the hard money system is not reintroduced at the federal level, then the next best thing would be to return to the gold standard, something that Alan Greenspan once advocated: "[U]nder the gold standard, a free banking system stands as the protector of an economy's stability and balanced growth."[1882]

Milton Friedman said, "If an automatic commodity standard were feasible, it would provide an excellent solution to the liberal's

---

[1879] Wolverton II, JD, Joe. "Tennessee Considering Bills Restoring Gold and Silver as Sound Money." *The New American*, 2 Feb. 2019, www.thenewamerican.com/usnews/constitution/item/31369-tennessee-considering-bills-restoring-gold-and-silver-as-sound-money.

[1880] Boldin, Michael. "Signed by the Governor: Arizona Law Treats Gold and Silver as Money." *Tenth Amendment Center*, 23 May 2017, blog.tenthamendmentcenter.com/2017/05/signed-by-the-governor-arizona-law-treats-gold-and-silver-as-money/.

[1881] Newman, Alex. "Washington State Considers Gold and Silver as Legal Tender." *The New American*, 31 Jan. 2012, www.thenewamerican.com/usnews/politics/item/9171-washington-state-considers-gold-and-silver-as-legal-tender.

[1882] Greenspan, Alan. "Gold and Economic Freedom." *Constitution Society*, www.constitution.org/mon/greenspan_gold.htm.

(i.e., classic liberal) dilemma: a stable monetary framework without danger of the irresponsible exercise of monetary powers. If, for example, an honest-to-goodness gold standard, in which 100 percent of the money in a country consisted literally of gold, were widely backed by the public at large, imbued with the mythology of a gold standard and with the belief that it is immoral and improper for government to interfere with its operation, it would provide an effective guarantee against governmental tinkering with the currency and against irresponsible monetary action."[1883]

"The world gold standard system worked very well, over a period of centuries prior to its dissolution in 1971, and we don't seem to have developed any viable alternatives since then."[1884] "Former Fed Chairman Alan Greenspan just provided a barely noticed Big Reveal. In an interview with the World Gold Council's *Gold Investor* Chairman Greenspan, stating 'I view gold as the primary global currency,' went on to explicitly reveal…that 'When I was Chair of the Federal Reserve I used to testify before US Congressman Ron Paul, who was a very strong advocate of gold. We had some interesting discussions. I told him that US monetary policy tried to follow signals that a gold standard would have created.' The period of 'following signals that a gold standard would have created,' called the Great Moderation under President Clinton, was one of the most equitably prosperous in modern American history. That era saw the creation of over 20 million jobs. Robust growth

---

[1883] "The 101 Best Gold Quotes From History – GoldSilver." *Gold Silver*, goldsilver.com/blog/101-best-gold-quotes-all-time/.

[1884] Lewis, Nathan. "The World Gold Standard System Will Rise Again — But, Not Yet." *Forbes*, 6 Dec. 2019, www.forbes.com/sites/nathanlewis/2019/12/06/the-world-gold-standard-system-will-rise-again---but-not-yet/#5474426235e6.

converted the federal deficit into a surplus. It was, if only virtually rather than institutionally, a golden age…"[1885]

"When the 'PhD Standard' is untempered by gold, it tends to lead to a decline in currency value. The dollar's value today vs. gold is less than one-thirtieth of its value during Bretton Woods… Another period of dollar decline, accompanied by all the various market interventionism common today and perhaps leading even to 'modern monetary theory' as a way to finance deficits, won't be much fun. It would produce…the urge to produce Stable Money once again. When that time comes, when the political support for Stable Money again forms, let's not fool around with temporary half-measures, but instead recreate a proper worldwide gold standard system, a modernized and updated version of the pre-1914 Classical Gold Standard system, appropriate for our times just as that was appropriate for theirs."[1886]

"It seems like today's national leaders are gradually reaching a consensus about how the world's monetary system should be structured. They are getting ready to return to a gold standard system…"[1887]   For example, "Malaysia's prime minister, Mohammad Mahathir, recently restated his long-held desire for an international currency system based on gold."[1888]

[1885] Benko, Ralph. "President Trump: Replace The Dollar With Gold As The Global Currency To Make America Great Again." *Forbes*, 25 Feb. 2017, www.forbes.com/sites/ralphbenko/2017/02/25/president-trump-replace-the-dollar-with-gold-as-the-global-currency-to-make-america-g r e a t - a g a i n / a m p / ? __&fbclid=IwAR08UD15lTTTpxe9ovabRK3ps1n5Vw7gcBV-SnZZUMQl8dmSasktRMFeFq.

[1886] Lewis, Nathan. "We Just Tested The Gold Standard -- It Still Works." *Forbes*, 8 Aug. 2019, www.forbes.com/sites/nathanlewis/2019/08/08/we-just-tested-the-gold-standard-it-still-works/#2044ef4c556b.

[1887] Lewis, Nathan. "The World Gold Standard System Will Rise Again — But, Not Yet." *Forbes*, 6 Dec. 2019, www.forbes.com/sites/nathanlewis/2019/12/06/the-world-gold-standard-system-will-rise-again---but-not-yet/#5474426235e6.

[1888] *Id.*

"Donald Trump shows a strong affinity for gold. He has also shown a keen intuitive grasp of how the gold standard was crucial to having made America great: Donald Trump: 'We used to have a very, very solid country because it was based on a gold standard...' But he said it would be tough to bring it back because 'we don't have the gold. Other places have the gold...' Trump's comment to *GQ*: "Bringing back the gold standard would be very hard to do, but boy, would it be wonderful. We'd have a standard on which to base our money."[1889] "His economic advisor Lawrence Kudlow, vice-president Mike Pence, and Trump-appointed World Bank president David Malpass, have also indicated their friendliness toward the idea."[1890]

"As Paul-Martin Foss of the Menger Center astutely points out, the Federal Reserve Board currently has three vacancies."[1891] "President Trump has consistently favored gold standard fans. He has nominated three — Stephen Moore, Herman Cain and Judy Shelton — to the Federal Reserve."[1892]

"[Judy] Shelton has argued for a gold-backed currency..."[1893] "To deal with perpetual inflation caused by the Fed's never-ending expansion of the monetary supply,...Shelton has

---

[1889] Benko, Ralph. "President Trump: Replace The Dollar With Gold As The Global Currency To Make America Great Again." *Forbes*, 25 Feb. 2017, www.forbes.com/sites/ralphbenko/2017/02/25/president-trump-replace-the-dollar-with-gold-as-the-global-currency-to-make-america-great-again/amp/?__&fbclid=IwAR08UD15lTTTpxe9ovabRK3ps1n5Vw7gcBV-SnZZUMQl8dmSasktRMFeFq.

[1890] *Id.*

[1891] *Id.*

[1892] *Id.*

[1893] Newman, Alex. "Trump Nominates Gold Advocate to Federal Reserve." *New American*, 7 Feb. 2020, www.thenewamerican.com/usnews/politics/item/34831-trump-nominates-gold-advocate-to-federal-reserve?fbclid=IwAR3wJ8NEBE-t0FNu6_UqzJ0bg2HrFwliT-0vFNfDJPC8MjiPxXQx83ON9Zs.

called for 'linking the supply of money and credit to gold.' That would severely limit the Fed's ability to quietly steal the savings of everyone holding U.S. dollars..."[1894] "If Trump were to fill those vacancies with three sophisticated gold standard advocates from the short list of Lewis E. Lehrman..., Dr. Judy Shelton (who served as an advisor on his presidential economic transition team), former presidential candidate Steve Forbes, and John Allison, former CEO of BB&T (preferably as vice chairman for regulation), the president would create a super 'beachhead team' at the Fed to seriously restore equitable prosperity."[1895] "These appointments would be the safe and sure first steps out of economic stagnation for America. Couple these with a White House 'Team B' to plan the enactment of the Jack Kemp Gold Standard Act and removal of the regulatory and tax barriers to using gold as currency. Then watch an American economic miracle take place..."[1896]

"With the IMF attempting to pull off a fiscal reckoning minus the US dollar, President Trump may (as his advisor Judy Shelton has advocated and as President Kennedy tried to do in 1963) pull off a global reckoning of his own, by issuing US Treasury Notes backed by gold."[1897] "The NEW dollars would be pegged to gold, possibly at a modest starting point of $10K or even higher, effectively

---

[1894] *Id.*

[1895] Benko, Ralph. "President Trump: Replace The Dollar With Gold As The Global Currency To Make America Great Again." *Forbes*, 25 Feb. 2017, www.forbes.com/sites/ralphbenko/2017/02/25/president-trump-replace-the-dollar-with-gold-as-the-global-currency-to-make-america-g r e a t - a g a i n / a m p / ? _ _ & f b c l i d = I w A R 0 8 U D 1 5 l T T T p x e 9 o v a b R K 3 p s 1 n 5 V w 7 g c B V-SnZZUMQl8dmSasktRMFeFq.

[1896] *Id.*

[1897] Anderson, Anthony. "New Dollar Backed by Gold Coming This October 2020?" *GSI Exchange*, 27 May 2020, gsiexchange.com/is-a-new-dollar-backed-by-gold-at-10000-per-ounce-coming-by-october-1st-2020/? fbclid=IwAR0JeJRf6pMwprbp4UUdETDxl4lQQg3Oek5XnXrk3CEAVjZ dWUbay6W6m28.

returning the Gold Standard. So, following a massive plunge in dollar values, we'd see a surge in gold prices and, with the new dollars, a surge in gold-backed dollar values as well."[1898]

Perhaps most importantly for gold, the big banking families "were...fanatical devotees of...the gold standard..."[1899]   If the prominent bankers support a return to the gold standard, then it is a likely outcome.   "Gold will become the new standard of international exchange (again) at some point in the next 10 years."[1900]

Some countries have already begun to prepare. For example, business commentator, Max Keiser, reported, "Russia has the best hand at the geopolitical poker table. The Kremlin, for 20 years, has been doing the opposite of everyone else by reducing their national debt to near zero, and buying thousands of tons of gold while simultaneously raising living standards... Moscow has been boosting its gold and foreign currency holdings in recent years to shield its economy against any turmoil. According to the latest data published by Russia's central bank, the reserves have recently eclipsed $580 billion."[1901]

[1898] *Id.*

[1899] "History of Banking and Money Key Excerpts From Carroll Quigley's Tragedy and Hope." *Wanttoknow.info*, www.wanttoknow.info/articles/ quigley_carroll.tragedy_hope_banking_money_history.

[1900] Stansberry, Porter. "How Paper Money Fails." *InflationData.com,* 11 Jul. 2010, inflationdata.com/articles/2010/07/11/how-paper-money-fails/.

[1901] Korotayev, Viktor. "Russia's gold & near-zero debt give it best chance of thriving in post-coronavirus apocalypse – Max Keiser." *RT*, 20 Mar. 2020, www.rt.com/business/483518-russia-best-position-crisis/? f b c l i d = I w A R 1 K 8 j n I j G w T N 4 5 F T 3 K - gCJHnjDPo4wiitY5VMJQmzjqOgLnmtv4ub4Z6F4. "Some people think that Muammar Qaddafi of Libya was deposed in part because he was aiming to establish a pan-African and pan-Islamic gold-based currency..." Lewis, Nathan. "The World Gold Standard System Will Rise Again — But, Not Yet." *Forbes*, 6 Dec. 2019, www.forbes.com/sites/nathanlewis/ 2019/12/06/the-world-gold-standard-system-will-rise-again---but-not-yet/ #5474426235e6.

Jim Rickards believes that if and when the monetary system collapses, there will be no choice but to go back to the gold standard.[1902] In this scenario, the price of gold would increase to match the amount of dollars in circulation, which could be a staggering $15,265 per ounce.[1903] Rickards bases this estimate on the M1 money supply (approximately $4 trillion) and number of ounce of gold (8,000 tons or 256 million ounces) and assumes a 100% gold standard.[1904] This result would vary depending on the percent of gold used to back the currency, and also whether the M2 money supply were included. Rickards thinks that the price of gold could conceivably go as high as $58,593/oz to $100,000/oz, depending on the circumstances.[1905]

The next chapter explores various methods to secure one's assets in turbulent economic times, including investment strategies and asset protection vehicles.

[1902] At 8. Gammon, George. "Jim Rickards: His Gold Price Prediction Explained...($50,000+ IS POSSIBLE!!)" *Youtube*, 6 Dec. 2019, www.youtube.com/watch?v=HpqJ-sFScxA.

[1903] *Id.*

[1904] *Id.*

[1905] At 8-11:30. *Id.*

Chapter 9

Cover Your Assets

In August 2019, fears of an impending recession were triggered when the yield curve inverted.[1906] "The yield curve is a graphical representation of yields on similar bonds across a variety of maturities."[1907] "The shape of the yield curve changes with the state of the economy. The normal or upward sloping yield curve occurs when the economy is growing."[1908] A yield curve inversion, aka a negative yield curve, is an abnormal situation that signals an economic recession will strike in the next year or two.[1909] The average recession lasts 18 months.[1910]

In the context of inverted yield curves, the yields on U.S. Treasury bonds are usually indicated — bonds that are guaranteed by the U.S. government.[1911] "A bond is like an IOU given to you by

---

[1906] Long, Heather. "Federal Reserve predicts no interest rate cuts in 2020, ignoring Trump's calls to boost the economy." *The Washington Post,* 11 Dec. 2019, www.washingtonpost.com/business/2019/12/11/federal-reserve-predicts-no-interest-rate-cuts-ignoring-trumps-calls-boost-economy/?wpisrc=al_news__alert-economy--alert-national&wpmk=1.

[1907] "Inverted Yield Curve." *Investopedia*, 7 Nov. 2019, www.investopedia.com/terms/i/invertedyieldcurve.asp.

[1908] *Id.*

[1909] *Id.* Amadeo, Kimberly. "Inverted Yield Curve and Why It Predicts a Recession." *The Balance,* 31 Oct. 2019, www.thebalance.com/inverted-yield-curve-3305856.

[1910] Amadeo, Kimberly. "Inverted Yield Curve and Why It Predicts a Recession." *The Balance,* 31 Oct. 2019, www.thebalance.com/inverted-yield-curve-3305856.

[1911] "Inverted Yield Curve: what is it and how does it predict disaster?" *I Will Teach You*, 10 Jun. 2019, www.iwillteachyoutoberich.com/blog/inverted-yield-curve/.

a bank. When you lend the bank money, it'll give you back that same amount at a later time, along with a fixed amount of interest…"[1912] "The U.S. Treasury Department sells them in 12 maturities They are: One-month, two-month, three-month, and six-month bills, One-year, two-year, three-year, five-year, and 10-year Treasury notes, and 30-year bonds."[1913]

In the normal situation, "[l]onger investments yield higher returns. The longer you're willing to wait on your bond typically means that you're going to have higher return rates…"[1914] Thus, "[y]ields are typically higher on fixed-income securities with longer maturity dates. Higher yields on longer-term securities are a result of the maturity risk premium. [T]he prices of bonds with longer maturities change more for any given interest rate change. That makes long-term bonds riskier, so investors usually have to be compensated for that risk with higher yields."[1915] That is why long-term bonds usually have higher yields than short-term bonds.[1916]

"A normal yield curve slopes upward, reflecting the fact that short-term interest rates are usually lower than long-term rates. That is a result of increased risk premiums for long-term investments."[1917] "In a normal yield curve, the short-term bills yield less than the long-term bonds. Investors expect a lower return when their money is tied up for a shorter period. They require a higher

---

[1912] *Id.*

[1913] Amadeo, Kimberly. "Inverted Yield Curve and Why It Predicts a Recession." *The Balance,* 31 Oct. 2019, www.thebalance.com/inverted-yield-curve-3305856.

[1914] "Inverted Yield Curve: what is it and how does it predict disaster?" *I Will Teach You,* 10 Jun. 2019, www.iwillteachyoutoberich.com/blog/inverted-yield-curve/.

[1915] "Inverted Yield Curve." *Investopedia,* 7 Nov. 2019, www.investopedia.com/terms/i/invertedyieldcurve.asp.

[1916] *Id.*

[1917] *Id.*

yield to give them more return on a long-term investment."[1918] "During healthy economic growth, the yield on a 30-year bond will be three points higher than the yield on a three-month bill..."[1919]

"An inverted yield curve represents a situation in which long-term debt instruments have lower yields than short-term debt instruments of the same credit quality."[1920] In other words. "short-term interest rates become higher than long-term rates."[1921]

"When a yield curve inverts, it's because investors have little confidence in the near-term economy. They demand more yield for a short-term investment than for a long-term one. They perceive the near-term as riskier than the distant future. They would prefer to buy long-term bonds and tie up their money for years even though they receive lower yields. They would only do this if they think the economy is getting worse in the near-term..."[1922] "They know that with a short-term bill, they have to reinvest that money in a few months. If they believe a recession is coming, they expect the value of the short-term bills to plummet soon."[1923] "What an inverted yield curve really means is that most investors believe interest rates are going to fall. As a practical matter, recessions usually cause interest rates to fall..."[1924]

[1918] Amadeo, Kimberly. "Inverted Yield Curve and Why It Predicts a Recession." *The Balance,* 31 Oct. 2019, www.thebalance.com/inverted-yield-curve-3305856.

[1919] *Id.*

[1920] *Id.* "Inverted Yield Curve." *Investopedia,* 7 Nov. 2019, www.investopedia.com/terms/i/invertedyieldcurve.asp.

[1921] "Inverted Yield Curve." *Investopedia,* 7 Nov. 2019, www.investopedia.com/terms/i/invertedyieldcurve.asp.

[1922] Amadeo, Kimberly. "Inverted Yield Curve and Why It Predicts a Recession." *The Balance,* 31 Oct. 2019, www.thebalance.com/inverted-yield-curve-3305856.

[1923] *Id.*

[1924] "Inverted Yield Curve." *Investopedia,* 7 Nov. 2019, www.investopedia.com/terms/i/invertedyieldcurve.asp.

Economists frequently use the spread between the yields of ten-year Treasuries and two-year Treasuries to determine if the yield curve is inverted.[1925] "The Federal Reserve Bank of Cleveland found that the spread between these two indicators is one of the best indicators of future recessions…"[1926]

"An inverted yield curve is most worrying when it occurs with Treasury yields. That's when yields on short-term Treasury bills, notes, and bonds are higher than long-term yields…[Investors] know that the Federal Reserve lowers the fed funds rate when the economy slows. Short-term Treasury bill yields track the fed funds rate. As investors flock to long-term Treasury bonds, the yields on those bonds fall. They are in demand, so they don't need as high of a yield to attract investors. The demand for short-term Treasury bills falls. They need to pay a higher yield to attract investors. Eventually, the yield on short-term Treasurys rises higher than the yield on long-term bonds and the yield curve inverts…If investors believe a recession is imminent, they'll want a safe investment for two years. They'll avoid any Treasurys with maturities of less than two years. That sends the demand for those bills down, sending their yields up, and inverting the curve."[1927]

"If there is a recession, then stocks become less attractive and might enter a bear market. That increases the demand for bonds, which raises their prices and reduces yields."[1928] "As more and more people begin to buy long-term bonds,…the Federal Reserve

---

[1925] *Id.*

[1926] Amadeo, Kimberly. "Inverted Yield Curve and Why It Predicts a Recession." *The Balance,* 31 Oct. 2019, www.thebalance.com/inverted-yield-curve-3305856.

[1927] *Id.*

[1928] "Inverted Yield Curve." *Investopedia,* 7 Nov. 2019, www.investopedia.com/terms/i/invertedyieldcurve.asp.

responds by lowering the yield rates for those securities."[1929] "If an investor thinks that yields are headed down, it is logical to buy bonds with longer maturities. That way, the investor gets to keep today's higher interest rates. The price goes up as more investors buy long-term bonds, which drives yields down."[1930] "Since people aren't buying a lot of short-term U.S. Treasury bonds, the Fed will make those yields higher to attract investors. This is basic supply and demand. The less people want a bond, the more financial institutions like the Fed are going to make that bond appealing to investors..."[1931] "When the yields for long-term bonds fall far enough, it produces an inverted yield curve..."[1932] "An inverted yield curve means investors believe they will make more by holding onto a longer-term Treasury than a short-term one."[1933]

"Inversions of the yield curve have preceded many recessions in the U.S."[1934] "The last seven recessions the country has seen were preceded by an inverted yield curve..."[1935] "The Treasury

---

[1929] "Inverted Yield Curve: what is it and how does it predict disaster?" *I Will Teach You*, 10 Jun. 2019, www.iwillteachyoutoberich.com/blog/inverted-yield-curve/.

[1930] "Inverted Yield Curve." *Investopedia*, 7 Nov. 2019, www.investopedia.com/terms/i/invertedyieldcurve.asp.

[1931] "Inverted Yield Curve: what is it and how does it predict disaster?" *I Will Teach You*, 10 Jun. 2019, www.iwillteachyoutoberich.com/blog/inverted-yield-curve/.

[1932] "Inverted Yield Curve." *Investopedia*, 7 Nov. 2019, www.investopedia.com/terms/i/invertedyieldcurve.asp.

[1933] Amadeo, Kimberly. "Inverted Yield Curve and Why It Predicts a Recession." *The Balance,* 31 Oct. 2019, www.thebalance.com/inverted-yield-curve-3305856.

[1934] "Inverted Yield Curve." *Investopedia*, 7 Nov. 2019, www.investopedia.com/terms/i/invertedyieldcurve.asp.

[1935] "Inverted Yield Curve: what is it and how does it predict disaster?" *I Will Teach You*, 10 Jun. 2019, www.iwillteachyoutoberich.com/blog/inverted-yield-curve/.

yield curve inverted before the recessions of 2001, 1991, and 1981."[1936] The ten and two year yield curve "indicator has 100% accuracy since 1968 — a perfect record in predicting a recession. A recession always followed a yield curve inversion. A recession never happened without the yield curve inverting."[1937] "Due to this historical correlation, the yield curve is often seen as a way to predict the turning points of the business cycle."[1938]

A yield curve inversion also predicted the 2008 financial crisis — "the worst recession since the Great Depression."[1939] The first inversion occurred on December 22, 2005, almost three years before the crash.[1940] The yield curve remained inverted during much of 2006.[1941] The events that led to this event were as follows: "The Fed raised the federal fund rate to 4.25%…Mainly, they were aware that there was a growing price bubble within certain assets like housing, and they were concerned that low interest rates were causing this. So when the fund rate was raised to 4.25% in 2005, it caused the two-year U.S. Treasury bond to yield 4.4% while the

---

[1936] For example, in "1998, the yield curve briefly inverted. For a few weeks, Treasury bond prices surged after the Russian debt default." "Inverted Yield Curve." *Investopedia*, 7 Nov. 2019, www.investopedia.com/terms/i/invertedyieldcurve.asp; Amadeo, Kimberly. "Inverted Yield Curve and Why It Predicts a Recession." *The Balance,* 31 Oct. 2019, www.thebalance.com/inverted-yield-curve-3305856.

[1937] Christy Ai at 0:55. RT America. "Why it's too late to avoid coming recession." *Youtube*, 19 Dec. 2019, www.youtube.com/watch?v=F2q6HfXH6nE.

[1938] "Inverted Yield Curve." *Investopedia*, 7 Nov. 2019, www.investopedia.com/terms/i/invertedyieldcurve.asp.

[1939] Amadeo, Kimberly. "Inverted Yield Curve and Why It Predicts a Recession." *The Balance,* 31 Oct. 2019, www.thebalance.com/inverted-yield-curve-3305856.

[1940] *Id.*

[1941] "Inverted Yield Curve." *Investopedia*, 7 Nov. 2019, www.investopedia.com/terms/i/invertedyieldcurve.asp.

longer term seven-year bond only yielded 4.39%. Soon the curve began to invert more and more as the recession began approaching and investors continued to invest more heavily into longer-term bonds...."[1942]   In 2008, "long-term Treasuries soared as the stock market crashed."[1943]   "The Fed continued to lower the rate 10 times until it reached zero by the end of 2008. The yield curve was no longer inverted, but it was too late."[1944]

More recently, "[a] series of interest rate hikes by the Federal Reserve in 2018 raised expectations of a recession. Those expectations eventually led the Fed to walk back the interest rate increases."[1945]   "On December 3, 2018, the Treasury yield curve inverted for the first time since the recession. The yield on the five-year note was 2.83. That's slightly lower than the yield of 2.84 on the three-year note. In this case, you want to look at the spread between the 3-year and 5-year notes. It was -0.01 points…The curve means investors were saying that the economy would be a bit better in five years than in three years…On March 22, 2019, the Treasury yield curve inverted more. The yield on the 10-year note fell to 2.44. That's 0.02 points below the three-month bill. On August 12, 2019, the 10-year yield hit a three-year low of 1.65%. That was below the 1-year note yield of 1.75%. On August 14 [2019], the 10-year yield briefly fell below that of the 2-year note. On August 15

[1942] "Inverted Yield Curve: what is it and how does it predict disaster?" *I Will Teach You*, 10 Jun. 2019, www.iwillteachyoutoberich.com/blog/inverted-yield-curve/.

[1943] "Inverted Yield Curve." *Investopedia*, 7 Nov. 2019, www.investopedia.com/terms/i/invertedyieldcurve.asp.

[1944] Amadeo, Kimberly. "Inverted Yield Curve and Why It Predicts a Recession." *The Balance,* 31 Oct. 2019, www.thebalance.com/inverted-yield-curve-3305856.

[1945] "Inverted Yield Curve." *Investopedia*, 7 Nov. 2019, www.investopedia.com/terms/i/invertedyieldcurve.asp.

[2019], the yield on the 30-year bond closed below 2% for the first time ever."[1946]

"[T]he Fed's proclamation that 'the financial system remains resilient,' when it released the results of the most recent bank stress tests in June 2019, strains credulity."[1947] "[T]he collapsing yield on the 10-year U.S. Treasury note is screaming that markets see a crisis in the offing..."[1948]   On March 5, 2020, the 10-year U.S. Treasury note was trading below a yield of one percent (at 0.9456) for the first time in 149 years.[1949]

"U.S. stocks endured their worst drop since 2008 on Monday [March 9, 2020] as a free fall in oil prices and mounting coronavirus cases frightened investors and pushed major indexes to the edge of a bear market...Monday's rout added to recent losses and left the broader stock market down nearly 20% – almost bear territory –

[1946] Amadeo, Kimberly. "Inverted Yield Curve and Why It Predicts a Recession." *The Balance*, 31 Oct. 2019, www.thebalance.com/inverted-yield-curve-3305856.

[1947] Long, Caitlin. "The Real Story Of The Repo Market Meltdown, And What It Means For Bitcoin." *Forbes*, 25 Sept. 2019, www.forbes.com/sites/caitlinlong/2019/09/25/the-real-story-of-the-repo-market-meltdown-and-what-it-means-for-bitcoin/#23f8ac237caa.

[1948] Martens, Pam and Russ Martens. "Demand for Fed's Repo Loans Surges Past $100 Billion a Day as 10-Year Treasury Hits Lowest Rate in 149 Years." *Wall Street on Parade*, 5 Mar. 2020, wallstreetonparade.com/2020/03/demand-for-feds-repo-loans-surges-past-100-billion-a-day-as-10-year-treasury-hits-lowest-rate-in-149-years/.

[1949] *Id.*

from its high in mid-February."[1950] "A bear market is confirmed when stocks reach 20 percent below record peak…"[1951]

On March 9, 2020, the Dow Jones Industrial Average (DJIA), which had been at an all time high just three weeks before, suffered its worst single-day point drop since October 2008 of 2,013.76 points, or 7.8%, to close at 23,851.02.[1952] Likewise, the Standard & Poor's 500 plunged "225.81 points, or 7.6%, to end at 2,746.56, its biggest one-day percentage decline since December 2008…"[1953]

[1950] Menton, Jessica. "Dow plummets 2,000 points, oil prices drop as global recession concerns mount." *USA Today*, 9 Mar. 2020, www.usatoday.com/story/money/2020/03/09/dow-oil-tumbles-global-recession-fears/4998613002/?fbclid=IwAR0-nu_ghM9t6mt9rWdK6498YrzkjReK0bjZoZEXtdEObacRWgIqtp0pL0Q.

[1951] McEnery, Thornton and Noah Manskar.. "Dow loses over 2,000 points, worst single-day drop ever, as oil prices crash." *New York Post,* 9 Mar. 2020, nypost.com/2020/03/09/dow-loses-over-2000-points-worst-single-day-drop-ever-as-oil-prices-crash/?utm_source=NYPFacebook&utm_medium=Native&utm_campaign=NYPFacebook&fbclid=IwAR2JITqZcWGqAFLCGShFmbGi6wZYuXw508E78pUpn3G66GKIf8Hv6KTiqQk.

[1952] *Id.* Menton, Jessica. "Dow plummets 2,000 points, oil prices drop as global recession concerns mount." *USA Today*, 9 Mar. 2020, www.usatoday.com/story/money/2020/03/09/dow-oil-tumbles-global-recession-fears/4998613002/?fbclid=IwAR0-nu_ghM9t6mt9rWdK6498YrzkjReK0bjZoZEXtdEObacRWgIqtp0pL0Q.

[1953] The S&P plummeted so dramatically "in the opening minutes of the trading session, triggering a New York Stock Exchange 'circuit breaker' that had halted trading for 15 minutes." Menton, Jessica. "Dow plummets 2,000 points, oil prices drop as global recession concerns mount." *USA Today*, 9 Mar. 2020, www.usatoday.com/story/money/2020/03/09/dow-oil-tumbles-global-recession-fears/4998613002/?fbclid=IwAR0-nu_ghM9t6mt9rWdK6498YrzkjReK0bjZoZEXtdEObacRWgIqtp0pL0Q; McEnery, Thornton and Noah Manskar.. "Dow loses over 2,000 points, worst single-day drop ever, as oil prices crash." *New York Post,* 9 Mar. 2020, nypost.com/2020/03/09/dow-loses-over-2000-points-worst-single-day-drop-ever-as-oil-prices-crash/?utm_source=NYPFacebook&utm_medium=Native&utm_campaign=NYPFacebook&fbclid=IwAR2JITqZcWGqAFLCGShFmbGi6wZYuXw508E78pUpn3G66GKIf8Hv6KTiqQk.

"The Nasdaq Composite dropped 624.94 points, or 7.3%, to finish at 7,950.68, putting the technology-heavy index 19% below last month's record…"[1954] The DJIA and "[t]he broad index, which is used as a benchmark for mutual funds," were also down about 19% from their record highs just weeks before.[1955] The S&P 500, meanwhile, was down about 18 to 19 percent below its all-time high set on February 19, 2020.[1956]

The sharp drop "ended the longest-ever bull market on the very day it turned 11. The bull market began on March 9, 2009, when stocks bottomed during the global financial crisis. The S&P 500 has risen more than 300% since then."[1957] According to MUFG economist, Chris Rupkey, "The recent decline in the markets has resurfaced concerns about a global economic slowdown. Business activity is going to hit the brakes…and stock markets around the world are in free-fall as the spread of this deadly pandemic virus has

---

[1954] Menton, Jessica. "Dow plummets 2,000 points, oil prices drop as global recession concerns mount." *USA Today*, 9 Mar. 2020, www.usatoday.com/story/money/2020/03/09/dow-oil-tumbles-global-recession-fears/4998613002/?fbclid=IwAR0-nu_ghM9t6mt9rWdK6498YrzkjReK0bjZoZEXtdEObacRWgIqtp0pL0Q.

[1955] *Id.*

[1956] McEnery, Thornton and Noah Manskar.. "Dow loses over 2,000 points, worst single-day drop ever, as oil prices crash." *New York Post,* 9 Mar. 2020, nypost.com/2020/03/09/dow-loses-over-2000-points-worst-single-day-drop-ever-as-oil-prices-crash/?utm_source=NYPFacebook&utm_medium=Native&utm_campaign=NYPFacebook&fbclid=IwAR2JITqZcWGqAFLCGShFmbGi6wZYuXw508E78pUpn3G66GKIf8Hv6KTiqQk; Davidson, Paul. "The odds of recession are rising but market sell-off doesn't mean it's inevitable." *USA Today*, 9 Mar. 2020, finance.yahoo.com/news/odds-recession-rising-market-sell-202721566.html.

[1957] Menton, Jessica. "Dow plummets 2,000 points, oil prices drop as global recession concerns mount." *USA Today*, 9 Mar. 2020, www.usatoday.com/story/money/2020/03/09/dow-oil-tumbles-global-recession-fears/4998613002/?fbclid=IwAR0-nu_ghM9t6mt9rWdK6498YrzkjReK0bjZoZEXtdEObacRWgIqtp0pL0Q.

the potential to slow the global economy to a crawl."[1958]   Peter Schiff maintained, "The bear market has already started"[1959]

"[O]f the 12 U.S. recession since 1945, eight were preceded by bear markets (a decline of at least 20% from a recent peak) and three were preceded by market corrections (a drop of at least 10% from peak), says Sam Stovall, chief investment strategist at CFRA Research."[1960]   "Anxieties over the possible damage to the economy have wiped out $5.3 trillion in stock value and raised fears of a recession."[1961]   "The yield on the 10-year Treasury note dropped to an unprecedented low of 0.408%, a possible signal that investors are expecting a recession."[1962]   In addition, "The CBOE Volatility index,

[1958] David, Javier E. "Stock market news live: Dow pares losses after Fed announces $500 billion in short-term bank funding." *Yahoo Finance*, 12 Mar. 2020, finance.yahoo.com/news/stock-market-news-live-march-12-013620137.html.

[1959] "Coronavirus to pop bubble greater than 2008; gold prices have 'nowhere to go but up.'" *Kitco News*, 12 Mar. 2020, www.kitco.com/news/2020-03-12/Coronavirus-to-pop-bubble-greater-than-2008-gold-prices-have-nowhere-to-go-but-up.html.

[1960] Davidson, Paul. "The odds of recession are rising but market sell-off doesn't mean it's inevitable." *USA Today*, 9 Mar. 2020, finance.yahoo.com/news/odds-recession-rising-market-sell-202721566.html.

[1961] Menton, Jessica. "Dow plummets 2,000 points, oil prices drop as global recession concerns mount." *USA Today*, 9 Mar. 2020, www.usatoday.com/story/money/2020/03/09/dow-oil-tumbles-global-recession-fears/4998613002/?fbclid=IwAR0-nu_ghM9t6mt9rWdK6498YrzkjReK0bjZoZEXtdEObacRWgIqtp0pL0Q.

[1962] Thorbecke, Catherine. "Dow sinks more than 2,000 points amid coronavirus uncertainty and plunging oil prices." *ABC News*, 9 Mar. 2020, abcnews.go.com/Business/dow-futures-plummet-1200-points/story?id=69481843&fbclid=IwAR0mvtFGb1J1E06BIMhbhOA_y8i5NQS47Xd5SFeiollmJgKJwgIw7oiynRs.

a gauge of investor anxiety, touched its highest level since December 2008."[1963]

A recent study from the National Association for Business Economics showed that 72% of economists now predict that a recession will occur between 2020 and the end of 2021.[1964] "'Bond king' Jeffrey Gundlach of DoubleLine Capital has said there's a 90% chance the United States will enter a recession by year-end [2020]."[1965] "Moody's Analytics recently raised its odds of a recession to 50% from about 33% just days ago. Grant Thornton also reckons there's a 50% chance of a slump."[1966] "Moody's Investor Services issued a revised economic outlook report Monday, warning that 'global recession risks have risen' and 'several unknowns make for a highly unpredictable environment…The fact that all economies, big and small, are simultaneously facing this

---

[1963] McEnery, Thornton and Noah Manskar.. "Dow loses over 2,000 points, worst single-day drop ever, as oil prices crash." *New York Post,* 9 Mar. 2020, nypost.com/2020/03/09/dow-loses-over-2000-points-worst-single-day-drop-ever-as-oil-prices-crash/?utm_source=NYPFacebook&utm_medium=Native&utm_campaign=NYPFacebook&fbclid=IwAR2JITqZcWGqAFLCGShFmbGi6wZYuXw508E78pUpn3G66GKIf8Hv6KTiqQk.

[1964] Jones, Stewart. "The Founders Warned Us About Central Banking." *Ron Paul Liberty Report,* 10 Oct. 2019, www.ronppaullibertyreport.com/archives/the-founders-warned-us-about-central-banking?fbclid=IwAR1GtgHBthCfZDgqhObnuqCX2hO9116CjGntgnKJ75rw5KXrb5U3mKOVFKI.

[1965] Stevens, Pippa. "Bank of America says the recession is already here: 'Jobs will be lost, wealth will be destroyed.'" *CNBC,* 19 Mar. 2020, www.cnbc.com/2020/03/19/bank-of-america-says-the-recession-is-already-here-jobs-will-be-lost-wealth-will-be-destroyed.html.

[1966] Davidson, Paul. "The odds of recession are rising but market sell-off doesn't mean it's inevitable." *USA Today,* 9 Mar. 2020, finance.yahoo.com/news/odds-recession-rising-market-sell-202721566.html.

same negative shock would reinforce the recessionary cycle.'"[1967] Minneapolis Federal Reserve president, Neel Kashkari, said in March 2020 that "his base case threat to the U.S. economy from the coronavirus pandemic is a mild recession."[1968]

"The US economy entered recession at the end of February, according to the economists who officially define such things... Geopolitics expert George Friedman noted recently that recessions are a cyclical financial process. They're painful, but the economy recovers. A depression is more than an especially severe recession. It changes the existential reality of daily life."[1969]

"Financial experts noted several ominous economic indicators, including skyrocketing student loans and U.S. household debts, that could predict a crash 'worse than the Great Depression...'"[1970] "At least one expert predicted that recent slides in housing and auto sales were the first step toward a U.S. recession...Murray Gunn, chief of global research at Elliott Wave International, told the *Post*, 'We think the major economies are on the cusp of turning into the worst recessions we have seen in 10 years...' The U.S. household debt of

[1967] Thorbecke, Catherine. "Dow sinks more than 2,000 points amid coronavirus uncertainty and plunging oil prices." *ABC News*, 9 Mar. 2020, abcnews.go.com/Business/dow-futures-plummet-1200-points/story? id=69481843&fbclid=IwAR0mvtFGb1J1E06BIMhbhOA_y8i5NQS47Xd 5SFeiollmJgKJwgIw7oiynRs.

[1968] Reuters. "Fed's Kashkari: Base case is mild recession like after 9/11." *Kitco*, 17 Mar. 2020, www.kitco.com/news/2020-03-17/Fed-s-Kashkari-Base-case-is-mild-recession-like-after-9-11.html.

[1969] Watson, Patrick W. "The Corona Depression Is Here." *Forbes*, 25 Jun. 2020, www.forbes.com/sites/patrickwwatson/2020/06/25/the-corona-depression-is-here/? fbclid=IwAR1uN8gUgewFfpUX-4UcWc_iVbs6uWDoHwhZ3qxMflOCU uk-5I3oJrvVKuY#44c7e99ddd91.

[1970] Fearnow, Benjamin. "There Could Be a Financial Crash Before End of Trump's First Term, Experts Say, Citing Looming Debts." *Newsweek*, 23 Sept. 2018, www.newsweek.com/stock-market-1134867? f b c l i d = I w A R 2 q Y X w u B p - gBoHWnz4O_28BsUBS4tVUldapK0ls2g5O0l3PrW202Lwb_G8.

$13.3 trillion is now far worse than it was during its 2008 peak, due primarily to mortgage lending. Outstanding student loan debts have simultaneously increased from $611 billion of unpaid debt in 2008 to more than $1.5 trillion today. Automobile loans have far exceeded their 2008 peaks, sitting at about $1.25 trillion today, and unpaid credit card balances are just as high as the years leading up to the Great Recession... Central bankers have also more than doubled global debt as they flooded national economies with cheap and easy money. In 2008, global debt sat at $177 trillion, in comparison to $247 trillion today [March 2020]."[1971] "Reducing interest rates to borrowers will ease the burden of existing debts slightly but is unlikely to spur the usual surge of borrowing as consumers and businesses batten down the hatches for a coming drop off in U.S. economic activity," according to Greg McBride, chief financial analyst at Bankrate.com.[1972] Meanwhile, Andy Brenner, warned, "The Fed's balance sheet is increasing at a 28% rate and the money supply at an 11% rate over the last three months. So, we see a lot of problems on the horizon."[1973] "'It's a perfect storm,' said Chris Zaccarelli, chief investment officer at Independent Advisor Alliance in Charlotte, North Carolina."[1974]

[1971] *Id.*

[1972] Bayly, Lucy. "Dow falls 2,200 points, trading halted, as rate cut fails to calm markets." *NBC News*, 16 Mar. 2020, www.nbcnews.com/business/ markets/dow-falls-2-200-points-trading-halted-rate-cut-fails-n1160246? fbclid=IwAR24696MUcBAcdGR3gAIl6YRnUqAlJxZWSwerePFTWZai8 lu68gJ7FjS1Nw.

[1973] At 8:20. Schiff, Peter. "Powell resurrecting the high inflation Volcker buried." *Youtube*, 11 Dec. 2019, www.youtube.com/watch? v=lWcLQFap2sQ.

[1974] McEnery, Thornton. "Dow loses over 2,000 points, worst single-day drop ever, as oil prices crash." *New York Post*, 9 Mar. 2020, nypost.com/ 2020/03/09/dow-loses-over-2000-points-worst-single-day-drop-ever-as-oil-prices-crash/?fbclid=IwAR2nfX-r6e_9icqr1BqOxbfYSjFRZfxYxrxb5VjXG7jaG19Kbp5ZTYoHGss.

As "the United States faces an historic collapse in GDP and mounting job losses," former White House Council of Economic Advisers Chairman, Kevin Hassett, issued a startling warning: "The widespread shutdown of the American economy because of the coronavirus could spark a repeat of the Great Depression..."[1975] Hassett also thinks "that the odds of a global recession are close to 100% right now."[1976] "The IMF describes a global recession as a sustained period when economic output falls and unemployment rises. It is simply an extended period of economic decline around the world...The world had last experienced recession between 2008 and 2009."[1977]

"A recession of a magnitude larger than the 2008 financial crisis is about to be triggered by the coronavirus, with problems rooted in excess levels of debt, this according to Peter Schiff, CEO

[1975] Egan, Matt. "Coronavirus could spark another Great Depression, former Trump adviser warns." *CNN*, 19 Mar. 2020, www.cnn.com/2020/03/19/business/great-depression-coronavirus-kevin-hassett/index.html?fbclid=IwAR28piMwTy6nFBwqzzXWS_08H44rYHGZ5lUJcSpno2rG7lACCWPtB6cgMag.

[1976] "We just ran the numbers carefully over the weekend, and we think second quarter's going to be about minus 5%, and we think the jobs number in early April might be as much as minus a million or so because ...nobody is going to get hired next week...You're going to have one really bad quarter. If you're going to have a recession, then you've got to have two bad quarters." Yilek, Caitlin. "Former Trump adviser: 'Odds of a global recession are close to 100%.'" *Washington Examiner*, 16 Mar. 2020, www.washingtonexaminer.com/news/former-trump-adviser-odds-of-a-global-recession-are-close-to-100?fbclid=IwAR0fxItrOZL-Pr-VobO2YQzhEDkOt4YrywCpb13Fsyy44fDXclmb8kd3hLc.

[1977] Bizimungu, Julius. "IMF officially declares global economic recession." *The New Times*, 27 Mar. 2020, www.newtimes.co.rw/news/imf-officially-declares-global-economic-recession?fbclid=IwAR0pEJQiDFplhokY8-Wpql7pgEgcTdE2kW1ZydtNSW1_CZjBPNFP6FZFQMo.

of Euro Pacific Capital."[1978] He said, "We won't be able to call it a recession, it's going to be worse than the Great Depression. The U.S. economy is in so much worse shape than it was a decade ago."[1979]

Scott Minerd, global chief investment officer at Guggenheim Investments, said that the European economy "is probably in a fairly severe recession," and that, "[i]f the United States is not already in a recession, it will enter one shortly… The risk is that for the first time since the 1930s we are facing the possibility of a downward spiral into something akin to a global recession. We have at least a 10% to 20% chance that that's the path we are on…"[1980]

Bank of America's top U.S. economist cautioned investors that the country is already in a recession.[1981] Michelle Meyer "warned investors that a coronavirus-induced recession is no longer avoidable — it's already here. 'We are officially declaring that the economy has fallen into a recession…joining the rest of the world,

---

[1978] "Coronavirus to pop bubble greater than 2008; gold prices have 'nowhere to go but up.'" *Kitco News*, 12 Mar. 2020, www.kitco.com/news/ 2020-03-12/Coronavirus-to-pop-bubble-greater-than-2008-gold-prices-have-nowhere-to-go-but-up.html.

[1979] Fearnow, Benjamin. "There Could Be a Financial Crash Before End of Trump's First Term, Experts Say, Citing Looming Debts." *Newsweek*, 23 Sept. 2018, www.newsweek.com/stock-market-1134867? fbclid=IwAR2qYXwuBp-gBoHWnz4O_28BsUBS4tVUldapK0ls2g5O0l3PrW202Lwb_G8.

[1980] Matthews, Chris. "U.S. businesses need a $2 trillion bailout fund to avoid a possible 'global depression,' says Guggenheim's Minerd." *Market Watch*, 18 Mar. 2020, www.marketwatch.com/story/us-businesses-need-a-2-trillion-bailout-to-avoid-a-possible-global-depression-says-guggenheims-minerd-2020-03-17? reflink=mw_share_facebook&fbclid=IwAR2DYUo5DrWOvyfu-sLPF608PpJbSgaqSvh8R2dYdgvzDSL3QrCmx7lFMqs.

[1981] Bowden, John. "Bank of America: The US is now in a recession." *The Hill*, 19 Mar. 2020, thehill.com/policy/finance/488388-bank-of-america-the-us-is-now-in-a-recession? fbclid=IwAR2wQSov4oS5TfkCbuTxpto0iXu8sKoJ7tsWU0xe3mkOopgK k26b8ZJN08c.

and it is a deep plunge…'"[1982] The cumulative decline in economic expansion will be severe, according to analysts: "We forecast the cumulative decline in GDP to be 10.4% and this will be the deepest recession on record, nearly five times more severe than the post-war average."[1983] "This recession could be the worst since World War II, Bank of America Global Research predicts."[1984]

World Bank president, David Malpass, wrote in a post on LinkedIn, "[W]e are expecting a major global recession."[1985] "'We are going into a global recession,' said Mohamed El-Erian, chief economic adviser at Allianz…'After what's been happening the last few days, we are going to see a spread of economic sudden stops…

[1982] Stevens, Pippa. "Bank of America says the recession is already here: 'Jobs will be lost, wealth will be destroyed.'" *CNBC*, 19 Mar. 2020, www.cnbc.com/2020/03/19/bank-of-america-says-the-recession-is-already-here-jobs-will-be-lost-wealth-will-be-destroyed.html.

[1983] DeCambre, Mark. "Brace for the 'deepest recession on record,' says BofA analysts, as jobless claims surge to 6.6 million." *Market Watch*, 2 Apr. 2020, www.marketwatch.com/story/brace-for-the-deepest-recession-on-record-says-bofa-analysts-as-jobless-claims-surge-to-66-million-2020-04-02?reflink=mw_share_facebook&fbclid=IwAR07I04dpmNf919IORdxeC1Ci3 V2yzx4DNwllgmEY03c-OpmIpg8lyPh1fs.

[1984] Katzeff, Paul. "Recession Ahead? Time To Shift Your Stock Mutual Funds To Cash?" *Investor's Business Daily*, 23 May 2020, www.investors.com/etfs-and-funds/personal-finance/retirement-savings-time-shift-mutual-funds-cash/?src=A00220&yptr=yahoo.

[1985] Shalai, Andrea. "IMF sees coronavirus-induced global downturn 'way worse' than financial crisis." *Reuters,* 3 Apr. 2020, uk.reuters.com/article/uk-health-coronavirus-imf/global-downturn-due-to-coronavirus-way-worse-than-global-financial-crisis-imf-idUKKBN21L328? fbclid=IwAR1UIBq5Mv2fCQrvdzrDzpXHb2BbcggPIwVhj0RnolpPjz4N KZWNgRnKqa4.

The trouble with economic sudden stops is it's not easy to restart an economy.'"[1986]

On March 27, 2020, "The International Monetary Fund (IMF) …officially declared that the global economy has entered recession as a result of the spread of the new coronavirus, which has shut down economic activities across the world. IMF's Managing Director, Kristalina Georgieva, said they have reassessed the prospect for growth for 2020 and 2021. 'It is now clear that we have entered a recession – as bad as or worse than in 2009.'"[1987] She asserted, "The coronavirus pandemic has brought the global economy to a standstill and plunged the world into a recession that will be 'way worse' than the global financial crisis a decade ago."[1988] Georgieva called it "humanity's darkest hour" and said, "This is a crisis like no other…We have witnessed the world economy coming to a standstill. We are now in recession. It is way worse than the global financial crisis" of 2008-2009.[1989]

"JPM's Bruce Kasman has also taken a flamethrower to his global economic forecasts, and the bank's head of economic policy now anticipates Europe to implode an unprecedented 22%,…he sees the global economy ex China contracting by a whopping

---

[1986] Imbert, Fred and Thomas Franck. "Stocks plummet again after Trump fails to quell virus fears." *MSN Money*, 12 Mar. 2020, www.msn.com/en-us/money/markets/stocks-plummet-again-after-trump-fails-to-quell-virus-fears/ar-BB112FMf?ocid=sf2.

[1987] Bizimungu, Julius. "IMF officially declares global economic recession." *The New Times*, 27 Mar. 2020, www.newtimes.co.rw/news/imf-officially-declares-global-economic-recession?fbclid=IwAR0pEJQiDFplhokY8-Wpql7pgEgcTdE2kW1ZydtNSW1_CZjBPNFP6FZFQMo.

[1988] Shalai, Andrea. "IMF sees coronavirus-induced global downturn 'way worse' than financial crisis." *Reuters,* 3 Apr. 2020, uk.reuters.com/article/uk-health-coronavirus-imf/global-downturn-due-to-coronavirus-way-worse-than-global-financial-crisis-imf-idUKKBN21L328?fbclid=IwAR1UIBq5Mv2fCQrvdzrDzpXHb2BbcggPIwVhj0RnolpPjz4N KZWNgRnKqa4.

[1989] *Id.*

-13.7%."[1990]   In the U.K., Chancellor Rishi Sunak warned that the country faced a "severe recession, the likes of which we haven't seen."[1991]

Some believe that events "will bring on MMT or helicopter money because it is the only way for the Fed to get the liquidity out of the financial economy and into the real economy…"[1992]   The U.S. central bank will continue until it causes severe inflation, if not hyperinflation.[1993]

Financial commentator and trader, Gregory Mannarino, maintains that this is by design: "The market is fake…We have a communist market…It's a managed market…The final solution of the world central banks is being fulfilled. They are being called on by world leaders…to issue more debt. That's their end game. This is their goal. They are serial bubble-blowers… They deliberately inflate bubbles — this one is a mega-bubble — then they deflate it. And they transfer wealth…This is a phenomenon that has been occurring over and over again…since before the 1929 crash, and it's going to continue. But this one is the all-encompassing bubble like we've never seen."[1994]

[1990] Durden, Tyler. "JPMorgan Now Expects A Global Depression In The Second Quarter." *ZeroHedge*, 18 Mar. 2020, www.zerohedge.com/economics/jpmorgan-now-expects-global-depression-second-quarter?fbclid=IwAR28Uak-h-A87LADh8EFvockAS47EoUjzZ1aCIB920ndvAGrjlkayhFVgro.

[1991] Nurse, Peter. "Dollar Climbs; Fed Minutes Offer Downbeat Outlook." *Yahoo Finance*, 20 May 2020, finance.yahoo.com/news/dollar-climbs-fed-minutes-offer-023949316.html.

[1992] At 11:40. Gammon, George. "Quantitative Easing: Will It Cause Hyperinflation? (ANSWER REVEALED)." *Youtube*, 19 Dec. 2019, www.youtube.com/watch?v=b7KafSma3xQ.

[1993] At 12:40. *Id.*

[1994] At 1:05. Mannarino, Gregory. "MARKETS: IMPORTANT UPDATES… By Gregory Mannarino." *Youtube*, www.youtube.com/watch?v=n6PCYssIR38.

"The system is winding down and the failures are becoming more evident."[1995]   Aaron Russo warmed, "[I]t's going to come crashing at some point. And they're going to try to hold [it] up as long as they can."[1996]   "All around us, we can see our society being thrown into convulsions as all of our systems begin to fail."[1997]   "For a very long time we have been warned that a U.S. economic collapse was inevitably coming, and now it is here. Fear of COVID-19 and unprecedented civil unrest in our major cities have combined to plunge us into a historic economic downturn, and nobody is exactly sure what is going to happen next...."[1998]   Peter Schiff predicted, "We have a bubble economy and the only thing keeping the air in the bubble is the Fed...That's why we are headed for a much larger economic crisis than in 2008. The Fed is powerless to do anything about it this time."[1999]

[1995] At 5:50. RonPaulLibertyReport. "Central Banking Is On The Ropes: Gold Will Survive & The Fed Will End." *Youtube*, 13 Dec. 2019, www.youtube.com/watch?v=Ndcb2SPRU7M.

[1996] "Aaron Russo: Reflections and Warnings - Full Transcript." *Matt Prather*, sites.google.com/site/themattprather/Reading/aaron-russo/reflections-and-warnings-full-transcript.

[1997] Durden, Tyler. "If You Feel Like Something Really, Really Bad Is About To Happen, You're Definitely Not Alone." *Zero Hedge*, 11 Sept. 2020, www.zerohedge.com/personal-finance/if-you-feel-something-really-really-bad-about-happen-youre-definitely-not-alone?utm_campaign=&utm_content=ZeroHedge%3A%20The%20Durden%20Dispatch&utm_medium=email&utm_source=zh_newsletter&fbclid=IwAR0GcPMLmadUb8gu1UkFCgGEX1CdoA06CObVf2Mp7jf-WX5aWJIpGjEjd-s.

[1998] Snyder, Michael. "We Are Experiencing Economic Devastation On A Scale That America Has Never Seen Before." *The Economic Collapse*, 30 Jul. 2020, theeconomiccollapseblog.com/archives/we-are-seeing-economic-devastation-on-a-scale-that-america-has-never-seen-before?fbclid=IwAR1me25eZmKq9vxntaeE5BLhs5QFSdQmaSOYvbc_XSr4jKpADZ55ztace-Q.

[1999] At 6. Schiff, Peter. "Powell resurrecting the high inflation Volcker buried." *Youtube*, 11 Dec. 2019, www.youtube.com/watch?v=lWcLQFap2sQ.

"The collapse of the developed world's sovereign borrowers, the demise of most of the triple-A-rated corporations in America, and the destruction of the U.S. consumer's balance sheet are all signposts to the end of the world's current monetary system."[2000] "[P]aper money systems fail...because, inevitably, far too much credit is created under the paper system. There's no fundamental limit to credit. Sooner or later, people realize the debts can't be carried, much less repaid. At that point, the system collapses – and not because the money becomes more valuable (i.e. deflation). It collapses because people suddenly decide any other asset is better to hold than the money the banks keep printing."[2001]   "Today, more than 60% of the world's banking reserves are U.S. dollars. When governments have to bail out their banks (and they will), they're going to need U.S. dollars to do it. And they're going to need massive quantities."[2002]

If the free market were allowed to function, the poorly-run financial institutions would collapse. Unfortunately, in a command economy run by private bankers, taxpayers or depositors are forced to prop them up. For this reason, the Federal Reserve implemented the bail-in rule, which took effect in January 2019.[2003] It is designed to help failing banks without resorting to government funding, which was unpopular with the voters.

In the bail-in scenario, a "systemically important bank" (a.k.a. "too big to fail") will not receive government aid to stay afloat. Instead, the bank will take whatever percentage of the depositors'

[2000] Stansberry, Porter. "How Paper Money Fails." *InflationData.com*, 11 Jul. 2010, inflationdata.com/articles/2010/07/11/how-paper-money-fails/.

[2001] *Id.*

[2002] *Id.*

[2003] Dodd-Frank Wall Street Reform and Consumer Act of January 2010. Kreiter, Marcy. "Too Big To Fail: US Federal Reserve Says No More Bailouts; Burden To Shift To Investors." *International Business Times*, 1 Nov. 2015, www.ibtimes.com/too-big-fail-us-federal-reserve-says-no-more-bailouts-burden-shift-investors-2164040.

money it needs to stabilize itself.[2004]   In other words, if the bank needs money, it will take it out of depositors' accounts. Essentially, "[c]ustomers who deposit money in banks are lending that money to the bank. Depositors are, in effect, unsecured creditors. If the bank fails, depositors get in line with other unsecured creditors to see how many cents on the dollar, if any, they can retrieve."[2005]

The bail-in rule was first implemented in Cyprus. "In spring of 2013, the failing European Bank of Cyprus performed a bail-in that required depositors to help save the bank by foregoing a large portion of the money they had deposited in the bank. In return…, depositors were given equity shares in the failing bank."[2006]   T h e banks that are allowed to take advantage of the bail-in rule are J.P. Morgan Chase, Bank of America, Citigroup, Wells Fargo, Capital One, Bank of N.Y. Mellon Corp, U.S. Bancorp, and PNC Financial Services Group.

Some people think that they can look to the Federal Deposit Insurance Corporation (FDIC), which has insured bank deposits since 1933 for up to $250,000, for reimbursement.   However, the FDIC is woefully underfunded to handle payouts in the event of massive bank failures.   Some estimate that the FDIC could cover $0.02 out of every $1 on deposit. "Contrary to what we have been led to believe, our bank deposits are not protected. We are told they are protected by the Federal Deposit Insurance Corporation (FDIC), but the FDIC is mandated by law to keep a balance equivalent to only 1.15% of insured deposits, which is only about

---

[2004] Cammarosano, Louis. "The U.S. Plans to Bail-In the Banks – Federal Reserve Vice Chairman." *Smaulgld*, smaulgld.com/u-s-plans-to-bail-in-t h e - b a n k s / ? utm_source=ReviveOldPost&utm_medium=social&utm_campaign=ReviveOldPost.

[2005] Duclos, Susan. "Surprise, Surprise! Did You Know That You Don't Own Your Bank Deposits Anymore?" *Internet Marketer*, 10 Jan. 2015, www.internetmarketer.com.au/bankruptcy/your-money-is-not-safe-in-the-bank-anymore-be-warned-watch-this-warning-video-now/.

[2006] *Id.*

$25 billion. In the event of a crisis, they would be unable to insure deposits for the remaining 98.85% of Americans. So there is a very high probability we would lose our deposits."[2007]

"Very challenging times are on the horizon, and what we have experienced so far is just the tip of the iceberg. More big corporations are going to go bankrupt, more businesses are going to fail, more workers are going to be laid off, and the financial dominoes are going to start to fall at a pace that is absolutely breathtaking…A great unraveling has begun, and it is imperative for all of us to find a way to survive the severe economic pain that is ahead of us."[2008]   Per Patrick M. Byrne, CEO of Overstock.com, "We are on a crazy strategy with our central bank. It's good to have alternative ecosystems. It's not that the dollar will go away, but we need other options if it crashes or wildly inflates."[2009]

Considering the dire predicament in which the economy finds itself, the prudent investor should consider ways to protect his assets, and, "[t]he time to prepare is before times get bad."[2010] Unfortunately, "[w]e live in difficult times for investors. Practically all major asset classes are richly valued in most developed markets. Yields are pathetic, or even negative. Underlying corporate profits aren't growing as before. Central banks and corporate managements

---

[2007] Bailey, James. "How to Withdraw Cash from the Bank Without Getting Arrested." *Z3 News*, 6 May 2015, z3news.com/w/how-to-withdraw-cash-from-the-bank-without-getting-arrested/.

[2008] Snyder, Michael. "We Are Experiencing Economic Devastation On A Scale That America Has Never Seen Before." *The Economic Collapse*, 30 Jul. 2020, theeconomiccollapseblog.com/archives/we-are-seeing-economic-devastation-on-a-scale-that-america-has-never-seen-before?fbclid=IwAR1me25eZmKq9vxntaeE5BLhs5QFSdQmaSOYvbc_XSr4jKpADZ55ztace-Q.

[2009] "Central Bank Quotes." *Brainy Quote*, www.brainyquote.com/quotes/patrick_m_byrne_851349?src=t_central_bank.

[2010] McMahon, Tim. "Surviving a Hyperinflation." *Financial Trend Forecaster*, 18 Jul. 2013, fintrend.com/2013/07/18/surviving-hyperinflation/.

rely on financial smoke and mirrors to maintain the mirage that all is well. So what should investors do to survive and thrive? Where should you put your money?"[2011]

Taking the precarious situation into account along with the new bail-in rule, one might want to move money out of the "too big to fail" corporate banks and into credit unions or even out of the banking system altogether.[2012] "Governments want to control cash flows, and that is why you should fear the confiscation of savings, as well as controls on the use of money...Furthermore, money withdrawals can be stopped or restrained within a matter of minutes."[2013] "Only the liquid savings are there for [the] taking. These are easy to confiscate. Tomorrow the government says that now 10% of all savings is the government's property, by calling it a 'crisis tax,' and the job is done!"[2014]

"Controls on money are not a potential future problem. Foreign currency controls, to a large or small extent, do already exist in almost every country. Almost everywhere, we see controls on: Transferring money to another country; Transferring money between different account holders; The amount of deposit currency that can be exchanged for cash...If these aren't foreign exchange controls, what are they? Foreign exchange controls will probably become stricter in the future..."[2015]

Author Nicole McKay suggested, "You could carve out the inside of a brick and hide your money in it for safe keeping. It's

---

[2011] Marstrand, Rob. "Where should you put your money?" *Of Wealth*, 29 Sept. 2016, www.ofwealth.com/where-should-you-put-your-money/ #.V_0bXJMrK9Y.

[2012] Marstrand, Bob. "Lies, damned lies and CPI." *Of Wealth,* 11 Oct. 2016, www.ofwealth.com/lies-damned-lies-cpi/.

[2013] Dirkmaat, Olav. "Do Not Worry about Gold Confiscation." *Gold Republic*, 16 Jun. 2015, www.goldrepublic.com/news/gold-confiscation.

[2014] *Id.*

[2015] *Id.*

certainly safer than keeping it in the bank!"[2016] Indeed, New York's elite in the Hamptons have been "going to banks and asking to withdraw large sums of cash."[2017] "According to reports, banks like Chase, JPMorgan and Bank of America (BoA) have been limiting withdrawals. This is because the rich from New York have been asking for $30-50K withdrawals so banks have created a limit between $3-10K in some areas. During the market massacre on March 12 [2020], Manhattan Bank temporarily ran low on $100 bills after a large rush for cash...Reports detail that a few German banks are imposing withdrawal limits and customers can only withdraw 1,000 euros per visit...'Bank runs are starting in Colorado,' another man from the U.S. tweeted on March 17 [2020]. 'Smaller towns and small cities are not allowing walk-ins [or] anyone, along with limits on cash withdrawals.'"[2018]

"If you do decide it's safer for you to keep your cash in a bank, then select a local/regional savings bank, with an AA or better rating, one that does NOT engage in or offer Investment Banking... Investment banks that take depositors cash and put it into the stock market automatically put your $ at risk, since what money you have deposited there is the Bank's money, you're legally lending it to them. A local bank that lends money to local business owners or home-buyers and does NOT offer equities investment services is your best bet..."[2019]

Either way, it would be prudent to hang on to some cash in case of an emergency. "[H]aving an emergency supply of cash

---

[2016] "Banks Quotes." *Good Reads*, www.goodreads.com/quotes/tag/banks.

[2017] "US Cash Crisis: Withdrawal Limits Spark Bank Run Fear." *Bitcoin.com*, 19 Mar. 2020, news.bitcoin.com/us-cash-crisis-withdrawal-limits-bank-run-fear/?fbclid=IwAR2BDF-W6lH4JqYuNm27x0PXTxDltJAwsY0btbf1pD03HE55KSV4tZOJVds.

[2018] *Id.*

[2019] Beck, Glenn. "Preparedness guide to the Marxist revolution." *Glennbeck.com*, 16 Jun. 2020, www.glennbeck.com/glenn-beck/preparedness-guide-for-the-american-collapse-reset.

should be at the top of our checklist to prepare for a financial crisis."[2020] "Cash is something everyone looks for during times of economic hardship…"[2021] "This is money you save away for financial disasters like medical emergencies, auto or home repairs. If you're ever in a situation where you lose your income or you run into a huge financial emergency, it's nice to have a safety net that you can fall back on… Calculate three to six months of expenses… This includes things like rent, mortgage payments, car payments, utilities, and groceries."[2022] Unfortunately, there is a growing trend to ban cash transactions.[2023]

Historically, the big "banking families…interests were almost exclusively in bonds and very rarely in goods, since they admired 'liquidity' and regarded commitments in commodities or even real estate as the first step toward bankruptcy…"[2024] However, nowadays, "[b]ubbly bonds and cash held for the long run (instead of as 'ammo') are bad places to be — unless the plan is to utilize the cash as dry powder to acquire income-producing assets when prices

[2020] Bailey, James. "How to Withdraw Cash from the Bank Without Getting Arrested." *Z3 News*, 6 May 2015, z3news.com/w/how-to-withdraw-cash-from-the-bank-without-getting-arrested/.

[2021] "US Cash Crisis: Withdrawal Limits Spark Bank Run Fear." *Bitcoin.com*, 19 Mar. 2020, news.bitcoin.com/us-cash-crisis-withdrawal-limits-bank-run-fear/?fbclid=IwAR2BDF-W6lH4JqYuNm27x0PXTxDltJAwsY0btbf1pD03HE55KSV4tZOJVds.

[2022] "Inverted Yield Curve: what is it and how does it predict disaster?" *I Will Teach You*, 10 Jun. 2019, www.iwillteachyoutoberich.com/blog/inverted-yield-curve/.

[2023] Dirkmaat, Olav. "Do Not Worry about Gold Confiscation." *Gold Republic*, 16 Jun. 2015, www.goldrepublic.com/news/gold-confiscation.

[2024] "History of Banking and Money Key Excerpts From Carroll Quigley's Tragedy and Hope." *Wanttoknow.info*, www.wanttoknow.info/articles/quigley_carroll.tragedy_hope_banking_money_history.

fall."[2025] "A down market (stock, bond, real estate) can actually be the best time to buy…"[2026]

"Cash loses value over time, after inflation, but it has no price volatility. So when (not if) there are stock market crashes…that's when it comes into play. It can be deployed quickly to pick up bargains as and when they arise. It's 'ammo' that can be fired off when there are juicy targets in the sights. And with stocks so expensive in many markets, it's also ballast that keeps your overall ship steady. The price of your stock positions could fall in the short run, but your overall portfolio will be insulated with a large allocation to cash…"[2027] "Markets fall sharply, but can also rebound quickly. No one knows when that comes and you don't want to be sitting on the sidelines when that happens."[2028]

Unfortunately, CFR members such as George Bush, Ben Bernanke, Barack Obama, Tim Geithner, Bill Clinton, David Rockefeller, and Dick Cheney "are pushing for the devaluation of the US Dollar."[2029] On May 21, 2009, the Macedonian International News Agency reported that "[a] new Kremlin report on

[2025] Marstrand, Bob. "Lies, damned lies and CPI." *Of Wealth,* 11 Oct. 2016, www.ofwealth.com/lies-damned-lies-cpi/.

[2026] Kiyosaki, Kim. "The (Many) Pros and (Few) Cons of Real Estate Investing." *RichDad.com*, 6 Jun. 2019, www.richdad.com/pros-and-cons-of-real-estate.

[2027] Marstrand, Rob. "Where should you put your money?" *Of Wealth*, 29 Sept. 2016, www.ofwealth.com/where-should-you-put-your-money/#.V_0bXJMrK9Y.

[2028] Thorbecke, Catherine. "Dow sinks more than 2,000 points amid coronavirus uncertainty and plunging oil prices." *ABC News*, 9 Mar. 2020, abcnews.go.com/Business/dow-futures-plummet-1200-points/story?id=69481843&fbclid=IwAR0mvtFGb1J1E06BIMhbhOA_y8i5NQS47Xd5SFeiollmJgKJwgIw7oiynRs.

[2029] Levis, Nick. "New World Disorder: Why Geithner's IMF SDR Plan For A Global Currency Looks a Bit Like High Treason." *Business Insider*, Business Insider, 20 Jul. 2011, www.businessinsider.com/new-world-disorder-why-geithners-imf-sdr-plan-for-a-global-currency-is-high-treason-2011-7.

the shadowy Bilderberg Group...states that the West's financial, political and corporate elite emerged from their conclave after coming to an agreement that, in order to continue their drive towards a New World Order dominated by the Western Powers, the US Dollar has to be 'totally' destroyed."[2030]   "Further, this same unconfirmed Kremlin report, stated that, 'most of the West's wealthiest elite convened at an unprecedented secret meeting in New York called for and led by' David Rockefeller, 'to plot the demise of the US Dollar.'"[2031]   George Soros argued that "the American government...should not resist the decline of the dollar, nor the decrease in living standards and the introduction of global currency...He added that the orderly decline of the dollar was 'desirable,' as it would allow the entire system to be reconstituted toward global currency..."[2032]

Lynette Zang, chief market analyst at ITM Trading, said, "I don't have any confidence in these central banks, and I certainly don't have any confidence in the fiat money. When I get it, I convert it into gold, into silver, into water, into food, into energy, into security, into whatever is bringing me more value..."[2033] "As we saw in Germany during hyperinflation, any real commodity will

---

[2030] Marshall, Andrew Gavin. "The Bilderberg Plan for 2009: Remaking the Global Political Economy." *Global Research,* 26 May 2009, www.globalresearch.ca/the-bilderberg-plan-for-2009-remaking-the-global-political-economy/13738.

[2031] *Id.*

[2032] Clabough, Raven. "George Soros Touts China as Leader of New World Order." *The New American,* 17 Nov. 2010, www.thenewamerican.com/world-news/north-america/item/10605-george-soros-touts-china-as-leader-of-new-world-order?fbclid=IwAR0lckBm-INZafvOcqeuUC9acGuyvLeoKR8otZP6073BqbLv3GyP5IieH3U#..

[2033] At 31. ITM Trading, Inc. "And Central Banks Using Up Their Ammo." *Youtube,* 18 Dec. 2018, www.youtube.com/watch?v=NvWm6Qkp5gU.

have value while almost all paper assets will evaporate."[2034]   "In Germany, farmers suffered the least because everyone including doctors and dentists were willing to accept eggs or butter in payment. Other items that might be useful (and valuable) would be gasoline, oil (motor or heating), propane, guns and ammunition for hunting, and even spare car parts."[2035]   "[C]opper and brass were also valuable."[2036]   During the period of hyperinflation in Zimbabwe, "eggs, butter, milk and cooking oil were all prized commodities.[2037] Thus, "in addition to precious metals...you should also stockpile useful commodities, such as canned food, grains and a grain mill, cooking oil, powdered or canned milk, etc. If you live outside a city and can produce your own food you will be that much better off during a hyperinflation."[2038]

Economist Antony C. Sutton said, "Those entrapped by the herd instinct are drowned in the deluges of history. But there are always the few who observe, reason, and take precautions, and thus escape the flood. For these few, gold has been the asset of last resort."[2039]   According to Peter Schiff, "Treasury bonds are not a safe haven. The Fed will own all the Treasury bonds, as well as most other U.S. dollar-denominated debt. The problem is that the tens of trillions of dollars the Fed will print to buy all those bonds will be

---

[2034] McMahon, Tim. "Surviving a Hyperinflation." *Financial Trend Forecaster*, 18 Jul. 2013, fintrend.com/2013/07/18/surviving-hyperinflation/.

[2035] *Id.*

[2036] *Id.*

[2037] *Id.*

[2038] *Id.*

[2039] "The 101 Best Gold Quotes From History – GoldSilver." *Gold Silver*, goldsilver.com/blog/101-best-gold-quotes-all-time/.

practically worthless. #Gold is the safe haven."[2040] "'In such an economic environment, with high inflationary expectations, gold looks set to shine,' Bitmex wrote."[2041]

The following sections will discuss the individual asset classes in more depth, starting with the yellow metal.

[2040] Schiffgold. "Peter Schiff: This Is Where the Problem Really Starts." *Schiffgold*, 25 Mar. 2020, schiffgold.com/peters-podcast/peter-schiff-this-is-where-the-problem-really-starts/?fbclid=IwAR3cIy0GtM1gWUF89rq33pe3iYdQWUjinWGge4H6GnhZhz8BIdOO7sC5y2I.

[2041] "US Cash Crisis: Withdrawal Limits Spark Bank Run Fear." *Bitcoin.com*, 19 Mar. 2020, news.bitcoin.com/us-cash-crisis-withdrawal-limits-bank-run-fear/?fbclid=IwAR2BDF-W6lH4JqYuNm27x0PXTxDltJAwsY0btbf1pD03HE55KSV4tZOJVds.

Gold

According to real estate tycoon, Robert Kiyosaki, "Commodities such as gold and silver have a world market that transcends national borders, politics, religions and race. A person may not like someone else's religion, but he'll accept his gold."[2042] "Gold is valuable everywhere in the world and is not dependent on political systems, any specific government policy or set of policies," per Roy Sebag.[2043] Ultimately, "[g]old and economic freedom are inseparable."[2044]

The yellow metal has long been valued for its unique properties, such as the fact that it does not corrode and can be melted over a flame, which makes it easy to work with.[2045] Gerald M. Loeb, a founding partner of E.F. Hutton & Co., opined, "The desire for gold is the most universal and deeply rooted commercial instinct of the human race."[2046] "People have been digging up and refining precious metals for more than 6,000 years. "[2047]

[2042] "The 101 Best Gold Quotes From History – GoldSilver." *Gold Silver*, goldsilver.com/blog/101-best-gold-quotes-all-time/.

[2043] *Id.*

[2044] Greenspan, Alan. "Gold and Economic Freedom." *Constitution Society*, www.constitution.org/mon/greenspan_gold.htm. Rep. Howard Buffett noted, "When you recall that one of the first moves by Lenin, Mussolini and Hitler was to outlaw individual ownership of gold, you begin to sense that there may be some connection between money, redeemable in gold, and the rare prize known as human liberty." "Money Quotes: What The Experts Say About Money." *Midas Gold Group*, 27 Aug. 2020, www.midasgoldgroup.com/money-quotes/.

[2045] Daltorio, Tony. "8 Reasons To Own Gold." *Investopedia*, 22 June 2019, www.investopedia.com/articles/basics/08/reasons-to-own-gold.asp.

[2046] "The 101 Best Gold Quotes From History – GoldSilver." *Gold Silver*, goldsilver.com/blog/101-best-gold-quotes-all-time/.

[2047] Becker, Sam. "Everything you need to know about investing in gold and precious metals." *Grow*, 13 Dec. 2019, grow.acorns.com/what-you-need-to-know-about-investing-in-gold-and-precious-metals/.

Gold was the first form of money, and was used to facilitate trade and store wealth.[2048] "In ancient times, gold's malleability and luster led to its use in jewelry and early coins."[2049] "Coins containing gold appeared around 800 B.C., and the first pure gold coins were struck during the reign of King Croesus of Lydia about 300 years later."[2050]

Gold is mined from the Earth, and is often found along with other metals, such as silver and copper.[2051] Thus, it is frequently a by-product of other mining operations.[2052]

The World Gold Council estimates that there are about 190,000 metric tons of gold above ground today and roughly 54,000 metric tons of gold that could still be mined using current technology.[2053] "Much of the supply of gold in the market since the 1990s has come from sales of gold bullion from the vaults of global central banks."[2054] However, this "selling by global central banks slowed greatly in 2008" when the financial crisis hit.[2055]

[2048] Brewer, Reuben Gregg. "The Beginner's Guide to Investing in Gold." *The Motley Fool*, 4 Sept. 2019, www.fool.com/investing/the-beginners-guide-to-investing-in-gold.aspx.

[2049] *Id.*

[2050] Daltorio, Tony. "8 Reasons To Own Gold." *Investopedia*, 22 June 2019, www.investopedia.com/articles/basics/08/reasons-to-own-gold.asp.

[2051] Brewer, Reuben Gregg. "The Beginner's Guide to Investing in Gold." *The Motley Fool*, 4 Sept. 2019, www.fool.com/investing/the-beginners-guide-to-investing-in-gold.aspx.

[2052] *Id.*

[2053] *Id.*

[2054] Daltorio, Tony. "8 Reasons To Own Gold." *Investopedia*, 22 Jun. 2019, www.investopedia.com/articles/basics/08/reasons-to-own-gold.asp.

[2055] *Id.*

The largest demand for gold is jewelry, which accounts for around 50% and remains fairly constant.[2056] "India is one of the largest gold-consuming nations in the world; it has many uses there, including jewelry. As such, the Indian wedding season in October is traditionally the time of the year that sees the highest global demand for gold…"[2057]

About 10% of demand for gold comes from people who see it as a finite resource with many industrial uses.[2058] Because gold is a good conductor of electricity, it is used to manufacture dentistry tools, heat shields, and technological gadgets.[2059]

The rest of demand (about 40%) "comes from direct physical investment in gold, including that used to create coins, bullion, medals, and gold bars."[2060] Investors, including individuals, central banks, and exchange-traded funds (ETFs), buy gold for three

---

[2056] "Bullion is a gold bar or coin stamped with the amount of gold it contains and the gold's purity. It is different than numismatic coins, collectibles that trade based on demand for the specific type of coin rather than its gold content." Brewer, Reuben Gregg. "The Beginner's Guide to Investing in Gold." *The Motley Fool*, 4 Sept. 2019, www.fool.com/investing/the-beginners-guide-to-investing-in-gold.aspx.

[2057] Daltorio, Tony. "8 Reasons To Own Gold." *Investopedia*, 22 June 2019, www.investopedia.com/articles/basics/08/reasons-to-own-gold.asp.

[2058] Amadeo, Kimberly. "Three Reasons to Invest in Gold According to Research." *The Balance*, 10 Jul. 2019, www.thebalance.com/why-invest-in-gold-3305651.

[2059] Brewer, Reuben Gregg. "The Beginner's Guide to Investing in Gold." *The Motley Fool*, 4 Sept. 2019, www.fool.com/investing/the-beginners-guide-to-investing-in-gold.aspx.

[2060] "Bullion is a gold bar or coin stamped with the amount of gold it contains and the gold's purity. It is different than numismatic coins, collectibles that trade based on demand for the specific type of coin rather than its gold content." *Id.*

reasons: As a hedge, as a safe haven, and as a direct investment.[2061] "Gold, silver, and other precious metals are, in many respects, the original investment."[2062] "Throughout the centuries, people have continued to hold gold for various reasons...It is the metal we fall back on when other forms of currency don't work, which means it always has some value as insurance against tough times."[2063]

Gold "creates a feeling of safety as a source of money that will always have value, no matter what."[2064] Because it is physical, and thus, can be stored at home, it cannot be hacked or deleted, and carries no counter-party risk, i.e. no risk that another party could default on their obligation, such as a bond-issuer failing to pay a bond-holder.[2065] The yellow metal is also considered to be a good way to pass on wealth to the next generation.[2066] "In China, where

---

[2061] Amadeo, Kimberly. "Three Reasons to Invest in Gold According to Research." *The Balance*, 10 Jul. 2019, www.thebalance.com/why-invest-in-gold-3305651. "For example, the SPDR Gold Trust, became one of the largest ETFs in the U.S., as well as one of the world's largest holders of gold bullion in 2008." Daltorio, Tony. "8 Reasons To Own Gold." *Investopedia*, 22 Jun. 2019, www.investopedia.com/articles/basics/08/reasons-to-own-gold.asp.

[2062] Becker, Sam. "Everything you need to know about investing in gold and precious metals." *Grow*, 13 Dec. 2019, grow.acorns.com/what-you-need-to-know-about-investing-in-gold-and-precious-metals/.

[2063] Daltorio, Tony. "8 Reasons To Own Gold." *Investopedia*, 22 June 2019, www.investopedia.com/articles/basics/08/reasons-to-own-gold.asp.

[2064] Amadeo, Kimberly. "Three Reasons to Invest in Gold According to Research." *The Balance*, 10 Jul. 2019, www.thebalance.com/why-invest-in-gold-3305651.

[2065] Becker, Sam. "Everything you need to know about investing in gold and precious metals." *Grow*, 13 Dec. 2019, grow.acorns.com/what-you-need-to-know-about-investing-in-gold-and-precious-metals/. "Why invest in gold?" *World Gold Council,* www.gold.org/what-we-do/investing-gold/why-invest-gold.

[2066] Daltorio, Tony. "8 Reasons To Own Gold." *Investopedia*, 22 June 2019, www.investopedia.com/articles/basics/08/reasons-to-own-gold.asp.

gold bars are a traditional form of saving, the demand for gold has been steadfast."[2067]

Unlike paper currency or some other "assets, gold has maintained its value throughout the ages," and is a good store of value.[2068] "Over time, fiat currencies — including the US dollar — tend to fall in value against gold."[2069] Alan Greenspan said, "Gold, unlike all other commodities, is a currency...and the major thrust in the demand for gold is not for jewelry. It's not for anything other than an escape from what is perceived to be a fiat money system, paper money, that seems to be deteriorating."[2070] "'Gold gives you a good perspective on things because in reality, long term, it's not the price of gold that goes up,' [Peter] Schiff said. 'The price of gold remains constant. It's the price of everything else that goes up... People like to say 200 years ago, 250 years ago, a man could buy a nice suit for an ounce of gold,...And that's the case today.'"[2071] For this reason, the yellow metal can serve as a hedge against inflation, deflation, and currency risk.[2072]

An example of gold maintaining its purchasing power is illustrated by the price of tuition at Yale University (in New Haven, Connecticut), which has remained the same over the years when

---

[2067] *Id.*

[2068] *Id.*

[2069] "Why invest in gold?" *World Gold Council,* www.gold.org/what-we-do/investing-gold/why-invest-gold.

[2070] Newman, Alex. "Greenspan: Gold is a Currency, Euro 'Breaking Down.'" *The New American,* 25 Aug. 2011, thenewamerican.com/greenspan-gold-is-a-currency-euro-breaking-down/.

[2071] Garber, Jonathan. "Coronavirus hyperinflation risk looms, buy gold: Peter Schiff." *Yahoo Finance,* 25 Mar. 2020, finance.yahoo.com/news/coronavirus-hyperinflation-looms-buy-gold-124257282.html.

[2072] "Why invest in gold?" *World Gold Council,* www.gold.org/what-we-do/investing-gold/why-invest-gold. Daltorio, Tony. "8 Reasons To Own Gold." *Investopedia,* 22 June 2019, www.investopedia.com/articles/basics/08/reasons-to-own-gold.asp.

priced in gold. "In 1932, the cost was $1,056 for a year. In 2015, the cost was $62,200. Yet the true cost, measured in gold, was the same: around 1,600 grams — about average for the 115 year period."[2073]

The cost of other commodities has also remained stable when priced in gold. Copper was "about the same price [in gold] in 2010 as in 1936. But because of the ongoing destruction of the US Dollar, it took 35 times as many dollars in 2010 to buy a pound of copper as it did in 1936!"[2074] Crude oil at two grams of gold "was about the same in 2010 as it was in the early 1950s; but if you measure the price in US dollars, you would get the impression that it was about 30 times more expensive."[2075]

Gold is a commodity that trades based on supply and demand, which ultimately determines its spot price.[2076] "As a general rule, reduction in the supply of gold increases gold prices."[2077] Some believe that supply constraints will continue to drive the price of gold up.[2078] Although gold is plentiful in nature, it can be difficult to obtain.[2079] For example, seawater contains gold, but in

---

[2073] "College Tuition." *Priced in Gold*, pricedingold.com/college-tuition/.

[2074] "Copper." *Priced in Gold*, pricedingold.com/copper/.

[2075] "Crude Oil." *Priced in Gold*, pricedingold.com/crude-oil/.

[2076] Brewer, Reuben Gregg. "The Beginner's Guide to Investing in Gold." *The Motley Fool*, 4 Sept. 2019, www.fool.com/investing/the-beginners-guide-to-investing-in-gold.aspx.

[2077] Daltorio, Tony. "8 Reasons To Own Gold." *Investopedia*, 22 June 2019, www.investopedia.com/articles/basics/08/reasons-to-own-gold.asp.

[2078] Amadeo, Kimberly. "Three Reasons to Invest in Gold According to Research." *The Balance*, 10 Jul. 2019, www.thebalance.com/why-invest-in-gold-3305651.

[2079] Brewer, Reuben Gregg. "The Beginner's Guide to Investing in Gold." *The Motley Fool*, 4 Sept. 2019, www.fool.com/investing/the-beginners-guide-to-investing-in-gold.aspx.

such small quantities that it would not be cost effective to extract it at current prices.[2080]

Demand from investors, including central banks, tends to inversely track the economy and investor sentiment.[2081]   When investors are worried about the economy, they often buy gold, and push its price higher.[2082]   Tom Cassidy, chief investment officer at Peoples Security Bank & Trust Company, said, "The value of gold is determined by supply and demand, which is very hard to predict. Demand typically goes up based on fear and not fundamentals."[2083]

"Gold prices climbed as investors sought a stable asset to hedge their portfolios against uncertainty and risk..."[2084]   In 1997, gold was $335 an ounce.[2085]   The price nearly tripled between 1998 and 2008, reaching $1,000-an-ounce in early 2008 and nearly doubling between 2008 and 2012, hitting the $1,800-$1,900 mark.[2086]   "Prices went from $869.75 in 2008 to...$1,895 on

---

[2080] *Id.*

[2081] *Id.*

[2082] *Id.*

[2083] Divine, John. "5 Reasons Not to Invest in Gold." *US News*, 10 Jul. 2018, money.usnews.com/investing/articles/2018-07-10/5-reasons-not-to-invest-in-gold.

[2084] Narayanan, Aparna. "Gold Stocks Shine As Viral Caution Ignites Gold Prices, But For How Long?" *Investors.com*, 22 May 2020, www.investors.com/news/gold-stocks-ride-gold-prices-higher-as-coronavirus-fuels-barrick-gold-stock-kinross-kirkland-lake/?src=A00220&yptr=yahoo.

[2085] Ganz, David L. "Gold Seizure." *USA Gold*, www.usagold.com/cpmforum/gold-seizure-ganz/.

[2086] "[T]he price of gold more than doubled between 2002 and 2007, from $347.20 to $833.75 an ounce. That's because the dollar's value as measured against the euro fell 40% during that same period." Daltorio, Tony. "8 Reasons To Own Gold." *Investopedia*, 22 June 2019, www.investopedia.com/articles/basics/08/reasons-to-own-gold.asp.

September 5, 2011."[2087]   In 2019, the price was mostly between $1,250 and $1,550 per ounce.[2088]   "Gold prices have shot up to a 7-1/2-year high as investors have fled other assets more sensitive to the economy…"[2089]   "This year [2020], gold prices have shot to record highs since September 2011, as investors fled to safe havens with the [Covid] pandemic showing no signs of abating and a crashing economy."[2090]   In March 2020, gold topped $1,700 per ounce for the first time in 12 years.[2091]   Gold exceeded $2,000 per ounce (at $2,021.30) for the first time in history in August 2020.[2092] "The sustained rally in gold has come as governments across the world have flooded their economies with financial aid to combat the

---

[2087] Amadeo, Kimberly. "Three Reasons to Invest in Gold According to Research." *The Balance*, 10 Jul. 2019, www.thebalance.com/why-invest-in-gold-3305651.

[2088] Becker, Sam. "Everything you need to know about investing in gold and precious metals." *Grow*, 13 Dec. 2019, grow.acorns.com/what-you-need-to-know-about-investing-in-gold-and-precious-metals/.

[2089] Narayanan, Aparna. "Gold Stocks Shine As Viral Caution Ignites Gold Prices, But For How Long?" *Investors.com,* 22 May 2020, www.investors.com/news/gold-stocks-ride-gold-prices-higher-as-coronavirus-fuels-barrick-gold-stock-kinross-kirkland-lake/?src=A00220&yptr=yahoo.

[2090] Tan, Weizhen. "Gold just hit a fresh record high — but some say silver is set to overtake." *CNBC*, 4 Aug. 2020, www.cnbc.com/2020/08/05/investing-in-precious-metals-silver-prices-set-to-outperform-gold-prices.html.

[2091] Authers, John. "A Shift in the Global Financial Order Is Upon Us." *Bloomberg Opinion*, 8 Mar. 2020, www.bloomberg.com/opinion/articles/2020-03-09/crash-in-oil-prices-bond-yields-marks-shift-in-global-order.

[2092] Tan, Weizhen. "Gold just hit a fresh record high — but some say silver is set to overtake." *CNBC*, 4 Aug. 2020, www.cnbc.com/2020/08/05/investing-in-precious-metals-silver-prices-set-to-outperform-gold-prices.html.

COVID-19 pandemic..."[2093] "Gold's 13.5% return so far this year has made it one of the best-performing asset classes, rivaling U.S. Treasurys and easily outperforming stocks in general."[2094]

"Russ Koesterich, portfolio manager for BlackRock's Global Allocation Fund, said that he sees three factors supporting gold going forward. 'With both nominal and real, i.e. inflation adjusted interest rates in free fall, gold is well positioned to do what it is intended to do: 'help insulate a portfolio...' A weakening U.S. dollar, falling global economic growth expectations and falling bond yields will help to push gold prices higher...'"[2095]

"A combination of disrupted supply chains, less travel and dented confidence [due to Covid-19] represents a threat, potentially a serious threat, to economic growth."[2096] "To the extent the coronavirus represents a threat to growth, gold should be a particularly effective hedge," Koesterich said.[2097] "Under these circumstances, investors may want to consider holding gold."[2098]

[2093] DeCambre, Mark. "Gold ends above $2,000 for the first time in history as U.S. dollar and bond yields recede." *MarketWatch*, 4 Aug. 2020, www.marketwatch.com/story/gold-prices-edge-higher-but-march-to-2000-hamstrung-by-rising-dollar-2020-08-04? reflink=mw_share_facebook&fbclid=IwAR3kMJFKUkS_YYs3VgKWB_ExX56L1jyb8PIKshDarrWLsNmmQREHPp3sYac.

[2094] Narayanan, Aparna. "Gold Stocks Shine As Viral Caution Ignites Gold Prices, But For How Long?" *Investors.com*, 22 May 2020, www.investors.com/news/gold-stocks-ride-gold-prices-higher-as-coronavirus-fuels-barrick-gold-stock-kinross-kirkland-lake/? src=A00220&yptr=yahoo.

[2095] Christensen, Niels. "Three factors supporting the gold price - Blackrock." *Kitco*, 13 Mar. 2020, www.kitco.com/news/2020-03-13/ Three-factors-supporting-gold-price-Blackrock.html.

[2096] *Id.*

[2097] *Id.*

[2098] *Id.*

"Interest rates historically are a major factor affecting gold prices."[2099] "Generally, there is some advantage to holding Treasuries in the fact that you get interest."[2100] "Typically, when rates rise, gold prices suffer. This is because gold doesn't pay interest or dividends and interest-bearing investments are more attractive."[2101] "But that's not the case right now. In fact, on short-term Treasuries, the yield is negative."[2102] On March 12, 2020, "as U.S. equity markets saw the biggest decline since the 1987 crash, the yield on 10-year U.S. Treasuries fell to its lowest point in history at 39 basis points...Koesterich noted that real interest rates, which include inflation, are negative 45 basis points. 'During the past decade, changes in real interest rates have explained more than 30% of the change in the price of gold. As a rough rule of thumb, every 0.10% drop in real rates coincides with about a 1.25% increase in gold.'"[2103] Thus, lower bond yields support gold prices.[2104] "The

---

[2099] CME Group. "What Can We Learn From Gold's Relationship To Other Assets?" *Yahoo Finance*, 21 May 2020, finance.yahoo.com/news/learn-golds-relationship-other-assets-152521709.html.

[2100] Schiffgold. "Peter Schiff: This Is Where the Problem Really Starts." *Schiffgold*, 25 Mar. 2020, schiffgold.com/peters-podcast/peter-schiff-this-i s - w h e r e - t h e - p r o b l e m - r e a l l y - s t a r t s / ? fbclid=IwAR3cIy0GtM1gWUF89rq33pe3iYdQWUjinWGge4H6GnhZhz8 BIdOO7sC5y2I.

[2101] CME Group. "What Can We Learn From Gold's Relationship To Other Assets?" *Yahoo Finance*, 21 May 2020, finance.yahoo.com/news/learn-golds-relationship-other-assets-152521709.html.

[2102] Schiffgold. "Peter Schiff: This Is Where the Problem Really Starts." *Schiffgold*, 25 Mar. 2020, schiffgold.com/peters-podcast/peter-schiff-this-i s - w h e r e - t h e - p r o b l e m - r e a l l y - s t a r t s / ? fbclid=IwAR3cIy0GtM1gWUF89rq33pe3iYdQWUjinWGge4H6GnhZhz8 BIdOO7sC5y2I.

[2103] Christensen, Niels. "Three factors supporting the gold price - Blackrock." *Kitco*, 13 Mar. 2020, www.kitco.com/news/2020-03-13/ Three-factors-supporting-gold-price-Blackrock.html.

[2104] *Id.*

fall in global interest rates over the last few years, including U.S. 10-year rates near historic lows, has also helped propel gold higher…"[2105]

"[C]hanges in the price of the U.S. dollar can dramatically affect the value of gold since gold is denominated in dollars. Typically, a strong U.S. dollar is negative for gold prices since it makes gold more expensive for investors and governments of other countries to purchase gold using their own currencies. If the U.S. dollar weakens, gold becomes less expensive for purchasers using foreign currencies and can push prices higher…"[2106] "Following a market downturn, an excess supply of capital is likely to flood the markets and drive up inflation, both of which would be bullish for gold," according to Peter Schiff.[2107] "The Federal Reserve has all but rubber stamped an extremely accommodative interest rate environment and has signaled that even solid growth will not lead to interest-rate hikes" in the near future.[2108]

Gold can protect against inflation because it is a store of value and maintains purchasing power.[2109] Along with stocks, it is the best inflation hedge for an investment portfolio.[2110] "Gold prices and the greenback have an inverse relationship. As the U.S.

[2105] CME Group. "What Can We Learn From Gold's Relationship To Other Assets?" *Yahoo Finance*, 21 May 2020, finance.yahoo.com/news/learn-golds-relationship-other-assets-152521709.html.

[2106] *Id.*

[2107] "Coronavirus to pop bubble greater than 2008; gold prices have 'nowhere to go but up.'" *Kitco News*, 12 Mar. 2020, www.kitco.com/news/2020-03-12/Coronavirus-to-pop-bubble-greater-than-2008-gold-prices-have-nowhere-to-go-but-up.html.

[2108] CME Group. "What Can We Learn From Gold's Relationship To Other Assets?" *Yahoo Finance*, 21 May 2020, finance.yahoo.com/news/learn-golds-relationship-other-assets-152521709.html.

[2109] Marstrand, Bob. "Lies, damned lies and CPI." *Of Wealth*, 11 Oct. 2016, www.ofwealth.com/lies-damned-lies-cpi/.

[2110] *Id.*

dollar has been falling against other currencies, the precious metal will become cheaper in other currencies, in turn spurring demand for gold and causing prices to go up."[2111] The price of gold (and silver) "soar[s] in the midst of a faltering global economy and a weakening U.S. dollar."[2112] "[W]hen fiat currency loses its purchasing power to inflation, gold tends to be priced in those currency units and thus tends to rise along with everything else."[2113] Indeed, "the gold price has comfortably beaten official inflation over the past 40 years…"[2114]

When the value of the dollar falls, this often prompts people to flock to the security of gold.[2115] "Many investors buy gold to hedge against the decline of a currency."[2116] ("Hedges are investments that offset losses in another asset class."[2117]) Thus, people may buy gold if they believe that their local currency is losing value, which raises gold prices.[2118] Koesterich said, "'While

[2111] Tan, Weizhen. "Gold just hit a fresh record high — but some say silver is set to overtake." *CNBC*, 4 Aug. 2020, www.cnbc.com/2020/08/05/investing-in-precious-metals-silver-prices-set-to-outperform-gold-prices.html.

[2112] *Id.*

[2113] Daltorio, Tony. "8 Reasons To Own Gold." *Investopedia*, 22 June 2019, www.investopedia.com/articles/basics/08/reasons-to-own-gold.asp.

[2114] Marstrand, Bob. "Lies, damned lies and CPI." *Of Wealth,* 11 Oct. 2016, www.ofwealth.com/lies-damned-lies-cpi/.

[2115] Daltorio, Tony. "8 Reasons To Own Gold." *Investopedia*, 22 June 2019, www.investopedia.com/articles/basics/08/reasons-to-own-gold.asp.

[2116] Amadeo, Kimberly. "Three Reasons to Invest in Gold According to Research." *The Balance*, 10 Jul. 2019, www.thebalance.com/why-invest-in-gold-3305651.

[2117] *Id.*

[2118] Daltorio, Tony. "8 Reasons To Own Gold." *Investopedia*, 22 June 2019, www.investopedia.com/articles/basics/08/reasons-to-own-gold.asp.

gold can do well even when the dollar is rallying, historically, its outperformance is strongest when the dollar is down."[2119]

Ned Naylor-Leyland, precious metals fund manager at Jupiter Asset Management, "pointed to factors 'tipping investors over the edge in their distrust of fiat currencies — especially the US dollar.' That includes monetary easing and the spike in government spending on managing the coronavirus outbreak…"[2120] "Looking at currency markets, Koesterich said that the U.S. dollar is down about 3% from its nearly three-year peak hit [in August 2020]."[2121]

"Gold giant Newmont expects prices to top $2,000 an ounce, thanks to massive global stimulus…"[2122] "Analysts at BofA [Bank of America] Global Research [Michael Widmer and Francisco Blanch] forecast that bullion will surge by 50% over the next 18 months to around $3,000 an ounce and see other precious metals benefiting in the COVID-19 environment."[2123] Peter "Schiff's

---

[2119] Christensen, Niels. "Three factors supporting the gold price - Blackrock." *Kitco*, 13 Mar. 2020, www.kitco.com/news/2020-03-13/Three-factors-supporting-gold-price-Blackrock.html.

[2120] Tan, Weizhen. "Gold just hit a fresh record high — but some say silver is set to overtake." *CNBC*, 4 Aug. 2020, www.cnbc.com/2020/08/05/investing-in-precious-metals-silver-prices-set-to-outperform-gold-prices.html.

[2121] Christensen, Niels. "Three factors supporting the gold price - Blackrock." *Kitco*, 13 Mar. 2020, www.kitco.com/news/2020-03-13/Three-factors-supporting-gold-price-Blackrock.html.

[2122] Narayanan, Aparna. "Gold Stocks Shine As Viral Caution Ignites Gold Prices, But For How Long?" *Investors.com,* 22 May 2020, www.investors.com/news/gold-stocks-ride-gold-prices-higher-as-coronavirus-fuels-barrick-gold-stock-kinross-kirkland-lake/?src=A00220&yptr=yahoo.

[2123] DeCambre, Mark. "Gold ends above $2,000 for the first time in history as U.S. dollar and bond yields recede." *MarketWatch*, 4 Aug. 2020, www.marketwatch.com/story/gold-prices-edge-higher-but-march-to-2000-hamstrung-by-rising-dollar-2020-08-04?reflink=mw_share_facebook&fbclid=IwAR3kMJFKUkS_YYs3VgKWB_ExX56L1jyb8PIKshDarrWLsNmmQREHPp3sYac.

minimum projection for the price of gold is $5,000 to $10,000 an ounce…"[2124]

When central banks start dumping dollars, they are going to buy gold.[2125] "[T]hey know the dollars are going to lose value because the Fed is going to flood the world with them. They just basically committed to doing that. They went all-in on QE and it's QE forever. They'll buy anything in any amount – unlimited amounts. And so, this is like OK, you got to get out. This is a giant sell signal," Peter Schiff wrote.[2126]

"In a note sent to clients on [March 24, 2020], Jeffrey Currie, global head of commodities, said it's 'time to buy the currency of last resort,' arguing that the world's shortage of dollars — which has buoyed the greenback's value — will come to an end under the Fed's 'open-ended' asset purchases. The situation resembles 2008, he said, when gold — a perceived safe-haven — fell 20 percent due to 'dollar strength and a run on cash' before the Fed's $600 billion quantitative easing program curbed the greenback's value and made gold more attractive."[2127]

The extreme measures taken by the U.S. government and the Federal Reserve to combat the COVID-19 pandemic, such as the $2 trillion relief package and the Fed's plan to "buy unlimited amounts of assets to support market functions and the economy" and cutting interest rates to almost zero, could drive "the U.S. into an

---

[2124] Garber, Jonathan. "Coronavirus hyperinflation risk looms, buy gold: Peter Schiff." *Yahoo Finance*, 25 Mar. 2020, finance.yahoo.com/news/coronavirus-hyperinflation-looms-buy-gold-124257282.html.

[2125] Schiffgold. "Peter Schiff: This Is Where the Problem Really Starts." *Schiffgold*, 25 Mar. 2020, schiffgold.com/peters-podcast/peter-schiff-this-is-where-the-problem-really-starts/?fbclid=IwAR3cIy0GtM1gWUF89rq33pe3iYdQWUjinWGge4H6GnhZhz8BIdOO7sC5y2I.

[2126] *Id.*

[2127] Garber, Jonathan. "Coronavirus hyperinflation risk looms, buy gold: Peter Schiff." *Yahoo Finance*, 25 Mar. 2020, finance.yahoo.com/news/coronavirus-hyperinflation-looms-buy-gold-124257282.html.

episode of hyperinflation and boost gold, according to Peter Schiff."[2128]

The first line of defense against hyperinflation is precious metals, especially gold.[2129] "[D]uring a hyperinflation, all commodity prices should increase relatively equally so whatever you could buy with 1 ounce today you could probably buy then..."[2130] "So if you had an ounce of gold and went to the grocery store, you would have to buy a lot of groceries or accept your change in rapidly depreciating paper putting you back in a bad situation. You might be thinking, ahhh but by then maybe bread will cost $2,000 a loaf. Yes, but in that case, since all commodities rise in a hyperinflation, an ounce of gold would probably be worth $2,000,000..."[2131] "[A]s the dollar goes to zero, the dollar-denominated value of gold heads toward infinity."[2132] "So, the key with one ounce gold bars or coins is to only use it for large purchases such as a house or car. For smaller purchases, you should have gold in smaller quantities such as 1/4 ounce or even 1/10th ounce."[2133] "[I]f there is no bread, milk, butter or cooking oil available you can't eat your gold. So in very extreme cases,

---

[2128] *Id.*

[2129] McMahon, Tim. "Surviving a Hyperinflation." *Financial Trend Forecaster*, 18 Jul. 2013, fintrend.com/2013/07/18/surviving-hyperinflation/.

[2130] *Id.*

[2131] *Id.*

[2132] Adams, Mike. "Analysis: Bitcoin could go to $100,000 as the fiat currency dollar collapses, but the 'value' won't be the fortune you're imagining." *Natural News*, 17 May 2020, www.naturalnews.com/2020-05-17-analysis-bitcoin-could-go-to-100000-as-fiat-currency-dollar-collapses.html.

[2133] McMahon, Tim. "Surviving a Hyperinflation." *Financial Trend Forecaster*, 18 Jul. 2013, fintrend.com/2013/07/18/surviving-hyperinflation/.

starving people might be willing to exchange an ounce of gold for a loaf of bread!"[2134]

"[W]hile hyperinflation wiped out most people's savings [in the Weimar Republic], turning wealthy citizens into poor ones literally overnight, those who had assets denominated in gold experienced no loss in purchasing power. In fact, their ability to purchase goods and services grew beyond the runaway prices they saw all around them."[2135] This is because the price of gold increased 1.8 times faster than the inflation during this five-year period.[2136] In January 1919, one ounce of gold traded for 170 *Reichsmarks*, but by November 1923, that same ounce was worth 87 trillion *Reichsmarks*.[2137]   During the Weimar hyperinflation, an entire city block of prime real estate in downtown Berlin was purchased for one ounce of gold.[2138]

"So, if you suspect hyperinflation on the horizon, you could take out a loan and buy 'real assets' almost any commodity would do, houses, gold, oil, whatever. Then at the peak of the hyperinflation when things are at their craziest, you sell a small portion and pay off all your loans..."[2139] Bear in mind, however,

[2134] *Id.*

[2135] Clark, Jeff. "How Does Gold Fare During Hyperinflation?" *InflationData.com*, 25 Jun. 2012, inflationdata.com/articles/2012/06/25/gold-hyperinflation/.

[2136] *Id.*

[2137] Mikhan, Alena and Jeff Clark. "Does Gold Keep Up In Hyperinflation?" *Casey Research*, 18 Jun. 2012, www.caseyresearch.com/does-gold-keep-hyperinflation/; Clark, Jeff. "How Does Gold Fare During Hyperinflation?" *InflationData.com*, 25 Jun. 2012, inflationdata.com/articles/2012/06/25/gold-hyperinflation/.

[2138] Durden, Tyler. "This Is What Happens To Gold In A Hyperinflationary Currency Crisis: Ukraine Edition." *Zero Hedge*, 25 Feb. 2012, archive.is/aiYLX.

[2139] McMahon, Tim. "Surviving a Hyperinflation." *Financial Trend Forecaster*, 18 Jul. 2013, fintrend.com/2013/07/18/surviving-hyperinflation/.

that "[d]uring times of hyperinflation it is unlikely you will find a loan. Because the loan industry will probably disappear. Who will loan you $100 today if in two weeks when you pay it back they couldn't buy a bar of soap? And even if they were to charge you an exorbitant amount of interest how would they know how much to charge? 100%, 1000% 1,000,000%? The problem with hyperinflation is the uncertainty. During hyperinflation if you already have a loan it is like a windfall. You can take your lunch money and pay off your house but obviously no one in their right mind is going to loan you any more money."[2140]

In addition to inflation, the yellow metal is also a way to combat against deflation, which is a period in which prices decrease, when business activity slows, and the economy is burdened by excessive debt.[2141] For example, during the Great "Depression, the relative purchasing power of gold soared while other prices dropped sharply. This is because people chose to hoard cash, and the safest place to hold cash was in gold and gold coin at the time."[2142]

"As a global store of value, gold can also provide financial cover during geopolitical and macroeconomic uncertainty."[2143] It is considered to be a safe-haven asset, which "protects investors against a possible catastrophe."[2144] The yellow metal is a way to diversify a portfolio and mitigate losses in times of market stress.[2145] "Research done by Trinity College found that gold is the best hedge

---

[2140] *Id.*

[2141] Daltorio, Tony. "8 Reasons To Own Gold." *Investopedia*, 22 June 2019, www.investopedia.com/articles/basics/08/reasons-to-own-gold.asp.

[2142] *Id.*

[2143] *Id.*

[2144] *Id.* Amadeo, Kimberly. "Three Reasons to Invest in Gold According to Research." *The Balance*, 10 Jul. 2019, www.thebalance.com/why-invest-in-gold-3305651.

[2145] "Why invest in gold?" *World Gold Council,* www.gold.org/what-we-do/investing-gold/why-invest-gold.

against a potential stock market crash."[2146] "When capital markets are in turmoil, gold often performs relatively well as investors seek out safe-haven investments."[2147] "Gold typically does not trade in tandem with the stock market and often the two have a negative correlation. Gold is supposed to act as a safety net when markets decline and vice versa. Gold's peak in the last two decades came during the Great Recession in August 2011, and the low over that period came in 1999 prior to the dot-com bubble. In the 2020 environment, with negative growth and negative real interest rates, gold has shined."[2148] Katie Brewer, a Dallas-based certified financial planner who runs the financial firm, Your Richest Life, explains, "[W]hen investors get spooked, they sell stocks and buy investments like precious metals. It's something people flock to when they're uncertain of the markets."[2149] For instance, between November 30, 2007 and June 1, 2009, the S&P 500 index fell 36%.[2150] During that same period, the price of gold rose 25%.[2151] "Year to date [2020] [gold] increased over 13% as of mid-May.

[2146] Amadeo, Kimberly. "Three Reasons to Invest in Gold According to Research." *The Balance*, 10 Jul. 2019, www.thebalance.com/why-invest-in-gold-3305651.

[2147] Brewer, Reuben Gregg. "The Beginner's Guide to Investing in Gold." *The Motley Fool*, 4 Sept. 2019, www.fool.com/investing/the-beginners-guide-to-investing-in-gold.aspx.

[2148] CME Group. "What Can We Learn From Gold's Relationship To Other Assets?" *Yahoo Finance*, 21 May 2020, finance.yahoo.com/news/learn-golds-relationship-other-assets-152521709.html.

[2149] Becker, Sam. "Everything you need to know about investing in gold and precious metals." *Grow*, 13 Dec. 2019, grow.acorns.com/what-you-need-to-know-about-investing-in-gold-and-precious-metals/.

[2150] Brewer, Reuben Gregg. "The Beginner's Guide to Investing in Gold." *The Motley Fool*, 4 Sept. 2019, www.fool.com/investing/the-beginners-guide-to-investing-in-gold.aspx.

[2151] *Id.*

Over the same period, the S&P 500 index declined over 9% and the Dow Jones Industrial Average (DJIA) declined about 15%..."[2152]

"Many investors bought gold during the [2008] financial crisis."[2153] Some investors hedged "against a dollar decline caused by...the quantitative easing program launched in December 2008. In that program, the Federal Reserve exchanged credit for bank Treasuries. The Fed simply created the credit out of thin air. Investors were concerned this increase in the money supply would create inflation."[2154] "[A]t the time, there were very real concerns about the viability of the global financial system."[2155] People "sought protection against a possible U.S. economic collapse."[2156]

Another concern "was record-level deficit spending that drove the debt-to-GDP ratio above the critical 77% level. That expansionary fiscal policy could create inflation. The increase in the nation's debt could also cause the dollar to decline."[2157] "The most significant supportive factor for gold is the 'amount of debt being created to fund the various global monetary and fiscal deficits,' says Peter Grosskopf, chief executive officer at Sprott Inc...Against that backdrop, gold is experiencing a broad rally, with 'participants

---

[2152] CME Group. "What Can We Learn From Gold's Relationship To Other Assets?" *Yahoo Finance*, 21 May 2020, finance.yahoo.com/news/learn-golds-relationship-other-assets-152521709.html.

[2153] Amadeo, Kimberly. "Three Reasons to Invest in Gold According to Research." *The Balance*, 10 Jul. 2019, www.thebalance.com/why-invest-in-gold-3305651.

[2154] *Id.*

[2155] Brewer, Reuben Gregg. "The Beginner's Guide to Investing in Gold." *The Motley Fool*, 4 Sept. 2019, www.fool.com/investing/the-beginners-guide-to-investing-in-gold.aspx.

[2156] Amadeo, Kimberly. "Three Reasons to Invest in Gold According to Research." *The Balance*, 10 Jul. 2019, www.thebalance.com/why-invest-in-gold-3305651.

[2157] *Id.*

ranging from state funds to pensions to [high-net-worth] clients to hedge funds.'"[2158]

"Gold retains its value not only in times of financial uncertainty, but in times of geopolitical uncertainty. It is often called the 'crisis commodity,' because people flee to its relative safety when world tensions rise; during such times, it often outperforms other investments...Its price often rises the most when confidence in governments is low."[2159] "Regardless of what happens to the domestic currency, gold will always be accepted internationally by creditors..."[2160]

It may seem odd that "[g]old prices have met resistance during the recent stock market selloff."[2161] "Typically, investors flock to gold during times of economic uncertainty, but in some instances, like the current global health crisis, even those assets that are considered safe-havens can see indiscriminate selling as investors seek to raise cash."[2162] "Early in an economic downturn, gold prices often plummet with the rest of the market. This is from investors selling gold to offset losses in shares and other assets. We

---

[2158] Saefong, Myra P. "Gold Prices Could Hit a Record High by Year End. Just Don't Expect an Easy Ride." *Barrons*, 22 May 2020, www.barrons.com/articles/how-to-instill-values-when-teaching-kids-about-money-51590192190.

[2159] Daltorio, Tony. "8 Reasons To Own Gold." *Investopedia*, 22 June 2019, www.investopedia.com/articles/basics/08/reasons-to-own-gold.asp.

[2160] Dirkmaat, Olav. "Do Not Worry about Gold Confiscation." *Gold Republic*, 16 Jun. 2015, www.goldrepublic.com/news/gold-confiscation.

[2161] "Coronavirus to pop bubble greater than 2008; gold prices have 'nowhere to go but up.'" *Kitco News*, 12 Mar. 2020, www.kitco.com/news/2020-03-12/Coronavirus-to-pop-bubble-greater-than-2008-gold-prices-have-nowhere-to-go-but-up.html.

[2162] Garber, Jonathan. "Gold drops but still has luster long term." *Fox Business*, 13 Mar. 2020, www.foxbusiness.com/markets/gold-price-drops-but-still-has-luster-long-term? fbclid=IwAR2R59v4DB4oqw8vea6qjJB7zPL-uw-nCIr5iwLSa1NiSAw0fk-HsnqpWtk.

saw this in March [2020], when gold fell 12% in two weeks, then quickly recovered…"[2163] "Gold prices plunged [March 12, 2020,] but experts say the dumping of the yellow metal is likely a short-term trade and the precious metal remains attractive. Amid extreme volatility, investors are being forced to cover losses in other corners of the market brought on by concerns over the escalating coronavirus outbreak."[2164] "The yellow metal spent some time trading lower for the year as investors sold gold in a bid for cash to cover losses in the stock market."[2165] "'Margin calls and losses in other markets are driving investors to search for cash, and gold happens to be the liquid position they are choosing to cash out on,' wrote Christopher Louney, commodity strategist at RBC Capital Markets."[2166] "Bullion owners in any form physical, paper or scrap, will probably continue to liquidate in order to boost capital levels the more protracted the Covid19 global lockdown extends."[2167]

[2163] Colvin, Chris. "How the US government seized all citizens' gold in 1930s." *Yahoo News*, 21 May 2020, news.yahoo.com/us-government-seized-citizens-gold-143231746.html?soc_src=community&soc_trk=fb.

[2164] Garber, Jonathan. "Gold drops but still has luster long term." Fox Business, 13 Mar. 2020, www.foxbusiness.com/markets/gold-price-drops-but-still-has-luster-long-term?fbclid=IwAR2R59v4DB4oqw8vea6qjJB7zPL-uw-nCIr5iwLSa1NiSAw0fk-HsnqpWtk.

[2165] Saefong, Myra P. "Gold Prices Could Hit a Record High by Year End. Just Don't Expect an Easy Ride." *Barrons*, 22 May 2020, www.barrons.com/articles/how-to-instill-values-when-teaching-kids-about-money-51590192190.

[2166] Garber, Jonathan. "Gold drops but still has luster long term." *Fox Business*, 13 Mar. 2020, www.foxbusiness.com/markets/gold-price-drops-but-still-has-luster-long-term?fbclid=IwAR2R59v4DB4oqw8vea6qjJB7zPL-uw-nCIr5iwLSa1NiSAw0fk-HsnqpWtk.

[2167] Innes, Stephen. "Currency Carnage: FX Market's Unhinged." *Yahoo Finance*, 18 Mar. 2020, finance.yahoo.com/news/currency-carnage-fx-market-unhinged-222325310.html.

"Gold has been hurt by 'forced selling' by investors needing cash due to weakness in equities and other markets, but that does not mean the precious metal has lost its safe-haven status, said Commerzbank analyst Carsten Fritsch. ..."[2168] "'The current preference for liquidity and the U.S. dollar is overshadowing gold's status as a safe haven,' Fritsch said. 'However, we do not share the view of those who believe that gold has already lost this status. We regard its current weakness as merely a temporary anomaly like in the autumn of 2008, when gold likewise came under pressure for several weeks but subsequently rose all the more sharply...'"[2169] For instance, after the drop, "the precious metal was still up 4.3 percent this year 2020..."[2170] Peter "Schiff said that gold will still retain its safe haven asset. 'Gold is going to be the only safe haven left standing.'"[2171]

George Milling-Stanley, chief gold strategist at State Street Global Advisors, opined, "'Gold will bounce back as central bank money floods into financial markets.' He added that once the panic is over, gold should resume its uptrend because of massive deficits and extremely loose monetary policies. In this environment, Milling-Stanley said that gold will not only shine as a safe-haven asset but it will be an important global currency. 'Deficits around the

---

[2168] Sykora, Allen. "Ommerzbank: gold has not lost its safe-haven status." *Kitco*, 23 Mar. 2020, www.kitco.com/news/2020-03-23/Commerzbank-gold-has-not-lost-its-safe-haven-status.html.

[2169] *Id.*

[2170] Garber, Jonathan. "Gold drops but still has luster long term." *Fox Business*, 13 Mar. 2020, www.foxbusiness.com/markets/gold-price-drops-but-still-has-luster-long-term?fbclid=IwAR2R59v4DB4oqw8vea6qjJB7zPL-uw-nCIr5iwLSa1NiSAw0fk-HsnqpWtk.

[2171] "Coronavirus to pop bubble greater than 2008; gold prices have 'nowhere to go but up.'" *Kitco News*, 12 Mar. 2020, www.kitco.com/news/2020-03-12/Coronavirus-to-pop-bubble-greater-than-2008-gold-prices-have-nowhere-to-go-but-up.html.

world are only going to get bigger and currency depreciation is what investors and markets should be looking at,' he said."[2172]

Billionaire investor, Thomas Kaplan, said, "If the world does well, gold will be fine. If the world doesn't do well, gold will also do fine…but a lot of other things could collapse."[2173] The financial writer, Richard Russell, predicted, "Gold will be around, gold will be money when the dollar and the euro and the yuan and the ringgit are mere memories."[2174] For these reasons, some experts advise "to keep your savings in gold…"[2175]

"'More investors need to add gold as a protection asset in their portfolios,' [Peter] Grosskopf says. That will 'create more demand than the market can handle,' he says, and with the increasing amounts of monetary accommodation and fiscal deficits, gold could move through its past highs…He refers to gold as a chameleon, as well as an 'anti-confidence thermometer' that 'attaches itself to themes and…does equally well during periods of extreme deflation and inflation…' Grosskopf says if more economies reopen and there's a strong recovery in China and elsewhere this year, there will be inflation, and gold 'will do well as bond markets get crushed.' On the other hand, if the coronavirus continues to spread and economies stay mostly shut, 'there will be more money printing and debasement, [which] is also good for

---

[2172] Christenson, Neils. "Gold price will bounce back after central banks flood markets – State Street Global Advisors." *Kitco,* 17 Mar. 2020, www.kitco.com/news/2020-03-17/Gold-price-will-bounce-back-after-central-banks-flood-markets-State-Street-Global-Advisors.html.

[2173] "The 101 Best Gold Quotes From History – GoldSilver." *Gold Silver*, goldsilver.com/blog/101-best-gold-quotes-all-time/.

[2174] *Id.*

[2175] Stansberry, Porter. "How Paper Money Fails." *InflationData.com,* 11 Jul. 2010, inflationdata.com/articles/2010/07/11/how-paper-money-fails/.

gold...While equity prices have risen, we continue to see gold as a good hedge given the uncertainty' in the markets, he says."[2176]

"Gold should be an important part of a diversified investment portfolio because its price increases in response to events that cause the value of paper investments, such as stocks and bonds, to decline."[2177] Jim Cramer, the host of CNBC's "Mad Money," suggested, "If you're looking for an insurance policy against volatility and economic uncertainty, gold is a great way to go. I always advocate owning at least a little as insurance against the unknown."[2178] Canadian businessman and author, Kevin O'Leary, said, "I like gold because it is a stabilizer; it is an insurance policy."[2179] "The real benefit, for new and experienced investors alike, comes from the diversification that gold can offer."[2180]

How much gold is enough? "Portfolio allocation analysis (based on the seminal work of Richard and Robert Michaud) indicates that investors who hold between 2% to 10% of their portfolio in gold can significantly improve performance. This is also true even when assuming a conservative average annual gold return of a modest 2% to 4% — well below its actual, long-term historical

----

[2176] Saefong, Myra P. "Gold Prices Could Hit a Record High by Year End. Just Don't Expect an Easy Ride." *Barrons*, 22 May 2020, www.barrons.com/articles/how-to-instill-values-when-teaching-kids-about-money-51590192190.

[2177] Daltorio, Tony. "8 Reasons To Own Gold." *Investopedia*, 22 June 2019, www.investopedia.com/articles/basics/08/reasons-to-own-gold.asp.

[2178] Becker, Sam. "Everything you need to know about investing in gold and precious metals." *Grow*, 13 Dec. 2019, grow.acorns.com/what-you-need-to-know-about-investing-in-gold-and-precious-metals/.

[2179] "The 101 Best Gold Quotes From History – GoldSilver." *Gold Silver*, goldsilver.com/blog/101-best-gold-quotes-all-time/.

[2180] Brewer, Reuben Gregg. "The Beginner's Guide to Investing in Gold." *The Motley Fool*, 4 Sept. 2019, www.fool.com/investing/the-beginners-guide-to-investing-in-gold.aspx.

performance."[2181]   On the other hand, some think that "[a]nything less than 5% will not offer you a sufficient level of protection in a high inflationary environment. Another way to look at it is this: How many ounces do you need to cover your monthly expenses? In Weimar Germany, inflation rose uncomfortably for two years – and then pinched harder, spiraling into a destructive hyperinflation for another two. Consider what it would take to maintain your standard of living for a couple years instead of just a couple months…"[2182]

There are numerous ways to invest in precious metals, both through the stock market, such as by investing in companies that finance gold miners, or by purchasing the physical metal itself.[2183]

One option is to buy gold bullion, bars, and coins. If acquired from the U.S. Mint, for example, they are generally 99.99% pure gold.[2184] However, the cost incurred to turn raw metal into a coin is usually passed on to the end user.[2185]

One can also purchase from a dealer — either in person or online.   Most coin dealers will add a markup to their prices to

---

[2181] "Why invest in gold?" *World Gold Council,* www.gold.org/what-we-do/investing-gold/why-invest-gold.

[2182] Clark, Jeff. "How Does Gold Fare During Hyperinflation?" *InflationData.com,* 25 Jun. 2012, inflationdata.com/articles/2012/06/25/gold-hyperinflation/.

[2183] Becker, Sam. "Everything you need to know about investing in gold and precious metals." *Grow,* 13 Dec. 2019, grow.acorns.com/what-you-need-to-know-about-investing-in-gold-and-precious-metals/; Brewer, Reuben Gregg. "The Beginner's Guide to Investing in Gold." *The Motley Fool,* 4 Sept. 2019, www.fool.com/investing/the-beginners-guide-to-investing-in-gold.aspx.

[2184] Becker, Sam. "Everything you need to know about investing in gold and precious metals." *Grow,* 13 Dec. 2019, grow.acorns.com/what-you-need-to-know-about-investing-in-gold-and-precious-metals/.

[2185] Brewer, Reuben Gregg. "The Beginner's Guide to Investing in Gold." *The Motley Fool,* 4 Sept. 2019, www.fool.com/investing/the-beginners-guide-to-investing-in-gold.aspx.

compensate them for acting as a middlemen.[2186] If one buys small amounts over time, there is the possibility to dollar-cost average down into a position.[2187]

Once the investor has acquired the physical metal, there are storage and security considerations. One could rent a safe deposit box from the local bank. However, this would incur ongoing storage fees. In addition, the gold may not be easily accessible should there be a bank holiday.

Another consideration is that "banks have been known to hypothecate gold, i.e. lend it out to someone other than its rightful owner, putting it at systemic risk. Just as importantly, during the modern 'bail-ins' we've seen in debt-stricken countries, banks were often working hand in hand with governments to seize assets long before citizens found out what was happening."[2188]

One way to get exposure to gold without physically owning it is via gold certificates, which are notes issued by a company that owns gold.[2189] These notes are usually for unallocated gold, which means that there is no specific gold associated with the certificate.[2190] One can also buy allocated gold certificates, which cost more.[2191] Unfortunately, the certificates are only as good as the company backing them.

[2186] *Id.*

[2187] *Id.*

[2188] Clark, Jeff and Mike Maloney. "Gold & Silver Confiscation: Can the Government Seize Assets? (Video)." *GoldSilver.com*, goldsilver.com/blog/gold-confiscation-history-myths-and-real-solutions/.

[2189] Brewer, Reuben Gregg. "The Beginner's Guide to Investing in Gold." *The Motley Fool*, 4 Sept. 2019, www.fool.com/investing/the-beginners-guide-to-investing-in-gold.aspx.

[2190] *Id.*

[2191] *Id.*

Another method to gain exposure to the metal is with an exchange-traded fund (ETF), such as SPDR Gold Shares (GLD).[2192] "An exchange-traded fund, or ETF, is a marketable security that tracks a certain index and trades on a major stock exchange. ETFs are available to invest in stocks, commodities, and bonds..."[2193] They are similar to mutual funds, but trade like common stock.[2194] The investor does not actually own the metal, but rather shares in a trust.[2195] For example, GLD purchases physical gold on behalf of its shareholders.[2196] Keep in mind that there are fees and commissions associated with trading ETFs.[2197]

Gold futures contracts are also a possibility, but they are highly leveraged and risky.[2198] "Futures contracts are a complex and time-consuming investment that can materially amplify gains and losses."[2199] "Essentially, a futures contract is an agreement between a buyer and a seller to exchange a specified amount of gold at a specified future date and price. As gold prices move up and down, the value of the contract fluctuates, with the accounts of the seller

---

[2192] *Id.*

[2193] Motley Fool Staff. "What Are Exchange-Traded Funds?" *The Motley Fool*, 19 Sept. 2016, www.fool.com/knowledge-center/what-are-exchange-traded-funds.aspx.

[2194] *Id.*

[2195] Becker, Sam. "Everything you need to know about investing in gold and precious metals." *Grow*, 13 Dec. 2019, grow.acorns.com/what-you-need-to-know-about-investing-in-gold-and-precious-metals/.

[2196] Brewer, Reuben Gregg. "The Beginner's Guide to Investing in Gold." *The Motley Fool*, 4 Sept. 2019, www.fool.com/investing/the-beginners-guide-to-investing-in-gold.aspx.

[2197] *Id.*

[2198] *Id.*

[2199] *Id.*

and buyer adjusted accordingly."[2200] "Futures contracts are usually bought with only a small fraction of the total contract cost. For example, an investor might only have to put down 20% of the full cost of the gold controlled by the contract. This creates leverage, which increases an investor's potential gains — and losses. And since contracts have specific end dates, you can't simply hold on to a losing position and hope it rebounds."[2201]

Some investors prefer mining stocks, as prices tend to track the price of the commodity.[2202] Because "miners are running businesses that can expand over time, investors can benefit from increasing production. This can provide upside that owning physical gold never will."[2203] In addition, most gold miners produce more than just gold, which can help diversify the portfolio.[2204] "However, running a business also comes with the accompanying risks. Mines don't always produce as much gold as expected, workers sometimes go on strike, and disasters like a mine collapse or deadly gas leak can halt production and even cost lives."[2205]

If one does not wish to research all of the mining stocks, then ETFs, such as VanEck Vectors Gold Miners ETF (GDX) and VanEck Vectors Junior Gold Miners ETF (GDXJ), can provide broadly diversified exposure with a single investment.[2206] However, Rick Santelli, the editor for the CNBC Business News network, warned, "If you trade in paper, the notion of many who trade gold...if the financial world comes to an end, they're going to

---

[2200] *Id.*

[2201] *Id.*

[2202] *Id.*

[2203] *Id.*

[2204] *Id.*

[2205] *Id.*

[2206] *Id.*

have the gold. If you're playing in ETFs, you're going to have a piece of paper."[2207]

Investors who prefer owning mining stocks can also invest in a mutual fund in order to own a portfolio of miners. Most major mutual fund houses offer open-end funds that invest in gold miners, such as the Fidelity Select Gold Portfolio (FSAGX) and Vanguard Precious Metals Fund (VGPMX).[2208] Bear in mind that "[f]ees for actively managed funds...can be materially higher than those of index-based products."[2209]

"For most investors, buying stock in a streaming and royalty company is probably the best all-around option for investing in gold. These companies provide miners with cash up front for the right to buy gold and other metals from specific mines at reduced rates in the future. They are like specialty finance companies that get paid in gold, allowing them to avoid many of the headaches and risks associated with running a mine."[2210] The benefits of such companies include "widely diversified portfolios, contractually built-in low prices that lead to wide margins in good years and bad, and exposure to gold price changes (since streaming companies make money by selling the gold they buy from the miners)..."[2211] "They provide exposure to gold, they offer growth potential via the investment in new mines, and their wide margins through the cycle provide some downside protection when gold prices fall."[2212] "[W]hile streaming companies avoid many of the risks of running a

---

[2207] "The 101 Best Gold Quotes From History – GoldSilver." *Gold Silver*, goldsilver.com/blog/101-best-gold-quotes-all-time/.

[2208] Brewer, Reuben Gregg. "The Beginner's Guide to Investing in Gold." *The Motley Fool*, 4 Sept. 2019, www.fool.com/investing/the-beginners-guide-to-investing-in-gold.aspx.

[2209] *Id.*

[2210] *Id.*

[2211] *Id.*

[2212] *Id.*

mine, they don't completely sidestep them: If a mine isn't producing any gold, there's nothing for a streaming company to buy."[2213]

There are some disadvantages associated with investing in gold. For example, "precious metal prices tend to be very volatile. Wild price fluctuations aren't uncommon."[2214] In addition, "there are no periodic cash flows made to the investor. Unlike most stocks and bonds, there are no regular cash dividends or coupon payments made to gold investors."[2215] Tom Cassidy explained, "Gold's return is solely based on the price going up. Thus, when you sell gold, you create a capital gain that in most cases will be taxed…"[2216]

Another concern involves the potential for gold confiscation. "During extreme crises, governments can…seize people's gold."[2217] "Historically, the government will seize gold when it's the most valuable, during times when its fiat currency has become utterly devalued."[2218] Mike Maloney wrote in *Guide to Investing in Gold and Silver,* "Confiscation all comes down to this: the government

[2213] *Id.*

[2214] Becker, Sam. "Everything you need to know about investing in gold and precious metals." *Grow,* 13 Dec. 2019, grow.acorns.com/what-you-need-to-know-about-investing-in-gold-and-precious-metals/.

[2215] Divine, John. "5 Reasons Not to Invest in Gold." *US News,* 10 Jul. 2018, money.usnews.com/investing/articles/2018-07-10/5-reasons-not-to-invest-in-gold.

[2216] "However, if one invests in gold in a tax-deferred account, the gains one receives will be taxed based on their income tax bracket, which is typically higher than their capital gains rate. So if an investor does want to own gold it should be done using taxable assets." Divine, John. "5 Reasons Not to Invest in Gold." *US News,* 10 Jul. 2018, money.usnews.com/investing/articles/2018-07-10/5-reasons-not-to-invest-in-gold.

[2217] Colvin, Chris. "How the US government seized all citizens' gold in 1930s." *Yahoo News,* 21 May 2020, news.yahoo.com/us-government-seized-citizens-gold-143231746.html?soc_src=community&soc_trk=fb.

[2218] Lewis, Tom. "Yes, The U.S Government Can Still Confiscate Gold." *The Gold Telegraph,* 4 May 2018, www.goldtelegraph.com/the-u.s-government-can-still-confiscate-gold.

makes the rules, changes the rules, and enforces the rules…The Constitution did not stop the government from taking people's gold in 1933."[2219]

Gold confiscation has "happened in the past enough times to make it a reasonable concern for those uneasy about unsolvable debt levels, runaway government spending, and continual central bank money creation."[2220] "There have been a few notable gold confiscations around the world. The specific circumstances varied, but there was one common thread to all of them: They all arose out of a financial crisis. As government coffers dwindled and reached emergency levels, politicians didn't hesitate to grab the net worth of private citizens."[2221] "In a true confiscation, your assets are seized with no compensation. Should a severe national crisis arise, it's certainly possible the government wouldn't be able to afford to pay investors the full value of their bullion."[2222] "Imagine having the forethought to buy gold to shield your finances from an economic or monetary crisis — only to have it taken away from you by your government."[2223] For example, "Germany has a history of banning personal ownership of gold from the 1920s to the 1950s."[2224] Thus, German investors in physical gold and silver are concerned about the risk of confiscation within the EU.[2225]

[2219] Clark, Jeff and Mike Maloney. "Gold & Silver Confiscation: Can the Government Seize Assets? (Video)." *GoldSilver.com*, goldsilver.com/blog/gold-confiscation-history-myths-and-real-solutions/.

[2220] *Id.*

[2221] *Id.*

[2222] *Id.*

[2223] *Id.*

[2224] Greyerz, Egon. "Gold Confiscation and Manipulation." *Gold Switzerland*, 15 Nov. 2018, goldswitzerland.com/gold-confiscation-and-manipulation/.

[2225] *Id.*

"Why do governments risk the bad publicity of restricting gold? This is linked to a cornerstone of macroeconomics known as the monetary policy trilemma. This states that countries must choose between two of the following and can't generally do all three at the same time: (1) setting fixed exchange rates; (2) allowing capital to move freely over international borders; and (3) being able to independently set interest rates and print money (in other words, control monetary policy)...In the 1930s system, countries generally chose fixed exchange rates linked to gold, plus free capital movement and sacrificed control of monetary policy. The system came under more and more pressure because too many investors were trading in their money for gold. One way for the US to take enough control of monetary policy to print more money was to impose various capital controls, including seizing gold."[2226]

In 1933, during the Great Depression, President Franklin Delano Roosevelt nationalized the gold holdings of U.S. citizens. During this period, the U.S. government could not make its debt payments.[2227] The Federal Reserve was prevented from increasing the money supply, a situation that they wanted to remedy.[2228] The only way to inflate the money supply was to confiscate gold, because, under the gold standard, the total number of dollars was tied to the amount of gold in the banking system.[2229] Under the 1913 Federal Reserve Act, the dollar had to be backed by 40 percent

---

[2226] Colvin, Chris. "How the US government seized all citizens' gold in 1930s." *Yahoo News*, 21 May 2020, news.yahoo.com/us-government-seized-citizens-gold-143231746.html?soc_src=community&soc_trk=fb.

[2227] Clark, Jeff and Mike Maloney. "Gold & Silver Confiscation: Can the Government Seize Assets? (Video)." *GoldSilver.com*, goldsilver.com/blog/gold-confiscation-history-myths-and-real-solutions/.

[2228] *Id.*

[2229] Dirkmaat, Olav. "Do Not Worry about Gold Confiscation." *Gold Republic*, 16 Jun. 2015, www.goldrepublic.com/news/gold-confiscation.

gold.[2230] As a consequence, the total number of dollars could not be increased without adding to the gold reserves.[2231]

"To ensure that the federal government would never have any problems paying for [its] new socialist, imperialist, and interventionist direction, the Roosevelt administration decreed an end to America's gold-coin standard. Gold ownership by Americans was made illegal."[2232] On April 5, 1933, President Roosevelt declared a national emergency, and, using the Trading with the Enemy Act of 1917, which states that "during the time of war…the President may regulate or prohibit the hoarding of gold or silver coin or bullion," issued Executive Order (EO) 6102.[2233] EO 6102 prohibited "the hoarding of gold coin, gold bullion, and gold certificates within the continental United States."[2234] It required that, "on or before May 1, 1933, all persons [U.S. citizens] in possession or control of gold coin, gold bullion, and gold certificates (i.e. paper currency redeemable in gold coin of the United States) to turn them in to any federal reserve bank or any 'member bank' of

---

[2230] Lewis, Tom. "Yes, The U.S Government Can Still Confiscate Gold." *The Gold Telegraph*, 4 May 2018, www.goldtelegraph.com/the-u.s-government-can-still-confiscate-gold.

[2231] Dirkmaat, Olav. "Do Not Worry about Gold Confiscation." *Gold Republic*, 16 Jun. 2015, www.goldrepublic.com/news/gold-confiscation.

[2232] Hornberger, Jacob. "Monetary Destruction in America." *Tenth Amendment Center*, 7 Jun. 2020, tenthamendmentcenter.com/2020/06/07/monetary-destruction-in-america/? fbclid=IwAR1qznHUtpPxV4SZfCJk0G9H9gTS2kepV1ZU5BKoX_o06D xBXusfHyCPK6s.

[2233] 50 U.S. Code §4305(b)(1)(A); Ganz, David L. "Gold Seizure." *USA Gold*, www.usagold.com/cpmforum/gold-seizure-ganz/. "Within the United States, only those who had special gold collections or needed the gold for industrial or professional use were allowed to retain quantities of the yellow metal." "The History of American Money." *CMI Gold $ Silver*, www.cmi-gold-silver.com/history-american-money/.

[2234] Clark, Jeff and Mike Maloney. "Gold & Silver Confiscation: Can the Government Seize Assets? (Video)." *GoldSilver.com*, goldsilver.com/blog/gold-confiscation-history-myths-and-real-solutions/.

the Federal Reserve system."[2235] EO 6102 forced Americans to sell their gold at $20.67 per ounce.[2236] Thus, it was not a "confiscation" per se, because people were compensated for the gold they turned over to the Federal Reserve (the 5th Amendment prohibits the government from taking property without just compensation).[2237] In exchange, citizens received Federal Reserve notes redeemable in silver.[2238] Unfortunately, the ownership of silver was made illegal a year later.[2239]

"On May 22, 1933, Congress enacted a law (48 Stat. 31) declaring all coin and currencies then in circulation to be legal tender, dollar for dollar, as if they were gold."[2240] "On June 5, 1933, Congress enacted a joint resolution (48 Stat. 112) that all gold clauses in contracts were outlawed and no one could legally demand gold in payment for any obligation due him."[2241]

President Roosevelt signed the Gold Reserve Act on January 30, 1934, "giving the Federal Reserve title to all the gold which had

---

[2235] Ganz, David L. "Gold Seizure." *USA Gold*, www.usagold.com/cpmforum/gold-seizure-ganz/.

[2236] Approximately $376.58 today. Dirkmaat, Olav. "Do Not Worry about Gold Confiscation." *Gold Republic*, 16 Jun. 2015, www.goldrepublic.com/news/gold-confiscation.

[2237] Clark, Jeff and Mike Maloney. "Gold & Silver Confiscation: Can the Government Seize Assets? (Video)." *GoldSilver.com*, goldsilver.com/blog/gold-confiscation-history-myths-and-real-solutions/.

[2238] "The History of American Money." *CMI Gold $ Silver*, www.cmi-gold-silver.com/history-american-money/.

[2239] Lewis, Tom. "Yes, The U.S Government Can Still Confiscate Gold." *The Gold Telegraph*, 4 May 2018, www.goldtelegraph.com/the-u.s-government-can-still-confiscate-gold.

[2240] "The History of American Money." *CMI Gold $ Silver*, www.cmi-gold-silver.com/history-american-money/.

[2241] *Id.*

been collected."[2242]   This was confirmed in 1982 when President Ronald Reagan appointed the Grace Commission to look into re-introducing the gold standard.[2243] They found that the U.S. Treasury owned no gold — all of the gold remaining at Fort Knox is being held as collateral by the Federal Reserve against the national debt.[2244]   "The Gold Reserve Act was the primary policy that, in fact, took the United States off the gold standard before it was utterly dissolved by President Nixon in 1971."[2245]   "[T]he Gold Reserve Act asserted that gold could no longer be privately owned. The law required that gold certificates held by the Federal Reserve through private ownership be surrendered and vested in the Department of the Treasury…Only licensed jewelers were allowed to have gold for sales purposes."[2246]

"Even though gold coins had been the official money established by the Constitution and had been the official money for more than 100 years, Roosevelt made it a felony offense for

---

[2242] *Id.*

[2243] "The Gold Commission Finds That The US Government Owns No Gold." *Mind Contagion*, www.mindcontagion.org/banking/hb1981.html; "Report to the Congress of the Commission on the Role of Cold in the Domestic and International Monetary Systems." *Fraser,stlouisfed.org*, Mar. 1982, fraser.stlouisfed.org/files/docs/historical/congressional/198203_usgcom_prtcomrolegold_v1.pdf.

[2244] *Id.*

[2245] Van, Germinal G. "The Gold Standard Didn't Create the Great Depression, the Federal Reserve Did." *FEE Freeman Article*, Foundation for Economic Education, 25 May 2019, fee.org/articles/the-gold-standard-didn-t-create-the-great-depression-the-federal-reserve-did/?fbclid=IwAR0vrzpM7GgbTDRu2mqA0EM_1vSSK_JaYKWsCWX7BlDGZ6PUxZhjt8niybw.

[2246] *Id.*

Americans to own non-numismatic gold coins."[2247] "The executive order provided for severe, Draconian criminal penalties for non-compliance: A $10,000 fine or 10 years imprisonment, or both."[2248] "Numerous individuals and companies were prosecuted."[2249] It was not until January 1, 1975 that U.S. citizens could own more than five ounces of gold again.[2250]

Roosevelt blamed the strong dollar for having caused the Great Depression, and thought that devaluing it was the answer.[2251] To that end, he devalued the dollar by raising the price of gold.[2252] The Gold Reserve Act raised the price of gold from $20.67 an ounce to $35 an ounce, which effectively devalued the dollar by 40% overnight.[2253] Thus, the dollars the ex-gold owners had received

---

[2247] Hornberger, Jacob. "Monetary Destruction in America." *Tenth Amendment Center*, 7 Jun. 2020, tenthamendmentcenter.com/2020/06/07/monetary-destruction-in-america/?fbclid=IwAR1qznHUtpPxV4SZfCJk0G9H9gTS2kepV1ZU5BKoX_o06DxBXusfHyCPK6s.

[2248] Ganz, David L. "Gold Seizure." *USA Gold*, www.usagold.com/cpmforum/gold-seizure-ganz/.

[2249] Clark, Jeff and Mike Maloney. "Gold & Silver Confiscation: Can the Government Seize Assets? (Video)." *GoldSilver.com*, goldsilver.com/blog/gold-confiscation-history-myths-and-real-solutions/.

[2250] *Id.*

[2251] Dirkmaat, Olav. "Do Not Worry about Gold Confiscation." *Gold Republic*, 16 Jun. 2015, www.goldrepublic.com/news/gold-confiscation.

[2252] *Id.*

[2253] Van, Germinal G. "The Gold Standard Didn't Create the Great Depression, the Federal Reserve Did." *FEE Freeman Article*, Foundation for Economic Education, 25 May 2019, fee.org/articles/the-gold-standard-didn-t-create-the-great-depression-the-federal-reserve-did/?fbclid=IwAR0vrzpM7GgbTDRu2mqA0EM_1vSSK_JaYKWsCWX7BlDGZ6PUxZhjt8niybw.

were devalued by 40%.[2254]   In other words, "all of the silver certificates the people had recently received for their gold now lost 40 percent of their value."[2255]   However, "the US government had a lot more funds than it had before."[2256]   In 1971, President Richard Nixon further devalued the dollar by raising the price of gold to $38 an ounce, and in 1973, it was raised to $42.22 an ounce.[2257]

"By August 1971, many of the European countries had collected so many billions in Eurodollars (foreign aid, money spent by the U.S. military abroad, etc.) that European banks had begun to get nervous about redeeming their money in gold. A threatened run on the U.S. Treasury resulted in the American gold window being slammed shut."[2258]   "[T]he federal government announced that it would no longer honor international obligations payable in gold. Instead, such obligations would be paid in irredeemable paper

[2254] Clark, Jeff and Mike Maloney. "Gold & Silver Confiscation: Can the Government Seize Assets? (Video)." *GoldSilver.com*, goldsilver.com/blog/gold-confiscation-history-myths-and-real-solutions/.

[2255] "The History of American Money." *CMI Gold $ Silver*, www.cmi-gold-silver.com/history-american-money/.

[2256] Lewis, Tom. "Yes, The U.S Government Can Still Confiscate Gold." *The Gold Telegraph*, 4 May 2018, www.goldtelegraph.com/the-u.s-government-can-still-confiscate-gold.

[2257] "The entire American gold reserve of 8,133.5 tonnes – 261 million troy ounces – is officially valued at $42.22 an ounce. That makes the American official gold reserves of gold about $11.019 billion – clearly an artificially low figure." Ganz, David L. "Gold Seizure." *USA Gold*, www.usagold.com/cpmforum/gold-seizure-ganz/. "The History of American Money." *CMI Gold $ Silver*, www.cmi-gold-silver.com/history-american-money/.

[2258] "The History of American Money." *CMI Gold $ Silver*, www.cmi-gold-silver.com/history-american-money/.

notes."[2259] "On March 16, 1973, Congress set the American dollar completely afloat with nothing to back it up but the declaration of the government that it was 'legal tender,' or fiat currency."[2260] "This resulted in [the] collapse of the dollar on the world market."[2261] Since then, the dollar "has fluctuated on the world market like any other commodity, since it is no longer redeemable in precious metal and therefore has no intrinsic value."[2262]

Other examples of gold confiscation abound. In Italy, Benito Mussolini, the fascist prime minister, introduced the "Gold for the Fatherland" initiative in 1935.[2263] The public was "encouraged" to "voluntarily donate" their gold rings, necklaces, and other forms of gold to the government.[2264] In return, they received a steel bracelet with the inscription, "Gold for the Fatherland."[2265] The government netted 35 tonnes (1.23 million ounces) of gold, which was melted down, made into bars, and then distributed to banks.[2266]

[2259] Hornberger, Jacob. "Monetary Destruction in America." *Tenth Amendment Center*, 7 Jun. 2020, tenthamendmentcenter.com/2020/06/07/monetary-destruction-in-america/?fbclid=IwAR1qznHUtpPxV4SZfCJk0G9H9gTS2kepV1ZU5BKoX_o06DxBXusfHyCPK6s.

[2260] "The History of American Money." *CMI Gold $ Silver*, www.cmi-gold-silver.com/history-american-money/.

[2261] *Id.*

[2262] *Id.*

[2263] Clark, Jeff and Mike Maloney. "Gold & Silver Confiscation: Can the Government Seize Assets? (Video)." *GoldSilver.com*, goldsilver.com/blog/gold-confiscation-history-myths-and-real-solutions/.

[2264] *Id.*

[2265] *Id.*

[2266] Saddam Hussein and Fidel Castro were dictators who confiscated gold, art, jewelry, etc. at the point of a sword or gun. Citizens were not compensated. Clark, Jeff and Mike Maloney. "Gold & Silver Confiscation: Can the Government Seize Assets? (Video)." *GoldSilver.com*, goldsilver.com/blog/gold-confiscation-history-myths-and-real-solutions/.

In Australia, the government nationalized gold in 1959.[2267] The Banking Act allowed gold to be seized from private citizens if the Governor determined it was "expedient so to do, for the protection of the currency or of the public credit of the Commonwealth."[2268] In exchange, people would be given paper currency.[2269] The country's Treasurer stated, "All gold (other than wrought gold and coins to a limited extent) had to be delivered to the Reserve Bank of Australia within one month of its coming into a person's possession."[2270] The law prohibited the sale of gold, except to the Reserve Bank of Australia (their central bank), and the export of gold without the bank's permission.[2271] This law stayed on the books until 1976 when it was "suspended."[2272]

Great Britain went off of the gold standard in 1931, which precipitated a slow decline in their currency.[2273] Many investors began to store gold overseas, worried their country might never recover.[2274] As a counter measure, the government prohibited private citizens from owning more than four precious metal coins in

---

[2267] *Id.*

[2268] *Id.*

[2269] *Id.*

[2270] *Id.*

[2271] *Id.*

[2272] *Id.*

[2273] *Id.*

[2274] *Id.*

1966.[2275] It also banned imports of gold coins.[2276] This law was on the books until 1979.[2277]

In Holland, the 1978 Noodwet financieel verkeer (Emergency Act Financial Transactions) is a reason for some investors to hide their gold in their backyards.[2278] This law refers to a situation termed "the crack-up boom," i.e. a total currency collapse.[2279] Chapter XII International Financial Transactions contains Article 26 of the Emergency Act, which states: "Our Minister is authorized…to demand gold coins, fine gold, gold alloys (unprocessed or semi-finished alloys) and foreign assets of inhabitants."[2280]

In the former Soviet Union, private ownership of gold and silver in any form — except jewelry and numismatic coins — was strictly forbidden.[2281] "People went to jail for owning a gold bar."[2282] Those laws are still on the books and "make it illegal to buy or sell bullion bars except at a bank that has a precious metals license…[I]t is a criminal offense to buy or sell a gold bar from a

---

[2275] "The only exemption to owning more than four coins was to prove you were a collector. You were required to apply for a license, and then an officer from the Bank of England would determine if you were a true collector or not. If not, we'll take your bullion, thank you very much." *Id.*

[2276] Clark, Jeff and Mike Maloney. "Gold & Silver Confiscation: Can the Government Seize Assets? (Video)." *GoldSilver.com*, goldsilver.com/blog/gold-confiscation-history-myths-and-real-solutions/.

[2277] *Id.*

[2278] Dirkmaat, Olav. "Do Not Worry about Gold Confiscation." *Gold Republic*, 16 Jun. 2015, www.goldrepublic.com/news/gold-confiscation.

[2279] *Id.*

[2280] *Id.*

[2281] Clark, Jeff and Mike Maloney. "Gold & Silver Confiscation: Can the Government Seize Assets? (Video)." *GoldSilver.com*, goldsilver.com/blog/gold-confiscation-history-myths-and-real-solutions/.

[2282] *Id.*

friend or relative...it is illegal to take bullion bars out of the country...buying and selling foreign-made bars is also illegal."[2283] Although it is possible to buy gold coins, they are few and of poor quality.[2284]

In 2020, "Venezuela...filed a $1bn lawsuit against the Bank of England over its refusal to release gold stashed in its vaults, as the government of Nicolás Maduro scrambles for funds to alleviate a deepening economic and health crisis."[2285]

"In sum, there's ample authority –– and many cases — allowing for seizure of gold coins and bullion."[2286] "It may be small solace that the government would have to pay just compensation" in fiat currency.[2287]

Many investors believe gold will not be confiscated today because it is not part of the monetary system as it was in 1933.[2288] "Gold no longer limits the power of governments and central banks

---

[2283] *Id.*

[2284] *Id.*

[2285] "It might strike many as odd that Venezuela, a country an ocean away from the UK with little in the way of historical ties, has its gold stashed in vaults deep underneath the City of London. Indeed it, and the New York Fed, have long been the biggest custodians of bullion in the world – a legacy of the gold standard and the proximity of both central banks to the world's most active markets for gold trading." Jones, Claire. "When gold and geopolitics clash, it's rarely pretty." *Yahoo Finance*, 21 May 2020, finance.yahoo.com/m/66217439-be36-3483-bc04-a44f62c17a35/when-gold-and-geopolitics.html.

[2286] Ganz, David L. "Gold Seizure." *USA Gold*, www.usagold.com/cpmforum/gold-seizure-ganz/.

[2287] *Id.*

[2288] Clark, Jeff and Mike Maloney. "Gold & Silver Confiscation: Can the Government Seize Assets? (Video)." *GoldSilver.com*, goldsilver.com/blog/gold-confiscation-history-myths-and-real-solutions/.

to spend, lend and inflate money…a government does not need to confiscate gold to devalue its currency."[2289]

However, there is historical precedence that gold may be confiscated even though it is not part of the monetary system.[2290] (As we have seen, Great Britain was not on a gold standard when it banned gold.)[2291] "The government is keeping afloat by printing as much fiat currency as it can. The more it prints, the less valuable the dollar becomes, while gold concurrently rises in value. A desperate government might very well begin to eye private gold as the solution to its problems."[2292] If there is "a complete collapse of the currency (a 'crack-up boom,' in the terminology of economist Ludwig von Mises)," a government may want to confiscate gold.[2293]

"Under extreme circumstances, the U.S. government can still keep you from 'hoarding' gold if it wishes to do so."[2294] The authority to confiscate gold "was derived from the Trading with the Enemy Act of 1917 and the Emergency Banking Act, found in Title

---

[2289] Dirkmaat, Olav. "Do Not Worry about Gold Confiscation." *Gold Republic*, 16 Jun. 2015, www.goldrepublic.com/news/gold-confiscation.

[2290] Clark, Jeff and Mike Maloney. "Gold & Silver Confiscation: Can the Government Seize Assets? (Video)." *GoldSilver.com*, goldsilver.com/blog/gold-confiscation-history-myths-and-real-solutions/.

[2291] *Id.*

[2292] Lewis, Tom. "Yes, The U.S Government Can Still Confiscate Gold." *The Gold Telegraph*, 4 May 2018, www.goldtelegraph.com/the-u.s-government-can-still-confiscate-gold.

[2293] Dirkmaat, Olav. "Do Not Worry about Gold Confiscation." *Gold Republic*, 16 Jun. 2015, www.goldrepublic.com/news/gold-confiscation.

[2294] Lewis, Tom. "Yes, The U.S Government Can Still Confiscate Gold." *The Gold Telegraph*, 4 May 2018, www.goldtelegraph.com/the-u.s-government-can-still-confiscate-gold.

12 of the U.S. Code in section 95."[2295] They are "still good law, and could still be used by the President of the United States, as FDR [Roosevelt] used it in 1933 to nationalize domestic gold and silver coin and bullion and JFK [Kennedy] used it during his administration to require Americans owning gold coin and bullion abroad to turn it all in."[2296] "The general consensus in the legal community is that a confiscation could happen again in the near future."[2297]

"Many dealers claim numismatic coins would be excluded, since there was an exception made for rare coin collectors in 1933. But as history will show, during past confiscations, the onus was on the investor to prove they were a coin collector and not a bullion buyer. Unless you owned a substantial amount of rare coins, you were automatically deemed a bullion owner, not a collector."[2298]

"When the gold investor considers the number of ways a confiscation could take place, how long it could last, how easily the government could change the rules and how deeply it could reach —

[2295] FDR's Emergency Banking Act of 1933 "vastly expanded the powers of the President and Federal Reserve. It gave the President the ability to declare a national emergency and have absolute control over the national finances and foreign exchange of the United States in the event of such an emergency." Quinn, Jim. "The Federal Reserve Must Die." *HCP Live*, 25 Aug. 2009, www.mdmag.com/medical-news/federal_reserve_must_die; Ganz, David L. "Gold Seizure." *USA Gold*, www.usagold.com/cpmforum/gold-seizure-ganz/. https://law.justia.com/codes/us/2000/title12/chap2/subchapiv/sec95a/; United States Code, 12 U.S.C.A. Sec 95a
(1) During the time of war, the President may, —
    (a) investigate, regulate, or prohibit,…the importing, exporting, hoarding, melting, or earmarking of gold or silver coin or bullion…

[2296] Ganz, David L. "Gold Seizure." *USA Gold*, www.usagold.com/cpmforum/gold-seizure-ganz/.

[2297] Read Professor Hank Holzer's article in the 1973 Brooklyn Law Review: "How Americans lost their right to own gold and became criminals in the process.") *Id.*

[2298] Clark, Jeff and Mike Maloney. "Gold & Silver Confiscation: Can the Government Seize Assets? (Video)." *GoldSilver.com*, goldsilver.com/blog/gold-confiscation-history-myths-and-real-solutions/.

all against the backdrop of an economic or monetary crisis — it underscores the need to put a viable strategy in place."[2299] "When a gold confiscation happens, there unfortunately aren't a lot of viable solutions. If your government declares it illegal to own a meaningful amount of bullion, you'd have little choice but to comply. Either that or play the role of a fugitive — with the prospects of financial penalties, forcible confiscation of your metal, and even jail time waiting for you."[2300] "What's really viable is a lesson best learned by the mistakes and successes of the past…"[2301]

There are a couple of strategies that have historically been effective in combating a gold confiscation order. Storing gold where a government is less able to reach it quickly and easily, such as keeping it outside of the banking system — even overseas — is a smart buffer to put in place.[2302] "[I]f you're worried about a gold confiscation, you can manage this risk by depositing your gold in different locations in the world… [Y]ou can spread your risks by diversifying; you can store several precious metals (gold, silver and platinum) in multiple safe locations…"[2303] "Without the ability to take quick possession, you have more time and distance to fight such an order."[2304]

Luckily, there are some countries that do not have a history of gold confiscation. For example, "Switzerland has never banned

---

[2299] *Id.*

[2300] *Id.*

[2301] *Id.*

[2302] *Id.*

[2303] "For investors with more modest means, it may be a smart thing to investigate the option to obtain a second passport as protection against future restrictions on our (economical and perhaps political) freedom." Dirkmaat, Olav. "Do Not Worry about Gold Confiscation." *Gold Republic*, 16 Jun. 2015, www.goldrepublic.com/news/gold-confiscation.

[2304] Clark, Jeff and Mike Maloney. "Gold & Silver Confiscation: Can the Government Seize Assets? (Video)." *GoldSilver.com*, goldsilver.com/blog/gold-confiscation-history-myths-and-real-solutions/.

or confiscated gold. Gold ownership is a long established tradition in Switzerland."[2305] Investors who are "worried about confiscation in Germany and the EU [are] interested in moving their gold and silver holdings to Switzerland and also to Singapore."[2306] Unfortunately, off-shore gold storage is not very handy at a time of urgent need.

Bear in mind that a desperate government could easily repatriate all personal gold holdings, regardless of location.[2307] "It'd be a spinoff of the old tax joke, 'How much gold do you own?...Give it to us.'"[2308] "If the company holding your metal is a domestic entity, they might be forced to comply anyway, at least in reporting your holdings so they can be taxed in lieu of surrender."[2309]

"Some suggest you should instead do business with a foreign company. But that adds a different risk, and one that comes with a dubious level of added protection. First, you give up access to the local rule of law. If a vault in Singapore swears your gold is there, what will you do if it ends up not being the case? When dealing with a domestic company, at least you can turn to the court system."[2310]

"Second, a foreign company can be compelled to cooperate with a big enough foreign government, like the US. As investors using private banking services in Switzerland discovered in recent years, the threat of being cut off from banking with the US will quickly convince a company, or its host government, to comply with

---

[2305] Greyerz, Egon. "Gold Confiscation and Manipulation." *Gold Switzerland*, 15 Nov. 2018, goldswitzerland.com/gold-confiscation-and-manipulation/.

[2306] *Id.*

[2307] Clark, Jeff and Mike Maloney. "Gold & Silver Confiscation: Can the Government Seize Assets? (Video)." *GoldSilver.com*, goldsilver.com/blog/gold-confiscation-history-myths-and-real-solutions/.

[2308] *Id.*

[2309] *Id.*

[2310] *Id.*

a confiscation order at least by reporting holdings. Even if it does not relent to pressure from abroad, the foreign entity would almost certainly refuse to deliver, buy, or sell precious metals in a jurisdiction where authorities have issued a confiscation order, leaving you only with the option to relocate elsewhere — hardly better, and often much worse than using a domestic provider you have real recourse against."[2311]

Historically, gold confiscations have targeted monetary metals, such as coins and bars, but not jewelry.[2312] The Trading with the Enemy Act and the Emergency Banking Act only apply to "gold or silver coin or bullion." Thus, jewelry is not implicated in the statute. (In other words, gold jewelry is an asset that is less appealing to grab.[2313]) Therefore, one option is to buy gold jewelry (at least 10 karats) if confiscation is a concern.[2314]

Originally, jewelry was a form a wearable wealth, which was meant to keep assets close at hand.[2315] Traditionally in Europe and Asia, gold jewelry was a portable outside-the-bank asset that held its value and was easily passed to the next generation.[2316] This tradition continues in India, China, and Thailand.[2317] For instance,

---

[2311] *Id.*

[2312] *Id.*

[2313] *Id.*

[2314] Pure gold is 24 karat.

[2315] Clark, Jeff and Mike Maloney. "Gold & Silver Confiscation: Can the Government Seize Assets? (Video)." *GoldSilver.com*, goldsilver.com/blog/gold-confiscation-history-myths-and-real-solutions/.

[2316] *Id.*

[2317] "The Thai currency, Baht, for example, is even named for a common jewelry style that pre-dates it." *Id.*

gold jewelry in India is viewed as an investment; the vast majority of gold in India is in the form of jewelry.[2318]

When the Hollywood actress, Elizabeth Taylor, traveled, she was able to walk right through customs wearing her jewelry.[2319] Passengers traveling abroad are required to complete customs forms "and declare large amounts of money they are carrying, anything over $10,000 for travel to/from the US, for example. The new rules specifically mention gold, and also that the price of the gold determines if you are at the reporting limit (not the face value on a coin). That means 7 ounces of gold would be the maximum you could carry at $1,300 gold. You'd be at risk with 5 coins when gold reaches $2,000/ounce."[2320] Since gold jewelry is not considered a financial asset under US law, it does not require reporting.[2321] Thus, Elizabeth Taylor did not need to declare her jewelry on the customs forms.[2322]

Unfortunately, mark-ups in the industry make jewelry an expensive way to invest in gold.[2323] In addition, its resale value is

---

[2318] "The Indian government has tried to crackdown on gold jewelry demand numerous times and in numerous ways. They currently have a 10% tariff on all gold imports in an attempt to curtail demand. They introduced a monetization scheme that would pay interest on the gold you "lent" them, also something they've tried several times. In fact, these attempts have been tried for decades, on both gold and silver." *Id.*

[2319] Clark, Jeff and Mike Maloney. "Gold & Silver Confiscation: Can the Government Seize Assets? (Video)." *GoldSilver.com*, goldsilver.com/blog/gold-confiscation-history-myths-and-real-solutions/.

[2320] *Id.*

[2321] *Id.*

[2322] *Id.*

[2323] "Mark-ups are easily two and three times the gold value, and it's not hard to find it four or even five times higher." *Id.*

likely to fall significantly after purchase.[2324] "Extremely expensive jewelry may hold its value, but more because it is a collector's item than because of its gold content."[2325]

Bullion-grade jewelry, such as the Gold Without Borders jewelry line, may be a viable alternative.[2326] These are investment grade 22-carat (91.6% gold, same as an American Eagle coin) and 24-carat (99.99% pure gold) pieces.[2327] Another option may be to have a jeweler fashion a pendant, pin, or bracelet out of a gold coin (or coins). Such jewelry is a real asset that can be worn and transported, and a confiscation order is not likely to apply.[2328]

The next section deals with gold's little brother, silver.

[2324] Brewer, Reuben Gregg. "The Beginner's Guide to Investing in Gold." *The Motley Fool*, 4 Sept. 2019, www.fool.com/investing/the-beginners-guide-to-investing-in-gold.aspx.

[2325] *Id.*

[2326] Clark, Jeff and Mike Maloney. "Gold & Silver Confiscation: Can the Government Seize Assets? (Video)." *GoldSilver.com*, goldsilver.com/blog/gold-confiscation-history-myths-and-real-solutions/.

[2327] *Id.*

[2328] *Id.*

Silver

Historically, the white precious metal has been used to coin money even more than gold has.[2329] As a portable, hard asset, silver facilitates private and confidential transactions.[2330] In this respect, it can "be viewed as an alternative currency to fiat currencies such as the U.S. dollar or euro."[2331]

Silver is a store of value and has retained its purchasing power over long periods of time.[2332] "Compared with stocks and paper investments...silver is still generally seen as a safe haven for investment during market instability."[2333] Unlike stocks and bonds, silver has no counter-party risk.[2334] Neither can the physical metal be hacked or deleted as can occur with digital assets.[2335]

Because silver maintains purchasing power, it is a way to protect against inflation.[2336] "Silver is known to be an inflation hedge...Since inflation means a decrease in the value of paper

---

[2329] Clark, Jeff. "Why Buy Silver? 10 Reasons to Invest in Silver Now (w/ Charts)." *GoldSilver.com*, goldsilver.com/blog/top-10-reasons-to-buy-silver/.

[2330] *Id.*

[2331] Carlson, Debbie. "How to Invest in Silver." *US News*, 1 Aug. 2019, money.usnews.com/investing/investing-101/articles/how-to-invest-in-silver.

[2332] "10 Reasons You Should Invest In Silver." *IRA Gold Advisor*, iragoldadvisor.com/silver-ira/10-reasons-you-should-invest-in-silver/.

[2333] Reed, Eric. "Investing in Silver: Four Ways to Invest and Why." *The Street*, 5 Nov. 2015, www.thestreet.com/markets/commodities/investing-in-silver-14767113.

[2334] Clark, Jeff. "Why Buy Silver? 10 Reasons to Invest in Silver Now (w/ Charts)." *GoldSilver.com*, goldsilver.com/blog/top-10-reasons-to-buy-silver/.

[2335] *Id.*

[2336] Marstrand, Bob. "Lies, damned lies and CPI." *Of Wealth,* 11 Oct. 2016, www.ofwealth.com/lies-damned-lies-cpi/.

money, unbacked by metal, when inflation rears its ugly head, smart investors turn to assets like silver, which has proven itself valuable throughout history."[2337]

"Most economic experts now agree that it is not a question of if, but when the next brutal economic crisis will hit."[2338] Adding silver to a portfolio diversifies investments and mitigates geopolitical, monetary and systemic risks.[2339] Investors can protect themselves and maintain their standard of living by acquiring silver — something with intrinsic value — to insulate themselves from the destructive policies of central bankers.[2340] "Because recent studies show that silver is one of the only asset classes that positively correlates with inflation, this is further evidence that investing in silver is a good way to protect your assets not only in times of economic turmoil but also against the ever-present long term threat of inflation."[2341] "If you're worried that an economic disaster might cause the dollar to plummet, you may be looking to commodities like silver as a safe haven."[2342]

"Market watchers see a positive environment for silver as the Federal Reserve cuts U.S. interest rates as a hedge against inflation and interest rates for German *bunds*, which are German government bonds; and other global fixed-income vehicles turn negative. Very low interest rates make precious metals such as silver and gold

---

[2337] "10 Reasons You Should Invest In Silver." *IRA Gold Advisor*, iragoldadvisor.com/silver-ira/10-reasons-you-should-invest-in-silver/.

[2338] *Id.*

[2339] *Id.*

[2340] *Id.*; Clark, Jeff. "Why Buy Silver? 10 Reasons to Invest in Silver Now (w/ Charts)." *GoldSilver.com*, goldsilver.com/blog/top-10-reasons-to-buy-silver/.

[2341] "10 Reasons You Should Invest In Silver." *IRA Gold Advisor*, iragoldadvisor.com/silver-ira/10-reasons-you-should-invest-in-silver/.

[2342] Josephson, Amelia. "Investing in Silver." *Smartasset*, 15 Aug. 2019, smartasset.com/investing/investing-in-silver.

attractive, since these assets act as a store of value, offsetting the fact [that] no yield is paid."[2343]

Recent studies have shown how silver is one of the only asset classes with a negative correlation to other asset classes, such as stocks and government bonds.[2344] In other words, silver "tends to perform counter-cyclically to the stock market."[2345] This makes the metal a good hedge in uncertain times or even in times of crisis.[2346] "Folks who invest in silver often say that doing so lets them hedge against the risk that their other investments might depreciate – and against the risk of catastrophic events. According to these investors, silver's intrinsic value and history of being used as a currency mean that even if the dollar's value drops, folks who hold silver will come out on top."[2347] "History shows us that those who come out on top after a recession are investors in precious metals, such as silver. When the inevitable coming economic collapse happens, investing in physical silver will not only protect your wealth, but allow it to appreciate significantly. Like an insurance policy, when fire strikes, the benefits outweigh the cost."[2348] "As a stabilizing asset, silver,

---

[2343] Carlson, Debbie. "How to Invest in Silver." *US News*, 1 Aug. 2019, money.usnews.com/investing/investing-101/articles/how-to-invest-in-silver.

[2344] "10 Reasons You Should Invest In Silver." *IRA Gold Advisor*, iragoldadvisor.com/silver-ira/10-reasons-you-should-invest-in-silver/.

[2345] Reed, Eric. "Investing in Silver: Four Ways to Invest and Why." *The Street*, 5 Nov. 2015, www.thestreet.com/markets/commodities/investing-in-silver-14767113.

[2346] "10 Reasons You Should Invest In Silver." *IRA Gold Advisor*, iragoldadvisor.com/silver-ira/10-reasons-you-should-invest-in-silver/; Clark, Jeff. "Why Buy Silver? 10 Reasons to Invest in Silver Now (w/ Charts)." *GoldSilver.com*, goldsilver.com/blog/top-10-reasons-to-buy-silver/.

[2347] Josephson, Amelia. "Investing in Silver." *Smartasset*, 15 Aug. 2019, smartasset.com/investing/investing-in-silver.

[2348] "10 Reasons You Should Invest In Silver." *IRA Gold Advisor*, iragoldadvisor.com/silver-ira/10-reasons-you-should-invest-in-silver/.

like gold, can give your portfolio a steady, diversified return compared to traditional stocks and mutual funds. In particular, they can do so while retaining much higher liquidity than many other forms of safe investment."[2349]

The price of silver is driven by market demand. Industry now accounts for more than half of all demand.[2350] "Industrial use and supply affect silver's value. It's one of the reasons why silver production depends on the health of the economy and the industrial sector."[2351]

Silver has hundreds of industrial and medical applications.[2352] According to author, Mike Maloney, "Of all the elements, silver is the indispensable metal. It is the most electrically conductive, thermally conductive, and reflective. Modern life, as we know it, would not exist without silver."[2353] It is used as a component in electronics and other consumer products, such as cellphones, cameras, laptops, mirrors, monitors, medical devices, solar panels, photovoltaic cells (the main constituents of solar panels), batteries,

---

[2349] Reed, Eric. "Investing in Silver: Four Ways to Invest and Why." *The Street*, 5 Nov. 2015, www.thestreet.com/markets/commodities/investing-in-silver-14767113.

[2350] Clark, Jeff. "Why Buy Silver? 10 Reasons to Invest in Silver Now (w/ Charts)." *GoldSilver.com*, goldsilver.com/blog/top-10-reasons-to-buy-silver/.

[2351] Carlson, Debbie. "How to Invest in Silver." *US News*, 1 Aug. 2019, money.usnews.com/investing/investing-101/articles/how-to-invest-in-silver.

[2352] "10 Reasons You Should Invest In Silver." *IRA Gold Advisor*, iragoldadvisor.com/silver-ira/10-reasons-you-should-invest-in-silver/.

[2353] Clark, Jeff. "Why Buy Silver? 10 Reasons to Invest in Silver Now (w/ Charts)." *GoldSilver.com*, goldsilver.com/blog/top-10-reasons-to-buy-silver/.

electrical switches, etc.[2354] Another common industrial use for silver is as a catalyst for the production of ethylene oxide (used in the production of plastics and chemicals).[2355] In the last two decades, usage has increased substantially to include an array of electronic and digital products, medical appliances due to its anti-microbial properties, and even clothing.[2356] For example, a cell phone contains about one-third of a gram of silver.[2357] The self-heating windshield in the new Volkswagen has an ultra-thin invisible layer of silver instead of tiny wires.[2358] The vehicles also have silver filaments at the bottom of the windshield to heat the wipers so they do not freeze to the glass.[2359]

"Due to its unique characteristics, industrial uses for silver continue to expand, which means we can reasonably expect this source of demand to remain robust."[2360] As our information age progresses and silver's chemical uniqueness is more fully

---

[2354] "10 Reasons You Should Invest In Silver." *IRA Gold Advisor*, iragoldadvisor.com/silver-ira/10-reasons-you-should-invest-in-silver/; Divine, John. "5 Reasons Not to Invest in Gold." *US News*, 10 Jul. 2018, money.usnews.com/investing/articles/2018-07-10/5-reasons-not-to-invest-in-gold; Carlson, Debbie. "How to Invest in Silver." *US News*, 1 Aug. 2019, money.usnews.com/investing/investing-101/articles/how-to-invest-in-silver; Clark, Jeff. "Why Buy Silver? 10 Reasons to Invest in Silver Now (w/ Charts)." *GoldSilver.com*, goldsilver.com/blog/top-10-reasons-to-buy-silver/.

[2355] Clark, Jeff. "Why Buy Silver? 10 Reasons to Invest in Silver Now (w/ Charts)." *GoldSilver.com*, goldsilver.com/blog/top-10-reasons-to-buy-silver/.

[2356] "10 Reasons You Should Invest In Silver." *IRA Gold Advisor*, iragoldadvisor.com/silver-ira/10-reasons-you-should-invest-in-silver/.

[2357] Clark, Jeff. "Why Buy Silver? 10 Reasons to Invest in Silver Now (w/ Charts)." *GoldSilver.com*, goldsilver.com/blog/top-10-reasons-to-buy-silver/.

[2358] *Id.*

[2359] *Id.*

[2360] *Id.*

understood, demand for this irreplaceable metal will continue to rise.[2361]

"While silver is technically a commodity, precious metals are somewhat different as an asset class. Unlike crude oil, corn or lumber, the value of silver isn't limited to its consumption uses. In fact, while silver does have industrial applications, most of its value comes from its status as an investment vehicle. Since silver is used relatively rarely compared to other industrial metals, it does not have production/consumption cycles of most commodities. Instead its value is chiefly driven by either long term investors or those seeking to ride out a down market."[2362] Edmund Moy, director of the U.S. Mint from 2006 to 2011, "told MarketWatch that the rise in silver bullion demand is 'just the beginning,' and is 'primarily driven by individual investors who see silver as an affordable safe haven and because of the lower prices, a buying opportunity.'"[2363]

"Global demand for silver is growing. Virtually all major government mints have seen record levels of sales, with most already operating at peak production."[2364] For example, "[o]n March 12, [2020.] the United States Mint…temporarily sold out of American Silver Eagle bullion coins. 'Our rate of sale in just the first part of March exceeds 300% of what was sold last month,' the

---

[2361] "10 Reasons You Should Invest In Silver." *IRA Gold Advisor*, iragoldadvisor.com/silver-ira/10-reasons-you-should-invest-in-silver/.

[2362] Reed, Eric. "Investing in Silver: Four Ways to Invest and Why." *The Street*, 5 Nov. 2015, www.thestreet.com/markets/commodities/investing-in-silver-14767113.

[2363] Saefong, Myra P. "Physical demand for silver spikes as price drops to an 11-year low." *Market Watch*, 19 Mar. 2020, www.marketwatch.com/story/physical-demand-for-silver-spikes-as-price-drops-to-an-11-year-low-2020-03-19?reflink=mw_share_facebook&fbclid=IwAR2asSl2TwNpIZg8AbtkjBdtyAW_ElE14NwK9FUyPCiFF4rE2OhCpk1RWyc.

[2364] Clark, Jeff. "Why Buy Silver? 10 Reasons to Invest in Silver Now (w/ Charts)." *GoldSilver.com*, goldsilver.com/blog/top-10-reasons-to-buy-silver/.

Mint said."²³⁶⁵ "Sales of the one-ounce American Silver Eagle coins were at 3.1 million so far this month, as of Wednesday, [March 18, 2020] compared with total sales of 650,000 in the month of February..."²³⁶⁶ However, "[s]urging demand is nowhere more evident than China and India. These two behemoth markets have long histories of cultural affinity toward precious metals. And with their populations growing, their tremendous appetite will continue."²³⁶⁷

"At the same time that demand is increasing, silver inventories are falling."²³⁶⁸ Most governments no longer hold stockpiles of silver because it is not used in coinage.²³⁶⁹ The "only countries that warehouse silver are the US, India, and Mexico."²³⁷⁰

Unlike gold, most industrial silver is consumed or destroyed during the fabrication process.²³⁷¹ The "silver is never replenished or returned to stockpiles."²³⁷² This is because it is not economically feasible "to recover every tiny flake of silver from millions of

---

²³⁶⁵ Saefong, Myra P. "Physical demand for silver spikes as price drops to an 11-year low." *Market Watch*, 19 Mar. 2020, www.marketwatch.com/story/physical-demand-for-silver-spikes-as-price-drops-to-an-11-year-low-2020-03-19?reflink=mw_share_facebook&fbclid=IwAR2asSl2TwNpIZg8AbtkjBdtyAW_ElE14NwK9FUyPCiFF4rE2OhCpk1RWyc.

²³⁶⁶ *Id.*

²³⁶⁷ Clark, Jeff. "Why Buy Silver? 10 Reasons to Invest in Silver Now (w/ Charts)." *GoldSilver.com*, goldsilver.com/blog/top-10-reasons-to-buy-silver/.

²³⁶⁸ *Id.*

²³⁶⁹ *Id.*

²³⁷⁰ *Id.*

²³⁷¹ *Id.*

²³⁷² "10 Reasons You Should Invest In Silver." *IRA Gold Advisor*, iragoldadvisor.com/silver-ira/10-reasons-you-should-invest-in-silver/.

discarded products."[2373] As a result, millions of ounces of silver are gone for good.[2374]

Adding to decreased amounts of silver is the fact that miners sometimes scale back the development of new silver mines to cut costs to turn a profit.[2375] About 70% of silver production is a byproduct of base metal mining (copper and zinc, for example).[2376] "Because silver is a by-product, base-metal miners are unlikely to ramp up production if silver demand suddenly spikes."[2377]

Unfortunately, "[t]he majority of the world's silver comes from nations marked with political turmoil, labor unrest, and undeveloped economies. Mexico and Peru account for the largest share of production, both of which have fragile political systems and primitive infrastructure. Geopolitical instability and poor infrastructure in turn significantly strains silver supplies, predicting a dramatic price increase in coming years."[2378] "These realities have set the stage for a peak in silver supply. If demand stays at current levels, it will be difficult for everyone who wants silver to get as much as they need."[2379]

[2373] Clark, Jeff. "Why Buy Silver? 10 Reasons to Invest in Silver Now (w/ Charts)." *GoldSilver.com*, goldsilver.com/blog/top-10-reasons-to-buy-silver/.

[2374] *Id.*

[2375] *Id.*

[2376] Carlson, Debbie. "How to Invest in Silver." *US News*, 1 Aug. 2019, money.usnews.com/investing/investing-101/articles/how-to-invest-in-silver.

[2377] *Id.*

[2378] "10 Reasons You Should Invest In Silver." *IRA Gold Advisor*, iragoldadvisor.com/silver-ira/10-reasons-you-should-invest-in-silver/.

[2379] Clark, Jeff. "Why Buy Silver? 10 Reasons to Invest in Silver Now (w/ Charts)." *GoldSilver.com*, goldsilver.com/blog/top-10-reasons-to-buy-silver/.

At present, however, silver (aka "poor man's gold") is one of the most undervalued assets.[2380] In fact, "[i]t's hard to find an asset with a greater distortion between price and fundamentals."[2381] The historical gold-to-silver ratio has averaged 12 to 1, i.e. 12 ounces of silver to one ounce of gold.[2382] The current gold to silver ratio is around 73:1.[2383] "The gold-to-silver ratio averaged 47:1 during the 20th century. It's averaged about 61:1 in the 21st century. So a ratio at or above 70...makes silver a good buy relative to the price of gold...[T]he ratio sank to almost 30 at the peak of the bull market in 2011. It reached as low as 17 in early 1980."[2384]

During the first quarter of 2020, "[s]ilver prices have seen sharp declines as 'institutions have dumped silver for cash to pay for margin calls and other obligation, as well as hoarding cash,' said Edmund Moy," who was the former Director of the United States Mint.[2385] "[W]hile silver's value as an industrial metal pressured prices on the heels of global economic weakness, an economic recovery may not offer an equal lift. The metal had been held back

---

[2380] "10 Reasons You Should Invest In Silver." *IRA Gold Advisor*, iragoldadvisor.com/silver-ira/10-reasons-you-should-invest-in-silver/.

[2381] Clark, Jeff. "Why Buy Silver? 10 Reasons to Invest in Silver Now (w/ Charts)." *GoldSilver.com*, goldsilver.com/blog/top-10-reasons-to-buy-silver/.

[2382] "10 Reasons You Should Invest In Silver." *IRA Gold Advisor*, iragoldadvisor.com/silver-ira/10-reasons-you-should-invest-in-silver/.

[2383] As of 25 Jan. 2021, the price of gold per ounce was approx. $1855 and the price of silver was $25.30 per troy ounce.

[2384] Clark, Jeff. "Why Buy Silver? 10 Reasons to Invest in Silver Now (w/ Charts)." *GoldSilver.com*, goldsilver.com/blog/top-10-reasons-to-buy-silver/.

[2385] Saefong, Myra P. "Physical demand for silver spikes as price drops to an 11-year low." *Market Watch*, 19 Mar. 2020, www.marketwatch.com/story/physical-demand-for-silver-spikes-as-price-drops-to-an-11-year-l o w - 2 0 2 0 - 0 3 - 1 9 ? reflink=mw_share_facebook&fbclid=IwAR2asSl2TwNpIZg8AbtkjBdtyA W_ElE14NwK9FUyPCiFF4rE2OhCpk1RWyc.

'precisely because of its industrial usage,' with investors anticipating a global slowdown selling every industrial commodity, said [Brien] Lundin [editor and publisher of Gold Newsletter]. Its industrial value 'acts more as a disadvantage than anything else,' offering a reason for 'selling in the advent of an economic slowdown.'"[2386]

However, the gold to silver ratio has always eventually reverted back to 12:1.[2387] With the compression of the gold:silver ratio at current levels, there may be tremendous upside potential for silver investors.[2388] "Eventually, low silver prices will catch up to limited physical supply and increased physical demand," according to Edmund Moy.[2389]

"At the current silver price level, the cost of insurance is tremendously cheap in relation to the wealth it would conserve" when the next financial crisis hits.[2390] In January 2020, "$1,000 [could] buy up to 50 ounces of silver but not even one ounce of gold."[2391] "An investor can buy more silver for less money, making

---

[2386] Saefong, Myra P. "Silver readies for biggest monthly gain in nearly 7 years." *Market Watch*, 22 May 2020, www.marketwatch.com/story/silver-readies-for-biggest-monthly-gain-in-nearly-7-years-2020-05-22?siteid=yhoof2&yptr=yahoo.

[2387] "10 Reasons You Should Invest In Silver." *IRA Gold Advisor*, iragoldadvisor.com/silver-ira/10-reasons-you-should-invest-in-silver/.

[2388] *Id.*

[2389] Saefong, Myra P. "Physical demand for silver spikes as price drops to an 11-year low." *Market Watch*, 19 Mar. 2020, www.marketwatch.com/story/physical-demand-for-silver-spikes-as-price-drops-to-an-11-year-low-2020-03-19?reflink=mw_share_facebook&fbclid=IwAR2asSl2TwNpIZg8AbtkjBdtyAW_ElE14NwK9FUyPCiFF4rE2OhCpk1RWyc.

[2390] "10 Reasons You Should Invest In Silver." *IRA Gold Advisor*, iragoldadvisor.com/silver-ira/10-reasons-you-should-invest-in-silver/.

[2391] *Id.*

it potentially popular choice for lower capitalization investors."[2392] "With the same amount of money, you can buy a lot more silver than gold. If you don't have a lot of extra money and you have your heart set on investing in a precious metal, silver may be a better place to start."[2393]

Conventional advice is for investors to buy low and sell high. However, "skittish investors tend to flock to both gold and silver when an economic crisis has already set in, the stock market is down and metal prices are up. If you jump on this bandwagon, you're committing the classic mistake of 'buying high,' investing in something when its price is already at or near peak."[2394] The time to buy insurance in the form of silver is before disaster strikes — while the prices are still relatively low.

"[D]uring the coming economic collapse, gold prices are expected to rise, but silver prices are expected to rise even more. During the economic crisis of the 1970's, the price of silver rose 3,800%, compared to 2,500% for gold."[2395] "'Silver has a well-documented habit of coming late to gold's party, only to then dramatically outperform the yellow metal,' said Brien Lundin, editor and publisher of Gold Newsletter... 'Once gold has somewhat run its course and starts to look expensive, a lot of people turn to the cheaper counterparty, namely silver, which has attracted fund and investor money,' said David Govett, head of precious metals at

---

[2392] Reed, Eric. "Investing in Silver: Four Ways to Invest and Why." *The Street*, 5 Nov. 2015, www.thestreet.com/markets/commodities/investing-in-silver-14767113.

[2393] Josephson, Amelia. "Investing in Silver." *Smartasset*, 15 Aug. 2019, smartasset.com/investing/investing-in-silver.

[2394] *Id.*

[2395] "10 Reasons You Should Invest In Silver." *IRA Gold Advisor*, iragoldadvisor.com/silver-ira/10-reasons-you-should-invest-in-silver/.

commodity brokerage Marex Spectron…"[2396] "For active investors, this can make silver a potentially lucrative investment, as its tendency toward price swings can lead to sharp upward movements."[2397] Thus, there may be the potential for substantial gains in the future.

"To find baseline silver prices, Peter Thomas, senior vice president of Zaner Precious Metals, says investors should look at the London Silver Fix. This price is updated twice daily and is carried on most precious metals dealers' websites. Dealers use that price to set their bid and offer [ask] prices on physical metals."[2398]

Because of its tendency to be volatile, one should not over-allocate a portfolio to silver. (Silver is about 1.5 times more volatile than gold.)[2399] "Much of this volatility comes from the fact that silver is a smaller market than gold, and that gold tends to draw more investors seeking more stability in uncertain markets."[2400] "Silver is a very small market — so small, in fact, that a little money moving into or out of the industry can impact the price to a much greater degree than other assets (including gold). This greater volatility means that in bear markets, silver falls more than gold. But in bull markets, silver will soar much farther and faster than

[2396] Saefong, Myra P. "Silver readies for biggest monthly gain in nearly 7 years." *Market Watch*, 22 May 2020, www.marketwatch.com/story/silver-readies-for-biggest-monthly-gain-in-nearly-7-years-2020-05-22?siteid=yhoof2&yptr=yahoo.

[2397] Reed, Eric. "Investing in Silver: Four Ways to Invest and Why." *The Street*, 5 Nov. 2015, www.thestreet.com/markets/commodities/investing-in-silver-14767113.

[2398] Carlson, Debbie. "How to Invest in Silver." *US News*, 1 Aug. 2019, money.usnews.com/investing/investing-101/articles/how-to-invest-in-silver.

[2399] *Id.*

[2400] Reed, Eric. "Investing in Silver: Four Ways to Invest and Why." *The Street*, 5 Nov. 2015, www.thestreet.com/markets/commodities/investing-in-silver-14767113.

gold."[2401] "Despite its volatility, investors will often move their money into precious metals at the beginning of a downturn... [S]ilver is seen as a more liquid, safe investment than other non-market options like government bonds. While the high volatility of silver can make selling more difficult, as you may have to wait for the price you want, it is still easier to end your position than in a Treasury bond, and often for a better (if still relatively low) return."[2402]

There are a number of ways to add silver to an asset portfolio. For most investors, this means the traditional buy-and-hold strategy using bullion (coins and/or bars).[2403] Other options are to invest in an exchange-traded fund backed by physical metal, or buy ETFs or mutual funds that include mining stocks.[2404]

Perhaps the simplest and most popular method to invest in silver is to purchase the physical metal itself. "Bullion silver is available in coin and bar form, and most coin dealers and precious metals dealers will offer silver bullion in various sizes and formats. Typically, you can find coins and bars as small as a single ounce, or large bullion bars as big as 1,000 ounces. Owning silver bullion has

---

[2401] Clark, Jeff. "Why Buy Silver? 10 Reasons to Invest in Silver Now (w/ Charts)." *GoldSilver.com*, goldsilver.com/blog/top-10-reasons-to-buy-silver/.

[2402] Reed, Eric. "Investing in Silver: Four Ways to Invest and Why." *The Street*, 5 Nov. 2015, www.thestreet.com/markets/commodities/investing-in-silver-14767113.

[2403] *Id.*; Carlson, Debbie. "How to Invest in Silver." *US News*, 1 Aug. 2019, money.usnews.com/investing/investing-101/articles/how-to-invest-in-silver.

[2404] Carlson, Debbie. "How to Invest in Silver." *US News*, 1 Aug. 2019, money.usnews.com/investing/investing-101/articles/how-to-invest-in-silver.

the advantage of having its value track the market price of silver directly."[2405]

"The easiest way to buy silver coins or bars is online through reputable dealers, says Terry Hanlon, president of Dillon Gage Metals, a metals trading firm in Dallas."[2406] "When it comes to pricing, bullion bars have the least amount of dealer premium, Thomas says, because these products are simply silver poured into a mold. 'It's not really labor intense [sic],' he says. 'You can sometimes buy them for 30 (or) 40 cents over spot price, which is really cheap.' Bullion coins have a higher premium over bars because of the labor that goes into making blanks, stamping them, inspecting and sealing them in a case, Thomas says. The most popular bullion coins with the lowest premiums are a 1-ounce Silver American Eagle from the U.S. Mint and a 1-ounce Canadian Maple Leaf from the Royal Canadian Mint."[2407] One can then sell it at any time for market price, typically minus a dealer commission.[2408]

"Silver dealers also sell bags of junk silver, which are pre-1965 U.S. currency that contain 90% silver such as Mercury Dimes, says Adrian Day, chairman and CEO of Adrian Day Asset Management. Investors can buy $100 or $1,000 in face value, but are priced by their silver content. Day says the rough price currently

---

[2405] Caplinger, Dan. "How to Invest in Silver the Right Way." *The Motley Fool*, 22 May 2017, www.fool.com/investing/2017/05/22/how-to-invest-in-silver-the-right-way.aspx.

[2406] "A good sign is if the dealer is a member of metals industry groups like the Industry Council for Tangible Assets or Professional Numismatists Guild. When researching prices, Hanlon says check a few dealers to get a sense of prevailing prices as most dealers should be competitive where they offer to buy or sell silver." Carlson, Debbie. "How to Invest in Silver." *US News*, 1 Aug. 2019, money.usnews.com/investing/investing-101/articles/how-to-invest-in-silver.

[2407] *Id.*

[2408] Reed, Eric. "Investing in Silver: Four Ways to Invest and Why." *The Street*, 5 Nov. 2015, www.thestreet.com/markets/commodities/investing-in-silver-14767113.

for $100 in old U.S. currency is $1,280 and contains about $1,190 in silver. While junk silver has the highest premium, he says the benefit is owners can sell off individual pieces."[2409] This makes them "very easy to use in emergency hyperinflation situations."[2410] Thus, "stocking up on 'junk' silver coins is a great way to be prepared for a hyperinflation..."[2411]

"Hanlon says most investors focus on bullion bars and coins, while numismatic coins are for collectors. Numismatic coins have a market value separate from bullion...For example, the U.S. Mint just offered a commemorative 2019 proof silver dollar to celebrate the 50th anniversary of Apollo II's moon landing. Those coins were sold at a high premium over the silver bullion price..."[2412]

If the investor chooses to hold physical metal, then he is responsible for storage, insurance and logistics, but one need not deal with any third parties.[2413] "Physical bullion can be stored in a home safe, but for quantities over 1,000 ounces, which weighs at least about 70 pounds, investors should consider depository

[2409] Carlson, Debbie. "How to Invest in Silver." *US News*, 1 Aug. 2019, money.usnews.com/investing/investing-101/articles/how-to-invest-in-silver.

[2410] McMahon, Tim. "Surviving a Hyperinflation." *Financial Trend Forecaster*, 18 Jul. 2013, fintrend.com/2013/07/18/surviving-hyperinflation/.

[2411] *Id.*

[2412] Carlson, Debbie. "How to Invest in Silver." *US News*, 1 Aug. 2019, money.usnews.com/investing/investing-101/articles/how-to-invest-in-silver.

[2413] Reed, Eric. "Investing in Silver: Four Ways to Invest and Why." *The Street*, 5 Nov. 2015, www.thestreet.com/markets/commodities/investing-in-silver-14767113.

storage…"[2414]   Thus, storing bullion may involve some logistical challenges and added costs.[2415]

"Silver can be included in individual retirement accounts, known as IRAs,…[b]ut the Internal Revenue Service has strict requirements on how these assets are stored and the type of coins – American Eagles and Maple Leafs are permitted. Silver coins must be sent straight from the dealer to an approved custodial depository."[2416]

There are a number of disadvantages associated with acquiring physical silver. One will typically pay a commission to buy and sell silver from dealers. "If you expect to hold on to your silver for a long time, then those costs aren't monumental, but for those who want to trade frequently, they're typically too costly to bear several times in close succession."[2417]

Frank Holmes, CEO and chief investment officer of U.S. Global Investors, said, "while he owns both silver coins and equities, he believes silver equities may have an advantage over coins in the current economic environment. He says when stocks are strong and interest rates are low, mining equities can outperform physical silver because of equities' leverage. He adds that's why precious metals prices and equities did so well during the 2002-2007 time frame. 'Commodities were up, stocks were up and interest rates

---

[2414] Carlson, Debbie. "How to Invest in Silver." *US News*, 1 Aug. 2019, money.usnews.com/investing/investing-101/articles/how-to-invest-in-silver.

[2415] Caplinger, Dan. "How to Invest in Silver the Right Way." *The Motley Fool*, 22 May 2017, www.fool.com/investing/2017/05/22/how-to-invest-in-silver-the-right-way.aspx.

[2416] Carlson, Debbie. "How to Invest in Silver." *US News*, 1 Aug. 2019, money.usnews.com/investing/investing-101/articles/how-to-invest-in-silver.

[2417] Caplinger, Dan. "How to Invest in Silver the Right Way." *The Motley Fool*, 22 May 2017, www.fool.com/investing/2017/05/22/how-to-invest-in-silver-the-right-way.aspx.

were falling,' he says. 'In an expanding economy, stocks outperform.'"[2418]

Commodities, futures and options contracts are a way to invest in the movement of the silver market.[2419] With these financial instruments, profit is derived not from the market price of silver, but from the price change.[2420] For instance, an investor can buy silver futures contracts and either go long (betting that its price will go up) or short (betting that its price will go down).[2421]

"Investors who want exposure to the silver price but do not necessarily want to own physical metal can buy silver ETFs."[2422] ETFs trade on a stock exchange and offer a high degree of liquidity.[2423] They "are made of bundled third party assets and your value comes from how those underlying assets perform. A silver ETF is built to track the market price of silver metal. It is often built around a specific quantity of silver or group of bullion assets."[2424] "Each share of a silver ETF corresponds to a certain notional amount of silver, and the prices of ETF shares typically track silver

---

[2418] Carlson, Debbie. "How to Invest in Silver." *US News*, 1 Aug. 2019, money.usnews.com/investing/investing-101/articles/how-to-invest-in-silver.

[2419] Reed, Eric. "Investing in Silver: Four Ways to Invest and Why." *The Street*, 5 Nov. 2015, www.thestreet.com/markets/commodities/investing-in-silver-14767113.

[2420] *Id.*

[2421] Josephson, Amelia. "Investing in Silver." *Smartasset*, 15 Aug. 2019, smartasset.com/investing/investing-in-silver.

[2422] Carlson, Debbie. "How to Invest in Silver." *US News*, 1 Aug. 2019, money.usnews.com/investing/investing-101/articles/how-to-invest-in-silver.

[2423] Josephson, Amelia. "Investing in Silver." *Smartasset*, 15 Aug. 2019, smartasset.com/investing/investing-in-silver.

[2424] Reed, Eric. "Investing in Silver: Four Ways to Invest and Why." *The Street*, 5 Nov. 2015, www.thestreet.com/markets/commodities/investing-in-silver-14767113.

prices fairly closely."[2425] "This is generally considered one of the best ways to own and trade silver with high liquidity and without the logistical challenges of owning the physical asset."[2426] For traders who just want to participate in the price movement, ETFs can be a handy substitute for owning bullion.[2427] "The biggest by assets under management is iShares Silver Trust (ticker: SLV), at $5.8 billion."[2428]

Some investors do not like ETFs because most do not allow for actual possession of silver.[2429] The exception is "Sprott Physical Silver Trust (PSLV), which allows owners to redeem their shares for physical metal."[2430]

"Like any mutual fund or ETF, silver ETFs have expenses that get charged through to shareholders, but they tend to be fairly modest. The iShares Silver ETF (SLV), for example, charges an annual expense ratio of 0.5%. In addition, ETF shares can trade at a

---

[2425] Caplinger, Dan. "How to Invest in Silver the Right Way." *The Motley Fool*, 22 May 2017, www.fool.com/investing/2017/05/22/how-to-invest-in-silver-the-right-way.aspx.

[2426] Reed, Eric. "Investing in Silver: Four Ways to Invest and Why." *The Street*, 5 Nov. 2015, www.thestreet.com/markets/commodities/investing-in-silver-14767113.

[2427] Caplinger, Dan. "How to Invest in Silver the Right Way." *The Motley Fool*, 22 May 2017, www.fool.com/investing/2017/05/22/how-to-invest-in-silver-the-right-way.aspx.

[2428] Carlson, Debbie. "How to Invest in Silver." *US News*, 1 Aug. 2019, money.usnews.com/investing/investing-101/articles/how-to-invest-in-silver.

[2429] Caplinger, Dan. "How to Invest in Silver the Right Way." *The Motley Fool*, 22 May 2017, www.fool.com/investing/2017/05/22/how-to-invest-in-silver-the-right-way.aspx.

[2430] Assuming it is available. Carlson, Debbie. "How to Invest in Silver." *US News*, 1 Aug. 2019, money.usnews.com/investing/investing-101/articles/how-to-invest-in-silver.

premium or discount to the actual value of silver, leading to some discrepancies depending on when you trade shares."[2431]

Another option is to buy stock in silver mining companies or firms that deal in the production, distribution and use of silver.[2432] "Silver mining stocks usually rise in value when silver prices go up and fall when silver performs poorly. Often, for a given price increase in silver bullion, mining stocks will climb several times that amount in percentage terms."[2433] "These stocks generally track the market value of silver but have value beyond pure supply and demand. As a result, they can be more reliable and less volatile than pure silver…"[2434] According to Adrian Day, miners who have silver production in their portfolio will benefit from silver price rises, and many of these company's current share price reflects the white metal's recent bounce.[2435] Some miners with significant silver production are Pan American Silver (PAAS) and Fortuna Silver Mines (FSM).[2436] However, there are often high fees and

---

[2431] Caplinger, Dan. "How to Invest in Silver the Right Way." *The Motley Fool*, 22 May 2017, www.fool.com/investing/2017/05/22/how-to-invest-in-silver-the-right-way.aspx.

[2432] Reed, Eric. "Investing in Silver: Four Ways to Invest and Why." *The Street*, 5 Nov. 2015, www.thestreet.com/markets/commodities/investing-in-silver-14767113.

[2433] Caplinger, Dan. "How to Invest in Silver the Right Way." *The Motley Fool*, 22 May 2017, www.fool.com/investing/2017/05/22/how-to-invest-in-silver-the-right-way.aspx.

[2434] Reed, Eric. "Investing in Silver: Four Ways to Invest and Why." *The Street*, 5 Nov. 2015, www.thestreet.com/markets/commodities/investing-in-silver-14767113.

[2435] Carlson, Debbie. "How to Invest in Silver." *US News*, 1 Aug. 2019, money.usnews.com/investing/investing-101/articles/how-to-invest-in-silver.

[2436] *Id.*

commissions associated with investing in individual silver stocks.[2437]

Another challenge with silver miners is that the investor not only runs the risk that the price of silver could fall, but also has to contend with the inherent risks of managing a mining company, such as business-related liabilities.[2438] "Sometimes, an accident at a mine or a bad result in exploring a potential property for silver will result in bad performance from a particular company, even if the silver market is generally strong."[2439] Hedging this risk by owning a basket of mining stocks can offer some protection.[2440]

For those seeking a return, mining stocks are more speculative, while streaming stocks offer more stability and often greater income.[2441] While most mining stocks do not pay dividends, most streaming companies do.[2442] "Silver streaming companies do not run mining operations themselves, but rather offer financing to miners, getting back a royalty or streaming interest in their production."[2443] "Usually, streaming companies are able to buy silver production from their mining partners at a fraction of the current market price, offering them a way to get paid back and earn a profit from their capital. Streaming company stocks therefore rise

[2437] Josephson, Amelia. "Investing in Silver." *Smartasset*, 15 Aug. 2019, smartasset.com/investing/investing-in-silver.

[2438] Reed, Eric. "Investing in Silver: Four Ways to Invest and Why." *The Street*, 5 Nov. 2015, www.thestreet.com/markets/commodities/investing-in-silver-14767113.

[2439] Caplinger, Dan. "How to Invest in Silver the Right Way." *The Motley Fool*, 22 May 2017, www.fool.com/investing/2017/05/22/how-to-invest-in-silver-the-right-way.aspx.

[2440] *Id.*

[2441] *Id.*

[2442] *Id.*

[2443] *Id.*

and fall with silver prices, but they're also affected by the quality of financing deals they can arrange."[2444]

When it comes to the matter of government confiscation of the white metal, "[s]ome investors assume silver would be exempt. That's usually because past confiscations mainly focused on gold, since silver wasn't part of the monetary system."[2445] "What is not well known is that President {Franklin} Roosevelt also confiscated silver, even though it was not legal tender at that time."[2446] "[A] year after the 1933 confiscation order, President Roosevelt signed Executive Order 6814 that 'required the delivery of all silver to the United States for coinage."[2447] The objective was the same: To achieve greater monetary inflation. In an attempt to increase the money supply, the confiscated silver was used to insert a new type of legal tender in the economy: silver coins and silver certificates. The 1934 confiscation of silver turned silver into a monetary precious metal again," which it would remain until the mid-1960s.[2448] Thus, if confiscation is a concern, then silver jewelry may be the solution.

The next section will focus on dividend stocks.

[2444] *Id.*

[2445] Clark, Jeff and Mike Maloney. "Gold & Silver Confiscation: Can the Government Seize Assets? (Video)." *GoldSilver.com*, goldsilver.com/blog/gold-confiscation-history-myths-and-real-solutions/.

[2446] Dirkmaat, Olav. "Do Not Worry about Gold Confiscation." *Gold Republic*, 16 Jun. 2015, www.goldrepublic.com/news/gold-confiscation.

[2447] Clark, Jeff and Mike Maloney. "Gold & Silver Confiscation: Can the Government Seize Assets? (Video)." *GoldSilver.com*, goldsilver.com/blog/gold-confiscation-history-myths-and-real-solutions/.

[2448] Dirkmaat, Olav. "Do Not Worry about Gold Confiscation." *Gold Republic*, 16 Jun. 2015, www.goldrepublic.com/news/gold-confiscation.

Dividend Stocks

Dr. Ron Paul complained that the Fed has "destroyed the most important financial price that people should have for investment, and that is the interest rates of money."[2449] "At the end of 2007, before the Wall Street crash in 2008, a senior citizen could invest $10,000 in a 10-year Treasury note and get $400 a year in income, or 4 percent. Today, that same $10,000 generates just 0.67 percent or $67. Seniors who were living on their Treasury income have experienced an 83 percent drop in income while food costs and pharmaceutical costs have soared…"[2450]

"Because yields on Treasury securities have collapsed by 83 percent since the financial crash, investors, including risk-adverse senior citizens, have been driven into the stock market in order to capture the higher dividends paid on stocks…"[2451] "Dividend paying stocks will, as a result, represent a more attractive alternative."[2452] Indeed, "dividends will be the key factor for retirees."[2453] "This

---

[2449] At 2. RonPaulLibertyReport. "Central Banking Is On The Ropes: Gold Will Survive & The Fed Will End." *Youtube*, 13 Dec. 2019, www.youtube.com/watch?v=Ndcb2SPRU7M.

[2450] Martens, Pam and Russ Martens. "The Federal Reserve Now Owns 15 Percent of the U.S. Treasury Market; At Its Current Rate, It Could Own the Whole Market in Less than Two Years." *Wall Street on Parade*, 28 Mar. 2020, wallstreetonparade.com/2020/03/the-federal-reserve-now-owns-15-percent-of-the-u-s-treasury-market-at-its-current-rate-it-could-own-the-whole-market-in-less-than-two-years/.

[2451] *Id.*

[2452] Carosa, Chris. "What Are 'Negative' Interest Rates And How Can You Make Money From Them?" *Forbes*, 20 Aug. 2019, www.forbes.com/sites/chriscarosa/2019/08/20/what-are-negative-interest-rates-and-how-can-you-make-money-from-them/#4766600a409b.

[2453] *Id.*

demand can then further push up the price of dividend paying stocks.""[2454]

"Historically speaking, few, if any, asset classes have outperformed the stock market over the long term."[2455] Warren Buffett, the CEO of Berkshire Hathaway (BRK.A, BRK.B), opined that gold investors are "right to be afraid of paper money. Their basic premise that paper money around the world is going to be worth less and less over time is absolutely correct. They have the correct basic premise. They should run from paper money, but where they run to is the mistake," implying that dividend stocks are preferable.[2456] Robert R. Johnson, principal at the Fed Policy Investment Research Group, wrote in the book, *Invest with the Fed*, "that gold underperforms equities in all interest rate environments, despite its celebrated popular status as a hedge against inflation..."[2457]

Over the long run, stocks have beaten inflation by a comfortable margin.[2458] "Including dividend reinvestment and inflation, the stock market has returned an average of 7% annually."[2459] "From 1972 through 2013, common stocks returned 14.68 percent in falling rate environments while gold futures returned 7.85 percent. In rising rate environments, stocks returned

---

[2454] *Id.*

[2455] Williams, Sean. "The 6 Biggest Risks to Bitcoin." *The Motley Fool*, 27 Nov. 2017, www.fool.com/investing/2017/11/27/the-6-biggest-risks-to-bitcoin.aspx.

[2456] Divine, John. "5 Reasons Not to Invest in Gold." *US News*, 10 Jul. 2018, money.usnews.com/investing/articles/2018-07-10/5-reasons-not-to-invest-in-gold.

[2457] *Id.*

[2458] Marstrand, Bob. "Lies, damned lies and CPI." *Of Wealth,* 11 Oct. 2016, www.ofwealth.com/lies-damned-lies-cpi/.

[2459] Williams, Sean. "The 6 Biggest Risks to Bitcoin." *The Motley Fool*, 27 Nov. 2017, www.fool.com/investing/2017/11/27/the-6-biggest-risks-to-bitcoin.aspx.

8.47 percent while gold only returned 4.86 percent. When rates were flat, stocks provided a gain of 10.61 percent and gold returned 8.61 percent."[2460]

"Stocks are considered to be the best hedge against inflation, as the rise in stock prices are inclusive of the effects of inflation. Since any increase in the cost of raw materials, labor, transport and other facets of operation leads to an increase in the price of the finished product a company produces, the inflationary effect gets reflected in stock prices."[2461] "As long as you can add brand-name businesses with superior yields to your portfolio, you should be able to generate income above and beyond the rate of inflation."[2462]

"One of the best things about stocks is their ability to produce income for the shareholder."[2463] "In the somewhat unlikely event that the Fed does choose to adopt negative interest rates, there's a pretty simple solution that should allow investors to generate real wealth and sleep well at night. This solution? Buy high-quality dividend stocks."[2464]

[2460] Divine, John. "5 Reasons Not to Invest in Gold." *US News*, 10 Jul. 2018, money.usnews.com/investing/articles/2018-07-10/5-reasons-not-to-invest-in-gold.

[2461] Fernando, Jason. "Inflation." *Investopedia*, 18 Nov. 2020, www.investopedia.com/terms/i/inflation.asp.

[2462] Williams, Sean. "3 Dangers of a Negative Interest Rate Policy." *The Motley Fool*, 20 Feb. 2016, www.fool.com/investing/general/2016/02/20/3-dangers-of-a-negative-interest-rate-policy.aspx.

[2463] Divine, John. "5 Reasons Not to Invest in Gold." *US News*, 10 Jul. 2018, money.usnews.com/investing/articles/2018-07-10/5-reasons-not-to-invest-in-gold.

[2464] Williams, Sean. "3 Dangers of a Negative Interest Rate Policy." *The Motley Fool*, 20 Feb. 2016, www.fool.com/investing/general/2016/02/20/3-dangers-of-a-negative-interest-rate-policy.aspx.

"Dividends are payments made by a corporation to its shareholders, typically as a form of profit-sharing."[2465]   Dividends are the most visible and direct way that corporations can share profits with stockholders.[2466]   "Dividend stocks distribute a portion of the company's earnings to investors on a regular basis. Most American dividend stocks pay investors a set amount each quarter, and the top ones increase their payouts over time, so investors can build an annuity-like cash stream…"[2467]   Depending on the company's policies, dividends can be paid on a monthly, quarterly, annual, or biannual basis.[2468]

"Dividend stocks are usually well-established companies with a track record of distributing earnings back to shareholders" in the form of dividends.[2469]   "Large corporations with a long history of financial stability and low volatility are the most likely to pay out dividends because they are more likely to be in a position where enough capital is stored to handle market fluctuations and keep day-to-day operations running in the event of a bad quarter or two."[2470]

"Although investing in the stock market involves more risk than investing in bonds, dividend-paying stocks offer modest

---

[2465] Horvath, Sarah. "How To Invest In Dividend-Paying Stocks." *Benzinga*, 25 Nov. 2019, www.benzinga.com/money/how-to-invest-in-dividend-stocks/.

[2466] *Id.*

[2467] Royal, James, PhD and Arielle O'Shea. "How to Invest in Dividend Stocks." *Nerdwallet*, 2 May 2019, www.nerdwallet.com/blog/investing/how-to-invest-dividend-stocks/.

[2468] Horvath, Sarah. "How To Invest In Dividend-Paying Stocks." *Benzinga*, 25 Nov. 2019, www.benzinga.com/money/how-to-invest-in-dividend-stocks/.

[2469] "Dividend Stocks." *Investopedia*, www.investopedia.com/dividend-stocks-4689744.

[2470] Horvath, Sarah. "How To Invest In Dividend-Paying Stocks." *Benzinga*, 25 Nov. 2019, www.benzinga.com/money/how-to-invest-in-dividend-stocks/.

income and the potential for longer-term capital appreciation. High-dividend stocks have become a more popular option for income-oriented investors in recent years since traditional fixed-income investments such as bank accounts, certificates of deposit, and U.S. Treasuries pay next to nothing. At a time of low bond yields, the typical 1.5%-5% yield you can get from dividend-paying stocks becomes much more attractive..."[2471]   The investor can "enjoy streams of passive income from his or her holdings..."[2472]   Over time, not only do you get to keep your equity in a growing company, but you get to receive the stock dividends paid out over the years, too."[2473]

"Many investors have done well for themselves by focusing on dividend stocks by using one of two strategies — dividend growth, which focuses on acquiring a diversified portfolio of companies that have raised their dividends at rates considerably above average and high dividend yield, which focuses on stocks that offer significantly above-average dividend yields as measured by the dividend rate compared to the stock market price..."[2474]   Dividend yield is "how much a company pays out in dividends each year

[2471] Thomas, Kenny. "The Basics of Investing in Dividend-Paying Stocks." *The Balance*, 31 May 2019, www.thebalance.com/the-basics-of-investing-in-dividend-paying-stocks-416832.

[2472] Kennon, Joshua. "Reasons to Consider Investing in Dividend Stocks." *The Balance*, 22 Jan. 2019, www.thebalance.com/consider-investing-in-dividend-stocks-4059284.

[2473] Divine, John. "5 Reasons Not to Invest in Gold." *US News*, 10 Jul. 2018, money.usnews.com/investing/articles/2018-07-10/5-reasons-not-to-invest-in-gold.

[2474] Kennon, Joshua. "Reasons to Consider Investing in Dividend Stocks." *The Balance*, 22 Jan. 2019, www.thebalance.com/consider-investing-in-dividend-stocks-4059284.

relative to its share price, and is usually expressed as a percentage."[2475]

"[D]ividend stocks tend to do better than the average stock over long periods of time…"[2476] "Historically, dividend-paying stocks also perform better than the overall market during times in which stock prices are weak."[2477] "Since stocks that pay dividends are generally more conservative and have stronger cash flows than those that do not, investors tend to gravitate toward dividend payers during times of trouble…"[2478]

There are two ways to collect dividends. One is a cash payment deposited directly into the brokerage account; the other is taking part in a dividend reinvestment plan (DRIP).[2479] A DRIP automatically reinvests dividend payments into buying more shares of the stock.[2480] According to Wharton professor, Dr. Jeremy Siegel, "investors who reinvest their dividends accumulate more shares

---

[2475] Royal, James, PhD and Arielle O'Shea. "How to Invest in Dividend Stocks." *Nerdwallet*, 2 May 2019, www.nerdwallet.com/blog/investing/how-to-invest-dividend-stocks/.

[2476] Kennon, Joshua. "Reasons to Consider Investing in Dividend Stocks." *The Balance*, 22 Jan. 2019, www.thebalance.com/consider-investing-in-dividend-stocks-4059284.

[2477] Thomas, Kenny. "The Basics of Investing in Dividend-Paying Stocks." *The Balance*, 31 May 2019, www.thebalance.com/the-basics-of-investing-in-dividend-paying-stocks-416832.

[2478] *Id.*

[2479] The dividend may also be mailed as a check, directly deposited into their checking or savings account, or sent to their broker for deposit in their brokerage account. Horvath, Sarah. "How To Invest In Dividend-Paying Stocks." *Benzinga*, 25 Nov. 2019, www.benzinga.com/money/how-to-invest-in-dividend-stocks/; Kennon, Joshua. "Reasons to Consider Investing in Dividend Stocks." *The Balance*, 22 Jan. 2019, www.thebalance.com/consider-investing-in-dividend-stocks-4059284.

[2480] Horvath, Sarah. "How To Invest In Dividend-Paying Stocks." *Benzinga*, 25 Nov. 2019, www.benzinga.com/money/how-to-invest-in-dividend-stocks/.

during stock market collapses as the dividend yield expanding allows them to gobble up more equity with each dividend check they shove back into their account or dividend reinvestment plan..."[2481] This is called the "Return Accelerator" or bear market protector.[2482]

Dividends are categorized as "qualified" or "nonqualified." "Most dividend stocks pay 'qualified' dividends, which receive special tax treatment. Depending on your tax bracket, qualified dividends are taxed at a rate of 0% to 20%, significantly lower than the ordinary income tax rates of 10% to 39.6%."[2483] Qualified dividends are "tax-free for those in the 10-15% tax brackets so long as the income from those dividends does not push the investor above that tax bracket. If it does, then dividend income is taxed at a 15% rate for those in the 25-35% tax brackets and 20% for those above it."[2484] High-earners pay an additional "3.8% tax on certain investment income, on top of their applicable tax rate."[2485]

[2481] Kennon, Joshua. "Reasons to Consider Investing in Dividend Stocks." *The Balance*, 22 Jan. 2019, www.thebalance.com/consider-investing-in-dividend-stocks-4059284.

[2482] *Id.*

[2483] "Of course, this doesn't apply if your dividend stocks are held in a tax-advantaged retirement account such as an IRA." Motley Fool Staff. "Dividend Investing for Beginners." *The Motley Fool*, 10 Apr. 2019, www.fool.com/how-to-invest/dividend-investing-for-beginners.aspx.

[2484] "Investors get a tax form at the end of the year showing how much they received in dividend income." "Dividends In Action: How They Work And What To Do With Them." *Future Advisor*, www.futureadvisor.com/content/resources/getting-started/portfolio-strategy/why-dividend-paying-stocks-have-advantages-long-term.

[2485] Motley Fool Staff. "Dividend Investing for Beginners." *The Motley Fool*, 10 Apr. 2019, www.fool.com/how-to-invest/dividend-investing-for-beginners.aspx.

Nonqualified dividends are taxed at regular income tax rates.[2486] "Real estate investment trusts, or REITs, are a good example of stocks whose dividends are generally considered ordinary income."[2487]

There are special classes of dividend stocks, which include master limited partnerships (MLPs), real estate investment trusts (REITs), and business development corporations (BDCs)."[2488] "All three are considered pass-through entities, which means that they must pay out 90% of their income as dividends."[2489] Because they are "required to pay out most of their net income as distributions, MLPs, REITs, and BDCs usually have higher dividends than typical stocks."[2490] They are also exempt from corporate taxes.[2491]

"MLPs are usually found in the oil and gas, real estate, and other natural-resource sectors, especially pipelines and storage entities that throw off predictable cash flow."[2492] "For MLPs, which are considered a partnership, distributions are often classified as a return of capital and aren't taxed as dividends. Rather, the return of capital lowers your tax basis, so investors often only pay taxes when

---

[2486] "Dividends In Action: How They Work And What To Do With Them." *Future Advisor*, www.futureadvisor.com/content/resources/getting-started/portfolio-strategy/why-dividend-paying-stocks-have-advantages-long-term.

[2487] Motley Fool Staff. "Dividend Investing for Beginners." *The Motley Fool*, 10 Apr. 2019, www.fool.com/how-to-invest/dividend-investing-for-beginners.aspx.

[2488] "Dividends In Action: How They Work And What To Do With Them." *Future Advisor*, www.futureadvisor.com/content/resources/getting-started/portfolio-strategy/why-dividend-paying-stocks-have-advantages-long-term.

[2489] *Id.*

[2490] *Id.*

[2491] *Id.*

[2492] *Id.*

they sell."[2493]   However, "MLPs tend to be in commodity-related businesses, which can be cyclical and somewhat risky."[2494]

"REITs are found in the real estate sector and can be either equity REITs or debt (mortgage) REITs. In addition to residential and commercial REITs, many REITs offer exposure to real estate within specific sectors, such as hospitals."[2495]

"BDCs mainly invest in a portfolio of debt securities but also some equity securities of small- and medium-sized businesses."[2496]

"[D]istributions from REITs and BDCs, which are corporations, are often taxed as ordinary income, which can be taxed at a higher rate — up to 39.6% — than the qualified dividends of traditional equities, which are taxed only up to 20%."[2497]

"All three asset classes are usually highly leveraged."[2498] In order to grow, MLPs, REITs, and BDCs often need to issue more equity or debt to fund it.[2499]   This allows for high dividend yields, but carries risk.[2500]

"In a nutshell, the best reason to invest in dividend stocks is to get rich slowly. Dividend-paying companies tend to be more mature and stable than their non-dividend counterparts, so while they aren't likely to skyrocket immediately, a solid portfolio of dividend stocks can create massive amounts of wealth over long periods of time... Since dividend stocks tend to be mature and profitable companies, they generally survive recessions and crashes better than non-

---

[2493] *Id.*

[2494] *Id.*

[2495] *Id.*

[2496] *Id.*

[2497] *Id.*

[2498] *Id.*

[2499] *Id.*

[2500] *Id.*

dividend stocks, and also tend to be less volatile…"[2501] "The companies that offer them don't like telling investors that they're not going to get them any longer, so the firms that tend to issue dividends – even on the lower end of the credit rating scale – are generally established, cash-rich and can ride out tough markets…"[2502] Benjamin Graham wrote, "The real money in investing will have to be made — as most of it has been in the past — not out of buying and selling, but out of owning and holding securities, receiving interest and dividends, and benefiting from their long-term increase in value."[2503]

In order to find a dividend-paying stock, start with a stock-screener that will identify which stocks pay dividends. This may be on an online broker's website, but free online tools include Zacks (https://www.zacks.com/screening/stock-screener) and Financial Visualization (https://finviz.com/screener.ashx).

"What you want to buy are high-quality stocks of companies that not only have enough cash on hand and future cash flow to ride out an economic storm but also have a history of increasing their dividend payouts each year, says Jay Sommariva, vice president and director of fixed income at Fort Pitt Capital Group…'Looking at historical dividend payers without decreases is a good place to start,' Sommariva says. But he notes that even these types of stocks are subject to large price drops in tough market environments, such as the panic-induced selloffs sparked by the coronavirus outbreak. As of early February [2020], 64 companies in the S&P 500 have

---

[2501] Motley Fool Staff. "Dividend Investing for Beginners." *The Motley Fool*, 10 Apr. 2019, www.fool.com/how-to-invest/dividend-investing-for-beginners.aspx.

[2502] "Dividends In Action: How They Work And What To Do With Them." *Future Advisor*, www.futureadvisor.com/content/resources/getting-started/portfolio-strategy/why-dividend-paying-stocks-have-advantages-long-term.

[2503] Kennon, Joshua. "Reasons to Consider Investing in Dividend Stocks." *The Balance*, 22 Jan. 2019, www.thebalance.com/consider-investing-in-dividend-stocks-4059284.

increased their dividend payouts to shareholders for 25 consecutive years or more, according to S&P Dow Jones Indices. These 'dividend aristocrats' include members of the Dow Jones industrial average, such as 3M, Coca-Cola, Johnson & Johnson, Procter & Gamble and Walmart. While tech stocks are new to the dividend-paying game, some tied to long-term growth trends, such as Big Data and digital communications, also offer plump yields without the risk of a dividend cut, says Matt Burdett, manager of Thornburg Investment Income Builder Fund. He cites Broadcom, a semiconductor and infrastructure software company, as an example. 'Broadcom is priced at a discount but is tied to the secular growth of more data and communications driving its cash flow,' Burdett says... Other big tech stocks that pay a fatter dividend than you can get on a 10-year Treasury include Apple, Microsoft, Intel, Cisco Systems and Qualcomm."[2504]

As long as a stock pays a reasonable dividend (for ex., 2%), there are other factors to consider. "Investors also look for companies with strong fundamentals backing up the dividend, such as robust earnings growth, solid balance sheets, and attractive valuations."[2505] In addition, "dividend consistency and growth are two things that are significantly more important for long-term investors than the stock's current yield..."[2506] For example, earnings-per-share (EPS) growth, i.e. whether the earnings are

---

[2504] Shell, Adam. "4 ways to invest when interest rates are plunging on coronavirus worries." *USA Today*, 9 Mar. 2020, www.usatoday.com/story/money/2020/03/09/interest-rates-plunge-on-coronavirus-fears-investing/4973410002/.

[2505] Thomas, Kenny. "The Basics of Investing in Dividend-Paying Stocks." *The Balance*, 31 May 2019, www.thebalance.com/the-basics-of-investing-in-dividend-paying-stocks-416832.

[2506] *Id.*

consistently growing, should be considered.[2507] This is a good indicator of whether a stock will continue to grow its dividend.[2508]

The total return is also useful to evaluate for an overall picture of the stock's performance.[2509] The total return is the appreciation of both dividends and share price.[2510] For instance, if a stock rises by 6% this year and pays a 3% dividend yield, its total return is 9%.[2511]

Once a potential dividend stock has been identified, assess the safety of that dividend. "A safe payout should be your top consideration in buying any dividend-paying investment…"[2512] "Companies are not required to pay their shareholders dividends — this means that a corporation can choose to raise, lower, or eliminate dividends at any time…"[2513] Therefore, look at its financial statements to make sure that the company can sustain its dividend. For that, investors should determine what the payout ratio or the cash dividend payout ratio is.[2514]

[2507] *Id.*

[2508] *Id.*

[2509] *Id.*

[2510] *Id.*

[2511] *Id.*

[2512] Royal, James, PhD and Arielle O'Shea. "How to Invest in Dividend Stocks." *Nerdwallet*, 2 May 2019, www.nerdwallet.com/blog/investing/how-to-invest-dividend-stocks/.

[2513] Consider selling the stock should dividends fall below a certain threshold. Horvath, Sarah. "How To Invest In Dividend-Paying Stocks." *Benzinga*, 25 Nov. 2019, www.benzinga.com/money/how-to-invest-in-dividend-stocks/.

[2514] Duberstein, Billy. "4 Dividend Investing Tips That Could Earn You Thousands." *The Motley Fool,* 7 Dec. 2019, www.fool.com/investing/2019/12/07/4-dividend-investing-tips-that-could-earn-you-thou.aspx.

The payout ratio shows what percentage of a company's net income is paid out as dividends.[2515] It "is the stock's dividend as a percentage of its earnings, and shows a stock's ability to continue to pay its dividend, even if profits drop."[2516] "For instance, a 25% payout ratio means that a company is paying out 25% of its net income as a dividend, with the remaining 75% available for reinvestment in growth, stock buybacks, or paying down debt."[2517] "The lower it is, the safer the dividend and the faster the dividend can grow over time. A payout ratio over 80% is generally a red flag…"[2518]

An even better metric for dividend safety is the cash dividend payout ratio, which is the payout ratio in relation to a company's free cash flow.[2519] "This is because net income may be misleading in certain circumstances. For instance, if a company has very high reinvestment needs, its capital expenditures may be much higher than its non-cash depreciation expenses. As such, the cash flow available for dividends may be lower than the company's headline net income figure."[2520]

[2515] Thomas, Kenny. "The Basics of Investing in Dividend-Paying Stocks." *The Balance*, 31 May 2019, www.thebalance.com/the-basics-of-investing-in-dividend-paying-stocks-416832.

[2516] *Id.*

[2517] Duberstein, Billy. "4 Dividend Investing Tips That Could Earn You Thousands." *The Motley Fool,* 7 Dec. 2019, www.fool.com/investing/2019/12/07/4-dividend-investing-tips-that-could-earn-you-thou.aspx.

[2518] Royal, James, PhD and Arielle O'Shea. "How to Invest in Dividend Stocks." *Nerdwallet*, 2 May 2019, www.nerdwallet.com/blog/investing/how-to-invest-dividend-stocks/.

[2519] Duberstein, Billy. "4 Dividend Investing Tips That Could Earn You Thousands." *The Motley Fool,* 7 Dec. 2019, www.fool.com/investing/2019/12/07/4-dividend-investing-tips-that-could-earn-you-thou.aspx.

[2520] "Net income can…be misleading for the MLP, REIT, and BDC structures…, because real estate often gets preferred tax treatment with large or accelerated depreciation expenses -- even though real estate tends to appreciate, not depreciate, over time." *Id.*

When buying a dividend stock, do not be a "yield pig," focusing only on the highest dividend yields.[2521] Generally, a higher dividend yield is preferable, but it can also be a red flag. The investor is cautioned that "anything above 3.5% should be examined more closely to assess the safety of the investment."[2522] "In some cases, an elevated dividend yield can serve as a warning that a stock's price might be depressed for a fundamental reason."[2523] "A high yield often signals that investors are skeptical of the company's ability to sustain the dividend and that it may be in danger of being cut. That skepticism drives down share price, and a lower share price pushes the yield ratio higher. If the market thinks the dividend will be cut and it is cut, the stock will go down and you'll lose money. Plus, you'll have a smaller dividend."[2524] "You don't want to simply go out and buy stocks with the highest yields, as those companies might be weaker financially and more apt to cut their dividends in tough times."[2525]

"[I]nvestors should assess the potential for their dividends to grow. To analyze the growth potential for the dividend, you not only have to analyze the company's payout ratios but also how much a company's free cash flow per share can grow over time. This comes down to an analysis of the growth prospects of the underlying

---

[2521] Royal, James, PhD and Arielle O'Shea. "How to Invest in Dividend Stocks." *Nerdwallet*, 2 May 2019, www.nerdwallet.com/blog/investing/how-to-invest-dividend-stocks/.

[2522] *Id.*

[2523] Thomas, Kenny. "The Basics of Investing in Dividend-Paying Stocks." *The Balance*, 31 May 2019, www.thebalance.com/the-basics-of-investing-in-dividend-paying-stocks-416832.

[2524] Royal, James, PhD and Arielle O'Shea. "How to Invest in Dividend Stocks." *Nerdwallet*, 2 May 2019, www.nerdwallet.com/blog/investing/how-to-invest-dividend-stocks/.

[2525] Shell, Adam. "4 ways to invest when interest rates are plunging on coronavirus worries." *USA Today*, 9 Mar. 2020, www.usatoday.com/story/money/2020/03/09/interest-rates-plunge-on-coronavirus-fears-investing/4973410002/.

business, which will require you to analyze a company's competitive advantages, total addressable market, potential for margin expansion, and management's capital allocation policies."[2526]

There are several important dates to be aware of when buying dividend-paying stocks. They will determine if and when the investor will receive the next dividend payment. For example, the trade date is the date the stock is bought.[2527] The settlement date is three business days after the trade date.[2528] This is the day that the purchase is finalized and the buyer becomes a "shareholder of record" on the company's books.[2529] The declaration date is the date when the company's board of directors declares its dividend. The ex-dividend date (or ex-date) is the first day a stock trades without its dividend.[2530] Traders must purchase the stock prior to the ex-date to receive the dividend payment. "If you buy shares before the ex-dividend date, you are entitled to that dividend payment. If you purchase the shares on or after this date, you won't get paid until the next dividend cycle."[2531] The record date is two business days after the ex-dividend date; it is the day when a company records current shareholders as eligible to receive the dividend.[2532] "This ensures that everyone who completed a trade

---

[2526] Duberstein, Billy. "4 Dividend Investing Tips That Could Earn You Thousands." *The Motley Fool,* 7 Dec. 2019, www.fool.com/investing/2019/12/07/4-dividend-investing-tips-that-could-earn-you-thou.aspx.

[2527] Thomas, Kenny. "The Basics of Investing in Dividend-Paying Stocks." *The Balance*, 31 May 2019, www.thebalance.com/the-basics-of-investing-in-dividend-paying-stocks-416832.

[2528] *Id.*

[2529] *Id.*

[2530] The ex-date is also the day when the stock price often drops in accord with the declared dividend amount. *Id.*

[2531] Thomas, Kenny. "The Basics of Investing in Dividend-Paying Stocks." *The Balance*, 31 May 2019, www.thebalance.com/the-basics-of-investing-in-dividend-paying-stocks-416832.

[2532] *Id.*

before the ex-dividend date becomes a shareholder of record on or before the record date."[2533]   The pay date is the day the dividend is disbursed to shareholders.[2534]

After examining a stock's dividend details, the next step is to look at the stock's quote, which is a summary of information on the stock. Free stock quotes are available on Google Finance, Yahoo Finance, NASDAQ.com, zacks.com, morningstar.com, and finviz.com.   In addition to dividend yield, other important considerations include the price to earnings (P/E) ratio, volume, and Money Flow Index (MFI).

The P/E ratio (aka the price multiple or the earnings multiple) is one of the most widely-used stock analysis tools to determine stock valuation.[2535]   It relates a company's share price to its earnings per share.[2536]   The P/E ratio helps investors ascertain the market value of a stock as compared to the company's earnings.[2537]   "The price-to-earnings ratio (P/E ratio) is the ratio for valuing a company that measures its current share price relative to its per-share earnings (EPS)..."[2538]   It is found by dividing the current stock price by the earnings per share (EPS).[2539] "P/E ratios are used by investors and analysts to determine the relative value of a company's shares in an apples-to-apples comparison. It can also be used to compare a company against its own historical record or to compare aggregate markets against one

---

[2533] *Id.*

[2534] *Id.*

[2535] "Price-to-Earnings Ratio – P/E Ratio." *Investopedia*, 11 Oct. 2019, www.investopedia.com/terms/p/price-earningsratio.asp.

[2536] *Id.*

[2537] *Id.*

[2538] *Id.*

[2539] *Id.*

another or over time..."[2540]   In short, the P/E ratio shows what the market is willing to pay today for a stock based on its past or future earnings.[2541]

"The average P/E for the S&P 500 has historically ranged from 13 to 15."[2542]   "A high P/E could mean that a stock's price is high relative to earnings and possibly overvalued."[2543]   On the other hand, a low P/E can indicate that a company's current stock price is low relative to earnings or that it is undervalued.[2544]   "Companies that have no earnings or that are losing money do not have a P/E ratio since there is nothing to put in the denominator..."[2545]   In this case, P/E will be shown as "N/A."   "[B]uy only when they're trading at attractive prices. Less than 10 times cash earnings is a good rule of thumb."[2546]

"Investors not only use the P/E ratio to determine a stock's market value, but also in determining future earnings growth. For example, if earnings are expected to rise, investors might expect the company to increase its dividends as a result. Higher earnings and rising dividends typically lead to a higher stock price."[2547] "[C]ompanies that grow faster than average typically have higher P/

[2540] *Id.*

[2541] *Id.*

[2542] Murphy, Chris B. "Using the Price-to-Earnings Ratio And PEG to Assess a Stock." *Investopedia*, 25 Jun. 2019, www.investopedia.com/ investing/use-pe-ratio-and-peg-to-tell-stocks-future/.

[2543] "Price-to-Earnings Ratio – P/E Ratio." *Investopedia*, 11 Oct. 2019, www.investopedia.com/terms/p/price-earningsratio.asp.

[2544] *Id.*

[2545] *Id.*

[2546] Stansberry, Porter. "How Paper Money Fails." *InflationData.com,* 11 Jul. 2010, inflationdata.com/articles/2010/07/11/how-paper-money-fails/.

[2547] Murphy, Chris B. "Using the Price-to-Earnings Ratio And PEG to Assess a Stock." *Investopedia*, 25 Jun. 2019, www.investopedia.com/ investing/use-pe-ratio-and-peg-to-tell-stocks-future/.

Es, such as technology companies. A higher P/E ratio shows that investors are willing to pay a higher share price today because of growth expectations in the future…For example, a company with a current P/E of 25, above the S&P average, trades at 25 times earnings. The high multiple indicates that investors expect higher growth from the company compared to the overall market."[2548] Thus, a high P/E does not necessarily mean a stock is overvalued."[2549] It could suggest that investors are expecting higher earnings growth in the future compared to companies with a lower P/E.[2550]

An'ther important matter is the stock's trading volume. "A stock's volume refers to the number of shares that are sold, or traded, over a certain period of time (usually daily)…"[2551] "Volume…represents the interest in the trading activity of said shares. Heavier volume indicates heavier interest and vice versa…"[2552] "For investors, it's helpful to know that volume generally gets higher when an investment's price is changing. Certain events, such as the company's earnings report or a major news release, can cause volume to spike and can lead to a large move in either the positive or negative direction. If the entire market is crashing or rising rapidly, it can also lead to higher volume across the market."[2553]

[2548] *Id.*

[2549] *Id.*

[2550] "Price-to-Earnings Ratio – P/E Ratio." *Investopedia*, 11 Oct. 2019, www.investopedia.com/terms/p/price-earningsratio.asp.

[2551] Motley Fool Staff. "What is Volume in Stock Trading?" *The Motley Fool*, 20 Jun. 2019, www.fool.com/knowledge-center/what-is-volume-in-stock-trading.aspx.

[2552] "Stock Volume." *Investors Underground*, www.investorsunderground.com/stock-volume/.

[2553] Motley Fool Staff. "What is Volume in Stock Trading?" *The Motley Fool*, 20 Jun. 2019, www.fool.com/knowledge-center/what-is-volume-in-stock-trading.aspx.

"From a chart analysis perspective, volume is critical."[2554] "All trading/charting platforms can visually display volume throughout the trading day usually at the bottom of the price chart. Volume is typically displayed as a vertical bar representing the total volume for the specific incremental charting time period. For example, a 5-minute price chart would display volume bars displaying the total trading volume for each 5-minute interval. Volume bars are usually colored green or red. Green represents net buying volume while red represents net selling volume…"[2555]

"[T]echnical analysts believe that volume precedes price; to confirm any trend, volume should increase in the direction of the trend. For instance, if a stock were to increase from $23 to $25 on high volume relative to the recent trend in volume for that stock, technical analysts would consider this to be a more sustainable bullish trend (i.e., the stock could keep going up over the short term) than if the same price increase were to occur on relatively low volume. If a stock were to decrease from $25 to $23 on relatively high volume, technical analysts would consider this to be a more sustainable bearish trend (i.e., the stock could keep going down over the short term) than if the same price decrease were to occur on relatively low volume. Price moves made on low volume may be said to 'lack conviction' and could be viewed as being less predictive of future returns."[2556]

Investors should be aware of the risks of trading in low-volume stocks, such as their lack of liquidity.[2557] "Liquidity refers

---

[2554] "Turn up the volume." *Fidelity*, 17 Oct. 2019, www.fidelity.com/viewpoints/active-investor/stock-volume.

[2555] "Stock Volume." *Investors Underground*, www.investorsunderground.com/stock-volume/.

[2556] "Turn up the volume." *Fidelity*, 17 Oct. 2019, www.fidelity.com/viewpoints/active-investor/stock-volume.

[2557] Seth, Shobhit. "The Risks of Trading Low-Volume Stocks." *Investopedia*, 10 Jan. 2018, www.investopedia.com/articles/active-trading/051415/risks-trading-lowvolume-stocks.asp.

to how much the market can absorb either buying or selling without making a market impact, i.e. changing the price."[2558] "When a stock is highly liquid, it is easier to enter and exit positions while having less impact on the stock's price..."[2559]

"For stocks, a good measure of liquidity is the average daily trading volume. In general, any stock that trades at fewer than 10,000 shares a day is considered a low-volume stock..."[2560] However, Investor's Business Daily (IBD) considers a stock that trades fewer than 400,000 shares per day to be thinly traded.[2561]

Low-volume stocks are usually ones that people do not want for a reason. "Thinly traded stocks tend to be extremely speculative and unpredictable."[2562] "Because there is such a limited number of shares, a large purchase by a mutual fund or another big investor can cause a huge spike in the price. By the same token, if the investor decides to sell, the share price will likely tank."[2563] "Trying to enter or exit a large position in a low dollar volume stock could result in the order moving the price substantially, something the investor doesn't want. Large orders in low volume stocks tend to result in

---

[2558] *Id.* "A stock that is trading at $25 per share should be easily bought or sold in large amounts (say 100,000 shares) while still maintaining the price of $25 per share." "Stock Volume." *Investors Underground*, www.investorsunderground.com/stock-volume/.

[2559] "Dollar Volume Liquidity." *Investopedia*, 21 Aug. 2019, www.investopedia.com/terms/d/dollar-volume-liquidity.asp.

[2560] Seth, Shobhit. "The Risks of Trading Low-Volume Stocks." *Investopedia*, 10 Jan. 2018, www.investopedia.com/articles/active-trading/051415/risks-trading-lowvolume-stocks.asp.

[2561] Gondo, Nancy. "How To Invest: Exactly How Much Daily Volume Should You Look For In A Great Stock?" *Investor's Business Daily*, 12 Nov. 2019, www.investors.com/how-to-invest/investors-corner/how-much-volume-should-a-stock-have/.

[2562] *Id.*

[2563] *Id.*

slippage."[2564]   "Their lack of liquidity makes them hard to sell even if the stock appreciates, susceptible to price manipulation, and attractive to scammers."[2565]

Another handy trading tool is the Money Flow Index (MFI), which "is a technical oscillator that uses price and volume for identifying overbought or oversold conditions in an asset."[2566] Because the MFI incorporates both price and volume data, some analysts call it the volume-weighted RSI (the Relative Strength Index (RSI) just uses price).[2567]

The MFI oscillator moves between 0 and 100.[2568]   An MFI above 80 is considered overbought, i.e. trading above its intrinsic value, while a value below 20 is considered to be oversold or below its intrinsic value.[2569]   However, the creators of the index, Gene Quong and Avrum Soudack, recommend using 90 and 10 to indicate overbought and oversold conditions.[2570]

MFI can also be used to spot divergences. For instance, if the oscillator moves in the opposite direction of the price, that is a sign of a potential reversal in the prevailing price trend.[2571]   In other

---

[2564] Slippage refers to the difference between the expected price of a trade and the price at which the trade is executed. "Dollar Volume Liquidity." *Investopedia*, 21 Aug. 2019, www.investopedia.com/terms/d/dollar-volume-liquidity.asp.

[2565] Seth, Shobhit. "The Risks of Trading Low-Volume Stocks." *Investopedia*, 10 Jan. 2018, www.investopedia.com/articles/active-trading/051415/risks-trading-lowvolume-stocks.asp.

[2566] "Money Flow Index - MFI Definition and Uses." *Investopedia*, 13 July 2019, www.investopedia.com/terms/m/mfi.asp.

[2567] *Id.*

[2568] *Id.*

[2569] *Id.*

[2570] *Id.*

[2571] *Id.*

words, this is a warning that the price could change.[2572]   "For example, if the indicator is rising while the price is falling or flat, the price could start rising…"[2573]   The extreme levels of 10 and 90 are rarely reached, but when they are, it often means the price could change direction.[2574] "Traders watch for the MFI to move back above 10 to signal a long trade, and to drop [back] below 90 to signal a short trade."[2575]

After evaluating the fundamental and technical aspects of the stock, decide how much to buy. Since diversification is desirable, determine what percent of the portfolio should be allocated to each stock.   Riskier stocks should probably comprise a smaller percentage of a portfolio than safer ones.

"Asked about stock volatility, [Suze] Orman   [financial advisor] recommended dollar-cost averaging. Dollar-cost averaging is when you invest a consistent dollar amount in a security but at regular intervals. This could mean buying fewer shares when a stock soars and buying more shares when a stock declines. The costs during both of these scenarios would amount to about the same. '[Y]ou should wish and pray and hope that these markets go down,' Orman said. 'These are the best things that could possibly happen to you if you are dollar-cost averaging, which means you take a specific amount of money every single month and you invest it.'"[2576]

It is not necessary to buy individual stocks to be a dividend investor. It may be easier to start with an ETF that specializes in dividend stocks. "A dividend ETF typically includes dozens, if not hundreds, of dividend stocks. That instantly provides you with

---

[2572] *Id.*

[2573] *Id.*

[2574] *Id.*

[2575] *Id.*

[2576] Singh, Dhara. "Suze Orman: The 60-40 portfolio 'is dead.'" *Yahoo Finance*, 26 Feb. 2020, finance.yahoo.com/news/you-should-have-a-threeyear-emergency-fund-172846902.html?guccounter=1.

diversification, which means greater safety for your payout: Even if a few of the fund's stocks cut their dividends, the effect will be minimal on the fund's overall dividend."[2577] "The biggest advantage for individual investors is that you can buy just one ETF and don't have to track dozens of companies, which is what you'd have to do if you buy dividend stocks yourself."[2578]

"Probably the safest choice is a low-cost fund that picks dividend stocks from the S&P 500 stock index. That offers a broadly diversified package of America's top companies..."[2579] There are a number of factors that the investor should evaluate, such as the ETF's 5-year returns — generally, higher is better.[2580] Another thing to consider is its expense ratio, which is the ETF's annual fee, which is paid out of your investment in the fund. The expense ratio should be 0.50% or lower.[2581] Finally, look at the stock size. "Dividend ETFs can be invested in companies with large, medium or small capitalization (referred to as large caps, mid caps and small caps). Large caps are generally the safest, while small caps are the riskiest."[2582]

"[T]he ETF dividend product line runs the gamut from investment grade credit to speculative grade credit...In the equity world, high yield dividends tend to have lower credit ratings, which is how they earned the term 'junk.' Depending on your appetite for

---

[2577] Royal, James, PhD and Arielle O'Shea. "How to Invest in Dividend Stocks." *Nerdwallet*, 2 May 2019, www.nerdwallet.com/blog/investing/how-to-invest-dividend-stocks/.

[2578] *Id.*

[2579] *Id.*

[2580] *Id.*

[2581] *Id.*

[2582] *Id.*

risk, however, this type of corporate equity has the potential for a higher yield."[2583]

Buying individual stocks, however, allows one to build a portfolio of dividend stocks that offers a higher yield than a dividend ETF.[2584] "Building a portfolio of individual dividend stocks takes time and effort, making it more complex than investing through a dividend ETF. But by picking and choosing your dividend stocks, you have the potential to personalize a portfolio and find higher dividends than in an ETF."[2585]

Some investors try to maximize the dividend payments via the dividend capture strategy, which is an income-focused stock trading strategy. In contrast to buying and holding stable dividend-paying stocks to generate a steady income stream, it is an active trading strategy that requires frequent buying and selling of shares, holding them for only a short period of time – just long enough to capture the dividend the stock pays. Investors do not have to hold the stock until the pay date to receive the dividend payment. The trader purchases shares of the stock before the ex-dividend date and sells the shares on the ex-dividend date or any time thereafter. Most often, a trader captures a substantial portion of the dividend despite selling the stock at a slight loss following the ex-dividend date. "It is often best to focus on mid-yielding (~3%) large-cap firms in order to minimize the risks associated with smaller companies while still realizing a noteworthy payout…"[2586]

[2583] "Dividends In Action: How They Work And What To Do With Them." *Future Advisor*, www.futureadvisor.com/content/resources/getting-started/portfolio-strategy/why-dividend-paying-stocks-have-advantages-long-term.

[2584] Royal, James, PhD and Arielle O'Shea. "How to Invest in Dividend Stocks." *Nerdwallet*, 2 May 2019, www.nerdwallet.com/blog/investing/how-to-invest-dividend-stocks/.

[2585] *Id.*

[2586] Pinkasovitch, Arthur. "How to Use the Dividend Capture Strategy." *Investopedia*, 9 Oct. 2019, www.investopedia.com/articles/stocks/11/dividend-capture-strategy.asp.

"Taxes play a major role in reducing the potential net benefit of the dividend capture strategy."[2587] "Dividends collected with a short-term capture strategy fail to meet the necessary holding conditions to receive the favorable tax treatment and are taxed at the investor's ordinary income tax rate. According to the IRS, in order to be qualified for the special tax rates, 'you must have held the stock for more than 60 days during the 121-day period that begins 60 days before the ex-dividend date."[2588] "However, it is important to note that an investor can avoid the taxes on dividends if the capture strategy is done in an IRA trading account."[2589]

Another strategy to maximize profits is to sell option contracts. "An equity option is a derivative instrument that acquires its value from the underlying security."[2590]

Selling put options is a way to buy stocks at a lower price than the current market price. When used correctly, this is a sophisticated and under-utilized way to enter equity positions.[2591] It is similar to a limit order, but has the advantage of paying a premium for the sale of the put.[2592] "You can name your own price…, and get paid to wait for the stock to dip to that level."[2593]

[2587] *Id.*

[2588] *Id.*

[2589] *Id.*

[2590] Gad, Sham. "How to Sell Put Options to Benefit in Any Market." *Investopedia*, 6 May 2019, www.investopedia.com/articles/optioninvestor/10/sell-puts-benefit-any-market.asp.

[2591] Alden, Lyn. "Selling Put Options: How to Get Paid for Being Patient." *Lynalden.com*, 4 Nov. 2019, www.lynalden.com/selling-put-options/.

[2592] "Selling Cash-Secured Puts on Stock You Want to Buy." *The Ally Invest Options Playbook*, www.optionsplaybook.com/rookies-corner/cash-secured-puts/.

[2593] Alden, Lyn. "Selling Put Options: How to Get Paid for Being Patient." *Lynalden.com*, 4 Nov. 2019, www.lynalden.com/selling-put-options/.

"When you sell a put option on a stock, you're selling someone the right, but not the obligation, to make you buy 100 shares of a company at a certain price (called the 'strike price') before a certain date (called the 'expiration date.')"[2594] The person who buys the option can "decide to sell you the shares at the strike price on or before the expiration date. As the [put] seller, you have the obligation to buy them at the strike price."[2595]

The smart play "here is to sell one or more cash-secured put options to take on the obligation to potentially buy the shares at a certain price before a certain date, and get paid money up front for taking on that obligation."[2596] This enables the investor to enter a stock position at the desired price. "Rather than buying shares at whatever the market currently offers, you can calculate exactly what you're willing to pay for them, and then sell the put option to get paid to wait until it dips to that level."[2597]

The put-seller receives a premium, and if the options are assigned, the premium can be subtracted from the purchase of the stock.[2598] If the stock does not dip below the strike price by expiration, the puts will not be assigned.[2599] Instead, the option(s) will expire worthless and the seller will still keep the premium.[2600]

[2594] *Id.*

[2595] *Id.*

[2596] *Id.*

[2597] *Id.*

[2598] "Selling Cash-Secured Puts on Stock You Want to Buy." *The Ally Invest Options Playbook*, www.optionsplaybook.com/rookies-corner/cash-secured-puts/.

[2599] *Id.*

[2600] *Id.*

"Selling put options can generate double-digit income and returns even in a flat, bearish, or overvalued market…"[2601]

In order to receive a desirable premium for out-of-the-money puts (i.e. the strike price is below the current stock price), the put should be sold anywhere from 30-60 days before expiration.[2602] This will enable the seller to take advantage of accelerating time decay on the option's price as expiration approaches, yet still provide enough premium to be worthwhile.[2603] When comparing 30 versus 60 days to expiration (DTE), "30 DTE has a higher theta decay. However, 60 DTE allows us to sell options farther out of the money" and the win rate is slightly higher.[2604] Some traders believe that 45 DTE is the sweet spot for selling options.[2605]

The two most important prices for option sellers are the strike and the bid. The strike price is the amount the put seller is obligated to buy the shares for if the option is exercised. The bid is the amount of premium per share the put seller can expect to receive up front.[2606] The ask price is what an option buyer will pay for that option.[2607] One should consider using the mid price to maximize profit and minimize expenses.

[2601] Alden, Lyn. "Selling Put Options: How to Get Paid for Being Patient." *Lynalden.com*, 4 Nov. 2019, www.lynalden.com/selling-put-options/.

[2602] "Selling Cash-Secured Puts on Stock You Want to Buy." *The Ally Invest Options Playbook*, www.optionsplaybook.com/rookies-corner/cash-secured-puts/.

[2603] *Id.*

[2604] Fabian, Josh. "Comparing 30 and 60 Days to Expiration." *Tasty Trade*, 15 Aug. 2016, tastytradenetwork.squarespace.com/tt/blog/comparing-30-and-60-days-to-expiration.

[2605] *Id.*

[2606] Alden, Lyn. "Selling Put Options: How to Get Paid for Being Patient." *Lynalden.com*, 4 Nov. 2019, www.lynalden.com/selling-put-options/.

[2607] The difference between "bid" and "ask" is the market maker's profit. The market maker is the middle man between option buyers and sellers that makes this a liquid market. *Id.*

Other items of interest include the change column, which shows the recent changes in the option prices. The volume is the number of option contracts at a particular strike price and expiration date sold that day. The open interest is the total number of options for a particular strike price and expiration that are currently in existence.[2608]

"Only two things can occur at expiration — either the price of the stock is above the chosen strike price or it's below. If the stock finishes above the strike price, then the trade is over and the option expires worthless. The option buyer walks away with nothing while the option seller gets to keep the upfront cash with no further obligations."[2609]   "Up to 90% of option contracts will expire worthless."[2610]   If the stock finishes below the strike price at expiration, the put option buyer will "exercise" his contractual right and require the put option seller to buy the stock at the strike price.[2611]

Selling puts is one of the most flexible and powerful tools for generating income and entering stock positions at a desired price.[2612] Selling puts at a strike price that is below the current market price of the stock is actually a more conservative strategy than buying shares of stock outright.[2613] "The downside risk is reduced in two ways: The buy price is below the current market price. In addition, the seller gets to keep the option premium, regardless of what happens

---

[2608] *Id.*

[2609] Lowell, Lee. "Selling Naked Put Options: Get Paid To Buy Stocks At A Discount." *Seeking Alpha*, 30 Apr. 2012, seekingalpha.com/article/541181-selling-naked-put-options-get-paid-to-buy-stocks-at-a-discount.

[2610] *Id.*

[2611] *Id.*

[2612] Alden, Lyn. "Selling Put Options: How to Get Paid for Being Patient." *Lynalden.com*, 4 Nov. 2019, www.lynalden.com/selling-put-options/.

[2613] *Id.*

after that."[2614]   The premium received from selling the put can be deducted from the cost of the shares, which lowers the cost basis of the stock.[2615] The net result is that the cost basis is lower than if the shares had been bought on the open market.[2616] Puts not only help to lower the cost basis of the stocks, but they can also give a portfolio 10% or more downside protection in the event of a market crash, depending on how low the strike price is below the current price.[2617]   For example, if the market drops 25%, and the strike prices are about 10% below current prices, then the investor's equity positions would likely only drop 15%.[2618]

It is advisable to only sell puts on the number of shares that the investor can afford to buy, as well as to have "a stop-loss plan in place, in case the stock goes completely in the tank."[2619]   Thus, a conservative investor always has cash available to buy the stocks that may be assigned (a "cash-secured" put.)[2620] "If you do not have the cash available, it would be called a 'naked' put, which is highly speculative" and risky.[2621]   This is because the broker can force the

---

[2614] *Id.*

[2615] "Selling Cash-Secured Puts on Stock You Want to Buy." *The Ally Invest Options Playbook*, www.optionsplaybook.com/rookies-corner/cash-secured-puts/.

[2616] Alden, Lyn. "Selling Put Options: How to Get Paid for Being Patient." *Lynalden.com*, 4 Nov. 2019, www.lynalden.com/selling-put-options/.

[2617] *Id.*

[2618] *Id.*

[2619] "Selling Cash-Secured Puts on Stock You Want to Buy." *The Ally Invest Options Playbook*, www.optionsplaybook.com/rookies-corner/cash-secured-puts/.

[2620] *Id.*

[2621] Alden, Lyn. "Selling Put Options: How to Get Paid for Being Patient." *Lynalden.com*, 4 Nov. 2019, www.lynalden.com/selling-put-options/.

investor to sell other holdings to buy the position, if there is not enough cash in the account.[2622]

If the trader is uncomfortable at any time prior to expiration, or decides he does not want to own the stock at the strike price, then he can unwind the trade. All he has to do is buy back the put option(s) that he sold to close the position prior to expiration.[2623] (The trader will be paying the ask price in this situation). This will remove any obligation to buy the stock. If the stock price has dropped, then it will be more expensive to buy the put back.[2624]

Once the investor has bought at least 100 shares in a stock, another option strategy is available (each option contract is for 100 shares).[2625] This involves selling covered calls, which "are a useful tool, and in the hands of a smart investor…, can be tremendously profitable."[2626] "If you already own a stock (or an ETF), you can sell covered calls on it to boost your income and total returns."[2627] Income from covered call premiums can be 2-3 times higher than dividends from that stock.[2628]

[2622] Gad, Sham. "How to Sell Put Options to Benefit in Any Market." *Investopedia*, 6 May 2019, www.investopedia.com/articles/optioninvestor/10/sell-puts-benefit-any-market.asp.

[2623] "The option price will fluctuate during the course of the trade. It may get cheaper or more expensive while you hold it." Lowell, Lee. "Selling Naked Put Options: Get Paid To Buy Stocks At A Discount." *Seeking Alpha*, 30 Apr. 2012, seekingalpha.com/article/541181-selling-naked-put-options-get-paid-to-buy-stocks-at-a-discount.

[2624] "Selling Cash-Secured Puts on Stock You Want to Buy." *The Ally Invest Options Playbook*, www.optionsplaybook.com/rookies-corner/cash-secured-puts/.

[2625] Alden, Lyn. "Covered Calls: A Step-by-Step Guide with Examples." *Lynalden.com*, 4 Nov. 2019, www.lynalden.com/covered-calls/.

[2626] *Id.*

[2627] *Id.*

[2628] *Id.*

"A call option is a contract that gives the buyer the legal right (but not the obligation) to buy 100 shares of the underlying stock… at the strike price any time on or before expiration."[2629] The call option buyer pays the call seller a premium for the right to buy shares at a predetermined price.[2630] "The premium is a cash fee paid on the day the option is sold and is the seller's money to keep, regardless of whether the option is exercised or not…"[2631]

Selling a call option obligates the seller to deliver 100 shares of a security at a predetermined price to the option buyer.[2632] "Covered call writing sells this right to someone else in exchange for cash, meaning the buyer of the option gets the right to own your security on or before the expiration date at a predetermined price called the strike price."[2633] The trader will continue to receive the dividends as long as he owns the stock (and perhaps some capital appreciation as well).[2634]

The two most important prices for option sellers are the strike and the bid. The strike is the agreed-upon amount to sell the shares if the option is exercised, and the bid is roughly the amount of premium per share the seller can expect to receive from the sale of the option.[2635] Option premiums can be affected by dividends,

---

[2629] Farley, Alan. "The Basics of Covered Calls." *Investopedia*, 25 Jun. 2019, www.investopedia.com/articles/optioninvestor/08/covered-call.asp.

[2630] *Id.*

[2631] *Id.*

[2632] Gad, Sham. "How to Sell Put Options to Benefit in Any Market." *Investopedia*, 6 May 2019, www.investopedia.com/articles/optioninvestor/10/sell-puts-benefit-any-market.asp.

[2633] Farley, Alan. "The Basics of Covered Calls." *Investopedia*, 25 Jun. 2019, www.investopedia.com/articles/optioninvestor/08/covered-call.asp.

[2634] Alden, Lyn. "Covered Calls: A Step-by-Step Guide with Examples." *Lynalden.com*, 4 Nov. 2019, www.lynalden.com/covered-calls/.

[2635] *Id.*

since stock prices usually drop by the amount of the dividend right after the dividend is paid.[2636]

If the seller of the call option owns the underlying security, the option is considered "covered" because he can deliver the shares without purchasing them on the open market upon option expiration. Since each option contract represents 100 shares, the trader must own at least 100 shares for every call contract he plans to sell. Thus, "[c]all sellers have to hold onto underlying shares or contracts or they'll be holding naked calls, which have theoretically unlimited loss potential if the underlying security rises..."[2637]

Investors are advised to sell calls that have a strike price that is about 10% higher than the current stock price.[2638] This is because premiums become negligible with a strike price higher than that.[2639] With a strike price lower than that, the odds of having the shares called away greatly increase.[2640] Therefore, choosing a strike price 10% over the current stock price appears to be optimal.[2641]

Selling covered call options can help offset downside risk, add to upside return, and reduce the cost basis.[2642] "A stock holding with a covered call on it is slightly less risky than holding the stock normally, because your downside potential is slightly reduced by an

---

[2636] *Id.*

[2637] Farley, Alan. "The Basics of Covered Calls." *Investopedia*, 25 Jun. 2019, www.investopedia.com/articles/optioninvestor/08/covered-call.asp.

[2638] Papadatos, Aristofanis. "Why You Should Not Sell Covered Call Options." *Seeking Alpha*, 16 May 2017, seekingalpha.com/article/4055775-why-you-should-not-sell-covered-call-options.

[2639] *Id.*

[2640] *Id.*

[2641] *Id.*

[2642] Farley, Alan. "The Basics of Covered Calls." *Investopedia*, 25 Jun. 2019, www.investopedia.com/articles/optioninvestor/08/covered-call.asp.

amount equal to the option premium."[2643] If "a portfolio has a poor selection of stocks, then the strategy will…mitigate capital losses by 1-3% per year."[2644] Selling calls on slow growth companies or over-valued stocks can maximize returns from a combination of dividends, call premiums, and capital appreciation.[2645] However, if the stock is already overvalued, then its price appreciation is probably limited.

The covered-call-writing strategy is also appropriate "in a rough market, as the shares are unlikely to be called away and the income from the option premiums will console investors for their capital losses…"[2646] "During periods of market overvaluation, where the market is likely to be flat or down for a while, you can generate a ton of income from options and dividends even in the face of a prolonged bear market."[2647] This strategy is primarily useful in flat markets or for overvalued holdings, because the total sum of option premiums and dividends can be quite high, giving the investor good returns while everyone else sits flat.[2648]

While it is true that selling covered calls generates an income stream, it comes at a high opportunity cost. Selling covered calls has the disadvantage of capping the potential profits when the stocks rally, so it is not a good idea to sell them when the stock (or market)

[2643] Alden, Lyn. "Covered Calls: A Step-by-Step Guide with Examples." *Lynalden.com*, 4 Nov. 2019, www.lynalden.com/covered-calls/.

[2644] Papadatos, Aristofanis. "Why You Should Not Sell Covered Call Options." *Seeking Alpha*, 16 May 2017, seekingalpha.com/article/4055775-why-you-should-not-sell-covered-call-options.

[2645] Alden, Lyn. "Covered Calls: A Step-by-Step Guide with Examples." *Lynalden.com*, 4 Nov. 2019, www.lynalden.com/covered-calls/.

[2646] Papadatos, Aristofanis. "Why You Should Not Sell Covered Call Options." *Seeking Alpha*, 16 May 2017, seekingalpha.com/article/4055775-why-you-should-not-sell-covered-call-options.

[2647] Alden, Lyn. "Covered Calls: A Step-by-Step Guide with Examples." *Lynalden.com*, 4 Nov. 2019, www.lynalden.com/covered-calls/.

[2648] *Id.*

is undervalued.[2649]   However, if the shares are called away, the investor can sell a put on the stock, and start the process over again.

In addition, the trader can buy the call back if he later decides he no longer wants to sell the underlying stock. "Depending on the price changes of the stock, the option could be cheaper to buy back than it was when you sold it, or it may be more expensive..."[2650]

"To purchase stocks, ETFs and other funds that can help to avoid the dangers of inflation, you'll likely need a brokerage account."[2651]   It is possible to buy stock through the company. "It's important to note that when you purchase stock directly through a company, you may be required to make a minimum investment between $25 to $500, depending on the corporation's policies and the price of each individual share. If you don't want to make a minimum investment or the stock you're looking to purchase is not currently offering direct purchase options," then a brokerage account is an alternative.[2652]

"There are a large number of brokerage firms operating online, each with their own set of minimum account balances, commissions, fees, and research tools...After you've opened an account with your broker's help, you can request a buy through your brokerage firm's website or mobile platform. Your broker will facilitate the transaction..."[2653]   Before trading options, the investor will need an approved "option trading account" with a broker.[2654]

[2649] *Id.*

[2650] *Id.*

[2651] Fernando, Jason. "Inflation." *Investopedia*, 18 Nov. 2020, www.investopedia.com/terms/i/inflation.asp.

[2652] Horvath, Sarah. "How To Invest In Dividend-Paying Stocks." *Benzinga*, 25 Nov. 2019, www.benzinga.com/money/how-to-invest-in-dividend-stocks/.

[2653] *Id.*

[2654] Interactive Brokers is one brokerage firm that will allow traders to sell put options.

"Naturally, there's no need to invest in just one asset class. Very often, a combination of these and other investments is necessary to generate the optimal combination of risk, total return potential, and yield...Investors can assemble a high-dividend portfolio in three ways: buy individual stocks, invest in dividend-focused mutual funds, or utilize the wide range of dividend ETFs that have been created in recent years."[2655] Some suggest to "[s]plit your financial investments as follows: 40-60% in stocks, but only where prices are sensible 30-40% in cash and bank deposits ('ammo') 10-20% in physical gold (coins or allocated bullion)."[2656]

The next section discusses investing in real estate.

[2655] Thomas, Kenny. "The Basics of Investing in Dividend-Paying Stocks." *The Balance*, 31 May 2019, www.thebalance.com/the-basics-of-investing-in-dividend-paying-stocks-416832.

[2656] Marstrand, Rob. "Where should you put your money?" *Of Wealth*, 29 Sept. 2016, www.ofwealth.com/where-should-you-put-your-money/#.V_0bXJMrK9Y.

Real Estate

"President Donald Trump made his name and fortune in real estate. He once said, 'It's tangible, it's solid, it's beautiful and it's artistic, from my standpoint. I just love real estate.'"[2657]

"The main reasons people invest in real estate are to diversify their investment portfolio, generate monthly income from rental cash flow, and benefit from long-term capital appreciation."[2658] "Having a more diversified investment portfolio can provide more security versus too narrow of a focus on a single investment domain."[2659]

Including real estate in one's portfolio can reduce overall investment risk, partly because it is considered to be less volatile (less extreme highs and lows) than stocks.[2660] "A cash-flowing property is not subject to the daily ups and downs of the markets because it is typically a longer-term play."[2661] It "provides more consistent ROI [return on investment]...an informed, long-term

[2657] Kiyosaki, Kim. "The (Many) Pros and (Few) Cons of Real Estate Investing." *RichDad.com*, 6 Jun. 2019, www.richdad.com/pros-and-cons-of-real-estate.

[2658] Lyons, Ruth. "Pros and Cons of Real Estate Investing: A Comprehensive Overview." *Investorjunkie*, 13 Dec. 2020, investorjunkie.com/real-estate/pros-and-cons/.

[2659] Memonen, Tarita. "The Pros and Cons of Real Estate Investing." *Mashvisor.com*, 13 Aug. 2019, www.mashvisor.com/blog/pros-and-cons-of-real-estate-investing/.

[2660] Edgar, Christy Murdoch. "The 5 Pros and 3 Cons of Real Estate Investing." *Roofstock*, learn.roofstock.com/blog/pros-and-cons-real-estate-investing; Lyons, Ruth. "Pros and Cons of Real Estate Investing: A Comprehensive Overview." *Investorjunkie*, 13 Dec. 2020, investorjunkie.com/real-estate/pros-and-cons/.

[2661] Kiyosaki, Kim. "The (Many) Pros and (Few) Cons of Real Estate Investing." *RichDad.com*, 6 Jun. 2019, www.richdad.com/pros-and-cons-of-real-estate.

strategy generally allows for temporary market corrections without damage to overall profitability."[2662]

Unlike some other asset classes, real estate will always have intrinsic value, which is derived from both the land and the improvements, i.e. buildings.[2663] "Overall market trends tend toward rising home values."[2664] This means that real estate, especially well-maintained properties with value-added improvements, usually appreciates significantly over time, "generally at a rate that far outpaces annual inflation."[2665]

"Inflation is the economic reality that prices increase over time due to the value of money decreasing…"[2666] "Investing in real estate offers great inflation protection," because it is one of the few assets that reacts proportionately to inflation.[2667] "Real estate investments keep pace with inflation. As the price of a loaf of bread goes up, so do rents and property values…As inflation pushes the

---

[2662] Edgar, Christy Murdoch. "The 5 Pros and 3 Cons of Real Estate Investing." *Roofstock*, learn.roofstock.com/blog/pros-and-cons-real-estate-investing.

[2663] Lyons, Ruth. "Pros and Cons of Real Estate Investing: A Comprehensive Overview." *Investorjunkie*, 13 Dec. 2020, investorjunkie.com/real-estate/pros-and-cons/.

[2664] Edgar, Christy Murdoch. "The 5 Pros and 3 Cons of Real Estate Investing." *Roofstock*, learn.roofstock.com/blog/pros-and-cons-real-estate-investing.

[2665] *Id.* Appreciation is how much the value the property has increased from the time it was bought. Although most properties will usually appreciate in value, it is possible that they could lose value or take many years to appreciate. Lyons, Ruth. "Pros and Cons of Real Estate Investing: A Comprehensive Overview." *Investorjunkie*, 13 Dec. 2020, investorjunkie.com/real-estate/pros-and-cons/.

[2666] Lyons, Ruth. "Pros and Cons of Real Estate Investing: A Comprehensive Overview." *Investorjunkie*, 13 Dec. 2020, investorjunkie.com/real-estate/pros-and-cons/.

[2667] Memonen, Tarita. "The Pros and Cons of Real Estate Investing." *Mashvisor.com*, 13 Aug. 2019, www.mashvisor.com/blog/pros-and-cons-of-real-estate-investing/.

cost of living higher, your cash flow increases. And inflation drives up the value of the property itself.."[2668]   Indeed, sales prices for homes in the U.S. have been on a continual rise for decades.[2669]

Historically, investors have seen an average annual rate of return between 5% and 9% on properties such as single- and multi-family properties, commercial and retail, and hospitality.[2670] Single-family rental homes, for instance, generate yearly returns of around 9%, and are "almost as… lucrative as stocks and considerably more so than bonds, deposit accounts and other conservative instruments."[2671]

Though real estate in general is a good hedge against inflation, rental properties that are re-leased every year are especially effective, since monthly rents can be adjusted upward in inflationary periods. "The one thing that doesn't increase is the monthly cost of a fixed-rate mortgage payment. So as your annual rental income

[2668] Lyons, Ruth. "Pros and Cons of Real Estate Investing: A Comprehensive Overview." *Investorjunkie*, 13 Dec. 2020, investorjunkie.com/real-estate/pros-and-cons/.

[2669] Landa, Allison. "5 Pros and Cons of Investing in Real Estate: Are You Ready for the Risk?" *HomeLight*, 31 Dec. 2018, www.homelight.com/blog/pros-and-cons-of-investing-in-real-estate/.

[2670] This includes storage facilities, warehouse, mobile homes, etc. Donohue, Kieran. "Considering Real Estate Investing? 5 Pros and Cons." *37th Parallel Properties*, 37parallel.com/considering-real-estate-investing/.

[2671] In August, the National Council of Real Estate Investment Fiduciaries found that returns for institutional real estate had hit their highest peak in more than two years, with the average quarterly return over the past five years at 9.85% annualized. According to Andrea Eisfeldt of UCLA's Anderson School of Management and Andrew Demers of Stamford, Conn.-based Structured Portfolio Management. Landa, Allison. "5 Pros and Cons of Investing in Real Estate: Are You Ready for the Risk?" *HomeLight*, 31 Dec. 2018, www.homelight.com/blog/pros-and-cons-of-investing-in-real-estate/.

increases, your cost of ownership doesn't."[2672]   For this reason alone, therefore, real estate is one of the best ways to hedge an investment portfolio against inflation.[2673]

There are many real estate investment strategies. Some are as simple as buying dividend-paying stocks in real estate investment trusts (REITs), which was discussed in the previous section. Another tactic is to buy and hold rental properties for cash flow and capital appreciation, which requires "active involvement and a fair amount of knowledge to be successful."[2674]

Probably the single best aspect of real estate investing is the ability to generate passive income. Rental properties provide a steady stream of monthly income, or "cashflow."   "By carefully analyzing the acquisition and carrying costs of your investment property, you can ensure ongoing cash flow that grows over time. With smart, cost-effective improvements, you can increase your property's market potential and maximize cash flow. Over time, you will find that smart refinancing will allow you to grow your margins each month. The faster you pay off that property, the faster you can look forward to maximizing its income potential — and your ability to expand your portfolio."[2675]   Positive cash flow (profit remaining

---

[2672] Lyons, Ruth. "Pros and Cons of Real Estate Investing: A Comprehensive Overview." *Investorjunkie*, 13 Dec. 2020, investorjunkie.com/real-estate/pros-and-cons/.

[2673] Memonen, Tarita. "The Pros and Cons of Real Estate Investing." *Mashvisor.com*, 13 Aug. 2019, www.mashvisor.com/blog/pros-and-cons-of-real-estate-investing/.

[2674] Lyons, Ruth. "Pros and Cons of Real Estate Investing: A Comprehensive Overview." *Investorjunkie*, 13 Dec. 2020, investorjunkie.com/real-estate/pros-and-cons/.

[2675] Edgar, Christy Murdoch. "The 5 Pros and 3 Cons of Real Estate Investing." *Roofstock*, learn.roofstock.com/blog/pros-and-cons-real-estate-investing.

after expenses have been met) from rentals can make the investor's finances secure, even in retirement.[2676]

Unfortunately, cash flow problems may arise if there are vacancies or tenants who do not pay their rent on time or cause damage to the property.[2677] Real estate agent, Christy Friesen, warned, "If you have a poor tenant in there who doesn't take care of the property, it really can become more of a money pit than a benefit. We have one who just moved out after two years; I think the total cash flow was $300 per month. Nothing to speak of. There was $15,000 worth of damage when he moved out."[2678]

Trying to evict tenants can cost the investor a lot of time and money (legal fees, court costs, lost income, etc.) Some states have "tenant-friendly" laws that make it difficult to evict tenants. In Maryland, for example, one must take a non-paying tenant to court three times before he or she can be evicted.[2679]

Another issue is rent control. For instance, "California lawmakers approved a statewide rent cap in November 2019. The bill limits annual rent increases to 5 percent after inflation and offers new barriers to eviction...In February [2019], Oregon lawmakers

---

[2676] Memonen, Tarita. "The Pros and Cons of Real Estate Investing." *Mashvisor.com*, 13 Aug. 2019, www.mashvisor.com/blog/pros-and-cons-of-real-estate-investing/.

[2677] One should bear in mind that up to 28% of rental-property applicants have a criminal hit on their record. according to TransUnion data and The Harvard Joint Center for Housing Studies and Pew Research. Landa, Allison. "5 Pros and Cons of Investing in Real Estate: Are You Ready for the Risk?" *HomeLight*, 31 Dec. 2018, www.homelight.com/blog/pros-and-cons-of-investing-in-real-estate/; Donohue, Kieran. "Considering Real Estate Investing? 5 Pros and Cons." *37th Parallel Properties*, 37parallel.com/considering-real-estate-investing/.

[2678] Landa, Allison. "5 Pros and Cons of Investing in Real Estate: Are You Ready for the Risk?" *HomeLight*, 31 Dec. 2018, www.homelight.com/blog/pros-and-cons-of-investing-in-real-estate/.

[2679] Lyons, Ruth. "Pros and Cons of Real Estate Investing: A Comprehensive Overview." *Investorjunkie*, 13 Dec. 2020, investorjunkie.com/real-estate/pros-and-cons/.

became the first to pass statewide rent control, limiting increases to 7 percent annually plus inflation...In New York City, where almost half of the rental stock is regulated, a board determines the maximum rent increases each year; this year it approved a 1.5 percent cap on one-year leases, considerably lower than the limits passed in Oregon and California. "[2680]

"Economists from both the left and the right have a well-established aversion to rent control, arguing that such policies ignore the message of rising prices, which is to build more housing. Studies in San Francisco and elsewhere show that price caps often prompt landlords to abandon the rental business by converting their units to owner-occupied homes...Jim Lapides, a vice president at the National Multifamily Housing Council, which opposes such restrictions [said,] 'But we're seeing folks turn to really shortsighted policy that will end up making the very problem worse.'"[2681]

Despite some risks, an important bonus associated with real estate is that the investor has more control than with other asset classes; he can decide for himself how to attract tenants and increase rental income.[2682] However, active real estate investing can be demanding and time-consuming. For example, the investor must monitor market conditions, find good deals, and become familiar "with a variety of legal, financial, and commercial" issues, such as

---

[2680] Dougherty, Conor and Luis Ferré-Sadurní. "California Approves Statewide Rent Control to Ease Housing Crisis." *New York Times*, 11 Sept. 2019, www.nytimes.com/2019/09/11/business/economy/california-rent-control.html?fbclid=IwAR3PhZHk2HWFvj6QoQZXYEc19rNPVY8qd-ZjanXS-1Pm8nXmt3uR2jsjpNA.

[2681] *Id.*

[2682] Lyons, Ruth. "Pros and Cons of Real Estate Investing: A Comprehensive Overview." *Investorjunkie*, 13 Dec. 2020, investorjunkie.com/real-estate/pros-and-cons/.

mortgage titles, insurance, contract negotiation, property management, etc.[2683]

In addition, real estate investing can be expensive to get started. It requires money for a down payment, closing costs, money to repair and maintain the property, money for mortgage payments, property taxes, insurance, etc.[2684]

One financing option available to real estate investors is to leverage debt, i.e. use borrowed capital to purchase property with minimal cash outlay. By leveraging other people's money (bank, lending institution, or a private lender), one can make money for himself via appreciation in property value and/or rental income.

For instance, using a long-term, fixed-rate mortgage, one can buy an investment property with a 20% down payment (closing costs will be an additional $5,000 or so).[2685] The bank, lending institution, or private party will provide the rest of the funding. With a down payment of $30,000, "you get the opportunity to control — and get all the benefits of owning — an asset worth $150,000."[2686] If one makes a larger down payment, then one can

---

[2683] Investors usually build a team of contractors, lenders, property managers, and other professionals who provide needed services.. Edgar, Christy Murdoch. "The 5 Pros and 3 Cons of Real Estate Investing." *Roofstock*, learn.roofstock.com/blog/pros-and-cons-real-estate-investing; Donohue, Kieran. "Considering Real Estate Investing? 5 Pros and Cons." *37th Parallel Properties*, 37parallel.com/considering-real-estate-investing/; Lyons, Ruth. "Pros and Cons of Real Estate Investing: A Comprehensive Overview." *Investorjunkie*, 13 Dec. 2020, investorjunkie.com/real-estate/pros-and-cons/.

[2684] Lyons, Ruth. "Pros and Cons of Real Estate Investing: A Comprehensive Overview." *Investorjunkie*, 13 Dec. 2020, investorjunkie.com/real-estate/pros-and-cons/.

[2685] Landa, Allison. "5 Pros and Cons of Investing in Real Estate: Are You Ready for the Risk?" *HomeLight*, 31 Dec. 2018, www.homelight.com/blog/pros-and-cons-of-investing-in-real-estate/.

[2686] Lyons, Ruth. "Pros and Cons of Real Estate Investing: A Comprehensive Overview." *Investorjunkie*, 13 Dec. 2020, investorjunkie.com/real-estate/pros-and-cons/.

lower the monthly payments, avoid mortgage insurance, and enjoy lower interest rates.[2687] "Contingent on a variety of factors, additional income generated from real estate investments may give you access to more credit. Generally, lending institutions lend more money to people who make more money. The additional income made from real estate investments may open broader credit lending doors."[2688]

Tenants then pay down the mortgage, increasing the investor's equity in the property.[2689] "When you use leverage wisely, your tenants are essentially buying the property for you. Rental income pays down your loan each month and builds equity for you…Today you might owe $200,000 on a rental property, but next year you might owe only $195,000 because the tenant is making the payment for you, making you $5,000 richer. Thirty years down the road (or whatever the term of your loan), it's paid down to $0. You own a significant asset that you can sell or continue renting, all thanks to your tenant paying the mortgage."[2690]

However, "financial institutions are more stringent about loaning for an investment property than for your primary residence," which can make securing financing difficult.[2691] "Although Fannie Mae and Freddie Mac typically offer generous loans to eligible

---

[2687] Neighborhood institutions (not big banks) often offer better rates. Landa, Allison. "5 Pros and Cons of Investing in Real Estate: Are You Ready for the Risk?" *HomeLight*, 31 Dec. 2018, www.homelight.com/blog/pros-and-cons-of-investing-in-real-estate/.

[2688] "The Advantages & Disadvantages of Investing in Real Estate." *SFGate*, homeguides.sfgate.com/advantages-disadvantages-investing-real-estate-1680.html.

[2689] Lyons, Ruth. "Pros and Cons of Real Estate Investing: A Comprehensive Overview." *Investorjunkie*, 13 Dec. 2020, investorjunkie.com/real-estate/pros-and-cons/.

[2690] *Id.*

[2691] Donohue, Kieran. "Considering Real Estate Investing? 5 Pros and Cons." *37th Parallel Properties*, 37parallel.com/considering-real-estate-investing/.

investors, not all investors meet eligibility requirements."[2692] "Check your credit score before applying Strong borrowers usually have a score of 740 or better."[2693] Consider alternative options: "If you've got a good prospect, consider getting a home equity line of credit or a personal loan to lock down the deal."[2694]

There is frequently a danger of becoming over-leveraged. One must be able to make mortgage, insurance, and property tax payments, etc., despite unexpected events such as market dips, tenant problems, vacancies, repairs, etc.[2695]

Happily, there is often "a chance to buy a quality property at a discount, make improvements to increase equity and eventually sell for a profit."[2696] "For example, some investors buy real estate they intend to flip. Flipping can result in huge profits for investors. The property may be in foreclosure, in danger of foreclosure or needs little or no repair. You may purchase the property for much less than its value, repair or update it, and resell or flip it at a much higher selling price."[2697]

"If you're thinking of flipping homes, consider this: it's not cheap. In fact, flipping is a high-cost business — a kitchen upgrade alone can run you anywhere from $35,000 to $60,000. In addition,

---

[2692] "The Advantages & Disadvantages of Investing in Real Estate." *SFGate*, homeguides.sfgate.com/advantages-disadvantages-investing-real-estate-1680.html.

[2693] Landa, Allison. "5 Pros and Cons of Investing in Real Estate: Are You Ready for the Risk?" *HomeLight*, 31 Dec. 2018, www.homelight.com/blog/pros-and-cons-of-investing-in-real-estate/.

[2694] *Id.*

[2695] Lyons, Ruth. "Pros and Cons of Real Estate Investing: A Comprehensive Overview." *Investorjunkie*, 13 Dec. 2020, investorjunkie.com/real-estate/pros-and-cons/.

[2696] *Id.*

[2697] "The Advantages & Disadvantages of Investing in Real Estate." *SFGate*, homeguides.sfgate.com/advantages-disadvantages-investing-real-estate-1680.html.

2018 saw a crash in the flipping industry, with returns dropping to an almost-four-year low."[2698] Christy Friesen cautioned, "If you go over budget and can't even sell it for what the agent thought you could, you have a problem. You just lost money to make a house pretty."[2699]   In addition, fluctuating demographics and volatile economies can reduce a property's value.[2700] Also bear in mind that transaction costs are high. "Unlike other types of investments, real estate transaction costs can significantly affect the value of the investment and make it more difficult to turn a profit."[2701]

Unfortunately, real estate is not a liquid asset, so it may not be easy to turn it into cash in an emergency.[2702]   "Should you find yourself short of cash, you'll need to develop a plan for either tapping into the home's equity or liquidating the asset. Should you have to sell the property, you could find yourself waiting weeks or months for a sale, especially if you have a tenant in place."[2703] "Offers, counters, appraisals, inspections, financing — they all take time."[2704] The investor is stuck with paying on the debt and with

---

[2698] Landa, Allison. "5 Pros and Cons of Investing in Real Estate: Are You Ready for the Risk?" *HomeLight*, 31 Dec. 2018, www.homelight.com/blog/pros-and-cons-of-investing-in-real-estate/.

[2699] *Id.*

[2700] Memonen, Tarita. "The Pros and Cons of Real Estate Investing." *Mashvisor.com*, 13 Aug. 2019, www.mashvisor.com/blog/pros-and-cons-of-real-estate-investing/.

[2701] *Id.*

[2702] "The Pros & Cons of Investing in Real Estate." *Smartmortgage.com*, smartmortgage.com/the-pros-cons-of-investing-in-real-estate/.

[2703] Edgar, Christy Murdoch. "The 5 Pros and 3 Cons of Real Estate Investing." *Roofstock*, learn.roofstock.com/blog/pros-and-cons-real-estate-investing.

[2704] Kiyosaki, Kim. "The (Many) Pros and (Few) Cons of Real Estate Investing." *RichDad.com*, 6 Jun. 2019, www.richdad.com/pros-and-cons-of-real-estate.

paying property taxes until the property finally sells.[2705] Real estate investors must be prepared to own a property for months or even years, especially if it will be leased out.[2706]

Most investors who choose to purchase rental properties will have to be landlords. In addition to the day to day management, it also requires one to "develop marketing expertise and an understanding of the rules and regulations in your area, including Fair Housing and other laws…In addition, late night phone calls and repair requests can be a time-consuming and frustrating part of the landlord lifestyle."[2707] Owners of rental property are responsible for timely repairs, which can be expensive. If repairs are not done in a "reasonable time frame," then the owner may be assessed significant fines.[2708] "If a tenant's water heater blows, it can't wait until you as the landlord return from vacation."[2709] Friesen reported, "The last (property) we renovated took us six months. We spent 40 to 50 hours at that house painting and making repairs on our own."[2710]

Luckily, property management can be outsourced. For example, "Roofstock is an online investment platform that lets you purchase turnkey rental properties…The service's certified property

---

[2705] "The Advantages & Disadvantages of Investing in Real Estate." *SFGate*, homeguides.sfgate.com/advantages-disadvantages-investing-real-estate-1680.html.

[2706] Memonen, Tarita. "The Pros and Cons of Real Estate Investing." *Mashvisor.com*, 13 Aug. 2019, www.mashvisor.com/blog/pros-and-cons-of-real-estate-investing/.

[2707] Edgar, Christy Murdoch. "The 5 Pros and 3 Cons of Real Estate Investing." *Roofstock*, learn.roofstock.com/blog/pros-and-cons-real-estate-investing.

[2708] "The Advantages & Disadvantages of Investing in Real Estate." *SFGate*, homeguides.sfgate.com/advantages-disadvantages-investing-real-estate-1680.html.

[2709] Landa, Allison. "5 Pros and Cons of Investing in Real Estate: Are You Ready for the Risk?" *HomeLight*, 31 Dec. 2018, www.homelight.com/blog/pros-and-cons-of-investing-in-real-estate/.

[2710] *Id.*

managers can do all of the work for you."[2711] However, property management companies collect 10% of the rent every month, so this will affect the cashflow.[2712]

Fortunately, the government offers tax incentives for owning investment property. For example, "[r]ental income is not subject to self-employment tax."[2713] In addition, it is often possible to deduct depreciation, mortgage interest, property taxes, operational expenses, property improvements, and travel expenses.[2714] "This annual deduction for depreciation means you can write off a certain percentage of the property value as an expense against revenues."[2715]

"Generally speaking, the government wants a piece of any 'capital gains' (aka profit) you make from selling off assets like stocks, bonds or property."[2716] "In terms of capital gains tax, real

---

[2711] Lyons, Ruth. "Pros and Cons of Real Estate Investing: A Comprehensive Overview." *Investorjunkie*, 13 Dec. 2020, investorjunkie.com/real-estate/pros-and-cons/.

[2712] Landa, Allison. "5 Pros and Cons of Investing in Real Estate: Are You Ready for the Risk?" *HomeLight*, 31 Dec. 2018, www.homelight.com/blog/pros-and-cons-of-investing-in-real-estate/.

[2713] Lyons, Ruth. "Pros and Cons of Real Estate Investing: A Comprehensive Overview." *Investorjunkie*, 13 Dec. 2020, investorjunkie.com/real-estate/pros-and-cons/.

[2714] *Id.* "The Tax Cuts and Jobs Act of 2017 has brought fresh opportunity for investors and property purchasers with a 100% first-year bonus depreciation deduction that will be in force until 2022." Edgar, Christy Murdoch. "The 5 Pros and 3 Cons of Real Estate Investing." *Roofstock*, learn.roofstock.com/blog/pros-and-cons-real-estate-investing; Landa, Allison. "5 Pros and Cons of Investing in Real Estate: Are You Ready for the Risk?" *HomeLight*, 31 Dec. 2018, www.homelight.com/blog/pros-and-cons-of-investing-in-real-estate/.

[2715] Memonen, Tarita. "The Pros and Cons of Real Estate Investing." *Mashvisor.com*, 13 Aug. 2019, www.mashvisor.com/blog/pros-and-cons-of-real-estate-investing/.

[2716] Landa, Allison. "5 Pros and Cons of Investing in Real Estate: Are You Ready for the Risk?" *HomeLight*, 31 Dec. 2018, www.homelight.com/blog/pros-and-cons-of-investing-in-real-estate/.

estate investment provides a significant advantage over other investment vehicles. There are a variety of ways to defer capital gains taxes on your rental property's appreciation, including a 1031 Exchange or a conversion of the investment property into a primary residence."[2717]   "A 1031 exchange allows investors to sell productive-use properties (meaning property you make money from, like apartments, rental homes, land, or office space) and buy another like-kind property (another investment property) while deferring payment of capital gains taxes."[2718] The "gains from the sale of real estate can be postponed indefinitely as long as the proceeds are reinvested in other real estate."[2719]

There are also usually tax credits for certain types of real estate investments, such as low-income housing and the rehabilitation of historical buildings.[2720]   These can be deducted from the taxes owed.[2721]

In addition, real estate may be willed to family members upon death. "Should you choose to make your portfolio part of your estate, your heirs will inherit at the stepped up value, allowing them to avoid taxation on the property's appreciation."[2722]

[2717] Edgar, Christy Murdoch. "The 5 Pros and 3 Cons of Real Estate Investing." *Roofstock*, learn.roofstock.com/blog/pros-and-cons-real-estate-investing.

[2718] Landa, Allison. "5 Pros and Cons of Investing in Real Estate: Are You Ready for the Risk?" *HomeLight*, 31 Dec. 2018, www.homelight.com/blog/pros-and-cons-of-investing-in-real-estate/.

[2719] Kiyosaki, Kim. "The (Many) Pros and (Few) Cons of Real Estate Investing." *RichDad.com*, 6 Jun. 2019, www.richdad.com/pros-and-cons-of-real-estate.

[2720] *Id.* Memonen, Tarita. "The Pros and Cons of Real Estate Investing." *Mashvisor.com*, 13 Aug. 2019, www.mashvisor.com/blog/pros-and-cons-of-real-estate-investing/.

[2721] *Id.*

[2722] Edgar, Christy Murdoch. "The 5 Pros and 3 Cons of Real Estate Investing." *Roofstock*, learn.roofstock.com/blog/pros-and-cons-real-estate-investing.

Unfortunately, the tax advantages are not available to all real estate investors. "At certain income levels, some of the tax benefits no longer apply."[2723] "If you counted on getting these tax benefits when budgeting your desired income level, this can be a big blow."[2724] Friesen said, "This is why we always have an accountant on hand…Some of these tax benefits — at certain income levels, they don't even work for you any more, if you make over a (certain) amount of dollars per year…It's not anything you can claim on your taxes. You just have to eat that loss."[2725]

Before taking the plunge, the investor should also be aware of the significant legal liability associated with being a property owner. If someone is injured on the property, the owner may be liable for damages in a personal injury or other tort cause of action. It would be wise to consult an attorney about devising a strategy to protect one's assets, such as setting up an LLC (which is discussed in the last chapter of this book.)

Despite the positive aspects of real estate, the big "banking families…interests were almost exclusively in bonds and very rarely in goods, since they admired 'liquidity' and regarded commitments in commodities or even real estate as the first step toward bankruptcy…"[2726] Bonds are the focus of the next section.

[2723] Lyons, Ruth. "Pros and Cons of Real Estate Investing: A Comprehensive Overview." *Investorjunkie*, 13 Dec. 2020, investorjunkie.com/real-estate/pros-and-cons/.

[2724] Memonen, Tarita. "The Pros and Cons of Real Estate Investing." *Mashvisor.com*, 13 Aug. 2019, www.mashvisor.com/blog/pros-and-cons-of-real-estate-investing/.

[2725] Landa, Allison. "5 Pros and Cons of Investing in Real Estate: Are You Ready for the Risk?" *HomeLight*, 31 Dec. 2018, www.homelight.com/blog/pros-and-cons-of-investing-in-real-estate/.

[2726] "History of Banking and Money Key Excerpts From Carroll Quigley's Tragedy and Hope." *Wanttoknow.info*, www.wanttoknow.info/articles/quigley_carroll.tragedy_hope_banking_money_history.

Bonds

"Governments and businesses issue bonds to raise funds from investors. Bonds pay regular interest, and bond investors get the principal back on maturity."[2727] "Bonds offer safety of principal and periodic interest income, which is the product of the stated interest rate or coupon rate and the principal or face value of the bond."[2728]

"Municipal bonds are issued by states and local entities to finance construction projects and provide services. The advantages include higher interest rates than U.S. Treasuries, relatively low risk, and certain tax advantages. Municipal bonds are exempt from federal income tax and from state and local taxes if you are a resident of the issuing state."[2729]

"Bonds, which are loans to governments and businesses that issue them, are often called good investments for older investors who need to rely on steady interest income."[2730] "Bonds are ideal investments for retirees who depend on the interest income for their living expenses and who cannot afford to lose any of their savings."[2731] "[I]nvestors nearing retirement might prefer bonds because they are interested in getting that regular, dependable interest income with less risk."[2732]

"The disadvantages of bonds include rising interest rates, market volatility and credit risk. Bond prices rise when rates fall and fall when rates rise. Your bond portfolio could suffer market price losses in a rising rate environment. Bond market volatility could

---

[2727] Basu, Chirantan. "Advantages and Disadvantages of Bonds." *Zack's*, 5 Mar. 2019, finance.zacks.com/advantages-disadvantages-bonds-2350.html.

[2728] *Id.*

[2729] *Id.*

[2730] *Id.*

[2731] *Id.*

[2732] *Id.*

affect the prices of individual bonds, regardless of the issuers' underlying fundamentals."[2733]

"Some bonds are riskier than others, and usually pay higher interest as a result."[2734] "Credit-rating agencies rate bonds based on creditworthiness. Low-rated bonds must pay higher interest rates to compensate investors for taking on the higher risk."[2735] "Credit risk means that issuers could default on their interest and principal repayment obligations if they run into cash-flow problems. Some bonds have call provisions, which give issuers the right to buy them back before maturity. Issuers are more likely to exercise their early-redemption rights when interest rates are falling, so you then might have to reinvest the principal at lower rates."[2736]

"Corporate bonds are usually riskier than government bonds. U.S. Treasury bonds are considered risk-free investments."[2737] Municipal "bonds are not risk-free. In periods of recession, some local governments have defaulted on their debt obligations because of slumping tax revenues."[2738]

Although they are touted as a "risk-free asset," Treasuries are not.[2739] This is because US Treasuries are "the most rehypothecated asset in financial markets…"[2740] "For every US Treasury security outstanding, roughly three parties believe they own it…Multiple

---

[2733] *Id.*

[2734] *Id.*

[2735] *Id.*

[2736] *Id.*

[2737] *Id.*

[2738] *Id.*

[2739] Long, Caitlin. "The Real Story Of The Repo Market Meltdown, And What It Means For Bitcoin." *Forbes*, 25 Sept. 2019, www.forbes.com/sites/caitlinlong/2019/09/25/the-real-story-of-the-repo-market-meltdown-and-what-it-means-for-bitcoin/#23f8ac237caa.

[2740] *Id.*

parties report that they own the very same asset, when only one of them truly does. To wit, the IMF has estimated that the same collateral was reused 2.2 times in 2018, which means both the original owner plus 2.2 subsequent re-users believe they own the same collateral (often a US Treasury security)…Financial regulators can't publicly admit to this, but big banks know it's true…"[2741]

"Real interest rates (nominal interest rates minus the inflation rate) determine the growth in real purchasing power from investing in bonds."[2742] "The inflation adjusted rate of interest or the 'real' rate is the number that investors care about since it is the nominal rate adjusted for changes in purchasing power, said Mike Davis, an economics professor at the Cox School of Business at Southern Methodist University in Dallas. If individuals earn a rate of 5% but prices go up by 3%, they have only earned 2%."[2743]

"Investors have good reason to be concerned by ZIRP and NIRP because starting yields predict future investment returns…the starting yield on the 10-year U.S. Treasury note has provided a highly accurate forecast of the subsequent 10-year return for those investing in the note. Consistent with this observation, zero real interest rates will predict zero real returns, and negative real interest rates will predict negative real returns…By our calculations, ZIRP and NIRP have depressed the expected real returns of core bond portfolios to within the narrow range of −1% to +1%…real yields on government bonds are being repressed by central bank

---

[2741] *Id.*

[2742] Brightman, Chris. "Negative Rates Are Dangerous to Your Wealth." *Research Affiliates*, Apr. 2016, www.researchaffiliates.com/en_us/ p u b l i c a t i o n s / a r t i c l e s / 542_negative_rates_are_dangerous_to_your_wealth.html.

[2743] Chang, Ellen. "How Do Negative Interest Rates Work?" *The Street*, 23 Feb. 2018, www.thestreet.com/how-to/how-negative-interest-rates-work-14492328.

policies…"[2744]   "The U.S. has been in a de facto negative interest rate environment for years such as when the Treasury Bill rate dropped below 1.5% for the past eight years…The real interest rate has been negative, given an average 1.5% to 2.0% inflation rate.:"[2745]   "Real cash rates have been negative across the developed world since the global financial crisis in 2008. Today, real bond yields are negative in longer maturities too: out to 5 years in the United States, past 10 years in the United Kingdom and the eurozone, and across the entire yield curve in Japan…"[2746]

"The yield on the 10-year Treasury (^TNX) dipped below 1% for the first time on record last week and continues to fall as coronavirus fears and an all-out oil price war grip investors. What does this mean for you? Any long-term loans tied to the bond are becoming increasingly cheap to borrow. But savers who want low-risk assets in their nest eggs may have to look elsewhere than bonds…With yields on all Treasuries below 1%, savers looking for conservative investments will need to find alternatives, such as certificates of deposit, or CDs, said Ken Tumin, founder of DepositAccounts.com."[2747]

"Financial advisors have long stood by the golden rule of having a portfolio of 60% stocks and 40% bonds, but Suze Orman

---

[2744] Brightman, Chris. "Negative Rates Are Dangerous to Your Wealth." *Research Affiliates*, Apr. 2016, www.researchaffiliates.com/en_us/ p u b l i c a t i o n s / a r t i c l e s / 542_negative_rates_are_dangerous_to_your_wealth.html.

[2745] Chang, Ellen. "How Do Negative Interest Rates Work?" *The Street*, 23 Feb. 2018, www.thestreet.com/how-to/how-negative-interest-rates-work-14492328.

[2746] Brightman, Chris. "Negative Rates Are Dangerous to Your Wealth." *Research Affiliates*, Apr. 2016, www.researchaffiliates.com/en_us/ p u b l i c a t i o n s / a r t i c l e s / 542_negative_rates_are_dangerous_to_your_wealth.html.

[2747] Herron, Janna. "'Money is on sale:' What does the historically low 10-year Treasury yield mean for your wallet?" *Yahoo Finance,* 10 Mar. 2020, finance.yahoo.com/news/treasury-yield-your-wallet-203628849.html? guccounter=1.

says the rule no longer applies. 'Actually, 60-40 is dead,' Orman, founder of the Suze Orman Financial Group, said…'It should probably be 75-25 stocks, believe it or not, stocks, if you also have enough cash to get you by.'"[2748] "Orman explained that with interest rates [being] low, bonds are now a less enticing diversification option for investors. 'Bonds will probably keep going down,' Orman said. 'So why not put your money in a high-yield savings account, where it's liquid, that's actually paying you more right now than 10-year treasury that's at 1.3%.'"[2749]

"Bonds are generally less volatile than stocks, but they underperform stocks over the long term. Since 1926, big company stocks have given investors an average annual return of 10%, while government bonds have averaged between 5% and 6%."[2750] "Stock prices generally go up faster than bond prices, but they're also usually riskier."[2751] "Stocks also often lose more money than bonds, particularly government bonds, in a bear market. Older investors relying on their investments for retirement don't necessarily have the luxury of waiting out the retirement before they need those funds, leading some advisors to encourage investors to buy more bonds before they plan to retire."[2752] "Bond prices sometimes benefit from safe-haven buying, which occurs when investors move funds from volatile stock markets to the relative safety of bonds."[2753]

[2748] Singh, Dhara. "Suze Orman: The 60-40 portfolio 'is dead.'" *Yahoo Finance*, 26 Feb. 2020, finance.yahoo.com/news/you-should-have-a-threeyear-emergency-fund-172846902.html?guccounter=1.

[2749] *Id.*

[2750] Basu, Chirantan. "Advantages and Disadvantages of Bonds." *Zack's*, 5 Mar. 2019, finance.zacks.com/advantages-disadvantages-bonds-2350.html.

[2751] *Id.*

[2752] *Id.*

[2753] *Id.*

"In my view, you should rule out bonds altogether. The only ones ever worth owning are the best quality ones, issued by developed country governments and rock solid corporations. In normal times, these act as a hedge against stock investments. When stocks crash, yields fall and bond prices rise. So there's an offsetting effect, and you can then sell some bonds to buy stocks when they're down, and cheap. This will improve returns over time. But nowadays, bonds are just risk without return..."[2754] However, should the investor so choose, "you can buy bonds directly through your broker or indirectly through bond mutual funds. You can also buy U.S. Treasury bonds directly from the department's TreasuryDirect website."[2755]

The next section deals with cryptocurrencies, such as Bitcoin.

[2754] Marstrand, Rob. "Where should you put your money?" *Of Wealth*, 29 Sept. 2016, www.ofwealth.com/where-should-you-put-your-money/#.V_0bXJMrK9Y.

[2755] Basu, Chirantan. "Advantages and Disadvantages of Bonds." *Zack's*, 5 Mar. 2019, finance.zacks.com/advantages-disadvantages-bonds-2350.html.

Cryptocurrencies

"Cryptocurrencies are peer-based money...[They are] based on electronic accounting entries that can be used as a medium of exchange."[2756] Cryptos are "an online exchange that is reliant on technology. Coins are digitally mined and exchanged via smart wallet..."[2757]

Bitcoin, the first cryptocurrency, was "created in January 2009. It follows the ideas set out in a white paper by the mysterious and pseudonymous developer, Satoshi Nakamoto, whose true identity" is a mystery.[2758] "Bitcoin is a decentralized digital currency that may be used to purchase goods and services online, or traded on online exchanges for conventional currencies, including the U.S. dollar. Bitcoin... has no single administrator, or central authority or repository."[2759] "Rather than relying on a central authority to transact money, a decentralized network of nodes all verify transactions. The process of adding verified transactions to

---

[2756] Brock, Thomas. "Money." *Investopedia*, 25 Dec. 2020, www.investopedia.com/terms/m/money.asp.

[2757] Herlean, Greg. "The Top 10 Risks Of Bitcoin Investing (And How To Avoid Them)." *Forbes*, 5 Dec. 2018, www.forbes.com/sites/forbesfinancecouncil/2018/12/05/the-top-10-risks-of-bitcoin-investing-and-how-to-avoid-them/#5f131fc52407.

[2758] Frankenfield, Jake. "Bitcoin." *Investopedia*, 30 Jan. 2021, www.investopedia.com/terms/b/bitcoin.asp. Mike Adams posits that "Satoshi Nakamoto is the NSA, which means he is either working for the NSA is is a sock puppet character created by the NSA..."; Adams, Mike. "Evidence points to Bitcoin being an NSA-engineered psyop to roll out one-world digital currency." *Natural News*, 10 Dec. 2017, www.naturalnews.com/2017-12-10-evidence-points-to-bitcoin-being-an-nsa-psyop-roll-out-one-world-digital-currency.html.

[2759] Flipside Crypto. "Cryptocurrency in Focus: Outbreak Takes Toll on Bitcoin." *The Street*, 11 Mar. 2020, www.thestreet.com/investing/cryptocurrency/cryptocurrency-in-focus-outbreak-takes-toll-on-bitcoin?fbclid=IwAR12wqco2v8bJF2MSpIkN2bHincr7Sn98JMzHWhyaXS7LRbAc7e6mvV-ujk.

the public ledger and unlocking new bitcoins as rewards is called 'mining,' and involves using computer power to solve complex mathematical puzzles, or hash functions."[2760] "Currently, there are more than 12.2 million bitcoins in circulation."[2761] "Since the release of bitcoin, over 6,000 'altcoins' — or alternative variants of bitcoin and other cryptocurrencies — have been created..."[2762]

"Digital currencies are expected to work just like regular coins and notes issued by central banks but exist entirely online."[2763] Thus, they have "no physical existence," and consist "of nothing but a digital record stored on computers" in various locations.[2764] "What makes cryptocurrencies different from ordinary bank accounts, which are also nothing but digital records, is that they don't reside on the servers of any particular financial institution."[2765] For example, "Bitcoins are held at, and sent to and from, bitcoin 'addresses.' A bitcoin 'wallet' is a software file that holds bitcoin addresses. Along with each bitcoin address, a bitcoin wallet stores the 'private key' for the address, essentially a password used by the holder to access the bitcoins held at the address, as well as the

---

[2760] *Id.*

[2761] *SEC. v. Shavers,* Case No. 4:13-CV-416 (E.D. Texas 2014).

[2762] Flipside Crypto. "Cryptocurrency in Focus: Outbreak Takes Toll on Bitcoin." *The Street,* 11 Mar. 2020, www.thestreet.com/investing/cryptocurrency/cryptocurrency-in-focus-outbreak-takes-toll-on-bitcoin?fbclid=IwAR12wqco2v8bJF2MSpIkN2bHincr7Sn98JMzHWhyaXS7LRbAc7e6mvV-ujk.

[2763] Bambrough, Billy. "China Could Force Donald Trump And The Fed To Destroy The U.S. Banking System." *Forbes,* 8 Jun. 2020, www.forbes.com/sites/billybambrough/2020/06/08/china-could-force-donald-trump-and-the-fed-to-destroy-the-us-banking-system/?fbclid=IwAR1QYQWgSJBQZJZQf_ou26oxLX2KD73xJ1H9rXTLHIznvrbtdKODhEDTspU#3aeed2b34f5f.

[2764] Krugman, Paul. "Bitcoin is basically a Ponzi scheme." *The Seattle Times,* 30 Jan. 2018, www.seattletimes.com/opinion/bitcoin-is-basically-a-ponzi-scheme/.

[2765] *Id.*

transaction history associated with the address. Whoever has the private key for a bitcoin address controls the bitcoins held at that address."[2766]

A drawback to Bitcoin is the danger that one could lose access to one's Bitcoins, as ownership is verified by a secret password (called a "key"), and not by establishing one's identity.[2767] "If you misplace or accidentally delete your 'key'...there is no 'forgot my password' option to help you."[2768]

Another fear is that the computer's hard drive on which the cryptocurrency details are stored may crash, which could delete the key file.[2769] In addition, the phone operating systems could become corrupted, which might delete a wallet from a user's phone."[2770] "If you do not back up the app and lose your phone, you're out of luck."[2771]

Although Bitcoin can be used to pay for purchases electronically, it has proven to be "a clunky, slow, costly means of

---

[2766] *SEC. v. Shavers,* Case No. 4:13-CV-416 (E.D. Texas 2014).

[2767] Krugman, Paul. "Bitcoin is basically a Ponzi scheme." *The Seattle Times*, 30 Jan. 2018, www.seattletimes.com/opinion/bitcoin-is-basically-a-ponzi-scheme/.

[2768] Blanco, Octavio. "Why Investing in Digital Currencies Like Bitcoin Is So Dangerous," *Consumer Reports*, 12 Jan. 2018, www.consumerreports.org/cryptocurrency/why-investing-in-digital-currencies-like-bitcoin-is-so-dangerous/.

[2769] Macwen, Urvish. "The Main Risks Of Investing In Bitcoin." *Finextra*, 19 Jun. 2019, www.finextra.com/blogposting/17390/the-main-risks-of-investing-in-bitcoin.

[2770] Blanco, Octavio. "Why Investing in Digital Currencies Like Bitcoin Is So Dangerous," *Consumer Reports*, 12 Jan. 2018, www.consumerreports.org/cryptocurrency/why-investing-in-digital-currencies-like-bitcoin-is-so-dangerous/.

[2771] *Id.*

payment."[2772] For instance, "before most people were thinking about trading bitcoin, a wallet transaction fee averaged around 6 cents…"[2773] That fee has since risen to as high as $55 per transaction.[2774] On top of that, "[a] potentially lengthy settlement period gives bitcoin time to move against the grain, which could mean converting bitcoin into a lot less cash than when a transaction was completed."[2775] Taking into account bitcoin's volatility, lack of being a store of value, and other concerns, "there's the real possibility that merchants could bow out of accepting the virtual currency…"[2776] Ironically, even Bitcoin conferences sometimes refuse to accept Bitcoins from attendees.[2777] "If brand-name merchants bail on the virtual currency, bitcoin's price could tumble."[2778]

People "buy and sell Bitcoin and other digital currencies on any of a number of popular online markets known as Bitcoin

---

[2772] Frankenfield, Jake. "Bitcoin." *Investopedia*, 30 Jan. 2021, www.investopedia.com/terms/b/bitcoin.asp.

[2773] Blanco, Octavio. "Why Investing in Digital Currencies Like Bitcoin Is So Dangerous," *Consumer Reports*, 12 Jan. 2018, www.consumerreports.org/cryptocurrency/why-investing-in-digital-currencies-like-bitcoin-is-so-dangerous/.

[2774] *Id.*

[2775] Williams, Sean. "The 6 Biggest Risks to Bitcoin." *The Motley Fool*, 27 Nov. 2017, www.fool.com/investing/2017/11/27/the-6-biggest-risks-to-bitcoin.aspx.

[2776] *Id.*

[2777] Krugman, Paul. "Bitcoin is basically a Ponzi scheme." *The Seattle Times*, 30 Jan. 2018, www.seattletimes.com/opinion/bitcoin-is-basically-a-ponzi-scheme/.

[2778] Williams, Sean. "The 6 Biggest Risks to Bitcoin." *The Motley Fool*, 27 Nov. 2017, www.fool.com/investing/2017/11/27/the-6-biggest-risks-to-bitcoin.aspx.

exchanges."[2779]   Investing money in Bitcoin is not for the risk-averse, however.[2780]   This is because the purchase and use of bitcoins is inherently risky.[2781]   Unlike gold, real estate, or stocks, "[t]he concept of a virtual currency is still novel and, compared to traditional investments, Bitcoin doesn't have much of a long-term track record or history of credibility to back it."[2782]   Another drawback is "bitcoin is ineligible to be included in any tax-advantaged retirement accounts; there are no good, legal options to shield investments from taxation."[2783]

"Investing in Bitcoin today is a very risky undertaking. There is no guarantee of minimum profitability or, at least, break-even investments."[2784] "With a constantly shifting market, no regulation and zero physical collateral, investors can end up losing everything they invest."[2785]   According to Jerry Brito, executive director of CoinCenter, a D.C.-based nonprofit research and advocacy group, "People are desperate for anything that can bring them instant wealth, but [cryptocurrencies] are very risky investments because

---

[2779] Frankenfield, Jake. "Bitcoin." *Investopedia*, 30 Jan. 2021, www.investopedia.com/terms/b/bitcoin.asp.

[2780] *Id.*

[2781] *Id.*

[2782] *Id.*

[2783] Frankenfield, Jake. "Bitcoin." *Investopedia*, 30 Jan. 2021, www.investopedia.com/terms/b/bitcoin.asp.

[2784] Macwen, Urvish. "The Main Risks Of Investing In Bitcoin." *Finextra*, 19 Jun. 2019, www.finextra.com/blogposting/17390/the-main-risks-of-investing-in-bitcoin.

[2785] Herlean, Greg. "The Top 10 Risks Of Bitcoin Investing (And How To Avoid Them)." *Forbes*, 5 Dec. 2018, www.forbes.com/sites/forbesfinancecouncil/2018/12/05/the-top-10-risks-of-bitcoin-investing-and-how-to-avoid-them/#5f131fc52407.

the technology is new and unproven."[2786]   Barry Silbert, CEO of Digital Currency Group, said, "It is pretty much the highest-risk, highest-return investment that you can possibly make."[2787]   Even the cofounder of the Bitcoin.com website warned that Bitcoin was "the riskiest investment you can make."[2788]   "With such an unpredictable market, there's no telling if you will get a return on your investment."[2789]   As with any investment, Jerry Brito advises, "You shouldn't invest in stuff you don't understand, and you shouldn't be investing money that you can't afford to lose."[2790]

Digital currencies are not backed by any physical collateral, have no intrinsic value, and are not a store of value.[2791]   "Unlike real currencies, cryptocurrencies…are not issued or backed by any

---

[2786] Blanco, Octavio. "Why Investing in Digital Currencies Like Bitcoin Is So Dangerous," *Consumer Reports*, 12 Jan. 2018, www.consumerreports.org/cryptocurrency/why-investing-in-digital-currencies-like-bitcoin-is-so-dangerous/.

[2787] Frankenfield, Jake. "Bitcoin." *Investopedia*, 30 Jan. 2021, www.investopedia.com/terms/b/bitcoin.asp.

[2788] "Bitcoin: Know the risks before you buy." *Al Jazeera*, 5 Feb. 2018, www.aljazeera.com/news/2017/12/bitcoin-buy-171219100738438.html.

[2789] Herlean, Greg. "The Top 10 Risks Of Bitcoin Investing (And How To Avoid Them)." *Forbes*, 5 Dec. 2018, www.forbes.com/sites/forbesfinancecouncil/2018/12/05/the-top-10-risks-of-bitcoin-investing-and-how-to-avoid-them/#5f131fc52407.

[2790] Blanco, Octavio. "Why Investing in Digital Currencies Like Bitcoin Is So Dangerous," *Consumer Reports*, 12 Jan. 2018, www.consumerreports.org/cryptocurrency/why-investing-in-digital-currencies-like-bitcoin-is-so-dangerous/.

[2791] Herlean, Greg. "The Top 10 Risks Of Bitcoin Investing (And How To Avoid Them)." *Forbes*, 5 Dec. 2018, www.forbes.com/sites/forbesfinancecouncil/2018/12/05/the-top-10-risks-of-bitcoin-investing-and-how-to-avoid-them/#5f131fc52407.

government or central bank."[2792]   Although the modern dollar is a fiat currency, "its value is ultimately backed by the fact that the U.S. government will accept it…in payment for taxes."[2793]   Russian President Vladimir Putin said, "It is known that the cryptocurrency is not backed by anything. It cannot be a store of value. No material valuables are behind it, and it is not secured by anything."[2794] Economist Mark Skousen warned, "Bitcoin is not an actual physical coin, and if computers are shut down, you can't buy or sell them."[2795]   Without technology, "cryptocurrency is worth nothing."[2796] "Bitcoin, like any cryptocurrency, goes to zero if the power grid collapses or the internet infrastructure stops functioning…"[2797]   For such reasons, renowned investor, Warren

---

[2792] "Bitcoin: Know the risks before you buy." *Al Jazeera*, 5 Feb. 2018, www.aljazeera.com/news/2017/12/bitcoin-buy-171219100738438.html; Frankenfield, Jake. "Bitcoin." *Investopedia*, 30 Jan. 2021, www.investopedia.com/terms/b/bitcoin.asp.

[2793] Krugman, Paul. "Bitcoin is basically a Ponzi scheme." *The Seattle Times*, 30 Jan. 2018, www.seattletimes.com/opinion/bitcoin-is-basically-a-ponzi-scheme/.

[2794] "Bitcoin: Know the risks before you buy." *Al Jazeera*, 5 Feb. 2018, www.aljazeera.com/news/2017/12/bitcoin-buy-171219100738438.html.

[2795] "The 101 Best Gold Quotes From History – GoldSilver." *Gold Silver*, goldsilver.com/blog/101-best-gold-quotes-all-time/.

[2796] Herlean, Greg. "The Top 10 Risks Of Bitcoin Investing (And How To Avoid Them)." *Forbes*, 5 Dec. 2018, www.forbes.com/sites/forbesfinancecouncil/2018/12/05/the-top-10-risks-of-bitcoin-investing-and-how-to-avoid-them/#5f131fc52407.

[2797] Adams, Mike. "Analysis: Bitcoin could go to $100,000 as the fiat currency dollar collapses, but the 'value' won't be the fortune you're imagining." *Natural News*, 17 May 2020, www.naturalnews.com/2020-05-17-analysis-bitcoin-could-go-to-100000-as-fiat-currency-dollar-collapses.html.

Buffett, has described Bitcoin as a "mirage, a soap bubble."[2798] Some even claim that "cyber currencies are 'imaginary money.'"[2799]

"Bitcoins are the epitome of 'thin air' investments. They represent nothing — not a piece of a company, or an ounce of precious metal or the faith in a country..."[2800] Because Bitcoin "is almost purely speculative," it is "incredibly volatile."[2801] "The price of bitcoin is constantly changing.[2802] "Bitcoin cost fluctuations are completely unpredictable in the short term, which only adds to the riskiness of this asset."[2803] "In a span of just five months, bitcoin has endured three bear-market-like crashes of 38%, 40%, and 29%, respectively."[2804]

[2798] Macwen, Urvish. "The Main Risks Of Investing In Bitcoin." *Finextra*, 19 Jun. 2019, www.finextra.com/blogposting/17390/the-main-risks-of-investing-in-bitcoin.

[2799] Ely, Bert. "Bitcoin is a Ponzi scheme, and it will collapse like one." *The Hill*, 11 Dec. 2017, thehill.com/opinion/finance/364306-bitcoin-is-a-ponzi-scheme-and-it-will-collapse-like-one.

[2800] Crudele, John. "The Bitcoin 'pyramid scheme' continues to collapse." *New York Post*, 26 Nov. 2018, nypost.com/2018/11/26/the-bitcoin-pyramid-scheme-continues-to-collapse/.

[2801] Krugman, Paul. "Bitcoin is basically a Ponzi scheme." *The Seattle Times*, 30 Jan. 2018, www.seattletimes.com/opinion/bitcoin-is-basically-a-ponzi-scheme/.

[2802] Herlean, Greg. "The Top 10 Risks Of Bitcoin Investing (And How To Avoid Them)." *Forbes*, 5 Dec. 2018, www.forbes.com/sites/forbesfinancecouncil/2018/12/05/the-top-10-risks-of-bitcoin-investing-and-how-to-avoid-them/#5f131fc52407.

[2803] Macwen, Urvish. "The Main Risks Of Investing In Bitcoin." *Finextra*, 19 Jun. 2019, www.finextra.com/blogposting/17390/the-main-risks-of-investing-in-bitcoin.

[2804] Williams, Sean. "The 6 Biggest Risks to Bitcoin." *The Motley Fool*, 27 Nov. 2017, www.fool.com/investing/2017/11/27/the-6-biggest-risks-to-bitcoin.aspx.

Bitcoin is highly sensitive to news.[2805] "Many of Bitcoin's wild price swings owe to retail investors' piling into or bailing out of bitcoin based on the latest news. It wouldn't take much for investor sentiment to shift and send bitcoin's value plummeting."[2806]

Since its introduction in 2009, Bitcoin's value has ranged from $2 per coin to $40,324.01 on January 7, 2021.[2807] On December 17, 2017, the price of Bitcoin topped $20,000.[2808] Days later, on the 24th, the price crashed 26% to $14,626.[2809] "If you had bought a bitcoin on December 19, 2017, you would have paid $18,936 for each coin. But if you wanted to sell it on December 23, buyers on the market were not willing to pay more than $14,048 — a loss of $4,888 for each coin."[2810] In January 2018, the price dropped again by more than 10%, down to $8,000 per coin.[2811] In March 2020, Bitcoin crashed, losing about half its value over a seven-day trading

---

[2805] Krugman, Paul. "Bitcoin is basically a Ponzi scheme." *The Seattle Times*, 30 Jan. 2018, www.seattletimes.com/opinion/bitcoin-is-basically-a-ponzi-scheme/.

[2806] Williams, Sean. "The 6 Biggest Risks to Bitcoin." *The Motley Fool*, 27 Nov. 2017, www.fool.com/investing/2017/11/27/the-6-biggest-risks-to-bitcoin.aspx.

[2807] Bovaird, Charles. "Bitcoin Breaks Through $40,000 To Notch A Fresh All-Time High." *Forbes*, 7 Jan. 2021, www.forbes.com/sites/cbovaird/2021/01/07/bitcoin-breaks-through-40000-to-notch-a-fresh-all-time-high/?sh=4418cf283a96.

[2808] Herlean, Greg. "The Top 10 Risks Of Bitcoin Investing (And How To Avoid Them)." *Forbes*, 5 Dec. 2018, www.forbes.com/sites/forbesfinancecouncil/2018/12/05/the-top-10-risks-of-bitcoin-investing-and-how-to-avoid-them/#5f131fc52407.

[2809] *Id.* "Bitcoin: Know the risks before you buy." *Al Jazeera*, 5 Feb. 2018, www.aljazeera.com/news/2017/12/bitcoin-buy-171219100738438.html.

[2810] "Bitcoin: Know the risks before you buy." *Al Jazeera*, 5 Feb. 2018, www.aljazeera.com/news/2017/12/bitcoin-buy-171219100738438.html.

[2811] *Id.*

period.[2812]   The bitcoin price fell "to lows of $3,850 per bitcoin on the Luxembourg-based Bitstamp exchange before rebounding somewhat to trade around $5,000..."[2813]   On January 7, 2021, Bitcoin shot up to $40,324, but plummeted back down to $32,716.91 by January 28, 2021.[2814] That is a drop of almost 19%.

"The value of cryptocurrencies may change significantly even in a single day."[2815]   According to the Consumer Financial Protection Bureau (CFPB), the price of Bitcoins fell by 61% in a single day in 2013, while the record for a one-day drop was 80% in 2014.[2816]   "The price of Bitcoin fell 5% in just 7 minutes" on December 16, 2019.[2817]   On March 12, 2020, "Bitcoin prices plummeted..., shedding approximately half of their value as global markets were afflicted by widespread panic and liquidity problems. The digital currency fell to as little as $3,867.09...At this point, the cryptocurrency had plunged 49.6% from its price of more than $7,600 at the start of the day..."[2818] "The CEO of Hong Kong-based crypto derivatives exchange FTX has speculated that if BitMEX had not gone offline on account of 'hardware issues' Friday morning [March 13, 2020], the price of Bitcoin could have crashed to zero.

[2812] Bambrough, Billy. "Devastating Bitcoin Wipeout Could See The Price Go 'Sub-$1,000.'" *Forbes*, 13 Mar. 2020, www.forbes.com/sites/billybambrough/2020/03/13/devastating-bitcoin-wipeout-could-see-the-price-go-sub-1000/#5b050f3480eb.

[2813] *Id.*

[2814] "Bitcoin." *Coindesk*, www.coindesk.com/price/bitcoin.

[2815] "Bitcoin: Know the risks before you buy." *Al Jazeera*, 5 Feb. 2018, www.aljazeera.com/news/2017/12/bitcoin-buy-171219100738438.html.

[2816] Krugman, Paul. "Bitcoin is basically a Ponzi scheme." *The Seattle Times*, 30 Jan. 2018, www.seattletimes.com/opinion/bitcoin-is-basically-a-ponzi-scheme/.

[2817] *Id.*

[2818] Bovaird, Charles. "Bitcoin Lost Roughly 50% Of Its Value In A Day." *Forbes*, 12 Mar. 2020, www.forbes.com/sites/cbovaird/2020/03/12/bitcoin-lost-roughly-50-of-its-value-in-a-day/#5a895433056a.

Sam Bankman-Fried, a.k.a. SBF, mused…that BitMEX may have pulled their exchange offline out of fear their liquidation engine could collapse the XBTUSD order book all the way down to zero…"[2819]

"Altcoin prices also took on heavy losses as Bitcoin price corrected. For the second time in 24-hours, notable daily losers were Ether (ETH) with a 43.06% loss, Bitcoin Cash (BCH) which has dropped 42.85%, ad XRP which now trades at $0.13, a multi-year low."[2820]

"There is also the risk of alternative technologies that could supersede existing cryptocurrencies and make them obsolete."[2821] "There is already plenty of competition, and though Bitcoin has a huge lead over the hundreds of other digital currencies that have sprung up,…a technological break-through in the form of a better virtual coin is always a threat."[2822] "[T]he Bitcoin blockchain suffers from important design limitations that make mining very expensive, slow down transaction throughput, and cause high volatility in price."[2823] "There was a time when John McAfee of

---

[2819] Emsley, Jonnie. "FTX CEO: Bitcoin price might have gone to zero if BitMEX hadn't gone offline." *Crytostate.com*, 13 Mar. 2020, cryptoslate.com/ftx-ceo-bitcoin-price-might-have-gone-to-zero-if-bitmex-hadnt-gone-offline/.

[2820] Hughes, Horus. "Crypto Market Meltdown Continues as Bitcoin Price Drops Below $5,000." *Cointelegraph*, 12 Mar. 2020, cointelegraph.com/news/crypto-market-meltdown-continues-as-bitcoin-price-drops-below-5-000.

[2821] "Bitcoin: Know the risks before you buy." *Al Jazeera*, 5 Feb. 2018, www.aljazeera.com/news/2017/12/bitcoin-buy-171219100738438.html.

[2822] Frankenfield, Jake. "Bitcoin." *Investopedia*, 30 Jan. 2021, www.investopedia.com/terms/b/bitcoin.asp.

[2823] Flipside Crypto. "Cryptocurrency in Focus: Outbreak Takes Toll on Bitcoin." *The Street*, 11 Mar. 2020, www.thestreet.com/investing/cryptocurrency/cryptocurrency-in-focus-outbreak-takes-toll-on-bitcoin?fbclid=IwAR12wqco2v8bJF2MSpIkN2bHincr7Sn98JMzHWhyaXS7LRbAc7e6mvV-ujk.

antivirus fame predicted that Bitcoin would reach $1 million by 2020. But he's since changed his mind and decided that Bitcoin will eventually reach $0 because the cryptocurrency is based on 'ancient' technology."[2824] "Bitcoin is ancient in that…it lacks features of scalability and functionality that have now become common in other, competing cryptocurrencies."[2825]

"Newer blockchains have privacy, smart contracts, distributed apps and more."[2826] For example, blockchain consortium Hyperledger, is working on the "eThaler using the ethereum blockchain to create a central bank digital currency (CBDC)…"[2827] "In June 2019, Facebook revealed its own plans to help launch a 'stablecoin' backed by a basket of global currencies…"[2828] However, the fact is that "every cryptocurrency becomes obsolete with the invention of large-scale quantum computing."[2829]

Unfortunately, Bitcoins can be used for black market transactions, money laundering, drug-trafficking, and tax

---

[2824] Huff, Ethan. "John McAfee just withdrew his famous 2020 prediction about Bitcoin, now says the cryptocurrency is essentially obsolete." *Natural News*, 12 Jan. 2020, www.naturalnews.com/2020-01-12-john-mcafee-withdrew-famous-2020-bitcoin-prediction-obsolete.html.

[2825] *Id.*

[2826] *Id.*

[2827] "eThaler gets its name from the thaler, a silver coin used throughout Europe for hundreds of years, from which the word 'dollar' is derived…" Del Castillo, Michael. "Trillion-Dollar Stimulus Jumpstarts Project To Issue Central Bank Currency On Ethereum." *Forbes*, 25 Mar. 2020, www.forbes.com/sites/michaeldelcastillo/2020/03/25/trillion-dollar-stimulus-jumpstarts-project-to-issue-central-bank-currency-on-ethereum/?fbclid=IwAR19L3HysNicGD7MrSHy0osbLVC4_pGgzT_ArXLK31ZH_r xBNtkHlXhLtIM#fc5153a47bc0.

[2828] *Id.*

[2829] Adams, Mike. "Evidence points to Bitcoin being an NSA-engineered psyop to roll out one-world digital currency." *Natural News*, 10 Dec. 2017, www.naturalnews.com/2017-12-10-evidence-points-to-bitcoin-being-an-nsa-psyop-roll-out-one-world-digital-currency.html.

evasion.[2830]   "In Egypt, the Grand Mufti said that cryptocurrency carried risks of 'fraudulence, lack of knowledge, and cheating.'"[2831]

Because Bitcoin and other crypto-currency exchanges are entirely digital, they are vulnerable to online fraud, cyber-attacks from hackers, malware, operational glitches, and even shut-downs.[2832]   Hackers can target Bitcoin exchanges, and gain access to thousands of accounts and digital wallets where Bitcoins are stored.[2833] If a hacker gains access to a Bitcoin owners computer hard drive and steals the private encryption key, he could transfer the Bitcoins to another account.[2834]   There is no way to retrieve the stolen Bitcoins.[2835]

One hacking incident took place in 2014, when Mt. Gox, a Bitcoin exchange in Japan that was handling about 70% of Bitcoin's

[2830] Macwen, Urvish. "The Main Risks Of Investing In Bitcoin." *Finextra*, 19 Jun. 2019, www.finextra.com/blogposting/17390/the-main-risks-of-investing-in-bitcoin.

[2831] "Bitcoin: Know the risks before you buy." *Al Jazeera*, 5 Feb. 2018, www.aljazeera.com/news/2017/12/bitcoin-buy-171219100738438.html.

[2832] Frankenfield, Jake. "Bitcoin." *Investopedia*, 30 Jan. 2021, www.investopedia.com/terms/b/bitcoin.asp; Herlean, Greg. "The Top 10 Risks Of Bitcoin Investing (And How To Avoid Them)." *Forbes*, 5 Dec. 2018, www.forbes.com/sites/forbesfinancecouncil/2018/12/05/the-top-10-risks-of-bitcoin-investing-and-how-to-avoid-them/#5f131fc52407.

[2833] Frankenfield, Jake. "Bitcoin." *Investopedia*, 30 Jan. 2021, www.investopedia.com/terms/b/bitcoin.asp.

[2834] *Id.*

[2835] Users can prevent this only if bitcoins are stored on a computer which is not connected to the internet, or else by choosing to use a paper wallet – printing out the Bitcoin private keys and addresses, and not keeping them on a computer at all. Herlean, Greg. "The Top 10 Risks Of Bitcoin Investing (And How To Avoid Them)." *Forbes*, 5 Dec. 2018, www.forbes.com/sites/forbesfinancecouncil/2018/12/05/the-top-10-risks-of-bitcoin-investing-and-how-to-avoid-them/#5f131fc52407; Frankenfield, Jake. "Bitcoin." *Investopedia*, 30 Jan. 2021, www.investopedia.com/terms/b/bitcoin.asp.

trading volume at the time, was hit by a crippling cyberattack.[2836] The exchange was forced to shut down after millions of dollars worth of bitcoins were stolen.[2837] "In the bankruptcy filing from Mt. Gox,…it cited the theft of 850,000 bitcoin…and cash."[2838]

Another example involved a prominent South Korean exchange that had to close after hackers stole cryptocurrencies.[2839] "On December 19, 2017, a South Korean cryptocurrency exchange said it would file for bankruptcy after it was hacked for the second time that year. Over $70m worth of bitcoins has reportedly been lost by several cryptocurrency exchanges and miners."[2840]

"In addition to hacking, there is a fair amount of fraud in the bitcoin market."[2841] Indeed, the crypto world is rife with scams. "Fraudsters may be attracted to using virtual currencies to perpetrate their frauds because transactions in virtual currencies supposedly have greater privacy benefits and less regulatory oversight than

---

[2836] Williams, Sean. "The 6 Biggest Risks to Bitcoin." *The Motley Fool*, 27 Nov. 2017, www.fool.com/investing/2017/11/27/the-6-biggest-risks-to-bitcoin.aspx.

[2837] Frankenfield, Jake. "Bitcoin." *Investopedia*, 30 Jan. 2021, www.investopedia.com/terms/b/bitcoin.asp.

[2838] Williams, Sean. "The 6 Biggest Risks to Bitcoin." *The Motley Fool*, 27 Nov. 2017, www.fool.com/investing/2017/11/27/the-6-biggest-risks-to-bitcoin.aspx.

[2839] Blanco, Octavio. "Why Investing in Digital Currencies Like Bitcoin Is So Dangerous," *Consumer Reports*, 12 Jan. 2018, www.consumerreports.org/cryptocurrency/why-investing-in-digital-currencies-like-bitcoin-is-so-dangerous/.

[2840] "Bitcoin: Know the risks before you buy." *Al Jazeera*, 5 Feb. 2018, www.aljazeera.com/news/2017/12/bitcoin-buy-171219100738438.html.

[2841] Herlean, Greg. "The Top 10 Risks Of Bitcoin Investing (And How To Avoid Them)." *Forbes*, 5 Dec. 2018, www.forbes.com/sites/forbesfinancecouncil/2018/12/05/the-top-10-risks-of-bitcoin-investing-and-how-to-avoid-them/#5f131fc52407.

transactions in conventional currencies…"[2842]   Scammers, for instance, have convinced "victims to invest millions in cryptocoins or blockchain-based products that would never come to exist."[2843]

Bitcoin is "highly susceptible to market manipulation. Back in 2013 fraudulent activities by a single trader appear to have caused a sevenfold increase in bitcoin's price…"[2844] Fraudsters depressed the price in 2019 when they sold off stolen Bitcoins on a Ponzi-scheme website called "PlusToken."[2845]   According to blockchain firm, Chainalysis, crooks sought to liquidate at least $2 billion worth of cryptocurrency.[2846]   It "tracked roughly 45,000 Bitcoin ($302 million) and 800,000 ETH ($102 million) sent from PlusToken's operational wallets to individual addresses owned by the scammers themselves. The firm noted…that 20,000 BTC (worth over $134 million) is still waiting to be dumped."[2847]   "It is estimated that 185

[2842] "Ponzi schemes Using virtual Currencies." *SEC*, www.sec.gov/investor/alerts/ia_virtualcurrencies.pdf.

[2843] Barber, Gregory. "This Alleged Bitcoin Scam Looked a Lot Like a Pyramid Scheme." *Wired*, 18 Dec. 2019, www.wired.com/story/alleged-bitcoin-scam-like-pyramid-scheme/.

[2844] Krugman, Paul. "Bitcoin is basically a Ponzi scheme." *The Seattle Times*, 30 Jan. 2018, www.seattletimes.com/opinion/bitcoin-is-basically-a-ponzi-scheme/.

[2845] At 0:05. Yahoo Finance. "Bitcoin sinks to lowest level since May after alleged Ponzi scheme." *Youtube*, 17 Dec. 2019, www.youtube.com/watch?v=TO2ccMrva1E; Canellis, David. "Bitcoin's failing price could be caused by $2B Chinese Ponzi scheme dumping its crypto." *Hard Fork*, 17 Dec. 2019, thenextweb.com/hardfork/2019/12/17/bitcoin-cryptocurrency-price-dump-ponzi-scheme-plustoken/.

[2846] Canellis, David. "Bitcoin's failing price could be caused by $2B Chinese Ponzi scheme dumping its crypto." *Hard Fork*, 17 Dec. 2019, thenextweb.com/hardfork/2019/12/17/bitcoin-cryptocurrency-price-dump-ponzi-scheme-plustoken/.

[2847] *Id.*

million in stolen Bitcoins have already been dumped, and more may still be dumped which may cause the price to fall farther."[2848]

Online exchanges can even be fake.[2849] "The Consumer Finance Protection Bureau and the Securities and Exchange Commission have warned against these transactions where unsuspecting investors are duped out of their bitcoins in fraudulent exchanges."[2850] "[R]egulators, including the Consumer Finance Protection Bureau and the Securities and Exchange Commission... have been warning that some exchanges are fake. Unsuspecting investors can easily open an account at a fraudulent exchange and submit money to buy, say, bitcoin. But the criminals steal the money and the investor never receives the bitcoin."[2851]

Scams involving mining pools in which customers participate in business ventures that effectively amount to money printing are also popular.[2852] For example, Japhet Mesa of Zambia outed a swindle involving the BitClub Network in 2018 via a Medium post.[2853] Consequently, "five men involved with BitClub Network

---

[2848] At 0:05. Yahoo Finance. "Bitcoin sinks to lowest level since May after alleged Ponzi scheme." *Youtube*, 17 Dec. 2019, www.youtube.com/watch?v=TO2ccMrva1E.

[2849] Herlean, Greg. "The Top 10 Risks Of Bitcoin Investing (And How To Avoid Them)." *Forbes*, 5 Dec. 2018, www.forbes.com/sites/forbesfinancecouncil/2018/12/05/the-top-10-risks-of-bitcoin-investing-and-how-to-avoid-them/#5f131fc52407.

[2850] *Id.*

[2851] Blanco, Octavio. "Why Investing in Digital Currencies Like Bitcoin Is So Dangerous," *Consumer Reports*, 12 Jan. 2018, www.consumerreports.org/cryptocurrency/why-investing-in-digital-currencies-like-bitcoin-is-so-dangerous/.

[2852] Barber, Gregory. "This Alleged Bitcoin Scam Looked a Lot Like a Pyramid Scheme." *Wired*, 18 Dec. 2019, www.wired.com/story/alleged-bitcoin-scam-like-pyramid-scheme/.

[2853] *Id.*

were accused of a $722 million scam" in December 2019.[2854] This scheme "allegedly preyed on victims who thought they were investing in a pool of bitcoin mining equipment...[which are] machines that produce bitcoin through a process called hashing. When those machines were turned on, all would (in theory) enjoy the spoils. The company also allegedly gave rewards to existing investors in exchange for recruiting others to join [all of the hallmarks of a classic pyramid scheme]. According to the complaint, the scheme began in April 2014...Matthew Brent Goettsche, Jobadiah Sinclair Weeks, and Silviu Catalin Balaci are accused of conspiracy to commit wire fraud and conspiracy to offer and sell unregistered securities. A fourth defendant, Joseph Frank Abel, faces only the latter charge...Internal messages between the conspirators give the impression of growing glee at the ease of taking advantage of investors, referring to 'building this whole model on the backs of idiots.' The men allegedly described their victims as 'dumb' investors and 'sheep...' In October 2014,...Goettsche allegedly posted about the need to 'fak[e] it for the first 30 days while we get going,' instructing a co-conspirator to do some 'magic' on the company's revenue numbers..."[2855]

In *SEC v. Shavers* (2014), "the organizer of an alleged Ponzi scheme advertised a Bitcoin 'investment opportunity' in an online Bitcoin forum. Investors were allegedly promised up to 7% interest per week and that the invested funds would be used for Bitcoin arbitrage activities in order to generate the returns. Instead, invested Bitcoins were allegedly used to pay existing investors and exchanged into U.S. dollars to pay the organizer's personal expenses."[2856]

Bitcoin (aka "Bitcon") and other cyber currencies are "a pyramid scheme. A fraud. But it is best described as a 'confidence

---

[2854] *Id.*

[2855] *Id.*

[2856] "Ponzi schemes Using virtual Currencies." *SEC*, www.sec.gov/investor/alerts/ia_virtualcurrencies.pdf.

game.'"[2857] A Ponzi scheme is "an investment scam that involves the payment of purported returns to existing investors from funds contributed by new investors."[2858] "Ponzi scheme organizers often solicit new investors by promising to invest funds in opportunities claimed to generate high returns with little or no risk."[2859] They "promise investors returns above what real investments yield, but the Ponzi scheme operator does little, if any, actual investing.[2860] Instead, "the fraudulent actors focus on attracting new money to make promised payments to earlier investors[2861] The "cash from new investors is paid to earlier investors to maintain the illusion that the scheme is earning real profits."[2862] Some of these "invested" funds are diverted for personal use.[2863] "All Ponzi schemes

---

[2857] Crudele, John. "The Bitcoin 'pyramid scheme' continues to collapse." *New York Post*, 26 Nov. 2018, nypost.com/2018/11/26/the-bitcoin-pyramid-scheme-continues-to-collapse/; Ely, Bert. "Bitcoin is a Ponzi scheme, and it will collapse like one." *The Hill*, 11 Dec. 2017, thehill.com/opinion/finance/364306-bitcoin-is-a-ponzi-scheme-and-it-will-collapse-like-one.

[2858] "Ponzi schemes Using virtual Currencies." *SEC*, www.sec.gov/investor/alerts/ia_virtualcurrencies.pdf; Herlean, Greg. "The Top 10 Risks Of Bitcoin Investing (And How To Avoid Them)." *Forbes*, 5 Dec. 2018, www.forbes.com/sites/forbesfinancecouncil/2018/12/05/the-top-10-risks-of-bitcoin-investing-and-how-to-avoid-them/#5f131fc52407.

[2859] *Id.*

[2860] Ely, Bert. "Bitcoin is a Ponzi scheme, and it will collapse like one." *The Hill*, 11 Dec. 2017, thehill.com/opinion/finance/364306-bitcoin-is-a-ponzi-scheme-and-it-will-collapse-like-one.

[2861] Krugman, Paul. "Bitcoin is basically a Ponzi scheme." *The Seattle Times*, 30 Jan. 2018, www.seattletimes.com/opinion/bitcoin-is-basically-a-ponzi-scheme/.

[2862] Ely, Bert. "Bitcoin is a Ponzi scheme, and it will collapse like one." *The Hill*, 11 Dec. 2017, thehill.com/opinion/finance/364306-bitcoin-is-a-ponzi-scheme-and-it-will-collapse-like-one.

[2863] Krugman, Paul. "Bitcoin is basically a Ponzi scheme." *The Seattle Times*, 30 Jan. 2018, www.seattletimes.com/opinion/bitcoin-is-basically-a-ponzi-scheme/.

eventually collapse…when sufficient amounts can no longer be raised from new investors to pay off earlier investors…"[2864]

Unfortunately, there is no consumer protection afforded to buyers.[2865] "Generally speaking, Bitcoin exchanges and Bitcoin accounts are not insured by any type of federal or government program…"[2866] "Many investor alerts have been issued by the Securities and Exchange Commission (SEC), the Financial Industry Regulatory Authority (FINRA), the Consumer Financial Protection Bureau (CFPB), and other agencies."[2867] Sadly, "[t]here is very little authorities can do to recover the funds."[2868] This is because "[a]ll Bitcoin transactions are permanent and irreversible.[2869] "…SEC chairman John Clayton warned investors that the regulator may not be able to effectively pursue bad actors or recover funds for investors, partly because these markets often operate outside of the United States."[2870] The only recourse is to try to convince the fund-

[2864] Ely, Bert. "Bitcoin is a Ponzi scheme, and it will collapse like one." *The Hill*, 11 Dec. 2017, thehill.com/opinion/finance/364306-bitcoin-is-a-ponzi-scheme-and-it-will-collapse-like-one.

[2865] Macwen, Urvish. "The Main Risks Of Investing In Bitcoin." *Finextra*, 19 Jun. 2019, www.finextra.com/blogposting/17390/the-main-risks-of-investing-in-bitcoin.

[2866] Frankenfield, Jake. "Bitcoin." *Investopedia*, 30 Jan. 2021, www.investopedia.com/terms/b/bitcoin.asp.

[2867] *Id.*

[2868] Blanco, Octavio. "Why Investing in Digital Currencies Like Bitcoin Is So Dangerous," *Consumer Reports*, 12 Jan. 2018, www.consumerreports.org/cryptocurrency/why-investing-in-digital-currencies-like-bitcoin-is-so-dangerous/.

[2869] Frankenfield, Jake. "Bitcoin." *Investopedia*, 30 Jan. 2021, www.investopedia.com/terms/b/bitcoin.asp.

[2870] Blanco, Octavio. "Why Investing in Digital Currencies Like Bitcoin Is So Dangerous," *Consumer Reports*, 12 Jan. 2018, www.consumerreports.org/cryptocurrency/why-investing-in-digital-currencies-like-bitcoin-is-so-dangerous/.

recipient to voluntarily return the payment.[2871] This is due to the fact that there is "no third party or a payment processor, as in the case of a debit or credit card – hence, no source of protection or appeal if there is a problem…"[2872]

In the case of crypto-investing, "people at the top [are] benefiting off the ignorance of others."[2873] Some worry that Bitcoin is "a giant bubble that will end in grief."[2874] "As more people buy into bitcoin, it creates a bubble economy. When the bubble bursts, bitcoin will essentially become useless; there will be many people holding onto cryptocurrency, intending to sell but unable to unload. There is no return on the investment, which can equal a very painful financial loss."[2875] "As Robert Shiller, the world's leading bubble expert, points out, asset bubbles are like 'naturally occurring Ponzi schemes.' Early investors in a bubble make a lot of money as new investors are drawn in, and those profits pull in even more people. The process can go on for years before something — a reality check, or simply exhaustion of the pool of potential marks — brings the party to a sudden, painful end."[2876]

[2871] Frankenfield, Jake. "Bitcoin." *Investopedia*, 30 Jan. 2021, www.investopedia.com/terms/b/bitcoin.asp.

[2872] *Id.*

[2873] Herlean, Greg. "The Top 10 Risks Of Bitcoin Investing (And How To Avoid Them)." *Forbes*, 5 Dec. 2018, www.forbes.com/sites/forbesfinancecouncil/2018/12/05/the-top-10-risks-of-bitcoin-investing-and-how-to-avoid-them/#5f131fc52407.

[2874] Krugman, Paul. "Bitcoin is basically a Ponzi scheme." *The Seattle Times*, 30 Jan. 2018, www.seattletimes.com/opinion/bitcoin-is-basically-a-ponzi-scheme/.

[2875] Herlean, Greg. "The Top 10 Risks Of Bitcoin Investing (And How To Avoid Them)." *Forbes*, 5 Dec. 2018, www.forbes.com/sites/forbesfinancecouncil/2018/12/05/the-top-10-risks-of-bitcoin-investing-and-how-to-avoid-them/#5f131fc52407.

[2876] Krugman, Paul. "Bitcoin is basically a Ponzi scheme." *The Seattle Times*, 30 Jan. 2018, www.seattletimes.com/opinion/bitcoin-is-basically-a-ponzi-scheme/.

"Bitcoin continues to be worth something only if its proponents can convince others to jump on board with the idea and bid up the price. That's the definition of a confidence game. You have to be confident that someone is dumb enough to keep investing in this scam..."[2877] Bitcoin "will stay afloat only as long as enough people buy the fiction that bitcoin represents real value."[2878]

Eventually, "[i]nvestors will pull back from buying cyber currencies, causing their prices to begin a sustained decline. That downward spiral will accelerate as cyber-currency 'investors' try to bail out before prices plunge even more."[2879] "The inability of cyber currencies to serve as a store of value and to efficiently function as a medium of exchange for buying and selling real goods and services will become increasingly evident [as prices approach zero]. Once that fiction is revealed, the game will be over for cyber currencies"[2880] Warren Buffett feels almost certain that putting money in the Bitcoin market "will come to a bad ending."[2881]

Indeed, "[t]he pyramid scheme that lured new money into this scam is collapsing."[2882] This is because fewer and fewer people have confidence that the price of this inherently worthless

[2877] Crudele, John. "The Bitcoin 'pyramid scheme' continues to collapse." *New York Post*, 26 Nov. 2018, nypost.com/2018/11/26/the-bitcoin-pyramid-scheme-continues-to-collapse/.

[2878] Ely, Bert. "Bitcoin is a Ponzi scheme, and it will collapse like one." *The Hill*, 11 Dec. 2017, thehill.com/opinion/finance/364306-bitcoin-is-a-ponzi-scheme-and-it-will-collapse-like-one.

[2879] *Id.*

[2880] *Id.*

[2881] Blanco, Octavio. "Why Investing in Digital Currencies Like Bitcoin Is So Dangerous," *Consumer Reports*, 12 Jan. 2018, www.consumerreports.org/cryptocurrency/why-investing-in-digital-currencies-like-bitcoin-is-so-dangerous/.

[2882] Crudele, John. "The Bitcoin 'pyramid scheme' continues to collapse." *New York Post*, 26 Nov. 2018, nypost.com/2018/11/26/the-bitcoin-pyramid-scheme-continues-to-collapse/.

cryptocurrency is going to continue to rise.[2883] "The only real explanation for Bitcoin's value to disappear is that the confidence game is falling apart."[2884] "Consequently, bitcoin and its ilk will collapse, just as earlier speculative bubbles did, going back to the plunge of tulip prices in 1637..."[2885]

"With bitcoin plummeting over 30% in a 24-hour period to trading levels of $5,683, the lowest level in 10 months, a longtime critic of the cryptocurrency said that the coin is showings its true colors...'We've now answered the question... as to whether or not bitcoin was a safe haven, a store of value, an asset that people would flock to in times of trouble and financial turbulence,' Peter Schiff, founder of EuroPacific Capital said..., 'The answer is, no, it's not a safe haven asset. It is a very risky asset. The price of bitcoin has collapsed by more than the stock market during the last several weeks and in fact, it's not even a non-correlated asset,' Schiff said...'When the stock market goes down, bitcoin goes down more. And then when the stock market goes up, bitcoin goes up, but it goes up less. So I don't really see what value bitcoin brings to a portfolio...[S]o it's trading the opposite of a safe haven. It's correlated to the risk assets only. There is no place in anybody's portfolio for bitcoin, it's nothing more than a giant pyramid scheme which is what I've been saying from the beginning,' Schiff said...'Bitcoin is supposed to be skyrocketing and instead, it is collapsing. And that's got to call into question the validity of holding on to this asset.'"[2886]

[2883] *Id.*

[2884] *Id.*

[2885] Ely, Bert. "Bitcoin is a Ponzi scheme, and it will collapse like one." *The Hill*, 11 Dec. 2017, thehill.com/opinion/finance/364306-bitcoin-is-a-ponzi-scheme-and-it-will-collapse-like-one.

[2886] Cambone, Daniela. "Bitcoin price comes crashing, when this should be glory days says Peter Schiff." *Kitco*, 12 Mar. 2020, www.kitco.com/news/2020-03-12/Bitcoin-Price-Comes-Crashing-When-This-Should-Be-Glory-Days-Says-Peter-Schiff.html.

Another problem for Bitcoin is that it can be considered "a rival to government currency."[2887] "Depending on the country, there are a variety of approaches to regulating Bitcoin."[2888] Some "governments may seek to regulate, restrict or ban the use and sale of bitcoins, and some already have."[2889] In January 2018, Vladimir Putin warned that Russia's central bank would have to regulate cryptocurrencies.[2890] "[B]oth China and South Korea nixed initial coin offerings, with China going a step further and announcing the eventual closure of domestic cryptocurrency exchanges."[2891]

Some countries are developing their own digital currencies to compete with Bitcoin. For example, "[t]he Bank of Canada is considering launching a digital currency that would help it combat cryptocurrencies…"[2892] "[T]he currency would…initially coexist with coins and paper money, eventually replacing them completely…"[2893]

[2887] Frankenfield, Jake. "Bitcoin." *Investopedia*, 30 Jan. 2021, www.investopedia.com/terms/b/bitcoin.asp.

[2888] Macwen, Urvish. "The Main Risks Of Investing In Bitcoin." *Finextra*, 19 Jun. 2019, www.finextra.com/blogposting/17390/the-main-risks-of-investing-in-bitcoin.

[2889] Frankenfield, Jake. "Bitcoin." *Investopedia*, 30 Jan. 2021, www.investopedia.com/terms/b/bitcoin.asp.

[2890] "Bitcoin: Know the risks before you buy." *Al Jazeera*, 5 Feb. 2018, www.aljazeera.com/news/2017/12/bitcoin-buy-171219100738438.html.

[2891] Williams, Sean. "The 6 Biggest Risks to Bitcoin." *The Motley Fool*, 27 Nov. 2017, www.fool.com/investing/2017/11/27/the-6-biggest-risks-to-bitcoin.aspx.

[2892] Schwartz, Zane. "Bank of Canada exploring digital currency that would replace cash, track how people spend money." *Financial Post*, 15 Oct. 2019, business.financialpost.com/technology/blockchain/bank-of-canada-exploring-digital-currency-that-would-replace-cash-track-how-people-spend-money?fbclid=IwAR265L-vijcJSOj2u_wmH3CT3D2EXEeW4LgdNrZoiKDILDgcP1w3yQoJncU.

[2893] *Id.*

China is in the final steps of launching its own digital coin.[2894] "China is poised to launch a digital version of its yuan…"[2895] "China has already begun trialling payments in its new digital currency in four major cities, local media reported at the end of April [2020]."[2896]

"US central bankers have explored the possibility of developing a digital currency that would be directly available to businesses and households…"[2897] "The Federal Reserve [in August 2020] announced it is building and testing a hypothetical digital currency, equivalent of cash…'"[2898]

"The Central Bank of Russia (CBR) is studying a proposal to create a gold-backed cryptocurrency, which could be used for cross-border settlements with other countries. The bold proposal was made by Russia's State Duma member Vladimir Gutenev. He has suggested initiating discussion to set up national cryptocurrency, denominated in gold…Gutenev explained that, unlike ordinary cryptocurrencies, which are not secure because they are not backed by anything, gold-backed cryptos have their value tied to a real

---

[2894] *Id.*

[2895] Bambrough, Billy. "China Could Force Donald Trump And The Fed To Destroy The U.S. Banking System." *Forbes* 8 Jun. 2020, www.forbes.com/sites/billybambrough/2020/06/08/china-could-force-donald-trump-and-the-fed-to-destroy-the-us-banking-system/?fbclid=IwAR04NRJnWpR0WBekOK1K_k6u2bSyanBBK61LeTTpTUVD jrkp_fxqBSu7A7U#10952b414f5f.

[2896] *Id.*

[2897] Heeb, Gina. "The Federal Reserve is looking into developing a digital currency in the US, Powell confirms." *Markets Insider*, 20 Nov. 2019, markets.businessinsider.com/news/stocks/the-federal-reserve-is-looking-into-developing-a-digital-currency-us-2019-11-1028705211.

[2898] Robb, Greg. "Fed says it is developing an experimental digital currency." *Market Watch*, 15 Aug. 2020, www.marketwatch.com/story/fed-says-it-is-developing-an-experimental-digital-currency-11597352302?fbclid=IwAR3OgT9nTgUpqZ3ho_ks3Po08ryIL89zriTkT4i1ezk5WN8RV QIZ61E0ncU.

asset. They would come in the form of a so-called stablecoin which is a type of cryptocurrency but offers price stability characteristics..."[2899]

"Bank of England President Mark Carney floated the idea of a 'synthetic hegemonic currency [SHC],' possibly based on new digital-asset technologies, to reduce the dollar's 'domineering influence' on global trade."[2900] Mark Carney said, "A central bank-supported digital currency could replace the dollar as the global hedge currency."[2901] "Carney suggested a number of possible replacements [for] the dollar,...most notably, a digital currency supported by an international coalition of central banks."[2902]

"Other countries around the world, including Norway, Sweden and Japan, are all working on digitalizing their own

---

[2899] May, Frank. "Russia bringing back the gold standard may kill US dollar & solve main problem of cryptocurrencies." *RT*, 13 Jun. 2019, www.rt.com/business/461752-russia-gold-dollar-cryptocurrencies/.

[2900] Keoun, Bradley. "After Coronavirus 'War,' Bretton Woods-Style Shakeup Could Dethrone the Dollar." *Yahoo Finance*, 27 Mar. 2020, finance.yahoo.com/news/coronavirus-war-bretton-woods-style-130000284.html.

[2901] De, Nikhilesh. "UK Central Bank Chief Sees Digital Currency Displacing US Dollar as Global Reserve." *Coindesk*, 23 Aug. 2019, www.coindesk.com/bank-of-england-governor-calls-for-digital-currency-replacement-to-the-dollar?fbclid=IwAR1JBToRF3ui7otU4G3VT5vmY0GwU5Au92wDa-HpwHvzJ0voY8pDh9oeraQ.

[2902] *Id.*

currencies…"[2903] Venezuela already has a state-run cryptocurrency called "Petros."[2904]

"Thus, my warning to anyone considering playing the Bitcoin roulette wheel during these times is that unless you time it just right, you might be left holding Bitcoin long past the peak and well into a sharp decline. This could happen literally overnight. For example, what happens if the U.S. government announces an oil-backed cryptocurrency that's also backed by the Fed? Or if China announces a gold-backed hybrid crypto solution? Literally in a matter of hours, you could see a mad rush away from Bitcoin into a new crypto that's backed by a government…"[2905]

Mike Adams, the Health Ranger, suggested that "Bitcoin may be a creation of the NSA [National Security Agency] and was rolled out as a 'normalization' experiment to get the public familiar with digital currency."[2906] He envisioned a dystopian scenario in which cash, gold, and silver will be outlawed, and the government-backed

[2903] Bambrough, Billy. "China Could Force Donald Trump And The Fed To Destroy The U.S. Banking System." *Forbes* 8 Jun. 2020, www.forbes.com/sites/billybambrough/2020/06/08/china-could-force-donald-trump-and-the-fed-to-destroy-the-us-banking-system/?fbclid=IwAR04NRJnWpR0WBekOK1K_k6u2bSyanBBK61LeTTpTUVDjrkp_fxqBSu7A7U#10952b414f5f.

[2904] Reuters Staff. "Venezuela sets new price controls, with eggs costing more than a month's wages." *Reuters*, 30 Apr. 2020, www.reuters.com/article/us-venezuela-economy-idUSKBN22D41S?fbclid=IwAR3uYQqYdAAzOmERb852Y7Mb9V0aEa6z7oIhgp8H5gQxbJgzHCMmeNFQuV8.

[2905] Adams, Mike. "Analysis: Bitcoin could go to $100,000 as the fiat currency dollar collapses, but the 'value' won't be the fortune you're imagining." *Natural News*, 17 May 2020, www.naturalnews.com/2020-05-17-analysis-bitcoin-could-go-to-100000-as-fiat-currency-dollar-collapses.html.

[2906] Adams, Mike. "Evidence points to Bitcoin being an NSA-engineered psyop to roll out one-world digital currency." *Natural News*, 10 Dec. 2017, www.naturalnews.com/2017-12-10-evidence-points-to-bitcoin-being-an-nsa-psyop-roll-out-one-world-digital-currency.html.

digital currency will be used to track all transactions, investments, and commercial activities.[2907]   Adams predicted that "the world's fiat currencies will be obliterated in an engineered debt collapse…, then replaced with a government approved cryptocurrency with tracking of all transactions…"[2908]   For example, "[t]he Bank of Canada is considering launching a digital currency that would help it… collect more information on how people spend money than is possible when people use cash. 'Personal details…could be shared with police or tax authorities.'"[2909]

Adams pointed to a 1997 paper entitled, "How to make a mint: the cryptography of anonymous electronic cash," which was authored by "mathematical cryptographers at the National Security Agency's Office of Information Security Research and Technology."[2910] "Much of the Bitcoin protocol is detailed in this document, including signature authentication techniques, eliminating cryptocoin counterfeits through transaction authentication and several features that support anonymity and untraceability of transactions."[2911]

[2907] *Id.*

[2908] *Id.*

[2909] Schwartz, Zane. "Bank of Canada exploring digital currency that would replace cash, track how people spend money." *Financial Post,* 15 Oct. 2019, business.financialpost.com/technology/blockchain/bank-of-canada-exploring-digital-currency-that-would-replace-cash-track-how-people-spend-money?fbclid=IwAR265L-vijcJSOj2u_wmH3CT3D2EXEeW4LgdNrZoiKDILDgcP1w3yQoJncU.

[2910] Adams, Mike. "Evidence points to Bitcoin being an NSA-engineered psyop to roll out one-world digital currency." *Natural News,* 10 Dec. 2017, www.naturalnews.com/2017-12-10-evidence-points-to-bitcoin-being-an-nsa-psyop-roll-out-one-world-digital-currency.html.

[2911] "The document even outlines the heightened risk of money laundering that's easily accomplished with cryptocurrencies. It also describes "secure hashing" to be "both one-way and collision-free…" *Id.*

The NSA was "the creator of the SHA-256 hash upon which every Bitcoin transaction depends."[2912] If the SHA-256 hash actually has a backdoor method for cracking the encryption, it would mean the NSA could take Bitcoins whenever it wants.[2913] Thus, the State would be able to confiscate a portion of one's crypto holdings as "automated taxation."[2914] In addition, automatic deductions could be instituted for traffic violations and such.[2915] In this way, the globalists could "seize total control over the world's money supply, savings, taxation and financial transactions while enslaving humanity."[2916] Mohit Kumar, the author of the creepy paper, admitted that this could be the case: "Possibly it [Bitcoin] was designed from day one as a tool to help maintain control of the money supplies of the world."[2917]

***

Ultimately, the investor should diversify his holdings with assets that are a store of value. "[T]oday's global capital markets provide ample opportunity for attractive long-term investment returns. Credit, non-U.S. equities, and alternative asset classes, such as commodities and REITS, provide investors the means to

---

[2912] "As The Hacker News explains. 'The integrity of Bitcoin depends on a hash function called SHA-256, which was designed by the NSA and published by the National Institute for Standards and Technology (NIST) …'" *Id.*

[2913] *Id.*

[2914] *Id.*

[2915] *Id.*

[2916] *Id.*

[2917] *Id.*

assemble a broadly diversified portfolio with a real expected long-term return of 5% or better."[2918]

Economist, Marc Faber, said that in a hyper-inflationary environment, good investments are gold, "commodities, real estate, art, collectibles and so forth, anything that essentially cannot be multiplied at the same rate as paper money, that is subject to the printing presses of Mr. Bernanke."[2919]   "Properly diversified investors combine gold with stocks and bonds in a portfolio to reduce the overall volatility and risk."[2920]   Even pick-up trucks, such as 1995-2002 Fords, should maintain their value, if they have low mileage and no rust.[2921]

"The key to diversification is finding investments that are not closely correlated to one another; [for ex.] gold has historically had a negative correlation to stocks and other financial instruments."[2922]

The next chapter talks about how to use limited liability companies for asset protection.

[2918] Brightman, Chris. "Negative Rates Are Dangerous to Your Wealth." *Research Affiliates*, Apr. 2016, www.researchaffiliates.com/en_us/ p u b l i c a t i o n s / a r t i c l e s / 542_negative_rates_are_dangerous_to_your_wealth.html.

[2919] Cox, Jeff. "Gold Is Still Cheap Despite Record Surge: Marc Faber." *CNBC*, 8 Apr. 2011, www.cnbc.com/id/42478554.

[2920] Daltorio, Tony. "8 Reasons To Own Gold." *Investopedia*, 22 June 2019, www.investopedia.com/articles/basics/08/reasons-to-own-gold.asp.

[2921] At 10:20. Gammon, George. "Asset Bubbles Explained: Simple And Fast! (COLLABORATION VIDEO)." *Youtube*, 13 Dec. 2019, www.youtube.com/watch?v=eyz7SeSIbqc.

[2922] Daltorio, Tony. "8 Reasons To Own Gold." *Investopedia*, 22 June 2019, www.investopedia.com/articles/basics/08/reasons-to-own-gold.asp.

Chapter 10

Limited Liability Company (LLC)

Nelson Rockefeller once said, "The secret to success is to own nothing, but control everything."[2923] What he was implying was the use of an asset-protection strategy. Suppose an investor is involved in a car accident, and his liability exceeds the limits of his auto insurance policy. In that case, his assets could be at risk. Removing assets from one's personal possession can shield them from creditors.

A typical asset protection plan involves the formation of a limited liability company (LLC). An LLC "is a hybrid or a cross between a partnership and a corporation. Limited Liability Companies were first developed in Wyoming in 1977 and spread to the rest of the United States during the 1990s..."[2924] They are among the most widely used and effective domestic asset protection vehicles.[2925] "LLCs are exceptionally beneficial when used to safeguard real estate or stock market investments."[2926]

"When you form an LLC, you establish a new business entity that's legally separate from its owners. This separation provides

---

[2923] Luster, Brian. "How To Protect Your Assets Without Giving Up Control." *Forbes*, 18 Mar. 2014, www.forbes.com/sites/brianluster/2014/03/18/why-forming-a-family-limited-partnership-means-less-stress-at-tax-time/#2ed697a68658.

[2924] "Limited Liability Company 101." *Assetprotection.com*, assetprotection.com/limited-liability-company/limited-liability-company-101/.

[2925] "Limited Liability Company (LLC) Asset Protection." *Asset Protection Planners*, www.assetprotectionplanners.com/services/llc/.

[2926] "Although real estate ownership creates potential liability with tenant and guest injuries, leases, contracts, environmental laws, mortgages and other laws, real estate investors prefer LLCs because they are advantageous when used to own assets that create passive income." *Id.*

what is called limited liability protection."[2927] "Limited liability means that there is a wall between your personal assets and your business assets. One type of creditor (e.g., business) cannot reach other types of assets (personal.)"[2928]

"In a typical situation, an LLC is formed in which you are the manager, and the assets that you want protected are contributed to the LLC. As the manager, you retain control over the assets in the LLC."[2929] "The manager of an LLC can be a member...or...a non-member. The members of a Limited Liability Company can be natural people, other LLCs, or even trusts and corporations."[2930]

LLCs "can shield the members from the liability related to business transactions."[2931] They "protect the personal assets of the company members (owners) if someone sues the business."[2932] "If your LLC is sued, the money that is in the LLC can be used to

---

[2927] Haskins, Jane. "LLC Asset Protection: How to Protect your Personal Assets as an LLC Owner." *Legal Zoom*, www.legalzoom.com/articles/llc-asset-protection-how-to-protect-your-personal-assets-as-an-llc-owner.

[2928] "Leveraging Limited Liability for Asset Protection." *Bizfilings.com*, www.bizfilings.com/toolkit/research-topics/running-your-business/asset-strategies/leveraging-limited-liability-for-asset-protection.

[2929] "With an irrevocable trust, you give up the ownership and control of the property transferred to the irrevocable trust and turn it over to the trustee of the irrevocable trust. Both of these techniques can shield the assets from creditors." "Asset Protection FAQs." *The Farrell Law Group*, www.farrell-lawgroup.com/Practice-Areas/Asset-Protection-Law/FAQs-Regarding-Asset-Protection.

[2930] "Limited Liability Company 101." *Assetprotection.com*, assetprotection.com/limited-liability-company/limited-liability-company-101/.

[2931] "Limited Liability Company (LLC) Asset Protection." *Asset Protection Planners*, www.assetprotectionplanners.com/services/llc/.

[2932] *Id.*

satisfy a creditor, but your personal assets usually cannot."[2933] "It provides this protection even for its managers. Plus, it offers asset protection services to its members regardless of the extent to which they participate in management and control of the company's business affairs."[2934] "The Limited Liability Company members can be active in the management of the Limited Liability Company and not take on any personal liability as a result of the management activity."[2935]

"Forming a limited liability company is an important first step to protect your personal assets from being used to pay business creditors."[2936] "If you decide to form a Limited Liability Company (LLC), one primary concern is liability protection for your personal assets from your LLC's creditors and legal liabilities. Excluding your financial contributions to your business, the general rule is that your LLC is considered a separate legal entity and as its owner, you are not personally liable for its debts or legal liabilities."[2937] "[I]f the LLC can't pay its debts, the LLC's creditors can go after the LLC's bank account and other assets, but the owners' personal assets such as cars, homes and bank accounts are safe."[2938]

[2933] Haskins, Jane. "LLC Asset Protection: How to Protect your Personal Assets as an LLC Owner." *Legal Zoom*, www.legalzoom.com/articles/llc-asset-protection-how-to-protect-your-personal-assets-as-an-llc-owner.

[2934] "Limited Liability Company (LLC) Asset Protection." *Asset Protection Planners*, www.assetprotectionplanners.com/services/llc/.

[2935] "Limited Liability Company 101." *Assetprotection.com*, assetprotection.com/limited-liability-company/limited-liability-company-101/.

[2936] Haskins, Jane. "LLC Asset Protection: How to Protect your Personal Assets as an LLC Owner." *Legal Zoom*, www.legalzoom.com/articles/llc-asset-protection-how-to-protect-your-personal-assets-as-an-llc-owner.

[2937] "Strategies to Strengthen LLC Asset Protection." *NOLO*, www.nolo.com/legal-encyclopedia/llcs-owner-liability-protection.html.

[2938] Haskins, Jane. "LLC Asset Protection: How to Protect your Personal Assets as an LLC Owner." *Legal Zoom*, www.legalzoom.com/articles/llc-asset-protection-how-to-protect-your-personal-assets-as-an-llc-owner.

"An LLC protects its members from liabilities generated by property owned by the LLC. For example, if an LLC is formed and a rental property is contributed to the LLC and later someone falls down the steps of the rental property and sues the owner, it is the LLC that gets sued. Any liability belongs to the LLC. Only the assets owned by the LLC, in this case, the rental property, are available to the plaintiff if the lawsuit is successful. The other assets owned by the members of the LLC are not available to the plaintiff."[2939]

It is advisable to not commingle dangerous assets with safe assets or other dangerous assets.[2940] Dangerous assets, such as rental real estate, commercial property, business assets, i.e. tools and equipment, and motor vehicles, entail a lot of potential legal liability to third parties.[2941] "Keeping ownership of dangerous assets separate limits exposure of loss to the individual asset."[2942] Stocks, bonds, and bank accounts are considered "safe" assets because they do not involve a high degree of inherent risk.[2943]

"Many individuals who own real estate establish a separate LLC for each property."[2944] Putting each rental property into separate LLCs protects them from the potential liabilities of all of

---

[2939] "Asset Protection FAQs." *The Farrell Law Group*, www.farrell-lawgroup.com/Practice-Areas/Asset-Protection-Law/FAQs-Regarding-Asset-Protection.

[2940] Rando, David. "Asset Protection for the Business Owner." *Investopedia*, 25 Jun. 2019, www.investopedia.com/articles/pf/08/asset-protection-business.asp.

[2941] *Id.*

[2942] *Id.*

[2943] *Id.*

[2944] "LLC Asset Protection Strategies: Everything You Need To Know." *Upcounsel.com*, www.upcounsel.com/llc-asset-protection-strategies.

the other properties.[2945] Thus, a lawsuit affecting one of the rental properties will not affect the others, as they are each held in a separate company.[2946] For instance, if someone falls down the stairs of a rental property and sues the LLC, the only assets available to the plaintiff are those owned by that particular LLC.[2947]

"Since you can obtain protection from your personal creditors for assets owned by your LLC, some business owners think that they should convert as many assets as possible into business assets."[2948] "However,…most business owners are more likely to face a business liability or judgment than a personal one. The business's assets, as opposed to the owner's personal assets outside of the business, are usually at the greatest risk of loss, which means this strategy actually increases the risk of loss."[2949] Because the LLC has unlimited liability for its debts, it can lose everything it owns.[2950] Even if "[a]n LLC owner only risks the amount of money he or she has invested in the business," it is wise to maintain as little capital as

---

[2945] "Asset Protection FAQs." *The Farrell Law Group*, www.farrell-lawgroup.com/Practice-Areas/Asset-Protection-Law/FAQs-Regarding-Asset-Protection.

[2946] "LLC Asset Protection Strategies: Everything You Need To Know." *Upcounsel.com*, www.upcounsel.com/llc-asset-protection-strategies.

[2947] "Asset Protection FAQs." *The Farrell Law Group*, www.farrell-lawgroup.com/Practice-Areas/Asset-Protection-Law/FAQs-Regarding-Asset-Protection.

[2948] "Leveraging Limited Liability for Asset Protection." *Bizfilings.com*, www.bizfilings.com/toolkit/research-topics/running-your-business/asset-strategies/leveraging-limited-liability-for-asset-protection.

[2949] *Id.*

[2950] *Id.*

possible in the business and pay the rest to the members.[2951] This will limit the number of assets that are exposed to liability.[2952]

"However, you should be aware that this strategy can trigger an exception to limited liability, in which a court 'pierces the veil' of limited liability and imposes unlimited, personal liability on the owners on the grounds that the capitalization was inadequate and was a fraudulent scheme against the business's creditors."[2953] Therefore, "[a] better approach would be to use two entities, an operating entity and a holding entity. In this way, you can protect your assets against the claims of both your business and your personal creditors."[2954]

"[T]he LLC can protect the assets of the business when someone sues a member."[2955] "[T]he assets owned by the LLC are protected from any liability of any member."[2956] "[A]n LLC's money or property cannot be taken by personal creditors of the LLC's owners to satisfy personal debts against the owner."[2957] "[T]he personal creditors of LLC owners cannot obtain full

---

[2951] *Id.* Haskins, Jane. "LLC Asset Protection: How to Protect your Personal Assets as an LLC Owner." *Legal Zoom*, www.legalzoom.com/articles/llc-asset-protection-how-to-protect-your-personal-assets-as-an-llc-owner.

[2952] "Leveraging Limited Liability for Asset Protection." *Bizfilings.com*, www.bizfilings.com/toolkit/research-topics/running-your-business/asset-strategies/leveraging-limited-liability-for-asset-protection.

[2953] *Id.*

[2954] *Id.*

[2955] "Limited Liability Company (LLC) Asset Protection." *Asset Protection Planners*, www.assetprotectionplanners.com/services/llc/.

[2956] "Asset Protection FAQs." *The Farrell Law Group*, www.farrell-lawgroup.com/Practice-Areas/Asset-Protection-Law/FAQs-Regarding-Asset-Protection.

[2957] Fishman, Stephen. "LC Asset Protection and Charging Orders: An Overview of State Laws." *Nolo*, www.nolo.com/legal-encyclopedia/llc-asset-protection-charging-orders.html.

ownership of an owner-debtor's membership interest. Instead, all states as part of their uniform LLC laws have adopted provisions limiting what action creditors can take against LLC owner/members for their personal debts."[2958] The statutes that govern LLCs prevent creditors from seizing the business or its assets.[2959] "[W]hen someone sues a member personally, there are provisions in the law that keep a creditor from seizing the assets inside of the company to satisfy a judgment."[2960] "For example,…two or more people have formed an LLC and it owns a rental property. Now, if one of the members runs a red light and causes an accident, the rental property will be protected. Although the creditor (in this case the 'victim' of the auto accident) can sue the member, the 'victim' cannot either take the member's interest in the LLC, or force him to sell it. The interest in the LLCs and the rental property are protected."[2961]

"In all states, personal creditors of an LLC owner/member are limited to one or more of the following remedies: Getting a court to order that the LLC pay to the creditor all the money due to the LLC owner/debtor from the LLC (this is called a charging order), foreclosing on the owner/debtor's LLC ownership interest, or getting a court to order the LLC to be dissolved."[2962]

"All states permit personal creditors of an LLC owner to obtain a charging order against the debtor-owner's membership

---

[2958] *Id.*

[2959] "LLC Asset Protection Strategies: Everything You Need To Know." *Upcounsel.com*, www.upcounsel.com/llc-asset-protection-strategies.

[2960] "Limited Liability Company (LLC) Asset Protection." *Asset Protection Planners*, www.assetprotectionplanners.com/services/llc/.

[2961] "Asset Protection FAQs." *The Farrell Law Group*, www.farrell-lawgroup.com/Practice-Areas/Asset-Protection-Law/FAQs-Regarding-Asset-Protection.

[2962] Fishman, Stephen. "LC Asset Protection and Charging Orders: An Overview of State Laws." *Nolo*, www.nolo.com/legal-encyclopedia/llc-asset-protection-charging-orders.html.

interest."[2963]   "A charging order is an order issued by a court directing an LLC's manager to pay to the debtor-owner's personal creditor any distributions of income or profits that would otherwise be distributed to the debtor-member."[2964]   "The charging order... directs distributions to the creditor rather than to the debtor-member..."[2965]   The charging order directs "the limited liability company to pay to the creditor any income distributions that would otherwise flow to the debtor-member..."[2966]   "It simply requires distributions to be paid to the creditor before they are paid to you as the owner."[2967]

In "most states, creditors with a charging order only obtain the owner-debtor's financial rights and cannot participate in management of the LLC."[2968]   "The creditor gains only the financial rights of the debtor-member, not control or ownership rights."[2969]

"The charging order does not entitle the creditor to become a member of the LLC" or give him voting rights.[2970]   "Creditors of a

---

[2963] *Id.*

[2964] *Id.*

[2965] "Overview of How an LLC Protects your Personal Assets." *The Presser Law Firm*, www.assetprotectionattorneys.com/ Domestic_Asset_Protection/Limited_Liability_Companies/ How_an_LLC_Protects_your_Personal_Assets.aspx.

[2966] *Id.*

[2967] "LLC Asset Protection Strategies: Everything You Need To Know." *Upcounsel.com*, www.upcounsel.com/llc-asset-protection-strategies.

[2968] Fishman, Stephen. "LC Asset Protection and Charging Orders: An Overview of State Laws." *Nolo*, www.nolo.com/legal-encyclopedia/llc-asset-protection-charging-orders.html.

[2969] "Overview of How an LLC Protects your Personal Assets." *The Presser Law Firm*, www.assetprotectionattorneys.com/ Domestic_Asset_Protection/Limited_Liability_Companies/ How_an_LLC_Protects_your_Personal_Assets.aspx.

[2970] *Id.*

limited liability company member cannot seize or force a sale of the member's interest. Nor can the member's creditor vote the interest of the debtor-member."[2971] "A creditor of a member of an LLC cannot take either the interest in the LLC or assets from the LLC."[2972] "As a result, LLC owners in most states are never at risk of having another LLC member's creditor step into the shoes of an LLC debtor/member and share in the management and control of the LLC."[2973]

A charging order may entitle a creditor to LLC distributions, but they are not enforceable and are subject to income tax when they are received.[2974] While the creditor is entitled to any distributions made by the LLC to the member until the judgment is paid in full, "the charging order will not...force the limited liability company manager to pay distributions to a member or his creditor."[2975] "The members of an LLC can determine among themselves how to distribute LLC profits and losses. Unlike a corporation where the profits and losses are fixed according to the percentage owned, in an

---

[2971] *Id.*

[2972] "Asset Protection FAQs." *The Farrell Law Group*, www.farrell-lawgroup.com/Practice-Areas/Asset-Protection-Law/FAQs-Regarding-Asset-Protection.

[2973] Fishman, Stephen. "LC Asset Protection and Charging Orders: An Overview of State Laws." *Nolo*, www.nolo.com/legal-encyclopedia/llc-asset-protection-charging-orders.html.

[2974] "LLC Asset Protection Strategies: Everything You Need To Know." *Upcounsel.com*, www.upcounsel.com/llc-asset-protection-strategies.

[2975] "Asset Protection FAQs." *The Farrell Law Group*, www.farrell-lawgroup.com/Practice-Areas/Asset-Protection-Law/FAQs-Regarding-Asset-Protection; "Overview of How an LLC Protects your Personal Assets." *The Presser Law Firm*, www.assetprotectionattorneys.com/ Domestic_Asset_Protection/Limited_Liability_Companies/ How_an_LLC_Protects_your_Personal_Assets.aspx.

LLC there is no such requirement."[2976] "[T]he creditor cannot order the LLC to make a distribution subject to its charging order. Frequently, creditors who obtain charging orders end up with nothing because they can't order the LLC to make any distributions..."[2977] "If you manage your limited liability company, you will decide if and when you will make distributions. Your judgment creditor cannot replace you as the manager because your creditor cannot vote. And for as long as your creditor has a charging order against you, you can refuse to pay distributions."[2978] "Be sure to take care when drafting the entity's documents to avoid making any distributions to the owner mandatory."[2979]

For example, "[o]ne of the members rear ends someone's car. The injured driver of the other automobile sues and gets a $1 million judgment. That member only has $500,000 in liability insurance. Next, the judgment creditor gets a judge to place a charging order on that member's interest in the LLC. So, let's say that member owns 25% of the company. The ruling says that all distributions to that member must now go to the creditor. However, LLC statutes do not allow the creditor to step into the shoes of a member or manager and order the payment of distributions. So, the management decides to

---

[2976] "Limited Liability Company 101." *Assetprotection.com*, assetprotection.com/limited-liability-company/limited-liability-company-101/.

[2977] Fishman, Stephen. "LC Asset Protection and Charging Orders: An Overview of State Laws." *Nolo*, www.nolo.com/legal-encyclopedia/llc-asset-protection-charging-orders.html.

[2978] "Overview of How an LLC Protects your Personal Assets." *The Presser Law Firm*, www.assetprotectionattorneys.com/Domestic_Asset_Protection/Limited_Liability_Companies/How_an_LLC_Protects_your_Personal_Assets.aspx.

[2979] "Leveraging Limited Liability for Asset Protection." *Bizfilings.com*, www.bizfilings.com/toolkit/research-topics/running-your-business/asset-strategies/leveraging-limited-liability-for-asset-protection.

keep the profits inside of the LLC."[2980]   "[I]f there are no distributions, there will be no payments."[2981]

There is also a tax liability associated with the charging order against a limited liability company interest, which is often called a "poison pill" provision.[2982]   "The charging order creditor may be required to pay your income tax on LLC profits. Since a limited liability company is ordinarily taxed as a partnership, its tax liability automatically passes to its members."[2983]   "According to Revenue Ruling 77-137, whoever has the right to the distributions must pay taxes on them."[2984]   "The charging order creditor…gets the tax bill for the debtor-member's share of LLC profits. This forces the member's creditor to pay taxes on the member's earnings, even if the creditor has not received any distributions."[2985]   "So, even if the managers keep the profits locked up in the company, the members still need to pay the tax. What that means, is that now the creditor receives a tax bill…but no money…Operated properly, the one who holds the charging order gets a tax bill but they do not get any

---

[2980] "Limited Liability Company (LLC) Asset Protection." *Asset Protection Planners*, www.assetprotectionplanners.com/services/llc/.

[2981] Fishman, Stephen. "LC Asset Protection and Charging Orders: An Overview of State Laws." *Nolo*, www.nolo.com/legal-encyclopedia/llc-asset-protection-charging-orders.html.

[2982] "Overview of How an LLC Protects your Personal Assets." *The Presser Law Firm*, www.assetprotectionattorneys.com/Domestic_Asset_Protection/Limited_Liability_Companies/How_an_LLC_Protects_your_Personal_Assets.aspx.

[2983] *Id.*

[2984] "Limited Liability Company (LLC) Asset Protection." *Asset Protection Planners*, www.assetprotectionplanners.com/services/llc/.

[2985] "Overview of How an LLC Protects your Personal Assets." *The Presser Law Firm*, www.assetprotectionattorneys.com/Domestic_Asset_Protection/Limited_Liability_Companies/How_an_LLC_Protects_your_Personal_Assets.aspx.

money to pay it."[2986] "[T]he fact the creditor will be taxed on the LLC's earnings, even though he or she receives nothing, usually will persuade the creditor to drop collection efforts to cut his or her losses."[2987]

"Although a charging order is often a weak remedy for a creditor, it is not necessarily toothless. The existence of a charging order can make it difficult or impossible for an LLC owner/debtor or the other owners (if any) to take money out of an LLC business without having to pay the judgment creditor first."[2988] "Nevertheless, you can pay yourself a salary for services and salaries cannot be seized through the charging order. Also, your creditor is not able to garnish loans or other forms of compensation that you may pay to yourself as a manager or member."[2989]

"In about two-thirds of the states, the charging order is the exclusive (only) legal remedy personal creditors of LLC members have…"[2990] "These states are the most debtor friendly; they provide the greatest protection for LLC owners against personal creditors. This protection extends to both the debtor/LLC member and any co-owners who would otherwise be at risk of having creditors take more aggressive action against the LLC, including possibly forcing

---

[2986] "Limited Liability Company (LLC) Asset Protection." *Asset Protection Planners*, www.assetprotectionplanners.com/services/llc/.

[2987] "Leveraging Limited Liability for Asset Protection." *Bizfilings.com*, www.bizfilings.com/toolkit/research-topics/running-your-business/asset-strategies/leveraging-limited-liability-for-asset-protection.

[2988] Fishman, Stephen. "LC Asset Protection and Charging Orders: An Overview of State Laws." *Nolo*, www.nolo.com/legal-encyclopedia/llc-asset-protection-charging-orders.html.

[2989] "Overview of How an LLC Protects your Personal Assets." *The Presser Law Firm*, www.assetprotectionattorneys.com/Domestic_Asset_Protection/Limited_Liability_Companies/How_an_LLC_Protects_your_Personal_Assets.aspx.

[2990] Fishman, Stephen. "LC Asset Protection and Charging Orders: An Overview of State Laws." *Nolo*, www.nolo.com/legal-encyclopedia/llc-asset-protection-charging-orders.html.

a dissolution of their LLC."[2991]   "Others states simply state that a charging order is an allowed remedy for creditors and also allow foreclosure or are silent as to what other remedies a creditor could pursue."[2992]

"In about one-third of the states, a creditor who obtains a charging order but is not paid by the LLC can have the court order that the debtor-owner's LLC membership interest be foreclosed upon. If this occurs, the creditor becomes the permanent owner of all the debtor-member's financial rights, including the right to receive money from the LLC. However, the creditor cannot participate in the management of the LLC. Thus, it can't force the LLC to pay money to it or anyone else."[2993]   "A foreclosure will not allow for a creditor to receive anything more than a right to distributions from the LLC, which the creditor will likely never receive. Furthermore, the receiver of a foreclosed interest will certainly be liable for the taxes on a distribution he will probably never see…"[2994]

"A handful of states permit personal creditors of LLC owners to obtain a court order that the LLC be dissolved. In this event, the LLC would have to cease doing business and sell all of its assets. This is the most extreme remedy allowed for personal creditors of LLC owners."[2995]   In many states, however, "these creditors will not

---

[2991] *Id.*

[2992] *Id.*

[2993] *Id.*

[2994] "Overview of How an LLC Protects your Personal Assets." *The Presser Law Firm*, www.assetprotectionattorneys.com/ Domestic_Asset_Protection/Limited_Liability_Companies/ How_an_LLC_Protects_your_Personal_Assets.aspx.

[2995] Fishman, Stephen. "LC Asset Protection and Charging Orders: An Overview of State Laws." *Nolo*, www.nolo.com/legal-encyclopedia/llc-asset-protection-charging-orders.html.

be able to foreclose on the interest and force a liquidation of the business."[2996]

As to ownership, Limited Liability Companies can have a single member or multiple members. Multi-member LLCs are stronger unless the LLC was formed in "a state that treats both single member and multi-member LLCs the same."[2997] "The reason personal creditors of individual LLC owners are limited to a charging order or foreclosure is to protect the other members (owners) of the LLC. It doesn't seem fair that they should suffer because a member incurred personal debts that had nothing to do with their LLC. Thus, personal creditors are not permitted to take over the debtor-member's LLC interest and join in the management of the LLC or have the LLC dissolved and its assets sold without the other members' consent."[2998] Therefore, the "LLC should have one or more members in addition to the one who is a lawsuit defendant. The courts are more hesitant to expand upon a creditor's remedy when other LLC members would be affected."[2999]

Some courts have applied different rules for single member LLCs (SMLLC) because there are no other LLC owner/members to protect. "Courts in a few states have found that the charging order protection that exists for LLCs does not apply with SMLLCs because there are no co-owners to protect. These cases created a

---

[2996] "Leveraging Limited Liability for Asset Protection." *Bizfilings.com*, www.bizfilings.com/toolkit/research-topics/running-your-business/asset-strategies/leveraging-limited-liability-for-asset-protection.

[2997] "Limited Liability Company 101." *Assetprotection.com*, assetprotection.com/limited-liability-company/limited-liability-company-101/.

[2998] Fishman, Stephen. "LC Asset Protection and Charging Orders: An Overview of State Laws." *Nolo*, www.nolo.com/legal-encyclopedia/llc-asset-protection-charging-orders.html.

[2999] "Overview of How an LLC Protects your Personal Assets." *The Presser Law Firm*, www.assetprotectionattorneys.com/Domestic_Asset_Protection/Limited_Liability_Companies/How_an_LLC_Protects_your_Personal_Assets.aspx.

great deal of uncertainty in other states with similar charging order protection laws. In response, several states amended their LLC laws to make it clear that SMLLCs are entitled to the same protection from creditors as multi-member LLCs. These include Delaware, Nevada, and Wyoming...Their laws now specifically state that charging orders are the exclusive remedy for creditors of both multi- and single-member LLCs. A few states, including Florida and New Hampshire, have gone the other way and changed their LLC laws to make it clear that a charging order is not the only remedy that can be used against an SMLLC. In these states, the SMLLC does not provide nearly as much liability protection as a multi-member LLC."[3000] "Some courts will liquidate an LLC for the benefit of a creditor when the debtor is the only member and no other members would be affected."[3001]

"The federal bankruptcy law says nothing about how LLCs should be treated. As a result, the bankruptcy courts are in the process of making up the rules as they go along."[3002] "Should a member file bankruptcy; recent case law has demonstrated that the bankruptcy trustee may also have considerably greater rights to claim the member's limited liability company ownership interest than could be obtained by a judgment creditor holding a charging

---

[3000] Fishman, Stephen. "LC Asset Protection and Charging Orders: An Overview of State Laws." *Nolo*, www.nolo.com/legal-encyclopedia/llc-asset-protection-charging-orders.html.

[3001] "Overview of How an LLC Protects your Personal Assets." *The Presser Law Firm*, www.assetprotectionattorneys.com/Domestic_Asset_Protection/Limited_Liability_Companies/How_an_LLC_Protects_your_Personal_Assets.aspx.

[3002] Fishman, Stephen. "LC Asset Protection and Charging Orders: An Overview of State Laws." *Nolo*, www.nolo.com/legal-encyclopedia/llc-asset-protection-charging-orders.html.

order."[3003]   "It is also possible that the ownership interest of a member of a multi-member LLC could be taken over by a bankruptcy trustee."[3004]

"The protection afforded by the LLC form can simply be ignored by the bankruptcy court where there is only one LLC owner."[3005]   "Several bankruptcy courts have held that when the owner of a SMLLC files for Chapter 7 bankruptcy the trustee appointed by the bankruptcy court becomes a substituted member of the LLC and can exercise all the owner's rights. This includes the right to manage the LLC and sell its assets (such as real estate) to pay off creditors..."[3006]

"A simple way to avoid the potential creditor and bankruptcy problems with SMLLCs is not to have one. Instead, make sure your LLC has at least two members. The second member could be your spouse or another relative. However, the spouse, relative, or any other second member must be a legitimate co-owner of the LLC. If the second person is a member only on paper, it's likely that a court would disregard his or her interest and find that you have a single-member LLC. To avoid this, the co-owner must pay fair market value for the interest acquired and otherwise be treated as a 'real' LLC member — hat is, receive financial statements, participate in decision making, and receive a share of the LLC profits equal to the membership percentage owned."[3007]

[3003] "Overview of How an LLC Protects your Personal Assets." *The Presser Law Firm*, www.assetprotectionattorneys.com/Domestic_Asset_Protection/Limited_Liability_Companies/How_an_LLC_Protects_your_Personal_Assets.aspx.

[3004] Fishman, Stephen. "LC Asset Protection and Charging Orders: An Overview of State Laws." *Nolo*, www.nolo.com/legal-encyclopedia/llc-asset-protection-charging-orders.html.

[3005] *Id.*

[3006] *Id.*

[3007] *Id.*

Setting up an LLC is fairly simple. "It is a matter of filing the proper paperwork with the Secretary of State's officer where the LLC is to be located. In some cases, the Secretary of State's pre-printed articles are filed, and in other cases, custom articles are filed. A name is required, as well as a [registered] agent. The [registered] agent is the representative for the LLC in the state where the entity is formed. If you live in the state of formation, then you can be your own [registered] agent. The [registered] agent is also the entity that receives and accepts any lawsuits that are filed against the Limited Liability Company."[3008]

"You do not have to form your LLC in your home state, even if it is the state where you live or do business. Thus, if your home state's LLC law does not provide all the protection from creditors you would like, you could form your LLC in a more debtor-friendly state."[3009] "Thus, forming an LLC in a state with a favorable LLC law could provide you with more limited liability."[3010] "As a general rule, the formation state's LLC law will govern your LLC."[3011] "The states that offer the highest level of asset protection for LLCs include Delaware, Nevada, and Wyoming."[3012]

Unfortunately, "there is no guarantee that courts in your home state or courts in other states will always apply the law of the state where you formed your LLC, rather than the less favorable LLC law

---

[3008] "Limited Liability Company 101." *Assetprotection.com*, assetprotection.com/limited-liability-company/limited-liability-company-101/.

[3009] "Limited Liability Company (LLC) Asset Protection." *Asset Protection Planners*, www.assetprotectionplanners.com/services/llc/.

[3010] *Id.*

[3011] *Id.*

[3012] "LLC Asset Protection Strategies: Everything You Need To Know." *Upcounsel.com*, www.upcounsel.com/llc-asset-protection-strategies.

of your home state."[3013]   In addition, "doing so will increase your costs because you'll have to pay the fees to form your LLC in the other state plus the fees to register to do business in your home state…Wyoming is the most cost-effective because the annual renewal fees are far lower."[3014]

The Internal Revenue Service (IRS) "allows LLCs to determine whether they will be taxed as a corporation or as a sole proprietorship."[3015]   "With two or more members, the IRS recognizes an LLC as a partnership for income tax purposes by default."[3016]   However, "if your LLC is classified as a corporation, you can help shield your personal assets from LLC debt and liabilities along with responsibility for unpaid LLC payroll and other taxes."[3017]   Using "IRS Form 8832, you can elect to operate as an S Corporation or a C Corporation."[3018]   Because a C Corp involves double taxation, it may be better to choose S corporation status by filing a 2553 tax form along with the 8832 form with the IRS.[3019]

"The profits and losses of the Limited Liability Company pass through to its members and they report the income on their personal tax returns. The LLC pays no federal income taxes. If a Limited Liability Company is owned by a single member or by a husband and wife in a community property state, then the IRS considers the

---

[3013] Fishman, Stephen. "LC Asset Protection and Charging Orders: An Overview of State Laws." *Nolo*, www.nolo.com/legal-encyclopedia/llc-asset-protection-charging-orders.html.

[3014] "Limited Liability Company (LLC) Asset Protection." *Asset Protection Planners*, www.assetprotectionplanners.com/services/llc/.

[3015] *Id.*

[3016] *Id.*

[3017] "Strategies to Strengthen LLC Asset Protection." *NOLO*, www.nolo.com/legal-encyclopedia/llcs-owner-liability-protection.html.

[3018] *Id.*

[3019] "Limited Liability Company (LLC) Asset Protection." *Asset Protection Planners*, www.assetprotectionplanners.com/services/llc/.

LLC to be a disregarded entity for tax purposes. So, no tax return needs to be filed."[3020]

A comprehensive operating agreement is important, especially for multi-member LLCs, since disputes may develop among the members.[3021]

The operating agreement should determine what happens if a member files bankruptcy or has a court judgment entered against him or her. "For example, the LLC members may wish to include a provision in their operating agreement allowing for the expulsion of any member who files for bankruptcy; or allowing them to purchase the interest of any member who becomes subject to a charging order."[3022] "Expulsion clauses can protect LLC from a member's bankruptcy."[3023] "This clause…severs the filing member from the contract and allows the remaining owners to regroup and continue the LLC without bankruptcy court interference."[3024] "The expulsion clause may further provide for a diminished payout (e.g., equal to book value, rather than fair market value) to an owner who is so expelled. The clause also can provide that the bankruptcy action amounts to a material breach of the agreement by the debtor/owner, entitling the LLC to recover damages from the owner. Further, the clause can provide that this diminished amount be reduced further

---

[3020] "Limited Liability Company 101." *Assetprotection.com*, assetprotection.com/limited-liability-company/limited-liability-company-101/.

[3021] A sample LLC operating agreement is included in the Appendix. Fishman, Stephen. "LC Asset Protection and Charging Orders: An Overview of State Laws." *Nolo*, www.nolo.com/legal-encyclopedia/llc-asset-protection-charging-orders.html.

[3022] *Id.*

[3023] "Note that this is the default rule under the Delaware LLC statute--one more reason to consider forming your LLC in Delaware." "Leveraging Limited Liability for Asset Protection." *Bizfilings.com*, www.bizfilings.com/toolkit/research-topics/running-your-business/asset-strategies/leveraging-limited-liability-for-asset-protection.

[3024] *Id.*

on account of the damages caused to the LLC by the breach. These provisions reduce any amount that would be paid into the debtor/ owner's bankruptcy estate and could persuade the trustee to abandon the executory contract."[3025]

"An LLC can have a buy-sell agreement as part of the operating agreement. This is a very powerful feature as it prohibits a creditor from gaining access even in the event of a charging order... The agreement can state that should any member get a charging order against them, then their interest will be held by the company for future distribution."[3026] Thus, the LLCs operating agreement can ensure that a creditor with a charging order gets nothing.

LLCs operating agreements can even be used for estate planning purposes. The operating agreement can provide that non-managing members become managers upon the incapacity or death of the parents.[3027] Thus, assets remain in the LLC when they are transferred, which virtually eliminates death taxes.[3028] "Moreover, you can establish limited liability company with perpetual duration. Therefore, it can provide security for generations to come."[3029]

In sum, "[t]he LLC offers asset protection benefits. Coupled with the tax benefits, these features makes it the preferred vehicle for real estate and stock market investments. This is because it combines liability protection with favorable sole proprietorship or partnership tax treatment."[3030] You worked hard to acquire your assets. Make sure to protect them.

[3025] *Id.*

[3026] "Limited Liability Company 101." *Assetprotection.com*, assetprotection.com/limited-liability-company/limited-liability-company-101/.

[3027] "Limited Liability Company (LLC) Asset Protection." *Asset Protection Planners*, www.assetprotectionplanners.com/services/llc/.

[3028] *Id.*

[3029] *Id.*

[3030] *Id.*

Conclusion

With the backdrop of a quickly deteriorating economy, this book has outlined defensive measures investors can take to protect themselves from financial ruin. As conditions worsen, people who are pre-positioned in anticipation of total systemic failure will be able to rest more easily than those who trusted central bankers to safeguard their wealth. When the dust settles, prudent investors who insured themselves against central bank policies will be the last men standing amongst the rubble of the former economy. Simply by acting upon some of the suggestions detailed in this book, anyone with any wealth to preserve can protect it. In the bigger picture, just keeping what wealth one has will put one in a much better position than will be the case for many poor souls, unfortunately.

It is with regret that this author reports on such a sorry state of affairs. However, an ounce of prevention is worth a pound of cure. In this case, being willing to take a hard look at the bleak economic future will put one in a position of strength. It is of no use to wear rose-colored glasses when surveying the economic landscape.

This book has attempted to lay bare the most probable outcome of central bank shenanigans. In addition, it has offered solutions that are most likely to succeed in preserving assets. While the suggestions are not meant to constitute financial or legal advice, they are measures that have worked in the past and that the author is personally taking. They have been offered to the reader for educational purposes only. Further research is recommended prior to embarking on any course of action, as well as consultation with a legal and/or financial expert.

Appendix

The following LLC Operating Agreement was drafted by Cynthia F. Hodges, JD, LLM, MA, licensed to practice law in Washington State. It is provided as an example only for how how to protect assets, incorporate estate planning, etc, into an operating agreement, and is geared toward Washington State law. Please consult with an attorney to draft an operating agreement that would suit your needs.

LLC OPERATING AGREEMENT OF
COMPANY NAME, LLC

Pursuant to RCW 25.15.018, this Operating Agreement is entered into by and between the following LLC members:
Name of Address, State, Zip; and
Name of Address, State, Zip (hereinafter known as "Members") on DATE.

WHEREAS the Member(s) desire to create a limited liability company ("LLC" or "Company") under the laws of the State of _____ and set forth the terms herein of the Company's operation and the relationship between Member(s).

NOW, THEREFORE, in consideration of the mutual covenants set forth herein and other valuable consideration, the receipt and sufficiency of which hereby are acknowledged, the Member(s) and the Company agree as follows:

ARTICLE I: DEFINITIONS

Definitions used in this Operating Agreement shall have the respective meanings set forth below unless otherwise provided.

1.1 "Assigning Member" means a Member who has assigned his or her Membership Interest.

1.2 "Capital Account" shall mean the Capital Contribution to the Company by a Member. It refers to the accounting of each member's contributed cash or property, i.e., the "running total" of the members' ownership and investment.

1.3 "Capital Contribution" shall mean any contribution to the capital of the Company in cash or property by a Member whenever made.

1.4 The term "capital transactions" shall mean any of the following: the sale of all or any part of the assets of the Company; the refinancing of mortgages or other liabilities of the Company; the receipt of insurance proceeds; and any other receipts or proceeds are attributable to capital.

1.5 The term "cash receipts" shall mean all cash receipts of the Company from whatever source derived, including without limitation, capital contributions made by the Member(s); the proceeds of any sale, exchange, condemnation or other disposition of all or any part of the assets of the Company; the proceeds of any loan to the Company; the proceeds of any mortgage or refinancing of any mortgage on all or any part of the assets of the Company; the proceeds of any insurance policy for fire or other casualty damage payable to the Company; and the proceeds from the liquidation of assets of the Company following termination.

1.6 "Company" means the *[Company Name]*, a Limited Liability Company created under the State of _____.

1.7 "Distributable Cash" shall mean all cash, revenues and funds received by the Company from Company operations, less the sum of the following to the extent paid or set aside by the Company: (i) all principal and interest payments on indebtedness of the Company and all other sums paid to lenders; (ii) all cash expenditures incurred in the normal operation of the Company's business; and (iii) such reserves as the Member - Managers deem reasonably necessary for the proper operation of the Company's business.

1.8 "Expenses" include counsel fees.

1.9 "Majority Interest" shall mean one or more interests of Members which in aggregate exceed fifty percent (50%) of all interests held in the Company.

1.10 "Manager" shall mean one or more Managers, elected by the Members. References to the Manager in the singular or as him, her, it, itself, or other like references shall also, where the context so requires, be deemed to include the plural or the masculine or feminine reference, as the case may be. References to the Manager in the plural shall, where the context so requires, be deemed to include the singular, or the masculine or feminine reference, as the case may be.

1.11 "Member" shall mean each of the parties who executes this Operating Agreement or its counterpart as a Member and each of the parties who may hereafter become Members. A Person is a Member immediately upon the purchase or other acquisition by such Person of an interest, such

Person shall have all the rights of a Member with respect to such purchased or otherwise acquired interest.

1.12 "Membership Interest" shall mean a Member's entire interest in the Company including such Member's economic, voting, and management interest.

1.13 "Net Income" means the net income of the Company computed in accordance with generally accepted accounting principles for federal income taxes under the Internal Revenue Code.

1.14 "Net Profits" and "Net Losses" shall mean the income, gain, loss, deductions and credits of the Company in the aggregate or separately stated, as appropriate, resulting from the conduct of the Company's business, after all expenses, including depreciation allowance, incurred in connection with the conduct of its business for which such expenses have been accounted. "Net Profits" and "Net Losses" shall be determined in accordance with generally accepted accounting principles employed under the cash method of accounting at the close of each fiscal year on the Company's tax return filed for federal income tax purposes.

1.15 "Net operating profit" for any accounting period shall mean the gross receipts of the Company for such period, less the sum of all cash expenses of operation of the Company, and such sums as may be necessary to establish a reserve for operating expenses.

1.16 "Notice" means a writing delivered a. by first class mail, addressed to the last address known to the sender, or b. to the recipient in person.

1.17 "Operating Agreement" means this Limited Liability Company Operating Agreement.

1.18 "Party" includes a person who was, is, or is threatened to be made a named defendant or respondent in a proceeding.

1.19 "Percentage Interest" shall mean the percentage of ownership interest in the Company for any Member of the Company as set forth in this Operating Agreement. It may be changed from time to time by the unanimous vote of the Members or pursuant to the terms hereof.

1.20 "Person" means any individual or entity (partnership, joint venture, association, corporation, limited liability company, unincorporated associations, trusts, estates and other types of entities) and the heirs, executors, administrators, legal representatives, successors, and assigns of such "Person" where the context so permits.

1.21 "Proceeding" means any threatened, pending, or completed action, suit, or proceeding, whether civil, criminal, administrative, or investigative and whether formal or informal.

1.22 "Profits," upon a dissolution event as determined in this Operating Agreement, are determined and allocated based on any reasonable estimate of profits from the date of the dissolution event to the projected termination of the Company, taking into account present and future allocations of profits under the Company agreement that is in effect as of the date of the dissolution event.

1.23 "Property" means anything of value.

1.24 "State" means the state in which the *Company Name* Limited Liability Company is formed (*State*), unless indicated otherwise.

1.25 "Substantial economic effect" shall be the same as the meaning of Section 704 of the Internal Revenue Code and Treas. Reg. Section 1.704-1 [IRC § 704(b)(2); Treas. Reg. § 1.704-1(b)(1)(I)]. Should the provisions of this Agreement be inconsistent with or in conflict with Section 704 of the Code or the Regulations thereunder, then Section 704 of the Code and the Regulations shall be deemed to override the contrary provisions thereof. If Section 704 or the Regulations at any time require that limited liability company operating agreements contain provisions which are not expressly set forth herein, such provisions shall be incorporated into this Agreement by reference and shall be deemed a part of this Agreement to the same extent as though they had been expressly set forth herein.

ARTICLE II: NAME, PLACE, PURPOSE, AND DURATION

2.1 Formation. The Company was formed when the Member(s) filed the Certificate of Formation with the office of the Secretary of State on [*Date*] pursuant to the statutes governing limited liability companies in the State of _____ (the "Statutes").

2.2 Name. The name of the Company shall be *Company Name*, LLC. However, this LLC may do business under a different name by complying with the state's fictitious or assumed business name statutes and procedures.

2.3 Purpose. The purpose of the Company is to engage in and conduct any and all lawful businesses, activities, or functions, and to carry on any other lawful activities in connection with or incidental to the foregoing, as the Member(s) in their discretion shall determine. This LLC has the same powers as an individual to do all things necessary or convenient to carry on its activities. (RCW 25.15.031 or other state law)

2.4 <u>Principal Place of Business.</u> The principal place of business of the Company shall be at <u>Address</u>, City of _____, County of _____, in the State of _____, or at such other place of business as the Member(s) shall determine.

2.5 <u>Registered Office and Agent.</u> The registered office of this LLC and the registered agent at this address are as follows:

Name
Physical Address
City, State, Zip

The registered office and registered agent may be changed by filing the address of the new registered office and/or the name of the new registered agent with the State. It shall not be necessary to amend this provision of the operating agreement if and when such a change is made.

2.6 <u>Term.</u> The term of the Company shall be perpetual, commencing on the filing of the Certificate of Formation of the Company, and continuing until terminated under the provisions set forth herein.

2.7 <u>Membership Voting.</u> Except as otherwise may be required by the Certificate of Formation, other provisions of this operating agreement, or under the laws of this state, each member shall vote on any matter submitted to the membership for approval in proportion to the member's percentage interest in this LLC. Further, unless defined otherwise for a particular provision of this operating agreement, the phrase "majority of members" means the vote of members whose combined votes equal more than 50% of the votes of all members in this LLC. In this agreement, the default voting standard is by percentage interest in this LLC.

This LLC does not recognize creditors as having voting rights.

In accordance with RCW 25.15.121(4), the following members may vote on a per capita basis:
Name 1 and *Name 2*. This voting procedure does not extend to transferees, unless all of the members agree to grant a member this voting status.

2.8 <u>Admission of New Members (RCW 25.15.116).</u> The Company may admit new Members (or transferees of any interests of existing Members) into the Company by the unanimous vote or consent of the Members.

(RCW 25.15.121(2)). Nothing in this agreement prohibits a previous member of the LLC from being re-admitted as a new member.

As a condition to the admission of a new Member, such Member shall execute and acknowledge such instruments, in form and substance satisfactory to the Company, as the Company may deem necessary or desirable to effectuate such admission and to confirm the agreement of such Member to be bound by all of the terms, covenants and conditions of this Agreement, as the same may have been amended. Such new Member shall pay all reasonable expenses in connection with such admission, including without limitation, reasonable attorneys' fees and the cost of the preparation, filing or publication of any amendment to this Agreement or the Certificate of Formation, which the Company may deem necessary or desirable in connection with such admission.

No new Member shall be entitled to any retroactive allocation of income, losses, or expense deductions of the Company. The Company may make pro rata allocations of income, losses or expense deductions to a new Member for that portion of the tax year in which the Member was admitted in accordance with Section 706(d) of the Internal Revenue Code and regulations thereunder.

In no event shall a new Member be admitted to the Company if such admission would be in violation of applicable Federal or State securities laws, or would adversely affect the treatment of the Company as an S Corporation for income tax purposes.

2.9 Mandatory capital contribution: A prospective new member must contribute $100,000 to the LLC in order to become a member, unless the existing members unanimously agree to waive this provision.

2.10 Residency Requirement. There is no residency requirement for members or managers. (RCW 25.15.054)

2.11 Representations of Members. Each of the Members represents, warrants and agrees that the Member is acquiring the interest in the Company for the Member's own account for investment purposes only and not with a view to the sale or distribution thereof; the Member, if an individual, is over the age of 21; if the Member is an organization, such organization is duly organized, validly existing and in good standing under the laws of its State of organization and that it has full power and authority to execute this Agreement and perform its obligations hereunder; the execution and performance of this Agreement by the Member does not conflict with, and will not result in any breach of, any law or any order, writ, injunction or decree of any court or governmental authority against or which binds the Member, or of any agreement or instrument to which the Member is a party; and the Member shall not dispose of such interest or any part thereof in any manner which would constitute a violation of the Securities Act of 1933, the Rules and Regulations of the Securities and Exchange Commission, or any applicable laws, rules or regulations of any State or other governmental authorities, as the same may be amended.

2.12 <u>Certificates Evidencing Membership</u>. This LLC may obtain and issue certificates representing or certifying membership interests in this LLC. Each certificate shall show the name of the LLC, the name of the member, and state that the person named is a member of the LLC and is entitled to all the rights granted members of the LLC under the Certificate of Formation or a similar organizational document, this operating agreement and provisions of law. Each membership certificate shall be consecutively numbered and signed by one or more managers of this LLC. The certificates may include any additional information considered appropriate for inclusion by the members on membership certificates. In addition to the above information, all membership certificates may bear a prominent legend on their face or reverse side stating, summarizing or referring to any transfer restrictions that apply to memberships in this LLC under Certificate of Formation or a similar organizational document and/or this operating agreement, and the address where a member may obtain a copy of these restrictions upon request from this LLC. The records book of this LLC shall contain a list of the names and addresses of all persons to whom certificates have been issued, show the date of issuance of each certificate, and record the date of all cancellations or transfers of membership certificates.

Should the LLC members vote to issue certificates of limited liability company interest under RCW 25.15.246(2), then every membership interest in the Company shall be evidenced by a Certificate of Membership issued by the Company. Each Certificate of Membership shall set forth the name of the Member holding the membership interest and the Member's Percentage Interest held by the Member, and shall bear the following legend:

"The membership interest represented by this certificate is subject to, and may not be transferred except in accordance with, the provisions of the Operating Agreement of *Company Name*, LLC, dated effective as of _____, 20___, as the same from time to time may be amended, a copy of which is on file at the principal office of the Company."

2.13 <u>Certificates in the Trust Name</u>. Should a qualified trust be formed for the benefit of Members' beneficiaries, then the Certificates of Membership may be issued in the name of the trust. In this event, the Certificates of Membership shall include: (1) the name of the trust, (2) Date of the trust – Under Agreement _____ (date), (3) *Name of Member* Trustee or TTEE. A Subchapter S qualified trust shall be the only type of trust to hold the LLC as long as it is taxed as an S Corp.

2.14 All Necessary Acts. The members, managers, and officers of this LLC are authorized to perform all acts necessary to perfect the organization of this LLC and to carry out its business operations expeditiously and efficiently. The Secretary of the LLC, or other officers, or all members of the LLC, may certify to other businesses, financial institutions and individuals as to the authority of one or more members or officers of this LLC to transact specific items of business on behalf of the LLC.

ARTICLE III: RIGHTS AND DUTIES OF MANAGERS

3.1 Management. The Company shall be managed by the Managers, who shall be elected, designated, or appointed to direct, manage, and control the business of the Company. (RCW 25.15.154) Manager(s) need not be a member of the LLC. The "manager" may consist of a board of directors, if the members unanimously consent or agree.

Manager(s) may be removed or replaced by a vote, approval, or consent of a majority of the members. Manager(s) holds office until a successor has been elected. This LLC does not recognize the authority of a creditor to remove a manager.

A majority of members may agree to change this LLC to member-managed (RCW 25.15.151).

3.2 Personal Bankruptcy. A member may file for personal bankruptcy and not be removed as a manager.

3.3 Number, Tenure and Qualifications. The Company shall initially have three (3) Managers (hereinafter referred to as Managers) elected by the Members. A Manager's right to act as a Manager shall terminate upon the earlier of the Manager's resignation or termination by unanimous vote of the Members. Upon the resignation or termination of a Manager's right to act as a Manager, Members shall have the right to appoint a new Manager. The Managers and their addresses are as follows:
Name of Address, and
Name of Address.

3.4 <u>Duties and Authority of Managers</u>. Except for situations in which the approval of the Members is expressly required by this Operating Agreement or by statute, the Managers shall have full and complete authority, power, and discretion to manage and control the business, affairs, properties, and investments of the Company, to make all decisions regarding those matters, and to perform any and all other acts or activities customary or incident to the management of the Company's business. Such activities include, without limitation, those referenced below:

a. To obtain, sell, convey, mortgage, encumber, lease, exchange, pledge, partition, plat, subdivide, improve, repair, surrender, abandon or otherwise deal with or dispose of any and all real property of whatsoever character and wheresoever situated at such time or times and in such manner and upon such terms as the Managers deem expedient and proper. To give options therefore, to execute deeds, transfers, leases, pledges, mortgages, and other instruments of any kind. Any leases and contracts may extend beyond the term of the Company.

b. To acquire any personal property for the use of the Company.

c. To purchase, invest in, or otherwise acquire, and to retain, any and all stocks, bonds, notes, or other securities, or any variety of real or personal property, including stocks or interests in investment trusts and common trust funds operated and managed by a corporate trustee.

d. To sell, transfer, assign, convey, lease, exchange, or otherwise dispose of any or all of the assets of the Company upon such terms and conditions as the Members deem advisable, including a deferred payment sale or an exchange for other assets of any kind.

e. To place record title to, or the right to use, Company assets in the name of a Manager or the name of the nominee for any purpose convenient or beneficial to the Company.

f. To open and to close checking accounts, savings accounts, and safety deposit boxes in banks or similar financial institutions, with or without indication of any fiduciary capacity. To deposit cash in and withdraw cash from such accounts and boxes, with or without any indication of any fiduciary capacity. To hold such accounts and securities in bearer form, or in the name of a Manager or in the name of a nominee, with or without indication of any fiduciary capacity.

g. To borrow money upon terms acceptable to the Managers from any person or entity, to pledge or mortgage any property as security therefore and to renew any indebtedness incurred by the Managers.

h. To employ brokers, consultants, attorneys, accountants, architects, engineers, property managers, leasing agents and other agents, persons or entities deemed appropriate to the conduct of the Company business, including, without limitation, any persons or entities related to a Manager or in which a Manager has an interest.

i. To adjust, arbitrate, compromise, sue, defend, settle, abandon, or otherwise deal with any and all claims in favor of or against the Company.

j. To acquire and enter into any contract of insurance which the Managers deem necessary and proper for the protection of the Company, for the conservation of its assets, or for any purpose convenient or beneficial to the Company.

k. To execute and deliver on behalf of the Company such documents or instruments as the Managers deem appropriate in the conduct of the Company business. No person, firm or corporation dealing with the Company shall be required to inquire into the authority of the Managers to take any action or make any decisions.

l. To make employment contracts, to pay pensions and to establish pension and other incentive plans of any or all of its employees, including Health Reimbursement Agreements (HRAs), and profit-sharing plans.

m. To establish, invest and maintain reserves for the benefit of the Company in such amounts as the Managers, in their sole discretion, shall determine, and to expend such reserves in such amounts and for such purposes as the Managers shall determine.

n. Managers shall prepare all Federal, State and local income tax and information returns for the Company, and shall cause such tax and information returns to be timely filed.

o. Managers shall establish and maintain all accounting, bookkeeping, cash management and financial systems and records relating to the Company's transactions and other matters in accordance with generally accepted accounting principles, standards and procedures. Managers shall prepare and furnish to the Members not later than fifteen (15) days after the close of each monthly accounting period monthly financial reports and statements which shall include an income statement for the month, a statement of cash flows for the month and a balance sheet dated as of the end of the month, and such other reports related to the Company as reasonably requested by a majority interest of the Members. Managers shall prepare and file, on the Company's behalf, all periodic reports and tax returns in respect of income of the Company attributable to the Members of the Company.

p. Each Manager may authorize any persons to act for him by proxy on all matters in which Manager is entitled to participate. Every proxy must be signed by the Manager or his attorney-in-fact. No proxy shall be valid after the expiration of eleven (11) months from the date thereof unless otherwise provided in the proxy. Every proxy shall be revocable at the pleasure of such Manager executing it. A Manager may change its representative and appoint a successor representative at any time by giving written Notice of such change to the other Managers.

q. The LLC manager shall deliver to the secretary of state for filing the initial and annual reports in accordance with RCW **23.95.255**.

r. Managers may supervise the establishment and maintenance of all other records relative to the operation of the Company and cause to be provided to the Members such reports or summaries, including any internal audit reports prepared by Managers, with respect to such records, as Members with a Majority Interest may from time to time reasonably request.

3.5 Standard of Care. Each Manager shall perform its duties as a Manager in good faith, in a manner it reasonably believes to be in the best interests of the Company, and with such care as an ordinarily prudent person in a like position would use under similar circumstances.

3.6 Managers Have No Exclusive Duty to Company. No Manager shall be required to manage the Company as its sole and exclusive function, and each Manager may have other business interests and engage in activities in addition to those relating to the Company. Neither the Company nor any Member shall have any right, by virtue of this Operating Agreement, to share or participate in such other investments or activities of any Managers, or to the income or proceeds derived therefrom.

3.7 Indemnity of the Managers, Employees and Other Agents. The Company shall, to the maximum extent permitted, indemnify and make advances for expenses to each Manager, its employees, and other agents.

3.8 Resignation. Any Manager may resign at any time by giving written Notice to the Members of the Company. The resignation of any Manager shall take effect upon receipt of Notice thereof or at such later date specified in such Notice. Unless otherwise specified therein, the acceptance of such resignation shall not be necessary to make it effective. The resignation of a Manager who is also a Member shall not affect the Manager's rights as a Member, and shall not constitute a withdrawal of a Member.

3.9 Vacancies. Any vacancy occurring for any reason in the position of Managers of the Company may be filled by the unanimous affirmative vote of Members holding an Interest. An increase in the number of Managers shall be permitted upon a unanimous affirmative vote of Members holding an Interest. Any Manager's position to be filled by reason of an increase in the number of Managers shall be filled by election at a meeting of Members called for that purpose or by the Members' unanimous written consent. A Manager elected to fill a vacancy shall be elected for the unexpired term of his predecessor in office and shall hold office until the expiration of such term and until his successor shall be elected and qualified or until his earlier death, resignation, or removal. A Manager chosen to fill a position resulting from an increase in the number of Managers shall hold office until his successor shall be elected and qualified, or until his earlier death, resignation or removal.

3.10 Annual Report. Managers may cause an annual report to be made available to the Members no later than ninety (90) days after the close of the fiscal year or the calendar year adopted by the Company. This annual report shall be made available at least 15 days before the annual meeting of Members to be held during the next fiscal year and in the manner specified in this Operating Agreement for giving Notice to the Members of the Company. The annual report may contain a balance sheet as of the end of the fiscal year and an income statement and statement of changes in financial position for the fiscal year, accompanied by any report of independent accounts or, if there is no such report, the certificate of a Manager that the statements were prepared without audit from the books and records of Company. Nothing herein shall be interpreted as prohibiting the Managers from issuing other reports to the Members.

3.11 Manager Liability. No Manager shall be liable to the Company or to any Member for any loss or damage sustained by the Company or any Member, unless the loss or damage shall have been the result of fraud, deceit, gross negligence, willful misconduct, or a wrongful taking by the Manager.

3.12 Officers. The LLC may designate one or more officers, such as a President, Vice President, Secretary and Treasurer. Persons who fill these positions need not be members of the LLC. Such positions may be compensated or non-compensated according to the nature and extent of the services rendered for the LLC as a part of the duties of each office. Any officer may be reimbursed by the LLC for out-of-pocket expenses paid by the officer in carrying out the duties of his or her office. Initial officers are as follows:

Name - President   Name - Vice President
Name - Treasurer   Name - Secretary

ARTICLE IV: RIGHTS AND OBLIGATIONS OF MEMBERS

4.1 Names and Addresses. The names and addresses of the original Members are set forth in this Operating Agreement. Upon the written request of any Member, the Managers shall provide a list showing the names, addresses, and percentage interests of all Members.

4.2 Non-liability of Members (RCW 25.15.126). This agreement incorporates by reference the limitations of liability as specified in RCW 25.15.038. The debts, obligations, and liabilities of this LLC, whether arising in contract, tort or otherwise, are solely the debts, obligations, and liabilities of this LLC; and no member or manager is obligated personally for any such debt, obligation, or liability of the LLC solely by reason of being or acting as a member or manager respectively of the limited liability company. No member or manager agrees to be obligated personally for any of the debts, obligations, and liabilities of the LLC.

4.3 <u>Liability of a Member to the Company</u>. A Member who receives a distribution or the return in whole or in part of its contribution is liable to the Company only to the extent provided by applicable law.

4.4 <u>Liability for improper distributions.</u> This LLC expressly relieves *Name 1* and *Name 2* of the authority and responsibility to consent to distributions. (RCW 25.15.236)

4.5 <u>Other Business by Members.</u> Each member shall agree not to own an interest in, manage or work for another business, enterprise or endeavor, if such ownership or activities would compete with this LLC's business goals, mission, profitability or productivity, or would diminish or impair the member's ability to provide maximum effort and performance in managing the business of this LLC.

4.6 <u>Deficit Balance</u>. No Member shall have any liability to restore all or any portion of a deficit balance in such Member's Capital Account.

4.7 <u>Company Books</u>. Each Member shall have the right upon a reasonable written request, at a time during ordinary business hours, as reasonably determined by the Managers, to inspect and/or copy (at the requesting Member's expense) the accounts, books, and other relevant Company documents. The Member shall maintain all such copied material as confidential.

4.8 <u>Priority and Return of Capital</u>. Except as may otherwise be provided herein, no Member shall have priority over any other Member, either as to the return of Capital Contributions or as to Net Profits, Net Losses or distributions, or allocations of the income, gains, losses, deductions, credits, or other items of the LLC. This section shall not apply to loans which a Member has made to the Company.

4.9 <u>Withdrawal and Reduction of Members' Contributions to Capital</u>. No Member shall be entitled to withdraw or borrow any amount from his Capital Account without the consent of a majority of the Managers.

4.10 <u>Member Sale, Assignment, or Exchange</u>. A Member or a Member's legal representative has the power to sell, assign, or exchange such

Member's Membership Interest only with the unanimous approval of the other Members.

4.11 Member Withdrawal. In order to withdraw from this LLC, a member must give written notice to all other members at least 20 days before the date the withdrawal is to be effective. However, no Member may voluntarily withdraw from the Company without a majority vote or consent of the Members.

4.12 Member Loan. Any Member may loan money to the Company. Such a loan to the Company shall be at a reasonable rate of interest. Except as provided by law, the lending Member has the same rights and risks as any person making a loan to the Company who is not a Member.

4.13 Reimbursement for Organizational Costs. Members shall be reimbursed by the LLC for organizational expenses paid by the members. The LLC shall be authorized to deduct organizational expenses and start-up expenditures ratably over a period of time as permitted by the Internal Revenue Code and as may be advised by the LLC's tax advisor.

4.14 Single Member LLC. Nothing in this Operating Agreement precludes this LLC from operating as a single member LLC in the future.

4.15 Active vs. passive members. The following members shall be considered active members who may receive early distributions of profits as a salary, if the majority of members agree:

Name 1's duties include, but are not limited to, research and advice on investments, assistance on tax preparation and book-keeping.

Name 2's duties include, but are not limited to, research on investments.

Name 3's duties include, but are not limited to, research and advice on investments, executing trades, maintenance of bank and brokerage accounts, distributions, book-keeping, tax preparation, legal advice and services, and partaking in continuing education in law and investing.

A majority of members may agree to change members' classification.

4.16 Compensation. Members may be paid for performing duties and services associated with management of the LLC, as well as for any services rendered for the LLC, whether as officers, employees, independent contractors, or otherwise.

The members shall receive such sums for compensation as Members of the Company as may be determined from time to time by the affirmative vote or consent of Members holding a majority of the Members' Percentage Interests.

ARTICLE V: MEETINGS OF MEMBERS

5.1 <u>Meetings (RCW 25.15.121(5))</u>. Member and/or manager meetings are not required for this LLC. (RCW 25.15.061). Unless otherwise provided by law, any action required to be taken at a meeting of the Members, or any other action that may be taken at a meeting of the Members, may be taken without a meeting. The Members may by resolution prescribe the time and place for the holding of regular meetings and may provide that the adoption of such resolution shall constitute notice of such regular meetings.

However, any member may call a meeting by communicating his or her wish to schedule a meeting to all other members. Such notification may be in person or in writing, or by telephone, email, facsimile machine, or other form of electronic communication reasonably expected to be received by a member, stating the place, day and hour of the meeting and, in the case of a special meeting, the purpose for which the meeting is called, Such notice shall be delivered not less than three days before the date of the meeting to each Member of record entitled to vote at such meeting. The other members shall then agree, either personally, in writing, or by telephone, email, facsimile machine or other form of electronic communication to the member calling the meeting, to meet at a mutually acceptable time and place. Notice of the business to be transacted at the meeting need not be given to members by the member calling the meeting, and any business may be discussed and conducted at the meeting. When all the Members of the Company are present at any meeting, agree in writing to the holding of the meeting without them, or if those not present sign a written waiver of notice of such meeting, or subsequently ratify all the proceedings thereof, the transactions of such meeting shall be valid as if a meeting had been formally called and notice had been given.

Members of the Company may participate in any meeting of the Members by means of conference telephone or similar communication if all persons participating in such meeting can hear one another for the entire discussion of the matters to be vote upon. Participation in a meeting pursuant to this paragraph shall constitute presence in person at such meeting.

If all members cannot attend a meeting and do not agree to the meeting being held without them or ratify the proceedings, the meeting shall be postponed to a date and time when all members can attend. If a meeting is postponed, and the postponed meeting cannot be held either because all members do not attend the postponed meeting or the non-attending members have not signed a written consent to allow the postponed meeting to be held without them, a second postponed meeting may be held at a date and time announced at the first postponed meeting. The date and time of the second postponed meeting shall also be communicated to any members not attending the first postponed meeting. The second postponed meeting may be held without the attendance of all members as long as a majority of the percentage interests of the membership of this LLC is in attendance at the second postponed meeting. Written notice of the decisions or approvals made at this second postponed meeting shall be mailed or delivered to each non-attending member within 3 days after the holding of the second postponed meeting. Written minutes of the discussions and proposals presented at a members' meeting, and the votes taken and matters approved at such meeting, shall be taken by one of the members or a person designated at the meeting. A copy of the minutes of the meeting shall be placed in the LLC's records book after the meeting.

A Member of the Company who is present at a meeting of the Members at which action on any matter is taken shall be presumed to have assented to the action taken, unless the dissent of such Member shall be entered in the minutes of the meeting or unless such Member shall file a written dissent to such action with the person acting as the secretary of the meeting before the meeting's adjournment. Such right to dissent shall not apply to a Member who voted in favor of such action.

5.2 Special Meetings. Special meetings of the Members, for any purpose or purposes, may be called by any Member (or such other number of Members as the Members from time to time may specify). Such requests shall be Noticed as required herein and shall state the purpose of the proposed meeting.

5.3 Place of Meetings. If a meeting is called, the place of meeting shall automatically be the principal place of business of the Company, unless the Manager and Members unanimously designate and give Notice to all Members and Managers of another place, either within or outside the state which is designated as the principal place of business for the Company. Members of the Company may participate in any meeting of the Members by means of conference telephone or similar communication if all persons participating in such meeting can hear one another for the entire discussion of the matters to be vote upon. Participation in a meeting pursuant to this paragraph shall constitute presence in person at such meeting.

5.4 Notice of Meetings. Oral or written Notice stating the place, day, and hour of the meeting and the purpose or purposes for which the meeting is called shall be delivered not less than three nor more than thirty days before the date of the meeting, either personally or by telephone, mail, email, or fax, by or at the direction of the Managers or Member or Members calling the meeting, to each Member entitled to vote at such meeting. If mailed, such Notice shall be deemed to be delivered five (5) calendar days after being deposited in the United States mail, addressed to the Member at its address as it appears on the books of the Company, with postage thereon prepaid.

5.5 <u>Meeting of All Members</u>. If all of the Members shall meet at any time or place, and consent to the holding of a meeting at such time and place, such meeting shall be valid without call or Notice, and at such meeting lawful action may be taken.

5.6 <u>Record Date</u>. For the purpose of determining Members entitled to Notice, or to vote at any meeting, or Members entitled to receive payment of any distribution, or in order to make a determination of Members for any other purpose, the date on which Notice of the meeting is mailed or the date on which the resolution is declared, shall be the record date for such determination of Members. When a determination of Members entitled to vote at any meeting of Members has been made as provided herein, such determination shall apply to any adjournment thereof.

5.7 <u>Quorum</u>. At any meeting of the Members, the presence of Members holding a majority of the Members' Percentage Interests, as determined from the books of the Company, represented in person or by proxy, shall constitute a quorum for the conduct of the general business of the Company.

However, if any particular action by the Company shall require the vote or consent of some other number or percentage of Members pursuant to this Agreement, a quorum for the purpose of taking such action shall require such other number or percentage of Members.

If a quorum is not present, the meeting may be adjourned from time to time without further notice, and if a quorum is present at the adjourned meeting any business may be transacted which might have been transacted at the meeting as originally notified. The Members present at a duly organized meeting may continue to transact business until adjournment, notwithstanding the withdrawal of enough Members to leave less a quorum.

5.8 <u>Manner of Acting</u>. If a quorum is present, the unanimous affirmative vote of Members holding an Interest shall be considered the act of the Members, unless the vote of a lesser proportion or number is otherwise required by the Act or by this Operating Agreement. Unless otherwise expressly provided herein or required under applicable law, only Members may vote or give consent upon any matter and their vote or consent, as the case may be, shall be counted in the determination of whether the matter was approved by the Members.

5.9 <u>Proxies</u>. At any or all meetings, any Member may be represented in person or by proxy or proxies executed in writing by the Member or by a duly authorized attorney-in-fact. Such proxy shall be filed with the Managers of the Company before or at the time of the meeting. No proxy shall be valid after eleven (11) months from the date of its execution, unless otherwise provided in the proxy.

5.10 <u>Waiver of Notice</u>. When any Notice is required to be given to any Member, a waiver thereof in writing signed by the person entitled to such Notice, whether before, at, or after the time stated therein, shall be equivalent to the giving of such Notice.

ARTICLE VI: CAPITAL CONTRIBUTIONS

6.1 <u>Member Capital Contributions</u>. Each Member has contributed the following capital amounts to the Company as set forth below. This amount forms the basis for his ownership interest. Members are not obligated to make any additional capital contributions, but may choose to do so. In that case, members may choose to re-allocate % interest by a majority vote.

Member	Contribution	% Interest
Name 1	$ Amount	___%
Name 2	Services (RCW 25.15.191)	___%

6.2 <u>Allocation of Profit and Losses</u>. All profits and losses of the Company and each item of income, gain, loss, deduction or credit entering into the computation thereof shall be allocated among and borne by the Members based on the Manager's discretion taking into consideration the Member's Percentage Interest as shown on the table in 6.1.

6.3 <u>Additional Capital Contributions</u>. From time to time a Member may be required to make additional Capital Contributions as shall be determined reasonably necessary to meet the expenses and obligations of the Company. Except as provided below, such additional Capital Contributions shall not affect the Members' relative Percentage Interest. In the event that any Member fails to make its required Capital Contributions and thereby defaults, then the non-defaulting Members, on a pro rata basis, shall have the right, exercisable in their sole discretion, to make the Capital Contribution that the defaulting Member failed to make. In such event, the relative Percentage Interest of the Members shall be adjusted such that each contributing, non- defaulting Member's Percentage Interest shall be increased, in respect to each defaulting Member's Percentage Interest.

6.4 Failure to Make Contributions. If a member fails to make a required capital contribution within the time agreed for a member's contribution, the remaining members may, by unanimous vote, agree to reschedule the time for payment of the capital contribution by the late-paying member, setting any additional repayment terms, such as a late payment penalty, rate of interest to be applied to the unpaid balance, or other monetary amount to be paid by the delinquent member, as the remaining members decide. Alternatively, the remaining members may, by unanimous vote, agree to cancel the membership of the delinquent member, provided any prior partial payments of capital made by the delinquent member are refunded promptly by the LLC to the member after the decision is made to terminate the membership of the delinquent member.

6.5 Return of Capital Contributions. Each Member irrevocably waives any statutory, equitable or other rights he or she may have to withdraw or demand the return of his or her Capital Contribution except as provided herein.

6.6 Consent to Capital Contribution Withdrawals and Distributions. Members may withdraw or reduce their contributions to the capital of the Company if a majority of members agree, or if the Company has been terminated.

6.7 No Interest on Capital Contributions. No interest shall be paid on funds or property contributed as capital to this LLC, or on funds reflected in the capital accounts of the members.

6.8 Distribution of Profits. During each fiscal year, the net profits and net losses of the Company (other than from capital transactions), and each item of income, gain, loss, deduction, or credit entering into the computation thereof, may be credited or charged, as the case may be, to the capital accounts of each Member in proportion to the Members' Percentage Interests.

Distributions to the Members of net operating profits of the Company may be made annually or monthly, except that earnings may be retained by the Company and transferred to Company capital for the reasonable needs of the Company as determined in the sole discretion of the Managers.

The net profits of the Company from capital transactions may be allocated in the following order of priority: (a) to offset any negative balance in the capital accounts of the Members in proportion to the amounts of the negative balance in their respective capital accounts, until all negative balances in the capital accounts have been eliminated; then (b) to the Members in proportion to the Members' Percentage Interests.

The net losses of the Company from capital transactions may be allocated in the following order of priority: (a) to the extent that the balance in the capital accounts of any Members are in excess of their original contributions, to such Members in proportion to the excess balances until all such excess balances have been reduced to zero; then (b) to the Members in proportion to the Members' Percentage Interests.

The cash receipts of the Company may be applied in the following order of priority: (a) to the payment of interest or amortization on any mortgages on the assets of the Company, amounts due on debts and liabilities of the Company other than those due to any Member, costs of the construction of the improvements to the assets of the Company and operating expenses of the Company; (b) to the payment of interest and establishment of cash reserves determined by the Members to be necessary or appropriate, including without limitation, reserves for the operation of the Company's business, construction, repairs, replacements, taxes and contingencies; and (d) to the repayment of any loans made to the Company by any Member. Thereafter, the cash receipts of the Company shall be distributed among the Members as provided.

Distributions are not mandatory, and nothing in this agreement should be interpreted as requiring mandatory distributions.

6.9 Allocation and Distribution of Cash to Members. Cash from LLC business operations, as well as cash from a sale or other disposition of LLC capital assets, may be distributed from time to time to members as may be decided by all of the members.

6.10 Allocation of Non-Cash Distributions. If proceeds consist of property other than cash, the managers shall decide the value of the property and allocate such value among the members as may be decided by all of the members. If such noncash proceeds are later reduced to cash, such cash may be distributed among the members as otherwise provided in this agreement.

6.11 Non-Pro Rata Distributions. Except as otherwise required by law, distributions of profits of the Company may be allocated among the Members in equal portions or other agreed upon amount may be distributed on a monthly basis (RCW 25.15.206). A majority of members may agree to make distributions according to ownership interest, or to suspend, or halt distributions to one or more members altogether. Non-pro rata distributions are allowed.

The manager may withhold distributions to a member charged with a charging order or whose interest has been foreclosed upon while making non-pro rata distributions to the other members.

Managers have the fiduciary duties enumerated in RCW 25.15.038, unless limited by this operating agreement. The manager has a fiduciary duty to not make a distributions in violation of the LLC agreement.

6.12 Distribution to Record Holder of Interest. The Company shall be entitled to treat the record holder of the interest of a Member as the absolute owner thereof, and shall incur no liability by reason of distributions made in good faith to such record holder, unless and until there has been delivered to the Company the assignment or other instrument of transfer and such other evidence as may be reasonably required by the Company to establish to the satisfaction of the Company that an interest has been assigned or transferred in accordance with this Agreement.

6.13 Federal Income Tax Elections. The Company shall be treated as an S-Corporation for federal income tax purposes. A majority of members may agree to change the tax treatment of this LLC by signing, or authorizing the signature of, IRS Form 8832, Entity Classification Election, and filing it with the IRS and, if applicable, the state tax department within the prescribed time limits.

All elections required or permitted to be made by the Company under the Internal Revenue Code, and the designation of a tax matters partner pursuant to Section 6231(a)(7) of the Internal Revenue Code for all purposes permitted or required by the Code, shall be made by the Company by the affirmative vote or consent of Members holding a majority of the Members' Percentage Interests.

6.14 Federal Income Tax Deductions. The Company shall elect to treat as an expense, for federal tax purposes, all amounts incurred for taxes, interest, and other fees, charges and expenses to the extent that such expenditures are permitted or required to be currently deductible expenses in accordance with applicable laws and regulations. The Members agree that no election shall be made under Section 761 of the Internal Revenue Code of 1954, as amended, to exclude the Company from application of any provisions of Subchapter K, Chapter 1, thereof.

6.15 <u>Annual Income Tax Returns and Reports</u>. The Company shall furnish each Member, within 75 days after the end of each fiscal year, an annual report of the Company including a balance sheet, a profit and loss statement a capital account statement; and the amount of such Member's share of the Company's income, gain, losses, deductions and other relevant items for federal income tax purposes.

Within 75 days after the end of each fiscal year, the Company shall forward to each person who was a Member during the preceding fiscal year a true copy of the Company's information return filed with the Internal Revenue Service for the preceding fiscal year.

6.16 <u>Tax Matters Partner</u>. If this LLC is required under Internal Revenue Code provisions or regulations, it shall designate from among its members a "tax matters partner" in accordance with Internal Revenue Code Section 6231 (a) (7) and corresponding regulations, who will fulfill this role by being the spokesperson for the LLC in dealings with the IRS as required under the Internal Revenue Code and Regulations, and who will report to the members on the progress and outcome of these dealings.

6.17 <u>Nature of Interests</u>. All property owned by the Company, whether real or personal, tangible or intangible, shall be deemed to be owned by the Company as an entity. No Member shall have any direct ownership of any Company property. Because no member has an interest in specific limited liability company property, such property may not be transferred. (RCW 25.15.246(1))

ARTICLE VII: CAPITAL ACCOUNTS

7.1 <u>Capital Account</u>. Each contribution to the capital account shall be itemized in terms of a dollar amount, reflecting the amount of cash or the fair market value of real property contributed. Capital accounts may be adjusted up or down to reflect profit, loss, contributions to, or withdrawals from the LLC.

7.2 <u>Separate Capital Accounts</u>. A separate Capital Account shall be maintained for each Member. The initial balance of the Capital Account of each Member shall be that Member's proportionate share of the total Capital Contributions.

The Capital Account of each Member: a. Shall be increased at the end of each taxable year by the amount of the Company's income and gain allocated to the Member for the taxable year, b. Shall be decreased at the end of each taxable year by the amount of the Company's deductions and losses allocated to the Member for that taxable year, and c. Shall be decreased at the time of any distributions by the amount of that distribution.

7.3 Determination of Profits and Losses. The profits and losses of the Company shall be the Net Profits or Net Losses of the Company for federal income tax purposes as determined by the Company's accountant in accordance with the accounting principles employed by the Company for federal tax purposes.

ARTICLE VIII: BOOKS, RECORDS AND ACCOUNTING

8.1 Accounting/Tax Year. The Company's fiscal year shall commence on January 1st of each year and shall end on December 31st of each year. Both the tax year and the accounting period of the LLC may be changed with the consent of a majority of the members if the LLC qualifies for such change, and may be effected by the filing of appropriate forms with the IRS and state tax authorities.

8.2 Method of Accounting. The Company may use a cash basis method of accounting and shall maintain its accounting records in accordance with generally accepted accounting principles employed for federal income tax purposes.

8.3 Books and Records. The Managers shall maintain the books and records of the Company at the principal place of business. Each Member shall have access to such books and records and shall be entitled to examine them at any time during the Company's ordinary business hours, provided that member give 3 days notice. Such records shall include:
a. A current list in alphabetical order of the full name and last known business street address of each Member;
b. A copy of the Certificate of Formation and all Certificates of Amendment to them;
c. A copy of the Company's federal, state, and local income tax returns and reports, for the three most recent years; and
d. A copy of the Company's Operating Agreement.

If one or more of the above items is included or listed in this operating agreement, it will be sufficient to keep a copy of this agreement at the principal business address of the LLC without having to prepare and keep a separate record of such item or items at this address.

8.4 Annual Statements. At the end of the year, the Managers may cause the Company's accountant to prepare a balance sheet setting forth the financial position of the Company and a statement of operations (income and expenses) for that year. The Managers may make available to each

Member a report of the financial position and operations of the Company no later than ninety (90) days from the end of the fiscal year. The report may contain a financial report showing the Company's profit or loss for the year and the allocation thereof among the Members, together with the applicable tax information of the Company. Copies of all income tax returns filed by the Company shall also be furnished to all Members upon request.

8.5 Member Objections. Each Member shall be deemed to have waived all objections to any transaction or other facts about the operation of the Company disclosed in the balance sheet, statement of operations, and income tax returns unless he or she notified the Managers in writing of his or her objections within sixty (30) days of the date on which each such document was mailed.

ARTICLE IX: DISSOLUTION OR TERMINATION OF THE COMPANY

9.1 Liquidation. The Company shall terminate upon the occurrence of any of the following : (i) the election by the Members to dissolve the Company made by the unanimous vote or consent of the Members, (ii) the occurrence of a Withdrawal Event with respect to a Member and the failure of the remaining Members to elect to continue the business of the Company within 90 days, (iii) entry of a decree of dissolution of the LLC under state law, or (iv) any other event which pursuant to this Agreement, as the same may hereafter be amended, shall cause a termination of the Company.

Notwithstanding a Withdrawal Event with respect to a Member, the Company shall not terminate, irrespective of applicable law, if within aforesaid 90 day period the remaining Members, by the unanimous vote or consent of the Members (other than the Member who caused the Withdrawal Event), shall elect to continue the business of the Company.

The company or any of its members may purchase the withdrawing Member's interest under 10.9 of this Agreement.

Dissolution and/or bankruptcy must be made by a unanimous vote of all Managers. No member who has a charging order can force the dissolution of the LLC.

In the event that all of the the Managers vote to dissolve the Company, then they shall immediately begin to wind up the affairs of the Company, complying with all requirements of applicable law pertaining to the winding up of the affairs of final distribution of Company assets.

9.2 <u>Liquidation Distributions</u>. Upon dissolution, an accounting shall be made by the Company's accountant of the Company's assets, liabilities and operations, from the date of the last previous accounting until the date of dissolution. The Managers shall:

a. Sell or otherwise liquidate all of the Company's assets as promptly as practicable (except to the extent the Managers may determine to distribute any assets to the Members in kind).

b. Allocate any profit or loss resulting from such sales to the Member's Capital Accounts as described herein. If there is a deficit in a Capital Account, no Member shall have any liability to restore all or any portion of a deficit balance in such Member's Capital Account.

c. Discharge all liabilities of the Company, including liabilities to Members who are creditors, to the extent otherwise permitted by law, other than liabilities to Members for distributions, and establish such reserves as may be reasonably necessary to provide for contingent liabilities of the Company (for purposes of determining the Capital Accounts of the Members, the amounts of such reserves shall be deemed to be an expense of the Company).

d. Distribute the remaining assets to the Members in accordance with their respective Percentage Interests. Members shall look solely to the assets of the Company for the return of its Capital Contribution. If the Company property remaining after the payment or discharge of the debts and liabilities of the Company is insufficient to return the cash contribution of one or more Members, such Members shall have no recourse against any other Member, except as otherwise provided by law. A Member shall not receive any distribution until all liabilities of the Company have been paid or there remains property of the Company sufficient to pay them.

The Company may offset damages for breach of this Operating Agreement by a Member whose interest is liquidated (either upon the withdrawal of the Member or the liquidation of the Company) against the amount otherwise distributable to such Member.

9.3 <u>Liquidating Agent</u>. The liquidation of the Company shall be conducted and supervised by a person designated for such purposes by the affirmative vote or consent of Members holding a majority of the Members' Percentage Interests (the "Liquidating Agent"). The Liquidating Agent hereby is authorized and empowered to execute any and all documents and to take any and all actions necessary or desirable to effectuate the dissolution and liquidation of the Company in accordance with this Agreement.

Promptly after the termination of the Company, the Liquidating Agent shall cause to be prepared and furnished to the Members a statement setting forth the assets and liabilities of the Company as of the date of termination. The Liquidating Agent, to the extent practicable, shall liquidate the assets of the Company as promptly as possible, but in an orderly and businesslike manner so as not to involve undue sacrifice.

9.4 Priority of Distribution Following Liquidation. The proceeds of sale and all other assets of the Company shall be applied and distributed in the following order of priority: (1) to the payment of the expenses of liquidation and the debts and liabilities of the Company, other than debts and liabilities to Members; (2) to the payment of debts and liabilities to Members; (3) to the setting up of any reserves which the Liquidating Agent may deem necessary or desirable for any contingent or unforeseen liabilities or obligations of the Company, which reserves may be paid over to licensed attorney to hold in escrow for a period of two years for the purpose of payment of any liabilities and obligations, at the expiration of which period the balance of such reserves shall be distributed as provided; (4) to the Members in proportion to their respective capital accounts until each Member has received cash distributions equal to any positive balance in their capital account, in accordance with the rules and requirements of Treas. Reg. Section 1.704-1(b)(2)(ii)(b); and (5) to the Members in proportion to the Members' Percentage Interests.

The liquidation shall be complete within the period required by Treas. Reg. Section 1.704-1(b)(2)(ii)(b).

9.5 Company Terminated. Upon completion of the winding up, liquidation, and distribution of the assets, the Company shall be deemed terminated. The Members shall no longer be Members, and the Company shall execute, acknowledge and cause to be filed any documents or instruments as may be necessary or appropriate to evidence the dissolution and termination of the Company pursuant to applicable law.

9.6 Withdrawal Events. The following shall be considered "Withdrawal Events": the death, retirement, withdrawal, expulsion, dissolution of a Member, incompetence (as found by a court of competent jurisdiction), an event of bankruptcy or insolvency, or the occurrence of any other event that terminates the continued membership of a Member in the Company pursuant to applicable law.

An "event of bankruptcy or insolvency" with respect to a Member shall occur if such Member: (1) applies for or consents to the appointment of a receiver, trustee or liquidator of all or a substantial part of their assets; or (2) makes a general assignment for the benefit of creditors; or (3) is adjudicated a bankrupt or an insolvent; or (4) files a voluntary petition in bankruptcy or a petition or an answer seeking an arrangement with creditors or to take advantage of any bankruptcy, insolvency, readjustment of debt or similar law or statute, or an answer admitting the material allegations of a petition filed against them in any bankruptcy, insolvency, readjustment of debt or similar proceedings; or (5) takes any action for the purpose of effecting any of the foregoing; or (6) an order, judgment or decree shall be entered, with or without the application, approval or consent of such Member, by any court of competent jurisdiction, approving a petition for or appointing a receiver or trustee of all or a substantial part of the assets of such Member, and such order, judgment or decree shall be entered, with or without the application, approval or consent of such Member, by any court of competent jurisdiction, approving a petition for or appointing a receiver or trustee of all or a substantial part of the assets of such Member, and such order, judgment or decree shall continue unstayed and in effect for thirty days.

9.7 <u>Successors in Interest</u>. In the event of a Withdrawal Event with respect to any Member, any successor in interest to such Member (including without limitation any executor, administrator, heir, committee, guardian, or other representative or successor) shall not become entitled to any rights or interests of such Member in the Company, other than the allocations and distributions to which such Member is entitled, unless such successor in interest is admitted as a Member in accordance with this Agreement.

9.8 <u>Capital Account</u>. Upon a dissolution event, as determined in this Operating Agreement, capital will be determined as of the date of the dissolution event. If Capital Accounts are determined and maintained through the date of the dissolution event in accordance with the Capital Accounting rules of §1.704-1(b)(2)(iv) of the Income Tax Regulations, then capital determined as of the date of the dissolution event represents the Capital Account balances determined on that date.

ARTICLE X: MISCELLANEOUS PROVISIONS

10.1 <u>Execution of Additional Instruments</u>. Each Member hereby agrees to execute such other and further statements of interest and holdings, designations, and other instruments necessary to comply with any laws, rules, or regulations.

10.2 <u>Construction</u>. Whenever the singular number is used in this Operating Agreement and when required by the context, the same shall include the plural and vice versa, and the masculine gender shall include the feminine and neuter genders and vice versa. All pronouns shall be deemed to be the masculine, feminine, neuter, singular or plural as the identity of the person or persons may require.

10.3 <u>Headings</u>. The headings and/or captions in this Operating Agreement are inserted for convenience only and are in no way intended to describe, interpret, define, or limit the scope, extent or intent of this Operating Agreement or any provision hereof.

10.4 <u>Waivers</u>. The failure of any party to seek redress for default of or to insist upon the strict performance of any covenant or condition of this Operating Agreement shall not prevent a subsequent act, which would have originally constituted a default, from having the effect of an original default.

10.5 <u>Rights and Remedies Cumulative</u>. The rights and remedies provided by this Operating Agreement are cumulative and the use of any one right or remedy by any party shall not preclude or waive the right to use any other remedy. Said rights and remedies are given in addition to any other legal rights the parties may have.

10.6 <u>Severability</u>. If any provision of this Operating Agreement or the application thereof to any person or circumstance shall be invalid, illegal, or unenforceable to any extent, the remainder of this Operating Agreement and the application thereof shall not be affected and shall be enforceable to the fullest extent permitted by law. To the extent any provision of this Agreement is prohibited or otherwise ineffective under the statutes, such provision shall be considered to be ineffective to the smallest degree possible in order to make this Agreement effective under the statutes.

10.7 <u>Heirs, Successors and Assigns</u>. Each and all of the covenants, terms, provisions and agreements herein contained shall be binding upon and inure to the benefit of the parties hereto and, to the extent permitted by this Operating Agreement, their respective heirs, legal representatives, successors and assigns.

10.8 <u>Creditors</u>. None of the provisions of this Operating Agreement shall be for the benefit of or enforceable by any creditor(s) of the Company or its Members or Managers.

10.9. <u>Charging Order Protection/Poison Pill Provision.</u> In accordance with RCW 25.15.256(3(a)-(c)), a transferable interest of any member charged with a charging order may be redeemed (prior to foreclosure) by the judgment debtor, or by one or more of the other members for $1 (if not LLC property) or, if LLC property, then for $1 with the consent of all members whose interests are not so charged.

The LLC or any of its members may purchase the interest of any member who files for bankruptcy for $1.

10.10 <u>Counterparts</u>. This Operating Agreement may be executed in counterparts, each of which shall be deemed an original but all of which shall constitute one and the same instrument.

10.11 <u>Company Agrees to Be Bound</u>. The *Company Name*, LLC hereby accepts the terms of this Operating Agreement and agrees to be bound thereby.

10.12 <u>Title to Assets</u>. All personal and real property of this LLC shall be held in the name of the LLC, not in the names of individual members.

10.13 <u>Partition of Assets.</u> No partition of LLC assets is allowed without the unanimous consent of all of the members.

10.14 <u>Amendments</u>. This Operating Agreement may be amended upon the unanimous vote of the Members. Each Member shall receive written Notice of any amendment within thirty (30) days following the amendment.

10.15 <u>Bank Accounts</u>. The LLC shall designate one or more banks or other institutions for the deposit of the funds of the LLC, and shall establish savings, checking, investment and other such accounts as are reasonable and necessary for its business and investments. One or more members of the LLC shall be designated with the consent of all members to deposit and withdraw funds of the LLC, and to direct the investment of funds from, into and among such accounts. The funds of the LLC, however and wherever deposited or invested, shall not be commingled with the personal funds of any members of the LLC.

10.16 <u>Assignment of Interests (RCW 25.15.121)</u>: Except as otherwise provided in this Agreement, no Member or other person holding any interest in the Company may transfer, assign, pledge, hypothecate, or otherwise dispose of all or any part of their interest in the Company (economic, voting, and/or management rights), including without limitation, the capital, profits, or distributions of the Company without the prior written consent of all other Members in each instance.

Further, no member may encumber a part or all of his or her membership in the LLC by mortgage, pledge, granting of a security interest, lien or otherwise, unless the encumbrance has first been approved in writing by all other members of the LLC.

A transfer of a member's interest in the LLC to a living trust or a wholly-owned business entity of a current member does not require the approval of members.

A transfer of a member's interest in the LLC to a member's spouse requires the consent of a majority of the members.

An assignment to a permitted assignee shall only entitle the permitted assignee to the allocations and distributions to which the assigned interest is entitled, unless such permitted assignee applies for admission to the Company and is admitted to the Company as a Member in accordance with this Agreement.

An assignment, pledge, hypothecation, transfer or other disposition of all or any part of the interest of a Member in the Company or other person holding any interest in the Company in violation of the provisions hereof shall be null and void for all purposes.

No assignment, transfer or other disposition of all or any part of the interest of any Member permitted under this Agreement shall be binding upon the Company unless and until a duly executed and acknowledged counterpart of such assignment or instrument of transfer, in form and substance satisfactory to the Company, has been delivered to the Company.

No assignment or other disposition of any interest of any Member may be made if such assignment or disposition, alone or when combine with other transactions, would result in the termination of the Company within the meaning of Section 708 of the Internal Revenue Code or under any other relevant section of the Code or any successor statute. No assignment or other disposition of any interest of any Member may be made without an opinion of counsel satisfactory to the Company that such assignment or disposition is subject to an effective registration under, or exempt from the registration requirements of, the applicable Federal and State securities laws. No interest in the Company may be assigned or given to any person below the age of 21 years or to a person who has been adjudged to be insane or incompetent.

10.17 <u>Transfer on Death.</u> The transfer of a member's ownership interest, including economic, voting, and management rights, in the LLC vests immediately upon a member's death in the name of the designated heir(s), who then becomes a member of the LLC, unless a majority of the members refuse consent. In that case, the members may agree to assign only the deceased member's economic interest to his heir(s) by a vote of the majority of members.

Name 1's designated heir is Name 2; secondary designated heir is Name 3.

Name 2's designated heir is Name 3; secondary designated heir is Name 1.

10.18 <u>Right of First Refusal.</u> If a Member desires to sell, transfer or otherwise dispose of all or any part of their interest in the Company, such Member (the "Selling Member") shall first offer to sell and convey such interest to the other Members before selling, transferring or otherwise disposing of such interest to any other person, corporation or other entity. Such offer shall be in writing, shall be given to every other Member, and shall set forth the interest to be sold, the purchase price to be paid, the date on which the closing is to take place (which date shall be not less than thirty nor more than sixty days after the delivery of the offer), the location at which the closing is to take place, and all other material terms and conditions of the sale, transfer or other disposition.

Within 20 days after the delivery of said offer the other Members shall deliver to the Selling Member a written notice either accepting or rejecting the offer. Failure to deliver said notice within said 20 days conclusively shall be deemed a rejection of the offer. Any or all of the other Members may elect to accept the offer, and if more than one of the other Members elects to accept the offer, the interest being sold and the purchase price therefore shall be allocated among the Members so accepting the offer in proportion to their Members' Percentage Interests, unless they otherwise agree in writing.

If any or all of the other Members elect to accept the offer, then the closing of title shall be held in accordance with the offer and the Selling Member shall deliver to the other Members who have accepted the offer an assignment of the interest being sold by the Selling Member, and said other Members shall pay the purchase price prescribed in the offer.

If no other Member accepts the offer, or if the Members who have accepted such offer default in their obligations to purchase the interest, then the Selling Member within 120 days after the delivery of the offer may sell such interest to any other person or entity at a purchase price which is not less than the purchase price prescribed in the offer and upon the terms and conditions which are substantially the same as the terms and conditions set forth in the offer, provided all other applicable requirements of this Agreement are complied with. An assignment of such interest to a person or entity who is not a Member of the Company shall only entitle such person or entity to the allocations and distributions to which the assigned interest is entitled, unless such person or entity applies for admission to the Company and is admitted to the Company as a Member in accordance with this Agreement.

If the Selling Member does not sell such interest within said 120 days, then the Selling Member may not thereafter sell such interest without again offering such interest to the other Members in accordance with this Agreement.

All business and/or investment deals must first be offered to the LLC for consideration before an owner or member may take the deal for himself.

10.18 <u>Indemnification.</u> This LLC incorporates by reference the indemnification provisions in RCW 25.15.041. This LLC may indemnify any member or manager from and against any judgments, settlements, penalties, fines, or expenses incurred in a proceeding, or obligate itself to advance, or reimburse expenses incurred in a proceeding to which a person is a party, because such person is, or was, a member or a manager, provided that no such indemnity shall indemnify a member or a manager from or on account of acts or omissions of the member or manager finally adjudged to be intentional misconduct or a knowing violation of law by the member or manager, or conduct of the member or manager adjudged to be in violation of RCW 25.15.231 (Limitations on distribution).

This LLC may indemnify and advance expenses to an officer, employee, or agent of the limited liability company who is not a member or manager to the same extent as to a member or manager.

10.19 <u>Business Transactions of Member or Manager with the LLC</u>. A member or manager may lend money to and transact other business with a limited liability company and, subject to other applicable law, has the same rights and obligations with respect to the loan or other transaction as a person who is not a member or manager. (RCW 25.15.036)

10.20 <u>Margin Trading.</u> The LLC is authorized to conduct margin trading when investing in equities, securities, options, and other investment vehicles in its brokerage account(s).

10.21 <u>Decanting Clause.</u> Assets may be transferred to another jurisdiction, if a majority of the members agree.

10.22 <u>Series LLCs</u>. This operating agreement allows for the formation of series LLCs, should the laws of the state of _____ allow for it.

10.23 <u>Governing Law</u>. This Agreement and the rights and liabilities of the parties hereunder shall be governed by and determined in accordance with the laws of the State of _____.

10.24 Third Parties. No provision of this Agreement is intended to be for the benefit of or enforceable by any third party.

10.25 Mediation and Arbitration of Disputes Among Members. In any dispute over the provisions of this operating agreement and in other disputes among the members, if the members cannot resolve the dispute to their mutual satisfaction, the matter may be submitted to mediation. The terms and procedure for mediation shall be arranged by the parties to the dispute. If good-faith mediation of a dispute proves impossible or if an agreed-upon mediation outcome cannot be obtained by the members who are parties to the dispute, the dispute may be submitted to arbitration in accordance with the rules of the American Arbitration Association. Any party may commence arbitration of the dispute by sending a written request for arbitration to all other parties to the dispute. The request shall state the nature of the dispute to be resolved by arbitration, and, if all parties to the dispute agree to arbitration, arbitration shall be commenced as soon as practical after such parties receive a copy of the written request. All parties shall initially share the cost of arbitration, but the prevailing party or parties may be awarded attorney fees, costs and other expenses of arbitration. All arbitration decisions shall be final, binding and conclusive on all the parties to arbitration, and legal judgment may be entered based upon such decision in accordance with applicable law in any court having jurisdiction to do so.

10.26 Entire Agreement. This Agreement sets forth the entire agreement of the parties hereto with respect to the subject matter hereof. This Agreement, and any amendments hereto may be executed in counterparts all of which taken together shall constitute one agreement. It is the intention of the Member(s) that this Agreement shall be the sole agreement of the parties, and, except to the extent a provision of this Agreement provides for the incorporation of federal income tax rules or is expressly prohibited or ineffective under the statutes, this Agreement shall govern even when inconsistent with, or different from, the provisions of any applicable law or rule.

10.27 Venue. Venue shall lie exclusively in the county of _____ in the state of _____.

Subject to the limitations on transferability set forth above, this Agreement shall be binding upon and inure to the benefit of the parties hereto and to their respective heirs, executors, administrators, successors, and assigns.

ARTICLE XI: SIGNATURES OF MEMBERS

IN WITNESS WHEREOF, the members of this LLC sign and adopt this agreement as the operating agreement of this LLC this 1st day of March, 2018.

Manager: Member:

_____   _____
Name 1   Name 1

_____   _____
Name 2   Name 2

References

"9 Insights About Negative Interest Rates." *Knowledge@Wharton High School*, kwhs.wharton.upenn.edu/2019/09/9-insights-negative-interest-rates.

"10 Reasons You Should Invest In Silver." *IRA Gold Advisor*, iragoldadvisor.com/silver-ira/10-reasons-you-should-invest-in-silver/.

12 U.S.C. s. 301, 341-361.

26 U.S. Code §1.

50 U.S. Code §4305.

"150+ New World Order Globalist Agenda Quotes." *Wake Up New Zealand*, www.wakeupkiwi.com/nwo-globalist-agenda-quotes.shtml.

"A Quote by Franklin D. Roosevelt." *Goodreads*, Goodreads, www.goodreads.com/quotes/162689-the-real-truth-of-the-matter-is-as-you-and.

"A Quote by Henry Ford." *Goodreads*, Goodreads, www.goodreads.com/quotes/852618-the-one-aim-of-these-financiers-is-world-control-by.

"Aaron Russo: Reflections and Warnings - Full Transcript." *Matt Prather*, sites.google.com/site/themattprather/Reading/aaron-russo/reflections-and-warnings-full-transcript.

Adams, Mike. "Analysis: Bitcoin could go to $100,000 as the fiat currency dollar collapses, but the 'value' won't be the fortune you're imagining." *Natural News*, 17 May 2020, www.naturalnews.com/2020-05-17-analysis-bitcoin-could-go-to-100000-as-fiat-currency-dollar-collapses.html.

Adams, Mike. "Evidence points to Bitcoin being an NSA-engineered psyop to roll out one-world digital currency." *Natural News*, 10 Dec. 2017, www.naturalnews.com/2017-12-10-evidence-points-to-bitcoin-being-an-nsa-psyop-roll-out-one-world-digital-currency.html.

Adams, Mike. "Urgent alert: Financial system collapsing, food supply collapsing, hyperinflation coming, guns and ammo wiped out, military martial law plans leaked... details." *Natural News*, 19 Mar. 2020, www.naturalnews.com/2020-03-19-urgent-alert-financial-system-collapsing-food-supply-hyperinflation.html.

Agarwai, Ruchir and Signe Krogstrup. "Cashing In: How to Make Negative Interest Rates Work." *IMF Blog*, 5 Feb. 2019, blogs.imf.org/2019/02/05/cashing-in-how-to-make-negative-interest-rates-work/.

Akiboh, Alvita. "Who is James K. Polk?: The Most Important President You Don't Remember." *U.S. History Scene*, ushistoryscene.com/article/james-k-polk/.

Alden, Lyn. "Covered Calls: A Step-by-Step Guide with Examples." *Lynalden.com*, 4 Nov. 2019, www.lynalden.com/covered-calls/.

Alden, Lyn. "Selling Put Options: How to Get Paid for Being Patient." *Lynalden.com*, 4 Nov. 2019, www.lynalden.com/selling-put-options/.

Allison, John A. "Market Discipline Beats Regulatory Discipline." *Cato Journal*, www.cato.org/sites/cato.org/files/serials/files/cato-journal/2014/5/cato-journal-v34n2-9.pdf.

Amadeo, Kimberly. "Explaining Quantitative Easing – QE." *The Balance*, 3 Sept. 2019, www.thebalance.com/what-is-quantitative-easing-definition-and-explanation-3305881.

Amadeo, Kimberly. "Federal Reserve Chairman Ben Bernanke." *The Balance*, 26 Jan. 2021, www.thebalance.com/federal-reserve-chairman-ben-bernanke-3306152.

Amadeo, Kimberly. "Inverted Yield Curve and Why It Predicts a Recession." *The Balance,* 31 Oct. 2019, www.thebalance.com/inverted-yield-curve-3305856.

Amadeo, Kimberly. "Liquidity: Its Gluts, Traps, Ratios, and How the Fed Manages It." *The Balance*, 30 Dec. 2020, www.thebalance.com/liquidity-definition-ratios-how-its-managed-3305939.
Amadeo, Kimberly. "Reserve Requirement and How It Affects Interest Rates." *The Balance*, 10 Feb. 2019, www.thebalance.com/reserve-requirement-3305883.

Amadeo, Kimberly. "Three Reasons to Invest in Gold According to Research." *The Balance*, 10 Jul. 2019, www.thebalance.com/why-invest-in-gold-3305651.

"America: Freedom to Fascism Quotes." *Quotes.net.* STANDS4 LLC, 2020, www.quotes.net/mquote/970882.

"An Essay On The History Of Banking." *The Banking Swindle,* criminalbankingmonopoly.wordpress.com/banking-essay/.

Anderson, Anthony. "New Dollar Backed by Gold Coming This October 2020?" *GSI Exchange*, 27 May 2020, gsiexchange.com/is-a-new-dollar-backed-by-gold-at-10000-per-ounce-coming-by-october-1st-2020/?fbclid=IwAR0JeJRf6pMwprbp4UUdETDxl4lQQg3Oek5XnXrk3CEAVjZdWUba y6W6m28.

Anderson, Anthony Allen. "States Where Gold and Silver Have Become Legal Tender." *GSI Exchange*, 25 Jul. 2019, gsiexchange.com/states-gold-silver-become-legal-tender/.

Anderson, William L. "The Costs Are Mounting in this Government-Imposed Economic Collapse." *Mises Institute*, 24 Mar. 2020, mises.org/wire/costs-are-mounting-government-imposed-economic-collapse? fbclid=IwAR1ggouFwQpu6uof_Wv_Ym_RPrzvgPkr5hoz7pXFE3MiK6RYNmIlJ Y2kqp0.

Arcadia Economics. "Michael Pento: "Interest Rates Will Probably Never Be Raised Again In Our Lifetime." *Youtube*. 12 Dec. 2019, www.youtube.com/watch? v=X3KYNZcvioY.

"Arnold J. Toynbee." *Wikiquote*, Wikimedia Foundation, Inc., en.wikiquote.org/wiki/Arnold_J._Toynbee.
Ashworth, Marcus. "What Is Really to Blame for the Repo Market Blowup." *The Washington Post*, 9 Dec. 2019, www.washingtonpost.com/business/what-is-really-to-blame-for-the-repo-market-blowup/2019/12/09/38d68258-1a83-11ea-977a-15a6710ed6da_story.html.

"Asset Protection FAQs." *The Farrell Law Group*, www.farrell-lawgroup.com/Practice-Areas/Asset-Protection-Law/FAQs-Regarding-Asset-Protection.

Atlas Grinned. "Russian Stocks A Bargain With Ruble On De Facto Gold Standard." *Seeking Alpha,* 27 Jun. 2019, seekingalpha.com/article/4272351-russian-stocks-bargain-ruble-on-de-facto-gold-standard.

"Attorney Tommy Cryer Beats the IRS in court; Jury says not guilty!" *Freedom Law School*, 12 Jul. 2007, web.archive.org/web/20170425083913/http://freedomlawschool.org/victories/attorney-beats-irs.html.

Authers, John. "A Shift in the Global Financial Order Is Upon Us." *Bloomberg Opinion*, 8 Mar. 2020, www.bloomberg.com/opinion/articles/2020-03-09/crash-in-oil-prices-bond-yields-marks-shift-in-global-order.

Authers, John. "New World Order Is Coming, Maybe in Helicopters." *Bloomberg*, 9 Mar. 2020, www.bloomberg.com/opinion/articles/2020-03-09/oil-crash-coronavirus-is-just-the-start-of-market-shocks?fbclid=IwAR2YtaU-DhkS0kI7-L6iJQzClEBvP7jXwE3M6uoLRXddmkFdUGWWUFuDACI.

Bailey v. Drexel Furniture Company, 259 U.S. 20, 42 S.Ct. 449 (1922).

Bailey, James. "How to Withdraw Cash from the Bank Without Getting Arrested." *Z3 News*, 6 May 2015, z3news.com/w/how-to-withdraw-cash-from-the-bank-without-getting-arrested/.

Bambrough, Billy. "China Could Force Donald Trump And The Fed To Destroy The U.S. Banking System." *Forbes*, 8 Jun. 2020, www.forbes.com/sites/billybambrough/2020/06/08/china-could-force-donald-trump-and-the-fed-to-destroy-the-us-banking-system/? fbclid=IwAR1QYQWgSJBQZJZQf_ou26oxLX2KD73xJ1H9rXTLHIznvrbtdKO DhEDTspU#3aeed2b34f5f.

Bambrough, Billy. "Devastating Bitcoin Wipeout Could See The Price Go 'Sub-$1,000.'" *Forbes*, 13 Mar. 2020, www.forbes.com/sites/billybambrough/2020/03/13/devastating-bitcoin-wipeout-could-see-the-price-go-sub-1000/#5b050f3480eb.

Bambrough, Billy. "Donald Trump And The Fed Are Destroying The U.S. Dollar." *Forbes*, 28 Mar. 2020, www.forbes.com/sites/billybambrough/2020/03/28/donald-trump-and-the-fed-are-destroying-the-us-dollar/?fbclid=IwAR0FVSZWzVX5vEiMO6JUKf9DUyHAIM9Hbr3mPA2ECTJxMTkz4c80Xz8NRlE#36964d106ebc.

Banerji, Rishabh. "These Are The 13 Families In The World That Apparently Control Everything." *India Times*, 9 Mar. 2018, www.indiatimes.com/culture/who-we-are/these-are-the-13-families-in-the-world-that-apparently-control-everything-from-politics-to-terrorism-257642.html?fbclid=IwAR1csUuCsRdOuzyAJRA3hUnL0K_EWRzTCIwj3EuJ2R2Rq3dIHcFO_sDyvOo.

"Bankers Manifesto of 1892." *Frank-Webb.com*, web.archive.org/web/20190227170038/www.frank-webb.com/bankers-manifesto-of-1892.html.

"Banks Quotes." *Good Reads*, www.goodreads.com/quotes/tag/banks.

"Banning cash so you pay the bank to hold your money is what the IMF wants." *MSN*, 25 Aug. 2019, www.msn.com/en-au/money/personalfinance/banning-cash-so-you-pay-the-bank-to-hold-your-money-is-what-the-imf-wants/ar-AAGjopy?fbclid=IwAR3azKMt8SEjVWBYhS_p6u0ZQIaY-IcLekCFi5K_A8CEThzwrEWGwugJnrc.

Barber, Gregory. "This Alleged Bitcoin Scam Looked a Lot Like a Pyramid Scheme." *Wired*, 18 Dec. 2019, www.wired.com/story/alleged-bitcoin-scam-like-pyramid-scheme/.

Basu, Chirantan. "Advantages and Disadvantages of Bonds." *Zack's*, 5 Mar. 2019, finance.zacks.com/advantages-disadvantages-bonds-2350.html.

Bayly, Lucy. "Dow falls 2,200 points, trading halted, as rate cut fails to calm markets." *NBC News*, 16 Mar. 2020, www.nbcnews.com/business/markets/dow-falls-2-200-points-trading-halted-rate-cut-fails-n1160246?fbclid=IwAR24696MUcBAcdGR3gAIl6YRnUqAlJxZWSwerePFTWZai8lu68gJ7FjS1Nw.

Bayly, Lucy. "Dow plummets, trading briefly suspended after Trump's coronavirus response sparks market sell-off." *NBC News*, 12 Mar 2020, www.nbcnews.com/business/markets/trading-wall-street-temporarily-suspended-after-trump-s-crisis-response-n1156406?fbclid=IwAR3SOc27oG8hUdoTBC2VIo_4k1Uh7DRKj88l3XMOM93Q86qZAcqHzgbFskI.

Bayly, Lucy. "Federal Reserve cuts rates to near zero in emergency action," *NBC News,* 16 Mar. 2020, www.nbcnews.com/business/economy/federal-reserve-cuts-rates-near-zero-emergency-action-n1159691? cid=sm_npd_nn_fb_np&fbclid=IwAR1vJryRucDUBNTzpbUGIUYzex1MRGoId YVa-f3V0KiwMLkY4XPquv3PBuE.

Beck, Glenn. "Preparedness guide to the Marxist revolution." *Glennbeck.com,* 16 Jun. 2020, www.glennbeck.com/glenn-beck/preparedness-guide-for-the-american-collapse-reset.

Becker, Sam. "Everything you need to know about investing in gold and precious metals." *Grow,* 13 Dec. 2019, grow.acorns.com/what-you-need-to-know-about-investing-in-gold-and-precious-metals/.

Belz, Sage and David Wessel. "Quantitative easing lowered interest rates. Why isn't quantitative tightening lifting them more?" Brookings, 3 Dec. 2018, www.brookings.edu/blog/up-front/2018/12/03/quantitative-easing-lowered-interest-rates-why-isnt-quantitative-tightening-lifting-them-more/.

Benko, Ralph. "President Trump: Replace The Dollar With Gold As The Global Currency To Make America Great Again." *Forbes,* 25 Feb. 2017, www.forbes.com/sites/ralphbenko/2017/02/25/president-trump-replace-the-dollar-with-gold-as-the-global-currency-to-make-america-great-again/amp/? __&fbclid=IwAR08UD15ITTTpxe9ovabRK3ps1n5Vw7gcBV-SnZZUMQl8dmSasktRMFeFqI.
Bernish, Claire. "8 Years Ago Today, The US Helped Murder Gaddafi to Stop the Creation of Gold-Backed Currency." *The Free Thought Project,* 20 Oct. 2017, thefreethoughtproject.com/8-years-ago-us-killed-gaddafi-gold/? fbclid=IwAR2i8YWZQmdUCYggA-vWrFUgoEB55CZq4qtj2HPxwj1nFotrlTLISVAt2es.

Bianco, Jim. "The Fed's Cure Risks Being Worse Than the Disease." *Yahoo Finance,* 27 Mar. 2020, finance.yahoo.com/news/feds-cure-risks-being-worse-110052807.html.

Bit Coin Exchange Guide News Team. "Economist's 30-Year Old Prediction for a Global Currency Arrives: is Crypto Going to Rule World?" *Bit Coin Exchange Guide,* 10 Oct. 2018, bitcoinexchangeguide.com/economists-30-year-old-prediction-for-a-global-currency-arrives-is-crypto-going-to-rule-world/.

"Bitcoin." *Coindesk,* www.coindesk.com/price/bitcoin.

"Bitcoin: Know the risks before you buy." *Al Jazeera,* 5 Feb. 2018, www.aljazeera.com/news/2017/12/bitcoin-buy-171219100738438.html.

Bizimungu, Julius. "IMF officially declares global economic recession." *The New Times,* 27 Mar. 2020, www.newtimes.co.rw/news/imf-officially-declares-global-

economic-recession?fbclid=IwAR0pEJQiDFp1hokY8-
Wpql7pgEgcTdE2kW1ZydtNSW1_CZjBPNFP6FZFQMo.

Blanco, Octavio. "Why Investing in Digital Currencies Like Bitcoin Is So Dangerous," *Consumer Reports*, 12 Jan. 2018, www.consumerreports.org/cryptocurrency/why-investing-in-digital-currencies-like-bitcoin-is-so-dangerous/.

Boesler, Matthew. "Fed Has Purchased $1.8 Billion of Corporate-Bond ETFs So Far." *Yahoo Finance*, 21 May 2020, finance.yahoo.com/news/fed-purchased-1-8-billion-204012560.html.

Boesler, Matthew. "Federal Reserve's Balance Sheet Tops $5 Trillion for First Time." *Yahoo Finance*, 26 Mar. 2020, finance.yahoo.com/news/federal-balance-sheet-tops-5-210123506.html.

Boldin, Michael. "Signed by the Governor: Arizona Law Treats Gold and Silver as Money." *Tenth Amendment Center*, 23 May 2017, blog.tenthamendmentcenter.com/2017/05/signed-by-the-governor-arizona-law-treats-gold-and-silver-as-money/.

Bomey, Nathan. "New York Federal Reserve injects $1.5 trillion into markets amid coronavirus chaos for stocks." *USA Today*, 12 Mar. 2020, www.usatoday.com/story/money/2020/03/12/coronavirus-new-york-federal-reserve-stock-market-liquidity/5032970002/?fbclid=IwAR3fKK3v5WH_miBv3irfIxdseJsUm5jRy5zelLOhEh8Crmy-MgDGCl_DfoM.

Boring, Perianne. "If You Want To Know The Real Rate Of Inflation, Don't Bother With The CPI." *Forbes*, 3 Feb. 2014, www.forbes.com/sites/perianneboring/2014/02/03/if-you-want-to-know-the-real-rate-of-inflation-dont-bother-with-the-cpi/#5f1504b9200b.

Borowski, Julie. "Top 10 Reasons to End the Federal Reserve." *FreedomWorks*, 1 Feb. 2012, www.freedomworks.org/content/top-10-reasons-end-federal-reserve.

Bovaird, Charles. "Bitcoin Breaks Through $40,000 To Notch A Fresh All-Time High." *Forbes*, 7 Jan. 2021, www.forbes.com/sites/cbovaird/2021/01/07/bitcoin-breaks-through-40000-to-notch-a-fresh-all-time-high/?sh=4418cf283a96.

Bovaird, Charles. "Bitcoin Lost Roughly 50% Of Its Value In A Day." *Forbes*, 12 Mar. 2020, www.forbes.com/sites/cbovaird/2020/03/12/bitcoin-lost-roughly-50-of-its-value-in-a-day/#5a895433056a.

Bowden, Ebony. "Coronavirus stimulus package to exceed $6T, Larry Kudlow says." *New York Post*, 24 Mar. 2020, nypost.com/2020/03/24/coronavirus-stimulus-package-to-exceed-6t-larry-kudlow-says/?fbclid=IwAR1qGgCnbIOr-In-YRUiSRMRDXKQOlEjMC-10MPhbFKVX5WH_K1ocakkU_k.

Bowden, John. "Bank of America: The US is now in a recession." *The Hill*, 19 Mar. 2020, thehill.com/policy/finance/488388-bank-of-america-the-us-is-now-in-a - r e c e s s i o n ? fbclid=IwAR2wQSov4oS5TfkCbuTxpto0iXu8sKoJ7tsWU0xe3mkOopgKk26b8Z JN08c.

Breuninger, Kevin. "Trump wants direct payments of $1,000 for adults, $500 for kids in coronavirus stimulus bill, Mnuchin says." *CNBC*, 19 Mar. 2020, www.cnbc.com/2020/03/19/coronavirus-trump-wants-payments-of-1000-for-a d u l t s - 5 0 0 - f o r - k i d s . h t m l ? fbclid=IwAR2SSdXREmF1PstXDgRUECgWplZjOSTDpoybLIOgwnCbAYmNZ qUtzA5VOz8.

Breuninger, Kevin. "White House won't explain how it would pay for Trump's proposed payroll tax holiday." *CNBC Markets*, 10 Mar. 2020, www.cnbc.com/2020/03/10/white-house-wont-explain-how-it-would-pay-for-trumps-proposed-p a y r o l l - t a x - h o l i d a y . h t m l ? fbclid=IwAR2tNNEKkY2lRaPuzzRjkg57AWcvLt8vhiYRxk52ojesigjP9UhKFAB D9Dc.

Brewer, Reuben Gregg. "The Beginner's Guide to Investing in Gold." *The Motley Fool*, 4 Sept. 2019, www.fool.com/investing/the-beginners-guide-to-investing-in-gold.aspx.

Brightman, Chris. "Negative Rates Are Dangerous to Your Wealth." *Research Affiliates*, Apr. 2016, www.researchaffiliates.com/en_us/publications/articles/542_negative_rates_are_dangerous_to_your_wealth.html.

Brinks Inc. v. Board of Governors of the Federal Reserve System, 466 F.Supp. 116 (D.D.C. 1979).

Brock, Thomas. "Money." *Investopedia*, 25 Dec. 2020, www.investopedia.com/terms/m/money.asp.

Brown, Ellen. "Revive Lincoln's Monetary Policy: An Open Letter to President Obama." *The Web of Debt*, 8 Apr. 2009, www.webofdebt.com/articles/lincoln_obama.php.

Brown, Ellen. "The Fed's baffling response to the Coronavirus explained." *Nexusnewsfeedf.com*, 12 Mar. 2020, www.nexusnewsfeed.com/article/geopolitics/the-fed-s-baffling-response-to-the-coronavirus-explained/? fbclid=IwAR3KdMgB13LT98gK8-5bQvXUM5mm5zjEiCDl6MIQ_4t74ad9X_V 05lU8ajY.

Brushaber v. Union P. R. Co., 240 U.S. 1 (1916).

Bryan, Bob. "Trump is meeting with an ex-bank CEO who wants to abolish the Federal Reserve and return to the gold standard." *Business Insider*, 28 Nov. 2016, www.businessinsider.com/trump-meeting-john-allison-bank-ceo-abolish-the-fed-g o l d - s t a n d a r d - 2 0 1 6 - 1 1 ?

fbclid=IwAR1EQE7q7kSztggK0rGULdVV1RZYSXJ8ezHbl3DJOJ11eNeGOu7 KvjNpqTk.

Bryan, Bob. "Trump's attacks on the Fed may be intense, but they're nothing compared to a wild new story about Ronald Reagan from former Fed Chairman Paul Volcker." *Business Insider,*. 24 Oct. 2018, www.businessinsider.com/ronald-reagan-fed-chair-volcker-trump-2018-10.

Buhler, Rich. "Abraham Lincoln Quote About Capitalism and Corruption-Correctly Attributed!" *Truthorfiction,* 26 Feb. 2016, www.truthorfiction.com/ abraham-lincoln-quote-about-capitalism-and-corruption/.

"Bush 'Out of these troubled times— a new world order.'" *The Washington Post,* www.washingtonpost.com/archive/politics/1990/09/12/bush-out-of-these-troubled-times-a-new-world-order/b93b5cf1-e389-4e6a-84b0-85f71bf4c946/.

Butchers' Union Co. v. Crescent City Co., 111 U.S. 746, 4 S.Ct. 652 (1884).

Buyniski, Helen. "Kissinger says 'even US' can't defeat Covid-19 alone. His solution? Global NWO government, of course." *RT,* 6 Apr. 2020, www.rt.com/op-ed/485127-kissinger-new-order-defeat-coronavirus/? fbclid=IwAR17vlVJHtqtx3kOOCMpeyMzWv1QsJmQJffn1YClUXKeKCtCPD-ZweMVBwM.

Cambone, Daniela. "Bitcoin price comes crashing, when this should be glory days says Peter Schiff." *Kitco,* 12 Mar. 2020, www.kitco.com/news/2020-03-12/ Bitcoin-Price-Comes-Crashing-When-This-Should-Be-Glory-Days-Says-Peter-Schiff.html.

Cammarosano, Louis. "The U.S. Plans to Bail-In the Banks – Federal Reserve Vice Chairman." *Smaulgld,* smaulgld.com/u-s-plans-to-bail-in-the-banks/? utm_source=ReviveOldPost&utm_medium=social&utm_campaign=ReviveOldPo st.

Canellis, David. "Bitcoin's failing price could be caused by $2B Chinese Ponzi scheme dumping its crypto." *Hard Fork,* 17 Dec. 2019, thenextweb.com/hardfork/ 2019/12/17/bitcoin-cryptocurrency-price-dump-ponzi-scheme-plustoken/.

Caplinger, Dan. "How to Invest in Silver the Right Way." *The Motley Fool,* 22 May 2017, www.fool.com/investing/2017/05/22/how-to-invest-in-silver-the-right-way.aspx.

Carlson, Debbie. "How to Invest in Silver." *US News,* 1 Aug. 2019, money.usnews.com/investing/investing-101/articles/how-to-invest-in-silver.

Carosa, Chris. "What Are 'Negative' Interest Rates And How Can You Make Money From Them?" *Forbes,* 20 Aug. 2019, www.forbes.com/sites/chriscarosa/ 2019/08/20/what-are-negative-interest-rates-and-how-can-you-make-money-from-them/#4766600a409b.

"CBO: Bank Bailout Cost Taxpayers $25 Billion." *CBN.com*, 30 Nov. 2010, web.archive.org/web/20110429163248/https://www1.cbn.com/cbnnews/finance/2010/november/cbo-tarp-bailout-cost-taxpayers-25-billion/.

"Central Banks Quotes." *AZ Quotes*, www.azquotes.com/quotes/topics/central-banks.html.

"Central Bank Quotes." *Brainy Quote*, www.brainyquote.com/quotes/g_edward_griffin_852221?src=t_central_bank.

"Central Bank Quotes." *Brainy Quote*, www.brainyquote.com/quotes/gerhard_schroder_239484?src=t_central_bank.

"Central Bank Quotes." *Brainy Quote*, www.brainyquote.com/quotes/patrick_m_byrne_851349?src=t_central_bank.

"Central Bank Quotes." *Brainy Quote*, www.brainyquote.com/quotes/ron_paul_396265?src=t_central_bank.
"Central Bank Quotes." *Brainy Quote*, www.brainyquote.com/topics/central-bank-quotes.

"Central Banks Quotes." *Good Reads*, www.goodreads.com/quotes/tag/central-banks.

Chambers, Clem. "How Quantitative Tightening Affects The Market." *Forbes*, 28 Feb. 2019, www.forbes.com/sites/investor/2019/02/28/how-quantitative-tightening-affects-the-market/#540069a0763c.

Chang, Ellen. "How Do Negative Interest Rates Work?" *The Street*, 23 Feb. 2018, www.thestreet.com/how-to/how-negative-interest-rates-work-14492328.

Chappell, Bill. "U.S. National Debt Hits Record $22 Trillion." *NPR*, 13 Feb. 2019, www.npr.org/2019/02/13/694199256/u-s-national-debt-hits-22-trillion-a-new-record-thats-predicted-to-fall.

Chappelow, Jim. "Demonetization." *Investopedia*, 20 Mar. 2020, www.investopedia.com/terms/d/demonetization.asp.

Chappelow, Jim. "Quantitative Easing." *Investopedia*, 6 Sept. 2019, www.investopedia.com/terms/q/quantitative-easing.asp.

"Charles Lindbergh Jr. Lucky Lindy Son of Congressman Charles Lindbergh Sr. (R-MN) Speech in Iowa on 9/11 September 11th 1941." *Americanbuilt.us*, americanbuilt.us/patriots/charles-lindbergh.shtml.

Cheung, Brian. "Federal Reserve slashes rates to zero, restarts QE." *Yahoo Finance*, 16 Mar. 2020, finance.yahoo.com/news/federal-reserve-cuts-rates-to-zero-restarts-quantitative-easing-qe-210001968.html.

Chorpenning, Ashley. "What Is Quantitative Tightening?" *Yahoo Finance*, 13 Nov. 2019, finance.yahoo.com/news/quantitative-tightening-211917762.html.

Christenson, Neils. "Gold price will bounce back after central banks flood markets – State Street Global Advisors." *Kitco*, 17 Mar. 2020, www.kitco.com/news/2020-03-17/Gold-price-will-bounce-back-after-central-banks-flood-markets-State-Street-Global-Advisors.html.

Christensen, Niels. "Three factors supporting the gold price - Blackrock." *Kitco*, 13 Mar. 2020, www.kitco.com/news/2020-03-13/Three-factors-supporting-gold-price-Blackrock.html.

Clabough, Raven. "George Soros Touts China as Leader of New World Order." *The New American*, 17 Nov. 2010, www.thenewamerican.com/world-news/north-america/item/10605-george-soros-touts-china-as-leader-of-new-world-order?fbclid=IwAR01ckBm-INZafvOcqeuUC9acGuyvLeoKR8otZP6073BqbLv3GyP5IieH3U#.

Clark, Jeff. "How Does Gold Fare During Hyperinflation?" *InflationData.com*, 25 Jun. 2012, inflationdata.com/articles/2012/06/25/gold-hyperinflation/.

Clark, Jeff. "Why Buy Silver? 10 Reasons to Invest in Silver Now (w/ Charts)." *GoldSilver.com*, goldsilver.com/blog/top-10-reasons-to-buy-silver/.

Clark, Jeff and Mike Maloney. "Gold & Silver Confiscation: Can the Government Seize Assets? (Video)." *GoldSilver.com*, goldsilver.com/blog/gold-confiscation-history-myths-and-real-solutions/.

CME Group. "What Can We Learn From Gold's Relationship To Other Assets?" *Yahoo Finance*, 21 May 2020, finance.yahoo.com/news/learn-golds-relationship-other-assets-152521709.html.

"College Tuition." *Priced in Gold*, pricingold.com/college-tuition/.

Colvin, Chris. "How the US government seized all citizens' gold in 1930s." *Yahoo News*, 21 May 2020, news.yahoo.com/us-government-seized-citizens-gold-143231746.html?soc_src=community&soc_trk=fb.
"Constitutional Amendment Process." *National Archives*, 15 Aug. 2016, www.archives.gov/federal-register/constitution.

"Constitutional Tender." *Tenth Amendment Center*, tenthamendmentcenter.com/legislation/constitutional-tender/.

"Continental Currency." *Encyclopedia.com*, 7 Nov. 2019, www.encyclopedia.com/history/encyclopedias-almanacs-transcripts-and-maps/continental-currency.

Convergence, www.channelingreality.com/TTT/Intro/Convergence.htm.

"Copper." *Priced in Gold*, pricedingold.com/copper/.

"Coronavirus to pop bubble greater than 2008; gold prices have 'nowhere to go but up.'" *Kitco News*, 12 Mar. 2020, www.kitco.com/news/2020-03-12/ Coronavirus-to-pop-bubble-greater-than-2008-gold-prices-have-nowhere-to-go-but-up.html.

Cortez, JP. "Fake Money, Sound Money and Government Malfeasance." *Tenth Amendment Center*, 28 Aug. 2018, tenthamendmentcenter.com/2018/08/28/fake-money-sound-money-and-government-malfeasance/.

Cox, Jeff. "Fed to pump in more than $1 trillion in dramatic ramping up of market intervention amid coronavirus meltdown." *CNBC*, 12 Mar. 2020, www.cnbc.com/ 2020/03/12/fed-to-pump-more-than-500-billion-into-short-term-bank-funding-expand-types-of-security-purchases.html? __source=iosappshare%7Ccom.apple.UIKit.activity.PostToFacebook&fbclid=Iw AR15uK1dO3bybc49XFX90ozIhLhZTroLUrUDsr_gEnJJ1tQL1voo1TkiwGA.

Cox, Jeff. "Gold Is Still Cheap Despite Record Surge: Marc Faber." *CNBC*, 8 Apr. 2011, www.cnbc.com/id/42478554.

Cox, Jeff. "Negative rates come to the US: 1-month and 3-month Treasury bill yields are now below zero." *CNBC*, 25 Mar. 2020, www.cnbc.com/2020/03/25/ negative-rates-come-to-the-us-1-month-and-3-month-treasury-bill-yields-are-now-negative.html? fbclid=IwAR2H7UYRDpI2yY35p104gy6Z63Eda4pWaswcKCOXdqNSgQo1CqT 3vrRzIZ8.

Cox, Jeff. "Powell says the Fed is 'strongly committed' to 2% inflation goal, a sign that rates are likely to hold steady." *CNBC*, 25 Nov. 2019, www.cnbc.com/ 2019/11/25/powell-says-the-fed-is-strongly-committed-to-meeting-its-inflation-goal.html.

Cox, Jeff. "Worries grow over the Fed's efforts to fix funding issues: 'This is all likely to get much worse.'" *CNBC*, 18 Oct. 2019, www.cnbc.com/2019/10/22/fed-repo-worries-continue-over-the-efforts-to-fix-funding-issues.html.

"Crude Oil." *Priced in Gold*, pricedingold.com/crude-oil/.

Crudele, John. "The Bitcoin 'pyramid scheme' continues to collapse." *New York Post*, 26 Nov. 2018, nypost.com/2018/11/26/the-bitcoin-pyramid-scheme-continues-to-collapse/.

Cryer, Tommy K. JD. "The Memorandum." *Internet Archive*, 2006, archive.org/ stream/pdfy-ulz6hPCb-iFD2xHK/ THE_MEMORANDUM%20IRS%20INCOME%20TAX%20_djvu.txt.

"Currency vs Money: What's the Difference?" *Schiff Gold*, 26 Oct. 2016, schiffgold.com/key-gold-news/currency-vs-money-whats-difference/.

Daltorio, Tony. "8 Reasons To Own Gold." *Investopedia*, 22 June 2019, www.investopedia.com/articles/basics/08/reasons-to-own-gold.asp.

David, Javier E. "Stock market news live: Dow pares losses after Fed announces $500 billion in short-term bank funding." *Yahoo Finance*, 12 Mar. 2020, finance.yahoo.com/news/stock-market-news-live-march-12-013620137.html.

Davidson, Jordan. "April Grocery Prices Jumped the Most in 46 Years." *Eco Watch*, 13 May 2020, www.ecowatch.com/april-grocery-prices-coronavirus-2645989811.html?rebelltitem=2#rebelltitem2.

Davidson, Paul. "The odds of recession are rising but market sell-off doesn't mean it's inevitable." *USA Today*, 9 Mar. 2020, finance.yahoo.com/news/odds-recession-rising-market-sell-202721566.html.

Davidson, Paul. "Trump wants Fed to cut interest rates to zero or below. Here's what it could mean for you." *USA Today*, 12 Sept. 2019, www.usatoday.com/story/money/2019/09/12/interest-rates-what-zero-negative-rates-would-mean-you/2293676001/.
Davies, Antony and James P. Harrigan. "Massive Inflation May Be Coming, Because the US Government Has Cornered Itself into a Fiscal End Game." *FEE*, 21 May 2020, fee.org/articles/massive-inflation-may-be-coming-because-the-us-government-has-cornered-itself-into-a-fiscal-end-game/?fbclid=IwAR2ECln-Wt7EXea4XZnzfkl3G9z8VtdguUeRjMqwCpjQJXZuVRnz6nairik.

Davies, Phil. "The Bank That Hamilton Built." *Federal Reserve Bank of Minneapolis*, 1 Sept. 2007, www.minneapolisfed.org/article/2007/the-bank-that-hamilton-built.

De, Nikhilesh. "UK Central Bank Chief Sees Digital Currency Displacing US Dollar as Global Reserve." *Coindesk*, 23 Aug. 2019, www.coindesk.com/bank-of-england-governor-calls-for-digital-currency-replacement-to-the-dollar?fbclid=IwAR1JBToRF3ui7otU4G3VT5vmY0GwU5Au92wDa-HpwHvzJ0voY8pDh9oeraQ.

DeCambre, Mark. "Brace for the 'deepest recession on record,' says BofA analysts, as jobless claims surge to 6.6 million." *Market Watch*, 2 Apr. 2020, www.marketwatch.com/story/brace-for-the-deepest-recession-on-record-says-bofa-analysts-as-jobless-claims-surge-to-66-million-2020-04-02?reflink=mw_share_facebook&fbclid=IwAR07I04dpmNf919IORdxeC1Ci3V2yzx4DNwllgmEY03c-OpmIpg8lyPh1fs.

DeCambre, Mark. "Gold ends above $2,000 for the first time in history as U.S. dollar and bond yields recede." *MarketWatch*, 4 Aug. 2020, www.marketwatch.com/story/gold-prices-edge-higher-but-march-to-2000-hamstrung-by-rising-dollar-2020-08-04?

reflink=mw_share_facebook&fbclid=IwAR3kMJFKUkS_YYs3VgKWB_ExX56
Lljyb8PIKshDarrWLsNmmQREHPp3sYac.

"Definition of 'Quantitative Easing.'" *The Economic Times,*
economictimes.indiatimes.com/definition/quantitative-easing.

Del Castillo, Michael. "Trillion-Dollar Stimulus Jumpstarts Project To Issue
Central Bank Currency On Ethereum." *Forbes*, 25 Mar. 2020, www.forbes.com/
sites/michaeldelcastillo/2020/03/25/trillion-dollar-stimulus-jumpstarts-project-to-
issue-central-bank-currency-on-ethereum/?
fbclid=IwAR19L3HysNicGD7MrSHy0osbLVC4_pGgzT_ArXLK31ZH_rxBNtk
HlXhLtIM#fc5153a47bc0.

"Denis Healey > Quotes > Quotable Quote." *Good Reads*, www.goodreads.com/
quotes/40800-world-events-do-not-occur-by-accident-they-are-made.

Derby, Michael S. "Fed Adds $82 Billion to Financial Markets." *The Wall Street
Journal*, 14 Jan. 2020, www.wsj.com/articles/fed-adds-82-billion-to-financial-
markets-11579016506.

Derby, Michael S,. "Fed's $100 Billion Repo Intervention Falls Short Of Bank
Demand." *The Wall Street Journal,* 4 Mar. 2020, www.wsj.com/articles/feds-100-
billion-repo-intervention-falls-short-of-bank-demand-11583332932?
fbclid=IwAR1J-
Zph20xp456s6uBSTArVVWXeV52Pd6EINx3Yqn4wRKS3cpZPD9EaUlQ.

Dirkmaat, Olav. "Do Not Worry about Gold Confiscation." *Gold Republic*, 16 Jun.
2015, www.goldrepublic.com/news/gold-confiscation.

"Dividends In Action: How They Work And What To Do With Them." *Future
Advisor*, www.futureadvisor.com/content/resources/getting-started/portfolio-
strategy/why-dividend-paying-stocks-have-advantages-long-term.

"Dividend Stocks." *Investopedia*, www.investopedia.com/dividend-
stocks-4689744.

Divine, John. "5 Reasons Not to Invest in Gold." *US News*, 10 Jul. 2018,
money.usnews.com/investing/articles/2018-07-10/5-reasons-not-to-invest-in-gold.

Dmitry, Baxter. "Soros and His Minions Are FURIOUS As Trump Uses
COVID-19 To End Globalism & Bring Jobs Back To US." *News Punch*, 21 Mar.
2020, newspunch.com/soros-and-minions-furious-trump-uses-covid-19-end-
globalism-bring-jobs-back-us/?fbclid=IwAR2OwnwijZrabO8EWe-
uMKhEQ9w0LhgOPV50UrytfsyhITBiSFa2pG7ZuDg.

Dokko, Jane, et al. "Monetary Policy and the Housing Bubble."
Federalreserve.gov, 22 Dec. 2009, www.federalreserve.gov/pubs/feds/
2009/200949/200949pap.pdf.

"Dollar Volume Liquidity." *Investopedia*, 21 Aug. 2019, www.investopedia.com/ terms/d/dollar-volume-liquidity.asp.

Donohue, Kieran. "Considering Real Estate Investing? 5 Pros and Cons." *37th Parallel Properties*, 37parallel.com/considering-real-estate-investing/.

Dorn, James A. "Ending Tax Socialism." *CATO Institute*, 13 Sept. 1996, www.cato.org/publications/commentary/ending-tax-socialism.

Dougherty, Conor and Luis Ferré-Sadurní. "California Approves Statewide Rent Control to Ease Housing Crisis." *New York Times*, 11 Sept. 2019, www.nytimes.com/2019/09/11/business/economy/california-rent-control.html? fbclid=IwAR3PhZHk2HWFvj6QoQZXYEc19rNPVY8qd-ZjanXS-1Pm8nXmt3uR2jsjpNA.

Doyle v. Mitchell Bros. Co., 247 U.S. 179, 185 (1918).

Duberstein, Billy. "4 Dividend Investing Tips That Could Earn You Thousands." *The Motley Fool,* 7 Dec. 2019, www.fool.com/investing/2019/12/07/4-dividend-investing-tips-that-could-earn-you-thou.aspx.

Duclos, Susan. "Surprise, Surprise! Did You Know That You Don't Own Your Bank Deposits Anymore?" *Internet Marketer*, 10 Jan. 2015, www.internetmarketer.com.au/bankruptcy/your-money-is-not-safe-in-the-bank-anymore-be-warned-watch-this-warning-video-now/.

Durden, Tyler. "If You Feel Like Something Really, Really Bad Is About To Happen, You're Definitely Not Alone." *Zero Hedge*, 11 Sept. 2020, www.zerohedge.com/personal-finance/if-you-feel-something-really-really-bad-about-happen-youre-definitely-not-alone? utm_campaign=&utm_content=ZeroHedge%3A%20The%20Durden%20Dispatch &utm_medium=email&utm_source=zh_newsletter&fbclid=IwAR0GcPMLmadU b8gu1UkFCgGEXlCdoA06CObVf2Mp7jf-WX5aWJIpGjEjd-s.

Durden, Tyler. "JPMorgan Now Expects A Global Depression In The Second Quarter." *ZeroHedge*, 18 Mar. 2020, www.zerohedge.com/economics/jpmorgan-now-expects-a-global-depression-second-quarter?fbclid=IwAR28Uak-h-A87LADh8EFvockAS47EoUjzZ1aCIB920ndvAGrjlkayhFVgro.

Durden, Tyler. "This Is What Happens To Gold In A Hyperinflationary Currency Crisis: Ukraine Edition." *Zero Hedge*, 25 Feb. 2012, archive.is/aiYLX.

Durden, Tyler. "WHO Urges People To Go Cashless Because 'Dirty Banknotes Can Spread The Virus.'" *Activist Post*, 4 Mar. 2020, www.activistpost.com/ 2020/03/who-urges-people-to-go-cashless-because-dirty-banknotes-can-spread-the-virus.html.

Earle, Geoff. "Trump wants IMMEDIATE cash handouts for Americans: Treasury Secretary Steven Mnuchin says everyone will get MORE THAN $1,000 within two weeks once he strikes Senate deal - and tax payments are deferred for 90 days too." *Daily Mail,* 17 Mar. 2020, www.dailymail.co.uk/news/article-8122293/ Donald-Trump-wants-checks-Americans-IMMEDIATELY.html? fbclid=IwAR2x8DfHeY7Heu8dVKQN9UlB3IRvTyiTRo-TRohKhkJXj_o90xdw-_NfGn4.

Edgar, Christy Murdoch. "The 5 Pros and 3 Cons of Real Estate Investing." *Roofstock,* learn.roofstock.com/blog/pros-and-cons-real-estate-investing.

Egan, Matt. "Coronavirus could spark another Great Depression, former Trump adviser warns." *CNN,* 19 Mar. 2020, www.cnn.com/2020/03/19/business/great-depression-coronavirus-kevin-hassett/index.html? fbclid=IwAR28piMwTy6nFBwqzzXWS_08H44rYHGZ5lUJcSpno2rG7IACCWP tB6cgMag.

Eisner v. Macomber, 252 U.S. 189, 207 (1920).

Ellis, Blake. "States seek currencies made of silver and gold." *CNN Money,* 3 Feb. 2012, money.cnn.com/2012/02/03/pf/states_currencies/index.htm.

Elmaazi, Mohammed. "Bill Gates and His 'War Against Cash' Are a Threat to Our Liberty, Economist Warns." *Sputnik News,* 9 May 2020, sputniknews.com/amp/ analysis/202005071079213583-bill-gates-and-his-war-against-cash-are-a-threat-to-our-liberty-economist-warns/? fbclid=IwAR0z0XbSa6efxLY10IKmklyX48piXi4XK66l8f0kWvR8syY4S4iADg TWH5k.

Ely, Bert. "Bitcoin is a Ponzi scheme, and it will collapse like one." *The Hill,* 11 Dec. 2017, thehill.com/opinion/finance/364306-bitcoin-is-a-ponzi-scheme-and-it-will-collapse-like-one.

Emsley, Jonnie. "FTX CEO: Bitcoin price might have gone to zero if BitMEX hadn't gone offline." *Crytostate.com,* 13 Mar. 2020, cryptoslate.com/ftx-ceo-bitcoin-price-might-have-gone-to-zero-if-bitmex-hadnt-gone-offline/.

English, Carleton and Nicholas Jasinski. "Dow Plunges 3,000 Points in Worst Selloff Since 1987." *Market Watch,* 16 Mar. 2020, www.marketwatch.com/ articles/wall-street-is-bracing-for-another-day-of-big-losses-in-the-dow-51584362387? reflink=share_barrons_facebook&fbclid=IwAR0RysDhnM6rURO9b77u8oR7Dsi SFRB6DeSLdaFwYYULAhEmnMPOiwrnVYE.

Evans v. Gore, 253 U.S. 245, 263 (1920).

Fabian, Josh. "Comparing 30 and 60 Days to Expiration." *Tasty Trade,* 15 Aug. 2016, tastytradenetwork.squarespace.com/tt/blog/comparing-30-and-60-days-to-expiration.

"Famous Grace Commission Quote." *Liberty Tree*, quotes.liberty-tree.ca/quote_blog/Grace.Commission.Quote.C455.

"Famous Quotes About International Bankers, the Federal Reserve and America." *4closurefraud.com*, 13 Mar. 2012, 4closurefraud.org/2012/03/13/famous-quotes-about-international-bankers-the-federal-reserve-and-america/.

Farley, Alan. "The Basics of Covered Calls." *Investopedia*, 25 Jun. 2019, www.investopedia.com/articles/optioninvestor/08/covered-call.asp.

Favocci, Christine. "Dr. Ron Paul hits nail on the head in no-nonsense coronavirus interview." *WND*, 30 Mar. 2020, www.wnd.com/2020/03/dr-ron-paul-hits-nail-head-no-nonsense-coronavirus-interview/?fbclid=IwAR1G9cb8BGg9RujH6DN7YqHkEjMRte5uRjoLceDDkl_-CZRrGi4sv2DInYo.

Fearnow, Benjamin. "There Could Be a Financial Crash Before End of Trump's First Term, Experts Say, Citing Looming Debts." *Newsweek*, 23 Sept. 2018, www.newsweek.com/stock-market-1134867?fbclid=IwAR2qYXwuBp-gBoHWnz4O_28BsUBS4tVUldapK0ls2g5O0l3PrW202Lwb_G8.

"February 3, 2007." *Matthew Books*, 3 Feb. 2007, www.matthewbooks.com/february-3-2007/.

"Fed reduces reserve requirement ratios to 0% - effective March 26." *Nexusnewsfeed.com*, www.nexusnewsfeed.com/article/geopolitics/fed-reduces-reserve-requirement-ratios-to-0-effective-march-26/?fbclid=IwAR0i-YjEgQ6HmkoohQjAuM9k68jijImT5GjpxccXF4weYvFs_UWJZBL2HD8.

"Federal Reserve Act (1913)." *American History: From Revolution to Reconstruction and Beyond*, www.let.rug.nl/usa/essays/general/a-brief-history-of-central-banking/federal-reserve-act-(1913).php.

"Federal Reserve issues FOMC statement of longer-run goals and policy strategy." *Board of Governors of the Federal Reserve System*, 25 Jun. 2012, www.federalreserve.gov/newsevents/pressreleases/monetary20120125c.htm.

"Federal Reserve Quotes." *Good Reads*, www.goodreads.com/quotes/tag/federal-reserve.

Federaljacktube. "Former KGB Agent Yuri Bezmenov Explains How to Brainwash a Nation (Full Length)." *Youtube,* 28 Dec. 2012, www.youtube.com/watch?v=5It1zarINv0.

Fernando, Jason. "Inflation." *Investopedia*, 18 Nov. 2020, www.investopedia.com/terms/i/inflation.asp.

Ferrechio, Susan and Nihal Krishan. "Senate GOP unveils $1,200 direct cash payments in massive stimulus proposal." *Washington Examiner*, 19 Mar. 2020, www.washingtonexaminer.com/news/congress/senate-gop-unveils-1-200-direct-cash-payments-in-massive-stimulus-proposal? utm_source=WEX_Breaking+News+Alert_03%2F19%2F2020&utm_medium=e mail&utm_campaign=WEX_Breaking+News&rid=24098895&fbclid=IwAR3TJ wtD_8r7Exl00wd4c2rniXXE6fe4bsW6hwPNn6vDehtS24kqjFX4CIw.

Fishman, Stephen. "LC Asset Protection and Charging Orders: An Overview of State Laws." *Nolo*, www.nolo.com/legal-encyclopedia/llc-asset-protection-charging-orders.html.

Flint v. Stone Tracy Co., 220 U.S. 107, 151-152 (1911).

Flipside Crypto. "Cryptocurrency in Focus: Outbreak Takes Toll on Bitcoin." *The Street*, 11 Mar. 2020, www.thestreet.com/investing/cryptocurrency/ cryptocurrency-in-focus-outbreak-takes-toll-on-bitcoin? fbclid=IwAR12wqco2v8bJF2MSpIkN2bHincr7Sn98JMzHWhyaXS7LRbAc7e6m vV-ujk.

Fox, F. Earle. "Conspiracy Theory: Fact or Fictionregarding the Federal Reserve & the IRS?" *Internet Archive Wayback Machine*, 17 July 2010, web.archive.org/ web/20170406104258/http://www.theroadtoemmaus.org/RdLb/21PbAr/Pl/Consp-Fed&IRS.htm.

Frankenfield, Jake. "Bitcoin." *Investopedia*, 30 Jan. 2021, www.investopedia.com/ terms/b/bitcoin.asp.

Freeman, Makia. "7 NWO Agendas Accompanying the Coronavirus Outbreak." *Activist Post*, 21 Feb. 2020, www.activistpost.com/2020/02/7-nwo-agendas-accompanying-the-coronavirus-outbreak.html? fbclid=IwAR07E5b6kYhq6hsL9N2raQ5zRCQvR2BkSlzptepMUAO9l0u-eZ_bnqAdmP4.

"From the Book LINCOLN MONEY MARTYRED." *Cyberclass.net*, www.cyberclass.net/lincoln.htm.

"From Thomas Jefferson to Albert Gallatin, 13 December 1803." *Founders Online, National Archives*, founders.archives.gov/documents/Jefferson/ 01-42-02-0100.

"From Thomas Jefferson to Richard Henry Lee, 17 June 1779." *Founders Online, National Archives*, founders.archives.gov/documents/Jefferson/01-02-02-0128.

Frost, Liam. "The Federal Reserve is printing $1 million every second." *Decrypt.com*, 27 Mar. 2020, decrypt.co/23805/the-federal-reserve-is-printing-1-million-every-second? fbclid=IwAR1D2kiJSMK8jcF2S0GprjdcMnVxZx5YKNrDZTNeMo7u6nF0nffvx 7-q47Q.

Fuerbringer, Jonathan. "Regan Criticizes Fed's Move." *The New York Times*, 20 Jan. 1982, www.nytimes.com/1982/01/20/business/reagan-criticizes-fed-s-move.html.

"Full text of 'Conspiracy Evidence Archives and Quotes.'" *Internet Archive*, archive.org/stream/NWOQuotes14/International%20Bankers-famous%20quotes%20about%20international%20bankers%20wordpress.com-13_djvu.txt.

"Full text of 'The Deep State.'" *Internet Archive*, 4 Jul. 2017, archive.org/stream/TheDeepState/The%20Deep%20State_djvu.txt.

Gad, Sham. "How to Sell Put Options to Benefit in Any Market." *Investopedia*, 6 May 2019, www.investopedia.com/articles/optioninvestor/10/sell-puts-benefit-any-market.asp.

Gadsen, Christopher. "The Stamp Act - A Letter from Christopher Gadsden." *The Royal Colony of South Carolina*, www.carolana.com/SC/Royal_Colony/stamp_act_gadsden_letter.html.

Gammon, George. "Asset Bubbles Explained: Simple And Fast! (COLLABORATION VIDEO)." *Youtube*, 13 Dec. 2019, www.youtube.com/watch?v=eyz7SeSIbqc.

Gammon, George. "CPI Tax Scam: YOU'RE GOING TO LOSE A LOT OF MONEY! (Discover How)." *Youtube*, 11 Dec. 2019, www.youtube.com/watch?v=RA8PX_T1Suw.

Gammon, George. "Dollar Collapse: Can It Happen Overnight? (ANSWERED!)" *Youtube*, 29 Nov. 2019, www.youtube.com/watch?v=P0K-9EQk1PA.

Gammon, George. "Federal Reserve: Discover Lies & Secrets They're Hiding From YOU!" *Youtube*, 27 Nov. 2019, www.youtube.com/watch?v=ha_MFJadAzA.

Gammon, George. "Jim Rickards: His Gold Price Prediction Explained... ($50,000+ IS POSSIBLE!!)" *Youtube*, 6 Dec. 2019, www.youtube.com/watch?v=HpqJ-sFScxA.

Gammon, George. "Quantitative Easing: Will It Cause Hyperinflation? (ANSWER REVEALED)." *Youtube*, 19 Dec. 2019, www.youtube.com/watch?v=b7KafSma3xQ.

Gammon, George. "Quantitative Easing Exposed: Discover How It DESTROYS A SOCIETY!" *Youtube*, 9 Dec. 2019, www.youtube.com/watch?v=d-ifzjfGTkM.

Gammon, George. "Repo Market: Will Year End Doomsday Trigger DOLLAR COLLAPSE?!?." *Youtube*, 27 Dec. 2019, www.youtube.com/watch?v=7jXN42_GxNQ.

Gammon, George. "Repo Market Update: Is The Entire Financial System Broken? (ANSWERED)." *Youtube*, 18 Dec. 2019, www.youtube.com/watch? v=vw6fymmI9B0.

Ganz, David L. "Gold Seizure." *USA Gold*, www.usagold.com/cpmforum/gold-seizure-ganz/.

Garber, Jonathan. "Coronavirus hyperinflation risk looms, buy gold: Peter Schiff." *Yahoo Finance*, 25 Mar. 2020, finance.yahoo.com/news/coronavirus-hyperinflation-looms-buy-gold-124257282.html.

Garber, Jonathan. "Dow plunges over 2,000 points, oil collapses amid price war and coronavirus." *Fox Business*, 9 Mar. 2020, www.foxbusiness.com/markets/us-markets-march-9-2020?fbclid=IwAR3Nf-EknmtR5bQ-ISRm568hH-og7H8_Gq2K34gAa4plAWm2mMH2Ryi-aWM.

Garber, Jonathan. "Gold drops but still has luster long term." *Fox Business*, 13 Mar. 2020, www.foxbusiness.com/markets/gold-price-drops-but-still-has-luster-long-term?fbclid=IwAR2R59v4DB4oqw8vea6qjJB7zPL-uw-nCIr5iwLSa1NiSAw0fk-HsnqpWtk.

"George Bankcroft Quote." *Liberty Tree*, libertytree.ca/quotes/ George.Bancroft.Quote.2BD3.

"George Washington Quote." *Liberty Tree*, libertytree.ca/quotes/ George.Washington.Quote.2BD2.

Glass, Andrew. "Congress issues Continental currency, June 22, 1775." *Politico*, 22 Jun. 2018, www.politico.com/story/2018/06/22/congress-issues-continental-currency-june-22-1775-652244.

"Global Centralization Is the Cause of Crisis - Not the Cure." *NaturalNews.com*, 20 Feb. 2020, www.naturalnews.com/2020-02-20-global-centralization-cause-of-crisis.html.

"Globalists Look To Exploit Coronavirus In Push For Global Government." *Prophecy News Watch*, www.prophecynewswatch.com/article.cfm? recent_news_id=3869&fbclid=IwAR2uc7HdPmGIuKsqSQ7Ayl8pB2K09hWJnB NtTSnZBbKFEM6LVFslmsp-EuE.

"Gold and Silver Bullion and Tax Laws in New Hampshire." *Sound Money Defense League*, www.soundmoneydefense.org/gold-silver-laws-new-hampshire.

"Gold and Silver Bullion and Tax Laws in Washington." *Sound Money Defense League*, www.soundmoneydefense.org/gold-silver-laws-washington.

Goldstein, Steve. "Britain sells its first bonds at a negative interest rate." *Market Watch*, 20 May 2020, www.marketwatch.com/story/britain-sells-its-first-bonds-at-a-negative-interest-rate-2020-05-20?siteid=yhoof2&yptr=yahoo.

Goldstein, Steve. "Swift market reaction to Fed may be more about what it didn't do than what it did, analysts say." *Market Watch*, 11 Jun. 2020, www.marketwatch.com/story/swift-market-reaction-to-fed-may-be-more-about-what-it-didnt-do-than-what-it-did-analysts-say-2020-06-11?siteid=yhoof2&yptr=yahoo.

Gomez, Christian. "EU Globalists and Chinese Communists Team Up To Protect NWO." *The New American*, 25 Jun. 2018, www.thenewamerican.com/world-news/europe/item/29379-eu-globalists-and-chinese-communists-team-up-to-protect-nwo#disqus_thread.

Gomez, Christian. "Senate Coronavirus Stimulus Swells to $2 Trillion; Final Vote on Monday." *The New American*, 21 Mar. 2020, www.thenewamerican.com/usnews/congress/item/35214-senate-coronavirus-stimulus-swells-to-2-trillion-final-vote-on-monday?fbclid=IwAR1KJyfp2ynnXGGKePC0A2G3873eBSbYaOI7BNSlQeplgEq2d1423WkLmBQ.

Gondo, Nancy. "How To Invest: Exactly How Much Daily Volume Should You Look For In A Great Stock?" *Investor's Business Daily*, 12 Nov. 2019, www.investors.com/how-to-invest/investors-corner/how-much-volume-should-a-stock-have/.

"Gordon Brown calls for global government to tackle coronavirus." *The Guardian*, www.theguardian.com/politics/2020/mar/26/gordon-brown-calls-for-global-government-to-tackle-coronavirus?fbclid=IwAR2tWJfhjwJ7VjVG4gSorvxAJOrCaNYGNXTGr1XUsgzIxNkrfOWZSMSVCMg.

"Greenback." *Investopedia*, 30 Apr. 2019, www.investopedia.com/terms/g/greenback.asp.

"Greenback." *Museum of American Finance*, www.moaf.org/exhibits/checks_balances/abraham-lincoln/greenback.

"Greenback Labor Party." *Ohio History Central*, ohiohistorycentral.org/w/Greenback_Labor_Party.

"Greenback movement." *Encyclopedia Brittanica*, 6 Dec. 2019, www.britannica.com/event/Greenback-movement.

"Greenbacks: Definition & History." *Study.com*, study.com/academy/lesson/greenbacks-definition-lesson.html.

Greenberg, Jay. "Pompeo: 'Something Not Quite Right' About Feinstein Praising China." *Neon Nettle*, Neon Nettle, 3 Aug. 2020, neonnettle.com/news/12194-pompeo-something-not-quite-right-about-feinstein-praising-china.

Greenley, Larry. "Next Step to World Government: Atlantic Union." *The New American*, 9 Mar. 2020, www.thenewamerican.com/print-magazine/item/34944-next-step-to-world-government-atlantic-union?fbclid=IwAR2u5WqOk-netjF2WHw3U0kIuZBLFk8jXgW_6eUrs2lUdyJ0olEVD0rMi0A.

Greenspan, Alan. "Gold and Economic Freedom." *Constitution Society*, www.constitution.org/mon/greenspan_gold.htm.

Greenwald, Glenn. "Top Senate Democrat: bankers 'own' the U.S. Congress." *Salon*, 30 Apr. 2009, www.salon.com/2009/04/30/ownership/.

Greyerz, Egon. "Gold Confiscation and Manipulation." *Gold Switzerland*, 15 Nov. 2018, goldswitzerland.com/gold-confiscation-and-manipulation/.

Griffin, G. Edward. "JFK And The Federal Reserve." *Freedom Force International*, 16 May 2017, freedomforceinternational.org/position-statements/jfk_and_fed/.

Griffith, Joel. "A Backdoor Central Bank Bailout of State Governments." *Real Clear Markets*, 2 May 2020, www.realclearmarkets.com/articles/2020/05/02/a_backdoor_central_bank_bailout_of_state_governments_490609.html?fbclid=IwAR2ram3WBD1YDtA-phyhdAVkT1c8kageamzMChCjYT3r4duZ2iMWycBEYOY.

Griffith, Keith. "Dow plunges 10% in Wall Street's worst trading day since 1987 despite Fed pumping $1.5 TRILLION into bond markets amid panic over Trump's European travel ban." *Dailymail.com*, 12 Mar. 2020, www.dailymail.co.uk/news/article-8104731/Dow-set-fall-1-200-points-S-P-500-points-bear-territory.html?fbclid=IwAR02Prew4tzJHUM_6MmzNhg7am1Fsw3HucIHfY98rMIifhE9OzcA3jZeiM0.

Grzeszczzak, Jocelyn. "Under Trump's Watch, America's National Debt Has Increased by $6.6 Trillion." *Newsweek*, 29 Jul. 2020, www.newsweek.com/under-trumps-watch-americas-national-debt-has-increased-66-trillion-1521418?utm_term=Autofeed&utm_medium=Social&utm_source=Facebook&fbclid=IwAR14ZF2HG9b1Xh-cF-TjIlG6PeU3Syf5l5xsXr8IVtgVkWDZcmm9aVD2JHc#Echobox=1596040317.

Haber, Bob. "The Fed Fires 'The Big One.'" *Forbes,* 16 Mar. 2020, www.forbes.com/sites/bobhaber/2020/03/16/the-fed-fires-the-big-one/?fbclid=IwAR0j5PP70PzRQM6lOpfHCaTaHkZQp4dYm4o1pNCazj2PX7aitN-uZ8mGmEU#6c90761e6aa8.

Hagopian, Joachim. "One World Governance and the Council on Foreign Relations. 'We Shall Have World Government...by Conquest or Consent.'"

Global Research, 24 Jan. 2021, www.globalresearch.ca/one-world-governance-and-the-council-on-foreign-relations-we-shall-have-world-government-by-conquest-or-consent/5541363.

Hale v. Henkel, 201 U.S. 43, 74 (1906).

Hamilton, Jesse and Rich Miller. "Fed Warns Prolonged Low Interest Rates Could Spark Instability." *Bloomberg*, 15 Nov. 2019, www.bloomberg.com/news/articles/2019-11-15/fed-warns-prolonged-low-interest-rates-could-spark-instability.

Hankoff, Nick. "Coronavirus Being Used to Scare You Away From Using Cash." *Advocate,* 24 Mar. 2020, www.theadvocates.org/2020/03/coronavirus-being-used-to-scare-you-away-from-using-cash/?fbclid=IwAR3iYN4Niwu8AawMIhSH8kbohngSlHRUmgK_gOdFAE-LFIz0RR3xRu5-Awg.

Haskins, Jane. "LLC Asset Protection: How to Protect your Personal Assets as an LLC Owner." *Legal Zoom*, www.legalzoom.com/articles/llc-asset-protection-how-to-protect-your-personal-assets-as-an-llc-owner.

Haskins, Justin. "Introducing the 'Great Reset,' World Leaders' Radical Plan to Transform the Economy." *MSN*, MSN, 25 June 2020, www.msn.com/en-us/news/politics/introducing-the-great-reset-world-leaders-radical-plan-to-transform-the-economy/ar-BB15XGsU?fbclid=IwAR0nHYaWwbRdVMkSXaHZtrRXG7XbRMRBS55XWIzGCMR6InTtHuuQAn8iiu0.

Haskins, Justin. "The Fed is pushing America dangerously close to socialism." *Glennbeck.com*, 23 Mar. 2020, www.glennbeck.com/blog/the-fed-is-pushing-america-dangerously-close-to-socialism.

Hatfield, Stuart. "Faking It: British Counterfeiting During the American Revolution." *Journal of the American Revolution,* 7 Oct. 2015, allthingsliberty.com/2015/10/faking-it-british-counterfeiting-during-the-american-revolution/.

Hawkins, Justin. "Al Gore, UN Secretary-General, others now demanding 'Great Reset''of global capitalism." *Fox Business,* 24 Jun. 2020, www.foxbusiness.com/markets/al-gore-un-secretary-general-great-reset-global-capitalism?fbclid=IwAR18gs71dBfqNO0dqMKpi0uM-pRdMlU8yL2qaF_F_n5n2Xo6usxpzcuo37Q.

Hayes, Adam. "Negative Interest Rate Policy (NIRP) Definition." *Investopedia*, 7 May 2019, www.investopedia.com/terms/n/negative-interest-rate-policy-nirp.asp.

Heeb, Gina. "The Federal Reserve is looking into developing a digital currency in the US, Powell confirms." *Markets Insider*, 20 Nov. 2019, markets.businessinsider.com/news/stocks/the-federal-reserve-is-looking-into-developing-digital-currency-us-2019-11-1028705211.

Held, Sergio. "Venezuela's currency: Worth more as craft paper than as money." *AJ Impact*, 24 Dec. 2019, www.aljazeera.com/ajimpact/venezuela-currency-worth-craft-paper-money-191224144545023.html.

Hendrickson, John. "Budget and Tax Lessons from President Calvin Coolidge." *Calvin Coolidge Presidential Foundation*, 10 Dec. 2014, www.coolidgefoundation.org/blog/budget-and-tax-lessons-from-president-calvin-coolidge/.

Henney, Megan. "Fed's Powell warns coronavirus recovery could stretch through end of 2021." *Fox Business*, 17 May 2020, www.foxbusiness.com/markets/federal-reserve-jerome-powell-coronavirus-pandemic-economic-recovery?fbclid=IwAR1bTP1DicnDOcd3ZPq_OKM1B6IAWKwxijeD3rtxddezBGBHtwlbMJ6cYqw.

"Here Come the Bailouts, Starting With the Airlines." *The New York Tims*, 17 Mar. 2020, www.nytimes.com/2020/03/17/business/dealbook/coronavirus-airline-bailouts.html?fbclid=IwAR0OsdRHoS5atSi4c6hYLNNIcFEiTo5c_fkTSxP2Kr_JY6QP3AJhYG1ThNM.

Herlean, Greg. "The Top 10 Risks Of Bitcoin Investing (And How To Avoid Them)." *Forbes*, 5 Dec. 2018, www.forbes.com/sites/forbesfinancecouncil/2018/12/05/the-top-10-risks-of-bitcoin-investing-and-how-to-avoid-them/#5f131fc52407.

Herron, Janna. "'Money is on sale:' What does the historically low 10-year Treasury yield mean for your wallet?" *Yahoo Finance*, 10 Mar. 2020, finance.yahoo.com/news/treasury-yield-your-wallet-203628849.html?guccounter=1.

Hill, Andrew T. "The Second Bank of the United States." *Federal Reserve History*, 5 Dec. 2015, www.federalreservehistory.org/essays/second_bank_of_the_us.

"History - Essays: Andrew Jackson, banks, and the Panic of." *The Lehrman Institute*, lehrmaninstitute.org/history/Andrew-Jackson-1837.html.

"History of Banking and Money Key Excerpts From Carroll Quigley's Tragedy and Hope." *Wanttoknow.info*, www.wanttoknow.info/articles/quigley_carroll.tragedy_hope_banking_money_history.

History.com Editors. "Andrew Jackson narrowly escapes assassination." *History*, 16 Nov. 2009, www.history.com/this-day-in-history/andrew-jackson-narrowly-escapes-assassination.

History.com Editors. "Andrew Jackson shuts down Second Bank of the U.S." *History*, 16 Nov. 2009, www.history.com/this-day-in-history/andrew-jackson-shuts-down-second-bank-of-the-u-s.

History.com Editors. "Calvin Coolidge." *History*, 27 Oct. 2009, www.history.com/topics/us-presidents/calvin-coolidge.

History.com Editors. "Congress issues Continental currency." *A&E Television Networks*, 13 Nov. 2019, www.history.com/this-day-in-history/congress-issues-continental-currency.

History.com Editors. "James K. Polk." *History*, 29 Oct. 2009, www.history.com/topics/us-presidents/james-polk.

Hitchcock, Andrew. "Historical Timeline of the Rothschild Dynasty - Part 3." *The Sirius Report*, 17 Aug. 2015, www.thesiriusreport.com/geopolitics/historical-timeline-rothschild-dynasty-3/.

Hitchcock, Andrew. "Historical Timeline of the Rothschild Dynasty - Part 4." *The Sirius Report*, 18 Aug. 2016, www.thesiriusreport.com/geopolitics/historical-timeline-rothschild-dynasty-part-4/.

Hitchcock, Andrew. "Historical Timeline of the Rothschild Dynasty – Part 5." *The Sirius Report*, 19 Aug. 2016, www.thesiriusreport.com/geopolitics/historical-timeline-rothschild-dynasty-5/.

Hitchcock, Andrew. "Historical Timeline of the Rothschild Dynasty – Part 6 (final)." *The Sirius Report*, 20 Aug. 2016, www.thesiriusreport.com/geopolitics/historical-timeline-rothschild-dynasty-6/.

Hodges, James P. PhD. "Federal Income Tax: 2nd Plank of Communism." *Leadership By George Washington*, 12 Nov. 2011, leadershipbygeorge.blogspot.com/2011/11/federal-income-tax-2nd-plank-of.html.

Hodges, James P. PhD and Cynthia F. Hodges, JD, LLM, MA. "FED Up: Founding Fathers, the Banking System, and the Federal Reserve." *Leadership By George Washington*, 21 Apr. 2010, leadershipbygeorge.blogspot.com/2010/04/fed-up-founding-fathers-banking-system.html.

Holland, Ben. "A 5,000-Year-Old Plan to Erase Debts Is Now a Hot Topic in America." *Bloomberg*, 10 Dec. 2019, www.bloomberg.com/news/articles/2019-12-10/a-5-000-year-old-plan-to-erase-debts-is-hot-topic-now-in-america?utm_campaign=pol&utm_medium=bd&utm_source=applenews.

Horan, Patrick. "5 Problems with MMT." *The Bridge*, 18 Mar. 2019, www.mercatus.org/bridge/commentary/5-problems-mmt.

Hornberger, Jacob. "Monetary Destruction in America." *Tenth Amendment Center*, 7 Jun. 2020, tenthamendmentcenter.com/2020/06/07/monetary-destruction-in-

a   m   e   r   i   c   a   /   ?
fbclid=IwAR1qznHUtpPxV4SZfCJk0G9H9gTS2kepV1ZU5BKoX_o06DxBXusf
HyCPK6s.

Horvath, Sarah. "How To Invest In Dividend-Paying Stocks." *Benzinga*, 25 Nov.
2019, www.benzinga.com/money/how-to-invest-in-dividend-stocks/.

Huang, Zheping. "Chinese President Xi Jinping Has Vowed to Lead the 'New
World Order.'" *Quartz*, Quartz, 22 Feb. 2017, qz.com/916382/chinese-president-
x i - j i n p i n g - h a s - v o w e d - t o - l e a d - t h e - n e w - w o r l d - o r d e r / ?
fbclid=IwAR3uEWMJb4jsExoUgiSFrffjwwFFOJTvnewTkCSNL5Pl4dbGDWu4
KeQmaNs.

Huff, Ethan. "John McAfee just withdrew his famous 2020 prediction about
Bitcoin, now says the cryptocurrency is essentially obsolete." *Natural News*, 12
Jan. 2020, www.naturalnews.com/2020-01-12-john-mcafee-withdrew-
famous-2020-bitcoin-prediction-obsolete.html.

Hughes, Horus. "Crypto Market Meltdown Continues as Bitcoin Price Drops
Below $5,000." *Cointelegraph*, 12 Mar. 2020, cointelegraph.com/news/crypto-
market-meltdown-continues-as-bitcoin-price-drops-below-5-000.
Imbert, Fred and Thomas Franck. "Stocks plummet again after Trump fails to
quell virus fears." *MSN Money*, 12 Mar. 2020, www.msn.com/en-us/money/
markets/stocks-plummet-again-after-trump-fails-to-quell-virus-fears/ar-
BB112FMf?ocid=sf2.

Inconvenient Truths, www.inconvenienttruths.net/.

"Independent Treasury System." *Encyclopedia.com*, 29 Feb. 2020,
www.encyclopedia.com/history/united-states-and-canada/us-history/independent-
treasury-system.

"Independent Treasury System: Creation of the System." *Infoplease*,
www.infoplease.com/encyclopedia/history/north-america/us/independent-
treasury-system/creation-of-the-system.

"Indexing Income Taxes for Inflation: Why It Matters." *ITEP*, 22 Aug. 2016,
itep.org/indexing-income-taxes-for-inflation-why-it-matters-1/.

"Inflation Calculator." *US Inflation Calculator*, www.usinflationcalculator.com.

Inman, Phillip. "Pandemic is chance to reset global economy, says Prince
Charles." *The Guardian,* 3 Jun. 2020, www.theguardian.com/uk-news/2020/jun/
03/pandemic-is-chance-to-reset-global-economy-says-prince-charles?
CMP=share_btn_fb&fbclid=IwAR2lvjSEa2foRKfNLamD0uZlwCKQr3WsdZg58
AZ7lLRbjURrukz7puuscjM.

Innes, Stephen. "Currency Carnage: FX Market's Unhinged." *Yahoo Finance*, 18 Mar. 2020, finance.yahoo.com/news/currency-carnage-fx-market-unhinged-222325310.html.

"Inverted Yield Curve." *Investopedia*, 7 Nov. 2019, www.investopedia.com/terms/i/invertedyieldcurve.asp.

"Inverted Yield Curve: what is it and how does it predict disaster?" *I Will Teach You*, 10 Jun. 2019, www.iwillteachyoutoberich.com/blog/inverted-yield-curve/.

ITM Trading, Inc. "And Central Banks Using Up Their Ammo." *Youtube,* 18 Dec. 2018, www.youtube.com/watch?v=NvWm6Qkp5gU.

ITM Trading, Inc. "Stocks, Cash, Debt… Q&A with Lynette Zang and Eric Griffin." *Youtube,* 2 Jan. 2020, www.youtube.com/watch?v=TMvw4jD0oO4.

Jackson, Andrew. "December 8, 1829: First Annual Message to Congress." *UVA Miller Center*, 8 Dec. 1829, millercenter.org/the-presidency/presidential-speeches/december-8-1829-first-annual-message-congress.

Jackson, Andrew. "The Project Gutenberg EBook of State of the Union Addresses of Andrew Jackson." *Gutenberg.org*, 21 Nov. 2014, www.gutenberg.org/files/5016/5016-h/5016-h.htm.

"Jackson Vetoes Re-Charter of the Second Bank of the US." *Museum of American Finance*, www.moaf.org/exhibits/checks_balances/andrew-jackson/broadsheet.

"James K Polk." *ESRI,* www.arcgis.com/apps/Cascade/index.html?appid=e8e9072ed87e41e985e8add9a1f28969.

"James K. Polk: Battle of the Bank." *Spark Notes*, www.sparknotes.com/biography/polk/section4/.

Jasper, William F. "Joe Biden on Creating a 'New World Order.'" *The New American*, 8 Apr. 2013, www.thenewamerican.com/usnews/politics/item/15036-joe-biden-on-creating-a-new-world-order?fbclid=IwAR1NnFrzxnXBi1mJKf94lRmSQQMCaoWo6ndOCvAlRB2JXmGWWBnV0OAyxlw.

"Jefferson on the Economy." *American Policy Roundtable*, web.archive.org/web/20170608041633/www.aproundtable.org/tps2.cfm?ID=1028&issuecode=taxes.

Jefferson, Thomas. "Opinion on the Constitutionality of the Bill for Establishing a National Bank." *National Archives*, founders.archives.gov/documents/Jefferson/01-19-02-0051.

Jefferson, Thomas. "TJ: Plan for Reducing the Circulating Medium, 23 Nov. 1819, 23 November 2019." *Founders Online*, National Archives and Records Administration, founders.archives.gov/documents/Jefferson/98-01-02-0909.

Jeffrey, Terence P. "Federal Debt Tops $26 Trillion for First Time; Jumps $2 Trillion in Just 63 Days." *CNS News*, 10 Jun. 2020, www.cnsnews.com/article/ washington/terence-p-jeffrey/federal-debt-tops-26-trillion-first-time-jumps-2-t r i l l i o n - j u s t ? fbclid=IwAR0I0e87psr963MMEXQboOmw8eIxy4fONPHhb8VsodVscYE1YN9 PMEv897c.

"John Maynard Keynes Quotes – Keynes Said It." *John Maynard Keynes*, www.maynardkeynes.org/keynes-quotes.html.

Jones, Claire. "When gold and geopolitics clash, it's rarely pretty." *Yahoo Finance*, 21 May 2020, finance.yahoo.com/m/66217439-be36-3483-bc04-a44f62c17a35/when-gold-and-geopolitics.html.

Jones, Collin. "United Nations comes out in support of Antifa." *The Post Millenial*, 20 Jun. 2020, thepostmillennial.com/un-comes-out-in-support-of-antifa?fbclid=IwAR2-Euv-btLPRgi0CcKwKvqdkViWhpkOGnlsSauTXTxnXK-s4jMwyyaynA0.

Jones, Stack. "An Essay On The History Of Banking." *The Banking Swindle*, 1 Jan. 2018, criminalbankingmonopoly.wordpress.com/.

Jones, Stewart. "The Founders Warned Us About Central Banking." *Ron Paul Liberty Report*, 10 Oct. 2019, www.ronpaullibertyreport.com/archives/the-f o u n d e r s - w a r n e d - u s - a b o u t - c e n t r a l - b a n k i n g ? fbclid=IwAR1GtgHBthCfZDgqhObnuqCX2hO9116CjGntgnKJ75rw5KXrb5U3m KOVFKI.

Josephson, Amelia. "Investing in Silver." *Smartasset*, 15 Aug. 2019, smartasset.com/investing/investing-in-silver.

Justice Clifford's dissent. *Legal Tender Cases*, 79 U.S. 457 (1870).

Kagan, Julia. "Fractional Reserve Banking." *Investopedia*, 18 Dec. 2020, www.investopedia.com/terms/f/fractionalreservebanking.asp.

Katzeff, Paul. "Recession Ahead? Time To Shift Your Stock Mutual Funds To Cash?" *Investor's Business Daily*, 23 May 2020, www.investors.com/etfs-and-funds/personal-finance/retirement-savings-time-shift-mutual-funds-cash/? src=A00220&yptr=yahoo.

Kaza, Greg. "The U.S. Presidents and the Money Issue." *FEE*, 1 Apr. 1996, fee.org/articles/the-us-presidents-and-the-money-issue/.

Kennon, Joshua. "Reasons to Consider Investing in Dividend Stocks." *The Balance*, 22 Jan. 2019, www.thebalance.com/consider-investing-in-dividend-stocks-4059284.

Kent, Simon. "U.N.'s Guterres Warns a 'New Model for Global Governance' Is Coming." *Breitbart*, 21 July 2020, www.breitbart.com/politics/2020/07/21/u-n-s-guterres-warns-new-model-for-global-governance-is-coming-to-redistribute-power-and-wealth/?fbclid=IwAR3iWpHvEbWjTz0adZkF0QBtiAnj8AmI-k0GD2bYlQaDLFVVF7B8z7edC6A.

Kenton, Will. "Bubble." *Investopedia*, 30 June 2019, www.investopedia.com/terms/b/bubble.asp.

Kentoni, Will. "Hyperinflation." *Investopedia*, 8 Jul. 2018, www.investopedia.com/terms/h/hyperinflation.asp.

Keoun, Bradley. "After Coronavirus 'War,' Bretton Woods-Style Shakeup Could Dethrone the Dollar." *Yahoo Finance*, 27 Mar. 2020, finance.yahoo.com/news/coronavirus-war-bretton-woods-style-130000284.html.

Keoun, Bradly. "Fed Considers Letting Inflation Run Hot, Vice Chair Clarida Says." *The Street*, 24 Feb. 2019, www.thestreet.com/markets/fed-considers-letting-inflation-run-hot-vice-chair-clarida-says-14875204.

Kilgore, Tomi. "'Bearmageddon' for stocks appears to be upon us, strategist says." *Market Watch*, 15 Mar. 2020, www.marketwatch.com/story/bearmageddon-for-stocks-appears-to-be-upon-us-strategist-says-2020-03-15?reflink=mw_share_facebook&fbclid=IwAR1v5viyQmNrbpheaogqtoBY8mq8C63Ma4nttdiyxO9A6xTWxJOqIVU3c-Q.

Kirgis, Frederic L. "International Agreements and U.S. Law." *Insights*, American Society of International Law, 27 May 1997, www.asil.org/insights/volume/2/issue/5/international-agreements-and-us-law.

Kissinger, Henry A. "The Coronavirus Pandemic Will Forever Alter the World Order." *The Wall Street Journal*, 3 Apr. 2020, www.henryakissinger.com/articles/the-coronavirus-pandemic-will-forever-alter-the-world-order/?fbclid=IwAR0TppEvo0h7SnGzo7ajGdasG46qNlS-AIIFjeXy6PKPfLrYux-z0vzKvcU.

Kiyosaki, Kim. "The (Many) Pros and (Few) Cons of Real Estate Investing." *RichDad.com*, 6 Jun. 2019, www.richdad.com/pros-and-cons-of-real-estate.

Klein, Peter G. "The Financial System Is Now Totally Dependent on Government Intervention." *Mises Institute*, 16 Mar. 2020, mises.org/power-market/financial-system-now-totally-dependent-government-intervention?fbclid=IwAR3eKYaKZMJqyM91joNY59D1nTY6LqHPhsz4iz1fQS2VowwbR5YGkAlOHPA.

Knight, David. "Fed Introduces Cashless Society." *Info Wars*, 6 Oct. 2020, www.infowars.com/posts/fed-introduces-cashless-society/.

Knowlton v. Moore, 178 U.S. 41, 47 (1900).

Knutson, Lawrence L. "Jackson's Ghost Looms Over Debt." *CBS News*, 7 Feb. 2020, www.cbsnews.com/news/jacksons-ghost-looms-over-debt/.

Korotayev, Viktor. "Russia's gold & near-zero debt give it best chance of thriving in post-coronavirus apocalypse – Max Keiser." *RT*, 20 Mar. 2020, www.rt.com/business/483518-russia-best-position-crisis/?fbclid=IwAR1K8jnIjGwTN45FT3K-gCJHnjDPo4wiitY5VMJQmzjqOgLnmtv4ub4Z6F4.

Kreiter, Marcy. "Too Big To Fail: US Federal Reserve Says No More Bailouts; Burden To Shift To Investors." *International Business Times*, 1 Nov. 2015, www.ibtimes.com/too-big-fail-us-federal-reserve-says-no-more-bailouts-burden-shift-investors-2164040.

Krugman, Paul. "Abraham Lincoln, Inflationist." *The New York Times*, 10 Feb. 2011, www.nytimes.com/2011/02/11/opinion/11krugman.html.

Krugman, Paul. "Bitcoin is basically a Ponzi scheme." *The Seattle Times*, 30 Jan. 2018, www.seattletimes.com/opinion/bitcoin-is-basically-a-ponzi-scheme/.

Kuepper, Justin. "What Negative Interest Rates Mean for Investors." *The Balance*, 30 Nov. 2019, www.thebalance.com/what-negative-interest-rates-mean-for-investors-1978886.

Lacalle, Daniel. PhD. "The Fed Panicked, and Its Rate Cut Is Making the Economy Worse." *Mises Institute*, 9 Mar. 2020, mises.org/wire/fed-panicked-and-its-rate-cut-making-economy-worse?fbclid=IwAR31Z6Qs6p8b9dRJ-_YZBaEuHz4Pq0SQoLzOH7W2TJlQ3G4vboe6ViwOuMI#.XmbHfDyEiq4.twitter.

Landa, Allison. "5 Pros and Cons of Investing in Real Estate: Are You Ready for the Risk?" *HomeLight*, 31 Dec. 2018, www.homelight.com/blog/pros-and-cons-of-investing-in-real-estate/.

Leachman, Michael and David A. Super. "States Likely Could Not Control Constitutional Convention on Balanced Budget Amendment or Other Issues." *Center on Budget and Policy Priorities*, 18 Jan. 2017, www.cbpp.org/research/states-likely-could-not-control-constitutional-convention-on-balanced-budget-amendment-or.

"Leveraging Limited Liability for Asset Protection." *Bizfilings.com*, www.bizfilings.com/toolkit/research-topics/running-your-business/asset-strategies/leveraging-limited-liability-for-asset-protection.

Levis, Nick. "New World Disorder: Why Geithner's IMF SDR Plan For A Global Currency Looks a Bit Like High Treason." *Business Insider*, Business Insider, 20 Jul. 2011, www.businessinsider.com/new-world-disorder-why-geithners-imf-sdr-plan-for-a-global-currency-is-high-treason-2011-7.

Lewis, Nathan. "The Problem With "Modern Monetary Theory" Is That It's True." *Forbes*, 21 Feb. 2019, www.forbes.com/sites/nathanlewis/2019/02/21/the-problem-with-modern-monetary-theory-is-that-its-true/#4fb22b0256fb.

Lewis, Nathan. "The World Gold Standard System Will Rise Again — But, Not Yet." *Forbes*, 6 Dec. 2019, www.forbes.com/sites/nathanlewis/2019/12/06/the-world-gold-standard-system-will-rise-again---but-not-yet/#5474426235e6.

Lewis, Nathan. "We Just Tested The Gold Standard -- It Still Works." *Forbes*, 8 Aug. 2019, www.forbes.com/sites/nathanlewis/2019/08/08/we-just-tested-the-gold-standard-it-still-works/#2044ef4c556b.

Lewis, Tom. "Yes, The U.S Government Can Still Confiscate Gold." *The Gold Telegraph*, 4 May 2018, www.goldtelegraph.com/the-u.s-government-can-still-confiscate-gold.

Lewis v. United States, 680 F.2d 1239 (1982).

Li, Yun. "The Fed may soon let inflation run a little hotter than usual, Goldman says." *CNBC*, 18 Mar. 2019, www.cnbc.com/2019/03/18/the-fed-may-soon-let-inflation-run-a-little-hotter-than-usual-goldman-says.html.

Libertytree.ca. "Quotation by Robert Hemphill." *LibertyQuotes*, libertytree.ca/quotes/Robert.Hemphill.Quote.CA66.

"Limited Liability Company (LLC) Asset Protection." *Asset Protection Planners*, www.assetprotectionplanners.com/services/llc/.

"Limited Liability Company 101." *Assetprotection.com*, assetprotection.com/limited-liability-company/limited-liability-company-101/.

Litle, Justice. "Postcards From Weimar Germany." *InflationData.com*, 20 Sept. 2010, inflationdata.com/articles/2010/09/20/hyperinflation-in-weimar-germany/.

"LLC Asset Protection Strategies: Everything You Need To Know." *Upcounsel.com*, www.upcounsel.com/llc-asset-protection-strategies.

Long, Caitlin. "The Real Story Of The Repo Market Meltdown, And What It Means For Bitcoin." *Forbes*, 25 Sept. 2019, www.forbes.com/sites/caitlinlong/2019/09/25/the-real-story-of-the-repo-market-meltdown-and-what-it-means-for-bitcoin/#23f8ac237caa.

Long, Heather. "2019: The year the Federal Reserve admitted it was wrong." *Washington Post*, 11 Dec. 2019, www.washingtonpost.com/business/2019/12/11/year-federal-reserve-admitted-it-was-wrong/.

Long, Heather. "Fed Chair Powell says U.S. economy deteriorating with alarming speed." *The Washington Post*, 9 Apr. 2020, www.msn.com/en-us/news/us/fed-chair-powell-says-us-economy-deteriorating-with-alarming-speed/ar-BB12o0Ak?

fbclid=IwAR1Jkd_mpgI3SL_nuwrXPsW3uQ8SRlr2MV5KnzeF6SAeVv6ZIMY
UVmWAH1w.

Long, Heather. "Federal Reserve predicts no interest rate cuts in 2020, ignoring Trump's calls to boost the economy." *The Washington Post,* 11 Dec. 2019, www.washingtonpost.com/business/2019/12/11/federal-reserve-predicts-no-interest-rate-cuts-ignoring-trumps-calls-boost-economy/?wpisrc=al_news__alert-economy--alert-national&wpmk=1.

Long, Heather. "Federal Reserve slashes interest rates to zero as part of wide-ranging emergency intervention." *The Washington Post,* 15 Mar. 2020, www.washingtonpost.com/business/2020/03/15/federal-reserve-slashes-interest-rates-zero-part-wide-ranging-emergency-intervention/.

"Louis Thomas McFadden Quotes," *AZ Quotes,* www.azquotes.com/quote/615209.

Lowell, Lee. "Selling Naked Put Options: Get Paid To Buy Stocks At A Discount." *Seeking Alpha,* 30 Apr. 2012, seekingalpha.com/article/541181-selling-naked-put-options-get-paid-to-buy-stocks-at-a-discount.

Ludwig, E. Jeffrey. "The UN Wants to Be Our World Government By 2030." *American Thinker,* 27 Oct. 2018, www.americanthinker.com/articles/2018/10/the_un_wants_to_be_our_world_government_by_2030.html.

Luster, Brian. "How To Protect Your Assets Without Giving Up Control." *Forbes,* 18 Mar. 2014, www.forbes.com/sites/brianluster/2014/03/18/why-forming-a-family-limited-partnership-means-less-stress-at-tax-time/#2ed697a68658.

Lyons, Ruth. "Pros and Cons of Real Estate Investing: A Comprehensive Overview." *Investorjunkie,* 13 Dec. 2020, investorjunkie.com/real-estate/pros-and-cons/.

M'Culloch v. Maryland, 17 US 316 (1819).

Macleod, Alan. "Big Banks Call for Wall Street Deregulation to 'Fight Coronavirus.'" *MPN News,* 6 Mar. 2020, www.mintpressnews.com/big-banks-call-wall-street-deregulation-fight-coronavirus/265558/?fbclid=IwAR1MtJpe2A_-nxjKHjOSu8YP3vLuZwRjOMbXCjWlOjIxo9A82UBzGypfrLs.

Macwen, Urvish. "The Main Risks Of Investing In Bitcoin." *Finextra,* 19 Jun. 2019, www.finextra.com/blogposting/17390/the-main-risks-of-investing-in-bitcoin.

Maharrey, Mike. "Enjoy That Stimulus: You're Going to Pay for It!" *Tenth Amendment Center,* 12 Jun. 2020, blog.tenthamendmentcenter.com/2020/06/enjoy-that-stimulus-youre-going-to-pay-for-it/?fbclid=IwAR19Z7wT2WimDrd0lKKYKML2cbNPnIAVfnN-0SlNoUC8WvjMQ7tuzdIpJqg.

Mannarino, Gregory. "MARKETS: IMPORTANT UPDATES... By Gregory Mannarino." *Youtube*, www.youtube.com/watch?v=n6PCYssIR38.

Marbury v. Madison, 5 U.S. 137 (1803).

Marshall, Andrew Gavin. "The Bilderberg Plan for 2009: Remaking the Global Political Economy." *Global Research*, 26 May 2009, www.globalresearch.ca/the-bilderberg-plan-for-2009-remaking-the-global-political-economy/13738.

Marstrand, Bob. "Lies, damned lies and CPI." *Of Wealth*, 11 Oct. 2016, www.ofwealth.com/lies-damned-lies-cpi/.

Marstrand, Rob. "Where should you put your money?" *Of Wealth*, 29 Sept. 2016, www.ofwealth.com/where-should-you-put-your-money/#.V_0bXJMrK9Y.

Martens, Pam and Russ Martens. "Bernie Sanders Hasn't Quite Captured What Wall Street Does: It's Actually a Fraud-Monetization System with a Money-Printing Unit Called the New York Fed." *Wall Street on Parade*, 21 Jan. 2020, wallstreetonparade.com/2020/01/bernie-sanders-hasnt-quite-captured-what-wall-street-does-its-actually-a-fraud-monetization-system-with-a-money-printing-unit-called-the-new-york-fed/.

Martens, Pam and Russ Martens. "BlackRock Authored the Bailout Plan Before There Was a Crisis – Now It's Been Hired by three Central Banks to Implement the Plan." *Wall Street on Parade*, 5 Jun. 2020, wallstreetonparade.com/2020/06/blackrock-authored-the-bailout-plan-before-there-was-a-crisis-now-its-been-hired-by-three-central-banks-to-implement-the-plan/?fbclid=IwAR0GVrMUHztEuheKbZMYB56sZEc2DwIiAQEYSUIy9qSSfuzEqPoHz_u7wqQ.

Martens, Pam and Russ Martens. "Demand for Fed's Repo Loans Surges Past $100 Billion a Day as 10-Year Treasury Hits Lowest Rate in 149 Years." *Wall Street on Parade*, 5 Mar. 2020, wallstreetonparade.com/2020/03/demand-for-feds-repo-loans-surges-past-100-billion-a-day-as-10-year-treasury-hits-lowest-rate-in-149-years/.

Martens, Pam and Russ Martens. "Fed Chair Powell Attempts to Blame U.S. Inequality on Globalization – Gets Smacked Down by Bloomberg Reporter." *Wall Street on Parade*, 11 Jun. 2020, wallstreetonparade.com/2020/06/fed-chair-powell-attempts-to-blame-u-s-inequality-on-globalization-gets-smacked-down-by-bloomberg-reporter/.

Martens, Pam and Russ Martens. "Fed Chair Powell Tells Whoppers This Morning on the Brookings Institution Webcast." *Wall Street on Parade*, 9 Apr. 2020, wallstreetonparade.com/2020/04/fed-chair-powell-tells-whoppers-this-morning-on-the-brookings-institution-webcast/.

Martens, Pam and Russ Martens. "Fed Repos Have Plowed $6.6 Trillion to Wall Street in Four Months; That's 34% of Its Feeding Tube During Epic Financial Crash." *Wall Street on Parade*. 27 Jan. 2020, wallstreetonparade.com/2020/01/fed-repos-have-plowed-6-6-trillion-to-wall-street-in-four-months-thats-34-of-its-feeding-tube-during-epic-financial-crash/.

Martens, Pam and Russ Martens. "Fed Sets Off Panic with Plan to Eliminate Reserves at Wall Street's Mega Banks." *Wall Street on Parade,* 16 Mar. 2020, wallstreetonparade.com/2020/03/fed-sets-off-panic-with-plan-to-eliminate-reserves-at-wall-streets-mega-banks/.

Martens, Pam and Russ Martens. "Fed's Balance Sheet Skyrockets to $4.7 Trillion." *Wall Street on Parade*, 19 Mar. 2020, wallstreetonparade.com/2020/03/feds-balance-sheet-skyrockets-to-4-7-trillion/?fbclid=IwAR2sB1L8ZLt0TTR04NQ8IbGBj3elYLb_W8xN4FHrMO39018KctJI9UoQs-A.

Martens, Pam and Russ Martens. "Federal Reserve Announces Unprecedented $1.5 Trillion in Loans to Wall Street Today and Tomorrow." *Wall Street on Parade*, 12 Mar. 2020, wallstreetonparade.com/2020/03/federal-reserve-announces-unprecedented-1-5-trillion-in-loans-to-wall-street-today-and-tomorrow.

Martens, Pam and Russ Martens. "Stimulus Bill Allows Federal Reserve to Conduct Meetings in Secret; Gives Fed $454 Billion Slush Fund for Wall Street Bailouts." *Wall Street on Parade*, 26 Mar. 2020, wallstreetonparade.com/2020/03/stimulus-bill-allows-federal-reserve-to-conduct-meetings-in-secret-gives-fed-454-billion-slush-fund-for-wall-street-bailouts/.

Martens, Pam and Russ Martens. "The Fed Has Pumped $9 Trillion into Wall Street Over the Past Six Months, But Mnuchin Says 'This Isn't Like the Financial Crisis.'" *Wall Street on Parade*, 14 Mar. 2020, wallstreetonparade.com/2020/03/the-fed-has-pumped-9-trillion-into-wall-street-over-the-past-six-months-but-mnuchin-says-this-isnt-like-the-financial-crisis/.

Martens, Pam and Russ Martens. "The Fed Is Killing the Two Main Functions of Wall Street: Price Discovery and Prudent Capital Allocation." *Wall Street on Parade*, 11 Apr. 2020, wallstreetonparade.com/2020/04/the-fed-is-killing-the-two-main-functions-of-wall-street-price-discovery-and-prudent-capital-allocation/.

Martens, Pam and Russ Martens. "The Federal Reserve Now Owns 15 Percent of the U.S. Treasury Market; At Its Current Rate, It Could Own the Whole Market in Less than Two Years." *Wall Street on Parade*, 28 Mar. 2020, wallstreetonparade.com/2020/03/the-federal-reserve-now-owns-15-percent-of-the-u-s-treasury-market-at-its-current-rate-it-could-own-the-whole-market-in-less-than-two-years/.

Martens, Pam and Russ Martens. "The Man Who Advises the New York Fed Says It and Other Central Banks Are 'Fueling a Ponzi Market.'" *Wall Street on Parade*,

22 Jan. 2020, wallstreetonparade.com/2020/01/the-man-who-advises-the-new-york-fed-says-it-and-other-central-banks-are-fueling-a-ponzi-market/.

Martens, Pam and Russ Martens. "The New York Fed, Owned by Multinational Banks, Is Nationalizing Capital Markets." *Wall Street on Parade*, 9 Apr. 2020, wallstreetonparade.com/2020/04/the-new-york-fed-owned-by-multinational-b a n k s - i s - n a t i o n a l i z i n g - c a p i t a l - m a r k e t s / ? fbclid=IwAR00mmnOvw5SRN1mRcHQYLxaEihytz1NcYQHvEtGyp63NJn7AJ _Y9zxVtOo.

Martens, Pam and Russ Martens. "U.S. Debt Crisis Comes into View as Fed's Balance Sheet Explodes Past $7 Trillion." *Wall Street on Parade*, 29 May 2020, wallstreetonparade.com/2020/05/u-s-debt-crisis-comes-into-view-as-feds-balance-sheet-explodes-past-7-trillion/.

"Martin Van Buren - The independent treasury." *World Biography: U.S. Presidents*, www.presidentprofiles.com/Washington-Johnson/Martin-Van-Buren-The-independent-treasury.html#ixzz6HdrZGav5.

Matthews, Chris. "U.S. businesses need a $2 trillion bailout fund to avoid a possible 'global depression,' says Guggenheim's Minerd." *Market Watch*, 18 Mar. 2020, www.marketwatch.com/story/us-businesses-need-a-2-trillion-bailout-to-avoid-a-possible-global-depression-says-guggenheims-minerd-2020-03-17? r e f l i n k = m w _ s h a r e _ f a c e b o o k & f b c l i d = I w A R 2 D Y U o 5 D r W O v y f u - sLPF608PpJbSgaqSvh8R2dYdgvzDSL3QrCmx7lFMqs.

May, Donald H. "Reagan Blasts Fed's Control of Money Supply." *UPI*, 9 Feb. 1982, www.upi.com/Archives/1982/02/09/Reagan-blasts-Feds-control-of-money-supply/3386382078800/.

May, Frank. "Russia bringing back the gold standard may kill US dollar & solve main problem of cryptocurrencies." *RT*, 13 Jun. 2019, www.rt.com/business/461752-russia-gold-dollar-cryptocurrencies/.

McClean, Dorothy Cummings. "Kissinger: Failure to establish post-COVID new world order 'could set the world on fire.'" *Lifesite,* 7 Apr. 2020, www.lifesitenews.com/news/kissinger-failure-to-establish-post-covid-new-world-o r d e r - c o u l d - s e t - t h e - w o r l d - o n - f i r e ? fbclid=IwAR01KwPV5QHTzd5qNdoauCAkk36U5W6mAHGq6Sd9-QRCorzF_DH-AA5wQZI.

McCollum, Jason. "Second Bank of the United States: Definition & Overview," *Study.com*, study.com/academy/lesson/second-bank-of-the-united-states-definition-overview.html.

McCormick, Emily. "Stock market news: Dow plunges 1,861 points, or 7%, for worst day since mid-March." *Yahoo Finance,* 11 Jun. 2020, finance.yahoo.com/news/stock-market-news-live-june-11-2020-222011316.html.

McCormick, Liz. "Repo Blowup Was Fueled by Big Banks and Hedge Funds, BIS Says." *Bloomberg,* 8 Dec. 2019, www.bloomberg.com/news/articles/2019-12-08/repo-blowup-was-fueled-by-big-banks-and-hedge-funds-bis-says.

McCullagh, Declan. "United Nations Proposes New 'Global Currency.'" *CBS News,* 9 Sept. 2009, www.cbsnews.com/news/united-nations-proposes-new-global-currency/?fbclid=IwAR1g6IOfuRyddIBwcHaLVJfzNzB3d9zujpQKzpoh4-Yimk_MvTuVGkBO6Oo.

McEnery, Thornton. "Dow loses over 2,000 points, worst single-day drop ever, as oil prices crash." *New York Post,* 9 Mar. 2020, nypost.com/2020/03/09/dow-loses-over-2000-points-worst-single-day-drop-ever-as-oil-prices-crash/?fbclid=IwAR2nfX-r6e_9icqr1BqOxbfYSjFRZfxYxrxb5VjXG7jaG19Kbp5ZTYoHGss.

McEnery, Thornton and Noah Manskar.. "Dow loses over 2,000 points, worst single-day drop ever, as oil prices crash." *New York Post,* 9 Mar. 2020, nypost.com/2020/03/09/dow-loses-over-2000-points-worst-single-day-drop-ever-as-oil-prices-crash/?utm_source=NYPFacebook&utm_medium=Native&utm_campaign=NYPFacebook&fbclid=IwAR2JITqZcWGqAFLCGShFmbGi6wZYuXw508E78pUpn3G66GKIf8Hv6KTiqQk.

McHarrey, Mike. "Now in Effect: Arizona Law Treats Gold and Silver as Money." *Tenth Amendment Center,* 9 Aug. 2017, blog.tenthamendmentcenter.com/2017/08/now-in-effect-arizona-law-treats-gold-and-silver-as-money/.

McMahon, Tim. "Surviving a Hyperinflation." *Financial Trend Forecaster,* 18 Jul. 2013, fintrend.com/2013/07/18/surviving-hyperinflation/.

McMahon, Tim. "What is Hyperinflation?" *InflationData.com,* inflationdata.com/articles/hyperinflation/.

McMahon, Tim. "What is Quantitative Tightening?" *InflationData.com,* inflationdata.com/articles/quantitative-tightening/.

McMaken, Ryan. "The Fed Announces Another Flood of Easy Money." *Mises Institute,* 12 Mar. 2020, mises.org/power-market/fed-announces-another-flood-easy-money.

McManus, John F. "The Power of the Federal Reserve." *The New American,* 27 Jun. 2020, www.thenewamerican.com/reviews/opinion/item/29397-the-power-of-the-federal-reserve.

Memonen, Tarita. "The Pros and Cons of Real Estate Investing." *Mashvisor.com,* 13 Aug. 2019, www.mashvisor.com/blog/pros-and-cons-of-real-estate-investing/.

Menton, Jessica. "Dow plummets 2,000 points, oil prices drop as global recession concerns mount." *USA Today,* 9 Mar. 2020, www.usatoday.com/story/money/

2020/03/09/dow-oil-tumbles-global-recession-fears/4998613002/?fbclid=IwAR0-nu_ghM9t6mt9rwdK6498YrzkjReK0bjZoZEXtdEObacRWgIqtp0pL0Q.

Mercenary Trader. "Weekender: The Trouble With Modern Monetary Theory (MMT)." *Business Insider*, 19 Dec. 2010, www.businessinsider.com/weekender-the-trouble-with-modern-monetary-theory-mmt-2011-1.

Messamore, Wesley. "100 Reasons to End the Fed." *Young Americans for Liberty*, yaliberty.org/news/100-reasons-to-end-the-fed/.

Meyer v. Nebraska, 262 U.S. 390, 43 S.Ct. 625 (1923).

Mikhan, Alena and Jeff Clark. "Does Gold Keep Up In Hyperinflation?" *Casey Research*, 18 Jun. 2012, www.caseyresearch.com/does-gold-keep-hyperinflation/.

"Milton Friedman > Quotes > Quotable Quote." *Good Reads*, www.goodreads.com/quotes/110844-only-a-crisis---actual-or-perceived---produces-real.

"Milton Friedman Quotations." *Memorablequotations.com*, www.memorablequotations.com/friedman.htm.

"Milton Friedman Quotes." *Brainy Quote*, www.brainyquote.com/quotes/milton_friedman_101538.

Misesmedia. "Money, Banking, and the Federal Reserve." *Youtube*, 22 Feb. 2006, www.youtube.com/watch?v=iYZM58dulPE&index=3&list=PLtft_2mpNiCvN-PRcAsLmGlMkUMhzjMuq.

Misesmedia. "The Corrupt Origins of Central Banking in America | Thomas J. DiLorenzo." *Youtube*, 26 Jul. 2014, www.youtube.com/watch?v=1a9DrLOsrlA.

Miupiu. "15 Quotes About New World Order - #1." *Steemit*, steemit.com/quotes/@miupiu/15-quotes-about-new-world-order-part-1.

"Modern Monetary Theory (MMT)." *Investopedia*. 24 Sept. 2019, www.investopedia.com/modern-monetary-theory-mmt-4588060.

Mogollon, Mery and Alexandra Zavis. "It costs $200 to buy a dozen eggs in Venezuela right now." *The Sydney Morning Herald*, 1 Jun. 2016, www.smh.com.au/world/it-costs-200-to-buy-a-dozen-eggs-in-venezuela-right-now-20160601-gp8qx5.html?fbclid=IwAR2HinM8aT4V1txOREInlXDg53S1xx77uIgcr94lyLVOj_sAYrOZgTrvlTE.

"Money Flow Index - MFI Definition and Uses." *Investopedia*, 13 July 2019, www.investopedia.com/terms/m/mfi.asp.

Den of Vipers

"Money Quotes: What The Experts Say About Money." *Midas Gold Group*, 27 Aug. 2020, www.midasgoldgroup.com/money-quotes/.

"Motion for Temporary Restraining Order Hearing Before the Honorable James C. Fox Senior United States District Court Judge." *Sullivan v. United States,* 03-1611 (4th Cir. 2003). www.whatreallyhappened.com/WRHARTICLES/SullivanVUSA.pdf.

Motley Fool Staff. "Dividend Investing for Beginners." *The Motley Fool*, 10 Apr. 2019, www.fool.com/how-to-invest/dividend-investing-for-beginners.aspx.

Motley Fool Staff. "What Are Exchange-Traded Funds?" *The Motley Fool*, 19 Sept. 2016, www.fool.com/knowledge-center/what-are-exchange-traded-funds.aspx.

Motley Fool Staff. "What is Volume in Stock Trading?" *The Motley Fool*, 20 Jun. 2019, www.fool.com/knowledge-center/what-is-volume-in-stock-trading.aspx.

Mullen, Tom. "'Inflation is low': The Federal Reserve's Scam of the Century." *Tommullen.com*, 31 Mar. 2020, www.tommullen.net/featured/inflation-is-low-the-federal-reserves-scam-of-the-century/?fbclid=IwAR1As6UZbfSEJ6I0-s3g2LyrUf5QFsB0HJ5yrSdRMxE9TDTtYjwGUitZATc.

Murphy, Chris B. "Using the Price-to-Earnings Ratio And PEG to Assess a Stock." *Investopedia*, 25 Jun. 2019, www.investopedia.com/investing/use-pe-ratio-and-peg-to-tell-stocks-future/.

"Murray Rothbard Quotes." *AZ Quotes*, www.azquotes.com/quote/962764.

Mutsaka, Farai. "'It's a nightmare': Zimbabwe struggles with hyperinflation." *AP*, 10 Oct. 2019, apnews.com/1ce81eed4b064a529163513931b30178.

Narayanan, Aparna. "Gold Stocks Shine As Viral Caution Ignites Gold Prices, But For How Long?" *Investors.com,* 22 May 2020, www.investors.com/news/gold-stocks-ride-gold-prices-higher-as-coronavirus-fuels-barrick-gold-stock-kinross-kirkland-lake/?src=A00220&yptr=yahoo.

Narron, James and David Skeie. "Crisis Chronicles: Not Worth a Continental—The Currency Crisis of 1779 and Today's European Debt Crisis." *Liberty Street Economics,* 11 Apr. 2014, libertystreeteconomics.newyorkfed.org/2014/04/crisis-chronicles-not-worth-a-continentalthe-currency-crisis-of-1779-and-todays-european-debt-crisis.html.

"National Bank Act of 1863." *Encyclopedia.com*, Encyclopedia.com, www.encyclopedia.com/history/encyclopedias-almanacs-transcripts-and-maps/national-bank-act-1863.

"Negative Interest Rate Definition." *Investopedia*, 17 Aug. 2019, www.investopedia.com/terms/n/negative-interest-rate.asp.

"New Order of Barbarians - Transcript of Tapes I-III." *100777.Com*, 22 May 2003, 100777.com/nwo/barbarians.

"New tax code = new price index – new tax bracket adjustments." *The Fred Blog*, 25 Jan. 2018, fredblog.stlouisfed.org/2018/01/new-tax-code-new-price-index new-tax-bracket-adjustments/.

"New World Order: 37 Quotes on The New World Order, One-World Government and One-World Religion." *End Times Prophecy Report*, 8 Aug. 2018, endtimesprophecyreport.com/2013/06/05/new-world-order-37-quotes-on-the-new-world-order/.

Newman, Alex. "Globalist Henry Kissinger Outlines 'New World Order.'" *The New American*, 1 Sept. 2014, www.thenewamerican.com/world-news/item/19030-globalist-henry-kissinger-outlines-new-world-order?fbclid=IwAR1AaSLqFfNV2ROqwV7bo5slhsdSVSJwYoGX3U7VRYo0FbMmTvTS8DkYFoM#.

Newman, Alex. "Gold, Silver Now Legal Tender in Utah." *The New American*, 29 Mar. 2011, www.thenewamerican.com/economy/markets/item/4604-gold-silver-now-legal-tender-in-utah.

Newman, Alex. "Greenspan: Gold is a Currency, Euro 'Breaking Down.'" *The New American*, 25 Aug. 2011, thenewamerican.com/greenspan-gold-is-a-currency-euro-breaking-down/.

Newman, Alex. "Trump Nominates Gold Advocate to Federal Reserve." *New American*, 7 Feb. 2020, www.thenewamerican.com/usnews/politics/item/34831-trump-nominates-gold-advocate-to-federal-reserve?fbclid=IwAR3wJ8NEBEt0FNu6_UqzJ0bg2HrFwliT-0vFNfDJPC8MjiPxXQx83ON9Zs.

Newman, Alex. "UN-Backed 'Great Reset' to Usher in New World Order." *The New American*, 15 July 2020, www.thenewamerican.com/world-news/europe/item/36379-un-backed-great-reset-to-usher-in-new-world-order?fbclid=IwAR20CLmHQsrwV0V7dk46O5yT2KjetreQXYFIivnu-wJa8YRevNaUz5A16Bw.

Newman, Alex. "Waking up to a World Currency." *The New American*, 15 Sept. 2010, www.thenewamerican.com/economy/economics/item/4498-waking-up-to-a-world-currency.

Newman, Alex. "Washington State Considers Gold and Silver as Legal Tender." *The New American*, 31 Jan. 2012, www.thenewamerican.com/usnews/politics/item/9171-washington-state-considers-gold-and-silver-as-legal-tender.

"None Dare Call It Conspiracy." *Whale.to*, www.whale.to/b/allen_b1.html#chapter4.

Norton v. Shelby County, 118 U.S. 425 (1886).

Nurse, Peter. "Dollar Climbs; Fed Minutes Offer Downbeat Outlook." *Yahoo Finance*, 20 May 2020, finance.yahoo.com/news/dollar-climbs-fed-minutes-offer-023949316.html.

O'Callaghan, Laura. "End of UK coins and banknotes? New measures mean Britain could be cashless in two years." *Express*, 6 May 2020, www.express.co.uk/news/uk/1278656/coronavirus-uk-cash-payments-stopped-cashless-society-two-years-atm-withdrawals?fbclid=IwAR2QnWDXKpMDOnkW38dYpGkX8wEoXEgBZpM-GijoIscUp9UdMHLj_ccluY8.

O'Gilvie v. United States, 519 U.S. 79, 84 (1996).

O'Halloran, Suzanne. "Dow drops 2,999 points on word coronavirus crisis could extend until August." *Fox Business*, 16 Mar. 2020, www.foxbusiness.com/markets/us-stocks-march-16-2020?fbclid=IwAR0SNQD4jbEe-BAjk1aR2HK3-xyaxoocArng4mpLYTRxeHxKL0Zqrtkwaus.

O'Reilly, Andrew and John Roberts. "Trump floats temporarily eliminating payroll tax to boost economy amid coronavirus fears." *Fox News*, 10 Mar. 2020, www.foxnews.com/politics/trump-floats-temporarily-eliminating-payroll-tax-boost-economy-amid-coronavirus-fears?fbclid=IwAR1_DGiGh0xDxmgVFZNnOzAQe8S-XOQMH_BfZAtlU7nLSs7Eo0DLp39Qku8.

Oh, Sunny. "Former IMF chief economist says Fed's bond-buying is 'smoke and mirrors,' doesn't solve U.S. debt problems" *Market Watch*, 20 May 2020, www.marketwatch.com/story/former-imf-chief-economist-says-feds-bond-buying-is-smoke-and-mirrors-doesnt-solve-us-debt-problems-2020-05-20?siteid=yhoof2&yptr=yahoo.

"Overview of How an LLC Protects your Personal Assets." *The Presser Law Firm*, www.assetprotectionattorneys.com/Domestic_Asset_Protection/Limited_Liability_Companies/How_an_LLC_Protects_your_Personal_Assets.aspx.

Palmer, Barclay. "Why the Consumer Price Index Is Controversial." *Investopedia*, 25 Jun. 2019, www.investopedia.com/articles/07/consumerpriceindex.asp.

Papadatos, Aristofanis. "Why You Should Not Sell Covered Call Options." *Seeking Alpha*, 16 May 2017, seekingalpha.com/article/4055775-why-you-should-not-sell-covered-call-options.

"Paper Money Collapse: The Folly of Elastic Money, 2nd Edition by Thomas Mayer, Detlev S. Schlichter." *O'Reilly*, www.oreilly.com/library/view/paper-money-collapse/9781118877364/xhtml/fm01.xhtml.

Patton, Mike. "Trump Administration Considers Reducing Payroll Tax To Zero." *Forbes*, 10 Mar. 2020, www.forbes.com/sites/mikepatton/2020/03/10/trump-administration-considers-reducing-payroll-tax-to-zero/?fbclid=IwAR2wNkXGZSe8bdjXd95Lis-NO3hO0b6neY0149I.JBJGR6z0_mlcjnzQvQj0#1825e5473188.

Paul, Ron. "Ron Paul: 'Forget the Russians: It's the Federal Reserve Seeking to Meddle in Our Elections.'" *The Free Thought Project*, 3 Sept. 2019, thefreethoughtproject.com/ron-paul-end-federal-reserve/?fbclid=IwAR1nGlN-ywVH6dp-4yR2CGmdisX6qSZxeBCo9nTDg-qmZ53-AvddeYuUpGw.

Paul, Ron. "Will Coronavirus End the Fed?" *Ron Paul Institute,* 30 Mar. 2020, www.ronpaulinstitute.org/archives/featured-articles/2020/march/30/will-coronavirus-end-the-fed/?fbclid=IwAR1_DnSktag1_IBqBrAw-pooprcz6AC8pikp2JA8npi-QGq5RtVRETCB5mc.

Peck & Co. v. Lowe, 247 U.S. 165 (1918).

Phoenix Capital Research. "We Are Now Approaching the 'Lehman' Event...Prepare NOW!" *ZeroHedge.com,* 17 Mar. 2020, www.zerohedge.com/news/2020-03-17/we-are-now-approaching-lehman-event-prepare-now.

Pinheiro, John C. "James K. Polk: Domestic Affairs." *UVA Miller Center,* millercenter.org/president/polk/domestic-affairs.

Pinkasovitch, Arthur. "How to Use the Dividend Capture Strategy." *Investopedia*, 9 Oct. 2019, www.investopedia.com/articles/stocks/11/dividend-capture-strategy.asp.

Pollock v. Farmers' Loan and Trust Company, 157 U.S. 429, 633 (1895).

Polumbo, Brad. "New Stanford Study Suggests Biden's Agenda Will Have 4 Devastating Economic Consequences." *Fee,* 19 Oct. 2020, fee.org/articles/new-stanford-study-suggests-bidens-agenda-will-have-4-devastating-economic-consequences/?fbclid=IwAR2rOrrbZGkhEeuAq8hp0pBLBGW6Bi-7N0msiCAfX7oBL-dVDHkxtglswWg.

Pongracic, Ivan Jr. "The Great Depression According to Milton Friedman." *FEE,* 1 Sept. 2007, fee.org/articles/the-great-depression-according-to-milton-friedman/.

Pons, Corina, et al. "Venezuela sets new price controls, with eggs costing more than a month's wages." *Reuters,* 30 Apr. 2020, www.reuters.com/article/us-venezuela-economy-idUSKBN22D41S?fbclid=IwAR1_kx90-m3ncyl1pv9nxXMCDZmrEENhFeemSCOhdvEUoYV11pzOwD2i7aI.

"Ponzi schemes Using virtual Currencies." *SEC*, www.sec.gov/investor/alerts/ia_virtualcurrencies.pdf.

"President Martin Van Buren's Independent Treasury Sparks Controversy within the Democratic Party." *The History Engine,* historyengine.richmond.edu/episodes/view/2190.

"Price-to-Earnings Ratio – P/E Ratio." *Investopedia,* 11 Oct. 2019, www.investopedia.com/terms/p/price-earningsratio.asp.

"Prominent Quotes." *The Liberty Dollar,* libertydollar.org/ld/press-kit/prominent-quotes.htm.

Quinn, Jim. "The Federal Reserve Must Die." *HCP Live,* 25 Aug. 2009, www.mdmag.com/medical-news/federal_reserve_must_die.

"Quotation by Benjamin Disraeli." *LibertyQuotes,* Libertytree.ca, 6 Dec. 2019, libertytree.ca/quotes/Benjamin.Disraeli.Quote.2E3D.

"Quotation by Louis McFadden." *LibertyQuotes,* libertytree.ca/quotes/Louis.McFadden.Quote.B24B.

"Quote: Napoleon Bonaparte: When a Government Is Dependent upon Bankers." *Truth11.Com,* 8 Aug. 2009, truth11.com/2009/08/08/quote-napoleon-bonaparte-when-a-government-is-dependent-upon-bankers/.

"Quote by John G. Adams." *Goodreads,* Goodreads, www.goodreads.com/quotes/697421-there-are-two-ways-to-conquer-and-enslave-a-nations.

"Quotes," *Your Dictionary,* quotes.yourdictionary.com/author/quote/556191.

"Quotes by Abraham Lincoln." *myqualitywriting.com,* www.myqualitywriting.com/QuotesbyAbrahamLincoln1.html.

"Quotes By Curtis Bean Dall." *AZ Quotes,* www.azquotes.com/author/41348-Curtis_Bean_Dall.

"Quotes from International Bankers." *Stopthecrime.net,* 25 Feb. 2019, stopthecrime.net/wp/2019/02/25/quotes-from-international-bankers/.

"Quotes On The New World Order." *Jesus-Is-Savior.com,* www.jesus-is-savior.com/False%20Religions/Illuminati/quotes_on_the_new_world_order.htm.

"Quotes On The New World Order And One-World Government." *American Freedom Party,* 29 June 2014, web.archive.org/web/20200201152435/american3rdposition.com/quotes-new-world-order/.

R. A. "What is quantitative easing?" *The Economist,* 9 Mar. 2015, www.economist.com/the-economist-explains/2015/03/09/what-is-quantitative-easing.

Rando, David. "Asset Protection for the Business Owner." *Investopedia*, 25 Jun. 2019, www.investopedia.com/articles/pf/08/asset-protection-business.asp.

Randow, Jana. "Europe Bonds Soar as Lagarde Pledges No Limits to ECB Action." *Bloomberg*, 18 Mar. 2020, www.bloomberg.com/news/articles/ 2020-03-18/ecb-announces-750-billion-euro-pandemic-bond-buying-program? cmpid=socialflow-facebook-business&utm_campaign=socialflow-organic&utm_source=facebook&utm_content=business&utm_medium=social&fb clid=IwAR2CYk9i5qj7xuvo0p7ROUw5k8HroHCHGhXrW2JVMQaYWf9CQ-GuBHMfzfc.

Randow, Jana and Yuko Takeo. "Negative Interest Rates." *Bloomberg*, 1 Nov. 2019, www.bloomberg.com/quicktake/negative-interest-rates.

Redman, Jamie. "Data Shows the US Economy Was Collapsing 5 Months Before the Coronavirus Outbreak." *Bitcoin.com*, 3 May 2020, news.bitcoin.com/data-shows-the-us-economy-was-collapsing-5-months-before-the-coronavirus-outbreak/?fbclid=IwAR3cgTDBLMYGIYpRAO_pGNc7V-boxoJX-FHsWpJYCoJ3UOxdU6DmCN3hh-Q.

Reed, Eric. "Investing in Silver: Four Ways to Invest and Why." *The Street*, 5 Nov. 2015, www.thestreet.com/markets/commodities/investing-in-silver-14767113.

Relman, Eliza. "The Senate is about to pass the 'largest relief package in history' amid the coronavirus-induced economic crisis, but progressives say it isn't enough." *Business Insider*, 21 Mar. 2020, www.businessinsider.com/coronavirus-progressives-say-13-trillion-stimulus-isnt-enough-2020-3? utm_source=yahoo.com&utm_medium=referral.

Reilly, Peter J. "Stimulus' Tax Benefits Heavily Weighted To Ultrawealthy." *Forbes*, 27 Mar. 2020, www.forbes.com/sites/peterjreilly/2020/03/27/cares-bills-tax-benefit-heavily-weighted-to-ultrawealthy/?fbclid=IwAR0XG59-ZKf_PfHjiggIdKZEvNh-5REJKaJNVCpYEh7v2ZlQl4436h_0wuU#5696e6c91c3 c.

"Report to the Congress of the Commission on the Role of Gold in the Domestic and International Monetary Systems." *Fraser,stlouisfed.org*, Mar. 1982, fraser.stlouisfed.org/files/docs/historical/congressional/ 198203_usgcom_prtcomrolegold_v1.pdf.

Repp, John M. "Opinion: UN Report Says US Is a 'Shithole Country.'" *Common Dreams*, 15 June 2018, www.commondreams.org/views/2018/06/15/un-report-says-us-shithole-country? utm_campaign=shareaholic&fbclid=IwAR3i8n-44579Pge2vqxSV65e6H9p_UMN zgCbAdB0TFeQaFi7UGxwMauQ-uc.

"Reserve Requirements." *Board of Governors of the Federal Reserve System*, www.federalreserve.gov/monetarypolicy/reservereq.htm.

Restuccia. Andrew, Andrew Duehren, and Lindsay Wise. "U.S. Seeks to Send Checks to Americans as Part of Stimulus Package." *The Wall Street Journal*, 17 Mar. 2020, www.wsj.com/articles/trump-administration-seeking-850-billion-stimulus-package-11584448802?mod=hp_lead_pos2.

Reuters. "Fed's Kashkari: Base case is mild recession like after 9/11." *Kitco*, 17 Mar. 2020, www.kitco.com/news/2020-03-17/Fed-s-Kashkari-Base-case-is-mild-recession-like-after-9-11.html.

Reuters Staff. "Venezuela sets new price controls, with eggs costing more than a month's wages." *Reuters*, 30 Apr. 2020, www.reuters.com/article/us-venezuela-economy-idUSKBN22D41S?fbclid=IwAR3uYQqYdAAzOmERb852Y7Mb9V0aEa6z7oIhgp8H5gQxbJgzHC MmeNFQuV8.

Richardson, Gary and Jessie Romero. "The Meeting at Jekyll Island." *Federal Reserve History*, 4 Dec. 2015, www.federalreservehistory.org/essays/jekyll_island_conference.

Richter, Wolf. "$1.5 Trillion Helicopter Money for Wall Street in 3 Weeks of Fed Bailouts." *Wolf Street*, 2 Apr. 2020, wolfstreet.com/2020/04/02/helicopter-money-for-wall-street-1-5-trillion-in-3-weeks-of-fed-bailouts/?fbclid=IwAR0netP-VVmUMDmbNvCjD1J-MvMz3V9N0GmTymCv3IyyOYBl4qKhwACpqnI.

Richter, Wolf. "As Everything Bubble Implodes, Frazzled Fed Rolls Out Fastest Mega-Money Printer Ever, up to $4.5 Trillion in Four Weeks." *Wolf Street*, 12 Mar. 2020, wolfstreet.com/2020/03/12/frazzled-fed-rolls-out-fastest-mega-money-printer-ever-up-to-4-5-trillion-in-four-weeks/?fbclid=IwAR0E7v8G2QZf2rVqoEUuYYAesDUZLOTEogiq6C2JvYmrjzVLbme M53FhlQc.

Rickards, James G. "New Gold Standard? Chaos." *Bullion Vault*, 1 Jan. 2020, www.bullionvault.com/gold-news/gold-standard-012120201.

Riquier, Andrea. "The Fed is going to buy ETFs. What does it mean?" *Market Watch*, 28 Mar. 2020, www.marketwatch.com/story/the-fed-is-going-to-buy-etfs-what-does-it-mean-2020-03-23?siteid=yhoof2&yptr=yahoo.

Robb, Greg. "Fed announces unlimited QE and sets up several new lending programs." *Market Watch*, 23 Mar. 2020, www.marketwatch.com/story/fed-announces-unlimited-qe-and-sets-up-several-new-lending-programs-2020-03-23?reflink=mw_share_facebook&fbclid=IwAR1ZuxKWVmG2oXcIZ8icAOkTG-w7aMpCqLIcIAK4ifd1EHELVjN6tyCMzxs.

Robb, Greg. "Fed balance sheet hits record, as Powell says there is no limit to lending power." *Market Watch*, 27 Mar. 2020, www.marketwatch.com/story/fed-balance-sheet-hits-record-as-powell-says-there-is-no-limit-to-lending-power-2020-03-26?

reflink=mw_share_facebook&fbclid=IwAR0xKgkn7vsS1QNY3i_ntdw10HBWey
-VfdGgoya_avJqEy-xLN6BApHWhcE.

Robb, Greg. "Fed says it is developing an experimental digital currency." *Market Watch*, 15 Aug. 2020, www.marketwatch.com/story/fed-says-it-is-developing-an-experimental-digital-currency-11597352302?
fbclid=IwAR3OgT9nTgUpqZ3ho_ks3Po08ryIL89zriTkT4i1ezk5WN8RVQIZ61E
0ncU.

Robb, Greg. "The Fed and Congress may need to do more to support economy, Clarida says." *Market Watch*, 21 May 2020, www.marketwatch.com/story/the-fed-and-congress-may-need-to-do-more-to-support-economy-clarida-says-2020-05-21?siteid=yhoof2&yptr=yahoo.

"Ronald Reagan Quotes." *AZ Quotes*, www.azquotes.com/quote/1216586.

RonPaulLibertyReport. "Central Banking Is On The Ropes: Gold Will Survive & The Fed Will End." *Youtube*, 13 Dec. 2019, www.youtube.com/watch?
v=Ndcb2SPRU7M.

Rothbard, Murray N. "Not Worth a Continental." *Mises Institute,* 17 Dec. 2018, mises.org/library/not-worth-continental.

Royal, James, PhD and Arielle O'Shea. "How to Invest in Dividend Stocks." *Nerdwallet*, 2 May 2019, www.nerdwallet.com/blog/investing/how-to-invest-dividend-stocks/.

RT America. "Why it's too late to avoid coming recession." *Youtube*, 19 Dec. 2019, www.youtube.com/watch?v=F2q6HfXH6nE.

Saefong, Myra P. "Gold Prices Could Hit a Record High by Year End. Just Don't Expect an Easy Ride." *Barrons*, 22 May 2020, www.barrons.com/articles/how-to-instill-values-when-teaching-kids-about-money-51590192190.

Saefong, Myra P. "Physical demand for silver spikes as price drops to an 11-year low." *Market Watch*, 19 Mar. 2020, www.marketwatch.com/story/physical-demand-for-silver-spikes-as-price-drops-to-an-11-year-low-2020-03-19?
reflink=mw_share_facebook&fbclid=IwAR2asSl2TwNpIZg8AbtkjBdtyAW_ElE1
4NwK9FUyPCiFF4rE2OhCpk1RWyc.

Saefong, Myra P. "Silver readies for biggest monthly gain in nearly 7 years." *Market Watch*, 22 May 2020, www.marketwatch.com/story/silver-readies-for-biggest-monthly-gain-in-nearly-7-years-2020-05-22?siteid=yhoof2&yptr=yahoo.

Sangster, Kalila. "Banknotes may be spreading coronavirus, World Health Organisation warns." *Yahoo Finance,* 3 Mar. 2020, finance.yahoo.com/news/who-world-health-organisation-coronavirus-banknotes-warning-111019361.html.

Saunders, Joe. "Trading Halted Market-Wide as S&P Plummets 7% in Minutes." *The Western Journal*, 9 Mar. 2020, www.westernjournal.com/trading-halted-m a r k e t - w i d e - s p - p l u m m e t s - 7 - m i n u t e s / ? utm_source=facebook&utm_medium=patriotupdate&utm_campaign=lminetwork & u t m _ c o n t e n t = 2 0 2 0 - 0 3 - 0 9 & f b c l i d = I w A R 3 x 1 T G v S y - NCnqsh4H0-2Pxmc5qXsll2XqsKv3TVSkWmngmSD3DuyaP2PI.

Schiff, Peter. "Ep. 520: Volcker Dies as Inflation Comes Back to Life." *Youtube*, 11 Dec. 2019, www.youtube.com/watch?v=bJrq2SA8PCw.

Schiff, Peter. "Powell resurrecting the high inflation Volcker buried." *Youtube*, 11 Dec. 2019, www.youtube.com/watch?v=lWcLQFap2sQ.

Schiffgold. "Peter Schiff: This Is Where the Problem Really Starts." *Schiffgold*, 25 Mar. 2020, schiffgold.com/peters-podcast/peter-schiff-this-is-where-the-problem-r e a l l y - s t a r t s / ? fbclid=IwAR3cIy0GtM1gWUF89rq33pe3iYdQWUjinWGge4H6GnhZhz8BIdOO 7sC5y2I.

Schilling, A. Gary. "Globalists May Soon Become an Extinct Species." *Bloomberg*, 16 Mar. 2020, www.bloomberg.com/opinion/articles/2020-03-16/ c o r o n a v i r u s - g l o b a l i s t s - m a y - s o o n - b e c o m e - a n - e x t i n c t - s p e c i e s ? f b c l i d = I w A R 2 M u n B P h H 4 e j T Z Q R _ h 1 t y U r A j H v V _ T x - MDCD4h1mfVRbD6DXtVAKmByVlU.

Schneider, Howard. "As virus threatens, U.S. embraces big government, for now." *MSN*, 28 Mar. 2020, www.msn.com/en-us/news/politics/as-virus-threatens-us-embraces-big-government-for-now/ar-BB11PDTL?ocid=sf2.

Schneider, Howard and Steve Holland. "Trump's coronavirus payroll tax cut would punch hole in Social Security, Medicare budgets." *Reuters*, 11 Mar. 2020, news.yahoo.com/trumps-radical-plan-waive-payroll-192517459.html.

Schrotenboer, Brent. "US is 'printing' money to help save the economy from the COVID-19 crisis, but some wonder how far it can go." *USA Today*, 13 May 2020, www.usatoday.com/in-depth/money/2020/05/12/coronavirushow-u-s-printing-d o l l a r s - s a v e - e c o n o m y - d u r i n g - c r i s i s - f e d / 3 0 3 8 1 1 7 0 0 1 / ? fbclid=IwAR1QWoknShih2gZvREvMBumaWN4FU_AIxlfr9j4nuclqnLkrLWW Mho7NXSA.

Schultz, Marisa. "Congress OKs $2T stimulus in historic coronavirus response, as rep's objections sidelined." *Fox News*, 27 Mar. 2020, www.foxnews.com/politics/ house-massie-bill-coronavirus?fbclid=IwAR1-rs9DPKVUQmBefH-YzfcctpSUcjaebg6S09RZV1-2hC3oenR43YAk5ME.

Schwartz, Zane. "Bank of Canada exploring digital currency that would replace cash, track how people spend money." *Financial Post*, 15 Oct. 2019, business.financialpost.com/technology/blockchain/bank-of-canada-exploring-digital-currency-that-would-replace-cash-track-how-people-spend-money?

f   b   c   l   i   d   =   I   w   A   R   2   6   5   L   -
vijcJSOj2u_wmH3CT3D2EXEeW4LgdNrZoiKDILDgcP1w3yQoJncU.

Scott, David. "There's a big problem with the last tool in the arsenal of the world's central banks." *Business Insider*, 17 Feb. 2016, www.businessinsider.com/theres-a-big-problem-with-negative-interest-rates-2016-2.

SEC. v. Shavers, Case No. 4:13-CV-416 (E.D. Texas 2014).

"Second Bank of the United States." *History Central*, www.historycentral.com/Ant/Economics/Second.html.

"Second Bank of the United States (1816-1836)." *American History: From Revolution to Reconstruction and Beyond*, www.let.rug.nl/usa/essays/general/a-brief-history-of-central-banking/second-bank-of-the-united-states-(1816-1836).php.

"Secret Banking Cabal Emerges From AIG Shadows: David Reilly." *Bloomberg*, 28 Jan. 2010, www.bloomberg.com/news/2010-01-28/secret-banking-cabal-emerges-from-aig-shadows-david-reilly.html.

"Selling Cash-Secured Puts on Stock You Want to Buy." *The Ally Invest Options Playbook*, www.optionsplaybook.com/rookies-corner/cash-secured-puts/.

Seth, Shobhit. "The Risks of Trading Low-Volume Stocks." *Investopedia*, 10 Jan. 2018, www.investopedia.com/articles/active-trading/051415/risks-trading-lowvolume-stocks.asp.

Shalai, Andrea. "IMF sees coronavirus-induced global downturn 'way worse' than financial crisis." *Reuters,* 3 Apr. 2020, uk.reuters.com/article/uk-health-coronavirus-imf/global-downturn-due-to-coronavirus-way-worse-than-global-financial-crisis-imf-idUKKBN21L328?fbclid=IwAR1UIBq5Mv2fCQrvdzrDzpXHb2BbcggPIwVhj0RnolpPjz4NKZWNgRnKqa4.

Shell, Adam. "4 ways to invest when interest rates are plunging on coronavirus worries." *USA Today*, 9 Mar. 2020, www.usatoday.com/story/money/2020/03/09/interest-rates-plunge-on-coronavirus-fears-investing/4973410002/.

Shimron, Leeor. "Fed Chairman Powell 60 Minutes Interview Highlights Bitcoin's Value Proposition." *Forbes,* 18 May 2020, www.forbes.com/sites/leeorshimron/2020/05/18/fed-chairman-powell-60-minutes-interview-highlights-bitcoins-value-proposition/?fbclid=IwAR2JqJiGeYtrtZjiBz1_g0h1b3f0KEB2DINl-U-kjFY5k0uxfdQvfkzBxsY#5938e6db4cdb.

Shostak, Frank. "The Bureaucrats Can't Fix This." *Mises Wire*, 2 Apr. 2020, mises.org/wire/bureaucrats-cant-fix?fbclid=IwAR2OMen14SwzJUDCyzsRcfiwXMu4TyXFXI1mBFkg-LykyllACwxQlhjMAXw.

"Silver Conversion." *Traditional Oven*, www.traditionaloven.com/metal/precious-metals/silver/convert-qty_371_25-grain-gr-of-silver-to-troy-ounce-tr-oz-silver.html.

Singh, Dhara. "Suze Orman: The 60-40 portfolio 'is dead.'" *Yahoo Finance*, 26 Feb. 2020, finance.yahoo.com/news/you-should-have-a-threeyear-emergency-fund-172846902.html?guccounter=1.

Smialek, Jeanne. "Bonds Hit Historic Lows, Prompting Fed to Ponder: What More Can We Do?" *The New York Times*, 6 Mar. 2020, web.archive.org/web/20200307035222/https://www.nytimes.com/2020/03/06/business/economy/fed-coronavirus-rate-cut-limited-ammunition.html?fbclid=IwAR3SK_H_SWIXSpNx1zwSJBw9PaIGqhYqinfg3OhbzANEZM_qY1OeWkN1-o4.

Smith, Brandon. "Global Centralization Is The Cause Of Crisis – Not The Cure." *Activist Post*, 19 Feb. 2020, www.activistpost.com/2020/02/global-centralization-is-the-cause-of-crisis-not-the-cure.html.

Smith, Charles Hughes. "Modern Monetary Theory." *InflationData.com*, 5 Nov. 2019, inflationdata.com/articles/2019/11/05/modern-monetary-theory/.

Smith, George Ford. "Thomas Paine on Paper Money and Morality." *Mises Institute*, 29 Jan. 2019, mises.org/wire/thomas-paine-paper-money-and-morality?fbclid=IwAR0W6lgaIIh5jxJ7gwTFzdRAa94LMpNXt0OJdGzxVvivyaxr9GFbvGxxrwM.

Smock, Geoff. "John Marchall: Hamilton 2.0." *Journal of the American Revolution*, 30 Jun. 2020, allthingsliberty.com/2020/06/john-marshall-hamilton-2-0/.

Snyder, Michael. "We Are Experiencing Economic Devastation On A Scale That America Has Never Seen Before." *The Economic Collapse*, 30 Jul. 2020, theeconomiccollapseblog.com/archives/we-are-seeing-economic-devastation-on-a-scale-that-america-has-never-seen-before?fbclid=IwAR1me25eZmKq9vxntaeE5BLhs5QFSdQmaSOYvbc_XSr4jKpADZ55ztace-Q.

South Carolina v. Baker, 485 U.S. 505, 524 (1988).

"Special Message to the Congress on Balance of Payments." *The American Presidency Project*, 18 Jul. 1963, www.presidency.ucsb.edu/documents/special-message-the-congress-balance-payments.

Spratt, Stephen and Liz Capo McCormick. "Fed's New Repo Measures Followed a $100 Billion Treasury Exodus." *Yahoo Finance*, 1 Apr. 2020, finance.yahoo.com/news/over-100-billion-treasuries-dumped-171106252.html.

Stansberry, Porter. "How Paper Money Fails." *InflationData.com,* 11 Jul. 2010, inflationdata.com/articles/2010/07/11/how-paper-money-fails/.

Stanton v. Baltic Mining Co., 240 U.S. 103 (1916).

Stevens, Pippa. "Bank of America says the recession is already here: 'Jobs will be lost, wealth will be destroyed.'" *CNBC,* 19 Mar. 2020, www.cnbc.com/2020/03/19/bank-of-america-says-the-recession-is-already-here-jobs-will-be-lost-wealth-will-be-destroyed.html.

"Stock Volume." *Investors Underground,* www.investorsunderground.com/stock-volume/.

Strain, Michael R. "'Modern Monetary Theory' Is a Joke That's Not Funny" *Bloomberg,* 17 Jan. 2019, www.bloomberg.com/opinion/articles/2019-01-17/modern-monetary-theory-would-sink-u-s-in-debt.

"Strategies to Strengthen LLC Asset Protection." *NOLO,* www.nolo.com/legal-encyclopedia/llcs-owner-liability-protection.html.

Sumner, Scott. "MMT is wrong." *The Library of Economics and Liberty,* www.econlib.org/mmt-is-wrong/.

Sumner, Scott. "Tax-and-spend progressives put faith in flawed policy theory." *The Hill,* 25 Jan. 2019, thehill.com/opinion/finance/426862-tax-and-spend-progressives-put-faith-in-flawed-policy-theory.

Sweet, Ken. "Filthy lucre: Paper money shunned for fear of virus sprea." *AP,* 20 Mar. 2020, apnews.com/167186097f44116220b757abebb49be3?fbclid=IwAR2-UVEZ7HPab0g9JHcEXEfCJ-Me3CjTVS0Y14CP8O4MFnSvLVl_GIWaXXk.

Sykora, Allen. "Ommerzbank: gold has not lost its safe-haven status." *Kitco,* 23 Mar. 2020, www.kitco.com/news/2020-03-23/Commerzbank-gold-has-not-lost-its-safe-haven-status.html.

Tan, Weizhen. "Gold just hit a fresh record high — but some say silver is set to overtake." *CNBC,* 4 Aug. 2020, www.cnbc.com/2020/08/05/investing-in-precious-metals-silver-prices-set-to-outperform-gold-prices.html.

"Tax Hero: Tommy Cryer Passes at 62." *Republic Magazine,* 2014, web.archive.org/web/20170729063103/http://www.republicmagazine.com/news/tax-hero-tommy-cryer-passes-at-62.html.

"Texas to Establish Bullion Depository with HB 3169." *Scottsdale Bullion & Coin,* 17 May 2017, www.sbcgold.com/blog/texas-establish-bullion-depository-hb-3169/.

"The 101 Best Gold Quotes From History – GoldSilver." *Gold Silver,* goldsilver.com/blog/101-best-gold-quotes-all-time/.

"The Advantages & Disadvantages of Investing in Real Estate." *SFGate*, homeguides.sfgate.com/advantages-disadvantages-investing-real-estate-1680.html.

The Associated Press. "Dow drops nearly 3,000 points, worse than any day during 1929 crash." *KGUN9.com*, 16 Mar. 2020, www.kgun9.com/news/national/coronavirus/world-markets-dow-futures-sliding-as-coronavirus-continues-to-s   p   r   e   a   d   ? fbclid=IwAR3OtCDohTBWOoL3t5pq9Il7opi_Ygyf7u4m4030w_dbtuJS7AeuyK6L-U0.

"The Bankers' Manifesto of 1892." *Pathway to Ascension*, www.pathwaytoascension.com/manifesto.htm.

"The Churchill You Didn't Know." *The Guardian*, Guardian News and Media, 27 Nov. 2002, www.theguardian.com/theguardian/2002/nov/28/features11.g21.

"The COVID-19 Trojan Horse Is Pushing Us Towards A One World Government." *Revelation Timeline Decoded*, revelationtimelinedecoded.com/covid-19-trojan-horse/?fbclid=IwAR1plZ4zfiOrSB0oUYGoex-A4Kfz1pJLeWsC1KWUwceRtYPuecHg1f0Aw0c.

The Editors of Encyclopedia Britannica. "Specie Circular." *Encyclopedia Britannica*, www.britannica.com/event/Specie-Circular.

"The First Bank of the United States." *Federal Reserve History*, www.federalreservehistory.org/essays/first_bank_of_the_us.

"The First Bank of the United States." *History, Art, and Archives*, history.house.gov/Historical-Highlights/1700s/1791_First_Bank/.

"The Gold Commission Finds That The US Government Owns No Gold." *Mind Contagion*, www.mindcontagion.org/banking/hb1981.html.

"The Great Economic Depression of 2020: No lessons learned as central banks' bazookas dribble or misfire." *RT*, 23 Mar. 2020, www.rt.com/op-ed/483845-great-economic-depression-2020/.

"The Greenback Question." *US History.com*, www.u-s-history.com/pages/h171.html.

"The History of American Money." *CMI Gold $ Silver*, www.cmi-gold-silver.com/history-american-money/.

"The History of Money Part 2." *XAT3*, www.xat.org/xat/usury.html.

"The House of Rothschild Excerpted from the Book The Secrets of the Federal Reserve by Eustace Mullins Bankers Research Institute, 1983, Paperback." *Third*

World Traveler, www.thirdworldtraveler.com/Banks/
House_Rothschild_TSOTFR.html.

"The Illuminati Plan to Enslave Americans (1969)." *HenryMakow.com*, 10 May 2016, www.savethemales.ca/confirmedrockefeller_plan_to_g.html.

"The Inflation CPI Lie : BLS Posers..." *Signals Matter*, 2 Oct. 2017, www.signalsmatter.com/inflation-cpi/.

"The International Bankers: Famous Quotes." *ConspiracyAnalyst.org*, 23 Dec. 2019, conspiracyanalyst.org/2013/03/01/the-international-bankers-famous-quotes/.

"The New World Order and the United States of America." *Philadelphians.50megs.Com*, philadelphians.50megs.com/nwo-us.html.

"The Pros & Cons of Investing in Real Estate." *Smartmortgage.com*, smartmortgage.com/the-pros-cons-of-investing-in-real-estate/.

"The Ratification of the 16th Amendment." *History, Art & Archives: United States House of Representatives*, history.house.gov/Historical-Highlights/1901-1950/The-ratification-of-the-16th-Amendment/.

"The U.S. Lies About Inflation: Here's The Inflation Secret The Government Doesn't Want You to Know." *Money Morning*, moneymorning.com/the-u-s-lies-about-inflation-heres-the-inflation-secret-the-government-doesnt-want-you-to-know/.

"Thomas Jefferson." Quotes of Famous People, *Quote Park*, quotepark.com/quotes/1806450-thomas-jefferson-i-sincerely-believe-that-banking-institutions-are/.

"Thomas Jefferson > Quotes > Quotable Quote." *Goodreads*, www.goodreads.com/quotes/708734-to-compel-a-man-to-subsidize-with-his-taxes-the.

"Thomas Jefferson Quotes," *AZ Quotes*, www.azquotes.com/quote/650804.

"Thomas Jefferson Quotes," *Your Dictionary*, quotes.yourdictionary.com/author/thomas-jefferson/166784.

"Thomas Jefferson To John Wayles Eppes, 6 November 1813." Founders Online, *National Archives*, founders.archives.gov/documents/Jefferson/03-06-02-0458.

"Thomas Jefferson To Thomas Cooper, 10 September 1814." Founders Online, *National Archives*, founders.archives.gov/documents/Jefferson/03-07-02-0471.

Thomas, Kenny. "The Basics of Investing in Dividend-Paying Stocks." *The Balance*, 31 May 2019, www.thebalance.com/the-basics-of-investing-in-dividend-paying-stocks-416832.

Thorbecke, Catherine. "Dow sinks more than 2,000 points amid coronavirus uncertainty and plunging oil prices." *ABC News*, 9 Mar. 2020, abcnews.go.com/ B u s i n e s s / d o w - f u t u r e s - p l u m m e t - 1 2 0 0 - p o i n t s / s t o r y ? id=69481843&fbclid=IwAR0mvtFGb1J1E06BIMhbhOA_y8i5NQS47Xd5SFeioll mJgKJwgIw7oiynRs.

Thornton, Mark. "The Fed Can't Save Us." *Mises Institute*, 12 Mar. 2020, mises.org/power-market/fed-cant-save-us.

Tilford, Cale. "Repo: How the financial markets' plumbing got blocked." *Financial Times*, 25 Nov. 2019, ig.ft.com/repo-rate/.

Todd, Timothy M. "A Win For The 5th Amendment At The Tax Court." *Forbes*, 16 Nov. 2015, www.forbes.com/sites/timtodd/2015/11/16/a-win-for-the-5th-amendment-at-the-tax-court/#55257b616ecd.

Torres, Craig and Rich Miller. "Fed Cuts Main Interest Rate to Near Zero, to Boost Assets by $700 Billion." *Bloomberg*, 15 Mar. 2020, www.bloomberg.com/ news/articles/2020-03-15/fed-cuts-main-rate-to-near-zero-to-boost-assets-by-700-billion?fbclid=IwAR0w3K1m_1_Hu_grpBM9r9WHlxy31AvzCQO3FQeBXA7-le6bWAmdEMpiFCw.

Trump, Donald. "Remarks by President Trump at the World Economic Forum." *U.S. Embassy in Switzerland and Liechtenstein*, 21 Jan. 2020, ch.usembassy.gov/ remarks-by-president-trump-at-the-world-economic-forum/.

Tsukanov, Ilya. "Belarus's President Warns Global Elites Using COVID-19 Crisis to Try to Reshape World Order." *Sputnik,* 3 Apr. 2020, sputniknews.com/europe/ 202004031078824468-belaruss-president-warns-global-elites-using-covid-19-c r i s i s - t o - t r y - t o - r e s h a p e - w o r l d - o r d e r / ? fbclid=IwAR2WWNitdFQVyOjMaP42h94LhgN2fj_gsG2MzES2SUjvErSWzxm6 3EOl9wM.

"Turn up the volume." *Fidelity*, 17 Oct. 2019, www.fidelity.com/viewpoints/ active-investor/stock-volume.

Ullman, Owen. "An unsung hero of the coronavirus crisis: The Federal Reserve." *USA Today*, 24 Mar. 2020, www.usatoday.com/story/opinion/2020/03/24/unsung-h e r o - c o r o n a v i r u s - c r i s i s - f e d e r a l - r e s e r v e / 2 9 0 2 6 8 1 0 0 1 / ? fbclid=IwAR0SEFozSpmbHUjG7yUxgLSfPrg1i9kKHH37qCTXY_gNJlkOfNE7 74yjGfs.

United States v. Troescher, 99 F.3d 933, 936 (9th Cir. 1996).

"US Cash Crisis: Withdrawal Limits Spark Bank Run Fear." *Bitcoin.com*, 19 Mar. 2020, news.bitcoin.com/us-cash-crisis-withdrawal-limits-bank-run-fear/? f b c l i d = I w A R 2 B D F - W6lH4JqYuNm27x0PXTxDltJAwsY0btbf1pD03HE55KSV4tZOJVds.

"US Debt Clock." *usdebtclock.org*, www.usdebtclock.org.
USMR Staff. "More States Standing Up for Gold & Silver! Is Yours Next?" *U.S. Money*, 22 Jun. 2017, www.usmoneyreserve.com/blog/states-standing-up-for-gold-silver/.

Van, Germinal G. "The Gold Standard Didn't Create the Great Depression, the Federal Reserve Did." *FEE Freeman Article*, Foundation for Economic Education, 25 May 2019, fee.org/articles/the-gold-standard-didn-t-create-the-great-depression-the-federal-reserve-did/?fbclid=IwAR0vrzpM7GgbTDRu2mqA0EM_1vSSK_JaYKWsCWX7BlDGZ6PUxZhjt8niybw.

Vardi, Nathan. "The Federal Reserve Moves To Buy Corporate Debt." *Forbes*, 23 Mar. 2020, www.forbes.com/sites/nathanvardi/2020/03/23/the-federal-reserve-moves-to-buy-corporate-debt/?fbclid=IwAR3v93Orsu2lTli0X0TpRNsG_E0fpFwqMsJLT7oUPe5xufkCPuPfIInQtyM#fab35304c47f.

Watson, Patrick W. "The Corona Depression Is Here." *Forbes*, 25 Jun. 2020, www.forbes.com/sites/patrickwwatson/2020/06/25/the-corona-depression-is-here/?fbclid=IwAR1uN8gUgewFfpUX-4UcWc_ivbs6uWDoHwhZ3qxMflOCUuk-5l3oJrvVKuY#44c7e99ddd91.
Watson, Paul Joseph. "Think Tank Complains 'Coronavirus Is Killing Globalization as We Know It.'" *Summit News*, 13 Mar. 2020, summit.news/2020/03/13/think-tank-complains-coronavirus-is-killing-globalization-as-we-know-it/.

Weinberg, John. "The Great Recession and its Aftermath." *Federal Reserve History*, 22 Nov. 2013, www.federalreservehistory.org/essays/great-recession-and-its-aftermath.

Weiner, Keith, PhD. "Flattening the Economy Because, Virus." *Keith Weiner Economics*, 18 Mar. 2020, keithweinereconomics.com/2020/03/18/flattening-the-economy-because-virus/.

"What Caused the Great Depression?" *FEE,* 2 Feb. 2018, fee.org/articles/what-caused-the-great-depression/.

Wheatley, Jonathan. "Emerging market central banks embark on radical stimulus policies." *Yahoo Finance*, 29 Mar. 2020, finance.yahoo.com/m/0475597d-5a09-3b22-b535-b561236876fc/emerging-market-central-banks.html.

"Who financed Lenin and Trotsky?" *Wildboar.net*, www.wildboar.net/multilingual/easterneuropean/russian/literature/articles/whofinanced/whofinancedleninandtrotsky.htm.

"Why did US bankers fund the Russian Revolution?" *Communism Made Easy,* communism-explained.blogspot.com/2010/05/why-did-us-bankers-fund-russian.html.

"Why invest in gold?" *World Gold Council,* www.gold.org/what-we-do/investing-gold/why-invest-gold.

"Why the repo market went awry...and how the Fed should fix it." *The Economist,* 2 Nov. 2019, www.economist.com/finance-and-economics/2019/11/02/why-the-repo-market-went-awry.

Williams, David Yoe. "Return to Tender: Why Arizona and Other States Are Choosing Gold." *Real Money,* 25 May 2017, realmoney.thestreet.com/articles/05/25/2017/return-tender-why-arizona-and-other-states-are-choosing-gold.

Williams, Kelsey. "Fed Action Accelerates Boom-Bust Cycle; Not A Virus Crisis." *Yahoo Finance,* 19 May 2020, finance.yahoo.com/news/fed-action-accelerates-boom-bust-065808585.html.

Williams, Kelsey. "Federal Reserve – Conspiracy Or Not?" *Kelsey's Gold Facts,* 22 Dec. 2018, www.kelseywilliamsgold.com/federal-reserve-conspiracy-or-not/.

Williams, Sean. "3 Dangers of a Negative Interest Rate Policy." *The Motley Fool,* 20 Feb. 2016, www.fool.com/investing/general/2016/02/20/3-dangers-of-a-negative-interest-rate-policy.aspx.

Williams, Sean. "The 6 Biggest Risks to Bitcoin." *The Motley Fool,* 27 Nov. 2017, www.fool.com/investing/2017/11/27/the-6-biggest-risks-to-bitcoin.aspx.

Winck. Ben. "The Fed has been injecting hundreds of billions into markets since September's rate crisis. Here's why it might not be enough to calm lending conditions." *Market Insider,* 30 Oct. 2019, markets.businessinsider.com/news/stocks/why-fed-repos-capital-injections-might-not-calm-liquidity-fears-2019-10-1028643549#a-bank-government-disconnect2.

Winck, Ben. "The Fed's recent repo crisis was the fault of big banks and hedge funds, new study finds." *Markets Insider,* 9 Dec. 2019, markets.businessinsider.com/news/stocks/fed-repo-crisis-fault-banks-hedge-funds-new-study-finds-2019-12-1028748492.

WND Staff. "'Free World' Needs to Blockade China's Expansionist Agenda." *WND,* WND, 9 Aug. 2020, www.wnd.com/2020/08/free-world-needs-blockade-chinas-expansionist-agenda/?fbclid=IwAR3Lt3ZjEEHmdM8boMkpvAW3NF7T0Ia0j-MO68vcEUGHLUMJEwUeJBmCXC0.

Wolverton, Joe, II, JD. "Tennessee Considering Bills Restoring Gold and Silver as Sound Money." *The New American,* 2 Feb. 2019, www.thenewamerican.com/

usnews/constitution/item/31369-tennessee-considering-bills-restoring-gold-and-silver-as-sound-money.

"Woodrow Wilson > Quotes > Quotable Quote." *Goodreads*, Goodreads, www.goodreads.com/quotes/162688-since-i-entered-politics-i-have-chiefly-had-men-s-views.

Woods, Thomas E. Jr. "The Revolutionary War and the Destruction of the Continental." *Mises Institute*, 11 Oct. 2006, mises.org/library/revolutionary-war-and-destruction-continental.

Yahoo Finance. "Bitcoin sinks to lowest level since May after alleged Ponzi scheme." *Youtube*, 17 Dec. 2019, www.youtube.com/watch?v=TO2ccMrva1E.

Yick Wo v. Hopkins, 118 U.S. 356 (1886).

Yilek, Caitlin. "Former Trump adviser: 'Odds of a global recession are close to 100%.'" *Washington Examiner*, 16 Mar. 2020, www.washingtonexaminer.com/news/former-trump-adviser-odds-of-a-global-recession-are-close-to-100? f b c l i d = I w A R 0 f x I t r O Z L - P r - VobO2YQzhEDkOt4YrywCpb13Fsyy44fDXclmb8kd3hLc.

Zulu, Blessing. "Zimbabwean Hyperinflation Officially Estimated At 2.2 Million Percent." *InflationData.com*, 15 Jul. 2008, inflationdata.com/articles/2008/07/16/zimbabwean-hyperinflation-officially-estimated-at-2-2-million-percent/.

Made in the USA
Coppell, TX
15 March 2021